# LABORATORY MANUAL
## TO ACCOMPANY

# PREGO!

**AN INVITATION TO ITALIAN** · THIRD EDITION

# LABORATORY MANUAL
## TO ACCOMPANY

# PREGO!

### AN INVITATION TO ITALIAN • THIRD EDITION

## GRAZIANA LAZZARINO
*University of Colorado, Boulder*

## GIOVANNA BELLESIA
*Smith College*

**McGraw-Hill Publishing Company**

New York   St. Louis   San Francisco   Auckland   Bogotá   Caracas
Hamburg   Lisbon   London   Madrid   Mexico   Milan   Montreal   New Delhi
Oklahoma City   Paris   San Juan   São Paulo   Singapore   Sydney   Tokyo   Toronto

This is an ⌐B⌐ book.

Laboratory Manual to accompany
Prego!
An Invitation to Italian

1 2 3 4 5 6 7 8 9 0 MAL MAL 9 5 4 3 2 1 0

ISBN 0-07-557430-6

This book was typed on a Macintosh SE20 in Avant Garde and Times by Byll Travis.
The editors were Leslie Berriman, Cathy de Heer, and Elizabeth McDevitt.
The production supervisor was Tanya Nigh.
Production and editorial assistance was provided by Marian Hartsough and Jane Parkinson.
Illustrations were by Stephanie O'Shaughnessy.
Malloy Lithographing, Inc. was printer and binder.

# Contents

# Preface

This *Laboratory Manual* accompanies *Prego! An Invitation to Italian,* Third Edition. It is coordinated with an audiocassette program for the preliminary chapter and the twenty regular chapters. Each chapter has thirty to forty minutes of recorded material.

Each chapter through Chapter 13 begins with a pronunciation section in which Italian sounds and intonation patterns are practiced. The material in each chapter then follows the sequence of material in the student text: *Vocabolario preliminare,* minidialogues and grammar material from *Grammatica,* and a recording of the main *Dialogo.* The dictation section (*Dettato*) provides careful listening practice. A section new to the third edition of the *Laboratory Manual, E ora ascoltiamo!,* has students listen to extended passages (such as conversations, recorded cinema listings, police reports, and so on) to improve global listening-comprehension skills. All exercises in the Laboratory Program are additional exercises that enhance the student text.

Answers to most exercises are given on tape to give students immediate confirmation of their responses. A handful of exercises requires written responses, and those answers appear at the back of the manual. Answers to the dictations are not provided in this manual; they appear in the *Tapescript* as part of the transcription of the complete recorded program. The *Tapescript* is available only to instructors.

The *Laboratory Manual* is a guide to the audiocassettes. It contains the text of the pronunciation sections, the minidialogues, and the main *Dialoghi.* Directions for all recorded exercises are provided, with a model given for most. In some cases, cues for exercises are given in the manual; at other times, cues appear only on tape.

We suggest that students listen to the recorded materials on a given vocabulary section or grammar point only after that material has been covered in class. We recommend that students spend not more than thirty minutes at a time in the laboratory. A total of sixty minutes a week should enable students to listen to all of the recorded material for one chapter at least once and still give them time to repeat parts on which they feel they need additional practice.

The speech on the audiocassettes represents that of many regions of Italy; the language is authentic Italian.

The authors would like to thank Leslie Berriman and Cathy de Heer of McGraw-Hill, and Marion Lignana Rosenberg for her many imaginative contributions to this edition of the Laboratory Program.

CAPITOLO
# PRELIMINARE

## A. Alfabeto e suoni

**A.** Repeat the following abbreviations or formulas after the speaker:

| | | |
|---|---|---|
| K.O. | P.S. | Raggi X |
| PR | S.O.S. | LSD |
| LP | D.C. | |
| $H_2O_2$ | $H_2O$ | |

**B.** Repeat each word after the speaker:

pazzo / pezzo / pizzo / pozzo / puzzo
lana / lena / Lina / luna
casa / case / casi / caso
auto / aiuto / iuta / uva / uova / Europa / aiuola

**C.** **C** and **g** each have two sounds in Italian. Their sound is hard (as in *cat* and *get*) when followed directly by **a, o, u,** or **h.** Their sound is soft (as in *chain* and *giraffe*) when followed directly by **e** or **i.** Repeat after the speaker:

gatta / cane                    gotta / cotta
getta / ghetta / ceto / cheto    gusto / custode
giro / ghiro / Cina / china

**D.** Practice the difference between single and double consonants. Repeat after the speaker:

casa / cassa                    sono / sonno
sete / setta                    palude / allude
Ciro / cirro

**E.** Repeat the following sentences after the speaker:

1. Giuliano, cosa vuol dire giugno?
2. È il nome di un mese dell'anno.
3. Dopo giugno viene luglio e prima c'è maggio.

**F.** Circle the word you hear. You will hear each word twice.

| | | | | | | | |
|---|---|---|---|---|---|---|---|
| 1. | a. regolare | b. regalare | | 6. | a. pulizia | b. polizia |
| 2. | a. pezzo | b. pizzo | | 7. | a. anelo | b. anello |
| 3. | a. ragione | b. regione | | 8. | a. poso | b. posso |
| 4. | a. pasta | b. posta | | 9. | a. lungi | b. lunghi |
| 5. | a. amore | b. umore | | 10. | a. cioccolato | b. coccolato |

**G.** Can you hear where the stress falls in an Italian word? Underline the stressed syllable in each of the following words. You will hear each word twice. The answers appear at the end of this manual.

1. grammatica
2. importanza
3. partire
4. partirò

5. musica
6. trentatrè
7. subito
8. umiltà

9. abitano
10. cantavano

**H.** You will hear each word twice. Write in an accent, if needed. Remember: in Italian, if written accents appear, they do so only on the last syllable. The answers appear at the end of this manual.

1. prendere
2. prendero
3. caffe

4. tre
5. quarantatre
6. civilta

7. virtu
8. tornare

# B. Come si dice… in italiano?

**A.** You will hear two dialogues from the main text. Repeat after the speaker, paying careful attention to rhythm and intonation:

1.     LAURA: Ciao, Roberto, come stai?
    ROBERTO: Bene, grazie, e tu?
    LAURA: Non c'è male, grazie.
    ROBERTO: Ciao, Laura!
    LAURA: Arrivederci!
2.   SIG.RA M.: Buon giorno, signor Rossi, come sta?
    SIG. ROSSI: Bene, grazie, e Lei?
    SIG.RA M.: Abbastanza bene, grazie.
    SIG. ROSSI: ArrivederLa, signora!
    SIG.RA M.: ArrivederLa!

**B.** What would you say in the situations listed below? You will hear a possible response; repeat it.

1. Greet your neighbor, Mr. Rossi.
2. Say good-bye to him.
3. Say hi to your friend Roberto.
4. Say good-bye to him.
5. Ask Mrs. Rossi how she is.
6. Tell Mrs. Rossi how you are doing.

# C. L'anno

**A.** You are playing a game with your little brother. When he tells you a number, tell him the corresponding month. Repeat the correct answer.

ESEMPIO: uno → gennaio
due → febbraio

1. …    2. …    3. …    4. …    5. …    6. …    7. …    8. …    9. …    10. …    11. …    12. …

**B. Che tempo fa? Che giorno è?** Take a look at the pictures and answer the questions. Repeat the correct response.

1.

2.

3.

4.

# D. Numeri da uno a cento

**A.** Write down in figures the numbers you hear. You will hear each number twice. The answers appear at the end of this manual.

ESEMPIO:   trentadue → 32

1. _____        4. _____        7. _____

2. _____        5. _____        8. _____

3. _____        6. _____

**B.** You will hear two numbers. Say the one that is smaller. Repeat the correct response.

ESEMPIO:   sei, sette → sei

1. ...    2. ...    3. ...    4. ...    5. ...    6. ...

# E. Vocabolario per la classe

You are now ready to answer the following questions! You will hear each one twice.

1. ...    2. ...    3. ...

# Dettato

You will hear each sentence three times. The first time, listen carefully. The second time, write what you hear. The third time, check what you have written.

1. _____

2. _____

3. _____

4. _____

CAPITOLO

# **|**

# Pronuncia:  The Sounds of the Letter **c**

As you learned in the *Capitolo preliminare,* **c** represents two sounds:  [k] as in the English word *cat* and [č] as in the English word *cheese.*

**A.** The sound [k].  This sound occurs when **c** is followed directly by **a, o, u, h,** or another consonant. Listen and repeat:

| | | |
|---|---|---|
| caldo | chi | fresche |
| come | clima | ics |
| cugina | crema | |
| che | macchina | |

Contrast the single and double sound of [k].  Listen and repeat:

amico / ammicco          eco / ecco          fichi / ficchi

**B.** The sound [č].  This sound occurs when **c** is followed directly by **e** or **i.**  Listen and repeat:

| | | |
|---|---|---|
| cena | ciuffo | diciotto |
| città | piacere | piaciuto |
| ciao | ricetta | |
| ciglio | aranciata | |

Contrast the single and double sound of [č].  Listen and repeat:

aceto / accetto          caci / cacci          cacio / caccio

Remember that **c** in Italian is never pronounced as in the English words *cent* or *city.*  The sound [s] is represented only by **s** in Italian.

**C.** Repeat the following sentences after the speaker.  You will hear each sentence twice.

1. Il cinema è vicino al supermercato.
2. Cameriere, una cioccolata ed un caffè, per piacere!
3. Come si pronuncia bicicletta?
4. Michelangelo è un nome, non un cognome.
5. Ciao Carlo, come va? —Così così.

# Vocabolario preliminare

Your friend Tommaso has a number of complaints today. Luckily, you have many good observations and suggestions for him. Circle the most logical response, as in the example.

ESEMPIO:  Non ho latte. → Ecco uno stadio!  (Ecco un supermercato!)

1.  Ecco un ristorante!          Ecco un ospedale!

2.  Ecco un negozio!            Ecco una banca!

3.  Ecco un museo!             Ecco un bar!

4.  Hai bisogno di una macchina!     Hai bisogno di una bicicletta!

5.  Ecco una chiesa!            Ecco un caffè!

# Grammatica

## A. Nomi: genere e numero

A. You will hear a dialogue from the main text. Repeat after the speaker, paying careful attention to rhythm and intonation:

**In una stazione italiana**

|  |  |
|---|---|
| VENDITORE: | Panini, banane, gelati, vino, caffè, aranciata, birra… |
| TURISTA AMERICANA: | Due panini e una birra, per favore! |
| VENDITORE: | Ecco, signorina! Diecimila lire. |
| TURISTA AMERICANA: | Ecco dieci dollari. Va bene? |

B. Give the plural form of each word you hear. You will hear each word twice. Repeat the correct response.

ESEMPIO:  panino → panini

1. …   2. …   3. …   4. …   5. …   6. …   7. …   8. …   9. …   10. …

C. Your friend is not sure she has heard you correctly. Answer her questions, as in the example, with **no** plus a singular noun.

ESEMPIO:  Hai detto «treni»? → No, «treno».

1. …   2. …   3. …   4. …   5. …   6. …   7. …   8. …

## B. Articolo indeterminativo e **buono**

A. You need a lot of things today. Say that you need the following items. Repeat the correct response.

ESEMPIO:

Ho bisogno di un cappuccino.

1.

2.

3.

4.

5.

6.

**B.** Your sister always exaggerates. Correct what she says, as in the example.

ESEMPIO:   Due panini? → No, un panino!

1. …   2. …   3. …   4. …   5. …   6. …   7. …   8. …

**C.** Life is treating you well! Answer your friend's questions, as in the example. Repeat the correct response.

ESEMPIO:   Hai un lavoro? → Sì, ho un buon lavoro.

1. …   2. …   3. …   4. …   5. …   6. …

# C. Pronomi soggetto e presente di **avere**

**A.** You will hear a dialogue from the main text. Repeat after the speaker, paying careful attention to rhythm and intonation:

LUIGINO:   E Lei, signora, ha parenti in America?
SIG.RA PARODI:   No, Luigino, non ho parenti, solo amici. E tu, hai qualcuno?
LUIGINO:   Sì, ho uno zio in California e una zia e molti cugini in Florida.

**B.** Create new sentences by substituting the word or phrase below. You will hear the correct response.

ESEMPIO:   (Io ho un cane.) Marco → Marco ha un cane.

1. tu
2. tu e Anna
3. loro

4. noi
5. Lei, Signora

**C.** You are in a terrible mood today and you answer every question you are asked in the negative. Repeat the correct response.

ESEMPIO:   Hai soldi? → No, non ho soldi.

1. …   2. …   3. …   4. …   5. …   6. …

**D.** Indicate whether the expressions you hear are questions or statements. Circle *q* (for question) or *s* (for statement).

1. q    s
2. q    s

3. q    s
4. q    s

5. q    s
6. q    s

## D. Espressioni idiomatiche con **avere**

**A. Come sta Gilda?** Look at the illustrations and say how your friend Gilda is doing today. Repeat the correct response.

ESEMPIO:

Gilda ha freddo!

1.

2.

3.

4.

5.

**B.** Circle the most logical conclusion to the sentences you hear. You will hear each sentence twice.

1. una Coca-Cola      un panino

2. Ha sei anni.      Ha quarantadue anni.

3. Ho fretta!      Ho paura!

4. un gelato      una birra

5. un supermercato      un caffè

# Dialogo

Listen carefully to the dialogue. Feel free to go back and listen as many times as you need to. Then answer the questions.

MARCELLA: Ciao, Vittoria, come va?
VITTORIA: Abbastanza bene, e tu?
MARCELLA: Bene, grazie.
VITTORIA: Novità?
MARCELLA: Sì: domani arriva Beppino.
VITTORIA: Beppino? E chi è Beppino?
MARCELLA: Un cugino texano!
VITTORIA: Arriva a cavallo?
MARCELLA: Spiritosa! Arriva in treno con un amico di New York: Pietro, Pietro Nicolosi.
VITTORIA: Quanti anni ha questo cow-boy?
MARCELLA: Beppino non è un cow-boy, è uno studente e vent'anni.
VITTORIA: Hai una foto?
MARCELLA: Sì, ecco!
VITTORIA: Non c'è male! Ma non pare americano, pare napoletano… A domani, allora.
MARCELLA: A domani. Ciao, Vittoria!
VITTORIA: Ciao, Marcella!

You will hear five incomplete statements based on the dialogue. You will hear each statement twice. Circle the word or phrase that best completes each one.

1. napoletano      texano

2. in treno      a cavallo

3. un cow-boy      uno studente

4. sedici anni      vent'anni

5. un'amica di New York      un amico di New York

# Dettato

You will hear a short dictation three times. The first time, listen carefully. The second time, write what you hear. The third time, check what you have written.

_____

_____

_____

_____

_____

_____

# E ora ascoltiamo!

You will hear a conversation and then five statements. You will hear everything twice. Circle *vero* if the statement is true or *falso* if it is false. Feel free to go back and listen to the dialogue as many times as you need to.

1. vero    falso          4. vero    falso

2. vero    falso          5. vero    falso

3. vero    falso

CAPITOLO

# 2

# Pronuncia:  The Sounds of the Letter s

The letter **s** represents two sounds in Italian:  [s] as in the English word *aside* and [z] as in the English word *reside*.

**A.** The sound [s].  This sound occurs in the following places:

1.  At the beginning of a word when followed by a vowel.  *Ascoltate e ripetete* (Listen and repeat):

| | |
|---|---|
| salute | soldi |
| sete | supermercato |
| simpatico | |

2.  When **s** is followed by **ca, co, cu,** or **ch,** or by the consonants **f, p, q,** or **t.**  *Ascoltate e ripetete* (Listen and repeat):

| | |
|---|---|
| scuola | spaghetti |
| schema | squisito |
| sfera | stadio |

3.  When **s** is doubled.  *Ascoltate e ripetete* (Listen and repeat):

| | |
|---|---|
| passare | grasse |
| basso | messicano |
| assumere | |

**B.** The sound [z].  This sound occurs in the following places:

1.  When **s** is followed by the consonants **b, d, g, l, m, n, r,** or **v.**  *Ascoltate e ripetete:*

| | |
|---|---|
| sbaglio | smog |
| sdraio | snob |
| sgobbare | sregolato |
| slogan | sveglio |

2.  When **s** appears between vowels.  *Ascoltate e ripetete:*

| | |
|---|---|
| casa | rose |
| uso | visitare |
| chiusura | |

Note that you may also hear the pronunciation [s] between vowels in certain regions, particularly central and southern Italy.

**C.** The sounds [s] and [z]. Contrast the pronunciation of single and double **s** in these pairs of words. *Ascoltate e ripetete:*

| | | |
|---|---|---|
| casa / cassa | leso / lesso | illuso / lusso |
| base / basse | risa / rissa | abusi / bussi |
| tese / tesse | poso / posso | |
| mesi / messi | rose / rosse | |

**D.** You will hear each sentence twice. *Ascoltate e ripetete le frasi:*

1. Sette studentesse sono snelle.
2. Sono dei grossi sbagli di pronuncia.
3. Tommaso ha sei rose rosse.
4. Gli studenti sbadigliano spesso.
5. Non siete stanchi di sgobbare?

# Vocabolario preliminare

You will hear a passage about a family twice. Listen, then answer the questions.

**A. Vero o falso?** Circle the correct answer.

1. vero     falso          3. vero     falso

2. vero     falso          4. vero     falso

**B.** Circle the correct answer.

1. Philip     Giovanna     Peter     Francesco

2. Philip     Giovanna     Peter     Francesco

3. Philip     Giovanna     Peter     Francesco

4. Philip     Giovanna     Peter     Francesco

# Grammatica

## A. Aggettivi

**A.** Sentirete un dialogo dal vostro testo. Ripetete durante le pause. Attenzione all'intonazione! (*You will hear a dialogue from your text. Repeat during the pauses. Pay attention to your intonation!*)

MARISA:   È una ragazza carina Giovanna?
FRANCA:   Sì, è molto carina: è alta e snella ed è anche molto intelligente e simpatica.
MARISA:   E Mario com'è?
FRANCA:   È un ragazzo piuttosto brutto, ma intelligente e simpatico.

**B.** Circle the number and gender of the phrases you hear. You will hear each phrase twice. Then you will hear the correct response.

1. singolare     plurale          maschile     femminile

2. singolare     plurale          maschile     femminile

3. singolare     plurale          maschile     femminile

4. singolare     plurale          maschile     femminile

5. singolare     plurale          maschile     femminile

6. singolare     plurale          maschile     femminile

**C.** Create new phrases by substituting the word or expression you hear. Make any necessary changes.

  ESEMPIO: un ragazzo italiano (un'università) → un'università italiana

1. ...  2. ...  3. ...  4. ...  5. ...  6. ...  7. ...  8. ...  9. ...  10. ...

  ESEMPIO: molti dollari (lire) → molte lire

1. ...  2. ...  3. ...  4. ...  5. ...  6. ...  7. ...  8. ...  9. ...  10. ...

**D. Qual è il contrario** (*What is the opposite*)? You will hear each expression twice. Give the opposite of each one. You will hear the correct response.

  ESEMPIO: antipatico → simpatico

1. ...  2. ...  3. ...  4. ...  5. ...  6. ...  7. ...  8. ...

**E. Dal femminile al maschile** (*from feminine to masculine*). Change each expression from feminine to masculine.

  ESEMPIO: una zia buffa → uno zio buffo

1. ...  2. ...  3. ...  4. ...  5. ...

# B. Presente di essere

**A.** Your housemate wants to know the nationalities of everyone who will be at tonight's gathering. Answer his questions, as in the example. Repeat the correct response.

  ESEMPIO: (Chi è francese?) Gianni → Gianni è francese.

1. noi
2. Claudio e Gina
3. io

4. tu e Franco
5. Mirella

**B.** You are in an enthusiastic mood today. Every time Marco makes a statement, repeat it with exuberance. Use subject pronouns to add emphasis. Repeat the correct response.

  ESEMPIO: Maria è bassa. → Sì, lei è bassa!

1. ...  2. ...  3. ...  4. ...  5. ...  6. ...  7. ...

# C. C'è e com'è

**A.** You are showing a friend a picture of the town where you stayed in Italy. Answer her questions, as in the example. Repeat the correct response. First, take a moment to look over the illustration.

ESEMPIO: C'è una banca? → No, ci sono due banche.

1. ...   2. ...   3. ...   4. ...   5. ...   6. ...

**B.** You are very much in agreement with Carla's statements. Express your enthusiasm! Repeat the response.

ESEMPIO: Patrizia è simpatica. → Sì, com'è simpatica Patrizia!

1. ...   2. ...   3. ...   4. ...   5. ...   6. ...

**C.** Answer these questions about your dorm room, house, or apartment. You will hear a possible response.

ESEMPIO: C'è una bicicletta? → No, non c'è una bicicletta.

1. ...   2. ...   3. ...   4. ...   5. ...

**D.** Your housemate is showing you pictures of her Italian friends. React as in the example, choosing from among the following adjectives. Repeat the correct response.

**Aggettivi:** allegro, alto, basso, grasso, magro, triste

ESEMPIO:

Alessia e Marco → Come sono allegri Alessia e Marco!

1.

LUISA  GIORGIO

2.

MARCO

3.

MARINA   PAOLO

4.

ANTONIO

5.

## D. Articolo determinativo

**A.** Sentirete un dialogo dal vostro testo. Ripetete durante le pause. Attenzione all'intonazione! (*You will hear a dialogue from your text. Repeat during the pauses. Pay attention to your intonation!*)

Marcella mostra a Vittoria una vecchia fotografia di famiglia.

MARCELLA: Ecco la nonna e il nonno, la zia Luisa e lo zio Massimo, papà e la mamma molti anni fa… Buffi, no?
VITTORIA: E i due in prima fila chi sono?
MARCELLA: Sono gli zii di Chicago.

**B.** Change the indefinite article to the definite article, as in the example. You will hear each item twice. Repeat the correct response.

ESEMPIO:  un film → il film

1. …   2. …   3. …   4. …   5. …   6. …   7. …   8. …

**C.** Give the plural of the following expressions. You will hear each item twice. Repeat the correct response.

> ESEMPIO: la stazione → le stazioni

1. ...   2. ...   3. ...   4. ...   5. ...   6. ...   7. ...   8. ...

**D.** You have just moved to a new city and are telling your friends about it. Describe the following people, places, and things. The adjectives appear below. Be sure to make all necessary changes. Repeat the correct response.

> ESEMPIO: (ragazzi) bello → I ragazzi sono belli.

| | | |
|---|---|---|
| 1. piccolo | 5. simpatico | 9. carino |
| 2. intelligente | 6. brutto | 10. famoso |
| 3. bello | 7. grande | |
| 4. nuovo | 8. vecchio | |

## E. **Bello** e **quello**

**A.** Give the singular form of the following expressions. You will hear each expression twice. You will hear the correct response.

> ESEMPIO: due bei ragazzi → un bel ragazzo

1. ...   2. ...   3. ...   4. ...   5. ...   6. ...

**B.** It's fun to explore a new city. Point out the places you've discovered to a visitor. Repeat the correct response.

> ESEMPIO: Quel teatro. → Quel bel teatro.

1. ...   2. ...   3. ...   4. ...   5. ...   6. ...

**C.** A careless merchant is helping you to get a few things. She always holds up the wrong item. Tell her you want the other one. Repeat the correct response.

> ESEMPIO: Questi panini. → No, quei panini.

1. ...   2. ...   3. ...   4. ...   5. ...   6. ...

# Dialogo

Ascoltate attentamente il dialogo. Poi rispondete alle domande. (*Listen carefully to the dialogue. Then answer the questions.*) Feel free to go back and listen as many times as you need to.

| | |
|---|---|
| SIG. PEPE: | Beppino, Beppino! Siamo qui... come stai? |
| BEPPINO: | Bene! Ciao, zio! Ciao, zia! E Marcella? Sei tu Marcella? |
| VITTORIA: | Ma no, io non sono Marcella, sono Vittoria, l'amica di Marcella. |
| MARCELLA: | Marcella sono io. Ciao, Beppino, come stai? E Pietro? Pietro non c'è? |
| BEPPINO: | No, Pietro è a Roma; arriva lunedì. |
| SIG.RA PEPE: | Caro ragazzo! Come sei bello! Come stai? Sei stanco? Hai fame? |
| BEPPINO: | No, zia, non sono stanco e non ho fame; però ho sete. |
| SIG. PEPE: | C'è un bar qui vicino... Una Coca-Cola o una birra? |
| BEPPINO: | Una birra, grazie! |

You will hear four incomplete statements based on the dialogue. You will hear each statement twice. Circle the word or phrase that best completes each one.

1. Marcella Beppino     3. a Roma a Firenze

2. cugine amiche      4. ha fame ha sete

## Dettato

Sentirete tre volte un breve dettato. La prima volta, ascoltate attentamente. La seconda volta, scrivete quello che sentite. La terza volta, correggete quello che avete scritto. (*You will hear a short dictation three times. The first time, listen carefully. The second time, write down what you hear. The third time, correct what you've written.*)

_____

_____

_____

_____

_____

_____

## E ora ascoltiamo!

Listen to the police report and guess who the murderer is! Put an *X* next to the person who matches the description. You will hear the report twice.

MASSIMO SASSI SILVIA SCOTTI ALESSIO CORSINI

CAPITOLO

# 3

# Pronuncia:  The Sounds of the Letter **g**

As you learned in the *Capitolo preliminare,* the letter **g** represents two sounds:  [g] as in the English word *go* and [ǧ] as in the English word *giant*.

**A.** The sound [g].  This sound occurs when **g** is followed directly by **a, o, u, h,** or another consonant. *Ascoltate e ripetete:*

| | | |
|---|---|---|
| gatto | ghiaccio | ragù |
| gondola | grasso | vaghe |
| guidare | spiegare | |
| ghetto | agosto | |

The clusters **gl** and **gn** are exceptions to this rule.  Most of the time, **gl** is pronounced like the **ll** in the English word *million*.  The sound of **gn** is similar to the first **n** in the English word *onion*.  *Ascoltate e ripetete:*

| | | |
|---|---|---|
| gli | gnocchi | gnomo |
| sbagliato | spagnolo | figlio |

Contrast the single and double sound of [g]. *Ascoltate e ripetete:*

| | | |
|---|---|---|
| fuga / fugga | lego / leggo | trago / traggo |

**B.** The sound [ǧ].  This sound occurs when **g** is followed directly by **e** or **i**.  *Ascoltate e ripetete:*

| | | |
|---|---|---|
| gennaio | giorno | mangiare |
| giro | giusto | germinare |
| giapponese | biologia | |

Contrast the single and double sound of [ǧ]. *Ascoltate e ripetete:*

| | | |
|---|---|---|
| regia / reggia | agio / maggio | pagina / paggio |

**C.** Ascoltate e ripetete le frasi:

1. Ecco gli insegnanti di psicologia.
2. Lo spagnolo e l'inglese sono due lingue.
3. Gli ingegneri giapponesi arrivano in agosto.
4. Giugno e luglio sono due mesi meravigliosi.
5. Giovanna e Gabriella sono giovani.

# Vocabolario preliminare

You will hear five incomplete statements. You will hear each statement twice. Circle the word or phrase that best completes the statement you hear.

1. lo spagnolo      il francese
2. la matematica      la letteratura
3. informatica      giapponese

4. l'economia      la storia dell'arte
5. chimica      scienze politiche

# Grammatica

## A. Presente dei verbi in -are

**A.** Sentirete un brano (*passage*) dal vostro testo. Ripetete durante le pause. Attenzione all'intonazione!

LUCIANO: Noi siamo una famiglia d'insegnanti e di studenti: la mamma insegna matematica in una scuola media, papà è professore di francese, Gigi e Daniela frequentano le elementari ed io frequento l'università (studio medicina). Tutti studiamo e lavoriamo molto. Soltanto il gatto non studia e non lavora. Beato lui!

**B. Non paghiamo!** You and your friends can be cheapskates at times! Look at the people listed below and tell who doesn't pay when you go out for pizza. Repeat the correct response.

ESEMPIO:   Marco → Marco non paga.

1. tu    2. Marco e Paolo    3. tu e Paolo    4. noi    5. Franca    6. io

**C.** Professor Ghezzi makes the following statements about himself. You can't believe what he says! Respond as in the example, using the subject pronoun to emphasize your amazement. You will hear the correct response.

ESEMPIO:   Parlo sette lingue. → Lei parla sette lingue?

1. ...    2. ...    3. ...    4. ...    5. ...    6. ...

**D.** You will hear a series of sentences. Circle the subject to which the sentences refer.

1. questa ragazza      queste ragazze
2. io      lui
3. voi      tu

4. il signor Rossi      la signora Rossi
5. noi      loro
6. io      noi

**E.** You will hear six short sentences. You will hear each sentence twice. Circle the best English equivalent for each one.

1. Cristina isn't dancing.      Cristina isn't beautiful.
2. Do you speak gladly?      Do you pay gladly?
3. How well we sing!      How well they sing!
4. You don't learn much.      You don't speak much.
5. Here's the difficult word!      Here are the difficult words!
6. What do they give?      What do they do?

## B. **Andare, dare, fare** e **stare**

**A.** Sentirete un dialogo dal vostro testo. Ripetete durante le pause. Attenzione all'intonazione!

CRISTINA: Patrizia, tu e Cesare andate a casa di Marcella stasera per la festa in onore di Beppino?
PATRIZIA: Purtroppo no: io ho un brutto raffreddore e così sto a casa e vado a letto presto; Cesare lavora...
CRISTINA: Ah sì? E che cosa fa?
PATRIZIA: Dà lezioni di karatè e fa un sacco di soldi!

**B. Come vanno?** Take a look at the drawings and tell how these people are getting about. Use the pronouns or names you hear. Repeat the correct response.

ESEMPIO:

(Giulia) in Italia → Giulia va in Italia in aereo.

1.

all'università

2.

a Roma

3.

a casa

4.

in centro

5.

a Firenze

**C.** Your aunt has the wrong idea about all of your friends and relatives. Correct her, as in the example. Repeat the correct response.

 ESEMPIO: Fa fotografie Stefania? → No, non fa fotografie.

1. ...   2. ...   3. ...   4. ...   5. ...   6. ...

**D.** You have just arrived in a new city. Some people who live there are listed below. Ask them where they go to do the following things. Repeat the correct response.

 ESEMPIO: Carlo (ballare) → Dove vai a ballare?

1. Signori Binni            3. Pierino              5. Carlo e Anna
2. ragazzi                  4. Signora Lodi         6. Signor Rossi

# C. L'ora

**A. Che ore sono?** Answer, using the 12-hour clock and the expressions **di mattina, del pomeriggio, di sera,** or **di notte.** You will hear the correct response.

 ESEMPIO:

Sono le otto meno dieci di mattina.
(*o* Sono le sette e cinquanta di mattina.)

1.     2.     3.

4.     5.     6.

**B.** Luigi's watch is ten minutes fast. When he tells you the time, correct him, as in the example. Repeat the correct response.

 ESEMPIO: Sono le tre. → No, sono le tre meno dieci.

1. ...   2. ...   3. ...   4. ...   5. ...   6. ...

## D. Aggettivi possessivi

**A.** Sentirete un dialogo dal vostro testo. Ripetete durante le pause. Attenzione all'intonazione!

GIANNI: Chi è il tuo professore preferito?
ROBERTO: Be', veramente ho due professori preferiti: il professore di biologia e la professoressa d'italiano.
GIANNI: Perchè?
ROBERTO: Il professore di biologia è molto famoso: i suoi libri sono usati nelle università americane. La professoressa d'italiano è molto brava; apprezzo la sua pazienza e il suo senso dell'umorismo.

**B.** You are showing some visiting friends around campus. You see some of your friends and professors in the distance. Point them out, as in the example. Repeat the correct response.

ESEMPIO: amico → Ecco il mio amico!

1. ...   2. ...   3. ...   4. ...   5. ...

**C.** You and your housemates are cleaning up after a party. Following the example, tell them who owns these various objects. Repeat the correct response.

ESEMPIO: (Di chi sono questi bicchieri?) io → Sono i miei bicchieri.

1. noi                    3. io                    5. lei
2. voi                    4. tu                    6. loro

**D.** Your mother is very curious about some photos you are showing her. Answer her questions in the affirmative. You will hear the correct response.

ESEMPIO: È il cane di Marco? → Sì, è il suo cane.

1. ...   2. ...   3. ...   4. ...   5. ...

# Dialogo

Ascoltate attentamente il dialogo. Poi rispondete alle domande.

MARCELLA: Cari signori Verdi, come stanno? Ecco Beppino, il cugino americano!
SIG.RA VERDI: Ah, Lei arriva dal Texas, non è vero? E a Firenze cosa fa? Studia, lavora?
BEPPINO: Per ora faccio fotografie, ma ho intenzione di studiare architettura o di andare all'Accademia di Belle Arti.
SIG. VERDI: Ma bravo! Alla facoltà di architettura c'è un mio vecchio amico, il professor Gallo: insegna industrial design...

VITTORIA: Ora metto un disco e balliamo: va bene, Beppino?
BEPPINO: Benone! Ora balliamo e poi mangiamo. Ci sono tante cose buone!
MARCELLA: Un momento, Vittoria! Paolo e Mario hanno la chitarra e cantano bene...
VITTORIA: Suoni la chitarra anche tu, Beppino?
BEPPINO: Sì, suono e canto anch'io: country music...
MARCELLA: State zitti, per favore... Signore e signori, attenzione: concerto di musica folk con Paolo Rossi e Mario Casini, famosi cantautori toscani e Beppino il texano...

You will hear six statements based on the dialogue. You will hear each one twice. Circle *vero* if the statement is true or *falso* if it is false.

1. vero   falso          3. vero   falso          5. vero   falso

2. vero   falso          4. vero   falso          6. vero   falso

# Dettato

Sentirete tre volte un breve dettato. La prima volta, ascoltate attentamente. La seconda volta, scrivete quello che sentite. La terza volta, correggete quello che avete scritto.

_____

_____

_____

_____

_____

_____

# E ora ascoltiamo!

You will hear a description of Lisa and then six statements. You will hear everything twice. Circle *vero* or *falso*. Feel free to go back and listen to the description as many times as you need to.

1. vero   falso       3. vero   falso       5. vero   falso

2. vero   falso       4. vero   falso       6. vero   falso

CAPITOLO

# 4

## Pronuncia: The Sounds of the Letters sc

The combination **sc** represents two sounds: [sk] as in the English word *sky* and [š] as in the English word *shy*.

**A.** The sound [sk]. This sound occurs when **sc** is followed directly by **a, o, u, h,** or another consonant. *Ascoltate e ripetete:*

| | | |
|---|---|---|
| scandalo | schifo | tedeschi |
| sconto | scrive | discutere |
| scusa | fresca | |
| schema | pesche | |

**B.** The sound [š]. This sound occurs when **sc** is followed directly by **e** or **i**. *Ascoltate e ripetete:*

| | | |
|---|---|---|
| sciare | sciupare | sceriffo |
| scienza | scivolare | prosciutto |
| sciopero | scena | |

**C.** Ascoltate e ripetete le frasi:

1. Cos'è il «Gianni Schicchi»? È un'opera; io ho il disco.
2. Tosca esce con uno scultore tedesco.
3. Perchè non pulisci le scarpe?
4. Posso lasciare i pesci con il prosciutto?
5. Francesco preferisce sciare con questi sci.
6. «Capire fischi per fiaschi» significa capire una cosa per un'altra.

## Vocabolario preliminare

**Che cosa fanno?** Take a look at the drawings and tell how these people pass their spare time. Repeat the correct response.

ESEMPIO:

Mauro → Mauro ascolta dischi.

1.

Marta e Riccardo

2.

Nina

3.

Filippo

4.

Arturo e Gabriele

5.

Elena e Luisa

6.

Laura

# Grammatica

## A. Presente dei verbi in **-ere** e **-ire**

**A.** Sentirete un brano dal vostro testo. Ripetete durante le pause. Attenzione all'intonazione!

È una serata come tutte le altre in casa Bianchi: la mamma e la nonna guardano la televisione, papà legge il giornale (lui non guarda mai la televisione, preferisce leggere), lo zio Tony scrive una lettera, Luigino dorme, Franca e Sergio ascoltano un disco.

**B.** You and your friends' daily routines overlap to a great degree. Tell about your common activities, using the subjects you hear and **anche.** Repeat the correct response.

ESEMPIO:  Io leggo il giornale. (Marco) → Anche Marco legge il giornale.

1. ...   2. ...   3. ...   4. ...

ESEMPIO:  Io pulisco la casa. (tu) → Anche tu pulisci la casa.

1. ...   2. ...   3. ...   4. ...

ESEMPIO:  Non dormo abbastanza. (Gina) → Anche Gina non dorme abbastanza.

1. ...   2. ...   3. ...   4. ...

**C. Com'è la Sua giornata?** Answer the following questions about your own daily routine. You will hear a possible response.

    ESEMPIO:  Quante ore dorme? → Dormo otto ore.

1. ...    2. ...    3. ...    4. ...    5. ...

## B. Dire, uscire e venire; dovere, potere e volere

**A.** Some people are a little grumpy in the morning. Say who never says *Buon giorno*. Repeat the correct response.

    ESEMPIO:  Giulio → Giulio non dice mai «Buon giorno».

1. ...    2. ...    3. ...    4. ...    5. ...

**B.** Say what night of the week you and your friends go out. Repeat the correct response.

    ESEMPIO:  (noi) il sabato → Noi usciamo il sabato.

| | | |
|---|---|---|
| 1. il lunedì | | 4. il mercoledì |
| 2. la domenica | | 5. il venerdì |
| 3. il giovedì | | |

**C.** There is a departmental reception this week, and you think it's going to be boring. Explain that you and your friends are coming out of a sense of duty. You will hear the correct response.

    ESEMPIO:  Perchè vieni? → Vengo perchè devo venire.

1. ...    2. ...    3. ...    4. ...

**D.** Francesco cannot believe that people ever skip fun activities because they want to study. Set him straight, as in the example. You will hear the correct response.

    ESEMPIO:  Perchè non andate a ballare? → Non possiamo andare a ballare; vogliamo studiare.

1. ...    2. ...    3. ...    4. ...

## C. *Presente* + da + *espressioni di tempo*

**A.** Sentirete un brano dal vostro testo. Ripetete durante le pause. Attenzione all'intonazione!

RICCARDO: Ho un appuntamento con Paolo a mezzogiorno in piazza. Vogliamo andare a mangiare insieme. Io arrivo puntuale ma lui non c'è. Aspetto e aspetto, ma lui non viene... Finalmente, dopo un'ora, Paolo arriva e domanda: «Aspetti da molto tempo?» E io rispondo: «No, aspetto solo da un'ora!»

**B.** Using the information given below, tell how long you and your friends have engaged in these activities. Repeat the correct response.

    ESEMPIO:  (Da quanto tempo disegnate?) molto tempo → Disegniamo da molto tempo.

| | | |
|---|---|---|
| 1. un mese | | 4. un anno |
| 2. tre settimane | | 5. tre anni |
| 3. cinque anni | | |

**C.** Say how long you personally have been doing the following things. You will hear a possible response.

1. ...    2. ...    3. ...    4. ...    5. ...

## D. Interrogativi

**Marco l'affascinante** (*The Charming*)! You have many questions about the new student, Marco. Ask the questions that produced these answers. You will hear the correct response.

ESEMPIO: Marco ha dischi. → Che cosa ha Marco?

1. ... 2. ... 3. ... 4. ... 5. ...

# Dialogo

Ascoltate attentamente il dialogo. Poi rispondete alle domande.

MARCELLA: Vittoria, oggi finalmente arriva Pietro da Roma!
VITTORIA: L'amico di Beppino? E com'è questo Pietro?
MARCELLA: Mah, Beppino dice che è un ragazzo in gamba. Lui e Pietro sono vecchi amici.
VITTORIA: Arriva stamattina?
MARCELLA: No, questo pomeriggio. Viene in macchina con un'amica americana, una certa Geraldine.
VITTORIA: Chi è? La sua ragazza?
MARCELLA: Perchè non vieni a casa mia stasera? Così vedi Pietro e Geraldine…
VITTORIA: Mi dispiace, ma non posso. Devo studiare per l'esame di storia moderna.
MARCELLA: Povera Vittoria! Hai l'esame con il professor Biagi? Un vero pignolo! Vuole sapere tutte le date, tutti i nomi, tutti i minimi particolari!
VITTORIA: Sì, è vero, ma io non ho paura: ho una buona memoria. Ora vado in biblioteca a studiare; e tu, che fai?
MARCELLA: Io? Vado a lezione di karatè.
VITTORIA: Prendi lezioni di karatè? E da quanto tempo?
MARCELLA: Da due settimane. Ora devo andare. Ciao e… in bocca al lupo!
VITTORIA: Crepi!

You will hear six statements based on the dialogue. You will hear each one twice. Circle *vero* or *falso*.

1. vero   falso          3. vero   falso          5. vero   falso

2. vero   falso          4. vero   falso          6. vero   falso

# Dettato

Sentirete tre volte un breve dettato. La prima volta, ascoltate attentamente. La seconda volta, scrivete quello che sentite. La terza volta, correggete quello che avete scritto.

_____

_____

_____

_____

_____

_____

_____

# E ora ascoltiamo!

You will hear a passage about Paola and Carla and then five questions. You will hear everything twice. Circle the correct answer. Feel free to go back and listen to the passage as many times as you need to.

1. a Milano        a Firenze
2. il golf          l'aerobica
3. da un mese     da molto tempo

4. Carla        Paola
5. lingue       chimica

CAPITOLO

# 5

## Pronuncia: The Sounds of the Letter Combinations **qu** and **cu**

The combination **qu** corresponds to the sound [kʷ] as in the English word *quick.* The combination **cu** followed by another vowel has this same sound. (The pronoun **cui,** though, represents one common exception to this rule.)

**A.** Ascoltate e ripetete:

| | | |
|---|---|---|
| quasi | quota | nacqui |
| questo | cuore | piacque |
| qui | cuoio | |

**B.** Contrast the single and double sound of [kʷ]. Ascoltate e ripetete:

aquilone / acqua                                    quadro / soqquadro

**C.** Ascoltate e ripetete le frasi:

1. Mia cugina ha comprato cinque quadri qui.
2. Sono quasi le quattro e un quarto.
3. La qualità di quest'acqua è cattiva.
4. Dove mangiamo di solito quelle quaglie squisite? Qui?

## Vocabolario preliminare

**Che cosa prendiamo?** You will hear five incomplete statements. You will hear each statement twice. Circle the word or phrase that best completes each one.

1. il limone           il pomodoro

2. il vino            il succo di carota

3. lo zucchero         le noccioline

4. il ghiaccio         la panna

5. il succo di pompelmo     la cioccolata

# Grammatica

## A. Preposizioni articolate

**A.** Sentirete un brano dal vostro testo. Ripetete durante le pause:

Le vie e le piazze delle città italiane sono sempre affollate: c'è molta gente nei caffè, all'interno o seduta ai tavolini all'aperto, nei negozi, per le strade, sugli autobus, sui filobus... E gli stranieri domandano: «Ma non lavora questa gente?»

**B. Niente ghiaccio!** One of your housemates is always using up the ice. Tell where it is this time, as in the example. Repeat the correct response.

　　ESEMPIO:　succo di pomodoro → Il ghiaccio è nel succo di pomodoro.

1. ...　2. ...　3. ...　4. ...　5. ...

**C. A che ora?** A friend of yours often gets mixed up about the time you agreed to meet. Tell him you meant *before* the hour, not *on* the hour. You will hear the correct response.

　　ESEMPIO:　Alle cinque? → No, prima delle cinque!

1. ...　2. ...　3. ...　4. ...　5. ...

**D.** Another friend confuses "coming" with "going." Straighten him out! You will hear the correct response.

　　ESEMPIO:　Vengono dallo stadio? → No, vanno allo stadio!

1. ...　2. ...　3. ...　4. ...　5. ...

## B. Il passato prossimo con **avere**

**A. Chi ha parlato italiano?** You and your fellow students have been talking up a storm in Italian. Mention everyone who has spoken Italian today. Repeat the correct response.

　　ESEMPIO:　Roberto → Roberto ha parlato italiano.

1. ...　2. ...　3. ...　4. ...　5. ...　6. ...

**B. Cosa hanno fatto?** Look over the drawings and tell what these people have done. The infinitives of the verbs are listed below. Repeat the correct response.

　　ESEMPIO:

(la signora Gilli) ordinare →
La signora Gilli ha ordinato le paste.

1.

scrivere

2.

mangiare

3.

comprare

4.

bere

5.

fare

**C. Già fatto!** Explain why some people don't do certain things. They have already done them! You will hear the correct response.

ESEMPIO: Perchè non mangia Barbara? → Perchè ha già mangiato.

1. ...   2. ...   3. ...   4. ...   5. ...   6. ...

## C.  Il passato prossimo con **essere**

**A.** Sentirete un dialogo dal vostro testo. Ripetete durante le pause:

MIRELLA:   Sei andata al cinema ieri sera, Carla?
CARLA:   No, Mirella. Gli altri sono andati al cinema; io sono stata a casa e ho studiato tutta la santa serata!

**B. Tutti arrivati!** Say how punctual you, your classmates, and your instructor are. You all made it to class at nine sharp (**in punto**)! Repeat the correct response.

ESEMPIO:   io → Io sono arrivata alle nove in punto.

1. ...   2. ...   3. ...   4. ...   5. ...

**C.** Explain why some people don't do certain things. They have never done them! You will hear the correct response.

ESEMPIO: Perchè non vanno in aeroplano? → Perchè non sono mai andati in aeroplano!

1. ...  2. ...  3. ...  4. ...  5. ...  6. ...

**D.** Circle *presente* or *passato* to indicate whether the sentences or questions you hear are in the present or the past tense. You will hear each item twice.

1. presente     passato

2. presente     passato

3. presente     passato

4. presente     passato

5. presente     passato

**E.** Indicate whether the sentences you hear refer to a singular or plural subject by circling *singolare* or *plurale*. You will hear each item twice.

1. singolare     plurale

2. singolare     plurale

3. singolare     plurale

4. singolare     plurale

5. singolare     plurale

**F.** You will hear five short sentences or questions. Circle the best English equivalent for each. You will hear each one twice.

1. You have no milk.        You haven't read.

2. Who came home?           Who saw the house?

3. They said these things.  They gave these things.

4. They did this.           This is a fact.

5. I didn't sleep well.     He didn't sleep well.

# D. Lasciare, partire, uscire e andare via

**A. Sono usciti!** Explain why the following people are not in. They have all gone out! Repeat the correct response.

ESEMPIO: La signora non c'è? → È uscita.

1. ...   2. ...   3. ...   4. ...

**B. Cosa fa Carla?** Your housemate is peppering you with questions about your new neighbor, Carla. Answer with the information given below. Repeat the correct response.

ESEMPIO: (Quando è partita per l'aeroporto?) molto presto →
         È partita per l'aeroporto molto presto.

1. alle cinque
2. il giornale
3. venerdì

4. Michele
5. no

**C.** Answer each question you hear using the appropriate form of the verb *to leave*. Repeat the correct response.

ESEMPIO:

Cosa fa Silvio? → Silvio lascia il cane in macchina.

1.

2.

3.

4.

5.

# Dialogo

Ascoltate attentamente il dialogo dal vostro testo. Poi rispondete alle domande.

BEPPINO: Tu hai soldi? Ho lasciato il portafoglio a casa!

PIETRO: Non ho una lira: ho solo traveler's checks. Ma ho dimenticato il passaporto.

BEPPINO: Che stupidi! E ora come facciamo? Chi paga?

PIETRO: Buona! Che fame! Stamattina ho dormito fino a tardi e non ho avuto il tempo di fare colazione.

BEPPINO: Ma che fai? Vuoi finire in prigione?

PIETRO: Figurati! Per due paste!

GERALDINE: Salve, ragazzi, come va?

BEPPINO: Va male: non abbiamo soldi per pagare le paste.

GERALDINE: Mi dispiace, ma neanch'io ho un soldo. Non sono ancora andata in banca.

BEPPINO: E ora come facciamo? Chi paga?

PIETRO: Guarda chi c'è: c'è Vittoria!

|  |  |
|---|---|
| VITTORIA: | Ragazzi, ho finito ora l'esame di storia. |
| BEPPINO: | Com'è andato? |
| VITTORIA: | Bene! Ho preso ventotto! |
| BEPPINO, PIETRO E GERALDINE: | Brava! Congratulazioni! |
| PIETRO: | Ora dobbiamo festeggiare il successo: Vittoria paga per tutti! |

You will hear six statements based on the dialogue. You will hear each one twice. Circle *vero* or *falso*.

1. vero    falso          3. vero    falso          5. vero    falso

2. vero    falso          4. vero    falso          6. vero    falso

# Dettato

Sentirete tre volte un breve dettato. La prima volta, ascoltate attentamente. La seconda volta, scrivete quello che sentite. La terza volta, correggete quello che avete scritto.

_____

_____

_____

_____

_____

_____

# E ora ascoltiamo!

You will hear three short conversations, each one twice. Circle the place where each one is taking place.

1. in un taxi          in un aereo

2. in un ristorante          in un bar

3. in un ufficio          in un autobus

CAPITOLO

# 6

## Pronuncia:  The Sounds of the Letter **z**

The letter **z** represents two sounds:  [ć] as in the English word *bats* and [ź] as in the English word *pads*.

**A.** At the beginning of a word, **z** is pronounced either [ć] or [ź] according to the regional usage.  Most Italians use [ź].  *Ascoltate e ripetete:*

| | |
|---|---|
| zampa | zona |
| zero | zucchero |
| zitto | |

**B.** In medial position, **z** may be pronounced as either single or double [ć] or [ź].  *Ascoltate e ripetete:*

The sound [ź]:
| | |
|---|---|
| azalea | mezzogiorno |
| ozelot | azzurro |
| azimut | |

The sound [ć]:
| | |
|---|---|
| alzare | mazzo |
| differenze | sozzura |
| Lazio | |

**C.** Ascoltate e ripetete le frasi:

1. Sai che differenza c'è tra *colazione* e *pranzo?*
2. Alla stazione di Venezia vendono pizze senza mozzarella.
3. Conosci molte ragazze con gli occhi azzurri?
4. A mezzogiorno ho lezione di zoologia.
5. C'è un negozio di calzature in Piazza Indipendenza.

## Vocabolario preliminare

**E ora mangiamo!**  You will hear five incomplete statements.  You will hear each statement twice.  Circle the word or phrase that best completes each one.

1. ha una fame da lupi      odia i dolci

2. è vegetariana      ha paura d'ingrassare

3. ci sono le olive      c'è il minestrone

4. un contorno      un primo piatto

5. la panna      il pesce

# Grammatica

## A. Pronomi diretti

**A.** Sentirete un dialogo dal vostro testo. Ripetete durante le pause:

ANNAMARIA: Clara, in casa tua chi lava i piatti?
CLARA: Che domanda! Li lava Benny!
ANNAMARIA: E chi pulisce la casa?
CLARA: La pulisce Benny!
ANNAMARIA: E chi fa il letto ogni mattina?
CLARA: Lo fa Benny!
ANNAMARIA: E la cucina? E le altre faccende?
CLARA: Le fa Benny! Le fa Benny!
ANNAMARIA: Che marito adorabile! Come deve amarti Benny... E tu che fai tutto il giorno?
CLARA: Io lavoro con i computer. Ho creato Benny!

**B. Ma che memoria!** You have a great memory. Tell your friend you remember all these people and places. Repeat the correct response.

    ESEMPIO: Ricordi Franco? → Sì, lo ricordo.

1. ...    2. ...    3. ...    4. ...    5. ...    6. ...

**C. Perchè no?** Explain to your friend that you don't do these things because you are unable to. Repeat the correct response.

    ESEMPIO: Perchè non lo fate? → Perchè non possiamo farlo.

1. ...    2. ...    3. ...    4. ...    5. ...    6. ...

## B. Conoscere e sapere

**A. Certo che li conosco!** A friend asks you whether you know certain people. You reply that you know them well. Repeat the correct response.

    ESEMPIO: Conosci Vittoria? → Sì, la conosco bene!

1. ...    2. ...    3. ...    4. ...    5. ...

**B. Ma che bravi!** You and your friends have many talents. Look at the drawings and tell who knows how to do what. Repeat the correct response.

    ESEMPIO:

(Piero e Anna) ballare → Piero e Anna sanno ballare il tango.

1.

fare

2.

andare

3.

lavorare

4.

leggere

5.

suonare

**C. Sapere o conoscere?** You are quite proud of all the people and things little Tonino knows. Tell about his accomplishments using either **conoscere** or **sapere.** Repeat the correct response.

ESEMPI:    dov'è Roma → Sa dov'è Roma.

il ragazzo di Laura → Conosce il ragazzo di Laura.

1. fare il letto
2. la nostra città
3. la professoressa Neri

4. coniugare i verbi
5. che cos'è l'informatica

# C. Pronomi indiretti

**A.** Sentirete un dialogo dal vostro testo. Ripetete durante le pause.

ALBERTO: Siamo quasi a Natale: cosa regaliamo quest'anno alla nonna?
ELISABETTA: Semplice: le regaliamo il dolce tradizionale, il panettone.
ALBERTO: Benissimo! E allo zio Augusto?
ELISABETTA: Perchè non gli diamo un libro di cucina? Cucinare è il suo hobby preferito.
ALBERTO: Buona idea! E tu, cosa vuoi?
ELISABETTA: Puoi comprarmi una macchina per fare la pasta: così ci facciamo delle belle spaghettate!

**B. Quando?** Your mother is after you to keep in touch with your relatives. Using the expressions listed below, tell her when you're planning to do so. Repeat the correct response.

> ESEMPIO: (Quando telefoni alla zia?) domani → Le telefono domani.

1. stasera
2. questo pomeriggio
3. tra un'ora

4. dopo gli esami
5. sabato mattina

**C. Come mai?** Your roommate's actions seem out of character today. React to her statements using the correct direct or indirect object pronoun. Repeat the correct response.

> ESEMPIO: Ho scritto al professore. → Come mai gli hai scritto?

1. ... 2. ... 3. ... 4. ... 5. ...

# D. Piacere

**A.** Sentirete un brano dal vostro testo. Ripetete durante le pause:

Gianni e Gianna hanno gusti completamente diversi. Per esempio, a Gianni piacciono i ravioli, a Gianna piacciono le lasagne. A Gianni piace la cucina messicana, a Gianna piace la cucina cinese. A Gianni piace la carne, Gianna preferisce il pesce. A Gianni piace fumare, Gianna odia le sigarette… Chissà perchè si sono sposati!

**B. I Suoi gusti.** Tell about your own personal likes and dislikes. You will hear a possible response.

> ESEMPIO: Le piacciono i salumi? → Sì, mi piacciono. (o No, non mi piacciono.)

1. ... 2. ... 3. ... 4. ... 5. ...

**C. Gli piace?** Take a look at the drawings and say if the people like or dislike the foods mentioned. You will hear the correct response.

ESEMPIO:

A Giulio piacciono le patatine? → Sì, gli piacciono.

1.

2.

3.

4.    5.

**D. Un nuovo ristorante.** A group of people tried a new neighborhood restaurant last night. Ask them how they liked various items on the menu. Repeat the correct response.

ESEMPIO:  Ho mangiato i tortellini. → Ti sono piaciuti?

1. ...   2. ...   3. ...   4. ...   5. ...

## E. Accordo del participio passato nel passato prossimo

**Già fatto!** Your mother reminds you about things you have to do. Tell her you've already done them. Repeat the correct response.

ESEMPIO:  Devi comprare il giornale. → L'ho già comprato.

1. ...   2. ...   3. ...   4. ...   5. ...   6. ...

# Dialogo

Ascoltate il dialogo dal vostro testo. Poi rispondete alle domande.

MARCELLA:  Cara zietta, come stai? Sempre in gamba, vero? Ti ho portato finalmente Beppino, il nostro grande texano.

ZIA LUISA:  Mamma mia, come sei lungo! Proprio un bel ragazzo. Ma un po' magro: hai bisogno d'ingrassare. Ti piacciono i tortellini al sugo?

BEPPINO:  Veramente non li ho mai mangiati; ho mangiato le lasagne, i ravioli e naturalmente gli spaghetti, ma non i tortellini.

MARCELLA:  Sono una specialità di Bologna, ma li facciamo bene anche in Toscana. Zietta, ho una fame da lupi: cosa ci hai preparato di buono?

ZIA LUISA:  Oh, le solite cose: roba semplice ma genuina. Per cominciare, crostini di fegatini di pollo; poi i tortellini, e dopo i tortellini, pollo e coniglio arrosto con patate al forno e insalata; e per concludere, la crostata e il caffè.

MARCELLA:  Hai sentito, Beppino? Io, dopo un pranzo così, non entro più nei jeans che mi hai regalato...

BEPPINO:  Zia, questa crostata mi piace molto: mi dai la ricetta, per favore?

ZIA LUISA:  Volentieri, ma tu sai cucinare?

BEPPINO:  Sicuro! Non voglio morire di fame: la mia ragazza non sa cucinare e io mi devo arrangiare.

ZIA LUISA:  Che bravi questi giovanotti che sanno cucinare! Ai miei tempi gli uomini non sapevano fare nulla.

You will hear five incomplete statements based on the dialogue, each one twice. Circle the word or phrase that best completes each one.

1. un po' grasso          un po' magro

2. di Bologna             di Firenze

3. molto                  poco

4. non piacciono          piacciono

5. ha la ragazza          non ha la ragazza

# Dettato

Sentirete tre volte un breve dettato. La prima volta, ascoltate attentamente. La seconda volta, scrivete quello che sentite. La terza volta, correggete quello che avete scritto.

_____

_____

_____

_____

_____

_____

_____

_____

# E ora ascoltiamo!

You will hear a conversation between Monica and Teresa. You will hear everything twice. Circle *vero* or *falso*.

1. vero     falso                    4. vero     falso

2. vero     falso                    5. vero     falso

3. vero     falso

CAPITOLO
# 7

# Pronuncia: The Sounds of the Letters l and gl

The letter **l** has a sound similar to the *l* in the English word *love*. Unlike the *l* in *alter* or *will*, however, the Italian [l] is a "clear" sound, articulated toward the front of the mouth, never in the back.

**A.** Ascoltate e ripetete:

| | | |
|---|---|---|
| lavarsi | loro | nocciolina |
| leggere | lunedì | salutare |
| lira | regalare | |

**B.** As you already learned in *Capitolo 3*, the sound of **gl** is different from the sound of **l**. Contrast the sounds in the following pairs of words. *Ascoltate e ripetete:*

| | |
|---|---|
| palliativo / paglia | belli / begli |
| veliero / veglie | olio / aglio |

**C.** Ascoltate e ripetete le frasi:

1. Come balla bene la moglie di Guglielmo! Glielo voglio dire.
2. Mi hai dato un biglietto da mille o da duemila?
3. Fa caldo a Milano in luglio?
4. Ecco il portafoglio di mio figlio.
5. Quella ragazza è alta e snella.
6. Vogliono il tè col latte o col limone?

# Vocabolario preliminare

You will hear five incomplete statements. You will hear each statement twice. Circle the word or phrase that best completes each one.

1. lavarmi          laurearmi

2. divertirci        diplomarci

3. vestirti          metterti

4. vi sentite male    vi sentite bene

5. si sono fermati qui   si sono sposati

# Grammatica

## A. Verbi riflessivi

**A.** Sentirete un dialogo dal vostro testo. Ripetete durante le pause:

SIG.RA ROSSI:    Nino è un ragazzo pigro: ogni mattina si sveglia tardi e non ha tempo di lavarsi e fare colazione. Si alza presto solo la domenica per andare in palestra a giocare al pallone.

SIG.RA VERDI:    Ho capito: a scuola si annoia e in palestra si diverte.

**B. Ci alziamo presto!** Using the subject you hear, tell who are early risers. Repeat the correct response.

    ESEMPIO:   noi → Noi ci alziamo presto.

1. ...   2. ...   3. ...   4. ...   5. ...

**C.** You will hear two sentences. You will hear each pair twice. Indicate which sentence contains a reflexive verb.

1. a    b                 4. a    b

2. a    b                 5. a    b

3. a    b

**D. Cos'ha fatto oggi?** Tell about your day. You will hear a possible response.

    ESEMPIO:   Come si sente oggi? → Oggi mi sento molto bene.

1. ...   2. ...   3. ...   4. ...   5. ...

## B. Costruzione reciproca

**A. Tutti si conoscono bene!** Tell about people who know each other well. Repeat the correct response.

    ESEMPIO:   noi → Noi ci conosciamo bene.

1. ...   2. ...   3. ...   4. ...

**B.** Due to a quarrel, some people didn't say "hello" to each other at the latest party. Tell who, as in the example. Repeat the correct response.

    ESEMPIO:   voi due → Voi due non vi siete salutati.

1. ...   2. ...   3. ...   4. ...

**C. Davide e Serena.** Davide and Serena are a devoted couple. Take a look at the drawings and tell what they are doing, after you hear the item number. You will hear the correct response.

    ESEMPIO:

Davide e Serena si guardano.

1.    2.    3.

4.    5.

## C. Possessivi con termini di parentela

**A. Non ricordo!** You're not very good with names or faces. Tell your friend you don't remember her relatives. Repeat the correct response.

ESEMPIO:   padre → Non ricordo tuo padre.

1. ...   2. ...   3. ...   4. ...   5. ...   6. ...

**B. Parliamo della famiglia!** You will hear five incomplete statements. You will hear each statement twice. Circle the answer that best completes each one.

1. la loro zia          la loro cugina          4. il mio nonno          la mia nonna

2. mia nipote          mio nipote          5. di mia figlia          dei miei nonni

3. le sue cugine          le sue nonne

## D. Numeri superiori a cento

Write down in figures the numbers you hear. You will hear each number twice. The answers appear at the end of this manual.

ESEMPIO:   millenovecentonovanta → 1990

1. _____   3. _____   5. _____

2. _____   4. _____   6. _____

# Dialogo

Ascoltate il dialogo dal vostro testo. Poi rispondete alle domande.

MIRELLA: Ciao, Pietro, sei pronto per uscire?

PIETRO: Figurati, sono ancora a letto!

MIRELLA: Ma come? Non ti sei ancora alzato, lavato e fatto la barba? Non hai fatto colazione?

PIETRO: Sono appena le otto e poi lo sai che ho fatto tardi ieri sera. Ma tu, ti svegli sempre così presto?

MIRELLA: Ma come, non ti ricordi che abbiamo un appuntamento questa mattina?

PIETRO: Dove e con chi?

MIRELLA: Dobbiamo andare dal dottor Bottino, il dentista. Abbiamo fissato l'appuntamento venti giorni fa!

PIETRO: Ah, è vero! Come sono smemorato! Ma, lo sai che ho paura dei dentisti.

MIRELLA: Che fifone! Il dottor Bottino è altamente qualificato. Si è specializzato ad Amsterdam. Sei in buone mani.

PIETRO: Va bene, va bene. Faccio in un minuto.

MIRELLA: Prendo l'automobile e sono a casa tua fra venti minuti.

PIETRO: D'accordo, allora!

DOTTORE: Avanti, si accomodi. Ah, Lei è il giovane americano di New York. La signorina mi ha parlato di Lei.

PIETRO: Sì, buon giorno, dottore; sa, io ho sempre avuto paura dei dentisti.

MIRELLA: Grande e grosso com'è, non è una vergogna, dottore?

DOTTORE: Ma su, non deve preoccuparsi! Ho fatto pratica in America. Lei, qui, è come a casa Sua!

You will hear eight statements based on the dialogue. You will hear each one twice. Circle *vero* or *falso*.

1. vero    falso          4. vero    falso          7. vero    falso

2. vero    falso          5. vero    falso          8. vero    falso

3. vero    falso          6. vero    falso

# Dettato

Sentirete tre volte un breve dettato. La prima volta, ascoltate attentamente. La seconda volta, scrivete quello che sentite. La terza volta, correggete quello che avete scritto.

_____

_____

_____

_____

_____

_____

_____

# E ora ascoltiamo!

You will hear a conversation between Maurizio and Elisabetta and then five statements. You will hear everything twice. Circle *vero* or *falso*.

1. vero    falso

2. vero    falso

3. vero    falso

4. vero    falso

5. vero    falso

CAPITOLO

# 8

# Pronuncia: The Sounds of the Letters **m** and **n**

**A.** The letter **m** is pronounced like *m* in the English word *mime. Ascoltate e ripetete:*

marito                                              moto
mese                                               musica
minuti

Contrast the single and double sound of [m]. *Ascoltate e ripetete:*

m'ama    mamma              some    somme                    fumo    fummo

**B.** The letter **n** is pronounced like *n* in the English word *nine. Ascoltate e ripetete:*

naso                                               noioso
neve                                               numeroso
nipoti

Contrast the single and double sound of [n]. *Ascoltate e ripetete:*

la luna    l'alunna                              noni    nonni
cane       canne                                 sano    sanno

**C.** As you learned in *Capitolo 3,* the sound of the letters **gn** is different from the sound of the letter **n.** Contrast the sounds in the following pairs of words. *Ascoltate e ripetete:*

campana    campagna          anello    agnello                    sono    sogno

**D.** Ascoltate e ripetete le frasi:

1. Guglielmo Agnelli è un ingegnere di Foligno.
2. Il bambino è nato in giugno.
3. Dammi un anello, non un agnello!
4. Buon Natale, nonna Virginia.
5. Anna è la moglie di mio figlio Antonio.

# Vocabolario preliminare

**I rapporti familiari.** You will hear five incomplete statements, each one twice. Circle the word or phrase that best completes each one.

1. mio genero                    mio cognato

2. non è nubile                   non è uno scapolo

3. di tua moglie        di tua sorella

4. vedova               vedovo

5. ha divorziato        è solo separato

# Grammatica

## A. Imperfetto

**A.** Sentirete un dialogo dal vostro testo. Ripetete durante le pause:

LUIGINO:   Papà, mi racconti una favola?
    PAPÀ:   Volentieri! C'era una volta una bambina che si chiamava Cappuccetto Rosso perchè portava
             sempre una mantella rossa col cappuccio. Viveva vicino a un bosco con la mamma...
LUIGINO:   Papà, perchè mi racconti sempre la stessa storia?
    PAPÀ:   Perchè conosco solo una storia!

**B. Troppi gelati!** Tell why you and your friends put on weight during your year abroad—you lived down the street from a great *gelateria* and overindulged. Repeat the correct response.

    ESEMPIO:   io → Io mangiavo sempre gelati.

1. ...    2. ...    3. ...    4. ...    5. ...

**C. Davide e Serena.** Davide and Serena were a devoted couple but . . . alas, no more. Restate Davide's statements in the *imperfetto*. Repeat the correct response.

    ESEMPIO:   Io le porto sempre i fiori. → Io le portavo sempre i fiori.

1. ...    2. ...    3. ...    4. ...    5. ...

**D. Tante volte!** When Simonetta asks if you ever did these things in Italy, tell her sure (**certo**)—you used to do them every day. Repeat the correct response.

    ESEMPIO:   Hai mai visto il duomo (*cathedral*)? → Certo, vedevo il duomo tutti i giorni.

1. ...    2. ...    3. ...    4. ...    5. ...

## B. Imperfetto e passato prossimo

**A.** Sentirete un brano dal vostro testo. Ripetete durante le pause:

Era una bella giornata: il sole splendeva e gli uccelli cantavano nel parco. Marco si sentiva felice perchè aveva un appuntamento con una ragazza che aveva conosciuto la sera prima. Purtroppo, però, la ragazza non è venuta; il tempo è cambiato ed ha cominciato a piovere. Marco è tornato a casa tutto bagnato e di cattivo umore.

**B. Non hanno potuto.** It's been a tough week. After you hear each item number, explain that you and your friends were unable to do what you wanted to do. Repeat the correct response.

    ESEMPIO:   le ragazze / venire → Le ragazze volevano venire, ma non hanno potuto.

1. noi / giocare a tennis                     4. tu e Gina / fare l'aerobica
2. tu / andare al museo                      5. io / divertirmi
3. Carlo / studiare

**C.** Giancarlo is telling you what he did yesterday. Say that those are all things you and your brothers and sisters used to do as children (**da piccolo/a/e/i**). You will hear the correct response.

> ESEMPIO: (Ieri ho mangiato molta pizza.) anche mia sorella →
> Anche mia sorella da piccola mangiava molta pizza.

1. anche mio fratello
2. anche le mie sorelle
3. anche i miei fratelli

4. anche noi
5. anch'io

## C. Trapassato

**Già fatto!** Explain that you and your friends didn't do these things because you had already done them. Repeat the correct response.

> ESEMPIO: Perchè non hai mangiato? → Non ho mangiato perchè avevo già mangiato.

1. ...   2. ...   3. ...   4. ...   5. ...

## D. **Dire, parlare** e **raccontare**

**A. Amici chiacchieroni** (*chatterbox*)! Your friends never keep quiet, and this makes for great parties! After you hear each item number, use **parlare** in the *passato prossimo* to tell about the various conversations at the latest party! Repeat the correct response.

> ESEMPIO: Francesca / di cinema → Francesca ha parlato di cinema.

1. tu / a mio fratello
2. loro / con mia nuora
3. io / dei miei studi

4. Carmela / italiano e spagnolo
5. voi due / di sport

**B. Dai parenti.** You attended a family gathering this weekend. After you hear each item number, tell what everyone was saying or talking about. Complete the sentence with the proper form of **dire, parlare** or **raccontare** in the *imperfetto*. Repeat the correct response.

> ESEMPIO: Stefania / molte cose interessanti → Stefania diceva molte cose interessanti.

1. il nonno Carlo / favole
2. tu / del tuo lavoro
3. i bambini / «Ciao» a tutti

4. mia suocera / inglese
5. io / un mio sogno
6. voi / di musica

## E. Suffissi per nomi e aggettivi

**A.** Holly does not understand suffixes in Italian. Answer her questions. You will hear the correct response.

> ESEMPIO: Una parolaccia è una bella parola o una brutta parola? → È una brutta parola.

1. ...   2. ...   3. ...   4. ...   5. ...

**B.** Take a look at each pair of drawings and circle the one that is indicated. You will hear each statement twice.

ESEMPIO: Ho ricevuto una letterona! →

a.

(b.)

1. a.

b.

2. a.

b.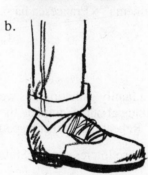

3. a.

b.

4. a.

b.

5. a.  b.

# Dialogo

Ascoltate il dialogo dal vostro testo. Poi rispondete alle domande.

VITTORIA: Hai foto della tua famiglia e della tua casa?
BEPPINO: Certo! Ora vado a prenderle.

BEPPINO: Ecco mio padre, mia madre e mia sorella Elena. Ed ecco la nostra casa e i miei due cani.
VITTORIA: E questo ragazzo chi è?
BEPPINO: Non mi riconosci?
VITTORIA: No davvero! Mamma mia, com'eri brutto! Quanti anni avevi?
BEPPINO: Grazie tanto! Avevo quattordici anni.
VITTORIA: No, non mi piaci in questa foto. Hai l'aria scema. E cosa facevi a quattordici anni?
BEPPINO: Boh, niente di speciale: andavo a scuola, ma non studiavo molto. Avevo insegnanti molto noiosi. Mi piacevano gli sport: giocavo a baseball e a tennis, e andavo a nuotare in piscina. Ah sì, suonavo anche la chitarra e cantavo. E tu, che facevi a quattordici anni?
VITTORIA: Anch'io andavo a scuola e mi annoiavo. Frequentavo anche una scuola di ballo; mi piaceva tanto ballare. Sognavo di diventare una grande ballerina…
BEPPINO: E poi, cos'è successo? Perchè non hai continuato?
VITTORIA: Perchè ho capito che non ero brava abbastanza. Ma non parliamo di malinconie! Devo tornare a casa: m'accompagni?
BEPPINO: Volentieri! Ma prima ti faccio una foto. La luce è proprio giusta e hai l'aria molto romantica.
VITTORIA: Una foto per il tuo album? Una foto per i tuoi amici e… le tue amiche del Texas? «Ecco una mia amica di Firenze; si chiamava Vittoria… era carina…»
BEPPINO: Vittoria, ti prego!
VITTORIA: No, no, andiamo. E poi la luce è andata via.

You will hear seven statements based on the dialogue. You will hear each one twice. Circle *vero* or *falso*.

1. vero    falso          5. vero    falso

2. vero    falso          6. vero    falso

3. vero    falso          7. vero    falso

4. vero    falso

# Dettato

Sentirete tre volte un breve dettato. La prima volta, ascoltate attentamente. La seconda volta, scrivete quello che sentite. La terza volta, correggete quello che avete scritto.

_____

_____

_____

_____

_____

_____

_____

_____

_____

# E ora ascoltiamo!

You will hear a conversation between Daniela and Giuseppe and then five statements. You will hear everything twice. Circle *vero* or *falso*.

1. vero    falso          4. vero    falso

2. vero    falso          5. vero    falso

3. vero    falso

CAPITOLO

# 9

## Pronuncia:  The Sounds of the Letter **r**

The sound of the letter **r** in Italian is completely different from English. The Italian **r** is pronounced with the tip of the tongue vibrating against the alveolar ridge—right behind your upper teeth.

**A.** Ascoltate e ripetete:

| | | |
|---|---|---|
| raccontare | romantico | mare |
| regalato | russo | proprio |
| riporta | arancia | |

**B.** Pay particular attention to the combination **tr** and to the sound of **r** in final position. *Ascoltate e ripetete:*

| | | |
|---|---|---|
| strada | centro | dir |
| treno | bar | amor |
| canestri | per | |

**C.** Contrast the single and double sound of [r]. *Ascoltate e ripetete:*

| | |
|---|---|
| sera / serra | cori / corri |
| spore / porre | caro / carro |

**D.** Ascoltate e ripetete le frasi:

1. La loro sorella preferisce vestirsi di marrone.
2. Trentatrè triestini tornavano da Trieste trotterellando.
3. Verrà stasera? Sì, ma telefonerà prima di venire.
4. Credo che preferirebbe comprare le arance dal fruttivendolo.
5. Corro perchè sono in ritardo per le prove del coro.

## Vocabolario preliminare

**Viva lo sport!**  You will hear five questions, each one twice.  Circle the correct answer or answers.

| 1. | pallacanestro | pattinaggio | ginnastica | tennis |
|---|---|---|---|---|
| 2. | sci | maratona | ciclismo | calcio |
| 3. | sci nautico | baseball | nuoto | jogging |
| 4. | baseball | equitazione | footing | basket |
| 5. | maratona | football | calcio | pattinaggio |

# Grammatica

## A. Pronomi tonici

**A.** Sentirete un dialogo dal vostro testo. Ripetete durante le pause:

MARINA: Riccardo, non sei venuto alla partita di pallacanestro? Abbiamo vinto: sessantotto a sessantacinque!

RICCARDO: Ma sì che son venuto! Non mi hai visto? Ti ho guardato tutta la serata!

MARINA: A dire la verità, ho visto te... ma tu non mi guardavi! Parlavi con Carlo e Stefania!

RICCARDO: Ma che dici! Non ho fatto altro che guardare te. Ho parlato con loro solo per dire come sei brava!

**B. Di ritorno.** You have just returned from Italy, and your mom wants to know if you managed to contact all your relatives there. Reassure her, as in the example. Repeat the correct response.

ESEMPIO: Gli hai scritto? → Sì, ho scritto proprio a lui.

1. ...   2. ...   3. ...   4. ...   5. ...

**C.** Your younger brother is asking you questions. Answer, using disjunctive pronouns. Repeat the correct response.

ESEMPIO: Esci con Mario? → Sì, esco con lui.

1. ...   2. ...   3. ...   4. ...   5. ...   6. ...

## B. Comparativi

**A. Una bella famiglia.** Everyone in your family got his or her good looks from your grandmother. Reminisce with them, as in the example. You will hear the correct response.

ESEMPIO: La zia Marcella → La zia Marcella era bella come la nonna.

1. ...   2. ...   3. ...   4. ...

**B. Il pattinaggio.** Describe how difficult skating is. Substitute the word or expression you hear. Repeat the correct response.

ESEMPIO: calcio → Il pattinaggio è più difficile del calcio.

1. ...   2. ...   3. ...   4. ...

**C.** Take a look at the following drawing and answer each question you hear. You will hear each question twice. You will hear the correct response.

GIORGIO   NINO   PIA   ROSA

    ESEMPIO:   Chi è meno alta di Giorgio? → Rosa è meno alta di Giorgio.

1. ...   2. ...   3. ...   4. ...   5. ...

**D.** After each comparison, you will hear a question. Circle the best answer. You will hear each item twice.

1. Luca      suo cugino            3. mia cognata      mio cognato

2. Piero    Luigi                     4. meno difficile      più difficile

# C.  Superlativi

**A. Claudio lo straordinario!** Claudio is one exceptional fellow. Tell how he stands out in his family, as in the example. Repeat the correct response.

    ESEMPIO:   simpatico → È il ragazzo più simpatico della famiglia.

1. ...   2. ...   3. ...   4. ...   5. ...

**B.** Francesca is overstating all your remarks about classmates. Correct her, as in the example. You will hear the correct response.

    ESEMPIO:   Hai detto che sono intelligentissime? →
                    No, ho detto solo che sono le più intelligenti della classe.

1. ...   2. ...   3. ...   4. ...   5. ...

# D.  Comparativi e superlativi irregolari

**A.** Sentirete un dialogo dal vostro testo. Ripetete durante le pause:

    MAMMA:    Ti senti meglio oggi, Carletto?
CARLETTO:    No, mamma, mi sento peggio.
    MAMMA:    Poverino! Ora ti do una medicina che ti farà bene.
CARLETTO:    Ha un buon sapore?
    MAMMA:    È migliore dello zucchero!

CARLETTO:    Mamma, hai detto una bugia! È peggiore del veleno!

**B.** You are a receptive critic! Everything you try you find to be the best of the year. Tell about your latest finds, as in the example. Repeat the correct response.

ESEMPIO: disco rock → È il migliore disco rock dell'anno!

1. … 2. … 3. … 4. … 5. …

**C.** You will hear five incomplete statements, each one twice. Circle the word that best completes each one.

1. migliori     migliore     meglio

2. migliori     migliore     meglio

3. peggiori     peggiore     peggio

4. peggiori     peggiore     peggio

5. migliori     migliore     meglio

# Dialogo

Ascoltate il dialogo dal vostro testo. Poi rispondete alle domande.

| | |
|---|---|
| VITTORIA: | Papà, ti presento Beppino Pepe, il cugino della mia amica Marcella. |
| SIG. PIATTELLI: | Piacere! Ti piace il calcio? Stasera ci sono i campionati mondiali. |
| BEPPINO: | Ho incominciato a interessarmi al calcio qui in Italia. Un gran bello sport! |
| SIG. PIATTELLI: | Uno sport molto antico e molto fiorentino. I fiorentini lo giocavano già nel Quattrocento e ogni occasione era buona per una partita. |
| SIG.RA PIATTELLI: | Finalmente ho il piacere di fare la tua conoscenza, Beppino. Ti posso dare del tu, vero? |
| BEPPINO: | Certamente, signora. Molto lieto di conoscerLa. |
| SIG.RA PIATTELLI: | Di dove sei, figliolo? |
| VITTORIA: | Mamma, te l'ho detto, è del Texas. |
| SIG.RA PIATTELLI: | Il Texas è così grande! Di dove nel Texas? |
| BEPPINO: | Sono di Houston. |
| SIG.RA PIATTELLI: | Ah, Houston! Ne ho sentito parlare. Una grande città, vero? E qual è quella città del Texas famosa per le missioni? |
| BEPPINO: | San Antonio. |
| SIG.RA PIATTELLI: | Bravi! Così anche voi texani onorate i santi! E da quanto tempo sei in Italia, Beppino? |
| BEPPINO: | Da un paio di mesi. |
| SIG.RA PIATTELLI: | E come ti trovi a Firenze? Ti piace? |
| VITTORIA: | Santo cielo, Mamma, quante domande! Vuoi proprio sapere vita, morte e miracoli di Beppino? |
| BEPPINO: | Che significa «vita, morte e miracoli»? |
| VITTORIA: | Significa «*life, death, and miracles*», cioè tutto di una persona, come nelle vite dei santi. Ecco San Beppino, famoso per la sua pazienza come Sant'Antonio! |
| SIG.RA PIATTELLI: | Ho capito, vi scoccio. E va bene, vi lascio in pace e vado in cucina a buttare giù la pasta. Tra dieci minuti porto in tavola. E tu, Attilio, stappa una bottiglia di vino! |

You will hear five incomplete statements based on the dialogue, each one twice. Circle the word or phrase that best completes each one.

1. in Italia          nel Texas                4. San Beppino        Sant'Antonio

2. da due secoli      da cinque secoli         5. gli dà del Lei     gli dà del tu

3. Houston            San Antonio

# Dettato

Sentirete tre volte un breve dettato. La prima volta, ascoltate attentamente. La seconda volta, scrivete quello che sentite. La terza volta, correggete quello che avete scritto.

_____

_____

_____

_____

_____

_____

_____

# E ora ascoltiamo!

You will hear a short radio broadcast about the latest news in sports and then five statements. You will hear everything twice. Circle *vero* or *falso*.

1. vero     falso                4. vero     falso

2. vero     falso                5. vero     falso

3. vero     falso

CAPITOLO

# 10

## The Sounds of the Letters **b** and **p**

**A.** The letter **b** is pronounced as in the English word *boy*. *Ascoltate e ripetete:*

bacio                    birra                    buono
bene                     bosco                    bravo

Contrast the single and double sound of [b]. *Ascoltate e ripetete:*

da basso / abbastanza        ebete / ebbene        cibi / nibbi

**B.** The letter **p** is pronounced as in the English word *pen*. *Ascoltate e ripetete:*

pattinare                posto
pensione                 progetto
piede

Contrast the single and double sound of [p]. *Ascoltate e ripetete:*

papa / pappa             capelli / cappelli        capi / cappi

**C.** Ascoltate e ripetete le frasi:

1. Paolo ha i capelli e i baffi bianchi.
2. Ho paura di guidare quando c'è la nebbia.
3. Non capisco perchè ti arrabbi sempre.
4. Hai già buttato giù la pasta?
5. Giuseppe, stappa una bottiglia di vino buono!

## Vocabolario preliminare

**Andiamo in vacanza!** You will hear five incomplete statements, each one twice. Circle the word or phrase that best completes each one.

1. doppia        singola                4. molto        molto poco

2. d'inverno     d'estate               5. una casa     una macchina

3. doccia        bagno

# Grammatica

## A. Futuro semplice

**A.** Sentirete un brano dal vostro testo. Ripetete durante le pause:

**Progetti per le vacanze**

JEFF: Alla fine di giugno partirò per l'Italia con i miei genitori e mia sorella. Prenderemo l'aereo a New York e andremo a Roma. Passeremo una settimana insieme a Roma, poi i miei genitori noleggeranno una macchina e continueranno il viaggio con mia sorella. Io, invece, andrò a Perugia dove studierò l'italiano per sette settimane. Alla fine di agosto ritorneremo tutti insieme negli Stati Uniti.

**B. A domenica!** Various family members are coming to town on Sunday for a wedding. Tell who, as in the example. Repeat the correct response.

    ESEMPIO: Stefania → Stefania arriverà domenica.

1. ...    2. ...    3. ...    4. ...    5. ...

**C. Le vacanze!** You're in on everyone's summer plans. Using the subjects listed below and the information you hear, tell who is doing what. Repeat the correct response.

    ESEMPIO: io (partire per le Bahamas) → Io partirò per le Bahamas.

1. i ragazzi
2. voi
3. tu
4. l'insegnante d'italiano
5. noi due
6. mio padre

## B. Usi speciali del futuro

**A. Verranno?** Your little sister wants the whole world to come to this week's Little League game, but everyone's plans are up in the air. Answer her questions, as in the example. Repeat the correct response.

    ESEMPIO: Verrai? → Verrò se potrò.

1. ...    2. ...    3. ...    4. ...

**B.** You are taking your neighbors' children to their grandparents' house by car. Assure them that you'll do various things when you get there. You will hear the correct response.

    ESEMPIO: Quando mangeremo? → Mangeremo quando arriveremo.

1. ...    2. ...    3. ...    4. ...

**C. Cosa faranno?** Giorgio has some questions, but you don't have all the information he asks for. Looking at the items listed below, offer an educated guess. You will hear the correct response.

    ESEMPIO: (Dov'è Mirella?) al cinema → Non so; sarà al cinema.

1. alle sette
2. panini
3. cinque dollari
4. in biblioteca
5. latte e frutta

## C. Futuro anteriore

**A.** Sentirete un dialogo dal vostro testo. Ripetete durante le pause:

BARBARA:   Dopo che avrete visitato Roma, tornerete negli Stati Uniti?
CRISTINA:   Solamente mio marito: lui tornerà a New York, ma io partirò per la Sicilia.
BARBARA:   Quanto tempo ti fermerai in Sicilia?
CRISTINA:   Dipende: se non avrò finito tutti i soldi, ci resterò un mese.

**B. Quando giocherete?** Silvia is a real tennis buff; she's anxious for everyone to play with her. Tell her you'll all play after you have studied. Repeat the correct response.

   ESEMPIO:   io → Io giocherò dopo che avrò studiato.

1. ...   2. ...   3. ...   4. ...

**C. Dopo la laurea.** Graduation has come and gone and now it's time to earn a living! Tell who will be happy when they find a job. Repeat the correct response.

   ESEMPIO:   io → Sarò contento quando avrò trovato un lavoro.

1. ...   2. ...   3. ...   4. ...   5. ...

**D.** React to Giulia's statements by saying what the people in question must have done. Use the appropriate forms of the expressions listed below. You will hear the correct response.

   ESEMPIO:   (Non vedo i Costa da tre giorni.) partire → Saranno partiti!

1.  capire male
2.  prenotare un albergo di lusso
3.  festeggiare senza di noi

4.  baciarsi
5.  andare alle Hawaii

## D. Usi dell'articolo determinativo

**A. Dove lavoravano?** Tell where various people used to work. Use the subjects listed below and the location you hear. Repeat the correct response.

   ESEMPIO:   (Stati Uniti) loro → Loro lavoravano negli Stati Uniti.

1.  tu
2.  io
3.  voi

4.  il signor Mauro
5.  i signori Bassani

**B.** Cinzia has finally come to visit you in the United States. You want to know what she likes. Ask her questions, as in the example. Repeat the correct response.

   ESEMPIO:   spaghetti e lasagne → Preferisci gli spaghetti o le lasagne?

1. ...   2. ...   3. ...   4. ...   5. ...   6. ...

**C. Cos'è importante?** Tell whether or not various things are important to you personally. You will hear a possible response.

   ESEMPIO:   lavoro → Per me, il lavoro è importante. (*o* Per me, il lavoro non è importante.)

1. ...   2. ...   3. ...   4. ...   5. ...

## E. Date

**A. Quanti ne abbiamo oggi?** After you hear each item number, express the date you see, as in the example. (Remember that in Italian the first number indicates the day!) You will hear the correct response.

ESEMPIO: 3/12 → Oggi è il tre dicembre.

1. 5/6
2. 27/12
3. 13/3
4. 1/10
5. 24/9
6. 18/1

**B.** Mariangela asks you questions about the United States. Answer her, as in the example. You will hear the correct response.

ESEMPIO: In Minnesota fa freddo d'inverno o d'estate? → D'inverno!

1. ...  2. ...  3. ...  4. ...  5. ...

# Dialogo

Ascoltate il dialogo dal vostro testo. Poi rispondete alle domande.

PAOLO: Quanto tempo resterai a Firenze, Geraldine?
GERALDINE: Ci resterò ancora un mese e poi partirò per il sud.
PAOLO: Dove andrai? Farai il solito giro turistico di Roma, Napoli e Capri?
GERALDINE: Neanche per idea! Conosco già bene quei posti. No, questa volta andrò a Metaponto, in Basilicata.
PAOLO: E perchè proprio a Metaponto?
GERALDINE: Perchè farò parte di una missione archeologica di professori e studenti americani che lavorano in quella zona.
PAOLO: Interessante! Ma non sarà troppo faticoso per te?
GERALDINE: E perchè? Perchè sono una donna? Scommetto che io sono forte quanto te! Guarda che muscoli! Io ho fatto sempre molto sport.
PAOLO: Per carità, non volevo offenderti. Quanti siete nel gruppo?
GERALDINE: Saremo circa quindici persone.
PAOLO: E quante ore al giorno lavorerete?
GERALDINE: Lavoreremo dalla mattina alle sei fino alle quattro del pomeriggio.
PAOLO: Caspita! Sempre a scavare? Ti verranno i calli alle mani, povera Geraldine, e hai delle manine così graziose...
GERALDINE: Senti, Paolino, a me i complimenti non interessano! E ora sarà meglio andare.
PAOLO: Mi piaci molto quando ti arrabbi. Quando potremo rivederci?
GERALDINE: Chi lo sa? Quando imparerai a non dire sciocchezze!

*Geraldine si allontana seguita da Paolo che canterella:*

> Sul ponte di Bassano,
> noi ci darem la mano,
> sul ponte di Bassano,
> noi ci darem la mano,
> noi ci darem la mano
> ed un bacin d'amor,
> ed un bacin d'amor,
> ed un bacin d'amor...

You will hear five questions based on the dialogue, each one twice.  Circle the best answer for each one.

1. un mese                 un anno

2. a Metaponto        a Roma

3. con un gruppo d'italiani      con un gruppo di americani

4. giocherà              scaverà

5. «Che bei muscoli hai!»      «Che belle mani hai!»

# Dettato

Sentirete tre volte un breve dettato.  La prima volta, ascoltate attentamente.  La seconda volta, scrivete quello che sentite.  La terza volta, correggete quello che avete scritto.

_____

_____

_____

_____

_____

_____

_____

# E ora ascoltiamo!

You will hear a conversation between Tony and Cristina and then six statements.  Circle *vero* or *falso*.

1. vero     falso         3. vero     falso         5. vero     falso

2. vero     falso         4. vero     falso         6. vero     falso

CAPITOLO

# 11

# The Sounds of the Letters **f** and **v**

**A.** The letter **f** is pronounced as in the English word *fine*. *Ascoltate e ripetete:*

| | | |
|---|---|---|
| favola | foto | portafoglio |
| festa | fumare | profumo |
| finire | frigo | |

Contrast the single and double sound of [f]. *Ascoltate e ripetete:*

da fare / daffare                    tufo / tuffo

**B.** The letter **v** is pronounced as in the English word *vine*. *Ascoltate e ripetete:*

| | | |
|---|---|---|
| vado | voglia | bevi |
| vedovo | vulcano | divorziato |
| vitello | lavare | |

Contrast the single and double sound of [v]. *Ascoltate e ripetete:*

piove / piovve                    bevi / bevvi

**C.** Ascoltate e ripetete le frasi:

1. Servo il caffè all'avvocato.
2. È vero che vanno in ufficio alle nove?
3. Pioveva e faceva freddo.
4. L'imperfetto dei verbi irregolari non è difficile.
5. Vittoria aveva davvero fretta.
6. Dove vendono questo profumo?

# Vocabolario preliminare

**Da chi o dove lo comprano?** Take a look at the drawings and tell from whom or in which store these people buy the items shown. Repeat the correct response.

ESEMPIO:

Da chi compra il pesce Sara? →
Lo compra dal pescivendolo.

1.

2.

3.

4.

5.

# Grammatica

## A. Ne

**A.** Sentirete un dialogo dal vostro testo. Ripetete durante le pause:

MAMMA:   Marta, per favore mi compri il pane?
MARTA:   Volentieri!  Quanto ne vuoi?
MAMMA:   Un chilo.  Ah sì, ho bisogno anche di prosciutto cotto.
MARTA:   Ne prendo due etti?
MAMMA:   Puoi prenderne anche quattro:  tu e papà ne mangiate sempre tanto!
MARTA:   Hai bisogno d'altro?
MAMMA:   No, grazie, per il resto vado io al supermercato.

**B. Domande personali.** Answer the following questions according to your own personal experiences. You will hear a possible response.

ESEMPIO:   Quanti corsi segue? → Ne seguo quattro.

1. ...   2. ...   3. ...   4. ...   5. ...

**C.** You are helping Marta set up for a party, but you cant't quite hear her because of the stereo.  Ask her to repeat the quantities she says, as in the example.  Repeat the correct response.

ESEMPIO:   Abbiamo comprato quattro meloni. → Quanti ne avete comprati?

1. ...   2. ...   3. ...   4. ...

## B. Usi di ci

**Delle domande in più.** Answer these questions based on your own personal experiences.  You will hear a possible response.

ESEMPIO:   Va in Italia quest'estate? → No, non ci vado quest'estate.

1. ...   2. ...   3. ...   4. ...   5. ...

## C. Pronomi doppi

**A.** Sentirete un dialogo dal vostro testo.  Ripetete durante le pause:

COMMESSA:   Allora, signora, ha provato tutto?  Come va?
CLIENTE:   La gonna è troppo stretta, ma la camicetta va bene.  La prendo.
COMMESSA:   Gliela incarto?
CLIENTE:   No, me la può mettere da parte?  Ora vado a fare la spesa e poi passo a prenderla quando torno a casa.
COMMESSA:   Va bene, signora, gliela metto qui, dietro al banco.

**B. Oggi no.** Everyone depends on you for small chores and favors, but today you're busy and can't help anyone out.  Answer the questions, as in the example.  You will hear the correct response.

ESEMPIO:   Puoi comprare il pane ai vicini (*neighbors*)? →
Mi dispiace; oggi non glielo posso comprare.

1. ...   2. ...   3. ...   4. ...   5. ...

**C.** You've had a productive day. Tell what you've gotten done, substituting double pronouns for the expressions indicated below. Repeat the correct response.

ESEMPIO: Ho parlato con Giovanni della macchina. → Gliene ho parlato.

1. le lettere agli amici
2. la camicetta a Silvia
3. ti, delle paste
4. vi, gli stivali

## D. Imperativo

**A.** You will hear six short sentences, each one twice. Circle the best English equivalent for each one.

1. I can't talk to you about it.    I can't bring you any.

2. When did you tell him?    When did you give it to him?

3. They don't want to go there.    They don't want to help you.

4. He goes there.    Go there!

5. I never go there.    He never sees us.

6. You are kind to everyone.    Be kind to everyone!

**B.** You are babysitting for two children. When they ask your permission to do something, answer in the affirmative, using **pure** and object pronouns in your response. Repeat the correct response.

ESEMPIO: Possiamo leggere la rivista? → Sì, leggetela pure!

1. …    2. …    3. …    4. …    5. …

**C.** You and Riccardo can't agree on anything today. When he gives an order, contradict him, as in the example. Use object pronouns whenever you can. Repeat the correct response.

ESEMPIO: Parliamo del film! → No, non parliamone!

1. …    2. …    3. …    4. …    5. …

# Dialogo

Ascoltate il dialogo dal vostro testo. Poi rispondete alle domande.

VENDITORE: Signorina, ha bisogno di nulla? Un bel vestitino, un bello scialle? Le faccio un buon prezzo!
GERALDINE: Quanto costa quel vestito verde?
VENDITORE: Glielo do per cinquantamila. È regalato!
GERALDINE: Cinquantamila? Mi sembra un po' caro! Che ne dici, Marcella?
MARCELLA: È troppo caro!
VENDITORE: Signorina, c'è l'inflazione, devo mangiare anch'io!
GERALDINE: E quella camicetta rossa quanto costa?
VENDITORE: Trentamila: gliela incarto?
GERALDINE: Se me la dà a ventimila, la prendo.
VENDITORE: E va bene, gliela do a ventimila e non ne parliamo più.

MARCELLA: Ha mozzarelle fresche?
SALUMIERE: Freschissime! Quante ne vuole?
MARCELLA: Ne prendo tre; e anche un pezzo di parmigiano, per favore.

SALUMIERE:  Quanti etti gliene do?
MARCELLA:  Due etti. E quella ricotta com'è?
SALUMIERE:  Da leccarsi i baffi, signorina. Se la compra, domani torna e ne compra di più!
MARCELLA:  E se non è buona, gliela riporto e Lei mi rende i soldi.
SALUMIERE:  Intesi! In tutti i modi domani La rivedo!

You will hear five questions based on the dialogue, each one twice. Circle the best answer for each one.

1. cinquantamila lire          ventimila lire

2. uno scialle                 una camicetta

3. salumi                      formaggio

4. tre                         un pezzo

5. riportarla al salumiere     dare un bacio al salumiere

# Dettato

Sentirete tre volte un breve dettato. La prima volta, ascoltate attentamente. La seconda volta, scrivete quello che sentite. La terza volta, correggete quello che avete scritto.

_____

_____

_____

_____

_____

_____

_____

_____

# E ora ascoltiamo!

You will hear a dialogue between Francesco and his mother and then six incomplete statements. You will hear each statement twice. Circle the word or phrase that best completes each one.

1. stasera          domani              4. la pizza       i dolci

2. carne            pesce               5. magro         grasso

3. dal macellaio    regione             6. sette anni    dieci anni

CAPITOLO

# 12

# Pronuncia: The Sounds of the Letter t

The Italian sound [t] is similar to the **t** in the English word *top*. It does not have the aspiration that characterizes English [t] at the beginning of a word. To pronounce it, place the tip of the tongue against the back of the upper teeth, but a bit lower than for a similar sound in English.

**A.** Contrast the sound of English and Italian **t**. *Ascoltate e ripetete:*

pretty / preti                      patty / patti
city / siti                         rotten / rotte
metro / metro                       tutti-frutti / tutti i frutti

**B.** Contrast the single and double sounds of **t**. *Ascoltate e ripetete:*

tuta / tutta                        mete / mette
fato / fatto                        riti / ritti

**C.** Ascoltate e ripetete le frasi:

1. Avete fatto tutto in venti minuti. Ottimo!
2. Mettete il latte nel tè?
3. Quanti tavolini all'aperto!
4. Il treno delle quattro e un quarto è partito in ritardo.
5. I salatini sono sul tavolino del salotto.

# Vocabolario preliminare

**Parliamo della casa.** Take a look at the drawing below, then write down the answer to the questions you hear. You will hear each question twice.

ESEMPIO:  Dove lascia la bici Mara?  Al pianterreno o al primo piano? → al pianterreno

1. _____     4. _____

2. _____     5. _____

3. _____

# Grammatica

## A. Aggettivi indefiniti

**A.** Sentirete un dialogo dal vostro testo.  Ripetete durante le pause:

> GIGI:   Ciao, Claudio!  Ho sentito che hai cambiato casa.  Dove abiti adesso?
> CLAUDIO:  Prima vivevo in un appartamentino in centro, ma c'era troppo traffico e troppo rumore; così sono andato a vivere in campagna.  Ho trovato una casetta che è un amore… È tutta in pietra, ha un orto enorme e molti alberi da frutta.
> GIGI:   Sono contento per te!  Sai cosa ti dico?  Alcune persone nascono fortunate!

**B.** You are taking a walk around campus with Nina, a bright young neighbor.  Indicate your agreement with her observations using **qualche** in your response.  You will hear the correct response.

ESEMPIO:  Alcuni studenti corrono. → È vero; qualche studente corre.

1. …   2. …   3. …   4. …

**C. Delle domande per Lei.**  Tell about your own life and experiences, using the partitive if your response is affirmative.  You will hear a possible response.

ESEMPIO:  Ha qualche disco? → Sì, ho dei dischi.  (*o* No, non ho dischi.)

1. …   2. …   3. …   4. …

**D. Conformisti!** Tell what everyone in the drawings is doing, using the subjects you hear and the verbs below. Use **tutti** or **tutte** in your response. Repeat the correct response.

ESEMPIO:

(ragazzi) correre → Tutti i ragazzi corrono.

1.

dormire

2.

cucinare

3.

cambiare casa

4.

sistemare i
mobili (*furniture*)

Now repeat the exercise, using **ogni.**

ESEMPIO: (ragazzo) correre → Ogni ragazzo corre.

## B. Pronomi indefiniti

**A.** Giulia and Tommaso have just returned from a fabulous trip to Tahiti. Ask them questions about it using the verbs listed below and the adjectives you hear. You will hear the correct response.

ESEMPIO: vedere (bello) → Avete visto qualcosa di bello?

1. fare
2. comprare

3. mangiare
4. provare

**B. Problemi di casa.** You will hear five quick exchanges about the housing woes of Giulia, Marta, and Cinzia. After each one, answer the question you hear. You will hear each exchange twice. You will hear the correct response.

**Espressioni utili:** qualcuno/a, alcuni/e, tutti/e, qualche cosa, tutto

1. ... 2. ... 3. ... 4. ... 5. ...

## C. Negativi

**A.** Sentirete un dialogo dal vostro testo. Ripetete durante le pause:

MARITO: Sento un rumore in cantina: ci sarà qualcuno, cara…
MOGLIE: Ma no, non c'è nessuno: saranno i topi!
MARITO: Ma che dici? Non abbiamo mai avuto topi in questa casa. Vado a vedere.

MOGLIE: Ebbene?
MARITO: Ho guardato dappertutto ma non ho visto niente di strano.
MOGLIE: Meno male!

**B. Arrivano le ragazze!** Franco is looking forward to meeting two young women you know from Italy. Answer his questions about them in the negative. Repeat the correct response.

ESEMPIO: Sono già arrivate? → No, non sono ancora arrivate.

1. … 2. … 3. … 4. … 5. …

**C.** You will hear six short statements, each one twice. Circle the best English equivalent for each one.

1. a. They are not buying any books.

   b. They don't buy just any kind of book.

2. a. They never come home.

   b. They don't come to my home.

3. a. I don't have more beds than he does.

   b. I don't read for him anymore.

4. a. We don't have a beautiful view.

   b. We haven't seen her.

5. a. We are still at the beach.

   b. We aren't at the beach yet.

6. a. I don't have any of them here or at home.

   b. He's neither here nor at home.

## D. Numeri ordinali

**A. Personaggi storici.** After you hear each item number, read the name you see. You will hear the correct response.

1. Luigi XIV
2. Giovanni XXIII
3. Enrico VIII

4. Carlo V
5. Vittorio Emanuele III

**B.** Give the ordinal form of each cardinal number you hear. Repeat the correct response.

ESEMPIO: 13 → tredicesimo

1. … 2. … 3. … 4. … 5. … 6. …

# Dialogo

Ascoltate il dialogo dal vostro testo.  Poi rispondete alle domande.

BEPPINO:  Prima di tutto, quanto costa quest'appartamento?
PIETRO:  Un milione al mese.
BEPPINO:  Sei matto?  È troppo caro!  E quante stanze ha?
PIETRO:  Due camere, più bagno e cucina.
BEPPINO:  Soltanto?  E in quale zona è?
PIETRO:  In centro; all'ultimo piano di una vecchia casa in Via del Corso.
BEPPINO:  All'ultimo piano?  E quanti scalini ci sono?
PIETRO:  Be', ce ne sono cento.
BEPPINO:  Benone!  Diecimila a scalino.  Ci sarà almeno l'ascensore?
PIETRO:  Veramente l'ascensore non c'è.  Ma cosa importa?  Sarà un ottimo esercizio.  Tu non cammini mai, non sali mai scale, non fai mai esercizio.  Se continui così, morirai d'infarto a cinquant'anni.
BEPPINO:  Ma che dici?  A Firenze non ho nemmeno la macchina: vado sempre a piedi.  Non prendo neanche l'autobus.  E a casa faccio molto sport:  jogging, tennis, nuoto.
PIETRO:  Insomma, t'interessa o no questo appartamento?  Se non t'interessa, troverò qualcun altro.
BEPPINO:  Mi puoi dare qualche altra informazione?  C'è almeno il frigorifero, il riscaldamento centrale?
PIETRO:  No, non c'è nè frigorifero nè riscaldamento centrale.
BEPPINO:  Ma non c'è nulla in questo appartamento!  Un milione per nulla!
PIETRO:  E invece c'è qualcosa di meraviglioso:  c'è una vista unica.  La cupola del Duomo e il Campanile di Giotto quasi a portata di mano, e tetti e terrazzini.  Vedrai che belle foto potrai fare!
BEPPINO:  E va bene, andiamo a vedere questo famoso appartamento.

You will hear six statements based on the dialogue, each one twice.  Circle *vero* or *falso*.

1.  vero     falso              3.  vero     falso              5.  vero     falso

2.  vero     falso              4.  vero     falso              6.  vero     falso

# Dettato

Sentirete tre volte un breve dettato.  La prima volta, ascoltate attentamente.  La seconda volta, scrivete quello che sentite.  La terza volta, correggete quello che avete scritto.

_____

_____

_____

_____

_____

_____

_____

_____

# E ora ascoltiamo!

You will hear three short conversations, each one twice. After each conversation, answer the question about it by circling the correct answer.

1. Did Giorgio go to the party Saturday night?

   a. No, he forgot about it.

   b. No, he wasn't invited.

   c. No, he wasn't feeling well.

   d. No, he decided to stay home and study instead.

2. What does the woman find out about Mr. Rossi?

   a. He has remarried.

   b. He had died.

   c. He has changed his name.

   d. He has moved.

3. What are the people planning?

   a. a shopping expedition

   b. the menu for a banquet

   c. a picnic

   d. an evening at a restaurant

CAPITOLO

# 13

## Pronuncia:  The Sounds of the Letter **d**

The letter **d** is pronounced like the *d* in the English word *tide*.  Unlike English, however, the Italian **d** is always pronounced the same way, regardless of position.

**A.** Contrast the English and Italian **d** in these pairs of words. *Ascoltate e ripetete:*

| | |
|---|---|
| ditto / dito | daddy / dadi |
| day / dei | wedding / vedi |

**B.** Ascoltate e ripetete:

| | | |
|---|---|---|
| dare | divieto | prendere |
| destra | durare | indovinare |

**C.** Contrast the single and double sound of **d.** *Ascoltate e ripetete:*

| | | |
|---|---|---|
| Ada / Adda | cade / cadde | cadi / caddi |

**D.** Ascoltate e ripetete le frasi:

1. Avete deciso dove andare questa domenica?
2. Fa freddo in dicembre?
3. Dammi i soldi che ti ho dato!
4. Non devi dare del tu a tutti.
5. Dieci più dodici fa ventidue.
6. Non so cosa dovrei dire al dottore.

## Vocabolario preliminare

You will hear five incomplete statements, each one twice.  Circle the word or phrase that best completes each one.

1. allacciare la cintura di sicurezza      controllare l'olio

2. prende la multa      rispetta i segnali

3. cambiare le gomme      fare l'autostop

4. la patente      un segnale

5. parcheggiare      controllare l'olio

# Grammatica

## A. Condizionale presente

**A.** Sentirete un dialogo dal vostro testo. Ripetete durante le pause:

SANDRO: Pronto, Paola? Senti, oggi sono senza macchina. È dal meccanico per un controllo. Mi daresti un passaggio per andare in ufficio?

PAOLA: Ma certo! A che ora devo venirti a prendere? Va bene alle otto e un quarto?

SANDRO: Non sarebbe possibile un po' prima: diciamo, alle otto? Mi faresti un vero piacere! Devo essere al lavoro alle otto e mezzo.

PAOLA: Va bene, ci vediamo giù al portone alle otto.

**B. Con un milione di dollari.** Take a look at the drawings and tell what these people would do with a million dollars. You will hear the correct response.

ESEMPIO:

(i signori Freni) fare il giro del mondo →
Con un milione di dollari farebbero il giro del mondo.

1.

comprare
uno yacht

2.

aiutare
i poveri

3.

andare a vivere
alle Hawaii

4.

scrivere il suo
romanzo

5.

mettersi solo vestiti di Gucci

**C. Qualcosa da bere?** When Paola offers you or your friends a drink, tell her you or your friends would prefer the items listed below. Repeat the correct response.

ESEMPIO: (Vuoi una birra?) un'aranciata → No, grazie, preferirei un'aranciata.

1. una cioccolata
2. una Coca-Cola
3. una limonata

4. un'acqua naturale (*uncarbonated*)
5. un tè freddo

**D.** You will hear several verb forms, each one twice. Indicate whether the verb is in the conditional or the future by circling *condizionale* or *futuro*.

1. condizionale     futuro
2. condizionale     futuro
3. condizionale     futuro

4. condizionale     futuro
5. condizionale     futuro
6. condizionale     futuro

# B. **Dovere, potere** e **volere** nel condizionale

**A.** You feel like giving advice to everybody today! React to each statement, as in the example. Repeat the correct response.

ESEMPIO: Vado in Italia. → Non dovresti andare in Italia!

1. …   2. …   3. …   4. …   5. …   6. …

**B.** Some of your friends find themselves in a jam today. Offer them one of your good suggestions—tell them what they could do instead! Follow the example and use the expressions listed below. Repeat the correct response.

ESEMPIO: (Sono quasi rimasto senza benzina.) fare il pieno più spesso →
Potresti fare il pieno più spesso!

1. chiedere un passaggio a Laura
2. rispettare i segnali
3. usare la benzina super

4. controllare l'olio
5. andare in bici

**C. Cosa vorrebbe Lei?** Answer the following questions according to your own personal desires. You will hear a possible response.

ESEMPIO: Che macchina vorrebbe? → Vorrei una Jaguar.

1. …   2. …   3. …   4. …

# C. Dimostrativi

**A.** Sentirete un dialogo dal vostro testo. Ripetete durante le pause:

SANDRO: Di chi è quell'automobile?
GABRIELLA: Quale? Quella targata Milano?
SANDRO: No, quella nera; quella che è parcheggiata in divieto di sosta…
GABRIELLA: Non sono sicura, ma deve essere la macchina del professor Ferrari, quello che è sempre così distratto…
SANDRO: Uno di questi giorni, gli daranno una multa o gli porteranno via la macchina, vedrai!

**B .** You have just witnessed a robbery! The police are questioning you, and they want to know who was there. Answer as in the example. You will hear the correct response.

    ESEMPIO:   Quel ragazzo alto? → Sì, proprio quello!

1. ...    2. ...    3. ...    4. ...    5. ...    6. ...

**C .** These people aren't satisfied with anything they have. They always think Laura's things are better! Follow the example. Repeat the correct response.

    ESEMPIO:   A Carlo non piacciono i suoi genitori. → Preferisce quelli di Laura.

1. ...    2. ...    3. ...    4. ...    5. ...    6. ...

## D. Pronomi possessivi

**A .** Ask Piero if the following objects belong to him, as in the example. Repeat the correct response.

    ESEMPIO:   questo disco → È tuo questo disco?

1. ...    2. ...    3. ...    4. ...    5. ...    6. ...

**B .** You and some former co-workers have managed to catch up with one another. Find out how everyone's family is doing, as in the example. You will hear the correct response.

    ESEMPIO:   (Mia moglie sta bene.) tu → Come sta la tua?

| | | |
|---|---|---|
| 1. voi | 3. lui | 5. loro |
| 2. noi | 4. io | 6. voi |

# Dialogo

Ascoltate il dialogo dal vostro testo. Poi rispondete alle domande.

MARCO: E allora, questo viaggio nell'estremo sud com'è andato?

GERALDINE: Non crederesti alle tue orecchie! Abbiamo avuto la prima avventura dopo appena tre ore di viaggio.

MARCO: Lasciami indovinare: sei rimasta senza benzina!

GERALDINE: No, caro mio, avevo fatto il pieno prima di partire. È successo questo: prima di arrivare in autostrada, ci eravamo fermate in un paesino per bere qualcosa. Siamo rimaste bloccate lì per oltre due ore perchè c'era la processione in onore del santo patrono del paese.

MARCO: E allora cosa avete fatto?

GERALDINE: Abbiamo aspettato e abbiamo fatto un sacco di fotografie!

MARCO: Me le farai vedere, spero!

GERALDINE: Certo! Ma lasciami continuare. La seconda avventura ci è capitata a Messina. Mentre giravamo per cercare un albergo, un vigile ci ha fermato.

MARCO: Scommetto che avevi superato il limite di velocità!

GERALDINE: Nossignore. Ci ha fermato perchè non avevamo allacciato le cinture di sicurezza.

MARCO: Quanto avete pagato di multa?

GERALDINE: Nemmeno un soldo! Il vigile ci ha detto: «Dovrei darvi la multa (sarebbero 12.000 lire), ma dato che siete due giovani simpatiche, per questa volta chiudo un occhio. Ma mi raccomando, rispettate i regolamenti!»

MARCO: Siete state fortunate!

GERALDINE: Ma non è finita. Due giorni dopo ci trovavamo a Palermo e ci siamo fermate per fare un po' di shopping. Abbiamo trovato subito un posto libero ed abbiamo parcheggiato.

MARCO: Sarà stato un parcheggio riservato.

GERALDINE: Questa volta hai quasi indovinato: era un parcheggio con divieto di sosta nei giorni pari e per combinazione quel giorno lo era proprio.

MARCO: Come ve la siete cavata?

GERALDINE: Abbiamo dovuto pagare. Venticinquemila lire! Però abbiamo avuto il tempo di comprarci due magliette che sono un sogno!

You will hear eight statements based on the dialogue, each one twice. Circle *vero* or *falso*.

1. vero    falso          4. vero    falso          7. vero    falso

2. vero    falso          5. vero    falso          8. vero    falso

3. vero    falso          6. vero    falso

# Dettato

Sentirete tre volte un breve dettato. La prima volta, ascoltate attentamente. La seconda volta, scrivete quello che sentite. La terza volta, correggete quello che avete scritto.

_____

_____

_____

_____

_____

_____

_____

_____

_____

# E ora ascoltiamo!

You will hear a dialogue and then six questions. You will hear everything twice. Circle the correct answer to each question.

1. bene                        male

2. centomila lire              ventimila lire

3. a meno di trenta all'ora    come un pazzo

4. un signore                  un vigile

5. bene                        male

6. sorpassi pericolosi         viaggi in macchina

CAPITOLO

# 14

## Vocabolario preliminare

**A. Film, teatro e musica.**  Take a look at the drawings and answer the questions you hear.  Repeat the correct response.

ESEMPIO:

Cosa guardano Nina e Franco? →
Guardano una tragedia.

1.

2.

3.

4.

5.

**B.** You will hear five incomplete statements, each one twice. Circle the word or phrase that best completes each one.

1. «Come sei cattivo!»   «Grazie.»

2. in inglese   in italiano

3. l'autrice   la produttrice

4. le tragedie   le commedie

5. cantare canzonette   diventare una famosa soprano

# Grammatica

## A. Condizionale passato

**A.** Sentirete un dialogo dal vostro testo. Ripetete durante le pause:

GIANCARLO:  Ciao, Paolo, speravo di vederti a Spoleto: come mai non sei venuto?
PAOLO:  Sarei venuto molto volentieri, ma purtroppo non ho trovato posto all'albergo.
GIANCARLO:  Peccato! Avresti dovuto prenotare la camera un anno fa, come ho fatto io.

**B.** A famous, very handsome movie star showed up at a local restaurant last night. Tell what you and your friends would have done if you had been there. Use the expressions listed below and the subjects you hear. Repeat the correct response.

ESEMPIO:  (noi) applaudire → Avremmo applaudito.

1. innamorarsi di lui
2. cercare di parlare con lui
3. offrirgli fiori
4. chiedergli l'autografo
5. partire, perchè odia la confusione

**C.** Everyone had plans to study this weekend . . . before Maurizio threw his beach party! Using the subjects you hear, tell what they said they would do on Friday. Repeat the correct response.

ESEMPIO:  Maria → Ha detto che avrebbe studiato.

1. ...   2. ...   3. ...   4. ...   5. ...   6. ...

## B. Pronomi relativi

**A.** Sentirete un dialogo dal vostro testo. Ripetete durante le pause:

ANGELA:  Vittoria, ben tornata! Ti sei divertita al Festival? Ho saputo che eri sempre in compagnia di un bellissimo ragazzo che fa l'attore, un Don Giovanni di cui tutte le donne s'innamorano.
VITTORIA:  I soliti pettegolezzi! Non bisogna credere a tutto quello che dice la gente!
ANGELA:  È vero. Però in ciò che dice la gente c'è spesso un granello di verità.

**B.** You have just picked up Lisa at the station. Following the example, point out various things to her as you drive home. Repeat the correct response.

ESEMPIO:  Studio con quel ragazzo. → Quello è il ragazzo con cui studio.

1. ...  2. ...  3. ...  4. ...  5. ...

**C.** Today you're finding everything you've misplaced! Tell what you've found, as in the example. You will hear the correct response.

ESEMPIO:  le chiavi → Ecco le chiavi che cercavo!

1. ...  2. ...  3. ...  4. ...

**D.** That Simone is an inscrutable fellow—you can never quite understand him. Following the example, create sentences using the expressions you hear. You will hear the correct response.

ESEMPIO:  dire → Non capisco quel che dice.

1. ...  2. ...  3. ...  4. ...

## C. Chi

**A. Generalità.** Restate the sentences you hear using **chi,** as in the example. Repeat the correct response.

ESEMPIO:  Le persone che parlano troppo non sono simpatiche. → Chi parla troppo non è simpatico.

1. ...  2. ...  3. ...  4. ...  5. ...

**B.** Find out who the culprit was! Following the example, ask questions, using the expressions given below. Repeat the correct response.

ESEMPIO:  mangiare tutto il gelato → Voglio sapere chi ha mangiato tutto il gelato!

1. baciare mia sorella
2. telefonare a mezzanotte
3. uscire con la sua ragazza
4. raccontare un pettegolezzo
5. perdere le mie chiavi

**C.** You will hear several definitions, each one twice. Circle the word that is defined.

1. il pittore       lo scultore
2. l'ascensore       le scale
3. l'autore       l'attore

4. il regista       il contadino
5. il frigo       il pesce

## Dialogo

Ascoltate una lettera dal vostro testo. Poi rispondete alle domande.

12 luglio

Cara mamma,

avrei voluto scriverti prima ma non ne ho avuto proprio il tempo. Una settimana fa sono partito con Marcella, Pietro, Vittoria ed altri amici che ho conosciuto a Firenze per il campeggio di cui ti avevo parlato nella mia lettera precedente. Ci troviamo ora in campagna vicino a Spoleto, che è una piccola città molto interessante dell'Italia centrale.

In questi giorni a Spoleto c'è il Festival dei due Mondi, di cui forse avrai sentito parlare dai giornali americani. Ogni sera c'è uno spettacolo diverso: un'opera o una commedia o un balletto, e di solito gli autori sono giovani e molto originali. La città intera è diventata un teatro: c'è gente di tutto il mondo, tra cui molti personaggi famosi, e ciò che mi sorprende soprattutto è il modo stravagante in cui tutti si vestono. Le boutique di moda creano infatti dei modelli speciali per quest'occasione e ognuno cerca di mettersi in mostra e di attirare l'attenzione su di sè. La città è piena come un'uovo ed è impossibile trovare una camera, ma noi per fortuna abbiamo la nostra tenda.

Vicino al campeggio c'è una fattoria che appartiene a una famiglia texana. Non ci credi? Ma è la verità, te lo giuro! Questi texani si chiamano Joe e Sally Brown, ma i contadini li hanno ribattezzati «sale e pepe». Durante il giorno noi li aiutiamo coi lavori della «farm» e così ci guadagniamo il pranzo.

Fra tre giorni partiremo per la Calabria e appena potrò ti scriverò di nuovo.

Un abbraccio affettuoso a te, papà e la sorellina.

Beppino

P.S. Accludo una foto del nostro gruppo: quei due al centro sono Joe e Sally e quella accanto a me è Vittoria. Non è carina?

You will hear six statements based on the dialogue, each one twice. Circle *vero* or *falso*.

1. vero    falso          3. vero    falso          5. vero    falso

2. vero    falso          4. vero    falso          6. vero    falso

# Dettato

Sentirete tre volte un breve dettato. La prima volta, ascoltate attentamente. La seconda volta, scrivete quello che sentite. La terza volta, correggete quello che avete scritto.

_____

_____

_____

_____

_____

_____

_____

_____

# E ora ascoltiamo!

**A.** The Cinema Excelsior is featuring a retrospective of classic American films. Listen to the recorded phone message and fill in the day and time that each movie is playing. You will hear the recorded message twice.

|  | GIORNI | SPETTACOLI |
|---|---|---|
| Via col vento (*Gone with the Wind*) | _____ | _____ |
| Il Padrino (*The Godfather*) | _____ | _____ |
| Il Mago di Oz | _____ | _____ |
| A qualcuno piace caldo | _____ | _____ |

**B.** Now listen to the announcement again and indicate whether the statements you hear are true or false. You will hear each statement twice.

1. vero    falso         4. vero    falso

2. vero    falso         5. vero    falso

3. vero    falso

CAPITOLO

# 15

## Vocabolario preliminare

**Le belle arti.** Take a look at the drawings and answer the questions you hear. You will hear each question twice. Repeat the correct response.

ESEMPIO:

Che tipo di quadro è questo? →
È un paesaggio.

1.

2.

3.

4.

5.

# Grammatica

## A. Passato remoto

**A.** Sentirete un brano dal vostro testo. Ripetete durante le pause:

La professoressa Marcenaro, docente di storia dell'arte al liceo Cristoforo Colombo di Genova, inizia la sua lezione su Michelangelo.

«Oggi vi parlerò di Michelangelo, di questo grandissimo artista che si affermò come pittore, scultore, architetto ed anche come poeta. Giovanissimo studiò con il Ghirlandaio e poi lavorò per principi, duchi, vescovi e papi. La sua opera più famosa sono gli affreschi della volta della Cappella Sistina. Pensate: questo immane lavoro che Michelangelo volle eseguire senza alcun aiuto durò ben quattro anni (1508–1512). Gli affreschi illustrano episodi tratti dal Vecchio Testamento e culminano con il Giudizio Universale...»

**B. Chi ebbe fortuna?** Tell who had good luck, as in the example. Repeat the correct response.

ESEMPIO:   lui → Lui ebbe fortuna.

1. ...   2. ...   3. ...   4. ...   5. ...

**C. Chi venne in America?** Tell who came to America, as in the example. Repeat the correct response.

ESEMPIO:   Sir Walter Raleigh → Sir Walter Raleigh venne in America.

1. ...   2. ...   3. ...   4. ...   5. ...

**D. Alcune date importanti.** Answer questions about Italian artists and writers using the information given below. Repeat the correct response.

ESEMPIO:   (Quando scolpì *Apollo e Dafne* Bernini?) dal 1622 al 1624 →
            Bernini scolpì *Apollo e Dafne* dal 1622 al 1624.

1. intorno al (*around*) 1310
2. nel 1452

3. nel 1527
4. dal 1813 al 1901

**E.** You will hear six statements, each one twice. Circle the tense of the verb you hear.

| | | |
|---|---|---|
| 1. futuro | condizionale presente | passato remoto |
| 2. futuro | condizionale presente | passato remoto |
| 3. futuro | condizionale presente | passato remoto |
| 4. futuro | condizionale presente | passato remoto |
| 5. futuro | condizionale presente | passato remoto |
| 6. futuro | condizionale presente | passato remoto |

## B. Ripasso dei tempi del passato

**A.** Sentirete un brano dal vostro testo. Ripetete durante le pause:

Due uomini viaggiavano insieme. Uno trovò una scure e l'altro disse: «Abbiamo trovato una scure.» «No», osservò il primo, «perchè dici *abbiamo trovato?* Devi dire *hai trovato*». Poco dopo si videro inseguiti da quelli che avevano perduto la scure, e quello che l'aveva disse al compagno, «Siamo rovinati!» «Non devi dire *siamo* rovinati», rispose il compagno, «devi dire *sono* rovinato».

**B.** Tell about you and your siblings' shenanigans on a famous afternoon many years ago. What did you do while your dad was napping? After you hear each item number, use the subjects and expressions listed below to tell the stories. Repeat the correct response.

> ESEMPIO:  noi / telefonare in Italia → Mentre papà dormiva noi telefonammo in Italia.

1. voi / mangiare tutti i cioccolatini (*chocolates*)
2. io / cercare di guidare la macchina
3. tu / tagliare le tendine (*cut the curtains*)
4. Piero / mettersi il frac (*tux*) di papà
5. Laura e Piero / dare del gelato al cane

**C. Perchè non scrissero?** Tell why the following people didn't write, using the expressions indicated below. You will hear the correct response.

> ESEMPIO:  (Gina) non avere tempo → Gina non scrisse perchè non aveva tempo.

1. non sapere il nostro indirizzo
2. non piacere scrivere
3. essere troppo occupata

4. non averne voglia
5. non amarmi più

## C. Avverbi

**A.** Change the adjectives you hear into adverbs. You will hear the correct response.

> ESEMPIO:  veri → veramente

1. ...    2. ...    3. ...    4. ...    5. ...    6. ...

**B.** You and Tommaso don't see eye to eye. Disagree with him, as in the example. Repeat the correct response.

> ESEMPIO:  Hanno risposto male. → No, hanno risposto bene.

1. ...    2. ...    3. ...    4. ...    5. ...    6. ...

# Dialogo

Ascoltate il dialogo dal vostro testo. Poi rispondete alle domande.

GERALDINE:  Che panorama incantevole! Sembra proprio un paesaggio da fiaba.
SALVATORE:  Mia cara, la Sicilia è un paese di fiabe e di tragedie. E io stasera vorrei raccontarti una piccola fiaba. Vuoi sentirla?
GERALDINE:  Volentieri. Ma dimmi: finisce bene o male?
SALVATORE:  Le fiabe di solito finiscono bene; ma questa, non so. La fine dovrai sceglierla tu... E ora ascoltami! C'era una volta una principessa bionda che viveva in un paese lontano lontano. Aveva un carattere allegro e voleva conoscere il mondo. Così un giorno salì su una grande aquila e attraversò l'oceano. Arrivò in un'isola dove la gente era molto diversa ma, per

fortuna, parlava una lingua che lei aveva imparato da bambina.  Nell'isola incontrò un
giovane nè bello nè brutto, un po' timido, che passava il tempo a leggere grossi libri.  Il
giovane s'innamorò di lei ma non aveva il coraggio di dirglielo.  E intanto il tempo
passava…  Come finisce la fiaba, Geraldine?  La bella principessa tornò al suo paese e il
giovane restò triste e solo con i suoi libri… o la fanciulla ricambiò il suo amore e i due si
sposarono, e vissero felici e contenti per tutta la vita?

GERALDINE:    Mio caro Salvatore, la tua fiaba è molto romantica e va bene per questa notte di luna; ma
domani, ci rideremo sopra tutt'e due!

You will hear seven statements based on the dialogue, each one twice.  Circle *vero* or *falso*.

1.  vero        falso                    5.  vero        falso

2.  vero        falso                    6.  vero        falso

3.  vero        falso                    7.  vero        falso

4.  vero        falso

# Dettato

Sentirete tre volte un breve dettato.  La prima volta, ascoltate attentamente.  La seconda volta, scrivete quello
che sentite.  La terza volta, correggete quello che avete scritto.

_____

_____

_____

_____

_____

_____

_____

_____

_____

# E ora ascoltiamo!

You will hear a story about a trip and then seven statements.  You will hear everything twice.  Circle *vero* or
*falso*.

1.  vero        falso                    5.  vero        falso

2.  vero        falso                    6.  vero        falso

3.  vero        falso                    7.  vero        falso

4.  vero        falso

CAPITOLO

# 16

## Vocabolario preliminare

You will hear five incomplete statements, each one twice. Circle the answer that best completes each statement.

1. un aumento               una riduzione

2. una chiesa              un partito politico

3. una riduzione          un aumento

4. le tasse                gli operai

5. un impiegato         un operaio

## Grammatica

### A. Congiuntivo presente

**A.** Sentirete un dialogo dal vostro testo. Ripetete durante le pause:

PENSIONATO 1: Tutti i giorni c'è uno sciopero; ho l'impressione che in Italia nessuno abbia più voglia di lavorare.

PENSIONATO 2: Però con gli scioperi i lavoratori ottengono gli aumenti di salario. Peccato che i pensionati non possano scioperare anche loro!

PENSIONATO 1: È necessario che i partiti ascoltino anche la nostra voce: dobbiamo organizzare una dimostrazione e farci sentire. Non siamo ancora morti!

**B. Non mi capisce nessuno!** Tell about all the people you think don't understand you. Use the subjects you hear. Repeat the correct response.

ESEMPIO: i miei genitori → Credo che i miei genitori non mi capiscano.

1. ... 2. ... 3. ... 4. ... 5. ...

**C. Le faccende di casa.** When Renata asks if you're doing certain things around the house, tell her you want the people listed below to do them instead. Repeat the correct response.

ESEMPIO: (Pulirai il frigo?) Paolo → No, voglio che Paolo pulisca il frigo!

1. voi                               4. Claudio
2. tu                                 5. tu e Claudio
3. gli altri

**D.** Your grandmother is very stubborn and lists all the things she doesn't want to do. Try to convince her to change her mind. You will hear the correct response.

ESEMPIO: Non voglio andare in Florida. → Ma è meglio che tu vada in Florida!

1. ...    2. ...    3. ...    4. ...    5. ...

# B. Verbi ed espressioni che richiedono il congiuntivo

**A.** Sentirete un dialogo dal vostro testo. Ripetete durante le pause:

CAMERIERE:   Professore, vuole che Le porti il solito caffè o preferisce un poncino?
PROFESSORE:   Fa un po' fresco... Forse è meglio che prenda un poncino. Scalda di più.
CAMERIERE:   Speriamo che questo sciopero finisca presto, professore.
PROFESSORE:   Certo; ma bisogna che prima gli insegnanti abbiano un miglioramento delle loro condizioni di lavoro.

**B.** Every time Roberta goes home her mother says Roberta's too thin. Take the part of Roberta's mother and complete the sentences you hear with the expressions listed below. Repeat the correct response.

ESEMPIO: (penso) essere troppo magra → Penso che tu sia troppo magra.

1. essere qui
2. avere fame
3. non cercare di dimagrire
4. mangiare di più
5. stare a dieta
6. ingrassare

**C. Congiuntivo o no?** Create new sentences by substituting the phrases you hear. Some require the subjunctive, some do not. Repeat the correct response.

ESEMPIO: preferisco → Preferisco che lei dorma.

1. ...    2. ...    3. ...    4. ...    5. ...

# C. Congiuntivo passato

**A. È strano.** A number of people didn't make it to class today. Express your surprise, as in the example. Repeat the correct response.

ESEMPIO: Paolo → È strano che Paolo non sia venuto.

1. ...    2. ...    3. ...    4. ...    5. ...

**B. Sciopero!** You are a great supporter of workers' rights. Express your approval of your friends' work actions, as in the example. Repeat the correct response.

ESEMPIO: Abbiamo fatto sciopero. → È bene che abbiate fatto sciopero!

1. ...    2. ...    3. ...    4. ...    5. ...

**C.** Anna asks you a lot of questions today but you're just not sure of the answers. Be honest with her, as in the example. You will hear the correct response.

ESEMPIO: È vero che Carlo ha scritto? → Non so, è possibile che Carlo abbia scritto.

1. ...    2. ...    3. ...    4. ...    5. ...

## D. Congiuntivo o infinito?

**A.** Sentirete un dialogo dal vostro testo. Ripetete durante le pause:

NUCCIA: Valentina, come mai in giro a quest'ora? Non sei andata in ufficio?
VALENTINA: Non lo sapevi? Mi sono licenziata sei mesi fa per avere più tempo per mio figlio.
NUCCIA: Sei contenta di fare la casalinga?
VALENTINA: Contentissima! E tutti in casa sono felici che io non vada fuori a lavorare!

**B.** You are looking for a roommate. Follow the example to create five basic questions to ask people over the phone before you decide to meet them. Use the expressions listed below with what you hear. Repeat the correct response.

ESEMPIO: (ti piace) alzarsi alle cinque → Ti piace alzarti alle cinque?

1. fumare in camera
2. andare a letto tardi
3. studiare molto
4. invitare amici ogni sera
5. arrabbiarsi facilmente

**C.** Create new sentences by beginning with the expressions you hear. Use **che** + *indicative*, **che** + *subjunctive*, or the infinitive with or without **di.** Follow the examples. Repeat the correct response.

ESEMPI: Marco è in sciopero.
è vero → È vero che Marco è in sciopero.
crediamo → Crediamo che Marco sia in sciopero.
Marco vorrebbe → Marco vorrebbe essere in sciopero.

Voto socialista.

1. ... 2. ... 3. ... 4. ...

Hanno avuto un aumento.

1. ... 2. ... 3. ... 4. ...

## E. Nomi e aggettivi in -a

**Chi sono?** Take a look at the drawings and tell who is depicted in each one. You will hear the correct response.

ESEMPIO:

Chi è? → È un turista.

1.

2.

3.

4.

5.

# Dialogo

Ascoltate il dialogo dal vostro testo. Poi rispondete alle domande.

PRIMO STUDENTE: Dite quello che volete, ma io credo che la DC, con tutti i suoi difetti, sia l'unico partito capace di garantire la democrazia in Italia.

SECONDO STUDENTE: Ma cosa dici! La DC garantisce solo gli interessi dei ricchi. Fa le riforme ma poi non le applica! Bisogna che anche il partito comunista entri a far parte del governo!

TERZO STUDENTE: Neanche per idea! È meglio che il PCI resti all'opposizione!

QUARTO STUDENTE: È ora che gli italiani capiscano che ci sono altre alternative. A me pare che gli altri partiti abbiano qualcosa da dire anche loro!

SECONDO STUDENTE: Quali altri partiti? Gli ultra-sinistra o quei fascisti del MSI?

QUARTO STUDENTE: Ma no! Parlo del partito socialista e del partito repubblicano; e, anche se tu non sei d'accordo, sono convinto che anche il vecchio partito liberale possa esercitare un suo ruolo.

UNA STUDENTESSA: Cari miei, sono stufa dei vostri grandi partiti che si ricordano delle donne soltanto quando vogliono il nostro voto: mio padre vuole che voti DC, il mio ragazzo esige che voti PCI; e io invece alle prossime elezioni voto radicale. È l'unico partito che abbia fatto qualcosa per noi donne!

BEPPINO: Com'è complicata la politica in Italia! Non ti pare che negli Stati Uniti le cose siano più semplici?

You will hear five incomplete statements based on the dialogue, each one twice. Circle the word or phrase that best completes each one.

1. a. fa parte del governo

   b. è all'opposizione

2. a. la Democrazia Cristiana e il Partito Comunista

   b. il Partito Socialista e il Partito Repubblicano

3. a. rappresentare un'alternativa

   b. garantire gli interessi delle donne

4. a. il Movimento Sociale Italiano

   b. il Partito Radicale

5. a. semplice

   b. complicata

## Dettato

Sentirete tre volte un breve dettato. La prima volta, ascoltate attentamente. La seconda volta, scrivete quello che sentite. La terza volta, correggete quello che avete scritto.

_____

_____

_____

_____

_____

_____

_____

_____

## E ora ascoltiamo!

You will hear a conversation between two friends and then five incomplete statements. You will hear each statement twice. Circle the word or phrase that best completes each one.

1. a. cercare un altro lavoro

   b. chiedere un aumento

2. a. Franco sia molto diligente

   b. Franco sia troppo aggressivo

3. a. non abbia tempo per parlargli

   b. non voglia parlare di questo soggetto

4. a. Franco non lavori abbastanza

   b. Franco sia molto bravo

5. a. Franco riceverà l'aumento

   b. gli diranno di no

CAPITOLO

## 17

## Vocabolario preliminare

You will hear a short passage and then five statements. You will hear everything twice. Circle *vero* or *falso*.

1. vero    falso
2. vero    falso
3. vero    falso

4. vero    falso
5. vero    falso

## Grammatica

### A. Congiunzioni che richiedono il congiuntivo

**A.** Sentirete un dialogo dal vostro testo. Ripetete durante le pause:

**Telefonata dagli Stati Uniti ad un'oreficeria di Arezzo**

SIG. GIANNINI: Pronto, pronto… è Lei la rappresentante di Maya Jewelers? Non deve preoccuparsi, ho già spedito le catene d'oro, arriveranno in settimana… a meno che la posta non abbia ritardi!

SIG.RA MAURI: Sarebbe possibile una seconda spedizione prima che finisca l'anno?

SIG. GIANNINI: Cara signora, non glielo posso promettere: per quanto i miei operai siano degli ottimi lavoratori, c'è sempre la possibilità di qualche sciopero…

SIG.RA MAURI: E il costo, sarà lo stesso?

SIG. GIANNINI: Be', no, in leggero aumento. Capirà i motivi senza che glieli spieghi: il prezzo dell'oro, il costo della mano d'opera, l'inflazione…

**B.** Your hard-working housemate Chiara is up and out long before the rest of you make it out of bed. Tell who she gets out of the house before, as in the example. Repeat the correct response.

ESEMPIO: io → Esce di casa prima che io mi alzi.

1. …    2. …    3. …    4. …    5. …

**C.** You don't approve of something Maria did. Explain to her how you're feeling. Use the expressions listed below to complete the sentences you hear. Repeat the correct response.

ESEMPIO: (Ti parlo affinchè…) tu / capire → Ti parlo affinchè tu capisca.

1. io / essere stanca
2. tu / non arrabbiarsi
3. non piacermi

4. tu / non farlo più
5. tu / non volere

**D.** You will hear five short statements or questions, each one twice. Circle the best English equivalent for each one.

1. a. She comes in without greeting anyone.

   b. She comes in without anyone greeting her.

2. a. Talk to me before getting mad.

   b. Tell me why you got mad before.

3. a. I'll do it because they're giving me two thousand dollars.

   b. I'll do it so that they give me two thousand dollars.

4. a. Why don't you call us before going out?

   b. Why don't you call us before we go out?

5. a. I help them without him knowing.

   b. I help them without their knowing it.

## B. Altri usi del congiuntivo

**A. Non dico niente!** You've decided to hold your tongue, no matter what the others do. Create new sentences using the expressions you hear. Repeat the correct response.

> ESEMPIO: Qualunque cosa facciano, io non dico niente. (preparare) →
> Qualunque cosa preparino, io non dico niente.

1. ...   2. ...   3. ...   4. ...

**B.** Ever since you started studying Italian, you've been bumping into Italians everywhere! Tell about your experiences, as in the example. Repeat the correct response.

> ESEMPIO: Dovunque tu vada, trovi italiani. (io) → Dovunque io vada, trovo italiani.

1. ...   2. ...   3. ...   4. ...

**C.** You are impressed with everything Mauro shows you. Tell him they are the most beautiful you've ever seen. You will hear the correct response.

> ESEMPIO: museo → È il museo più bello che io abbia visto.

1. ...   2. ...   3. ...   4. ...

**D.** You are in a bad mood. After you hear each item number, tell everything that's missing in your life using the expressions listed below. You will hear the correct response.

> ESEMPIO: nessuno / amarmi → Non c'è nessuno che mi ami.

1. niente / interessarmi
2. nessuno / volere studiare con me
3. niente / piacermi nel frigo
4. nessuno / farmi regali

**E.** You will hear five statements, each one twice. Indicate whether the sentences refer to a known or imaginary person or object.

1. known   imaginary        3. known   imaginary        5. known   imaginary

2. known   imaginary        4. known   imaginary

## C. Costruzioni con l'infinito

**A.** How does Cinzia feel about work? Create new sentences by substituting the expression you hear. Repeat the correct response.

   ESEMPIO:  Crede di lavorare molto.  (le piace) → Le piace lavorare molto.

1. ...    2. ...    3. ...    4. ...    5. ...

**B. Delle domande per Lei.** Answer these questions according to your own feelings and experiences. You will hear a possible response.

   ESEMPIO:  Che cosa ha bisogno di fare? → Ho bisogno di fare più ginnastica.

1. ...    2. ...    3. ...    4. ...    5. ...

## D. Le forme **Lei** e **Loro** dell'imperativo

**A.** Sentirete un dialogo dal vostro testo. Ripetete durante le pause:

   SEGRETARIA:  Dottoressa, il signor Biondi ha bisogno urgente di parlarLe: ha già telefonato tre volte.

   DOTTORESSA CADOPPI:  Che seccatore! Gli telefoni Lei, signorina, e gli dica che sono già partita per Chicago.

   SEGRETARIA:  Pronto!... Signor Biondi?... Mi dispiace, la dottoressa è partita per un congresso a Chicago. Come dice?... L'indirizzo? Veramente, non glielo saprei dire: abbia pazienza e richiami tra dieci giorni!

**B.** Tell your professor to do these things if she/he wants to. Repeat the correct response.

   ESEMPIO:  entrare → Se vuole entrare, entri!

1. ...    2. ...    3. ...    4. ...    5. ...

**C.** Now tell two of your professors not to do these things if they are unable to. Repeat the correct response.

   ESEMPIO:  pagare → Se non possono pagare, non paghino!

1. ...    2. ...    3. ...    4. ...    5. ...

## E. La formazione dei nomi femminili

**A.** Sentirete un dialogo dal vostro testo. Ripetete durante le pause:

CLAUDIO:  Ieri al ricevimento dai Brambilla c'era un sacco di gente interessante.

MARINA:  Ah sì? Chi c'era?

CLAUDIO:  Il pittore Berardi con la moglie, pittrice anche lei; dicono che è più brava del marito... la professoressa di storia dell'arte Stoppato, il poeta Salimbeni con la moglie scultrice, un paio di scrittori e scrittrici di cui non ricordo i nomi...

MARINA:  Che ambiente intellettuale! Ma i Brambilla cosa fanno?

CLAUDIO:  Beh, lui è un grosso industriale tessile e lei è un'ex-attrice.

**B.** Your Aunt Elsa is a bit behind the times and assumes that only men have certain roles and positions. Set her straight, as in the example. Repeat the correct response.

   ESEMPIO:  Hai detto due dottori alti? → No, due dottoresse alte!

1. ...    2. ...    3. ...    4. ...    5. ...

# Dialogo

Ascoltate il dialogo dal vostro testo. Poi rispondete alle domande.

MARCELLA: Ormai l'inverno è vicino; vorrei comprarmi un cappotto prima che incominci a fare veramente freddo.

VITTORIA: Io ho bisogno di tante cose: un paio di camicette, una gonna, una giacca di lana; ma soprattutto vorrei un paio di stivali... purchè non costino troppo!

MARCELLA: C'è un negozio in Via Calzaioli che ha gli stivali più belli che abbia mai visto. Ma i prezzi...

VITTORIA: Non me ne parlare! Io in quel negozio non ci metto piede... a meno che non trovi lavoro e faccia un po' di quattrini. Sai, c'è la possibilità che dei compratori americani mi assumano come interprete per la prossima sfilata di moda a Palazzo Pitti.

MARCELLA: Davvero? Come hai saputo di questo lavoro?

VITTORIA: Me l'ha detto una zia che lavora in una casa di moda a Roma; figurati che, senza che io glielo abbia chiesto, ha fatto il mio nome a questi compratori.

MARCELLA: Che fortuna! Speriamo che ti vada bene!

VITTORIA: Anche tu a far compere? Caspita! Questo è un negozio di miliardari. Su chi vuoi far colpo?

BEPPINO: Te lo dirò a patto che tu non lo dica in giro.

VITTORIA: Bionda o bruna?

BEPPINO: Biondissima e fatale! Domani vado a Milano a trovarla... Sul serio, ragazze, a Milano ci vado davvero per un colloquio con una ditta di arredamenti che esporta negli Stati Uniti. Può darsi che mi assumano come fotografo. Così ho comprato una cravatta per l'occasione. Eccola! Vi pare che sia adatta?

MARCELLA: Pura seta, disegno di buon gusto ma non chiassoso. Ottima scelta, Beppino. Allora buon viaggio e in bocca al lupo!

You will hear six statements based on the dialogue, each one twice. Circle *vero* or *falso*.

1. vero    falso          3. vero    falso          5. vero    falso

2. vero    falso          4. vero    falso          6. vero    falso

# Dettato

Sentirete tre volte un breve dettato. La prima volta, ascoltate attentamente. La seconda volta, scrivete quello che sentite. La terza volta, correggete quello che avete scritto.

_____

_____

_____

_____

_____

_____

_____

_____

# E ora ascoltiamo!

You will hear a letter from Mirella to her fiancé Roberto and then five statements. You will hear everything twice. Circle *vero* or *falso*.

1. vero     falso

2. vero     falso

3. vero     falso

4. vero     falso

5. vero     falso

CAPITOLO

# 18

# Vocabolario preliminare

You will hear five incomplete statements, each one twice. Circle the word or expression that best completes each one.

1. la giustizia sociale          l'ingiustizia sociale

2. il razzismo          l'uguaglianza

3. antiche          moderne

4. della protezione dell'ambiente          dell'inquinamento

5. dovremmo aiutarlo          andiamo in macchina con lui

# Grammatica

## A. L'imperfetto del congiuntivo

**A.** Sentirete un dialogo dal vostro testo. Ripetete durante le pause:

CINZIA: Così tuo padre voleva che tu facessi l'ingegnere?
MAURIZIO: Sì, perchè sperava che poi lavorassi con lui nella sua azienda.
CINZIA: E tua madre?
MAURIZIO: Mia madre, invece, desiderava che studiassi medicina.
CINZIA: E tu cosa hai deciso di fare?
MAURIZIO: Sono diventato scultore.

**B.** Piera is telling you about her problems with her parents. Show your support for her by telling her it would be better if her parents didn't do those things. Repeat the correct response.

ESEMPIO: Interferiscono sempre! → Sarebbe meglio che non interferissero.

1. ...    2. ...    3. ...    4. ...

**C.** You've just returned from visiting your uncle Carlo, who is very old-fashioned. After you hear each item number, use the expressions indicated below to tell all the things he couldn't believe about your life. You will hear the correct response.

ESEMPIO: dividere un appartamento con gli amici →
Non credeva che io dividessi un appartamento con gli amici.

1. guadagnarsi da vivere a 20 anni
2. volere studiare invece di sposarsi subito
3. lavorare per proteggere l'ambiente
4. essere felice della mia vita

**D.** You and Maurizio are having a serious talk with your housemates. When Maurizio tells them what he wants them to do, add that you, too, were hoping they would do those things. Repeat the correct response.

ESEMPIO: Voglio che facciate i letti! → Anch'io speravo che faceste i letti.

1. ...   2. ...   3. ...   4. ...

## B. Il trapassato del congiuntivo

**A.** A recent party didn't go so well because you and your friends got your signals crossed. When Silvia tells you what had actually happened, tell her what your assumption was. Repeat the correct response.

ESEMPIO: Non ero andata al mercato. → Boh, pensavo che tu fossi andata al mercato.

1. ...   2. ...   3. ...   4. ...   5. ...

**B.** Your Aunt Matilda was a great believer in the philosophy that "one is never too old!" List a few of the things she did, completing each sentence you hear with **benchè non,** as in the example. You will hear the correct response.

ESEMPIO: A ottant'anni scrisse un libro... → benchè non avesse mai scritto prima.

1. ...   2. ...   3. ...   4. ...   5. ...

## C. Correlazione dei tempi nel congiuntivo

**A.** Sentirete un dialogo dal vostro testo. Ripetete durante le pause:

LAURA:  Mamma, ho deciso di accettare quel lavoro a New York.
MADRE:  Ma non sarebbe meglio che tu restassi qui a Torino, vicino alla famiglia, agli amici? A New York c'è il problema della violenza e della droga: non voglio che ti capiti qualcosa di brutto...
LAURA:  Mamma, vorrei che tu non interferissi così! Ormai le decisioni me le devo prendere da me: non ho bisogno di qualcuno che mi protegga.
MADRE:  Cara, voglio solo che tu sia felice!

**B.** You and Ruggero are discussing important social and political issues. Complete each sentence you hear with the expressions listed below. Repeat the correct response.

ESEMPIO: (vorrei che) il razzismo / non esistere → Vorrei che il razzismo non esistesse.

1. la gente / cercare di eliminare l'inquinamento
2. i genitori / apprezzare le idee dei giovani
3. la gente / prendere sul serio i problemi degli anziani
4. il governo / lavorare per eliminare la povertà

**C.** Giuseppe and Franca have just purchased a new car. When Giuseppe tells you about his and Franca's thoughts on the matter, tell him that you share his convictions. Repeat the correct response.

ESEMPIO: Speriamo di avere fatto bene. → Anch'io spero che abbiate fatto bene.

1. ...   2. ...   3. ...   4. ...   5. ...

**D.** You will hear five short statements, each one twice. Circle the best English equivalent for each one.

1.  a.  He was talking as if he were making a decision.

    b.  He was talking as if he had made a decision.

2.  a.  I thought they would arrive tired.

    b.  I thought they had arrived tired.

3. a. I was hoping they would pay.

   b. I was hoping they had paid.

4. a. You are happy that they rested.

   b. Be happy that they rested!

5. a. Nobody believes we have arrived.

   b. Nobody believes they have arrived.

## D. Riassunto dei plurali irregolari

**A.** Sentirete un dialogo dal vostro testo. Ripetete durante le pause:

GUIDO:    Dimmi, Alberto: hai molti amici a Firenze?
ALBERTO:    Sì, ne ho diversi; e alcuni molto simpatici.
GUIDO:    E… amiche?
ALBERTO:    Certo; e una, specialmente, tanto carina, intelligente e simpatica.
GUIDO:    Ho capito: l'amica del cuore!

**B. Cosa sono?** Take a look at the drawings below and answer the questions you hear. Repeat the correct response.

ESEMPIO:

È una valigia? → No, sono due valige.

1.

2.

3.

4.

5.

6.

**C.** You will hear several expressions, each one twice. Write down the plural form if the expression is singular or the singular form if it is plural. The answers appear at the end of this manual.

ESEMPIO: occhio grigio → occhi grigi

1. _____     4. _____

2. _____     5. _____

3. _____

# Dialogo

Ascoltate il dialogo dal vostro testo. Poi rispondete alle domande.

MARCELLA: Speriamo che il libro sui disegni di Leonardo piaccia al tuo babbo: dato che è ingegnere, dovrebbe interessargli.

PIETRO: Già, lui crede che i pittori siano una razza a parte da scienziati e ingegneri. Lo sai che si era messo in testa che facessi l'ingegnere come lui?

MARCELLA: E tu invece cosa vuoi fare? Il pittore?

PIETRO: Non lo so ancora: è per questo che sono venuto in Italia... Mi pareva che mio padre fosse un tipo troppo autoritario e avevo paura che prendesse tutte le decisioni per me.

MARCELLA: E io che credevo che i padri americani fossero diversi da quelli italiani e non interferissero nella vita dei figli...

PIETRO: Ma lui è d'origine siciliana; benchè sia vissuto negli Stati Uniti trent'anni, è rimasto un padre all'antica, un «padre padrone».

MARCELLA: Ma a te piacerebbe rimanere in Italia?

PIETRO: Magari fosse possibile! Ma ormai ho finito i miei risparmi. L'Italia è stata per me un'esperienza straordinaria: nessuno che mi dicesse quello che dovevo fare; ho dipinto, ho viaggiato, ho letto i libri che mi interessavano senza che nessun professore mi obbligasse a scrivere «papers» e poi mi desse un voto!

MARCELLA: Insomma, un bell'interludio, una fuga dal quotidiano. Potessi farlo anch'io! Ma lo sai dove vorrei andare io? A New York!

PIETRO: Dici sul serio? E allora andiamoci insieme!

MARCELLA: Magari! Ma tu cosa farai quando torni a casa?

PIETRO: Chi lo sa! Può darsi che finisca per fare l'ingegnere...

You will hear five incomplete statements based on the dialogue, each one twice. Circle the word or phrase that best completes each one.

1. a. perchè il padre è pittore

   b. perchè il padre è ingegnere

2. a. in Sicilia

   b. in America

3. a. facesse l'ingegnere

   b. facesse il pittore

4. a. permissivi

   b. autoritari

5. a. non ha più soldi

   b. suo padre vuole che lui torni a casa

# Dettato

Sentirete tre volte un breve dettato. La prima volta, ascoltate attentamente. La seconda volta, scrivete quello che sentite. La terza volta, correggete quello che avete scritto.

_____

_____

_____

_____

_____

_____

_____

_____

_____

# E ora ascoltiamo!

You will hear a telephone conversation bewteen Piero and Nina and then six statements. You will hear everything twice. Circle *vero* or *falso*.

1. vero    falso        3. vero    falso        5. vero    falso

2. vero    falso        4. vero    falso        6. vero    falso

CAPITOLO

# 19

# Vocabolario preliminare

You will hear six incomplete statements, each one twice. Circle the word or phrase that best completes each one.

1. i libri              i racconti

2. un'intervista        un interprete

3. una recensione       una novella

4. il soggetto          i protagonisti

5. un riassunto         una novella

6. il libro             un brano

# Grammatica

## A. Il periodo ipotetico con l'indicativo

**A.** Sentirete un brano dal vostro testo. Ripetete durante le pause:

Secondo molte persone, i proverbi non sono pure e semplici curiosità; sono una forma di letteratura. I proverbi riflettono la filosofia, la cultura e le esperienze di intere generazioni e rappresentano una chiave per la comprensione d'un popolo.

Un proverbio cinese dice: «Se vuoi essere felice per un'ora, ubriacati. Se vuoi essere felice per tre giorni, sposati. Se vuoi essere felice per otto giorni, uccidi il tuo maiale e mangialo. Ma se vuoi essere felice per sempre, diventa giardiniere.»

**B. Niente gelato!** Swimsuit season approaches and you and your friends are avoiding *gelato*. Tell why, using the subjects you hear. Repeat the correct response.

   ESEMPIO:  io → Se mangio gelato, ingrasso.

1. ...    2. ...    3. ...    4. ...

**C.** Tell Maria that you and your friends will do the things she asks if you are able to. Repeat the correct response.

   ESEMPIO:  Mi darai un passaggio? → Lo farò se potrò.

1. ...    2. ...    3. ...    4. ...

**D. Delle domande per Lei.** Answer the questions you hear according to your own feelings and experiences. You will hear a possible response.

ESEMPIO:   Se ha fame, cosa fa? → Se ho fame, mi preparo un panino.

1. ...   2. ...   3. ...   4. ...

## B. Il periodo ipotetico con il congiuntivo

**A. Se avessimo tempo...** Tell what these people would do if they had more time. Use the subjects you hear and the expressions listed below. Repeat the correct response.

ESEMPIO:   (Mauro) fare da mangiare → Se Mauro avesse tempo farebbe da mangiare.

1. giocare a tennis
2. scrivere un romanzo
3. viaggiare

4. non correre
5. imparare a memoria (*memorize*) una poesia

**B.** Time to repent! Tell what got you into trouble. Complete the sentences you hear, using the expressions listed below. Repeat the correct response.

ESEMPIO:   (Se non avessi scherzato...) lui / non arrabbiarsi →
                 Se non avessi scherzato non si sarebbe arrabbiato.

1. io / arrivare puntuale
2. io / non ubriacarmi
3. loro / credermi

4. io / studiare di più
5. io / non dovere stare a dieta

## C. Fare + *infinito*

**A.** Sentirete un dialogo dal vostro testo. Ripetete durante le pause:

MICHELE:   L'hai poi finita quella traduzione tecnica dal giapponese?
   LINA:   Non me ne parlare! Mi ha fatto diventare matta!
MICHELE:   Lo so che sei sempre stata una perfezionista...
   LINA:   Perfezionista fino a un certo punto. Ci ho lavorato due settimane, ma mi sono resa conto che ancora non va: dovrò farmi aiutare da qualcun altro più bravo di me.
MICHELE:   Sta' tranquilla: te la faccio riguardare dalla mia amica Ako, che è un'ottima traduttrice.

**B.** Things have been breaking down around your house lately. Take a look at the drawings below and tell what these people need to have fixed. Use the subject you hear. Repeat the correct response.

ESEMPIO:

Roberta →
Deve fare riparare il televisore.

1.

2.

3.

4.

5.

**C.** You and some friends are babysitting for Nina and Tonio. When their parents call to check in, you ask them what to have the children do so they'll behave. Relay their commands to your friends using the information given below. Repeat the correct response.

ESEMPIO: (Fatelo leggere!) un libro → Fategli leggere un libro!

1. un latte caldo
2. un panino
3. un disco

4. la TV
5. un racconto

**D.** Barbara cannot believe you manage to have your housemates do all these things for you. Tell her about your power, as in the example. Repeat the correct response.

ESEMPIO: Fai stirare (iron) i vestiti a Piero? → Sì, glieli faccio stirare!

1. ...    2. ...    3. ...    4. ...

# D. Lasciare e i verbi di percezione + infinito

**A.** Mauro wants to know if you saw and heard all the action at the campus talent show. Tell him you did, as in the example. Repeat the correct response.

ESEMPIO: Hai sentito cantare Mirella? → Sì, l'ho sentita cantare.

1. ...    2. ...    3. ...    4. ...

**B.** What do you let your housemates get away with? After you hear each item number, follow the example and use the expressions indicated below. Repeat the correct response.

ESEMPIO: voi / cantare nella doccia → Vi lascio cantare nella doccia.

1. Maurizio / dormire fino a tardi
2. le ragazze / fare l'aerobica in cucina
3. tu / baciare mia sorella
4. voi / mangiare tutti i salumi

Now restate your sentences using the expression **lascio che.** Repeat the correct response.

ESEMPIO: voi / cantare nella doccia → Lascio che cantiate nella doccia.

## E. Plurali irregolari e nomi invariabili

**A.** Sentirete un dialogo dal vostro testo. Ripetete durante le pause:

GABRIELLA: Come stai, nonna?
   NONNA: Male, figlia mia! Il solito attacco di artrite; mi fanno male le braccia, le giunture delle ginocchia, le dita delle mani. Insomma, ho le ossa rotte!
GABRIELLA: E il dottore, che dice?
   NONNA: Ah, quell'uomo è impossibile! Dice di prendere un paio di aspirine e di mangiare frutta e verdura, poca carne e poche uova. Bella vita!

**B.** Give the plural of the following expressions. You will hear the correct response.

ESEMPIO: il dito lungo → le dita lunghe

1. ...   2. ...   3. ...   4. ...   5. ...

**C.** Give the singular of the following expressions. You will hear the correct response.

ESEMPIO: le crisi economiche → la crisi economica

1. ...   2. ...   3. ...   4. ...   5. ...

# Dialogo

---

Ascoltate il dialogo dal vostro testo. Poi rispondete alle domande.

      PAOLO: Come vanno gli studi? Fai progressi?
GERALDINE: Così così: ora studiamo l'uso del condizionale e del congiuntivo nel periodo ipotetico; questa grammatica italiana è più difficile di quanto credessi.
      PAOLO: Se vuoi, ti aiuto io. Ecco subito un bell'esempio: Se Geraldine mi amasse, sarei un uomo felice.
GERALDINE: Il solito spiritoso! Se davvero vuoi aiutarmi, sii più serio!
      PAOLO: Tu non ricordi le regole di grammatica perchè le frasi dei libri di testo sono noiose. Ora t'illustro io la regola con una poesia che pare fatta apposta. Stammi a sentire:
                S'io fossi foco, arderei 'l mondo;
                S'io fossi vento, lo tempesterei;
                S'io fossi acqua, i' l'annegherei;
                S'i fossi Dio, lo manderei in profondo...
      Oh Dio, non ricordo il resto! Solo l'ultima terzina che è un capolavoro:
                S'i fossi Cecco, come sono e fui,
                Torrei le donne giovani e leggiadre
                E vecchie e laide lascerei altrui.

GERALDINE: Tipico maschio italiano anche questo poeta… Chi era?

PAOLO: Un senese naturalmente: un certo Cecco Angiolieri che visse nel tredicesimo secolo e scherzava su tutto per non piangere.

GERALDINE: Mi pare che sia una vostra abitudine anche oggi.

PAOLO: Già, noi non vogliamo sembrare sentimentali e così prendiamo in giro tutto ciò che gli altri prendono sul serio.

GERALDINE: Ma non siete mai seri?

PAOLO: Certo! Più si scherza e più si è seri!

GERALDINE: Ah, se vi capissi, sarei contenta!

PAOLO: Brava! Vedi che hai già imparato la regola di grammatica? Se continuerai a stare in mia compagnia, imparerai tutte le regole! E anche a trasgredirle…

GERALDINE: Buffone!
          S'io fossi Geraldine, com'io sono e fui,
          Tutti i maschi italiani impiccherei…
     Ciao, scappo!

PAOLO: Ciao, bella! E se hai bisogno di altre lezioni, telefonami!

You will hear six statements based on the dialogue. You will hear each one twice. Circle *vero* or *falso.*

1. vero   falso        3. vero   falso        5. vero   falso

2. vero   falso        4. vero   falso        6. vero   falso

# Dettato

Sentirete tre volte un breve dettato. La prima volta, ascoltate attentamente. La seconda volta, scrivete quello che sentite. La terza volta, correggete quello che avete scritto.

_____

_____

_____

_____

_____

_____

_____

# E ora ascoltiamo!

You will hear Massimo's diary entry for today and then five statements. You will hear everything twice. Circle *vero* or *falso.*

1. vero   falso               4. vero   falso

2. vero   falso               5. vero   falso

3. vero   falso

CAPITOLO
# 20

## Vocabolario preliminare

Take a moment to look over the list of words on the right. You will hear five definitions. After each one, choose the word defined from the column on the right.

1. _____

2. _____

3. _____

4. _____

5. _____

   a.  gli antenati
   b.  gli stereotipi
   c.  le radici
   d.  immigrare
   e.  sognare
   f.  ricordare
   g.  la tradizione

## Grammatica

### A. La forma passiva del verbo

**A.** Sentirete un dialogo dal vostro testo. Ripetete durante le pause:

GIACOMO: Signora Bertucci, che buon pasto! Le tagliatelle erano squisite. Mi dica, dove le ha comprate?

SIG.RA BERTUCCI: Figlio mio, da noi, la pasta è sempre fatta in casa…

GIACOMO: E la tavola! Proprio un sogno.

ANGELA: Sai, Giacomo, la tovaglia l'ha fatta la nonna. E i tovaglioli…

SIG.RA BERTUCCI: Sono stati ricamati dalla zia Maria quando aveva solo quindici anni.

GIACOMO: Che belle queste tradizioni di famiglia!

**B.** Bob has just arrived in Rome for a study abroad program, and you are showing him around. When he asks who sells certain items, answer him as in the example, using the information given below. Repeat the correct response.

ESEMPIO: (Chi vende i formaggi?) il lattaio → I formaggi sono venduti dal lattaio.

1. il pasticciere
2. il fruttivendolo
3. il panettiere

4. il salumiere
5. il macellaio

**C. Chi è stato invitato?** Tell Pierina who has been invited to dinner. Repeat the correct response.

ESEMPIO: Hanno invitato Mirella? → Sì, Mirella è stata invitata.

1. …   2. …   3. …   4. …

# B. Il **si** impersonale

**A.** Sentirete un dialogo dal vostro testo. Ripetete durante le pause:

> ADA: Nonna, sei arrivata negli Stati Uniti nel 1930? Com'eri giovane! E avevi già un bambino!
> NONNA LILÌ: Figlia mia, erano tempi diversi… Ci si sposava giovani, e si doveva lavorare sodo per guadagnarsi il pane.
> ADA: Povera nonna! Non sarai stata molto felice.
> NONNA LILÌ: No, cara, tutt'altro: ci si voleva bene in famiglia e ci si divertiva con cose semplici. Certi valori si sono perduti con il passar degli anni…

**B.** Silvia's mother has just arrived in the United States for the first time and she is surprised at some aspects of the American lifestyle. Agree with her statements, as in the example. You will hear the correct response.

ESEMPIO:   Mangiate molta carne qui in America! → È vero; si mangia molta carne.

1. …   2. …   3. …   4. …   5. …

**C. Delle domande per Lei.** Answer the questions you hear according to your own experiences. You will hear a possible response.

ESEMPIO:   Dove si comprano i dischi nella Sua città? → I dischi si comprano da Tower Records.

1. …   2. …   3. …   4. …

**D. Cosa si è fatto in Italia?** You have just returned from a year in Italy and are telling your friends about your experiences there. After you hear each item number, use the expressions given below and the **si** construction. Repeat the correct response.

ESEMPIO:   alzarsi presto ogni mattina → Ci si è alzati presto ogni mattina.

1. andare in bici per un'ora
2. fare colazione
3. andare all'università
4. studiare nel pomeriggio
5. farsi da mangiare
6. andare a letto presto

# C. Il gerundio e i tempi progressivi

**A.** You can't avoid Cinzia today! Tell all the places you ran into her, as in the example. Use the expressions listed below. Repeat the correct response.

ESEMPIO:   passeggiare → Passeggiando, ho incontrato Cinzia.

1. ritornare a casa
2. fare la spesa
3. entrare al bar
4. uscire dalla banca
5. camminare in Via Roma

**B. Cosa si sta facendo?** Take a look at the drawings and tell what these people are doing right now. Repeat the correct response.

ESEMPIO:

Mirella → Sta uscendo di casa.

1.

2.

3.

4.

5.

Now repeat the exercise, telling what these people *were* doing when the pictures were made. Repeat the correct response.

    ESEMPIO:   Mirella → Stava uscendo di casa.

C. You will hear five short statements, each one twice. Circle the best English equivalent for each one.

1.  a.  Since she speaks Italian she doesn't find it difficult.

    b.  She doesn't find speaking Italian difficult.

2.  a.  Going to the movies is fun.

    b.  Going to the movies I had fun.

3.  a.  Did you meet him while he was coming out of the library?

    b.  Did you meet him while you were coming out of the library?

4.  a.  Having written a lot I felt tired.

    b.  Writing a lot makes me tired.

5.  a.  Since I'm doing this excercise I am bored.

    b.  Doing this excercise is very boring.

# Dialogo

Ascoltate il dialogo dal vostro testo. Poi rispondete alle domande.

GERALDINE: Scusa se ti interrompo, mi chiamo Geraldine. Sei italiana?

SILVIA: Piacere, sono Silvia. Sì, sono italiana ma studio in California da sei anni.

GERALDINE: E ogni anno torni in Italia?

SILVIA: Sì, voglio vedere i miei amici e la mia famiglia almeno una volta all'anno. Abbiamo sempre tante cose da raccontarci... come si sta negli Stati Uniti... cos'è cambiato in Italia... gli americani sono così... gli italiani invece...

GERALDINE: Ho capito... e tu ti trovi nel mezzo a dire: «Ma no, non è vero che gli americani sono superficiali, individualisti, che pensano solo ai soldi e a divertirsi. Ci sono anche gli americani che pensano ai problemi sociali e che non si occupano solo della loro carriera... »

SILVIA: Esattamente, e quando sono qui è la stessa cosa con gli italiani. Molti americani pensano che gli italiani siano tutti *Latin lovers* pronti ad assaltare le turiste, senza rispetto per la vita privata, estroversi, sempre pronti a ridere e a cantare... Tantissimi italiani invece sono introversi, odiano le feste e le canzonette, non si occupano della moda e non hanno mai fatto la pasta in casa.

GERALDINE: Sembra che gli stereotipi e i miti siano duri a morire.

SILVIA: Secondo me è tutta questione di pigrizia. Invece di cercare di conoscere le persone è più facile dire: «Ah! È americano, allora si occuperà solo di sport. È italiano, allora la sua passione sarà la cucina.» Se poi si fanno i confronti: «Le donne americane sono più emancipate delle donne italiane!» «Ma scherzi? Le donne italiane sono molto più emancipate delle donne americane!»

GERALDINE: Beh, su questo punto credo che potremmo discutere per qualche ora!

SILVIA: Di sicuro. Infatti io veramente penso che le donne italiane siano molto più indipendenti delle donne americane... per esempio...

GERALDINE: Ah, no!... Su questo io non sono assolutamente d'accordo!

You will hear six statements based on the dialogue. You will hear each one twice. Circle *vero* or *falso*.

1. vero   falso          3. vero   falso          5. vero   falso

2. vero   falso          4. vero   falso          6. vero   falso

# Dettato

Sentirete tre volte un breve dettato. La prima volta, ascoltate attentamente. La seconda volta, scrivete quello che sentite. La terza volta, correggete quello che avete scritto.

_____

_____

_____

_____

_____

_____

_____

_____

# Answers Not Appearing on Tape

## CAPITOLO PRELIMINARE
### A. Alfabeto e suoni
G. 1. grammatica 2. importanza 3. partire 4. partirò 5. musica 6. trentatrè 7. subito 8. umiltà 9. abitano 10. cantavano H. 1. prendere 2. prenderò 3. caffè 4. tre 5. quarantatrè 6. civiltà 7. virtù 8. tornare

### D. Numeri da uno a cento
A. 1. 12 2. 21 3. 97 4. 17 5. 50 6. 5 7. 76 8. 100

## CAPITOLO 7
### D. Numeri superiori a cento
A. 1. 3,600 2. 410 3. 12,300 4. 1,618 5. 1,000,500 6. 860

## CAPITOLO 18
### D. Riassunto dei plurali irregolari
C. 1. programma lungo 2. farmacie francesi 3. mance generose 4. nemici antipatici 5. paese natio

# Fundamentals of Economics

# Fundamentals of Economics

**THIRD EDITION**

**William Boyes**
*Arizona State University*

**Michael Melvin**
*Arizona State University*

**Houghton Mifflin Company**   Boston   New York

*To our families*
W.B.   M.M.

*Vice President, Publisher:* Charles Hartford
*Vice President, Editor-in-Chief:* George Hoffman
*Senior Sponsoring Editor:* Ann West
*Senior Project Editor:* Nancy Blodget
*Editorial Assistant:* Sean McGann
*Senior Composition Buyer:* Sarah Ambrose
*Art and Design Manager:* Gary Crespo
*Manufacturing Coordinator:* Chuck Dutton
*Senior Marketing Manager:* Todd Berman

Cover and part opener photos: *(left)* © Digital Vision; *(center)* © Andrew Ward/Life File/ Getty Images; *(right)* © Sami Sarkis/Getty Images

PHOTO CREDITS

p. 10, © Tom Stewart/The Stock Market/Corbis; p. 12, © Cameramann/The Image Works; p. 15, *(left)* © Paul Chesley, *(right)* © Cameramann; p. 34, © Jeff Greenberg/PhotoEdit; p. 37, © Chip East/Reuters/Corbis; p. 67, © Andy Freeberg; p. 73, Getty Images; p. 77, © Ferdinando Scianna/Magnum Photos; p. 90, © David R. Frazier Photo Library; p. 105, © David Young-Wolff/PhotoEdit; p. 108, AP/Wide World Photos; p. 132, © Reuters NewMedia Inc./Corbis; p. 133, AP/Wide World Photos; p. 153, © Lisa Quinones/Black Star; p. 166, © Jonathan Nourok/Stone/Getty Images; p. 168, © Nicolas Reynard; p. 221, © Norm Rowan/The Image Works; p. 229, © Jean-Claude N-Diaye/Imapress/The Image Works; p. 242, © Margaret Bourke White/*Life Magazine*/Getty Images; p. 245, © Gilles Mingasson; p. 278, © David R. Frazier Photo Library; p. 296, © Bob Daemmrich/The Image Works; p. 324, AP/Wide World Photos; p. 341 *(two photos)*, Charlotte Miller; p. 342, © Reuters NewMedia Inc./Corbis; p. 381, © Owen Franken/Stock Boston; p. 382, © Patrick Robert/Corbis Sygma; p. 393, © Jean-Leo Dugast/Panos Pictures; p. 417, © AFP/Getty Images; p. 424, © Jose Fuste Raga/Corbis

Printed in the U.S.A.

Library of Congress Control Number: 2004114089

ISBN: 0-618-49630-0

1 2 3 4 5 6 7 8 9–WB–09 08 07 06 05

# Brief Contents

# Contents

# Preface

As the title of the first chapter in this text makes clear, economics can be found all around you—in your everyday life, in the decisions you make, and in the news. We invite you to join us as we explore the economic landscape—the concepts and issues that confront us on a daily basis. We will consider fundamental questions such as:

- Why study economics? (Chapter 1)
- How does a market work? (Chapter 2)
- Why do people earn different incomes, and why do different jobs pay different wages? (Chapter 3)
- How do firms make money? (Chapter 4)
- What are the benefits of competition? (Chapter 6)
- Why does the government intervene in the affairs of business? (Chapter 7)
- Why are incomes not equally distributed? (Chapter 8)
- How is money traded internationally? (Chapter 10)
- What is a business cycle? (Chapter 11)
- How do banks create money? (Chapter 14)
- What is the Federal Reserve? (Chapter 15)
- Are business cycles related to political elections? (Chapter 16)
- Why do countries restrict international trade? (Chapter 17)
- What is globalization? (Chapter 18)

To help you understand these and other issues, we've tried to boil down economics to its fundamentals—the core concepts. Rather than focusing on formal economic theories, we have chosen to emphasize relevant applications and policy issues—the same issues you read about in today's newspapers.

## OUR GOALS IN WRITING THE TEXT

This book is intended for a one-term course in economics, a course that covers the fundamentals of micro- and macroeconomics. The text was written with several objectives in mind. First, one of our goals is to demonstrate the value of economic analy-

sis in explaining daily events. We also want to show how economic analysis can help us understand why individuals, business firms, and even governments behave as they do. To accomplish this, we relate each concept to the individual. For example, we show what *diminishing marginal returns* means to you and how money supply affects your paycheck. We believe that using real-world examples as illustrations of economic concepts is a more effective learning approach than relying on examples of hypothetical products, firms, and people.

Second, we want to present the world as a global economic environment and to present the tools you need in order to understand and live in this environment. While other texts ignore or isolate international coverage, we fully integrate a global perspective within our discussion of the traditional fundamentals of economics. Topics such as the creation of the European Central Bank, the change in the value of the dollar, and the effect of an exchange rate on firms, prices, and employees are all discussed within the context of economic analysis.

A third, overarching goal is to engage students with concepts that are currently meaningful. We want our readers to learn the fundamentals and to develop an economic way of thinking about issues that confront them. We strive to present only the essential topics rather than force readers to delve into abstract topics so that they become lost in the "forest" and lose sight of the "trees."

## A Focus on Fundamental Questions

Earlier, we introduced some of the fundamental questions considered in the text. These questions and others provide the organizing framework for the text and its accompanying ancillary package. *Fundamental Questions*, in fact, open and organize each chapter, highlighting the critical issues. Students should preview the chapters with these questions in mind, reading actively for understanding and retention. Each related *Fundamental Question* also appears in the margin next to the text discussion and, with brief answers, in the chapter summaries. Finally, *Fundamental Questions* are used as the integrating framework for the text and the entire ancillary package.

For example, brief paragraph answers to each of the questions are found on the student textbook website.

## An Integration of International Issues

As previously noted, the text incorporates a global perspective. In addition to two international chapters—Chapter 17, *Issues in International Trade and Finance,* and Chapter 18, *Globalization*—every chapter incorporates global examples to provide a more realistic picture of the economy. Topics include the following:

- gains from trade (Chapter 1)
- the effects of exchange rates on the demand and supply of individual markets (Chapter 2)
- the issue of price discrimination on an international basis (Chapter 4)
- comparative analysis of fiscal policies in different countries (Chapter 4)
- "global money" and international reserve currencies, including a new section on informal financial markets and a *Global Business Insight* box on Islamic banking (Chapter 14)
- foreign exchange market intervention as part of central bank policy (Chapter 15)
- business cycles and economic growth issues as important macroeconomic policy issues (Chapter 16)

## A Real-World Framework

We have developed a real-world framework that shows how markets work, focusing on competition and the behavior of firms. Instead of becoming bogged down in a theoretical discussion of each market structure model, students learn how businesses behave, compete, create profit, and attempt to sustain profits over time. They learn what business competition means and how it affects their daily lives.

To further connect the text to the real world, we incorporate *Economic Insight* and *Global Business Insight* boxes, which focus on the policies of today's leaders and the business decisions of real companies and governments from around the world. The goal is to help students think critically about news stories and to respond to them with greater insight. Some examples are:

- *Global Business Insight: "Free" Air?* (Chapter 1)
- *Global Business Insight: Jobs Moving Offshore* (Chapter 3)
- *Economic Insight: eBay and Online Markets* (Chapter 7)
- *Economic Insight: The Official Poverty Rate* (Chapter 8)

# CHANGES TO THE THIRD EDITION

## New, Built-in Study Guide

With this edition, we have attempted to provide a truly integrated learning experience for students by including a robust set of study materials after each text chapter. This *Chapter Study Guide* provides an opportunity for students to review and practice using key terms from the chapter, check their understanding of key concepts, and work on applying their new knowledge to short-answer questions and problems. Several application questions end each of these *Study Guide* sections. Answers to all the *Study Guide* questions are included at the back of the book so that students can see how they did and where they may need to review again. Each chapter also contains a complete set of *Exercises* that instructors can assign for homework. Answers to these *Exercises* are included in the instructor supplements only.

## Content Changes

While the organizational structure of the text itself remains similar to the last, the third edition contains a new Chapter 18 on *Globalization* and has been updated to include the latest available macroeconomic data and real-world examples. The text has been revised in response to the many helpful comments and suggestions we received from adopters and reviewers. All of the changes can be found in the Transition Guide, available on the Boyes/Melvin, *Fundamentals of Economics*, 3e website at **http://college.hmco.com** (and on the HM ClassPrep® CD-ROM for instructors), but a few of the more important changes are highlighted here:

- Chapter 1, *Economics and the World Around You.* New discussion has been added on what economists do and why one might want to study economics. In addition, the discussion of gains from trade has been expanded.
- Chapter 3, *Applications of Demand and Supply.* A new section has been added on tariffs and the effects of tariffs on supply and demand.
- Chapter 7, now titled *Competition, Cooperation, and the Government.* This chapter now includes expanded discussion of the functioning of markets with an example of low-carb diets. In addition, this chapter has an expanded discussion of cost/benefit analysis.
- Chapter 8, *Social Issues.* The discussion of minimum wages, illegal drugs, and the war on drugs has been expanded.
- Chapter 9, *An Overview of the National and International Economies.* Discussion of income distribution and poverty has been expanded.

- Chapter 10, *Macroeconomic Measures*. Presentation of the balance of payments has been simplified, eliminating the emphasis on double-entry bookkeeping of the previous edition.
- Chapter 11, *Unemployment, Inflation, and Business Cycles*. A new discussion of how the NBER identifies business cycle turning points has been added.
- Chapter 15, *Monetary Policy*. A new section on inflation targeting as a means of directing central bank policy has been added. This includes a recent policy directive from the FOMC as an example of how the Federal Reserve conducts U.S. policy.
- Chapter 18, *Globalization*. This new chapter discusses the arguments for and against globalization and includes coverage of recent financial crises.

## A COMPLETE TEACHING AND LEARNING SYSTEM

### Proven Pedagogical Features

Reviewers and adopters of the first and second editions have commented very favorably on the learning aids within each chapter. All of these features—along with the new, built-in *Study Guides*—aim to make learning easier by providing a consistent set of signposts to guide readers along the way.

**In-text Referencing System.** Sections are numbered for easy reference and to reinforce hierarchies of ideas. The numbering system serves as an outline of the chapter, allowing instructors flexibility in assigning reading, and making review easy for students.

**Fundamental Questions.** As described above, the *Fundamental Questions* provide an organizing framework for the text and ancillary package. They have been carefully reviewed and, in some cases, revised for this edition in order to reflect the essential points for each chapter.

**Recaps.** Briefly listing the main points covered, a *Recap* appears at the end of each major section. Students are able to quickly review what they have just read before going on to the next section.

**Now You Try It.** First introduced in the second edition to help students master some of the analytical techniques introduced in the text, this feature has been expanded in the third edition. Now even more of these checkpoint questions provide an opportunity for students to practice a technique when it is first introduced. Answers are provided at the back of the book so that students can immediately check their work and go back to the relevant text discussion if necessary.

**Key Terms.** Key terms appear boldfaced in the text where they are first introduced, and they are defined in the margin alongside the appropriate text discussion. They are also listed at the end of each chapter. A complete *Glossary* covering all the key terms and their definitions appears at the end of the book for easy reference.

**Summary.** The *Summary* at the end of each chapter is organized according to the list of *Fundamental Questions*. It includes a brief synopsis of the discussion, which helps students answer those questions.

**End-of-Chapter Exercises.** A full set of exercises at the end of each chapter (10–20 per chapter) provides the student with many additional opportunities for practice—and homework. Answers to these exercises are provided in the *Instructor's Resource Manual* and on the instructor's Boyes/Melvin, *Fundamentals of Economics*, 3e website.

**Internet Exercises.** Each chapter ends with a reference to the chapter-related *Internet Exercises* provided on the Boyes/Melvin website. Many of these exercises link students to real data in, for example, the *Economic Report of the President*, World Trade Organization publications, or a company's annual report.

### A Pedagogically Sound Art Program

Economics can be intimidating, which is why we've incorporated a number of pedagogical devices to help students read and interpret graphs. Annotations on the art point out areas of particular concern or importance. For example, students can see at a glance what parts of the graph illustrate a shortage or a surplus, a change in consumption, or consumer surplus.

Tables that provide data from which graphs are plotted are paired with their graphs. A good example is Figure 6 in Chapter 2. There, color is used to show correlations between the art and the table, and captions clearly explain what is shown in the figure, linking them to the text discussion.

### A Well-Integrated Ancillary Package

One goal for this revision was to make it easier for students to practice and apply the new information they were learning. Thus, they can review as they read a chapter, review again at the end of a chapter, and go to the student website for additional practice and review questions. Our instructor's materials support this student-centered approach. To foster the development of consistent teaching strategies well integrated with the text, the instructor supplements follow the same pedagogical format as the text, incorporating the *Fundamental Questions* throughout.

**Instructor's Resource Manual** by Davis Folsom, University of South Carolina, Beaufort, follows the *Fundamental Questions* framework. Each chapter contains a Lecture Outline and Teaching Strategies, Opportunities for Discussion, Answers to End-of-Chapter Exercises, and Internet Exercises. Each chapter also includes an Active-Learning Exercise that instructors can assign as homework or conduct in class. Available on the instructor website and HM ClassPrep CD.

**Test Bank,** developed by the text authors and Davis Folsom, University of South Carolina, Beaufort, includes over 1700 questions with a mix of difficulty levels and types—multiple-choice, true-false, and essay. All the questions are also referenced according to the in-text numbering system, so instructors can conveniently test down to the paragraph level.

**Houghton Mifflin ClassPrep® and Computerized Testing CD** contains an electronic version of the *Instructor's Resource Manual* (including teaching objectives, lecture outlines, discussion questions, and active-learning exercises) plus a complete set of test questions and HM Testing™ software. In addition, the CD contains a set of PowerPoint slides based on the artwork from the text.

**Instructor and Student Websites** (located at **http://college.hmco.com**) provide a rich store of teaching resources and an extended learning environment. For the instructor, we offer economic and teaching resource links, teaching tips, assignment ideas, and downloadable PowerPoint slides. Students will find Internet Exercises linked to the text, key economic resources for every chapter, additional online (ACE) practice tests, and e-Flash cards.

## ACKNOWLEDGMENTS

We are grateful to our friends and colleagues who have so generously given their time, creativity, and insight to help us create and revise this text. In particular, we would like to thank Cynthia Conrad, University of Hartford; Simeon J. Crowther, California State University, Long Beach; Davis Folsom, University of South Carolina, Beaufort; Arthur J. Janssen, Emporia State University; Wade E. Martin, Colorado School of Mines; Roger Riefler, University of Nebraska; Denise L. Stanley, University of Tennessee; and Eugene Elander, Plymouth State University, for their many constructive comments along the way. Chin-Chyuan Tai from Averett University provided critical feedback in the later stages of the book's production. We would also like to thank Andrea Worrell of ITT Education Services, Inc. for inspiring us to write the text with students like hers in mind. We are grateful to Davis Folsom for his work on the *Instructor's Resource Manual* and *Test Bank* questions and to Melissa Hardison and Eugenio Suarez, who worked with us in developing the *Test Bank* for the first edition. We would also like to thank Janet Wolcutt and Jim Clark for their work in developing strong in-text *Study Guides*.

Finally, we want to thank the staff at Houghton Mifflin Company for their support and publishing expertise—specifically, Ann West, Tonya Lobato, Nancy Blodget, Jim Dimock, and Sean McGann.

# Fundamentals of Economics

# Part One

The Price System

# Chapter 1

# Economics and the World Around You

**?** **Fundamental Questions**

1. **Why study economics?**
2. **What are opportunity costs?**
3. **How are specialization and opportunity costs related?**
4. **Why does specialization occur?**
5. **What are the benefits of trade?**

## Preview

Two women duked it out. Two men crashed their cars. One woman wrote a letter to her grandmother and read 150 pages in a paperback while sitting for $3\frac{1}{2}$ hours. Why? Cheap gas. To announce the grand opening of Circle K's first new stores in five years, the company sold gasoline between 10 AM and noon on a Saturday for the price of $.49 per gallon. Whitney Hamilton got in line at 6:30 AM. "I was in line before there was a line. I've never seen gas prices this low. I don't think I'll ever see them this low again." Vera Lujan drove the 15 or so miles from her home, arriving at 8 AM. Seven cars were ahead of her. "I was already on empty, so I put in $1 and drove over," Lujan said. A 15-gallon limit on the fill-ups was enforced. "I think I burned more gas than I'm going to get," Ben Valdez said as he approached the pumps after waiting 90 minutes. A fistfight broke out when one woman tried to cut in front of another. John Fecther came for the gas but saw the long lines and tried to make a U-turn away from the area. He was hit by another vehicle. "I was going to get the heck out of here," he said as he filled out a police report. "People are crazy. You're only going to save a little."

The people in this story decided to purchase 15 gallons of gas at the very low price of $.49 per gallon. In so doing they had to wait in line more than an hour and in some cases travel several miles to the store. At the time, gas was $1.20 per gallon, so paying the $.49 per gallon saved about $10. But don't forget the time spent and the gas consumed while waiting. These are costs as well. Nevertheless, comparing the costs to the savings, many people decided it was worthwhile to make the trip, wait in line, and purchase the gas. And had the price of gas been $2.00 per gallon, more people would have decided to wait in line.

To some of us, the decision to purchase the gas might seem silly. To others, it is very reasonable. But for all of us, the process of deciding whether to purchase the gas or not is basically the same. *We compare the costs of the decision to the benefits.*

We all have to make choices all the time. Why? Because we don't have everything we want, and we can't get everything we want. Since you are reading this text, you are most likely taking some type of post–high school economics class. Are you at the same time working 40 hours a week, playing tennis or golf, cycling, surfing, watching a movie, reading a novel, and socializing with friends? Probably not. You simply don't have time to do it all. You have to select some of these activ-

**1. Why study economics?**

ities and forgo others. This is what economics is about—trying to understand why people do what they do.

Why are you studying economics? Is it because you are required to, because you have an interest in it, or because you are looking for a well-paying job? All of these are valid reasons. The college degree is important to your future living standards; economics is a fascinating subject, as you will see; and an economics degree can lead to a good job. What is the difference between a high school diploma and a medical degree? About $3.2 million (U.S.), according to the U.S. Census Bureau. Someone whose education does not go beyond high school and who works full-time can expect to earn about $1.2 million between the ages of 25 and 64. Graduating from college and earning advanced degrees translate into much higher lifetime earnings: an estimated $4.4 million for doctors, lawyers, and others with professional degrees; $2.5 million for those with master's degrees; and $2.1 million for college graduates. These are average figures and do not take into account the value of different majors, but there aren't very many majors that provide a higher income than economics. In the business fields economics ranks below accounting but above marketing, management, and human resources in terms of starting salaries. Economics is the highest-paying social science, higher than sociology, psychology, and others. The median base salary of business economists in 2003 was around $83,000, with benefits and other income bringing the median compensation to over $90,000 per year. The highest salaries are earned by those who have a PhD.

A bachelor's degree in economics prepares you for a career in any number of fields—business, banking, the nonprofit sector, journalism, international relations, education, and government. An economics degree is also excellent preparation for graduate study—in law, business, economics, government, public administration, environmental studies, health-care administration, labor relations, urban planning, diplomacy, and other areas.

The reason studying economics can be so useful is that there is a certain logic in economics that enables the economist to solve complex problems, problems that can be of great importance to society. Economists are concerned with why the world is what it is. They examine how individuals and firms make decisions about work, consumption, investment, hiring, and pricing goods and services. They study how entire economies work and how economies interact, why recessions occur at certain times and why economies grow at other times, why some countries have much higher living standards than other countries, and why some people are poor and others rich. They explore the reasons that baseball players earn multimillion-dollar salaries while teachers earn less than $50,000. Studying economics may not provide a student with training to work in a specific trade like accounting or nursing, but it provides a broad base of skills on which to build. Economics sheds light on how the world—and corporations—work, but more importantly, it teaches a student how to think.

An old and tired joke about economists says that if you laid all the economists head to toe across the country, they still wouldn't come to an agreement. Another joke along the same lines is the one about a President wanting a one-handed economic advisor because economists were always saying, "On the one hand this result and on the other hand that result." It is true that the general public often believes that economists don't agree about anything and that, therefore, the subject of economics has nothing of importance to tell them. The problem is that economists don't talk much in public about what they agree on, which is almost everything involving the logic of economics, but instead emphasize their disagreements. Understandably, the general public and government officials who do not understand economics conclude that their own instincts are as good as anyone else's. Thus, the public and government administrators generalize from personal experience, which often leads them to commit errors of thinking such as the **fallacy of composition.** The fallacy of composition is the faulty logic that maintains that what's true for the individual or the single business is true for the whole economy. For instance, standing up at a concert to get a better view is good for one individual, so everyone's standing up must be better for everyone; restricting free trade is good for some workers, so such restrictions have to be good for all workers; providing free health care is good for some people, so offering free health care for everyone must be good for a nation as a whole.

**fallacy of composition:** the mistake of assuming that what applies to one applies to all

As you will learn in your study of economics, these conclusions are faulty; what's good for one is not necessarily good for many. Economics is often counterintuitive. In fact, economics is probably best defined as the study of unintended consequences. When you study economics, you learn that there are costs to everything—"there is no free lunch." This is the logic of economics that is often lost among members of the general public or government ministers and representatives. The logic for the individual is obvious: If you spend more on one thing, you have less to spend on something else. The logic for nations should be just as obvious: If the United States, Mexico, or any other country is going to spend more on the military, it has to give up spending more on something else. Why, then, do countries seemingly spend more on some government programs without giving up spending on anything else? You will discover how to analyze questions like this one during your study of economics.

The environmentalists who organized and protested at international meetings such as the European Economic Summit in April 2004 and the G8 Meeting in Savannah/Sea Island, Georgia, in June 2004 argue that the world is being overrun by greedy corporations that destroy the environment, create global warming, and destroy rain forests. They maintain that there should be no pollution and no harvesting of trees in the rain forests. Perhaps their arguments have some validity, but the environmentalists forget the unintended consequences of the policies they desire—there are costs to following these policies. People lose jobs, standards of living decline, the poor become even poorer, and so on. It is up to the economist to indicate these consequences. People with good intentions argued that asbestos can be damaging to people's health. Consequently, the government imposed strict rules regarding the use and removal of asbestos. These rules were supposed to save ten lives each year. The cost of implementing the rules per life saved is about $144 million per year. The general public might say that a life is worth an infinite amount of money, but the economist would point out that spending more than a billion dollars a year to reduce asbestos damage has had other consequences. In fact, the consequences of that expenditure may harm society more than they help it. The money spent on asbestos removal has to come from somewhere; that means there has to be less spending on other things such as safer cars, better health care, and leisure activities. As a consequence of reduced spending in other areas, more people could die than the number of people that the spending on asbestos removal and restricted use have saved. Many people argue that wealthy nations need to provide more aid to poorer nations, that such aid will save many destitute people from starvation and disease. The economist has to say, "Let's look at the costs and benefits of this policy. Such aid could have unintended consequences."

Perhaps you can see that your study of economics will be interesting and provocative. It will challenge some beliefs you now hold. It will also help you build skills that will be valuable to your life and in whatever occupation you choose. ■

# 1. THE DEFINITION OF ECONOMICS

**2. What are opportunity costs?**

Why are diamonds so expensive while water and air—necessities of life—are nearly free? The reason is that diamonds are relatively scarcer; that is, relative to the available quantities, more diamonds are wanted than water or air. Of course, water is far from free these days. Some people regularly spend over $6 a gallon on bottled drinking water, and most homeowners must pay their local government for tap water. Even air is not always cheap or free, as noted in the Global Business Insight feature: " 'Free' Air?"

## 1.a. Scarcity and Opportunity Costs

**scarcity:** occurs when the quantity people want is greater than the quantity available

The study of economics begins with scarcity. **Scarcity** refers to the idea that there is not enough of something to satisfy everyone who would like that something. People have unlimited wants—they always want more than they have or can

## "Free" Air?

**A**lthough air might be what we describe as a free good, quality, breathable air is not free in many places in the world. In fact, breathable air is becoming a luxury in many places. Consider the Opus Hotel in Vancouver, British Columbia. It is the first North American hotel to offer hand-held oxygen dispensers in every room. These oxygen canisters are small enough to fit into a purse or briefcase and hold enough air for twelve minutes of breathing time. Breathing oxygen is said to increase energy, improve cognitive performance, and reduce the effects of hangovers. Opus charges $9.40 for the use of the canisters.

An oxygen bar where you can inhale 95 percent pure $O_2$ is the latest craze to hit Dublin, Ireland, and other large cities around the world. Sniffing concentrated, flavored oxygen is a big hit in the United States.

Although these "luxury" purchases of oxygen are increasing, less developed countries find their sales of oxygen to be more a matter of necessity. In Mexico City, clean, breathable air is hard to find. In this city of 19 million people and more than 3 million cars, dust, lead, and chemicals make the air unsafe

### Global Business Insight

to breathe more than 300 days a year. Beijing is no different. A few entrepreneurs have opened oxygen boutiques, where someone strolling along the walkway can drop in and for a few pesos or RMB (renminbi) breathe some clean oxygen.

purchase with their incomes. Whether they are wealthy or poor, what they have is never enough. Since people do not have everything they want, they must use their limited time and income to select those things they want most and forgo the rest. The choices they make and the manner in which the choices are made explain much of why the real world is what it is.

A choice is simply a comparison of alternatives. For instance if you were deciding whether to buy a new car, what would your alternatives be? They would be other makes of automobiles, trucks, even bicycles. They also would be virtually anything else on which the money could be spent. When you choose one thing, the benefits you might get from other things are forgone. Economists refer to the forgone benefits of the next best alternative as **opportunity costs**—the highest-valued alternative that must be forgone when a choice is made.

Opportunity costs are part of every decision and activity. Your opportunity costs of reading this book are whatever else you could be doing—perhaps watching TV, talking with friends, working, or listening to music.

### 1.a.1. The Opportunity Cost of Going to School

Suppose you decided to attend a school where the tuition and other expenses add up to $4,290 per year. Are these your total costs? If you answer yes, you are ignoring opportunity costs. If instead of going to school you would have chosen to work full-time, then the benefits of full-time employment are your opportunity costs. If you could have obtained a position with an annual income of $20,800, the actual cost of school is the $4,290 of direct expenses plus the $20,800 of forgone salary, or $25,090.

Each term you must decide whether to register for school. You could work full-time and not attend school, attend school and not work, or work part-time and attend school. The time you devote to school will decrease as you devote more time to work. You trade off hours spent at work for hours spent in school. If you went to school full-time, you might earn the highest grades. As you work more hours, you gain additional income but might earn lower grades. If this situation occurs, we say that you trade off grades and income.

Societies, like individuals, face scarcities and must make choices, that is, have **tradeoffs.** Because resources are scarce, a nation cannot produce as much of everything as it wants. When it produces more health care, it must forgo the production of education, automobiles, or military hardware. When it devotes more of its resources to the military, fewer resources are available to devote to health care, education, or consumer goods.

## 1.b. Resources and Income

Some goods are used to produce other goods. For instance, to make chocolate chip cookies we need flour, sugar, chocolate chips, butter, our own labor, and an oven. To distinguish between the ingredients of a good and the good itself, we call the ingredients **resources.** (Resources are also called factors of production and inputs; the terms are interchangeable.) The ingredients of the cookies are the resources, and the cookies are the goods.

As illustrated in Figure 1(a), economists have classified resources into three general categories: land, labor, and capital.

1. **Land** includes all natural resources, such as minerals, timber, and water, as well as the land itself.
2. **Labor** refers to the physical and intellectual services of people and includes the training, education, and abilities of the individuals in a society.
3. **Capital** refers to products such as machinery and buildings that are used to produce other goods and services. You will often hear the term *capital* used to describe the financial backing for some project to finance some business. Economists refer to funds used to purchase capital as **financial capital.**

---

**opportunity costs:** the highest-valued alternative that must be forgone when a choice is made

**tradeoffs:** what must be given up to acquire something else

**resources:** inputs used to create goods and services

**land:** the general category of resources encompassing all natural resources, land, and water

**labor:** the general category of resources encompassing all human activity related to the productive process

**capital:** the equipment, machines, and buildings used to produce goods and services

**financial capital:** the stocks and bonds used to purchase capital

Figure 1

**Flow of Resources and Income**

Three types of resources are used to produce goods and services: land, labor, and capital. See 1(a). The owners of resources are provided income for selling their services. Landowners are paid rent, laborers receive wages, and capital receives interest. See 1(b). Figure 1(c) links Figures 1(a) and 1(b). People use their resources to acquire income with which they purchase the goods they want. Producers use the money received from selling the goods to pay for the use of the resources in making goods. Resources and income flow between certain firms and certain resource owners as people allocate their scarce resources to best satisfy their wants.

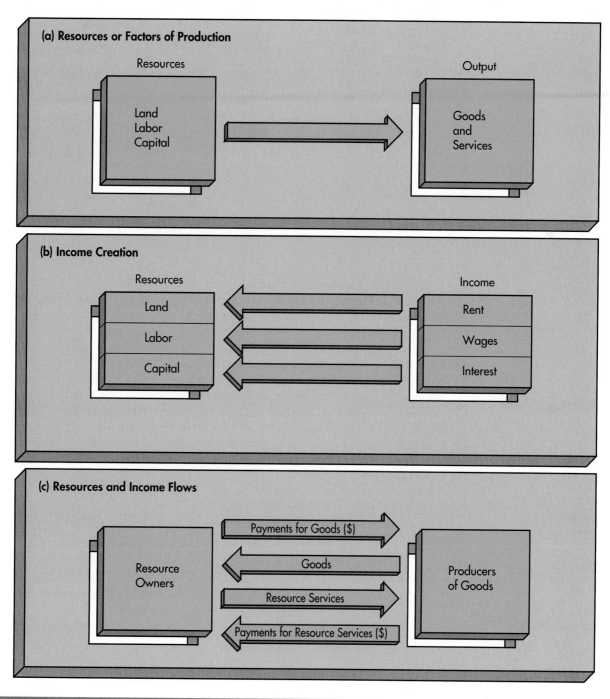

Income is based on the value of resources you own. People choose to attend college for many reasons, but primarily because their income is likely to be higher with a college degree than without one. Choosing to attend college means choosing not to work full-time or not to obtain a vocational training degree. Every choice involves opportunity costs—even attending class and taking notes has opportunity costs. It means not watching TV, sleeping in, eating, or participating in activities or work.

People obtain income by selling their resources or the use of their resources, as illustrated in Figure 1(b). Economists define payment to the owners of land as rent, payment to people who provide labor services as wages, and payment to owners of capital as interest.

Figures 1(a) and 1(b) are linked because the income that resource owners acquire from selling the use of their resources provides them the ability to buy goods and services. And producers use the money received from selling their goods to pay for the resource services. In Figure 1(c), the flows of money are indicated along the outside arrows, and the flows of goods or resource services are indicated along the inside arrows. The resource services flow from resource owners to producers of goods in return for income; the flows of goods go from the producers of the goods to resource owners in return for the money payment for these goods.

RECAP

1. Scarcity exists when people want more of an item than exists at a zero price.

2. Choices have to be made because of scarcity. People cannot have or do everything they desire all the time. Economics is the study of how people choose to use their scarce resources in an attempt to satisfy their wants.

3. Opportunity costs are the benefits that are forgone due to a choice. When you choose one thing you must give up—forgo—others.

4. Opportunity cost is an individual concept but can be used to demonstrate scarcity and choice for a society as a whole.

5. Goods are produced with resources (also called factors of production and inputs). Economists have classified resources into three categories: land, labor, and capital.

6. Income comes from the ownership of resources.

## 2. SPECIALIZATION AND EXCHANGE

Are you good with computers or reading or writing? Are you a good golfer or tennis player? Can you fix electrical or plumbing problems or work on large appliances? Even if you are good at all these things, do you do them all? At any moment in time individuals are endowed with certain resources and abilities. People can choose to be self-sufficient—using their resources and producing what they want and need themselves—or they can choose to exchange goods and services with others. By trading, they get more than they can by being self-sufficient.

### 2.a. Production Possibilities

Consider a very simple example of the benefits of trade. Suppose two people, Maria and Able, have the ability to carry out two types of tasks, solving math problems and solving economics problems. As shown in Table 1, the two tasks take different time and effort from Maria and Able. We will assume that the quality of their work is the same—just the quantity differs. If Maria does nothing but work on math, she is able to solve 10 problems in an hour; and if she does nothing but economics, she is able to solve 10 economics problems in an hour. Her opportunity cost of doing the 10 math problems is the 10 economics problems she could have done. Able, on the other hand, can solve the 10 math problems in an hour but is only able to solve 5 economics problems in that time. Able's opportunity cost of doing the 10 math problems is the 5 economics problems he could have done instead.

Suppose Maria and Able would each like to solve 5 math problems, as shown in Table 2. Maria would be able to solve 5 math and 5 economics problems while

**Table 1**

**Production Possibilities and Trade**

| Percent of Resources Devoted to | | | | | |
|---|---|---|---|---|---|
| | | Maria | | Able | |
| Math | Economics | Math | Economics | Math | Economics |
| 100 | 0 | 10 | 0 | 10 | 0 |
| 0 | 100 | 0 | 10 | 0 | 5 |

**Table 2**

**Choices and Trade**

| Trading Situation | Maria's Choices | | Able's Choices | | Gain from Trade |
|---|---|---|---|---|---|
| | Math | Economics | Math | Economics | |
| Alone, no trade | 5 | 5 | 5 | 2.5 | none |
| Trade 1 math problem for 1 economics problem | 5 | 5 | 5 | 5 | Able 2.5 |
| Trade 2 math problems for 1 economics problem | 5 | 7.5 | 5 | 2.5 | Maria 2.5 |

Able would be able to solve 5 math and 2.5 economics problems. This is shown in Table 2 under "Alone, no trade." Notice that together Maria and Able are able to produce 10 math problems and 7.5 economics problems.

## 2.b. Specialization and Comparative Advantage

Now, suppose Maria and Able decide to exchange answers in order to get more done than if each were to work alone. But who will do what? The answer is that the person who sacrifices the fewest economics problems to do math problems does math problems and the person who sacrifices the fewest math problems to do economics problems does economics problems. In other words, the person with the lowest opportunity cost in an activity performs that activity. Even though Maria can do math equally as well as Able and can do economics more efficiently than Able, Able gives up less by specializing in math. Able only has to give up or forgo half an economics problem for each math problem he does while Maria has to give up one economics problem for each math problem she does. As a result, they will do better having Maria specialize in economics. We say that Able has a **comparative advantage** in math because his opportunity cost in math is lower than Maria's, and Maria has a comparative advantage in economics because her opportunity cost in economics is lower than Able's.

## 2.c. Gains from Trade

Since Maria, by herself, can do one math problem at the same rate as she can do one economics problem, she will require at least one economics answer from Able to be willing to give him one math answer. Able can solve two math problems for each economics problem, so he will have to get at least half an economics answer from Maria to give her a math answer.

If they should exchange one math answer for one economics answer, then, as shown in row 2 (1:1) of Table 2, Maria and Able are each able to get five math and five economics answers. Although Maria is no better off than if she had done her own work, Able is 2.5 economics answers better off. These additional 2.5 answers are called the **gains from trade**.

**3. How are specialization and opportunity costs related?**

**4. Why does specialization occur?**

**comparative advantage:** the situation where one individual's opportunity cost is relatively lower than another's

### Now You Try It

**Assume that Maria and Able decide to exchange one math answer for three-quarters of an economics answer. Who gains and by how much?**

**gains from trade:** the additional amount one can consume by trading

The fruit of the prickly pear cactus is popular in salads and drinks. Recently, the extract from the cactus leaves has been found to relieve some of the symptoms of diabetes. Physicians in Mexico and Japan prescribe the extract as a substitute for insulin in some cases and as an enhancement to insulin in others. Though the prickly pear cactus grows in the southwestern United States as well, the harvesting of the cacti occurs mainly in Mexico because most of the prickly pear cactus forests are in Mexico, and the labor-intensive harvesting process is less costly in Mexico than it would be in the United States. Mexico has a comparative advantage in the harvesting of the cacti.

If, instead of one for one, they agree to exchange two math answers for each economics answer, then, as shown in row 3 (2:1) of Table 2, Maria gains 2.5 economics answers while Able is no better off than if he had done the problems himself. At any rate of exchange between 1:1 and 2:1, both Maria and Able will gain from specializing and exchanging answers.

In virtually every trading situation, both parties gain from voluntary exchange; the amount each party gains—that is, the amount both parties together get that is larger than the sum of what each could have produced without trade—is called the gains from trade.

This simple example illustrates how the real world works. People focus on what they do best and then trade with others. You cook and your roommate cleans; you work on computers and let someone else fix your car; you purchase groceries, letting someone else grow the food. Why do specialization and trade occur? Because people always want more than they currently have, and specializing and then trading enable them to get more than not specializing and trading. This is one of the fundamental assumptions of economics: people behave in ways that give them the greatest benefit—the greatest happiness—given their limited resources. In doing this, people compare the costs and benefits of an action and choose to undertake the action if, in their opinion, the benefits exceed the costs. Thus, people will look at making a trade if what they give up (their costs) is less than what they gain (their benefits).

We have to decide how to use our own scarce resources. We must choose where to devote our energies. Few of us are jacks-of-all-trades. Nations, similarly, have limited amounts of resources and must choose where to devote those resources.

**(?)**

**5. What are the benefits of trade?**

Specializing in those activities that require us to give up the smallest amount of other things—in other words, where we have a comparative advantage—enables us to obtain more than trying to do everything ourselves. A plumber does plumbing and leaves teaching to the teachers. The teacher teaches and leaves electrical work to the electrician. Grenada specializes in spice production and leaves manufacturing to the United States. But if we specialize, how do we get the other things we want? The answer is that we trade.

**RECAP**

1. Exchange occurs because all parties involved believe the exchange can be beneficial.

2. Opportunity cost is the amount of one good or service that must be given up to obtain one additional unit of another good or service.

3. The rule of specialization is that the individual (firm, region, or nation) will specialize in the production of the good or service that has the lowest opportunity cost.

4. Specialization and trade enable individuals, firms, and nations to get more than they could without specialization and trade.

5. By specializing in an activity one does relatively better than other activities, one can trade with others and gain more than if one carried out all activities oneself. This additional amount is referred to as gains from trade.

## 3. TRADE

Trade occurs because it makes people better off. Trade or exchange occurs among people within a family when someone cooks, someone else cleans, and another shovels snow or mows the lawn. Trade occurs within a neighborhood or town when people purchase goods and services at stores. People trade their money for the goods and services provided by the stores. When people go to work, they provide their services in return for money paid by employers. These voluntary exchanges would not occur if they did not make each trader better off. Trade among nations (or international trade) occurs because it makes the citizens of those nations better off than they would be if they could consume only domestically produced products.

## 3.a. Trade Patterns

Table 3 shows the amount of trade taking place between the United States and its top ten trading partners. Canada and Mexico are the United States' top trading partners. Part of the reason for this is their proximity. Another is that the three countries have formed the North American Free Trade Alliance (NAFTA), which reduces barriers to trade within the alliance. Japan continues to be a major trading partner of the United States, and the United States is purchasing more and more from China. Although just a few years ago it was only a minor trading partner with the United States, China has rapidly advanced to become its third largest partner. The Global Business Insight box entitled "Trade with China" goes into more detail about United States–China trade.

## 3.b. Barter and Money

By specializing in activities in which opportunity costs are lowest and then trading, each trader (individual, country) will end up with more than if each had tried to produce everything. Specialization and trade enable nations to acquire combinations of goods that are greater than what their own resource capabilities would allow, just as specialization and trade enable people to acquire combinations of goods that are greater than what they alone could produce. Even though one person, one firm, or one nation is limited to the combinations of goods it can produce using its own resources, through specialization and trade more goods can be acquired. This is why people, firms, and nations trade.

Traders are simply buyers and sellers. When you go to the store to purchase groceries, you are trading money for groceries. When you purchase your textbooks, you are trading money for textbooks. The McDonald's employee acts as a middleman for the firm and trades the hamburger, fries, and shake for money. The employee is trading his or her time for money.

Table 3

**Top Ten Countries with Which the United States Trades, August 2003**

| Country Name | 2003 (billions of U.S.$) |
| --- | --- |
| Canada | 393.65 |
| Mexico | 235.53 |
| China | 180.80 |
| Japan | 170.09 |
| Germany | 96.89 |
| United Kingdom | 76.56 |
| South Korea | 61.06 |
| Taiwan | 49.09 |
| France | 46.29 |
| Italy | 36.01 |

The total values given are for imports and exports added together. These countries represent 69.84 percent of U.S. imports, and 68.12 percent of U.S. exports. Source: U.S. Department of Commerce.

## Trade with China

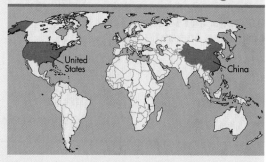

Trade between the United States and China has been increasing very rapidly. In 1998, the United States purchased $71 billion of products from China. By 2002, it was purchasing more than $125 billion. In 1998, China purchased $14 billion from the United States and in 2002, $22 billion. Thus, while sales of products from China to the United States had increased by 76 percent, sales from the United States to China had increased by 56 percent.

The items most purchased by the United States from China are miscellaneous manufactured articles (such as toys and games), office machines, telecommunications equipment, sound recording equipment (such as televisions and VCRs), electrical ma-

chinery, and footwear. The items most purchased by China from the United States are transport equipment (aircraft and parts), electrical machinery, office machines (mainly computers), and industrial machinery and equipment. Interestingly, the largest firms selling goods to the United States from China are U.S. firms—Motorola and Dell.

China currently has the world's largest mobile phone network, with 145 million cellular phone users, even though only 13 percent of the population uses mobile phones. China is a huge demander of com-

mercial aircraft equipment, and that demand will continue rising during the next 20 years. In 2002, China replaced Japan as the world's second largest PC market, and it became the world's second largest Internet user (after the United States). Demand for autos in China is rising more rapidly than anywhere else in the world, 20 to 30 percent per year.

---

**barter:** trade without the use of money

In some cases, people trade goods or services for goods or services and no money changes hands. These cases are referred to as **barter** trades. In most instances, barter is too complicated to serve as a means of trade. Let's say you needed a textbook. In a barter world, you would have to find someone with the textbook who also wanted something you had. If you did not have what he wanted, then you would have to find another person who wanted what you had and had what the textbook owner wanted. Then you would have to make two trades to get the textbook. This type of world would get very complicated quickly. That is why money has

Trade between the United States and the Asian nations has been growing for several years even though some of the Asian nations attempt to restrict the sale of foreign goods in their country or to otherwise limit trade. In the photo on the left, it is clear that Coca Cola has been able to enter the Korean market, dominating its soft drink industry. The United States has been relatively open to foreign goods. Although the United States threatens to impose trade sanctions against Japan or China at times, citizens of the United States clamor for goods made in other nations. In the photo on the right, seamstresses in Korea prepare clothes for major distributors in the United States.

| Country | Currency Name | Currency Symbol | Value of Currency in U.S.$ |
|---|---|---|---|
| Australia | Dollar | A$ | .7132 |
| Britain | Pound | £ | 1.8265 |
| Canada | Dollar | C$ | .7409 |
| Japan | Yen | ¥ | .0090 |
| Mexico | Peso | Ps | .0875 |
| European Union (EU) | Euro | € | 1.2237 |

arisen in virtually every society from the beginning of time. There are reports of rocks and shells being used for money in primitive societies, and gold and silver have been used in modern times. Today, most monies are printed or coined out of inexpensive materials.

Each nation has its own money or currency, so currencies have to be exchanged in order for nations to trade. The price at which currencies are exchanged is called the **exchange rate.** For instance, the exchange rates existing on August 11, 2004, between the U.S. dollar and a few currencies are listed in Table 4. According to the data, the Australian dollar was worth a little more than $.71, the British pound was worth a little less than $1.83, and so on. Exchange rates are reported daily in most newspapers.

**exchange rate:** the price at which one currency is exchanged for another

If in August 2004, a U.S. buyer wanted to purchase a pair of Doc Martens shoes priced at £80 from a British seller, the buyer would have had to first exchange enough dollars to get £80. Since 1 pound was worth 1.83 dollars, the buyer would need $1.83 \times 80 = 146.4$ dollars. For another example, suppose that in August 2004, a Canadian couple wanted to spend some winter months in Arizona. The rent the couple would have to pay in Arizona was 800 U.S. dollars per month. That doesn't sound too bad, but when the couple converted to their currency, the rent was quite high. Since 1 Canadian dollar was worth only .7409 U.S. dollars, the rent was $800 \times 1/.7409 = 1,079.77$ Canadian dollars. Yet this rent was better for the Canadian couple than what had been the case a year prior because the value of the dollar had fallen relative to the value of many other currencies, including the Canadian dollar. In March 2003, the Canadian dollar was worth just $.64, or one U.S. dollar equaled 1.56 Canadian dollars. So the $800 rent in Arizona would have cost 1,248 Canadian dollars.

RECAP

1. Trade is typically carried out using money; however, some trades are goods or services for goods or services. These are called barter trades.

2. International trade requires that the currencies of the trading nations be converted from one to another. The price at which the currencies are exchanged is the exchange rate.

# SUMMARY

### ? Why study economics?

1. The objective of economics is to understand why the real world is what it is.

2. Economics is the study of how people choose to allocate scarce resources to satisfy their unlimited wants.

3. Scarcity is universal; it applies to anything people would like more of than is available at a zero price. Because of scarcity, choices must be made.

### ? What are opportunity costs?

4. Opportunity costs are the forgone opportunities of the next best alternative. Choice means both gaining something and giving up something. When you choose one option, you forgo all others. The benefits of the next best alternative are the opportunity costs of your choice.

### ? How are specialization and opportunity costs related?

5. Comparative advantage is when one person (one firm, one nation) can perform an activity or produce a good with fewer opportunity costs than someone else.

### ? Why does specialization occur?

6. Comparative advantage accounts for specialization. We specialize in the activities in which we have the lowest opportunity costs, that is, in which we have a comparative advantage.

### ? What are the benefits of trade?

7. Specialization and trade enable those involved to acquire more than they could by not specializing and engaging in trade. The additional amount acquired from trade is called the gains from trade.

8. Trade can be made using barter—trading goods or services for goods or services—or using money.

9. If international trade occurs and the countries have different monies, or currencies, then the currencies have to be convertible. The rate at which currencies are convertible is called the exchange rate.

# KEY TERMS

scarcity

opportunity costs

tradeoffs

resources

land

labor

capital

financial capital

comparative advantage

gains from trade

barter

exchange rate

# EXERCISES

1. Explain why each of the following is or is not an economic good.
   a. Steaks      d. Garbage
   b. Houses      e. T-shirts
   c. Cars

2. It is well documented in scientific research that smoking is harmful to our health. Smokers have higher incidences of coronary disease, cancer, and other catastrophic illnesses. Knowing this, about 30 percent of young people begin smoking and about 25 percent of the U.S. population smokes. Are the people who choose to smoke irrational? What do you think of the argument that we should ban smoking in order to protect these people from themselves?

3. Use economics to explain why diamonds are more expensive than water when water is necessary for survival and diamonds are not.

4. Use economics to explain why people leave tips in the following two cases: (a) at a restaurant they visit often; (b) at a restaurant they visit only once.

5. Use economics to explain why people contribute to charities.

6. In presidential campaigns, candidates always seem to make more promises than they can fulfill. In their first campaign, Bill Clinton and Al Gore promised more and better health care; a better environment; only minor reductions in defense; better education; better

roads, bridges, sewer systems, and water systems; and so on. What economic concept did the critics claim Clinton and Gore ignored?

7. Perhaps you've heard of the old saying "There is no such thing as a free lunch." What does it mean? If someone invites you to a lunch and offers to pay for it, is it free for you?

8. During China's Cultural Revolution in the late 1960s and early 1970s, many people with a high school or college education were forced to move to farms and work in the fields. Some were common laborers for eight or more years. What does this policy say about specialization? Would you predict that the policy would lead to an increase in output?

9. Use Table 4 to calculate the U.S. dollar price of:
   a. A shirt manufactured in Mexico and selling there for 5,000Ps
   b. A boomerang selling in Australia for 40A$
   c. A box of tea selling in Britain for 5£
   d. A car selling in Japan for 50,000¥
   e. A loaf of bread selling in France for 1€

## Internet Exercise

**Use the Internet to examine U.S. international trade.**

Go to the Boyes/Melvin, *Fundamentals of Economics* website accessible through **http://college.hmco.com** and click on the Internet Exercise link for Chapter 1. Now answer the questions found on the Boyes/Melvin website.

# Study Guide for Chapter 1

## Key Term Match

**Match each term with its correct definition by placing the appropriate letter next to the corresponding number.**

A. fallacy of composition
B. scarcity
C. opportunity costs
D. tradeoffs
E. resources
F. land
G. labor
H. capital
I. financial capital
J. comparative advantage
K. gains from trade
L. barter
M. exchange rate

_____ 1. the amount that trading partners benefit beyond the sum of what each could have produced without the trade

_____ 2. the physical and intellectual services of people, including the training, education, and abilities of the individuals in a society

_____ 3. goods used to produce other goods—i.e., land, labor, and capital

_____ 4. products such as machinery and equipment that are used in production

_____ 5. the shortage that exists when less of something is available than is wanted at a zero price

_____ 6. the direct exchange of goods and services without the use of money

_____ 7. the rate at which monies of different countries are exchanged

_____ 8. the ability to produce a good or service at a lower opportunity cost than it would cost someone else to produce it

_____ 9. all natural resources, such as minerals, timber, and water, as well as the land itself

_____10. the highest-valued alternative that must be forgone when a choice is made

_____11. funds used to purchase capital

_____12. the giving up of one good or activity in order to obtain some other good or activity

_____13. the mistake of assuming that what is good for one is good for all

## Quick-Check Quiz

1 Ecomomics is the study of the relationship between
   a. people's unlimited wants and their scarce resources.
   b. people's limited wants and their scarce resources.
   c. people's limited wants and their infinite resources.
   d. people's limited income and their scarce resources.
   e. human behavior and limited human wants.

2 The heart of the economic problem is to
   a. provide for full employment.
   b. eliminate scarcity.
   c. increase our standard of living.
   d. allocate limited resources among unlimited uses.
   e. increase leisure.

3 Janine is an accountant who makes $30,000 a year. Robert is a college student who makes $8,000 a year. All other things being equal, who is more likely to stand in a long line to get a cheap concert ticket?
   a. Janine; her opportunity cost is lower
   b. Janine; her opportunity cost is higher
   c. Robert; his opportunity cost is lower
   d. Robert; his opportunity cost is higher
   e. Janine; because she is better able to afford the cost of the ticket

4 Which of the following should *not* be considered an opportunity cost of attending college?
   a. money spent on living expenses that are the same whether or not you attend college
   b. lost salary
   c. business lunches
   d. interest that could have been earned on your money had you put the money into a savings account instead of spending it on tuition
   e. opportunities sacrificed in the decision to attend college

5 Exchange among people occurs because
   a. everyone involved believes they will gain.
   b. one person gains, and the others lose.
   c. only one person loses while everyone else gains.
   d. people have no other choices.
   e. the government requires it.

6 You have a comparative advantage in producing something when you
   a. have a higher opportunity cost than someone else.
   b. have a special talent.
   c. have a lower opportunity cost than someone else.
   d. have learned a useful skill.
   e. have the same opportunity cost as someone else.

**7** Which of the following statements is true?

    a. Individuals, firms, and nations specialize in the production of the good or service that has the highest opportunity cost.

    b. An individual, firm, or nation first must be able to produce more of a good or service before it can have a comparative advantage in the production of that good or service.

    c. Comparative advantage exists whenever one person, firm, or nation engaging in an activity incurs the same costs as some other individual, firm, or nation.

    d. An individual, firm, or nation gains when it specializes according to comparative advantage.

    e. An individual, firm, or nation should trade with parties that have the same opportunity costs for the goods and services produced.

**8** Why do nations trade with each other?

    a. Trade makes people worse off.

    b. Trade makes people better off.

    c. Trade provides less to consume but more to produce.

    d. Trade provides less to consume and less to produce.

    e. Governments insist on it.

**Use the following table to answer study questions 9 through 13.**

On a 10-acre farm, one farmer can produce these quantities of corn or wheat in Alpha and Beta.

|  | Corn | Wheat |
|---|---|---|
| **Alpha** | 200 | 400 |
| **Beta** | 100 | 300 |

**9** The opportunity cost of corn in Beta is

    a. 300 wheat.

    b. 1 wheat.

    c. 3 wheat.

    d. 100 corn.

    e. .5 corn.

**10** The opportunity cost of corn in Alpha is

    a. 400 wheat.

    b. 2 wheat.

    c. 4 wheat.

    d. 100 corn.

    e. .5 corn.

**11** The opportunity cost of wheat in Beta is

    a. .333 corn.

    b. 1 wheat.

    c. 3 wheat.

    d. 300 wheat.

    e. .5 corn.

**12** The opportunity cost of wheat in Alpha is

    a. 400 wheat.

    b. 2 wheat.

    c. 4 wheat.

    d. 100 corn.

    e. .5 corn.

**13** Which of the following statements is (are) true?

    a. Alpha has a comparative advantage in corn, and Beta has a comparative advantage in wheat.

    b. Alpha has a comparative advantage in wheat, and Beta has a comparative advantage in corn.

    c. Alpha has a comparative advantage in both corn and wheat.

    d. Beta has a comparative advantage in both corn and wheat.

    e. Neither has a comparative advantage in anything.

## Practice Questions and Problems

**1** List the three categories of resources and the payments associated with each.

_____

_____

_____

**2** Janine decides to buy a ticket to a classical music concert. The ticket costs $10. She spends 30 minutes driving to the ticket office, 60 minutes waiting in line, and 30 minutes eating a snack after buying the ticket. List her opportunity costs of getting the ticket.

_____

**3** Exchange occurs because _____ (one person, everyone involved) believes the exchange can be beneficial.

**4** It is in your best interest to specialize in the area in which your opportunity costs are _____ (highest, constant, lowest).

Figure 4

**The Production Possibilities Curve**

With a limited amount of resources, only certain combinations of defense and nondefense goods and services can be produced. The maximum amounts that can be produced, given various tradeoffs, are represented by points $A_1$ through $E_1$. Point $F_1$ lies inside the curve and represents the underutilization of resources. More of one type of good and less of another could be produced, or more of both types could be produced. Point $G_1$ represents an impossible combination. There are insufficient resources to produce quantities lying beyond the curve.

| Combination | Defense Goods and Services (millions of units) | Nondefense Goods and Services (millions of units) |
|---|---|---|
| $A_1$ | 200 | 0 |
| $B_1$ | 175 | 75 |
| $C_1$ | 130 | 125 |
| $D_1$ | 70 | 150 |
| $E_1$ | 0 | 160 |
| $F_1$ | 130 | 25 |
| $G_1$ | 200 | 75 |

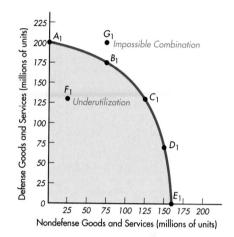

If all resources are allocated to producing defense goods and services, then 200 million units can be produced, but the production of nondefense goods and services will cease. The combination of 200 million units of defense goods and services and 0 units of nondefense goods and services is point $A_1$, a point on the vertical axis. At 175 million units of defense goods and services, 75 million units of nondefense goods and services can be produced (point $B_1$). Point $C_1$ represents 125 million units of nondefense goods and services and 130 million units of defense goods. Point $D_1$ represents 150 million units of nondefense goods and services and 70 million units of defense goods and services. Point $E_1$, a point on the horizontal axis, shows the combination of no production of defense goods and services and total production of nondefense goods and services.

The PPC is a picture of the tradeoffs facing society. A production possibilities curve shows that more of one type of good can be produced only by reducing the quantity of other types of goods that are produced; it shows that a society has scarce resources.

### 2.a. Interpreting Graphs: Points Inside the Production Possibilities Curve

Suppose a nation produces 130 million units of defense goods and services and 25 million units of nondefense goods and services. That combination, point $F_1$ in Figure 4, lies inside the production possibilities curve. A point lying inside the production possibilities curve indicates that resources are not being fully or efficiently used. If the existing work force is employed only 20 hours per week, it is not being fully used. If two workers are used when one would be sufficient—say, two people in each Domino's Pizza delivery car—then resources are not being used efficiently. If there are resources available for use, society can move from point $F_1$ to a point on the PPC, such as point $C_1$. The move would gain 100 million units of nondefense goods and services with no loss of defense goods and services.

## 2.b. Interpreting Graphs: Points Outside the Production Possibilities Curve

Point $G_1$ in Figure 4 represents the production of 200 million units of defense goods and services and 75 units of nondefense goods and services. Point $G_1$, however, represents the use of more resources than are available; it lies outside the production possibilities curve. Unless more resources can be obtained or the quality of resources improved so that the nation can produce more with the same quantity of resources, there is no way the society can currently produce 200 million units of defense goods and 75 million units of nondefense goods.

## 2.c. Shifts of the Production Possibilities Curve

As we have seen, graphs can be used to illustrate the effects of a change in a variable not explicitly shown on the graph. For instance, if a nation obtains more resources, points outside its current production possibilities curve become attainable. Suppose a country discovers new sources of oil within its borders and is able to greatly increase its production of oil. Greater oil supplies would enable the country to increase production of all types of goods and services.

Figure 5 shows the production possibilities curve before ($PPC_1$) and after ($PPC_2$) the discovery of oil. Curve $PPC_1$ is based on the data given in the table in Figure 4. Curve $PPC_2$ is based on the data given in the table in Figure 5, which shows the increase in the production of goods and services that results from the increase in oil supplies. The first combination of goods and services on $PPC_2$, point $A_2$, is 220 million units of defense goods and 0 units of nondefense goods. The second point, $B_2$, is a combination of 200 million units of defense goods and 75 million units of nondefense goods. Points $C_2$ through $F_2$ are the combinations shown in the table of Figure 5. Connecting these points yields the bowed-out curve, $PPC_2$. Because of the availability of new supplies of oil, the nation is able to increase the production of all goods, as shown by the shift from $PPC_1$ to $PPC_2$. A comparison

Figure 5

**A Shift of the Production Possibilities Curve**

Whenever everything else is not constant, the curve shifts. In this case, an increase in the quantity of a resource enables the society to produce more of both types of goods. The curve shifts out, away from the origin.

| Combination | Defense Goods and Services (millions of units) | Nondefense Goods and Services (millions of units) |
|---|---|---|
| $A_2$ | 220 | 0 |
| $B_2$ | 200 | 75 |
| $C_2$ | 175 | 125 |
| $D_2$ | 130 | 150 |
| $E_2$ | 70 | 160 |
| $F_2$ | 200 | 165 |

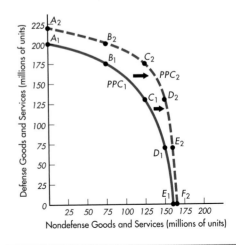

of the two curves shows that more goods and services for both defense and nondefense are possible along $PPC_2$ than along $PPC_1$.

The outward shift of the PPC can be the result of an increase in the quantity of resources, but it also can occur because the quality of resources improves. For instance, a technological breakthrough could conceivably improve the way that communication occurs, thereby requiring fewer people and machines and less time to produce the same quantity and quality of goods. The work force could become more literate, thereby requiring less time to produce the same quantity and quality of goods. Each of these quality improvements in resources could lead to an outward shift of the PPC.

Curves shift when things that affect the relationship between the variables measured on the graphs change. The PPC measures combinations of two different types of products that a country could produce. When technology improves, then the combinations of the two goods that could be produced changes, and the PPC shifts.

## 2.d. Gains from Trade

Let's use the trading problem between Maria and Able discussed in Chapter 1 to illustrate the use of the PPC graph. Review Table 1 Production Possibilities on page 11.

Figure 6 shows Maria's and Able's production possibilities curves based on the information given in the table. The output per day has been plotted for each. Maria's PPC is given in the graph on the left. It indicates that she can solve 10 economics problems and no math problems, 10 math problems and no economics problems, or any combination lying along the line. Able, similarly, can produce those combinations shown along the line in the figure on the right. Maria can produce only those combinations along her production possibilities line or combinations inside the line. Able can also produce only those combinations along or inside his production possibilities line. The production possibility curves in this example are actually straight lines. For our purposes, the difference between a straight line PPC and a bowed PPC does not matter. Both shapes illustrate the idea that the combinations of two products along the PPC are the maximum a person or a nation can produce given current limited resources.

Figure 6

**Gains from Trade**

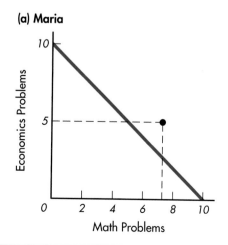

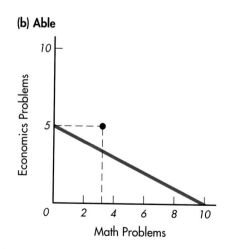

Maria and Able could each solve both the economics and the math problems, or one could solve economics problems, and the other could do the math problems. Remember, if each specializes in an area in which each has a comparative advantage (Maria solves the economics problems, and Able completes the math problems), they can then trade to get what they want.

Suppose Able agrees to do math problems for Maria if she will do economics problems for him. Then Maria ends up with more completed math and economics problems for herself than she could do alone, while Able also gets more math and economics problems than he alone could do. Gains from trade are shown by the combinations of economics and math problems that lie above the production possibility curves.

# SUMMARY

1. Most economic data are positive numbers, so often only the upper right quadrant of the coordinate system is used in economics.

2. A curve on a graph shifts—changes position—when something other than the two variables measured on the axes affects the relationship between the two variables.

3. The production possibilities curve shows all possible combinations of two products that a nation can produce at any given time given the quantity of resources and the use of those resources.

# KEY TERMS

production possibilities curve (PPC)

# EXERCISES

1. Plot the data listed in the table below.
   a. Measure price along the vertical axis and quantity along the horizontal axis and plot the first two columns.
   b. Show what quantity is sold when the price is $550.
   c. Directly below the graph in part a, plot the data in columns 2 and 3. In this graph, measure quantity on the horizontal axis and total revenue on the vertical axis.
   d. What is total revenue when the price is $550? Will total revenue increase or decrease when the price is lowered?

| Price | Quantity Sold | Total Revenue |
|-------|---------------|---------------|
| $1,000 | 200 | 200,000 |
| 900 | 400 | 360,000 |
| 800 | 600 | 480,000 |
| 700 | 800 | 560,000 |
| 600 | 1,000 | 600,000 |
| 500 | 1,200 | 600,000 |
| 400 | 1,400 | 560,000 |
| 300 | 1,600 | 480,000 |
| 200 | 1,800 | 360,000 |
| 100 | 2,000 | 200,000 |

2. Listed below are the production possibility curves for two countries producing health care and food. If they devote all resources to health care, Haiti can care for 1,000 people a month, while Cuba can care for 500. If they split their resources 50-50, Haiti can care for 500 people and produce 7 tons of food, while Cuba can care for 250 and produce 3 tons of food. Putting all resources into food, Haiti can produce 10 tons, while Cuba can produce 7.

| Percent of Effort Devoted to Health Care | Haiti | | Cuba | |
|---|---|---|---|---|
| | Health Care | Food | Health Care | Food |
| 100 | 1,000 | 0 | 500 | 0 |
| 50 | 500 | 7 | 250 | 3 |
| 0 | 0 | 10 | 0 | 7 |

   a. Plot their production possibility curves.
   b. Can you see any possible gains from trade that might occur?
   c. What would Haiti specialize in? What would Cuba specialize in?

3. Plot the PPC given by the following data.

| Combination | Health Care | All Other Goods |
|---|---|---|
| A | 0 | 100 |
| B | 25 | 90 |
| C | 50 | 70 |
| D | 75 | 40 |
| E | 100 | 0 |

    a. Calculate the opportunity cost of each combination compared to the combination before. Compare A to B, B to C, C to D, and D to E.

    b. What is the opportunity cost of combination C?

c. Suppose a second nation has the following PPC. Plot the PPC and then determine which nation has a comparative advantage in which activity. Show whether the two nations can gain from specialization and trade.

| Combination | Health Care | All Other Goods |
|---|---|---|
| A | 0 | 50 |
| B | 20 | 40 |
| C | 40 | 25 |
| D | 60 | 5 |
| E | 65 | 0 |

## Chapter 2

# Markets and the Market Process

## ? Fundamental Questions

1. How are goods and services allocated?
2. How does a market process work?
3. What is demand?
4. What is supply?
5. How is price determined by demand and supply?
6. What causes price to change?
7. Why isn't the market used to allocate everything?

## Preview

People (and firms and nations) can get more if they specialize in certain activities and then trade with one another to acquire the goods and services they desire. But how are the specialized producers to get together or to know who specializes in what? We could allow the government to decide, or we could rely on first-come, first-served, or even simply luck. Typically it is the market mechanism—buyers and sellers interacting via prices—we rely on to ensure that gains from trade occur. To see why, consider the following situation and then carry out the exercise.

I. At a sightseeing point, reachable only after a strenuous hike, a firm has established a stand where bottled water is sold. The water, carried in by the employees of the firm, is sold to thirsty hikers in six-ounce bottles. The price is $1 per bottle. Typically only 100 bottles of the water are sold each day. On a particularly hot day, 200 hikers want to buy at least one bottle of water. Indicate what you think of each of the following means of distributing the water to the hikers:

1. Increasing the price until the quantity of water bottles hikers are willing and able to purchase exactly equals the number of water bottles available for sale

   a. agree completely
   b. agree with slight reservation
   c. disagree
   d. strongly disagree
   e. totally unacceptable

2. Selling the water for $1 per bottle on a first-come, first-served basis

   a. agree completely
   b. agree with slight reservation
   c. disagree
   d. strongly disagree
   e. totally unacceptable

3. Having the local authority (government) buy the water for $1 per bottle and distribute it according to its own judgment

   a. agree completely
   b. agree with slight reservation
   c. disagree

not able to purchase a membership. Though willing, she is not able. At a price of $5,000, however, she is willing and able to purchase a membership.

The third phrase points out that the demand for any good is defined for a specific period of time. Without reference to a time period, a demand relationship would not make any sense. For instance, the statement that "at a price of $3 per Happy Meal, 13 million Happy Meals are demanded" provides no useful information. Are the 13 million meals sold in one week or one year? Think of demand as a rate of purchase at each possible price over a period of time—two per month, one per day, and so on.

The fourth phrase points out that price and quantity demanded move in opposite directions; that is, as the price rises, the quantity demanded falls, and as the price falls, the quantity demanded rises.

The final phrase, "everything else held constant," ensures that things or events that affect demand other than price do not change. The demand for a good or service depends on the price of that good or service but also on income, tastes, prices of related goods and services, expectations, and the number of buyers. If any one of these changes, demand changes.

### 3.b. The Demand Schedule

**demand schedule:** a table listing the quantity demanded at each price

A **demand schedule** is a table or list of the prices and the corresponding quantities demanded of a particular good or service. The table in Figure 2 is a demand schedule for DVD rentals (movies). It shows the number of DVDs that a consumer named Bob would be willing and able to rent at each price during the year, everything else held constant. As the rental price of the DVDs gets higher relative to the prices of other goods, Bob would be willing and able to rent fewer DVDs.

At the high price of $5 per DVD, Bob indicates that he will rent only 10 DVDs during the year. At a price of $4 per DVD, Bob tells us that he will rent 20 DVDs during the year. As the price drops from $5 to $4 to $3 to $2 to $1, Bob is willing

---

Figure 2

**Bob's Demand Schedule and Demand Curve for DVDs**

The number of DVDs that Bob is willing and able to rent at each price during the year is listed in the table, or demand schedule. The demand curve is derived from the combinations given in the demand schedule. The price-quantity combination of $5 per DVD and 10 DVDs is point A. The combination of $4 per DVD and 20 DVDs is point B. Each combination is plotted, and the points are connected to form the demand curve.

| Combination | Price per DVD (constant-quality units) | Quantity Demanded per Year (constant-quality units) |
|---|---|---|
| A | $5 | 10 |
| B | 4 | 20 |
| C | 3 | 30 |
| D | 2 | 40 |
| E | 1 | 50 |

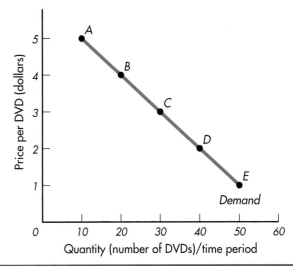

and able to rent more DVDs. At a price of $1, Bob would rent 50 DVDs during the year, nearly 1 per week.

### 3.c. The Demand Curve

**demand curve:** a graph showing the law of demand

A **demand curve** is a graph of the demand schedule. The demand curve shown in Figure 2 is plotted from the information given in the demand schedule. Price is measured on the vertical axis, quantity per unit of time on the horizontal axis. Point *A* in Figure 2 corresponds to combination *A* in the table: a price of $5 and 10 DVDs demanded. Similarly, points *B, C, D,* and *E* in Figure 2 represent the corresponding combinations in the table. The line connecting these points is Bob's demand curve for DVDs.

### 3.d. From Individual Demand Curves to a Market Curve

**market demand:** the sum of the individual demands

Unless Bob is the only renter of the DVDs, his demand curve is not the total, or market demand, curve. **Market demand** is the sum of all individual demands. To derive the market demand curve, then, the individual demand curves of all consumers in the market must be added together. The table in Figure 3 lists the demand schedules of three individuals, Salman, Akira, and Elena. Because in this example the market consists only of Salman, Akira, and Elena, their individual demands are added together to derive the market demand. The market demand is the last column of the table.

Salman's, Akira's, and Elena's demand schedules are plotted as individual demand curves in Figure 3(a). In Figure 3(b) their individual demand curves have been added together to obtain the market demand curve. (Notice that we add in a horizontal direction; that is, we add quantities at each price, not the prices at each quantity.) At a price of $5, we add the quantity Salman would buy, 10, to the quantity Akira would buy, 5, to the quantity Elena would buy, 15, to get the market demand of 30. At a price of $4, we add the quantities each of the consumers is willing and able to buy to get the total quantity demanded of 48. At all prices, then, we add the quantities demanded by each individual consumer to get the total, or market quantity, demanded.

---

### Now You Try It

Using the demand schedule for two individuals, Andrea and Rene, compute the market demand if these two are the only consumers.

| Price | 10 | 8 | 6 | 4 |
|---|---|---|---|---|
| **Quantity Andrea is willing and able to purchase** | 5 | 7 | 8 | 9 |
| **Quantity Rene is willing and able to purchase** | 3 | 4 | 6 | 7 |

---

### 3.e. Changes in Demand and Changes in Quantity Demanded

**quantity demanded:** the amount of a product that people are willing and able to purchase at a specific price

Economists distinguish between the terms *demand* and *quantity demanded.* When they refer to the **quantity demanded,** they are talking about the amount of a product that people are willing and able to purchase *at a specific price.* When they refer to demand, they are talking about the amount that people would be willing and able to purchase *at every possible price.* Thus, the statement that "the demand for U.S. white wine rose after a 300 percent tariff was applied to French white wine" means that at each price for U.S. white wine, more people were willing and able to purchase U.S. white wine. And the statement that "the quantity demanded of white

## 4.c. From Individual Supply Curves to the Market Supply

To derive market supply, the quantities that each producer supplies at each price are added together, just as the quantities demanded by each consumer are added together to get market demand. The table in Figure 5 lists the supply schedules of three DVD stores: MGA, Motown, and Blockmaster. For our example, we assume that these three are the only DVD stores offering DVDs. (We are also assuming that the brand names are not associated with quality or any other differences.)

The supply schedule of each producer is plotted in Figure 5(a). Then in Figure 5(b) the individual supply curves have been added together to obtain the market supply curve. At a price of $5, the quantity supplied by MGA is 60, the quantity supplied by Motown is 30, and the quantity supplied by Blockmaster is 12. This means a total quantity supplied in the market of 102. At a price of $4, the quantities supplied are 50 by MGA, 25 by Motown, and 9 by Blockmaster for a total market quantity supplied of 84. The market supply schedule is the last column in the table. The plot of the price and quantity combinations listed in this column is the market supply curve.

## 4.d. Changes in Supply and Changes in Quantity Supplied

When we draw the supply curve, we allow only the price and quantity supplied of the good or service we are discussing to change. Everything else that might affect supply is assumed not to change. If any of the determinants of supply—the prices of resources used to produce the product, technology and productivity, expectations of producers, number of producers in the market, and prices of related goods and services—changes, the supply schedule changes and the supply curve shifts.

*Prices of Resources*   If labor costs—one of the resources used to produce DVDs—rise, higher prices will be necessary to induce each store to offer as many DVDs as it did before the cost of the resource rose. Conversely, if resource prices decline, then supply of DVDs would increase.

*Technology and Productivity*   If resources are used more efficiently in the production of a good or service, more of that good or service can be supplied for the same cost; supply will rise.

*Expectations of Producers*   Sellers may choose to alter the quantity offered for sale today because of a change in expectations regarding the determinants of supply.

*Number of Producers*   When more producers decide to offer a good or service for sale, the market supply increases.

*Prices of Related Goods or Services*   The opportunity cost of producing and selling any good or service is the forgone opportunity to produce any other good or service. If the price of an alternative good changes, then the opportunity cost of producing a particular good changes. This could cause the supply curve to change.

## 4.e. International Effects

Many firms purchase supplies from firms in other nations or even locate factories and produce in other nations. Events in other parts of the world can influence their costs and thus the amounts they are willing and able to supply. Nike purchases its shoes from manufacturers in other parts of the world, particularly Asia, and then sells them primarily in the United States. The Thai currency, the baht, was worth $.028 in January 2002. If it cost Nike 261 bahts to get a pair of shoes manufactured in Thailand, then in dollar terms it cost Nike $7.30 (261 × $.028). In January of

Figure 5

**The Market Supply Schedule and Curve for DVDs**

The market supply is derived by summing the quantities that each producer is willing and able to offer for sale at each price. In this example, there are three producers: MGA, Motown, and Blockmaster. The supply schedules of each are listed in the table and plotted as the individual supply curves in part (a). By adding the quantities supplied at each price, we obtain the market supply curve shown in part (b). For instance, at a price of $5, MGA offers 60 units, Motown 30 units, and Blockmaster 12 units, for a market supply quantity of 102. The market supply curve reflects the quantities that all producers are able and willing to supply at each price.

| Price per DVD | MGA | | Motown | | Blockmaster | | Market Supply |
|---|---|---|---|---|---|---|---|
| | | | Quantities Supplied per Year by | | | | |
| $5 | 60 | + | 30 | + | 12 | = | 102 |
| 4 | 50 | | 25 | | 9 | | 84 |
| 3 | 40 | | 20 | | 6 | | 66 |
| 2 | 30 | | 15 | | 3 | | 48 |
| 1 | 20 | | 10 | | 0 | | 30 |

**(a) Individual Supply Curves**

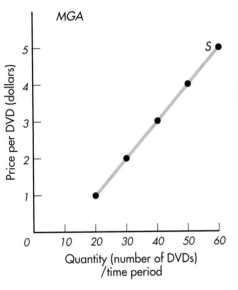
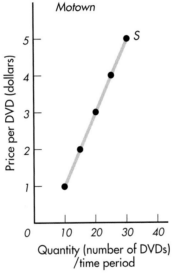
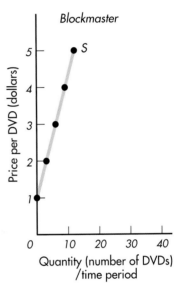

**(b) Market Supply Curve**

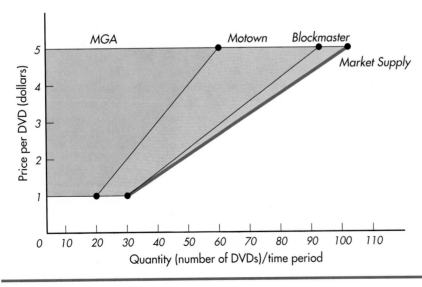

2004, the baht was worth \$.025. As a result, the cost to Nike declined to \$6.52 per unit. Thus, simply because the exchange rate changed, Nike's costs fell, and the quantity of shoes Nike was willing and able to offer for sale at each price declined.

**RECAP**

1. According to the law of supply, the quantity supplied of any good or service is directly related to the price of the good or service, during a specific period of time, everything else held constant.

2. Market supply is found by adding together the quantities supplied at each price by every producer in the market.

3. Supply changes if prices of relevant resources change, if technology or productivity changes, if producers' expectations change, if the number of producers changes, or if prices of related goods and services change.

4. Changes in supply are reflected in shifts of the supply curve. Changes in the quantity supplied are reflected in movements along the supply curve.

## 5. EQUILIBRIUM: PUTTING DEMAND AND SUPPLY TOGETHER

The demand curve shows the quantity of a good or service that buyers are willing and able to purchase at each price. The supply curve shows the quantity that producers are willing and able to offer for sale at each price. Only where the two curves intersect is the quantity supplied equal to the quantity demanded. This intersection is the point of **equilibrium.**

**equilibrium:** the price and quantity at which quantity demanded equals quantity supplied

**5. How is price determined by demand and supply?**

**surplus:** the quantity demanded is less than the quantity supplied

**shortage:** the quantity demanded is greater than the quantity supplied

### 5.a. Determination of Equilibrium

Figure 6 brings together the market demand and market supply curves for DVDs. The supply and demand schedules are listed in the table, and the curves are plotted in the graph in Figure 6. Notice that the curves intersect at only one point, labeled *e,* a price of \$3 and a quantity of 66. The intersection point is the equilibrium price, the only price at which the quantity demanded and quantity supplied are the same.

Whenever the price is greater than the equilibrium price, a **surplus** arises. For example, at \$4, the quantity of DVDs demanded is 48, and the quantity supplied is 84. Thus, at \$4 per DVD there is a surplus of 36 DVDs; that is, 36 DVDs are not purchased. Conversely, whenever the price is below the equilibrium price, the quantity demanded is greater than the quantity supplied, and there is a **shortage.** For instance, if the price is \$2 per DVD, consumers will want and be able to pay for more DVDs than are available. As shown in the table in Figure 6, the quantity demanded at a price of \$2 is 84, but the quantity supplied is only 48. There is a shortage of 36 DVDs at the price of \$2.

Neither a surplus nor a shortage exists for long if the price of the product is free to change. Producers who are stuck with DVDs sitting on the shelves getting out of date will lower the price and reduce the quantities they are offering for sale in order to eliminate a surplus. Conversely, producers whose shelves are empty as consumers demand DVDs will acquire more DVDs and raise the price to eliminate the shortage. Surpluses lead to decreases in the price and the quantity supplied and increases in the quantity demanded. Shortages lead to increases in the price and the quantity supplied and decreases in the quantity demanded.

Figure 6

**Equilibrium**

Equilibrium is established at the point where the quantity that suppliers are willing and able to offer for sale is the same as the quantity that buyers are willing and able to purchase. Here, equilibrium occurs at the price of $3 per DVD and the quantity of 66 DVDs. It is shown as point e at the intersection of the demand and supply curves. At prices above $3, the quantity supplied is greater than the quantity demanded, and the result is a surplus. At prices below $3, the quantity supplied is less than the quantity demanded, and the result is a shortage. The area shaded yellow shows all prices at which there is a surplus—where quantity supplied is greater than the quantity demanded. The surplus is measured in a horizontal direction at each price. The area shaded blue represents all prices at which a shortage exists—where the quantity demanded is greater than the quantity supplied. The shortage is measured in a horizontal direction at each price.

| Price per DVD | Quantity Demanded per Year | Quantity Supplied per Year | Status |
|---|---|---|---|
| $5 | 30 | 102 | Surplus of 72 |
| 4 | 48 | 84 | Surplus of 36 |
| 3 | 66 | 66 | Equilibrium |
| 2 | 84 | 48 | Shortage of 36 |
| 1 | 102 | 30 | Shortage of 72 |

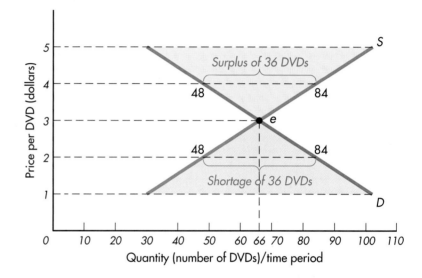

Sometimes people confuse scarcity with shortage. Scarcity occurs for almost everything. It refers to the idea that something is not free; there is not enough of that item to satisfy everyone who would want it if it cost nothing. Shortage refers to a specific price; there is not enough of the item available at a specific price to satisfy everyone who would be willing and able to purchase the item at that specific price. A shortage exists only if more is demanded than supplied *at a specific price* whereas scarcity exists if more is wanted than is available at a zero price. A shortage is eliminated by the price being driven up. Scarcity always exists.

## 5.b. Changes in the Equilibrium Price: Demand Shifts

Once a market is in equilibrium, there is no incentive for producers or consumers to move away from it. An equilibrium price changes only when demand or supply changes, that is, when the determinants of demand or the determinants of supply change.

Let's consider a change in demand and what it means for the equilibrium price. Suppose that experiments on rats show that watching DVDs causes brain damage. As a result, a large segment of the human population decides not to watch DVDs. Stores find that the demand for videos decreases, as shown in Figure 7 by a leftward shift of the demand curve, from curve $D_1$ to curve $D_2$.

6. **What causes price to change?**

e. The quantity of coffee demanded will decrease, and the demand for tea will increase.

5 Japanese producers of a type of microchip offered such low prices that U.S. producers of the chip were driven out of business. As the number of producers decreased,

   a. the market supply of microchips increased—that is, the supply curve shifted to the right.

   b. the market supply of microchips increased—that is, the supply curve shifted to the left.

   c. the market supply of microchips decreased—that is, the supply curve shifted to the right.

   d. the market supply of microchips decreased—that is, the supply curve shifted to the left.

   e. there was no change in the supply of microchips. (This event is represented by a movement from one point to another on the same supply curve.)

6 Electronics firms can produce more than one type of good. Suppose that electronics firms are producing both military radios and microchips. A war breaks out, and the price of military radios skyrockets. The electronics firms throw more resources into making military radios and fewer resources into making microchips. Which of the statements below is true?

   a. The supply of microchips has decreased, and the quantity of military radios supplied has increased.

   b. The supply of microchips has decreased, and the supply of military radios has increased.

   c. The quantity of microchips supplied has decreased, and the supply of military radios has decreased.

   d. The quantity of microchips supplied has decreased, and the quantity of military radios supplied has decreased.

   e. There has been no change in the supply of microchips or in the supply of military radios.

7 Suppose that automakers expect car prices to be lower in the future. What will happen now?

   a. Supply will increase.

   b. Supply will decrease.

   c. Supply will not change.

   d. Demand will increase.

   e. Demand will decrease.

8 Utility regulators in some states are considering forcing operators of coal-fired generators to be responsible for cleaning up air and water pollution resulting from the generators. Utilities in these states currently do not pay the costs of cleanup. If this law goes into effect,

   a. demand for electricity will increase, and price and quantity will increase.

   b. demand for electricity will decrease, and price and quantity will decrease.

   c. the supply of electricity will decrease, and price and quantity will decrease.

   d. the supply of electricity will increase, price will decrease, and quantity will decrease.

   e. the supply of electricity will decrease, price will increase, and quantity will decrease.

9 Medical research from South Africa indicates that vitamin A may be useful in treating measles. If the research can be substantiated, the

   a. supply of vitamin A will increase, causing equilibrium price and quantity to increase.

   b. supply of vitamin A will increase, causing equilibrium price to fall and quantity to increase.

   c. demand for vitamin A will increase, causing equilibrium price and quantity to increase.

   d. demand for vitamin A will increase, causing equilibrium price to rise and quantity to fall.

   e. supply of vitamin A will increase, causing equilibrium price to rise and quantity to fall.

10 Since 1900, changes in technology have greatly reduced the costs of growing wheat. The population also has increased. If you know that the changes in technology had a greater effect than the increase in population, then since 1900, the

   a. price of wheat has increased, and the quantity of wheat has decreased.

   b. price and quantity of wheat have increased.

   c. price and quantity of wheat have decreased.

   d. price of wheat has decreased, and the quantity of wheat has increased.

   e. quantity of wheat has increased, and you haven't got the faintest idea what happened to the price.

11 An increase in demand

   a. shifts the demand curve to the left.

   b. causes an increase in equilibrium price.

   c. causes a decrease in equilibrium price.

   d. causes a decrease in equilibrium quantity.

   e. does not affect equilibrium quantity.

12 Which of the following is *not* a determinant of demand?

   a. income

   b. tastes

   c. prices of resources

   d. prices of complements

   e. consumers' expectations

13 Which of the following is *not* a determinant of supply?

    a. prices of resources
    b. technology and productivity
    c. prices of complements
    d. producers' expectations
    e. the number of producers

## Practice Questions and Problems

1 Write the type of allocation method each example represents. Choose from the following: random allocation; market allocation; first-come, first-served allocation; or government allocation.

a. _____ Winning a lottery

b. _____ The high bidder at an auction gets a valuable painting.

c. _____ The mayor of a city decides who will be hired.

d. _____ Students at Big Football U. can park on campus without charge, but there aren't enough parking spaces for all students.

2 List six determinants of demand.

_____ _____

_____ _____

_____ _____

3 An increase in income _____ (increases, decreases) the _____ (demand, quantity demanded) for haircuts.

4 Many Americans have decreased their consumption of beef and switched to chicken in the belief that eating chicken instead of beef lowers cholesterol. This change in tastes has _____ (increased, decreased) the _____ (demand, quantity demanded) for beef and _____ (increased, decreased) the _____ (demand, quantity demanded) for chicken.

5 If a crisis in the Middle East causes people to expect the price of gasoline to increase in the future, then demand for gasoline today will _____ (increase, not change, decrease).

6 If the price of Pepsi increases, the demand for Coke and other substitutes will _____.

7 People in Mexico buy software produced in the United States. If the Mexican peso increased in value relative to the dollar, U.S. software in Mexico would _____ (increase, decrease) in price. Mexicans would then buy _____ (more, less) U.S. software, which would _____ (increase, decrease) the demand for U.S. software.

8 List the five determinants of supply.

_____ _____

_____ _____

_____ _____

9 Suppose that a crisis in the Middle East cuts off the supply of oil from Saudi Arabia. If $S_1$ is the original market supply of oil, draw another supply curve, $S_2$, on the graph to show the effect of Saudi Arabia's departure from the market. The _____ (quantity supplied, supply) has _____ (increased, decreased).

10 If the price of tomato sauce increases, the _____ (supply, quantity supplied) of pizza will _____ (increase, decrease).

11 A new process for producing microchips is discovered that will decrease the cost of production by 10 percent. The supply of microchips will _____ (increase, decrease, not change), which means the sup-

ply curve will _____ (shift to the right, shift to the left, not change).

**12** A paper manufacturer can produce notebook paper or wedding invitations. If the price of wedding invitations skyrockets, we can expect the supply of _____ (notebook paper, wedding invitations) to _____ (increase, decrease).

**13** A U.S. construction company buys lumber to build houses from a supplier in Canada. If the value of the Canadian dollar decreases relative to the U.S. dollar, it will cost the U.S. company _____ (more, fewer) U.S. dollars to buy a truckload of lumber. This will _____ (increase, decrease) the cost of building a house and _____ (increase, decrease) the supply of new houses.

**14** Shortages lead to _____ (increases, decreases) in price and quantity supplied and to _____ (increase, decrease) in quantity demanded.

**15** Surpluses lead to _____ (increases, decreases) in price and quantity supplied and to _____ (increase, decrease) in quantity demanded.

**16** As long as supply does not change, a change in equilibrium price and quantity is in the _____ (same, opposite) direction as a change in demand.

**17** Balloon manufacturers are nervous about a children's movement that may affect their product. The children are lobbying state legislatures to ban launchings of more than ten balloons at a time, citing the danger that balloons can pose to wildlife. If the children are successful, we can expect the _____ (demand for, supply of) balloons to _____ (increase, decrease), causing the equilibrium price to _____ and the equilibrium quantity to _____.

**18** If design changes in the construction of milk cartons cause the cost of production to decrease, we can expect the _____ (demand for, supply of) cartons to _____ (increase, decrease), the equilibrium price to _____, and the equilibrium quantity to _____.

**19** The following graph shows the market for corn. The equilibrium price is _____, and the equilibrium quantity is _____. If the price of corn is $14, the quantity demanded will be _____, and the quantity supplied will be _____. A(n) _____ of _____ units will develop, causing the price and quantity supplied to _____, and the quantity demanded to _____. If the price is $4, the quantity demanded will be _____, and the quantity supplied will be _____. A(n) _____ of _____ units will develop, causing the price and quantity supplied to _____ and the quantity demanded to _____.

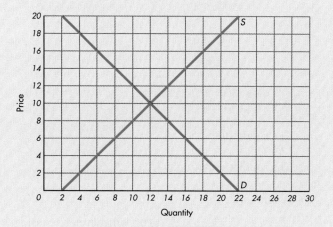

**20** If your car produces so much pollution that it causes other people to have to buy medicines so they can breathe, your car is creating a _____ (positive, negative) externality.

**21** If you are a parent and get your child immunized against certain diseases, other children are also less likely to get sick. This is an example of a _____ (positive, negative) externality.

**22** When there are positive externalities, the market system will produce _____ (too much, too little) of a product because the buyers and sellers are not receiving or paying all the _____ (benefits, costs) of producing and consuming the product.

**23** When there are negative externalities, the market system will produce _____ (too much, too little) of a product because the buyers and sellers are not receiving or paying all _____ (benefits, costs) of producing and consuming the product.

**Use the following table to answer questions 24 through 27.**

| Price | Quantity Demanded | Quantity Supplied |
|-------|-------------------|-------------------|
| $0 | 24 | 0 |
| 1 | 20 | 2 |
| 2 | 16 | 4 |
| 3 | 12 | 6 |
| 4 | 8 | 8 |
| 5 | 4 | 10 |
| 6 | 0 | 12 |

**24** The equilibrium price is _____.

**25** The equilibrium quantity is _____.

**26** If the price is $2, a _____ of _____ units will develop, causing the price to _____.

**27** If the price is $5, a _____ of _____ units will develop, causing the price to _____.

## Exercises and Applications

**I The Market for Battery-Operated Dancing Flowers**
For each event listed below, indicate whether it affects the demand or supply of battery-operated dancing flowers and the direction (increase or decrease) of the change. Also indicate what will happen to equilibrium price and quantity. Remember, the determinants of demand are income, tastes, prices of related goods or services, consumers' expectations, number of buyers, and exchange rates. The determinants of supply are prices of resources, changes in technology or productivity, producers' expectations, number of producers, and prices of related goods or services (goods that are substitutes in production).

a. There is a change in tastes toward battery-operated dancing gorillas.
b. The price of plastic falls.
c. A technological breakthrough makes it cheaper to produce plastic flowers.
d. Consumers' incomes rise.
e. The price of battery-operated dancing gorillas rises.
f. The price of plastic for making flowers skyrockets.
g. A fire destroys a major production facility for dancing flowers.
h. Consumers expect lower prices for dancing flowers in the future.

| | Demand | Supply | Price | Quantity |
|------|--------|--------|-------|----------|
| a. | ____ | ____ | ____ | ____ |
| b. | ____ | ____ | ____ | ____ |
| c. | ____ | ____ | ____ | ____ |
| d. | ____ | ____ | ____ | ____ |
| e. | ____ | ____ | ____ | ____ |
| f. | ____ | ____ | ____ | ____ |
| g. | ____ | ____ | ____ | ____ |
| h. | ____ | ____ | ____ | ____ |

**11  Drinking and Cancer**   A recent study suggests that the anticancer benefit of eating lots of fruits and vegetables is lost if you wash them down with more than two drinks of alcohol.

If people believe this study, you would expect the

_____ (demand, supply) for alcoholic

drinks will _____ (increase, not change, decrease). The equilibrium price will

_____ (increase, not change, decrease),

and the equilibrium quantity will _____ (increase, not change, decrease).

Assume that the market for alcoholic drinks was in equilibrium before the study, as shown. Illustrate the effects of the research linking the loss of anticancer benefits with alcohol. Be sure your graph matches your previous answers.

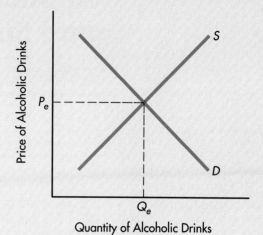

Now that you've completed the Study Guide for this chapter, you should have a good sense of the concepts you need to review. If you'd like to test your understanding of the material again, go to the Practice Tests on the Boyes/Melvin *Fundamentals of Economics,* 3e website, **economics.college.hmco.com/students.**

## Chapter 3

# Applications of Demand and Supply

**? Fundamental Questions**

1. In a market system, who determines what is produced?
2. Why do different people earn different incomes, and why do different jobs pay different wages?
3. When the government intervenes in the market by providing a subsidy, what is the result?
4. When the government intervenes in the market by setting a price floor or price ceiling, what is the result?
5. When the government intervenes in the market with a tariff, what is the result?

## Preview

A recent newspaper article noted that the city commission that oversees the rents at mobile home parks approved a 4 percent rent increase at the Soledad Trailer Lodge rather than the 13.7 percent hike the manager proposed. The higher increase was rejected because management had failed to take good care of the park, panel member Leslee Bowman said. "It's a slum," she said. "The roads are cracking, the septic tanks are leaking. The wiring appears to be inadequate." The landlord claims that he is losing money and yet continues to maintain facilities as much as he can.

What is the reason the landlord and tenants are fighting? What are their incentives? What do they want? The landlord wants to make money—as much as possible. The renters want quality housing that is cheap—the cheapest possible. It seems there is a conflict. But such conflicts occur all the time in a market system. Customers want quality products at low prices, and suppliers want to make huge profits. When you purchase a book, you want a quality book at a low price. When the book publishers offer their books for sale, they want to get a very high price for the books. You pay what you have to pay to get the book, and the publishers sell for the prices that the books will sell at. Buyers and sellers want different things, but the result of their conflicts is a price at which the product sells.

In a market system, the interaction of buyers and sellers determines the price of products being traded. As we noted in the previous chapter, sometimes people don't like the market outcome and seek another way to allocate the same resources. In the landlord-tenant case, the market is not allowed to work to find equilibrium price and quantity. The government controls rents. Why? Because some people did not like the market outcome. What's the result of interfering with the market, that is, switching to the government as the allocator? We'll return to this question later in the chapter. Before we do that, we have to understand how markets work. This means examining demand and supply.

In the previous chapter we examined a hypothetical market for DVD rentals in order to represent what goes on in real markets. We established that the rental price of the DVD is defined by equilibrium between demand and supply. We found that an equilibrium could be disturbed by a change in demand or a change in supply. Let's now look to some real markets and examine how they function. ∎

## 1. THE MARKET FOR LOW-CARB FOODS

1. In a market system, who determines what is produced?

In the 1980s, Americans learned the terms *low-fat, nonfat,* and *fat-free.* Food companies scrambled to create low-fat alternatives to our favorite foods. In 2004, a new term appeared: *low-carb.* It's now everywhere from TV beer commercials to the ice cream freezer of the local grocer. During January 2004, representatives of 450 companies, including Kraft, Con-Agra, and Wal-Mart, gathered at the two-day LowCarbiz Summit in Denver to discuss ways to take advantage of what some predict will be a $25 billion market for low-carb products.

Sales of white rice, pasta, breads, and *high-carb* fruit juices have dropped by as much as 5 percent, and manufacturers have begun formulating low-carb products to offset their loss of sales. Food makers such as Stouffer's, Sara Lee, Coors, and Hershey's have come up with their own low-carb products. Even Nabisco SnackWells, once marketed as fat-free, are now sold as a low-carb product. Burger King, Subway, Baja Fresh, Hardee's, Blimpie's, TGIF, Ruby Tuesday's, and Applebee's have low-carb options. The supermarket is rapidly filling with new low-carb products as well. A low-carb Sara Lee white bread might be teamed with Skippy "Carb Options" peanut butter, or a burger with Heinz's One-Carb Ketchup might be served with a low-carb Michelob Ultra and low-carb Tostitos.

Businesses are responding to what consumers are willing and able to buy. And when some 30 million or more consumers want low-carb options, these options are provided. Consumers have switched their purchases from high-carb but low-fat foods like pasta and bread to low-carb foods like meat and soy. Businesses have responded by producing more low-carb foods and fewer low-fat, high-carb foods. Resources have been reallocated from one food type to another.

To illustrate how resources get allocated in the market system, let's look at the market for low-fat and low-carb foods. Figure 1 shows the market for low-fat

### Figure 1

**A Demand Change in the Market for Low-Fat Food**

In Figure 1(a), the initial market-clearing price ($P_1$) and market-clearing quantity ($Q_1$) are shown. In Figure 1(b), the market-clearing price and quantity change from $P_1$ and $Q_1$ to $P_2$ and $Q_2$ as the demand curve shifts to the left because of a change in tastes. The result of decreased demand is a lower price and a lower quantity produced.

**(a) Low-Fat Food Market**

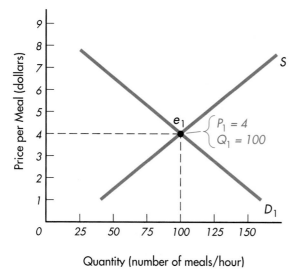

**(b) The Effect of a Change in Tastes**

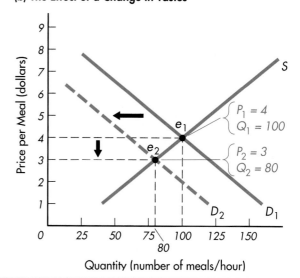

meals. The demand curve, $D_1$, shows that as the price of a low-fat meal declines, the quantity of low-fat meals demanded rises. The supply curve, $S$, shows that restaurants and supermarkets are willing to offer more low-fat meals as the price of a low-fat meal rises. The demanders are the consumers, the people who want low-fat food. The suppliers are the firms—Taco Bell, McDonald's, Burger King, and so on. With these demand and supply curves, the equilibrium price ($P_1$) is $4, and the equilibrium quantity ($Q_1$) is 100 units (low-fat meals) per hour. At this price-quantity combination, the number of low-fat meals demanded equals the number of low-fat meals sold; equilibrium is reached.

The second part of the figure shows what happens when consumer tastes change; people preferred to have low-carb food rather than low-fat food. This change in tastes caused the demand for low-fat meals to decline and is represented by a leftward shift of the demand curve, from $D_1$ to $D_2$, in Figure 1(b). The demand curve shifted to the left because fewer low-fat meals were demanded at each price. Consumer tastes, not the price of low-fat meals, changed first. (Remember: A price change would have led to a change in the quantity demanded and would be represented by a move along demand curve $D_1$, not a shift of the demand curve.) The shift from $D_1$ to $D_2$ created a new equilibrium point. The equilibrium price ($P_2$) decreased to $3, and the equilibrium quantity ($Q_2$) decreased to 80 units (low-fat meals) per hour.

While the market for low-fat meals was changing, so was the market for low-carb food. People substituted low-carb meals for low-fat meals. Figure 2(a) shows the original demand for low-carb food. Figure 2(b) shows a rightward shift of the demand curve, from $D_1$ to $D_2$, representing increased demand for low-carb meals. This demand change resulted in a higher market-clearing price for low-carb meals, from $5 to $6.

The changing profit potential of the two markets induced existing firms to switch from low-fat foods to low-carb foods and for new firms to offer low-carb foods from the start. The changing profit potential of the two markets induced

Figure 2

**A Demand Change in the Market for Low-Carb Food**

In Figure 2(a), the initial market-clearing price ($P_1$) and quantity ($Q_1$) are shown. In Figure 2(b), the demand for low-carb food increases, thus driving up the market-clearing price ($P_2$) and quantity ($Q_2$), as the demand curve shifts to the right, from $D_1$ to $D_2$.

**(a) Delivery Market**

**(b) The Effect of a Change in Tastes**

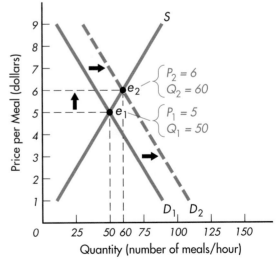

existing firms to switch from low-fat foods to low-carb foods and for new firms to offer additional low-carb foods.

As the market-clearing price of low-fat food fell (from $6 to $5 in Figure 1[b]), the quantity of low-fat meals sold also declined (from 100 to 80) because the decreased demand, lower price, and resulting lower profit induced some firms to decrease production. In the low-carb business, the opposite occurred. As the market-clearing price rose (from $5 to $6 in Figure 2[b]), the number of low-carb meals also rose (from 50 to 60). The increased demand, higher price, and resulting higher profit induced firms to increase production.

Why did the production of low-carb foods increase while the production of low-fat foods decreased? Not because of government decree. Not because of the desires of the business sector. The consumer made all this happen. Businesses that failed to respond to consumer desires and provide the desired good at the lowest price failed to survive. Why does the consumer wield such power? The name of the game for business is profit, and the only way business can make a profit is by satisfying consumer wants. In the market system, the consumer, not the politician or the business firm, ultimately determines what is to be produced. A firm that produces something that no consumers want will not remain in business very long. Consumer sovereignty—the authority of consumers to determine what is produced through their purchases of goods and services—dictates what goods and services will be produced.

After demand shifted to low-carb food, the resources that had been used in the low-fat food preparation and sale were available for use elsewhere. Some of the equipment used for preparing low-fat foods—ovens, pots, and pans—was purchased by the low-carb firms, and some was sold as scrap or to restaurants. Even ingredients that previously would have gone to the low-fat foods were bought by the firms producing low-carb foods. In other words, the resources moved from an activity in which their value was relatively low to an activity in which they were more highly valued. No one commanded the resources to move. They moved because they could earn more in some other activity.

Markets allocate scarce goods and resources to the place where they have the highest value. Markets exist not only for products but also for resources—land, labor, and capital. Let's discuss a few examples of this allocation process. Let's turn now to the market for labor.

RECAP

1. The market price is the equilibrium price, established where demand and supply are equal.

2. If demand or supply changes, then the equilibrium price and the quantity purchased will change.

3. When demand changes, the price changes, and the quantity produced and purchased changes, and thus the resources that are used to produce and sell the product change.

2. Why do different people earn different incomes, and why do different jobs pay different wages?

## 2. THE LABOR MARKET

Older workers tend to earn higher wages than younger workers, males earn more than females, whites earn more than African Americans and Latinos, and unionized workers earn more than nonunionized workers. Why? The answer is given in the labor market. The labor market consists of the demand for and the supply of labor.

Labor demand depends on the value of workers to the firm. How many workers does a firm hire? Those that bring in at least as much revenue for the firm as they cost the firm in wages and salaries would be valuable to the firm; they would be hired.

## Jobs Moving Offshore

One of the major issues of the 2004 presidential campaign in the United States was the movement of jobs offshore—the flow of certain types of businesses and their associated jobs to other countries. The U.S. Department of Labor estimates, based on trends noted in 2003 and 2004, that 3.3 million jobs currently in the United States will be moved out of the United States by 2015.

| Type | 2005 | 2015 |
| --- | --- | --- |
| Business | 61,252 | 348,028 |
| Computer | 108,991 | 472,632 |
| Management | 37,477 | 288,281 |
| Architecture | 32,202 | 184,347 |
| Office | 295,034 | 1,659,310 |
| All Other | 52,636 | 367,615 |
| Total | 587,592 | 3,320,213 |

Resources flow to where they have the highest value. If the resources cannot flow—for example, if workers in China or India cannot move to the United States, then the uses of the resources will go to where the costs are lowest; in other words, the jobs flow to the workers. The movement of resources occurs within a country just as it does among countries. The graph above shows how the U.S. economy has shifted from manufacturing to services over the past several decades. An economy in which voluntary trade occurs will see a constant shift of uses of resources. As it does, jobs will disappear in some uses and

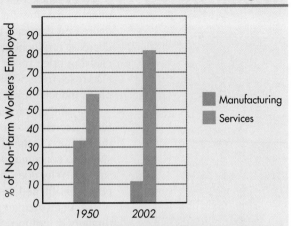

increase in others. The buggy whip manufacturers disappeared as the auto appeared; the slide rule manufacturers disappeared as the calculator and then the PC appeared. In each case, workers displaced by the changes were hurt; the new jobs created benefited those who had acquired the skills necessary to get one of the newly created jobs.

The higher the price of labor (the more it costs the firm), the less labor that the firm will demand. Thus, the labor demand curve slopes down.

The labor supply comes from households. People decide whether to work and how many hours to work at each possible wage. The higher the hourly wage, the more hours that people are willing and able to work, at least up to a point. In addition, some people who would not be willing to work at a low wage may decide to enter the labor force if the wage gets high enough. This means that the labor supply curve slopes up.

The labor demand and labor supply curves are shown in Figure 3. The intersection of the labor demand and labor supply curves determines the equilibrium wage ($W_e$) and the quantity of hours people work at this equilibrium wage ($Q_e$).

The labor market pictured in Figure 3 suggests that as long as workers are the same and jobs are the same, there will be one equilibrium wage. In fact, workers are not the same, jobs are not the same, and wages are definitely not the same. College-educated people earn more than people with only a high school education, and people with a high school education earn more than those with only a grammar school education. Riskier jobs pay more than less risky jobs. There is, in reality, a labor market for each type of worker and each type of job.

Some jobs are quite unpleasant because they are located in undesirable locations or are dangerous or unhealthy. How does a firm get someone to take a dangerous or unhealthy job? People choose to work in unpleasant occupations because they earn more money. Workers mine coal, clean sewers, and weld steel beams fifty stories off the ground because, compared to alternative jobs for which they could qualify, these jobs pay well.

In Figure 4, two labor markets are represented: one for a risky occupation and one for a less risky occupation. At each wage rate, fewer people are willing and able to work in the risky occupation than in the less risky occupation. Thus, if the demand curves were identical, the supply curve of the risky occupation would be above (to the left of) the supply curve of the less risky occupation. Fewer people are willing to

4. A common feature of skiing is waiting in lift lines. Does the existence of lift lines mean that the price is not working to allocate the scarce resource? If so, what should be done about it?

5. Many restaurants don't take reservations. You simply arrive and wait your turn. If you arrive at 7:30 in the evening, you have at least an hour wait. Notwithstanding that fact, a few people arrive, speak quietly with the maitre d', hand him some money, and are promptly seated. At some restaurants that do take reservations, there is a month wait for a Saturday evening, three weeks for a Friday evening, two weeks for Tuesday through Thursday, and virtually no wait for Sunday or Monday evening. How do you explain these events using demand and supply?

6. Give an example of a compensating wage differential in your community. What does it mean?

7. The federal government is trying to change Medicare because it is too expensive. Yet many senior citizens are upset because the government is trying to change matters. Why would the senior citizens be upset? Using demand and supply, explain what would happen if the government reduced how much it would pay for medical care.

8. Using demand and supply, illustrate the effects of a tariff imposed on foreign automobiles by the U.S. government.

9. Using demand and supply, illustrate the effects of a tariff imposed by the Canadian government on U.S. wheat. Show the U.S. wheat market and the Canadian wheat market.

## Internet Exercise

**Use the Internet to find current information about U.S. labor markets.**

Go to the Boyes/Melvin, *Fundamentals of Economics* website accessible through **http://college.hmco.com** and click on the Internet Exercise link for Chapter 3. Now answer the questions that appear on the Boyes/Melvin website.

## Study Guide for Chapter 3

## Key Term Match

**Match each term with its correct definition by placing the appropriate letter next to the corresponding number.**

A. compensating wage differential    D. price floor
B. subsidy    E. tariff
C. price ceiling

_____ 1. a situation in which the price is not allowed to rise above a certain level
_____ 2. wage differences that make up for the higher risk or poorer working conditions of one job over another
_____ 3. a tax on exports or imports
_____ 4. payments made by government to domestic firms to encourage exports
_____ 5. a situation in which the price is not allowed to decrease below a certain level

## Quick-Check Quiz

1. A change in tastes away from a good or service causes a(n) _____ in _____.
   - a. increase; demand
   - b. decrease; demand
   - c. increase; supply
   - d. decrease; supply
   - e. increase; quantity supplied

2. A decrease in demand results in a(n) _____ in quantity demanded at the original price. A _____ develops, causing the equilibrium price to _____.
   - a. increase; shortage; increase
   - b. increase; surplus; decrease
   - c. decrease; shortage; increase
   - d. decrease; surplus; decrease
   - e. decrease; surplus; increase

3. An increase in demand results in a(n) _____ in quantity demanded at the original price. A _____ develops, causing the equilibrium price to _____.
   - a. increase; shortage; increase
   - b. increase; surplus; decrease
   - c. decrease; shortage; increase
   - d. decrease; surplus; decrease
   - e. decrease; surplus; increase

4. The change in tastes away from low-fat meals initially resulted in a(n)
   - a. decrease in the demand for low-fat meals.
   - b. increase in the supply of low-fat meals.
   - c. increase in the quantity supplied of low-fat meals.
   - d. decrease in the quantity supplied of low-fat meals.
   - e. increase in the supply of low-carb foods.

5. Which of the following statements is false?
   - a. The demand for labor slopes down.
   - b. The supply of labor slopes up.
   - c. Younger workers earn higher wages than older workers.
   - d. Riskier jobs pay more than less risky jobs.
   - e. Males earn more than females.

6. Which statement is true?
   - a. The supply of workers in a less risky occupation is less than the supply of workers in a risky occupation.
   - b. The supply of workers in a less risky occupation is greater than the supply of workers in a risky occupation.
   - c. Firms will employ more people or hire people to work more hours as the wage rate increases.
   - d. Equilibrium-compensating wage differentials attract more workers from the less risky occupations to the risky ones.
   - e. The lower the hourly wage, the more hours that people are willing and able to work.

7. Which of the following caused the demand for health care to increase in recent years?
   - a. The percentage of elderly in the population is greater than before.
   - b. The cost of medical care has increased.
   - c. Government programs enable many people to get medical care without having to pay for it.
   - d. All of the above caused the demand for health care to increase in recent years.
   - e. Only *a* and *c* are reasons for the increase in the demand for health care in recent years.

8. A price ceiling
   - a. is a minimum price.
   - b. will cause a shortage if the ceiling is set above the equilibrium price.
   - c. will cause a shortage if the ceiling is set below the equilibrium price.
   - d. will cause a surplus if the ceiling is set above the equilibrium price.

e. will cause a surplus if the ceiling is set below the equilibrium price.

9   A price floor

   a. is a maximum price.
   b. will cause a shortage if the floor is set above the equilibrium price.
   c. will cause a shortage if the floor is set below the equilibrium price.
   d. will cause a surplus if the floor is set above the equilibrium price.
   e. will cause a surplus if the floor is set below the equilibrium price.

10   Which of the following statements is true?

   a. Governments impose price ceilings because the equilibrium price is perceived as being too high.
   b. Governments impose price floors because the equilibrium price is perceived as being too high.
   c. Governments impose price ceilings because the equilibrium price is perceived as being too low.
   d. Price ceilings always result in surpluses.
   e. Price floors always result in shortages.

11   If a price ceiling is set above the equilibrium price,

   a. a shortage will occur.
   b. a surplus will occur.
   c. the demand for the good or service will increase.
   d. the supply for the good or service will increase.
   e. the equilibrium price and quantity will prevail.

## Practice Questions and Problems

1   In the market system, the _____ ultimately determines what is to be produced.

2   The authority of consumers to determine what is produced through their purchases of goods and services is called _____.

3   Business firms respond to changes in consumers' tastes because they want to make _____.

4   When the demand for a good or service changes, resources move from an activity in which their value is relatively _____ to an activity in which their value is relatively _____.

5   In any labor market, the wage rate and number of jobs depend on the _____ and _____ curves for labor.

6   _____ (Business firms, Households) demand labor.

7   _____ (Business firms, Households) supply labor.

8   The demand for labor slopes _____, showing that the higher the price of labor, the _____ (more, less) labor the firm will demand.

9   The supply of labor slopes _____, showing that the higher the hourly wage, the _____ hours people are willing to work.

10   Health care expenditures have increased so much because the _____ for health care services has increased relative to the _____.

11   _____ and _____ are government programs that pay for medical services.

12   The emergence of Medicare and Medicaid in 1966 caused the _____ (demand, supply) for health care services to _____ (increase, decrease).

13   Because Medicare and Medicaid reduce the cost of purchasing health care, they are examples of _____.

14   A price ceiling will cause a shortage only if it is set _____ (above, equal to, below) the equilibrium price.

15   A price floor will cause a surplus only if it is set _____ (above, equal to, below) the equilibrium price.

**16** A price ceiling will have no effect if it is set _____ (above, equal to, below) the equilibrium price.

**17** Usury laws restricted banks and other lending institutions from charging interest rates higher than some legal maximum. Usury laws create price _____ (ceilings, floors) and may result in _____ (shortages, surpluses).

**18** If the U.S. government decided to impose a tariff on imports of televisions into the United States, you could predict that the tariff would _____ (increase, decrease) the cost of importing televisions, which would _____ (increase, decrease) the _____ (demand, supply) of imported televisions, in turn _____ (increasing, decreasing) the price of imported televisions and _____ (increasing, decreasing) the quantity of televisions imported into the United States.

## Exercises and Applications

**I** **Price Controls and Medical Care** As the price of health care rises, politicians may consider price controls on certain medical procedures to keep costs down.

1. Would the price controls take the form of a price ceiling or a price floor? _____
2. What do you think would happen in the market for these medical procedures if price controls were adopted? _____

**II** **Wooden Bats Versus Metal Bats** The supply of wooden bats is shown as $S_w$ on the following graph. It has a steeper slope than the supply of metal bats, $S_m$, reflecting the fact that it is easier to produce additional metal bats than additional wooden bats.

1. Assume $D_m$ is the demand for metal bats. Suppose baseball purists are willing to pay more for a "sweet crack" sound than for a dull, metallic "ping" when they connect with a fastball. Draw a demand curve for wooden bats and label it $D_w$.

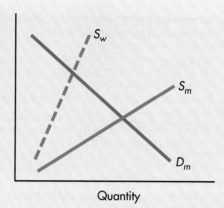

Quantity

2. What are the consequences for the relative prices of wooden and metal bats?

_____

_____

_____

**III** **Contests and CEO Pay** In many American firms, the pay of the person running the company (the chief executive officer, or CEO) is a hundred times higher than the pay received by most company employees. It's hard to believe that these CEOs are so special that their value to the firm is so much greater than that of regular workers. Does this mean that there's no economic logic behind what companies pay CEOs?

Not necessarily. One way to look at CEO pay is that it's the "prize" for winning a contest among potential CEOs. A high prize not only rewards the current CEO for his or her success but also acts as an incentive to other executives to work harder and more productively, in the hope that someday they will do well enough to "win" and become CEOs themselves.

Let's look at a different kind of contest to see how this idea works. Suppose someone in your town is sponsoring a road race for the ten best runners in town and has decided to offer $10,000 in prizes to the ten runners. The people organizing the race are considering two different ways to award the $10,000 in prizes:

**Method 1:** Pay each runner $1,000 for participating in the race.

**Method 2:** Pay the winner $7,000, the second-place finisher $2,000, and the other eight runners $125 for participating.

Figure 1

**Average and Marginal Revenue**

The average-revenue (demand) and marginal-revenue curves are plotted here. As price declines, per unit revenue (the average-revenue) declines. The downward-sloping marginal-revenue curve lies below the average-revenue curve.

| (1)<br>Total<br>Quantity<br>(Q) | (2)<br><br>Price<br>(P) | (3)<br>Total<br>Revenue<br>(TR) | (4)<br>Average<br>Revenue<br>(AR) | (5)<br>Marginal<br>Revenue<br>(MR) |
|---|---|---|---|---|
| 1 | $1,700 | $1,700 | $1,700 | $1,700 |
| 2 | 1,600 | 3,200 | 1,600 | 1,500 |
| 3 | 1,500 | 4,500 | 1,500 | 1,300 |
| 4 | 1,400 | 5,600 | 1,400 | 1,100 |
| 5 | 1,300 | 6,500 | 1,300 | 900 |
| 6 | 1,200 | 7,200 | 1,200 | 700 |
| 7 | 1,100 | 7,700 | 1,100 | 500 |
| 8 | 1,000 | 8,000 | 1,000 | 300 |
| 9 | 900 | 8,100 | 900 | 100 |
| 10 | 800 | 8,000 | 800 | −100 |

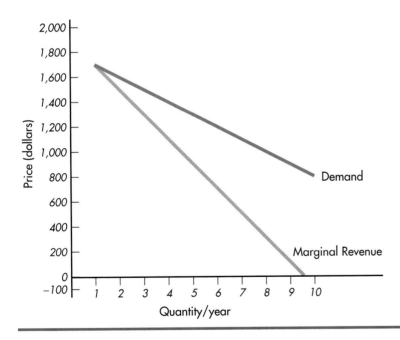

You might have noticed that average revenue is just price: compare columns 2 and 4 and you'll see that they are the same. So demand provides a great deal of information. It tells us what total revenue is—it is average revenue—and it allows us to calculate marginal revenue.

**Marginal revenue (MR)** is the incremental revenue, the additional revenue from selling one more unit of output. Marginal revenue is listed in column five. The marginal revenue of the first bike sold is the *change* in revenue that the firm receives for increasing its sales from 0 to 1 unit. When sold, the first bike brings in $1,700 in revenue, so the marginal revenue is $1,700. The marginal revenue of the

**marginal revenue:**
incremental revenue, change in total revenue divided by change in quantity

$$MR = \frac{\text{change in } TR}{\text{change in } Q}$$

second bike sold is the *change* in revenue that the firm receives for increasing its sales from 1 to 2 bikes. The second bike brings in an additional $1,500 in revenue, so the marginal revenue of the second bike is $1,500. The third bike brings in an additional $1,300 in revenue, so the marginal revenue of the third bike is $1,300.

You may have wondered why a firm would care about its average or marginal revenue. It is because, as you'll see in the next chapter, average and marginal revenues help determine the price to charge and the quantity to offer for sale.

The average- and marginal-revenue schedules are plotted in Figure 1. The average-revenue (demand) curve slopes down, indicating that as the price declines, the per-unit revenue declines. The marginal-revenue curve also slopes down. It is steeper than the average-revenue curve and lies below it.

## Now You Try It

**If the price of a good or service is $10 per unit no matter how many units are sold, calculate average total revenue and marginal revenue at each quantity.**

**RECAP**

1. Total revenue is the quantity sold multiplied by the price at which each unit sold.

2. Average revenue (per-unit revenue) is the total revenue divided by the number of units sold.

3. Marginal revenue is the incremental revenue, the additional revenue obtained by selling one more unit of output.

4. Average revenue is the same as price.

## 2. HOW DOES A FIRM LEARN ABOUT ITS DEMAND?

Demand provides a great deal of information to a business and is something the firm has to know about. There are several ways that a business can learn about the demand for its goods and services. One approach you have probably run across is a survey. Polling organizations are hired by firms to ask consumers questions about demand. You may see the surveys conducted in malls where passersby are asked a series of questions about a product, or you may get a phone call—usually at dinner time—from a telemarketer.

Another type of survey is called the focus group. A focus group usually consists of several randomly chosen shoppers who are paid to spend a few minutes completing questionnaires or answering questions.

Another approach to obtaining information about demand is to use actual experience. A firm that has been in business for a period of time can use its actual experience to map out its demand—comparing past prices and quantities demanded, levels of income, number of customers, changes in the season, and so on. A new firm might have to rely on the experiences of other firms, using the prices and quantities demanded of a firm with a similar product that has been in business for a period of time. A firm offering a new product might do a test trial, introducing the product in just one city. This allows the firm to learn about the relationship between price and quantity demanded before it introduces the product nationwide.

Many firms have instituted information retrieval or inventory control systems that record demand information on a continuous basis. Wal-Mart was one of the first firms to do this. Its scanning devices at the checkout register are connected to a computer that communicates with another computer at central headquarters. The system keeps track of sales and prices and orders more inventory when necessary.

7. The price elasticity of demand is always a negative number because of the law of demand; when price goes up, quantity demanded goes down, and vice versa. As a result, we typically ignore the negative sign when speaking of the price elasticity of demand.

8. If the price elasticity of demand is greater than 1, demand is price-elastic. In this case, total revenue and price changes move in opposite directions. An increase in price causes a decrease in total revenue, and vice versa. If demand is inelastic, then price changes and total revenue move in the same direction.

9. Firms use price elasticity to set prices. In some cases, a firm will charge different prices to different sets of customers for an identical product. This is called price discrimination.

10. The greater the number of close substitutes, the greater the price elasticity of demand.

11. The greater the proportion of a household's budget a good constitutes, the greater the household's price elasticity of demand for that good.

12. The demand for most products over a longer time period has a greater price elasticity than the same product demand over a short time period.

## KEY TERMS

total revenue

average revenue (AR)

marginal revenue (MR)

price elasticity of demand

elastic

unit elastic

inelastic

perfectly elastic

perfectly inelastic

price discrimination

## EXERCISES

1. Use the table below to complete the following exercise. Plot the price and quantity data. Indicate the price elasticity value at each point. What happens to the elasticity value as you move down the demand curve?

| Price | % Change in Price | Quantity Demanded | % Change in Quantity |
|---|---|---|---|
| $ 5 | | 100 | |
| 10 | 100 | 80 | −20 |
| 15 | 66 | 60 | −25 |
| 20 | 33 | 40 | −33 |
| 25 | 25 | 20 | −50 |
| 30 | 20 | 0 | −100 |

2. Below the demand curve plotted in exercise 1, plot the total-revenue curve, measuring total revenue on the vertical axis and quantity on the horizontal axis.

3. What would a 10 percent increase in the price of movie tickets mean for the revenue of a movie theater if the price elasticity of demand was, in turn, 0.1, 0.5, 1.0, and 5.0?

4. Suppose the price elasticity of demand for movies by teenagers is 0.2 and that by adults is 2.0. What policy would the movie theater implement to increase total revenue?

5. Explain why senior citizens often obtain special price discounts.

6. Using the following data, calculate total, average, and marginal revenues:

| Price | Quantity Sold |
|---|---|
| $100 | 200 |
| 90 | 250 |
| 80 | 300 |
| 70 | 350 |
| 60 | 400 |
| 50 | 450 |
| 40 | 500 |
| 30 | 550 |
| 20 | 600 |

7. In recent years, U.S. car manufacturers have charged lower car prices in western states in an effort to offset the competition by the Japanese cars. This two-tier pricing scheme has upset many car dealers in the eastern states. Many have called it discriminatory and illegal. Can you provide another explanation for the two-tier pricing scheme?

## Internet Exercise

**Use the Internet to calculate point price elasticity on the About Economics website.**

Go to the Boyes/Melvin, *Fundamentals of Economics* website accessible through **http://college.hmco.com** and click on the Internet Exercise link for Chapter 4. Now answer the questions that appear on the Boyes/Melvin website.

## Key Term Match

**Match each term with its correct definition by placing the appropriate letter next to the corresponding number.**

A. total revenue
B. average revenue (AR)
C. marginal revenue (MR)
D. price elasticity of demand
E. elastic demand
F. unit elastic demand
G. inelastic demand
H. perfectly elastic demand
I. perfectly inelastic demand
J. price discrimination

_____ 1. incremental revenue, change in total revenue divided by change in quantity
_____ 2. price elasticity greater than 1
_____ 3. price times quantity sold
_____ 4. price elasticity less than 1
_____ 5. zero price elasticity
_____ 6. price elasticity equal to 1
_____ 7. per-unit revenue, total revenue divided by quantity
_____ 8. different prices charged to different customers
_____ 9. infinite price elasticity
_____10. the percentage change in quantity demanded divided by the percentage change in price

## Quick-Check Quiz

1 One day while you are in a shopping mall, someone comes up to you and asks you questions about a product. What is the firm that is paying someone to ask the questions probably trying to get information about?
   a. its supply
   b. its demand
   c. its production costs
   d. the quality of its management
   e. its negative revenue

2 What method for learning about demand for a product can only be used by a firm that has been making the product for a period of time?
   a. shopping mall surveys
   b. telephone surveys
   c. the firm's actual experience
   d. doing a test trial in one or two cities
   e. using focus groups

3 When price elasticity is greater than 1, total revenue increases if price
   a. decreases.
   b. increases.
   c. holds constant.

4 A business knows that it has two sets of customers, one of which has a much more elastic demand than the other. If the business uses price discrimination, which set of customers should receive a lower price?
   a. Both sets should receive the same price.
   b. It doesn't matter to the business which gets a lower price.
   c. The set with the more price elastic demand should receive a lower price.
   d. The set with the less elastic demand should receive a lower price.

5 The price elasticity of demand for a product is largest when there
   a. are no good substitutes for the product.
   b. is only one good substitute for the product.
   c. are two or three good substitutes for the product.
   d. are many good substitutes for the product.

6 The price elasticity of demand for a product is largest when the
   a. product constitutes a large portion of the consumer's budget.
   b. product constitutes a small portion of the consumer's budget.
   c. time period under consideration is very short.

7 The price elasticity of demand for a product is largest when the
   a. time period under consideration is long.
   b. time period under consideration is very short.
   c. product constitutes a small portion of the consumer's budget.

8 Suppose you are the city manager of a small Midwestern city. Your city-owned bus system is losing money, and you have to find a way to take in more revenue. Your staff recommends raising bus fares, but bus riders argue that reducing bus fares to attract new riders would increase revenue. You conclude that
   a. your staff thinks that the demand for bus service is elastic whereas the bus riders think that demand is inelastic.
   b. your staff thinks that the demand for bus service is inelastic whereas the bus riders think that demand is elastic.
   c. both your staff and the bus riders think that the demand for bus service is elastic.
   d. both your staff and the bus riders think that the demand for bus service is inelastic.

e. both your staff and the bus riders think that the demand for bus service is unit elastic.

9   Airlines know from experience that vacation travelers have an elastic demand for air travel whereas business travelers have an inelastic demand for air travel. If an airline wants to increase its total revenue, it should

a. decrease fares for both business and vacation travelers.

b. increase fares for both business and vacation travelers.

c. increase fares for business travelers and decrease fares for vacation travelers.

d. decrease fares for business travelers and increase fares for vacation travelers.

e. leave fares the same for both groups.


## Practice Questions and Problems

1   The equation for calculating total revenue is

_____.

2   The equation for calculating average revenue is

_____.

3   The equation for calculating marginal revenue is

_____.

4   Incremental revenue is another term for

_____.

5   Average revenue is the same as _____.

6   Use the following demand schedule to calculate total revenue, average revenue, and marginal revenue.

| Price | Quantity | Total Revenue | Average Revenue | Marginal Revenue |
|-------|----------|---------------|-----------------|------------------|
| $10   | 1        | _____        | _____          | _____           |
| 9     | 2        | _____        | _____          | _____           |
| 8     | 3        | _____        | _____          | _____           |
| 7     | 4        | _____        | _____          | _____           |

7   The equation used to calculate the price elasticity of demand is

$$e_d = \frac{\text{percentage change in } \rule{2cm}{0.4pt}}{\text{percentage change in } \rule{2cm}{0.4pt}}$$

8   Use the following demand schedule to calculate total revenue, average revenue, and marginal revenue.

| Price | Quantity | Total Revenue | Average Revenue | Marginal Revenue |
|-------|----------|---------------|-----------------|------------------|
| $5    | 1        | _____        | _____          | _____           |
| 5     | 2        | _____        | _____          | _____           |
| 5     | 3        | _____        | _____          | _____           |
| 5     | 4        | _____        | _____          | _____           |

How does the relationship between price and marginal revenue differ between problem 6 and problem 8?

_____

_____

9   Use the following demand schedule to calculate total revenue, average revenue, and marginal revenue. Be careful doing this one—remember the exact definition of marginal revenue.

| Price | Quantity | Total Revenue | Average Revenue | Marginal Revenue |
|-------|----------|---------------|-----------------|------------------|
| $20   | 100      | _____        | _____          | _____           |
| 18    | 200      | _____        | _____          | _____           |
| 16    | 300      | _____        | _____          | _____           |
| 14    | 400      | _____        | _____          | _____           |

10   List four methods besides experience that firms use to gain information about what consumers say they will do in different circumstances.

_____   _____

_____   _____

11   If $e_d$ is less than 1, demand is _____.

12   If $e_d$ is greater than 1, demand is _____.

13   If $e_d$ is equal to 1, demand is _____.

14   If a 5 percent change in the price of movies causes a 10 percent change in the number of movie tickets sold, $e_d$ equals _____ and demand is _____ (elastic, inelastic, unit elastic).

15   If a 6 percent change in the price of coffee causes a 3 percent change in the quantity of coffee bought, $e_d$

equals _____ and demand is _____ (elastic, inelastic, unit elastic).

**16** If a 2 percent change in the price of wine causes a 2 percent change in the number of bottles of wine bought, $e_d$ equals _____ and demand is _____ (elastic, inelastic, unit elastic).

**17** If a 5 percent change in the price of heroin causes no change in the amount of heroin bought, $e_d$ equals _____ and demand is _____ (perfectly elastic, perfectly inelastic).

**18** a. Demand is elastic. The percentage change in _____ (quantity, price) is larger than the percentage change in _____ (quantity, price).

b. When price decreases, quantity demanded increases and total revenue _____ (increases, decreases).

**19** a. Demand is inelastic. The percentage change in _____ (quantity, price) is larger than the percentage change in _____ (quantity, price).

b. When price decreases, quantity increases and total revenue _____ (increases, decreases).

**20** Complete the following table.

| Demand Elasticity | Price Change | Effect on Total Revenue (Increase, Decrease, Unchanged) |
|---|---|---|
| Elastic | Increase | _____ |
| Elastic | Decrease | _____ |
| Inelastic | Increase | _____ |
| Inelastic | Decrease | _____ |
| Unit elastic | Increase | _____ |
| Unit elastic | Decrease | _____ |

**21** List the three determinants of the price elasticity of demand.

_____

_____

_____

**22** A product with _____ (many, few) good substitutes would have a more elastic demand than a product with _____ (many, few) good substitutes.

**23** The demand for new cars is likely to be _____ (more, less) elastic than the demand for new Chevrolet cars.

**24** The demand for paperback novels is likely to be _____ (more, less) elastic than the demand for required college textbooks.

**25** A product that takes a _____ (large, small) portion of a consumer's budget has a more elastic demand than a product that takes a _____ (large, small) portion.

**26** When consumers have a _____ (long, short) time to react to price changes, demand is more elastic than when consumers have a _____ (long, short) period of time to react.

## Exercises and Applications

**1** **Taxing Tobacco** According to the law of demand, taxes that increase the price of a product are expected to reduce consumption of the product. Several years ago, California increased its cigarette tax by $.25 a pack; by the next year, cigarette purchases in California had declined by 10 percent. For simplicity, assume that all of this decrease was caused by the price of cigarettes increasing $.25 as a result of the tax increase. Use this information to answer the following questions.

1. Cigarettes back then cost $1 per pack before the tax increase and $1.25 after. The demand elasticity for cigarettes over this price range is

_____. Demand for this product is _____ (elastic, inelastic).

2. Use the determinants of demand elasticity discussed in Section 3 of the chapter to explain why you would expect the demand for cigarettes to be inelastic.

_____

_____

3. One billion (1,000,000,000) packs of cigarettes were sold in California before the tax increase.

After the tax went into effect, _____ packs were sold, and the state earned

_____ in tax revenue.

**II**  **Price Discrimination in Airline Fares** Several years ago Northwest Airlines cut fares 35 percent for summer travel. There were some restrictions:

Travel must begin on or after May 27 and be completed by September 15.

The nonrefundable tickets require 14-day advance purchase.

Travelers must stay at their destination over a Saturday night.

People taking a plane trip for a vacation usually can plan their trip far in advance and don't mind spending a weekend at their vacation destination. Business travelers, on the other hand, frequently have to travel without much advance notice and want to be back home on weekends.

1. The main customers for Northwest's discounted tickets will be _____ (business, vacation) travelers.

2. Does Northwest think the demand for airline tickets for vacation travel is elastic, inelastic, or unit elastic? Explain your answer.

_____

_____

_____

3. Based on the restrictions it sets and the effects of those restrictions on business and vacation travelers, Northwest must think that

_____ (business, vacation) travelers have a higher price elasticity of demand.

| Chapter 5 | # Costs and Profit Maximization |
|---|---|

**? Fundamental Questions**

1. **What is the relationship between costs and output in the short run?**
2. **Why is the difference between economic profit and accounting profit important?**
3. **Why is profit maximized when** *MR = MC*?

*Preview*

We would all enjoy getting the things we purchase at lower prices. But a firm can't supply goods and services for very long if it can't sell them for at least what it costs the firm to supply them. A firm hires labor; purchases or leases equipment, buildings, and land; and acquires raw materials. What it pays for these resources are the firm's costs. The firm must decide how many resources it needs and then what is the least costly way to acquire and use these resources. Once the firm figures out its costs, it can compare the costs with the revenues to see if it can make a profit.

In this chapter, we first discuss costs, and then we combine costs and revenue to see how the firm earns a profit. ■

## 1. COSTS

The costs of producing and selling goods and services are the costs of the resources used (i.e., the cost of land, labor, and capital). Total cost is $C \times Q$—the cost of each quantity of output supplied multiplied by the quantity supplied.

What happens to costs as output rises? Since more resources are required to sell more output, it would seem logical that costs would rise as output rises. This is the case; costs do rise as output rises, but each unit increase in output does not increase costs the same amount. As output rises unit by unit, costs rise relatively slowly at first but then increase more and more rapidly. The reason is that at first one additional resource can do a lot. For example, hiring another employee can allow the firm to deal with several more customers. But eventually it takes an increasing amount of additional resources to increase output another unit. With too many salespeople, each customer has to wait until his or her salesperson can get access to a cash register, for example. Thus, if there is only one salesclerk, to increase sales by $100 an hour might require only one additional register. But, if there are 20 clerks around the store, to increase sales by $100 an hour might require ten more registers. This means that costs rise by increasingly large amounts for each additional $100 of sales.

### 1.a. Total, Average, and Marginal Costs

Let's use the table in Figure 1 to discuss costs for the same bicycle store from Chapter 4. The costs for the bicycle firm, Pacific Bikes, to sell bicycles each week are shown. Column 1 lists the total quantity (*Q*) of output—the number of bikes

## Figure 1

### Average Total and Marginal Costs

The curves for average total and marginal costs in the short run are U-shaped. Every firm, no matter what it does and no matter what its size, has cost curves that look like those shown here. For every firm, as output rises, per-unit and incremental costs initially fall but eventually rise.

| (1)<br>Total<br>Output<br><br>(Q) | (2)<br>Total<br>Cost<br><br>(TC) | (3)<br>Average<br>Total<br>Cost<br>(ATC) | (4)<br>Marginal<br>Cost<br><br>(MC) |
|---|---|---|---|
| 0 | 1,000 | – | – |
| 1 | 2,000 | 2,000 | 2,000 |
| 2 | 2,800 | 1,400 | 800 |
| 3 | 3,500 | 1,167 | 700 |
| 4 | 4,000 | 1,000 | 500 |
| 5 | 4,500 | 900 | 500 |
| 6 | 5,200 | 867 | 700 |
| 7 | 6,000 | 857 | 800 |
| 8 | 7,000 | 875 | 1,000 |
| 9 | 9,000 | 1,000 | 2,000 |

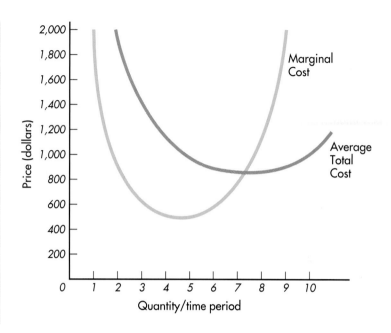

offered for sale each week. Column 2 lists the total costs (*TC*) of providing each output level; it is the total cost schedule.

Column 3 lists **average total costs (*ATC*).** Average total costs are derived by dividing the total costs by the quantity of output, in this case the number of bicycles. Average total costs inform the manager what the costs of producing each unit of output are.

**Marginal costs *(MC),*** the additional costs that come from selling an additional unit of output, are listed in column 4. Marginal costs are the incremental costs, the change in costs resulting from a small decline or increase in output. Marginal costs inform the manager whether the last unit of output offered for sale increased costs a huge amount, a small amount, or not at all.

The average and marginal cost schedules are plotted in the graph in Figure 1. The *ATC* curve declines until 7 bicycles and then rises. The *MC* curve begins below the *ATC* curve and declines until 4 bicycles, stays the same for the 5th, and then begins to climb. The *MC* curve passes through the *ATC* curve at the minimum point of the *ATC* curve.

**average total costs:** per-unit costs, total costs divided by quantity

$$ATC = \frac{TC}{Q}$$

**marginal costs:** incremental costs, change in total costs divided by change in quantity

$$MC = \frac{\text{change in } TC}{\text{change in } Q}$$

### Now You Try It

Using the data, calculate average total cost and marginal cost at each quantity.

| Quantity | 100 | 200 | 300 | 400 | 500 | 600 |
|---|---|---|---|---|---|---|
| Total Cost | $2,000 | $2,900 | $3,700 | $4,400 | $5,000 | $6,200 |

**1. What is the relationship between costs and output in the short run?**

**short run:** a period of time just short enough so that at least one resource is fixed

**long run:** period of time just long enough so that everything can be changed

## 1.b. Why Are the Cost Curves U-Shaped?

Both the curves for average and marginal costs are described as U-shaped; as output rises, per-unit and incremental costs initially fall but eventually rise. The shape of these curves is quite important because every firm, no matter what it does and no matter what its size, has cost curves that look like those in Figure 1 in the short run. The **short run** is a period of time just short enough so that at least one of the resources can't be changed. How long is this? It depends on the type of business. An airline may have year-long leases on equipment and year-long contracts with employees. In such a case, the short run would be anything less than one year. A basket weaver may have no leases and may be able to alter all of its resources within a week's time. In this case, the short run would be anything less than one week.

It is important to distinguish between the short run and the long run. The **long run** is a period of time just long enough so that everything can be changed. In the short run, the firm has fewer options. It cannot expand or contract its entire operation. It can change only some of its resources, the resources referred to as variable. For instance, for the bike shop, the number of employees can be changed quite readily, probably within a day or two. But it would take a long time to change the size of the building and the number of cash registers, display areas, and repair stations. It is this fact that gives us the U-shaped cost curves. To understand why, let's look more closely at the operations of the bicycle shop.

The number of bicycles that can be assembled or repaired and then offered for sale during 1 week is shown in Table 1. One employee can put together and sell 3 bicycles if the bike store has 1 station for assembling the bikes, 10 bicycles if the bike store has 2 repair stations, 25 bicycles if the bike store has 3 stations, and so on. With a second employee, output is increased with each quantity of repair stations: 2 employees and 1 repair station now generate 6 bicycles, and so on.

In the long run every possible combination is an option for the firm. But suppose that Pacific Bikes had previously constructed one repair station and cannot change the number for at least a year. The firm is operating in the short run because it cannot change the size of the building or the number of repair stations. In this case, the number of repair stations is the fixed resource. The options open to Pacific Bikes in the short run are only those under column 1. Pacific Bikes can vary the number of employees but not the number of repair stations in the short run.

As the first units of the variable resource (employees) are hired, each additional employee can prepare and sell many bicycles. But after a time, there are too many employees in the store ("too many chefs stirring the broth"), and each additional employee adds only a little to total bicycles offered for sale. If the employees must

Table 1

**Output with Different Combinations of Resources**

| Number of Employees | Capital (number of repair stations and cash registers) | | | | | | |
|---|---|---|---|---|---|---|---|
| | 1 | 2 | 3 | 4 | 5 | 6 | 7 |
| 0 | 0 | 0 | 0 | 0 | 0 | 0 | 0 |
| 1 | 3 | 10 | 25 | 34 | 41 | 40 | 39 |
| 2 | 6 | 25 | 36 | 45 | 52 | 53 | 50 |
| 3 | 10 | 36 | 48 | 57 | 61 | 62 | 61 |
| 4 | 13 | 44 | 58 | 64 | 69 | 70 | 69 |
| 5 | 13 | 50 | 65 | 71 | 76 | 77 | 77 |
| 6 | 11 | 54 | 70 | 76 | 80 | 82 | 84 |
| 7 | 10 | 55 | 72 | 79 | 82 | 85 | 89 |
| 8 | 8 | 54 | 68 | 80 | 83 | 86 | 90 |

**2. Why is the difference between economic profit and accounting profit important?**

**2.a.4. Accountants and Economic Profit** Accountants do not present economic profit in financial statements, and firms usually don't report it in their annual reports. Why not? Partly because they have not been convinced it is necessary and partly because of the difficulty of calculating the cost of capital. The cost of (equity) capital is the amount that the investors would have to be paid not to move their funds to another firm—that is, the opportunity cost to investors of leaving their money with a particular firm. That amount is sure to vary from investor to investor. My opportunity cost is not the same as yours. This problem could be ignored by focusing on the average investor; however, until the last four or five years, few firms have thought that reporting economic profit was important. In the past few years, investors have begun to realize that having some information about economic profit helps to distinguish between successful and not-so-successful firms. As a result, more and more firms are beginning to offer investors some information on economic profit.

**RECAP**

1. Accounting profit is total revenue minus total costs. It does not include the opportunity cost of the owner's capital, however.

2. Economic profit is accounting profit minus the opportunity cost of the owner's capital.

3. Economic profit can be positive, negative, or zero. A positive economic profit means that the revenue exceeds the full costs of inputs, that is, that inputs are earning more than their opportunity costs. A negative economic profit means that inputs are not earning their opportunity costs. A zero economic profit means that inputs are just earning their opportunity costs.

4. Economic profit is not straightforward to measure because the opportunity cost of capital depends on investor alternatives.

5. The cost of capital is the amount a firm would have to pay investors to have them invest in it rather than in another firm.

## 3. THE PROFIT-MAXIMIZING RULE: *MR = MC*

**3. Why is profit maximized when *MR = MC*?**

We know what profit is. The question now facing us is how do we know what quantity to sell and what price to charge in order to maximize profit. As we will see in this section, the answer is quite simple; all we have to do is find the price and quantity at which marginal revenue equals marginal costs.

### 3.a. Graphical Derivation of the *MR = MC* Rule

*Now You Try It*

Using Figure 2, find the profit-maximizing output level if price is a constant $800 no matter how many units are sold.

Profit is maximized at the price and quantity at which *MR = MC*. Marginal costs are the additional costs of producing one more unit of output. Marginal revenue is the additional revenue obtained from selling one more unit of output. If the production of one more unit of output increases costs less than it increases revenue—that is, if marginal costs are less than marginal revenue—then producing (and selling) that unit of output will increase profit. Conversely, if the production of one more unit of output costs more than the revenue obtained from the sale of that unit, then producing that unit of output will decrease profit. *When marginal revenue is greater than marginal cost, producing more will increase profit. Conversely, when marginal revenue is less than marginal cost, producing more will lower profit. Thus, profit is at a maximum when marginal revenue equals marginal cost: MR = MC.*

Figure 2

**Revenue, Costs, and Profit**

When marginal revenue is greater than marginal cost, there is less output and some profit that could be earned is not. When marginal revenue is less than marginal cost, there is more output and profit is reduced.

| (1)<br>Total<br>Output<br><br>(Q) | (2)<br>Price<br><br><br>(P) | (3)<br>Total<br>Revenue<br><br>(TR) | (4)<br>Average<br>Revenue<br><br>(AR) | (5)<br>Marginal<br>Revenue<br><br>(MR) | (6)<br>Total<br>Cost<br><br>(TC) | (7)<br>Average<br>Total<br>Cost<br>(ATC) | (8)<br>Marginal<br>Cost<br><br>(MC) | (9)<br>Total<br>Profit<br><br>(TR – TC) | |
|---|---|---|---|---|---|---|---|---|---|
| 0 | 0 | 0 | 0 | 0 | $1,000 | — | — | –$1,000 | |
| 1 | $1,700 | 1,700 | 1,700 | 1,700 | 2,000 | 2,000 | 2,000 | –300 | |
| 2 | 1,600 | 3,200 | 1,600 | 1,500 | 2,800 | 1,400 | 800 | 400 | |
| 3 | 1,500 | 4,500 | 1,500 | 1,300 | 3,500 | 1,167 | 700 | 1,000 | |
| 4 | 1,400 | 5,600 | 1,400 | 1,100 | 4,000 | 1,000 | 500 | 1,600 | |
| 5 | 1,300 | 6,500 | 1,300 | 900 | 4,500 | 900 | 500 | 2,000 | |
| 6 | 1,200 | 7,200 | 1,200 | 700 | 5,200 | 867 | 700 | 2,000 | Profit Maximum |
| 7 | 1,100 | 7,700 | 1,100 | 500 | 6,000 | 857 | 800 | 1,700 | |
| 8 | 1,000 | 8,000 | 1,000 | 300 | 7,000 | 875 | 1,000 | 1,000 | |
| 9 | 900 | 8,100 | 900 | 100 | 9,000 | 1,000 | 2,000 | –900 | |

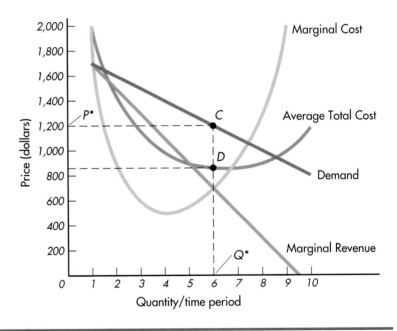

Consider Figure 2, in which the curves of average total and marginal cost from Figure 1 are drawn along with the curves of demand and marginal revenue from the previous chapter. Figure 2 illustrates the fundamental decisions made by all business managers and owners. The profit-maximizing rule, *MR* = *MC*, is illustrated in the table of Figure 2, which lists output, total revenue, total costs, marginal revenue, marginal cost, and profit for Pacific Bikes. The first column is the total quantity (*Q*) of bikes sold. Column 2 is the price (*P*) of each bike. Column 3 is the total revenue (*TR*) generated by selling each quantity. Column 4 is average revenue (*AR*) (which is the same as demand)—total revenue divided by quantity. Column 5 lists marginal revenue (*MR*)—the change in total revenue that comes with the sale of an additional bike.

Total costs (*TC*) are listed in column 6. You might note that costs are $1,000 even when no bikes are sold. Costs that have to be paid even when production is zero are called **fixed costs.** Fixed costs are items like the lease on the building and the payment on the loans used to construct repair stations. Other costs, referred to as **variable costs,** change as output changes. Variable costs include the costs of employees, electricity, water, and materials—items that change as quantity changes.

Average total cost (*ATC*) is listed in column 7; it is total cost divided by quantity. Marginal cost (*MC*), the additional cost of selling an additional bike, is listed in column 8. The marginal cost of the first bike is the additional cost of offering the first bike for sale, $1,000; the marginal cost of the second bike is the increase in costs that results from offering a second bike for sale, $800. Total profit, the difference between total revenue and total costs (*TR* − *TC*), is listed in the last column.

The first bike costs an additional $1,000 to sell; the marginal cost (additional cost) of the first bike is $1,000. When sold, the bike brings in $1,700 in revenue, so the marginal revenue is $1,700. Since marginal revenue is greater than marginal cost, the firm is better off selling that first bike than not selling it.

The second bike costs an additional $800 (column 8) to sell and brings in an additional $1,500 (column 5) in revenue when sold. With the second bike, marginal revenue exceeds marginal cost. Thus, the firm is better off producing two bikes than none or one.

Profit continues to rise until the sixth bike is sold. The marginal cost of selling the seventh bike is $800 while the marginal revenue is $500. Thus, marginal cost is greater than marginal revenue. Profit declines if the seventh bike is sold. The firm can maximize profit by selling six bikes, the quantity at which marginal revenue and marginal cost are equal.

We can easily find the profit-maximizing price and quantity in Figure 2. Profit is maximized at the point at which *MR* = *MC*. The quantity the firm should sell to maximize profit is given by dropping a line down to the horizontal axis from the *MR* = *MC* point, a quantity of *Q*\* = 6. The price that the firm should charge to sell this quantity is given by extending the vertical line from the *MR* = *MC* point up to the demand curve. The demand curve tells us how much consumers are willing and able to pay for the quantity *Q*\*. Then, we draw a horizontal line over to the vertical axis, the price axis, at *P*\* = $1,200.

Total revenue is given by the rectangle 06CP\*. The total cost is found by multiplying average total cost by quantity. We draw a vertical line from *Q*\* = 6 up to the average-total-cost curve; it intersects at point *D*. This gives us the per-unit costs of selling six bikes. We then draw a horizontal line over to the vertical axis; this represents multiplying *ATC* by *Q*\* = 6. The resulting rectangle 06D$867 is the total cost. Total profit, then, is the difference between total revenue and total cost. Total profit is given by the rectangle $867DCP\*.

Figure 2 provides a great deal of information about business behavior. The demand curve may be different (steeper or flatter) depending on the price elasticity of demand, or the position of the cost curves might be different depending on cost conditions; but irrespective, profit is maximized when *MR* = *MC*. Every decision a manager or owner makes comes down to comparing marginal revenue and marginal cost. Should the firm increase advertising expenditures? If the *MR* from doing so is greater than the *MC*, then yes. Should the firm hire another employee? If the *MR* from doing so exceeds the *MC*, then yes. This decision-making approach shouldn't be any surprise to you. It is how you make decisions as well. You compare your marginal revenue (your additional benefits) of doing something to your marginal costs. If your marginal revenue exceeds your marginal cost, you do it.

fixed costs: costs of fixed resources; costs that do not change as output changes

variable costs: costs that vary as output varies

Nike used to have a slogan, "Just Do It." What they ought to have said is, "If *MR* exceeds *MC*, then do it."

### 3.b. What Have We Learned?

We have covered a great deal of territory. We have learned how firms select the price to charge and quantity to sell to maximize profit. A firm will supply the quantity and charge a price given by the point at which $MR = MC$. Marginal revenue depends on demand, that is, on consumers. The firm must know what the consumer likes and what prices the consumer is willing and able to pay. It must supply its goods and services at those prices if it is to maximize its profit.

For-profit firms behave so as to maximize profit and thus sell a quantity and set a price determined by the point at which $MR = MC$. So if we know marginal revenue and marginal cost, determining the quantity to sell and the price to charge is trivial. The problem is that marginal revenue and marginal cost are typically not known. All opportunity costs are not reported in accounting statements. Moreover, accountants allocate costs among activities or across departments; they do not calculate the *incremental* cost of producing one more unit or the *incremental* revenue from selling one more unit. As a result, it is often said that marginal cost and marginal revenue are not really useful. Why, then, do we pay so much attention to the rule $MR = MC$?

Although accountants do not provide marginal cost information and although executives say they pay no attention to marginal cost or marginal revenue, these concepts are critical aspects of their decision making. Consider, for instance, how an airline decides to price its services. The price of seats varies considerably depending on the time one flies, whether a Saturday night stay occurs, and when one purchases a ticket. Often an airline flying with some empty seats will sell the seats at the last moment very inexpensively. In fact, the price of the seat is often below the average cost of flying the plane. The average total cost (per passenger cost) for Southwest Airlines is about $.07 per mile. Yet Southwest will often sell some of its seats on distances of 1,000 miles for $25. Why? Because $25 is significantly more than $0. The marginal cost of adding one more passenger is nearly zero. Thus, the additional (marginal) revenue of the seat, $25, is greater than the marginal cost. The executives of Southwest know that they are better off selling the seat than not selling it. They know this not because they have calculated marginal revenue and marginal cost but because they know they make more profit by doing so. The profit-maximizing rule, $MR = MC$, may not be on executives' lips or in their manuals, but it does describe their behavior. It provides a framework for understanding business behavior. Thus, it is a very important part of understanding why the world looks and acts as it does.

RECAP

1. The profit-maximizing rule is to produce the quantity at which marginal revenue equals marginal cost, $MR = MC$, and to sell that quantity at the price given by demand.

# SUMMARY

### ? What is the relationship between costs and output in the short run?

1. The short run is a period of time just short enough so that the quantity of at least one of the resources cannot be altered.

2. Average total costs are the costs per unit of output—total costs divided by the quantity of output sold.

3. As quantity rises, total costs rise. Initially, as quantity rises, total costs rise slowly. Eventually, as quantity rises, total costs rise more and more rapidly.

4. According to the law of diminishing marginal returns, when successive equal amounts of a variable resource are combined with a fixed amount of another resource, the additional output will initially rise but will eventually decline.

5. The U shape of short-run, average-total-cost curves is due to the law of diminishing marginal returns.

6. The objective of firms is to make a profit. The difference between sales, or the value of output, and the input costs (including the opportunity costs) is called economic profit.

### ? Why is the difference between economic profit and accounting profit important?

7. Accountants do not measure all opportunity costs. Accounting profit does not include the opportunity cost of the owner's capital. Economists take into account all opportunity costs.

8. Normal accounting profit is a zero economic profit. Positive economic profit occurs when revenue is greater than all opportunity costs. Negative economic profit occurs when revenue is less than total opportunity costs.

### ? Why is profit maximized when *MR* = *MC*?

9. Profit is maximized at the output level at which total revenue exceeds total costs by the greatest amount, at the point at which $MR = MC$.

10. The supply rule for all firms is to supply the quantity at which the firm's marginal revenue and marginal costs are equal and to charge a price given by the demand curve at that quantity.

# KEY TERMS

average total costs (*ATC*)

marginal costs (*MC*)

short run

long run

law of diminishing marginal returns

cost of capital

debt

equity

economic profit

accounting profit

negative economic profit

zero economic profit

normal accounting profit

positive economic profit

fixed costs

variable costs

# EXERCISES

1. Use the table below and find average total costs and marginal costs.

| Output | Costs | ATC | MC |
|--------|-------|-----|-----|
| 0 | $100 | | |
| 1 | 175 | | |
| 2 | 225 | | |
| 3 | 255 | | |
| 4 | 300 | | |
| 5 | 400 | | |

2. Use the completed table to do a and b.
   a. Plot each of the cost curves.
   b. At what quantity of output do marginal costs equal average total costs?

3. Describe the relation between marginal and average total costs.

4. In the following figure, if the firm has average total costs $ATC_1$, which rectangle measures total profit? If the firm has average costs $ATC_2$, what is total profit?

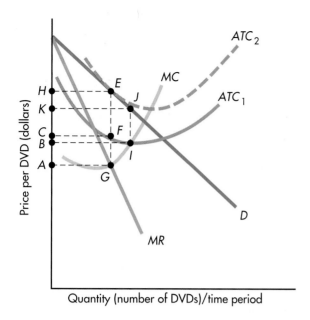

Price per DVD (dollars)

Quantity (number of DVDs)/time period

5. Using the following demand schedule, compute marginal and average revenue:

| Price | $100 | $95 | $88 | $80 | $70 | $55 | $40 | $22 |
|---|---|---|---|---|---|---|---|---|
| Quantity | 1 | 2 | 3 | 4 | 5 | 6 | 7 | 8 |

6. Suppose the marginal costs of producing the good in exercise 5 is a constant $10 per unit of output. What quantity of output will the firm sell?

7. What follows is some accounting information for each of the firms shown. Can you tell which firm is the most successful? Explain.

| | Boeing | Goodyear | Liz Claiborne | Circuit City |
|---|---|---|---|---|
| Sales | $5,601 | $423 | $622 | $1,767 |
| Profits | $254 | $26.9 | $56.2 | $31.6 |

8. A cost of capital figure for each of the firms is listed below. Explain what this figure means.

| | |
|---|---|
| Motorola | 11.6 |
| Hershey Foods | 12.8 |
| Home Depot | 12.2 |
| Dillard Department Stores | 10.5 |
| Coca-Cola | 12.0 |

9. Can accounting profit be positive and economic profit negative? Can accounting profit be negative and economic profit positive? Explain.

10. Use the following information to calculate accounting profit and economic profit:

| | |
|---|---|
| Sales | $100 |
| Employee expenses | 40 |
| Inventory expenses | 20 |
| Value of owner's labor in any other enterprise | 40 |

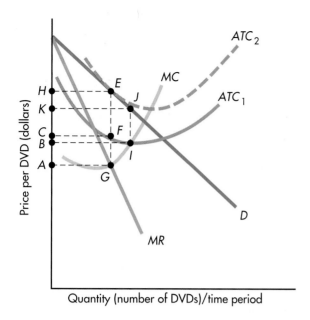

Internet Exercise

**Use the Internet to experiment with marginal cost and marginal revenue and think about how managers make decisions every day.**

Go to the Boyes/Melvin, *Fundamentals of Economics* website accessible through **http://college.hmco.com** and click on the Internet Exercise link for Chapter 5. Now answer the questions that appear on the Boyes/Melvin website.

## Key Term Match

Match each term with its correct definition by placing the appropriate letter next to the corresponding number.

A. average total costs (ATC)
B. marginal costs (MC)
C. short run
D. long run
E. law of diminishing marginal returns
F. cost of capital
G. debt
H. equity
I. economic profit
J. accounting profit
K. negative economic profit
L. zero economic profit
M. normal accounting profit
N. positive economic profit
O. fixed costs
P. variable costs

_____ 1. loans
_____ 2. costs that have to be paid even when production is zero
_____ 3. per unit cost; total cost divided by the total output
_____ 4. revenue less all costs, including the opportunity cost of the owner's capital
_____ 5. shares of stock; ownership of a piece of a company
_____ 6. zero economic profit
_____ 7. the additional cost of producing one more unit of output
_____ 8. total revenue that is less than total costs when total costs include all opportunity costs
_____ 9. a period of time short enough so that the quantities of at least one of the resources cannot be varied
_____10. profit that occurs when total revenue is greater than total opportunity costs
_____11. profit that occurs when total revenue equals total opportunity costs
_____12. costs that change relative to output
_____13. total revenue less total costs, except the opportunity cost of the owner's capital
_____14. declining marginal increases in output attributed to combining equal additional amounts of a variable resource with a fixed amount of another resource
_____15. the opportunity cost of the funds used to purchase capital; the cost of debt plus the cost of equity
_____16. a period of time in which everything can be changed

## Quick-Check Quiz

1. According to the law of diminishing marginal returns, as successive units of a variable resource are added to some fixed resources, the additional output will

   a. initially rise but will eventually decline.
   b. initially decline but will eventually rise.
   c. continually rise.
   d. continually decline.
   e. remain constant.

2. The primary objective of business firms is to

   a. sell as much as possible.
   b. keep their total costs to the minimum.
   c. keep their marginal costs to the minimum.
   d. maximize profit.
   e. pay their employees more than other workers earn.

3. The factor that makes accounting profit different from economic profit is

   a. opportunity cost of debt capital.
   b. opportunity cost of equity capital.
   c. opportunity cost of labor.
   d. opportunity cost of land.
   e. all opportunity costs.

4. A firm is getting normal accounting profit when

   a. revenue just pays all opportunity costs.
   b. it has a zero economic profit.
   c. revenue just pays the cost of capital.
   d. all of the above are true.
   e. only a and b are true.

5. A firm can increase its profit by producing another unit of output when

   a. total revenue is more than total cost.
   b. total revenue is less than total cost.
   c. total revenue is equal to total cost.
   d. marginal revenue is more than marginal cost.
   e. marginal revenue is less than marginal cost.

6. The profit-maximizing rule for a firm is to set the price and sell the quantity at which

   a. $MC = ATC$.
   b. $MR = MC$.
   c. $AR = ATC$.
   d. $TR = TC$.
   e. $MR = ATC$.

## Practice Questions and Problems

1. You calculate average total costs (ATC) by using this equation: _____.

**2** You calculate marginal costs (*MC*) by using this equation: _____.

**3** The short run is a period of time just short enough so that _____ of the resources is _____.

**4** Diminishing marginal returns happen in any type of business firm because the efficiency of variable resources depends on the _____ of the _____.

**5** Use the following total cost table for Joe's Gourmet Hamburgers to calculate Joe's *ATC* and *MC*. Then plot the *TC* curve on graph (a) below, and the *ATC* and *MC* curves on graph (b).

| *Burgers* | *TC* | *ATC* | *MC* |
|---|---|---|---|
| 0 | $5.50 | $_____ | $_____ |
| 1 | 9.00 | _____ | _____ |
| 2 | 10.00 | _____ | _____ |
| 3 | 10.50 | _____ | _____ |
| 4 | 11.50 | _____ | _____ |
| 5 | 13.00 | _____ | _____ |
| 6 | 15.00 | _____ | _____ |
| 7 | 17.50 | _____ | _____ |
| 8 | 20.50 | _____ | _____ |
| 9 | 24.00 | _____ | _____ |
| 10 | 28.00 | _____ | _____ |

**6** The *ATC* and *MC* curves are shaped like the letter _____.

**7** Business firms try to maximize _____, which is also known as _____.

**8** Capital can be acquired through either _____ or _____.

**9** The cost of debt is the _____ that is paid on the debt.

**10** The cost of equity is the _____ that the owners or investors could have gotten if they had put their money into some other investment.

**11** Accounting profit = _____ costs of inputs: _____, _____, and _____.

**12** Economic profit = accounting profit − _____.

**13** Economic profit is always _____ (larger, smaller) than accounting profit.

**14** If accounting profit is more than the cost of equity capital, the firm is receiving _____ (negative, positive, zero) economic profits.

**(a) Total Costs**

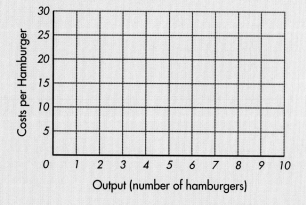

**(b) Unit Costs**

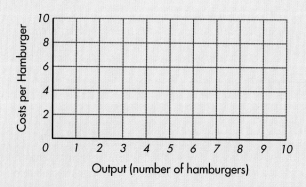

**15** If accounting profit is less than the cost of capital, the firm is receiving _____ (negative, positive, zero) economic profits.

**16** If accounting profit is equal to the cost of capital, the firm is receiving _____ (negative, positive, zero) economic profits.

**17** a. If Joe's Gourmet Hamburgers and other similar restaurants are currently receiving a _____ (negative, positive, zero) economic profit, other people are likely to open similar restaurants.

b. If Joe's Gourmet Hamburgers and other similar restaurants are currently receiving a _____ (negative, positive, zero) economic profit, other people are *not* likely to want to open similar restaurants.

**18** Last year, the accountant for Joe's Gourmet Hamburgers gave Joe the following information:

| | |
|---|---|
| Revenues | $200,000 |
| Labor costs | 140,000 |
| Land costs | 10,000 |
| Debt costs | 20,000 |
| Equity costs | 50,000 |

a. Joe's accounting profit was _____.

b. Joe's economic profit was _____.

c. Joe received a _____ (negative, positive, zero) economic profit.

d. Based on Joe's results, other people are _____ (likely, unlikely) to open new restaurants like Joe's.

e. How much more revenue does Joe need to receive a normal profit (assuming his costs don't change)? _____

**19** If the marginal revenue from selling another unit of output is _____ (more, less) than the marginal cost, the firm should produce another unit.

**20** If the marginal revenue from selling another unit of output is _____ (more, less) than the marginal cost, the firm should not produce another unit.

**21** Sally Smith is a world-famous artist who carves exquisite models of birds out of rare, expensive woods. Sally knows that if she carves only one bird per month, her customers will pay a high price for it because of its rarity. If she makes more birds per month, people will only be willing to pay lower prices. Moreover, when she carves more birds per month, her hands get very sore, and she has to spend money having them massaged.

a. The following table lists the price Sally can charge for different numbers of birds sold per month and her total costs for making different numbers of birds per month. Calculate Sally's total revenue, marginal revenue, marginal cost, and profit for each output level.

| Q | P | TR | TC | MR | MC | Profit |
|---|---|---|---|---|---|---|
| 0 | — | $ 0 | $ 500 | — | — | $ ____ |
| 1 | $2,000 | ____ | 700 | $ ____ | $ ____ | ____ |
| 2 | 1,800 | ____ | 1,100 | ____ | ____ | ____ |
| 3 | 1,600 | ____ | 1,700 | ____ | ____ | ____ |
| 4 | 1,400 | ____ | 2,500 | ____ | ____ | ____ |
| 5 | 1,200 | ____ | 3,500 | ____ | ____ | ____ |
| 6 | 1,000 | ____ | 4,700 | ____ | ____ | ____ |

b. Sally's profit is at its maximum at an output level of _____ bird(s).

c. Sally's marginal revenue equals her marginal cost at an output level of _____ bird(s).

d. On the following graph a, plot Sally's profit at each output level. On the following graph b, plot Sally's marginal cost and marginal revenue. As you can see, profit is maximized at the output level at which $MR = MC$ (4 birds).

**(a) Sally's Profit**

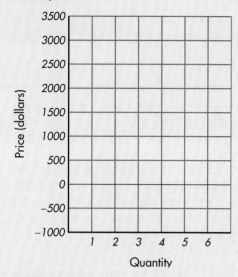

**(b) Sally's MR and MC**

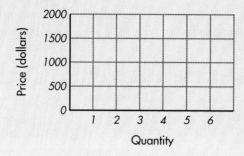

## Exercises and Applications

**Profit Maximization and Pollution Reduction** The ideas of profit maximization and of comparing marginal revenue and marginal cost to find the profit-maximizing output level can be useful even for organizations that are not involved in profit maximization. All organizations need to find the most effective ways of reaching their goals.

Suppose you are the head of the Environmental Protection Agency (EPA), and you have to decide how much, if any, pollution a particular water treatment plant should be allowed to produce. Right now, the plant produces 4 tons of pollutants per day. The plant is owned by the federal government, so any cleanup costs will be paid through taxes. Let's assume that the EPA knows what the benefits and costs (in dollars) are from reducing pollution by various amounts. Using the benefits and costs in the following table, find the amount of pollution reduction that provides people with the biggest "profit." Profit in this case is the net value people get from pollution reduction: the total benefits minus the total costs.

| Pollution Improvement: Tons Reduced per Day | Marginal Benefits | Marginal Costs |
|---|---|---|
| 1 | $ 10 million | $ 1 million |
| 2 | 5 million | 4 million |
| 3 | 2 million | 10 million |
| 4 | 1 million | 30 million |

**1** The plant should reduce pollution by _____ tons per day.

**2** Explain why you chose this amount.

_____

_____

_____

ACE self-test

Now that you've completed the Study Guide for this chapter, you should have a good sense of the concepts you need to review. If you'd like to test your understanding of the material again, go to the Practice Tests on the Boyes/Melvin *Fundamentals of Economics,* 3e website, **economics.college.hmco.com/students.**

## Chapter 6

# Competition and Market Structures

### ? Fundamental Questions

1. **What is a market structure, and what can it tell us about how a firm will behave?**
2. **Do all firms maximize profit when *MR* = *MC*?**
3. **Is it possible to earn positive economic profit in the long run?**
4. **What are the benefits of competition?**
5. **Why does it matter whether there are barriers to entry?**

*Preview*

We know that every firm, no matter its size, no matter its location, no matter what it does, has a relationship in the short run between costs and output dictated by the law of diminishing marginal returns. Thus, the cost curves can have only one shape—the U shape. Demand is another matter. Every single firm has a unique demand curve for its goods and services. But the similarities of the shapes of the demand curve for similar-type firms enable us to discuss just four very general market structures and, thus, four general demand curves—perfect competition, monopolistic competition, oligopoly, and monopoly. In this chapter we discuss the market structures and firm behavior in each case. We find that an especially important attribute of a market is how difficult it is for competitors to enter the market and begin competing with the incumbent firms. ■

## 1. CHARACTERISTICS OF THE MARKET STRUCTURES

A market structure is a *model*—a simplification of reality. Few, if any, industries fit neatly into one market structure or another. Economists use models of market structures to describe how firms might behave under certain conditions. They can then modify the models to improve their understanding of how firms behave in real life.

The market structure in which a firm produces and sells its product is defined by three characteristics:

- The number of firms that make up the market
- The ease with which new firms may enter the market and begin producing the good or service
- The degree to which the products produced by the firms are different

In some industries, such as agriculture, there are millions of individual firms. In others, such as photofinishing supplies, there are very few firms. It is relatively easy and inexpensive to enter the desktop publishing business, but it is much more costly and difficult to start a new airline.

Table 1 summarizes the characteristics of the four market structures.

**1. What is a market structure, and what can it tell us about how a firm will behave?**

| Table 1 | Characteristics | | | |
|---|---|---|---|---|
| **Summary of Market Structures** | Market Structure | Number of Firms | Entry Condition | Product Type |
| | Perfect competition | Very large number | Easy | Standardized |
| | Monopoly | One | No entry possible | Only one product |
| | Monopolistic competition | Large number | Easy | Differentiated |
| | Oligopoly | Few | Difficult | Standardized or differentiated |

## 1.a. Perfect Competition

**perfect competition:** a market structure characterized by such a large number of firms that no *one* firm has an effect on the market

**Perfect competition** is a market structure characterized by a very large number of firms, so large that whatever any *one* firm does has no effect on the market; firms that produce an identical (standardized or nondifferentiated) product; and easy entry. Because of the large number of firms, consumers have many choices of where to purchase the good or service, and there is no cost to the consumer of going to a different store. Because the product is standardized, consumers do not prefer one store to another or one brand to another. In fact, there are no brands—only identical, generic products. Because each firm is such a small part of the market, each is unable to do anything other than choose how much to sell at the prevailing market price. In other words, the demand curve for the individual firm in perfect competition is a horizontal line. Figure 1(a) shows how the individual firm's demand is given by the market price established by the equilibrium between market demand and market supply. The market demand is the sum of the demands by all consumers, and the market supply is the sum of the supplies by all firms. The equilibrium establishes the market price, which becomes the individual firm's demand.

## 1.b. Monopoly

**monopoly:** a market structure in which there is just one firm, and entry by other firms is not possible

**Monopoly** is a market structure in which there is just one firm, and entry by other firms is not possible. Because there is only one firm, consumers have only one place to buy the good, and there are no close substitutes.

The demand curve facing the single firm in a monopoly is the market demand curve because the firm is the only supplier in the market. Figure 1(b) shows the demand curve facing the firm in a monopoly. Being the only producer, the firm in a monopoly must carefully consider what price to charge. Unlike a price increase in a perfectly competitive market, a price increase in a monopoly will not drive every customer to another producer. But if the price rises too high, revenue will decline as consumers decide to forgo the product supplied by that one firm.

## 1.c. Monopolistic Competition

**monopolistic competition:** a market structure characterized by a large number of firms, easy entry, and differentiated products

The market structure of a **monopolistic competition** is characterized by a large number of firms, easy entry, and differentiated products. Product differentiation distinguishes a perfectly competitive market from a monopolistically competitive market (in both, entry is easy, and there are a large number of firms).

Figure 1

**The Demand Curve Facing an Individual Firm in Each of the Three Market Structures**

The demand curve for the individual firm in perfect competition is a horizontal line at the market price, as shown in Figure 1(a).

Figure 1(b) shows the market demand, which is the demand curve faced by the monopoly firm. The firm is the only supplier and thus faces the entire market demand. Figure 1(c) shows the downward-sloping demand curve faced by the firm in monopolistic competition. The curve slopes downward because of the differentiated nature of the products in the industry.

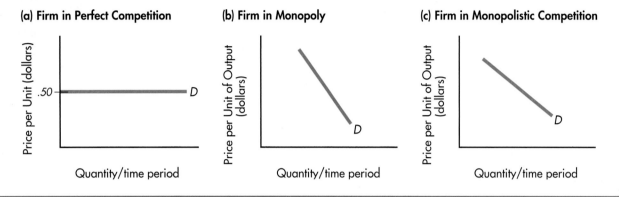

(a) Firm in Perfect Competition

(b) Firm in Monopoly

(c) Firm in Monopolistic Competition

Even though there are many firms in a monopolistically competitive market structure, the demand curve faced by *any one firm* slopes downward, as in Figure 1(c). Because each product is slightly different from all other products, each firm is like a mini-monopoly—the only producer of that specific product. The greater the differentiation among products, the less price-elastic the demand.

### 1.d. Oligopoly

**oligopoly:** a market structure in which there are few enough firms that each firm alone can affect the market

In an **oligopoly,** there are few firms—more than one but few enough so that each firm alone can affect the market. Automobile producers constitute one oligopoly, steelmakers another. Entry into an oligopoly is more difficult than entry into a perfectly competitive or monopolistically competitive market, but in contrast to monopoly, entry can occur. The products offered by the firms in an oligopoly may be differentiated or nondifferentiated. Oligopolistic firms are *interdependent,* and this interdependence distinguishes oligopoly from the other market structures.

The oligopolist faces a downward-sloping demand curve, but the shape of the curve depends on the behavior of its competitors. Oligopoly is the most complicated of the market structure models to examine because there are so many behaviors firms may display. Because of its diversity, many economists describe oligopoly as the most realistic of the market structure models.

*Now You Try It*

**What type of market structure does Microsoft Corporation belong to?**

**2. Do all firms maximize profit when *MR = MC*?**

### 1.e. Demand and Profit Maximization

Does a perfectly competitive firm maximize profit in a different manner than a monopolist or monopolistically competitive firm? The answer is not really. Each firm maximizes profit by finding the quantity at which marginal revenue equals marginal costs (*MR = MC*) and then setting the price according to demand. The difference is that the perfectly competitive firm has no choice about the price. The only decision for the perfectly competitive firm is what quantity to produce; price is determined by the entire market (all firms and all consumers). As with all

## The American Girls Phenomenon

For many years the parents of daughters complained about the dearth of toys available to them. Other than Barbie, what was there? Then came the American Girls, a collection of historical dolls made by Pleasant Company, each with a series of books describing each girl's place in history. Girls love the dolls; nearly 4 million of them were sold in the past 11 years. In addition to the dolls, the Pleasant Company sold clothes, accessories, furniture, craft kits, and even matching clothes in real-girl sizes.

The Pleasant Company dolls were so successful that competitors began to offer their own collections, each with a distinct twist. Like the American Girls, the dolls are sold exclusively by mail order, and each comes with its own predetermined, fantasy history. There's Global Friends, which spins stories about girls from different cultures. Just Pretend offers Laurel the Woodfairy with her own trellis and lute and Alissa the Princess with an armoire and a throne. My Twinn dolls are custom-made to match

photographs of their owners, down to the shape of their eyebrows and placement of freckles. Savannah and her friends from Storybook Heirlooms each have a distinct personality.

Many of these dolls are sized just differently enough so that their expensive clothes won't fit on dolls from rival collections. The 18-inch American Girls dolls, for example, are too chubby to fit into the clothes made for the more svelte 18-inch Magic Attic Club dolls. The Little Women dolls are 16 inches tall. My Twinn is 23 inches. Global Friends dolls are only 14 inches.

The economic profit of these doll companies seems to have been driven to zero and, as a result, additional companies are not entering the market. American Girls and Mattel's Barbie control more than 40 percent of the U.S. market. Barbie's annual sales of almost $900 million are more than three times larger than those of Pleasant Company's American Girls, which in turn overshadow the sales of its competitors.

The doll story illustrates the market process. For years, there was only Barbie—a doll with dimensions that no real person could achieve and which focused on no intellectual aspects. Then an entrepreneur (Pleasant Company) comes up with a new product— American Girls dolls and the whole package of highly readable, fictionalized history books, clothes, and accessories—and is very successful. Other entrepreneurs see the success and want to get in on the good thing. They begin copycat companies, but to be successful, they have to be slightly different. In this case, the dolls are different sizes and have different stories than those of the American Girls. The success of Pleasant Company attracted new resources to the market—new companies. New companies with different approaches continued to enter the doll market until the potential for success looked no better than that for other industries, and the market topped out.

---

firms, the perfectly competitive firm selects to produce and offer for sale the amount at which the *MC* curve crosses the *MR* curve. The difference is that for the perfectly competitive firm, marginal revenue, demand, and price are identical. For firms in all other market structures, the process of maximizing profit is what we described earlier. The firm finds the quantity at which $MR = MC$. It then determines what price consumers are willing and able to pay to purchase the quantity of output offered by the firm (indicated by tracing a vertical line up to demand).

Consider Table 2. Marginal revenue is a constant $80 since a perfectly competitive firm has a perfectly elastic demand, which is the same as the marginal revenue—a constant amount equal to the price. If 1 unit of output is produced and sold, the firm in Table 2 experiences a cost of $30 and a revenue of $80; clearly, it makes sense to produce that unit. Similarly, it makes sense to produce and sell the second and third units. But the fourth unit brings in only $80 while it costs $120; that fourth unit will not be produced. Profit is maximized when $MR = MC = \$80$, so the firm will produce 3 units. Compare this to the firm whose demand is downward sloping—the monopolist, monopolistic competitor, or oligopolist.

Consider the data shown in Table 3. Column 1 is output, column 2 is the marginal cost of each output level, and column 3 is the marginal revenue.

| Output | MC | MR |
|---|---|---|
| **Table 2** | | |
| **Marginal Revenue and Marginal Cost for the Perfectly Competitive Firm** | | |
| 0 | | |
| 1 | $ 30 | $ 80 |
| 2 | 50 | 80 |
| 3 | 80 | 80 |
| 4 | 120 | 80 |
| 5 | 170 | 80 |

| Output | MC | MR |
|---|---|---|
| **Table 3** | | |
| **Marginal Revenue and Marginal Cost** | | |
| 0 | | |
| 1 | $ 30 | $100 |
| 2 | 50 | 90 |
| 3 | 80 | 80 |
| 4 | 120 | 70 |
| 5 | 170 | 60 |

The first unit of output costs $30 and, when sold, brings in $100, so the firm earns a profit of $70 on the first unit. The second unit costs $50 and brings in $90 when sold, so the second unit increases profit by $40. The third unit costs $80 and brings in $80 when sold. The third unit neither increases nor decreases profit. The fourth unit costs $120 but brings in only $70 when sold, and the fifth unit would cost $110 more than the revenue the firm would obtain by selling it. The firm makes additional profit by producing and selling units 1 and 2 and makes no additional profit but loses nothing producing and selling the third unit. The fourth and fifth units take profit away. The firm clearly will produce and sell either 2 or 3 units. If the firm produced 2 units and saw the additional profit of that second unit, it would produce the second unit. When the firm saw that the additional profit of the third unit was zero, it would know that to produce the fourth unit would reduce profit. Thus, the firm produces 3 units—the quantity at which $MR = MC$.

The point of Tables 2 and 3 is to demonstrate that profit is maximized when $MR = MC$ for all firms. Only when marginal revenue and marginal costs are the same is profit at a maximum. This is the case for perfectly competitive firms just as it is for firms in the other market structures.

In the previous chapter we illustrated the non-perfectly competitive firm maximizing profit in Figure 2. The comparable illustration for the perfectly competitive firm is shown in Figure 2 in this chapter. With a price of $1 per unit, the individual firm producing wheat maximizes profit by producing 9 units. We can illustrate how much profit or loss the individual firm in perfect competition makes by calculating total costs at the quantity at which $MR = MC$ and comparing that with total revenue. The price per unit of $1 exceeds the cost per unit (average total costs, $.8733) by the distance $BC$ ($.1267) when 9 units are produced. This amount ($.1267) is the profit per unit. The total profit is the rectangle $ABCD$ (highlighted in the table of Figure 2).

Compare Figure 2 with Figure 2 in the previous chapter. You can see that the only difference is the demand curve. In perfect competition, the firm's demand is a horizontal line at the market price. In the other market structures, the individual firm's demand curve is downward sloping.

## Figure 2

### Profit Maximization

The profit-maximization point for a single firm is shown for a price of $1 per bushel. Marginal revenue and marginal cost are equal at the profit-maximization point, 9 bushels. At quantities of fewer than 9 bushels, marginal revenue exceeds marginal cost, so increased production would raise profits. At quantities greater than 9, marginal revenue is less than marginal cost, so reduced production would increase profits. The point at which profit is maximized is shown by the highlighted row in the table. The profit per unit is the difference between the price line and the average-total-cost curve at the profit-maximizing quantity. Total profit ($1.14) is the rectangle *ABCD*, an area that is equal to the profit per unit times the number of units.

| Total Output (Q) | Price (P) | Total Revenue (TR) | Total Cost (TC) | Total Profit (TR − TC) | Marginal Revenue (MR) | Marginal Cost (MC) | Average Total Cost (ATC) |
|---|---|---|---|---|---|---|---|
| 0 | $1 | $ 0 | $ 1.00 | −$1.00 | | | |
| 1 | $1 | $ 1 | $ 2.00 | −$1.00 | $1 | $1.00 | $2.00 |
| 2 | $1 | $ 2 | $ 2.80 | −$ .80 | $1 | $ .80 | $1.40 |
| 3 | $1 | $ 3 | $ 3.50 | −$ .50 | $1 | $ .70 | $1.1667 |
| 4 | $1 | $ 4 | $ 4.00 | $ .00 | $1 | $ .50 | $1.00 |
| 5 | $1 | $ 5 | $ 4.50 | $ .50 | $1 | $ .50 | $ .90 |
| 6 | $1 | $ 6 | $ 5.20 | $ .80 | $1 | $ .70 | $ .8667 |
| 7 | $1 | $ 7 | $ 6.00 | $1.00 | $1 | $ .80 | $ .8571 |
| 8 | $1 | $ 8 | $ 6.86 | $1.14 | $1 | $ .86 | $ .8575 |
| 9 | $1 | $ 9 | $ 7.86 | $1.14 | $1 | $1.00 | $ .8733 |
| 10 | $1 | $10 | $ 9.36 | $ .64 | $1 | $1.50 | $ .936 |
| 11 | $1 | $11 | $12.00 | −$1.00 | $1 | $2.64 | $1.09 |

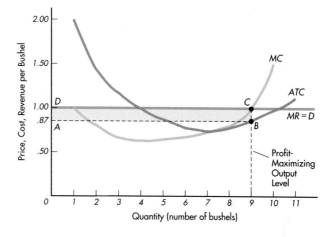

RECAP

1. Economists classify selling environments into four market structures: perfect competition, monopoly, monopolistic competition, and oligopoly.

2. Perfect competition is a market structure in which many firms are producing a nondifferentiated product, and entry is easy.

3. Monopoly is a market structure in which only one firm supplies the product, and entry cannot occur.

4. Monopolistic competition is a market structure in which many firms are producing differentiated products, and entry is easy.

5. Oligopoly is a market structure in which a few firms are producing either standardized or differentiated products, and entry is possible but not easy. The distinguishing characteristic of oligopoly is that the firms are interdependent.

6. No matter the market structure, when *MR* is less than *MC*, the firm is not maximizing profit; when *MR* is greater than *MC*, the firm is not maximizing profit; only when *MR* = *MC* is the firm maximizing profit.

## 2. FIRM BEHAVIOR IN THE LONG RUN

In the short run, at least one of the resources cannot be altered. This means that new firms cannot be organized and begin producing. Thus, the supply of firms in an industry is fixed in the short run. In the long run, of course, all quantities of resources can be changed. Buildings can be built or purchased and machinery accumulated and placed into production. New firms may arise as entrepreneurs not currently in the industry see that they could earn more than they are currently earning and decide to expand into new businesses.

Entry and exit can both occur in the long run. How does exit occur? Entrepreneurs may sell their businesses and move to another industry, or they may use the bankruptcy laws to exit the industry. A sole proprietor or partnership may file what is called a Chapter 13 personal bankruptcy; a corporation may file Chapter 7 bankruptcy or a Chapter 11 reorganization; a farmer may file Chapter 12. From the mid-1970s to the present, the average birthrate for all industries (the percentage of total businesses that begin during a year) has been just over 11.2 percent, and the average death rate (the percentage of total businesses that disappear during a year) has been 9.6 percent.

3. Is it possible to earn positive economic profit in the long run?

### 2.a. Normal Profit in the Long Run: Perfect Competition

One of the principal characteristics of the perfectly competitive market structure is that entry and exit can occur easily. Thus, entry and exit occur whenever firms are earning more or less than a *normal profit* (zero economic profit). When a normal profit is being earned, there is no entry or exit. This condition is the long-run equilibrium.

The process of establishing the long-run position is shown in Figure 3. The market demand and supply curves for corn are shown in Figure 3(a), and the cost and revenue curves for a representative firm in the industry are shown in Figure 3(b). Let's assume that the market price is $1. Let's also assume that at $1 per bushel, the demand curve facing the individual farm (the price line) is equal to the minimum point of the *ATC* curve. The quantity produced is 9 bushels. The individual farm and the industry are in equilibrium. There is no reason for entry or exit to occur, and no reason for individual farms to change their scale of operation.

To illustrate how the process of reaching the long-run equilibrium occurs in the perfectly competitive market structure, let's begin with the market in equilibrium at $S_1 = D_1$. Then let's suppose a major agricultural disaster strikes Russia, and Russia turns to the United States to buy agricultural products. As a result of the increased Russian demand, the total demand for U.S. corn increases, as shown by the rightward shift of the demand curve to $D_2$ in Figure 3(a). In the short run, the market price rises to $1.50 per bushel, the point at which the new market demand curve intersects the initial market supply curve $S_1$. This raises the demand curve for the individual farm to the horizontal line at $1.50 per bushel. In the short run, the individual farms in the industry increase production (by adding variable inputs) from 9 bushels to 10 bushels, the point in Figure 3(b) at which $MC = MR_2 = \$1.50$, and earn economic profit of the amount shown by the orange rectangle.

The above-normal profit attracts others to the farming business. The result of the new entry and expansion is a rightward shift of the market supply curve. How far does the market supply curve shift? It shifts until the market price is low enough that firms in the industry earn normal profit. Let us suppose that the costs of doing business do not rise as the market expands. Then, if the market supply curve shifts to $S_2$, the new market price, $1.25, is less than the former price of $1.50 but still high enough for firms to earn above-normal profits. These profits are sufficient inducement for more firms to enter, causing the supply curve to shift farther right. The supply curve continues to shift until there is no incentive for additional firms to enter, that is, until firms are earning the normal profit, when price is equal to the

Figure 3

## Economic Profit in the Long Run

Market demand and supply determine the price and the demand curve faced by the single perfectly competitive firm. At a price of $1 per bushel, the individual firm is earning normal profit. After an agricultural disaster in Russia increases the demand for U.S. corn, the price rises to $1.50. At $1.50 per bushel, the single firm makes a profit equal to the yellow rectangle. Above-normal profits induce new firms to begin raising corn and existing firms to increase their production.

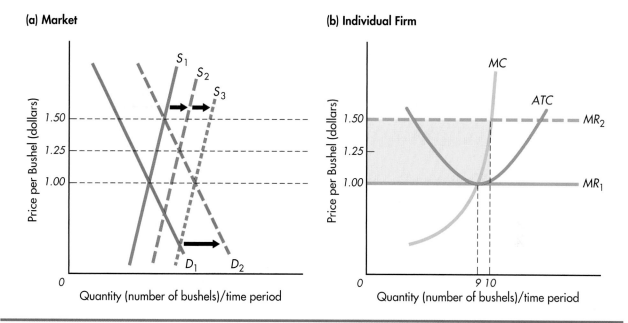

**(a) Market**

**(b) Individual Firm**

minimum *ATC*, shown as $S_3$ in Figure 3(a). When the adjustment stops, firms are just earning the normal profit.

According to the model of perfect competition, whenever above-normal profits are earned by existing firms, entry occurs until a normal profit is earned by all firms. Conversely, whenever economic losses occur, exit takes place until a normal profit is made by all remaining firms.

It is so important to keep in mind the distinctions between economic and accounting terms that we repeatedly remind you of them. A *zero economic profit* is a *normal accounting profit,* or just *normal profit.* It is the profit just sufficient to keep a business owner or investors in a particular line of business, the point at which revenue exactly equals total opportunity costs. Business owners and investors earning a normal profit are earning enough to cover their opportunity costs—they could not do better by changing—but are not earning more than their opportunity costs. A *loss* refers to a situation in which revenue is not sufficient to pay all of the opportunity costs. A firm can earn a positive accounting profit and yet be experiencing a loss, not earning a normal profit.

The long-run equilibrium position of the perfectly competitive market structure shows firms producing at the minimum point of their long-run average-total-cost curves. If the price is above the minimum point of the *ATC* curve, then firms are earning above-normal profit and entry will occur. If the price is less than the minimum of the *ATC* curve, exit will occur. Only when price equals the minimum point of the *ATC* curve will neither entry nor exit take place.

Producing at the minimum of the *ATC* curve means that firms are producing with the lowest possible costs. They could not alter the way they produce and

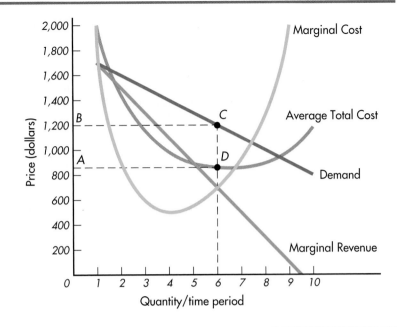

**Figure 4**

**Revenue, Costs, and Profit**

This figure is the same as Figure 2 in the previous chapter. Profit is maximized at the point at which the marginal revenue and marginal cost are equal. If there were less output, marginal revenue would exceed marginal cost, and some profit that could be earned would not be earned. If there were greater output, marginal cost would exceed marginal revenue, and profit would be reduced.

produce less expensively. They could not alter the resources they use and produce less expensively.

Firms produce at a level at which marginal cost and marginal revenue are the same. Since marginal revenue and price are the same in a perfectly competitive market, firms produce when marginal cost equals price. This means that firms are employing resources until the marginal cost to them of producing the last unit of a good just equals the price of the last unit. Moreover, since price is equal to marginal cost, consumers are paying a price that is as low as it can get; the price just covers the marginal cost of producing that good or service. There is no waste; no one could be made better off without making someone else worse off.

## 2.b. Normal Profit in the Long Run: Monopolistic Competition

Figure 4 illustrates a monopolistically competitive firm. Profit is the rectangle *ADCB*, and it is a positive economic profit. If a firm is making a positive economic profit, the owners of the firm are doing better than they could expect to do by putting their money into any other activity. In fact, other investors want to get in on the good thing. In the long run, new firms enter the market to compete for profits with the original firm.

When a new firm begins competing with the original firm, the new firm takes some business away from that firm. This causes the demand curve for the original firm to shift down. New firms continue to enter the market as long as economic profits are positive. Each entry causes the original firm's demand curve to shift down farther. Eventually, profits are driven down to the point at which only a normal accounting profit (zero economic profit) is earned. This is shown in Figure 5, where, at $900 for 3 units, the average revenue (demand) equals average total cost, and total revenue is equal to total cost, rectangle *OGEF*. At this point there is no reason that additional firms would wish to enter.

It is clear from this illustration that a firm cannot earn positive economic profit very long when there is free entry. Free entry drives the economic profit to zero. If new firms cannot enter very easily or at all, then the story is different. The demand curve is not forced down, and economic profit does not decline. The incumbent firm can earn positive economic profit as long as entry is restricted.

2. Producer surplus is a bonus of the market system that goes to firms. It is the difference between the price at which the producers are willing and able to supply a good or service and the price that the producers actually receive.

3. Economic profit induces entry and new competition, which drives economic profit to zero unless there are barriers.

4. Barriers to entry include brand name and reputation, and unique resources and size can serve as a barrier to entry in certain circumstances.

5. The long run is a period just long enough so that all resources are variable; there are no fixed resources.

6. Economies of scale occur when the per-unit costs decline as all resources (the size of the firm) increase in the long run.

7. If an industry is characterized by economies of scale, then the large firm can produce at lower per-unit costs than the small firm can. To enter this industry, a firm must be large.

8. Whether economies of scale give a cost advantage to a large firm depends on the extent of the market. If demand is sufficiently large so that a large firm can realize economies of scale, then firm size is a distinct advantage.

9. Diseconomies of scale occur when as the size of the firm increases, the per-unit costs rise.

## SUMMARY

### ❓ What is a market structure, and what can it tell us about how a firm will behave?

1. A market structure is a model of the producing and selling environments in which firms operate. The three characteristics that define market structure are the number of firms, the ease of entry, and whether the products are differentiated.

2. A perfectly competitive market is one in which a very large number of firms are producing an identical product, and entry is easy.

3. A monopoly is a market in which there is only one firm, and entry cannot occur.

4. A monopolistically competitive market is a market in which a large number of firms are producing differentiated products, and entry is easy.

5. An oligopoly is a market in which there are only a few firms, and entry is difficult.

6. The demand curve of an individual firm, except for a perfectly competitive firm, is downward sloping, indicating that the firm can sell more only by lowering its price. The demand curve for a perfectly competitive firm is a horizontal line at the market price.

### ❓ Do all firms maximize profit when $MR = MC$?

7. All firms, no matter the market structure, maximize profit by producing the quantity at which $MR = MC$

and charging a price at that quantity given by the demand.

### ❓ Is it possible to earn positive economic profit in the long run?

8. If entry is easy, it is not possible for a firm to earn positive economic profit in the long run. If a firm earns positive economic profit, others see that the firm is earning more than its opportunity costs and want to get in on the good thing as well. More firms enter, thereby driving profit to zero.

9. If entry is difficult or not possible, a firm can earn positive economic profit for as long as entry does not occur.

### ❓ What are the benefits of competition?

10. Size can serve as a barrier to entry in certain circumstances.

11. The long run is a period just long enough so that all resources are variable; there are no fixed resources.

12. Economies of scale occur when the per-unit costs decline as all resources (the size of the firm) increase in the long run.

13. If an industry is characterized by economies of scale, then the large firm can produce at lower per-unit costs than the small firm can. To enter this industry requires that a firm be large.

14. Entry defines whether a firm can keep or sustain the positive economic profit it earns. If entry occurs, competition will drive profit down to a normal accounting profit, or zero economic profit.

15. Consumer surplus is the bonus the market provides to consumers. It is the difference between the price the consumer would be willing and able to pay for a product and the price the consumer actually has to pay.

16. Producer surplus is the bonus market exchange provides to firms. It is the difference between the price at which the firm would be willing and able to supply a good or service and the price the firm actually receives for selling the good or service.

17. Deadweight loss is the benefits of market exchange that are lost when entry is restricted.

18. Activities such as advertising, brand name creation, and sunk cost expenditures may be effective barriers to the entry of other firms.

19. Size can serve as a barrier to entry in certain circumstances. Those circumstances depend on whether there are economies or diseconomies of scale.

20. Whether economies of scale give a cost advantage to a large firm depends on the extent or size of the market and whether the industry also experiences diseconomies of scale. If demand is sufficiently large so that a large firm can realize economies of scale, then firm size is a distinct advantage.

## KEY TERMS

perfect competition

monopoly

monopolistic competition

oligopoly

consumer surplus

producer surplus

deadweight loss

sunk cost

economies of scale

diseconomies of scale

## EXERCISES

1. Which type of market structure would characterize most businesses operating in the United States today? Explain.

2. What market structure would you classify each of the following as?
   a. airlines
   b. fast food
   c. computer chips
   d. Internet service providers
   e agricultural products
   f. diamonds

3. Since a monopoly has no competitors, does the monopolist set exorbitantly high prices?

4. Advertising to create brand preferences would be most common in which market structure?

5. Give ten examples of differentiated products. Then list as many nondifferentiated products as you can.

6. Why will a firm not produce quantities for which $MR$ is greater than $MC$?

7. Use the information in the table to calculate total revenue, marginal revenue, and marginal costs. Indicate the profit-maximizing level of output. What

market structure is this firm operating in? What would change if the structure were monopolistic competition?

| Output | Price | Total Costs | Total Revenue $(P \times Q)$ |
|--------|-------|-------------|------------------------------|
| 1 | $5 | $10 | |
| 2 | 5 | 12 | |
| 3 | 5 | 15 | |
| 4 | 5 | 19 | |
| 5 | 5 | 24 | |
| 6 | 5 | 30 | |
| 7 | 5 | 45 | |

8. Draw a perfectly elastic demand curve on top of a standard U-shaped, average-total-cost curve. Now add in the marginal-cost and marginal-revenue curves. Find the profit-maximizing point, $MR = MC$. Indicate the firm's total revenue and total costs.

9. Describe profit maximization in terms of marginal revenue and marginal costs.

10. Using demand curves, illustrate the effect of product differentiation on haircutters.

11. Why might society prefer a situation in which entry can occur to a situation in which entry is restricted?

12. Under what circumstances would a large size provide an advantage to a firm? How could it serve as a barrier to entry?

---

## Internet Exercise

**Use the Internet to examine why Americans are paying more for health care but not living longer.**

Go to the Boyes/Melvin, *Fundamentals of Economics* website accessible through **http://college.hmco.com** and click on the Internet Exercise link for Chapter 6. Now answer the questions that appear on the Boyes/Melvin website.

## Key Term Match

**Match each term with its correct definition by placing the appropriate letter next to the corresponding number.**

A. perfect competition
B. monopoly
C. monopolistic competition
D. oligopoly
E. consumer surplus
F. producer surplus
G. deadweight loss
H. sunk cost
I. economies of scale
J. diseconomies of scale

_____ 1. a market structure characterized by a large number of firms, easy entry, and differentiated products

_____ 2. a market structure in which there is more than one firm, but few enough so that each firm can affect the market

_____ 3. a market structure characterized by such a large number of firms that no one firm has an effect on the market

_____ 4. the loss of consumer and producer surplus when entry is restricted

_____ 5. the difference between what suppliers are willing to supply some item for and the price they actually receive

_____ 6. cost that cannot be recouped

_____ 7. a market structure in which there is just one firm, and entry by other firms is not possible

_____ 8. the decreases in per-unit costs when all resources are increased

_____ 9. the difference between what consumers are willing to pay and what they have to pay to purchase some item

_____ 10. the increases in per-unit costs when all resources are increased

## Quick-Check Quiz

**1** Which of the following market characteristics are *not* used to define market structures?

  a. the number of firms in the market
  b. the ease of entry into the market by new competitors
  c. the percentage of the firm's income that is paid in taxes
  d. the type of product produced (identical or differentiated)
  e. All of the above characteristics are used to define market structures.

**2** Regardless of market structure, a firm maximizes its profits by producing the quantity of output at which

  a. $P = MR$.
  b. $P = MC$.
  c. $MR = MC$.
  d. $MC = D$.
  e. $D = MR$.

**3** When the owner of a firm is getting zero economic profit,

  a. the owner should exit that market in the short run.
  b. the owner should exit that market in the long run.
  c. the owner cannot make any more money by exiting the market and doing something else with her resources.
  d. the owner is not receiving any income from owning the firm.
  e. the owner is getting rich.

**4** In which market structures do firms receive just a normal profit in the long run?

  a. monopoly and perfect competition
  b. monopolistic competition and perfect competition
  c. monopoly and monopolistic competition
  d. monopoly and oligopoly
  e. monopolistic competition and oligopoly

**5** What is the most important determinant of whether or not firms receive economic profits in the long run?

  a. how easy it is for new firms to enter the market
  b. the size of the firms in a market
  c. the size of the market overall
  d. the amount of taxes firm owners pay
  e. the amount of taxes the firms' customers pay

**6** The total benefits that come from an exchange in a market are

  a. producer surplus minus consumer surplus.
  b. producer surplus plus consumer surplus.
  c. consumer surplus minus producer surplus.
  d. only producer surplus.
  e. only consumer surplus.

**7** Consumer surplus will be higher when

  a. consumers dislike a product.
  b. consumers like a product.
  c. entry is free than when entry is restricted.

# 1. PRICE STRATEGIES FOR INDEPENDENT FIRMS

Firms maximize profit by selling the quantity of their goods and services at the price customers are willing and able to pay for that quantity of goods and services as determined by $MR = MC$. However, if you ask sole proprietors or managers in large corporations if they determine how much to sell and at what price on the basis of setting $MR$ equal to $MC$, their response will be no. They may say they add a markup to their costs or simply match what their competitors are charging to set prices. However, although they may say this and believe it, the end result of their actions is for the price and quantity to be determined as if marginal revenue were being set equal to marginal cost. Think about it—what would happen if a firm set a price based on its costs and thought that it might be leaving some money on the table? The firm would change the price to capture more of that profit. As a firm makes those adjustments, it moves closer and closer to the point at which $MR = MC$. Therefore, it is not a stretch to assume that the adjustment process has taken place and that the firm operates at the point where $MR = MC$. This simple rule holds for every firm in every circumstance: Profit is maximized when $MR = MC$.

It can get complicated trying to determine $MR$ or $MC$ as firms sell more than one product, operate in more than one market, deal with varied consumers, and interact with rivals. Nevertheless, as was stated above, it is not unreasonable to assume that firms are pricing and operating at the point at which $MR = MC$. In the previous chapter we noted that firms that are able to create barriers to entry or to differentiate products are able to take some of the consumer surplus for themselves, that is, to increase their profit over what they would get if there were free entry or no differentiation. One way in which firms attempt to collect that extra profit is to define customers according to their price elasticities of demand and to set $MR = MC$ for each different demand. Some of the more common applications of this are price discrimination, peak load pricing, the use of coupons, bundling, and rebates. Let's begin with the situation in which a firm has many rivals or substitutes, but each firm is able to differentiate itself or its products. In this situation the firm can pretty much ignore its rivals; it can set a price without regard to what its rivals do.

## 1.a. Price Discrimination

Price discrimination is the practice of charging different buyers different prices for the same good or service when the different prices are not associated with differences in costs. The seller must be able to separate buyers into distinct groups, each having different price elasticities of demand. It is relatively easy for a movie theater to separate customers by age. Similarly, it is easy for airlines to separate buyers into business travelers and tourists. The seller must also be able to keep those buyers who get the lower prices from selling their good or service to those buyers who pay the higher prices. A senior citizen could not sell his or her ticket to a middle-aged adult; the tickets are different colors. Travelers cannot change names on airline tickets; IDs are required.

When the price elasticity of demand differs from buyer to buyer, then the firm will maximize profit by charging each customer a different price. Profit maximization occurs when $MR = MC$, but in this case, there is a different $MR$ for each buyer. The firm thus equates $MC$ with each $MR$; $MC = MR_1, MR_2$, and so on, depending on how many buyers there are. The buyers with higher price elasticities get lower prices.

Price discrimination can be effective only if different sets of customers have different price elasticities of demand, and the various sets of customers can be separated and easily distinguished. Suppose a movie theater decided to give a discount to people with Irish ancestry but not to people with eastern European ancestry. This would be an impossible task. It would cost the movie theater too much to force the customers to prove their ancestry.

*Now You Try It*

**What do California pistachio producers mean when they say the Iranian producers are dumping pistachios in the U.S. market?**

## Dumping

**D**umping means that a firm sells its products for less than its cost of production or, in other words, sells at a loss. Why would a firm sell at a loss? One reason could be that a firm would sell in one market at a loss so that it could run other firms out of that market and then control the market. Of course, this strategy would be a success only if once the firm had control of the market, it could keep others from entering that market. Thus, dumping is a difficult thing to carry out. What appears to be dumping can often merely be price discrimination. A firm charges a lower price in another country than it does for the same product in its home country. This would be a perfectly logical strategy if the consumers in the home country have a lower price elasticity of demand than consumers in the foreign country. In this case,

the firm would increase revenue by setting a higher price in the home country and a lower one in the foreign country. This pricing strategy would be no different than charging senior citizens lower prices for movie tickets than the general population is charged.

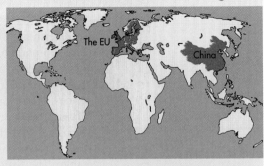

This is not to say that there are no legitimate cases of dumping, but many cases involve government subsidies and taxes rather than competition among firms. One case of dumping occurred with sugar produced in the European Union (EU) and sold in China. The EU provides subsidies and protection to sugar producers, who then can sell their sugar at prices that are below production costs. China pointed out that the average produc-

tion cost of sugar in Guangxi is 2,230 yuan per ton compared with 5,623 yuan per ton in the EU. But when the EU provides a subsidy of 4,127 per ton, the EU sugar exporters can sell for as low as 1,429 yuan and as high as 2,230 yuan and drive Chinese sugar producers out of the market. The result of the dumping is that sugar prices in China have dropped by 35 percent, and the amount of sugar produced in China has declined significantly.

---

What is the purpose of price discrimination? It is to enable a firm to collect as much of the consumer surplus as possible. If a firm could sell each customer a product at the highest price the customer was willing and able to pay, the firm would collect the entire consumer surplus. This would be perfect price discrimination—each customer would pay a different price. This is what some selling tactics are designed to do. Many purchases of automobiles involve hours of negotiation between dealer and customer. The dealer is trying to find the very highest price the customer is willing and able to pay. That price will differ from customer to customer, so the dealer is price discriminating.

### 1.b. Peak Load Pricing

Price discrimination requires that the firm determine the different price elasticities of demand of the different customers or sets of customers. Sometimes the firm is unable to determine the different price elasticities of demand. So the firm creates a situation in which the customer essentially self-selects according to her or his price elasticity of demand. In the case of peak load pricing, the customer chooses at what time to consume the product. Peak load pricing involves charging a higher price to customers who purchase the product during periods of *peak* demand and a lower price for those who purchase during periods of *off-peak* demand.

The pricing of long-distance telephone calls is a good example of peak load pricing. Most long-distance calls are placed on weekday afternoons while fewer calls are placed late at night and on weekends. In addition, just as the demand for telephone calls differs by the time of day, so does the cost of producing them. The switching facilities and lines provided by the telephone companies are designed to meet demand during peak times. As a result, marginal cost is low during off-peak times when much of the firm's capacity sits idle and high during peak times when capacity is strained. The firm equates *MR* and *MC* for the two time periods, generating higher prices during peak times and lower prices during off-peak times. Electric utilities use peak load pricing. They charge a higher rate for electric use during seasons and times of the day when the usage is greatest. Peak load pricing is a commonly used pricing strategy in tourism businesses as well. Resort hotels charge more during busy times than during the off-season. Renegade Golf Course in Phoenix, Arizona, has green fees of $250 in February and $80 in July.

### 1.c. Discount Coupons

Businesses in the United States have distributed more than 300 billion coupons with a face value of $200 billion a year, either as hard copy or via the Internet. Of these, consumers have redeemed only 6 billion coupons worth about $4 billion a year. If only a small percentage of the coupons are redeemed, why do firms offer coupons? Why don't sellers simply cut the price? One reason is that the coupon is a way to discriminate among buyers. The more valuable a consumer's time, the higher the cost of redeeming a coupon will be. By issuing coupons, a seller can provide a lower price to those with higher price elasticities of demand—people willing to spend the time collecting coupons.

### 1.d. Bundling

Bundling is combining two or more products and selling the bundle for a single price. Cable television providers make extensive use of bundling in their pricing. The cable television providers offer a set of channels for a single price. The channels are bundled; a consumer cannot simply buy one of the channels. Why does the cable provider bundle the channels together rather than offer each one at a distinct price? The reason is primarily cost. The marginal cost of providing separate channels or separate packages of channels to each and every customer would be high since different customers prefer different channels. The cable company determines which set of channels satisfies most of the customers. It then determines the marginal revenue on the bundle and sets price where $MR = MC$.

### 1.e. Rebates and Other Price Strategies

Let's begin this section with a quiz.

1. Who is happier: person A, who wins the office football pool for $100 on the same day she ruins the carpet in her apartment and must pay the landlord $75, or person B, who wins the office football pool for $25?

2. Who is happier: person A, who ruins the carpet in her apartment and must pay the landlord $100, or person B, who ruins the carpet in his apartment and must pay the landlord $75 and also scratches the front door and must pay the landlord $25?

In both cases, most people believe person A is happier even though A and B end up with the same gain or loss. The difference in the two cases is the way the gains and losses are presented. In the first case, A has a gain ($100) and a loss ($75) together while B has just a gain ($25). In the second case, A has a loss ($100) while B has two losses ($25 + $75). If a comparison of alternatives involves a gain, people prefer to have the results of the actions presented separately—a $100 gain and a $25 loss rather than a $75 gain. This result is characterized by the lesson: "Don't wrap all the Christmas presents in one box." But if the comparison involves losses, people prefer to have the losses combined or shown just once—a $100 loss rather than separate losses of $25 and $75.

Our analysis of the quiz states that prospective buyers are happier if multiple gains are offered separately and if multiple losses are combined. Instead of offering an additional discount for new subscribers, a sports magazine will add a video of sports highlights. The television shopping networks encourage you to buy now, and if you do, you get several other attachments and related products. The separate gain means more to prospective buyers than a larger price discount on the subscription would or a reduction of the price of the item being sold on television.

Automobile manufacturers use price rebates to stimulate sales. Why don't the manufacturers simply discount the price instead? Because buyers seem to prefer a separate rebate payment—separating gains from losses.

Whereas consumers like their gains to be separated, they do not like to have losses offered separately. The price elasticity of demand is higher for separate purchases than if the same purchases are bundled together. For instance, it is easier to induce someone to buy a car stereo or other options at the time of a car purchase than to make the same sale separately. Most computer and appliance stores and most automobile dealerships offer extended warranty plans at the time the product is purchased. People are more likely to purchase savings bonds and insurance through payroll deductions. Paying for these by slightly reducing a large gain is much more palatable than incurring the cost outright.

**2. What is the difference in rivalry between those firms that are interdependent and those that are not?**

interdependence: a situation in which the best strategy for one firm depends on what another firm does

## 2. FIRM BEHAVIOR WHEN THERE ARE FEW RIVALS

The pricing strategies we have discussed so far focus on a firm in isolation not really considering how other firms behave. Most firms have to consider the behavior of other firms when choosing their own strategies; most firms are interdependent. **Interdependence** between firms occurs when what is best for A depends on what B does, and what is best for B depends on what A does. The setting is much like a card game—bridge, say—in which strategies are designed depending on the cards the players are dealt. Underbidding, overbidding, bluffing, deceit, and other strategies are carried out. This is what much of business is about. In this section, we discuss some of the ways that firms interact.

### 2.a. The Kinked Demand Curve

Firms often have to predict how their competitors will respond to a price change in order to know what their demand curve looks like. Let's consider the auto industry. Suppose General Motors's costs have fallen (its marginal-cost curve has shifted down), and the company is deciding whether to lower the prices on its cars. If GM

Figure 1

**The Kinked Demand Curve**

In Figure 1(a), a firm ignores other firms. In Figure 1(b), rivals follow price declines but not price increases. Since rivals follow price decreases, the firm does not gain as much when it lowers its price as it would if the rivals did

not match the price decrease. Thus, the actual demand curve is $D_2$, not $D_1$, below the price $P_1$. This puts a kink in the demand curve.

**(a) Competitors Follow Price Changes**

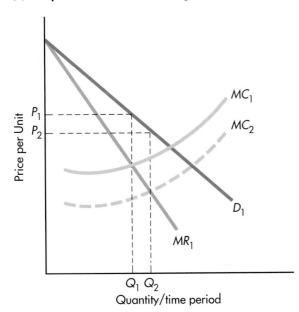

**(b) Competitors Do Not Follow Price Changes**

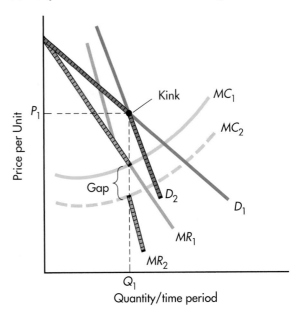

did not have to consider how the other car companies would respond, it would simply lower the price from $P_1$ to $P_2$, as illustrated in Figure 1(a). But GM suspects that the demand and marginal-revenue curves in Figure 1(a) do not represent its true market situation. It believes that if it lowers the prices on its cars from their current level of $P_1$, the other auto companies will follow suit. In other words, GM does not capture more of the market, as indicated in Figure 1(b) by $D_1$, but instead finds the quantity demanded increasing along $D_2$ (below price $P_1$). Also, GM suspects that should it increase the price of its cars, none of the other auto companies would raise theirs. In this case, the price increase would mean substantially reduced sales for GM. The quantity demanded decreases, as indicated along $D_1$. Consequently, the demand curve for GM is a combination of $D_1$ and $D_2$. It is $D_1$ above $P_1$ and $D_2$ below $P_1$—a demand curve with a kink.

What should GM do? It should price where $MR = MC$. But the resulting marginal-revenue curve is given by a combination of $MR_1$ and $MR_2$. The $MR_1$ curve slopes down gently until reaching the quantity associated with the kink. Below the kink, $MR_2$ becomes the appropriate marginal-revenue curve. Thus, the striped portions of the two marginal-revenue curves combine to give the firm's marginal-revenue curve. Notice how GM's marginal-cost curves $MC_1$ and $MC_2$ intersect the combined $MR$ curves at the same price $P_1$ and quantity $Q_1$. Thus, GM's strategy is to do nothing, to not change price even though costs have changed.

## 2.b. Price Wars

Firms often find themselves in a price war (constantly lowering prices) even though the war hurts all the competitors who are involved in it. Why engage in a price war when it is harmful? Consider the situation in which firms must decide whether to

Figure 2

**Price Wars**

The best strategy for firm A is to lower price, no matter what firm B does. The best strategy for firm B is to lower price, no matter what firm A does. The result is that both lower price.

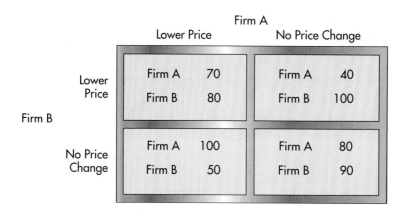

lower the price or to keep it the same. The situation facing two firms is illustrated in Figure 2. This is referred to as a payoff matrix; it shows what each firm can expect in profit under its own actions and those of its rival. Each firm looks over this payoff matrix and decides which action to take. Consider firm A first. If firm B lowers price, then firm A can earn 70 by also lowering price, or it can earn 40 by not lowering price. If firm B does not lower price, firm A earns 100 by lowering price but only 80 by not lowering price. No matter what firm B does, firm A is better off lowering price. Turning the situation around and looking at firm B's decision, we see it is the same as firm A's in that firm B is better off lowering price no matter what firm A does. The result is that both firms lower price—a price war.

Although both firms acted in what each perceived to be its best interest, both ended up in worse shape than if they had not changed price. This type of situation, referred to as a **prisoner's dilemma,** occurs quite often in business. Firms taking what they think is their best action relative to the actions of their rivals end up in a poorer situation than if they had acted differently. Consider another such case, that of advertising.

**2.b.1. Advertising Wars** The prisoner's dilemma occurs in more than pricing issues. Consider the situation in which firms must decide whether to devote more resources to advertising. When a firm in any given industry advertises its product, its demand increases for two reasons. First, people who had not used that type of product before learn about it, and some will buy it. Second, other people who already consume a different brand of the same product may switch brands. The first effect boosts sales for the industry as a whole whereas the second redistributes existing sales within the industry.

Consider the cigarette industry as an example and assume that the matrix in Figure 3 illustrates the possible actions that two firms might undertake and the results of those actions. The top left rectangle represents the payoffs, or results, if both A and B advertise; the bottom left is when A advertises but B does not; the top right represents when B advertises but A does not; and the bottom right shows the payoffs if neither advertises. If firm A can earn higher profits by advertising than by not advertising, whether or not firm B advertises, then firm A will surely advertise. This is referred to as a **dominant strategy**—a strategy that produces the best results, no matter what strategy the opposing player follows. Firm A compares the

**prisoner's dilemma:** a situation in which the best outcome is not selected because actions depend on other firms

*Now You Try It*

Two firms must decide what price to advertise for their products in the weekly newspaper. If each charges a low price, each earns zero profit. If each charges a high price, each earns a profit of $3. If they each advertise different prices, the one advertising the lower price has a $5 profit, and the other has a $5 loss. What is the outcome?

**dominant strategy:** an alternative that is better than other alternatives, no matter what rivals do

Figure 3

**Dominant Strategy Game**

The dominant strategy for firm A is to advertise. No matter what firm B does, firm A is better off advertising. Similarly, firm B is better off advertising, no matter what firm A does. Both A and B have dominant strategies—to advertise.

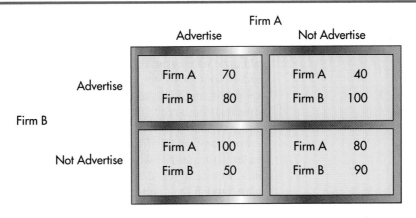

*Now You Try It*

Fox and NBC are determining the upcoming season of shows. If they use more reruns and fewer new shows, they make more money. Set up their choices in a payoff matrix; can you create a prisoner's dilemma?

**3. Why and under what conditions do firms cooperate rather than compete?**

left side of the matrix to the right side and sees that it earns more by advertising, no matter what firm B does. If B advertises and A advertises, then A earns 70; but if A does not advertise, it earns 40. If B does not advertise, then A earns 100 by advertising and only 80 by not advertising. The dominant strategy for firm A is to advertise.

The dominant strategy for firm B also is to advertise, according to Figure 3. Firm B will earn 80 by advertising and 50 by not advertising if A advertises. Firm B will earn 100 by advertising but only 90 by not advertising if A does not advertise. But notice that both firms would be better off if neither advertised; firm A would earn 80 instead of 70, and firm B would earn 90 instead of 80. Yet the firms cannot afford not to advertise because each would lose more if the other firm advertised and it did not.

None of the cigarette manufacturers wants to do much advertising, yet they must. Firm A advertises, so firm B does also. Each ups the advertising ante.

## 2.c. Cooperation

If the firms could come to some cooperative agreement, they would all be better off. For instance, the airlines might agree not to lower fares. Or cigarette companies might agree not to advertise. Cooperation is an integral part of business when a few firms dominate the market. In the case of the advertising wars just described, the cigarette companies were able to enlist the help of government to eliminate the prisoner's dilemma. The government passed a law banning cigarette advertising on television, something that saved each of the companies a great deal of money and eliminated the possibility that they would enter an advertising war. Why go through the roundabout way of eliminating the advertising war by getting a law passed? Why don't the executives of the firms simply call each other up and say, "Let's agree not to advertise" or "Let's agree not to lower price"? The reason is that it is illegal to do this; the government does not allow firms to cooperate in this manner, reasoning that it would harm the consumer by reducing competition. Firms, therefore, have to find other ways to generate the cooperation.

### 2.c.1. Price Leadership

One way for firms to cooperate is to allow one firm to be the leader in changes in price or advertising activities. Once the leader makes a change, the others duplicate what the leader does. This action enables all firms to know exactly what the rivals will do. It eliminates a kink in the demand curve because both price increases and price decreases will be followed, and it avoids the situation in which excessive expenses are made on advertising or other activities. This type of behavior is called *price leadership*.

The steel industry in the 1960s is an example of a dominant-firm price leadership. For many years, steel producers allowed United States Steel to set prices for the entire industry. The cooperation of the steel companies probably led to higher profits than would have occurred with rivalry. However, the absence of rivalry is said to be one reason for the decline of the steel industry in the United States. Price leadership removed the need for the firms to compete by maintaining and upgrading equipment and materials and by developing new technologies. As a result, foreign firms that chose not to behave as price followers emerged as more-sophisticated producers of steel than U.S. firms.

For many years, airlines also relied on a price leader. In many cases, the price leader in the airlines was not the dominant airline but one of the weaker or new airlines. In recent years, airlines have communicated less through a price leader and more through their computerized reservation system.

### 2.c.2. Collusion, Cartels, and Other Cooperative Mechanisms

Acting jointly allows firms to earn more profits than if they act independently or against each other. Firms may collude or come to some agreement about price and output levels. Typically these agreements provide the dominant firms in the market with higher profits and thus raise prices to consumers. Collusion, which leads to secret cooperative agreements, is illegal in the United States, although it is acceptable in many other nations.

**cartel:** An organization of independent producers that dictates the quantities produced by each member of the organization

A **cartel** is an organization of independent firms whose purpose is to control and limit production and maintain or increase prices and profits. A cartel can result from either formal or informal agreement among members. Like collusion, cartels are illegal in the United States but occur in other countries. The cartel most people are familiar with is the Organization of Petroleum Exporting Countries (OPEC), a group of nations rather than a group of independent firms. During the 1970s, OPEC was able to coordinate oil production in such a way that it drove the market price of crude oil from $1.10 to $32 a barrel. For nearly eight years, each member of OPEC agreed to produce a certain limited amount of crude oil as designated by the OPEC production committee. Then in the early 1980s, the cartel began to fall apart as individual members began to cheat on the agreement. Members began to produce more than their allocation in an attempt to increase profit. As each member of the cartel did this, the price of oil fell, reaching $12 per barrel in 1988. Oil prices rose again in 1990 when Iraq invaded Kuwait, causing widespread damage to Kuwait's oil fields. But as repairs were made to Kuwait's oil wells, Kuwait was able to increase production, and oil prices dropped.

Production quotas are not easy to maintain among different firms or different nations. Most cartels do not last very long because the members cheat on the agreements. If each producer thinks that it can increase its own production, and thus its profits, without affecting what the other producers do, all producers end up producing more than their assigned amounts; the price of the product declines, and the cartel falls apart.

Even though cartels are illegal in the United States, a few have been sanctioned by the government. The National Collegiate Athletic Association (NCAA) is a cartel of colleges and universities. It sets rules of behavior and enforces those rules through a governing board. Member schools are placed on probation or their programs are dismantled when they violate the agreement. The citrus cartel, composed of citrus growers in California and Arizona, enforces its actions through its governing board. Sunkist Growers, a cooperative of many growers, represents more than half of the California and Arizona production and also plays an important role in enforcing the rules of the cartel.

### 2.c.3. Facilitating Practices

Actions by firms can contribute to cooperation and collusion even though the firms do not formally agree to cooperate. Such

## eBay and Online Markets

Internet auctions are attracting increasing numbers of buyers and sellers. The most well-known company in this online market arena is eBay, founded in 1995. On any given day, there are millions of items listed across thousands of categories. Sellers list an item for a small fee, and buyers bid for that item. The auctions typically last three or four days, and at the end of the auction time, the high bidder receives the item. eBay is far from the only company offering online auctions. The biggest growth area for the online auctions is that between

businesses. The auto companies purchase supplies through an online auction; John Deere and other manufacturers purchase supplies through online auctions. New business-to-business auctions are being created every day. The online auctions focus most attention on price; customers view or read about the product and the product's features and then offer a price. The result is that prices are driven to their lowest possible level—much like the model of perfect competition.

What does the online auction mean for businesses wedded to

buildings and face-to-face contact with customers? When Wal-Mart located in a small town, the local businesses were hard-pressed to compete with it. They could not offer the variety or the low prices that Wal-Mart offered. In town after town, local businesses attempted to keep Wal-Mart from entering. Think about what an online auction could do. eBay is a rival to virtually every store in your city or neighborhood, and there is no way to keep eBay from entering.

---

**facilitating practices:** actions that lead to cooperation among rivals

**cost-plus markup pricing:** a price set by adding an amount to the per unit cost of producing and supplying a good or service

---

### Now You Try It

A firm has a 30 percent markup on average costs of $300 as its price. What is the price? Is this profit maximizing?

---

**most-favored customer:** a commitment that the customer will receive a lower price if anyone else receives a lower price

---

actions are called **facilitating practices.** Pricing policies can leave the impression that firms are explicitly fixing prices, or cooperating, when in fact they are merely following the same strategies. For instance, the use of **cost-plus markup pricing** tends to bring about similar if not identical pricing behavior among rival firms. If firms set prices by determining the average cost of an item and adding a 50 percent markup to the cost, they would be cost-plus pricing. If all firms face the same cost curves, then all firms will set the same prices. If costs decrease, then all firms will lower prices the same amount and at virtually the same time. Such pricing behavior is common in the grocery business.

Another practice that leads to implicit cooperation is the most-favored-customer policy. Often the time between purchase and delivery of a product is quite long. To avoid the possibility that customer A purchases a product at one price and then learns that customer B purchased the product at a lower price or benefited from product features unavailable to customer A, a producer will guarantee that customer A will receive the lowest price and all features for a certain period of time. Customer A is thus a **most-favored customer (MFC).**

The most-favored-customer policy actually gives firms an incentive not to lower prices even in the face of reduced demand. A firm that lowers the price of its product must then give rebates to all most-favored customers; this forces all other firms with most-favored-customer policies to do the same. In addition, the MFC policy allows a firm to collect information on what its rivals are doing. Customers will return products for a rebate when another firm offers the same product for a lower price.

Consider the behavior of firms that produced antiknock additives for gasoline from 1974 to 1979. Lead-based antiknock compounds had been used in the refining of gasoline since the 1920s. From the 1920s until 1948, the Ethyl Corporation was the sole domestic producer of the compounds. In 1948, Du Pont entered the industry; PPG Industries followed in 1961, and Nalco in 1964. Beginning in 1973, the demand for lead-based antiknock compounds decreased dramatically. However, because each company had most-favored-customer clauses, high prices were maintained even as demand for the product declined.

A most-favored-customer policy discourages price decreases because it requires producers to lower prices retroactively with rebates. If all rivals provide all buyers with most-favored-customer clauses, a high price is likely to be stabilized in the industry.

We've seen that firm behavior can be understood as an attempt to maximize profit. But firms are not always free to do what they believe will maximize profit. The government defines rules of behavior and limits many actions that firms would otherwise undertake. In the next section we discuss the involvement of government in the affairs of business.

**RECAP**

1. Most business is carried out by large firms.

2. The shape of the demand curve and the marginal-revenue curve may depend on how rival firms react to changes in price and product.

3. The kinked demand curve is one example of how firms may react to price changes. The kink occurs because rivals follow price cuts but not price increases.

4. A prisoner's dilemma occurs when the actions of rivals lead them to a result that is worse for all of them than would be the case if they did not undertake these actions.

5. Price leadership occurs when one firm determines the price and quantity of the good or service, knowing that all other firms will follow suit. The price leader is usually the dominant firm in the industry.

6. Firms often have incentives to cooperate. Collusion, making a secret cooperative agreement, is illegal in the United States. Cartels, also illegal in the United States, rest on explicit cooperation achieved through formal agreement.

7. Facilitating practices implicitly encourage cooperation in an industry.

## 3. GOVERNMENT AND FIRMS

**4. Why does government intervene in the affairs of business?**

In the previous chapter, we saw that the large firm could have a cost advantage over smaller firms. When a firm dominates a market and does not fear entry, it can charge higher prices and earn higher profits. In the previous sections, we discussed several business strategies. The objective of the strategies is to take the consumer surplus and collect it as producer surplus—to earn positive economic profit. Are these behaviors fair? Are they legal?

**antitrust laws:** laws enacted to maintain competition by limiting the behavior of large firms

The government makes the rules that define business behavior. **Antitrust laws,** enforced by the Justice Department and the Federal Trade Commission (FTC), determine which types of contracts are legal, who can participate in certain markets, when firms can merge, and in general how firms *should* behave. These rules focus primarily on the large firm because of the potential of the large firm to charge excessive prices and earn excessive profits.

### 3.a. Antitrust Laws

**monopolization of a market:** market dominance by one firm gained unfairly

The government—specifically the Justice Department and the Federal Trade Commission—attempts to maintain competition in markets by monitoring and controlling the activities of large firms and by setting the rules of behavior for large businesses. The government may not allow large firms to merge or to carry out certain activities. The government may take large firms to court and attempt to penalize them for what is called **monopolization of a market**—the attempt to unfairly

the chip directly to manufacturers like IBM and Macintosh under your own firm's label?

2. Explain when it might make sense to bundle two products together and charge a single price for the two. Would you charge more or less than the total of each one separately?

3. Explain how negotiating over the price of an automobile is an attempt by the auto dealer to extract your consumer surplus.

4. Time-of-day pricing is a strategy of charging a different price for a good or service depending on the time of day. Explain what this and peak-load pricing have in common.

5. In a situation that occurs only once, if you advertise and your rival advertises, you will each earn $5 million in profits. If neither of you advertises, your rival will make $4 million, and you will make $2 million. If you advertise and your rival does not, you will make $10 million, and your rival will make $3 million. If your rival advertises and you do not, you will make $1 million, and your rival will make $3 million.
   a. Set up the situation in a matrix form.
   b. Do you have a strategy that you will choose, no matter what your rival does?
   c. Does your rival have a strategy that he will choose, no matter what you do?
   d. What is the solution or equilibrium?
   e. How much would you be willing to pay your rival not to advertise?
   f. Find the equilibrium when there are no repeated transactions.
   g. Now, suppose there are repeated transactions. If the interest rate is 10 percent, what will be the outcome?

6. You and your rival must simultaneously decide what price to advertise in the weekly newspaper. If you each charge a low price, you each earn zero profits. If you each charge a high price, you each earn profits of $3. If you charge different prices, the one charging the higher price loses $5, and the one charging the lower price makes $5. Explain what you would do in this case.

7. You are the owner-operator of a gas station in a small town. Over the past twenty years, you and your rival have successfully kept prices at a very high level. You recently learned that your rival is retiring and closing her station in two weeks. What should you do today?

8. What is meant by interdependence? How does the kinked demand curve describe interdependence?

9. What are the costs to a firm that fails to take rivals' actions into account? Suppose the firm operates along demand curve $D_1$, shown below, as if no firms will follow its lead in price cuts or price increases. In fact, however, other firms do follow the price cuts, and the true demand curve below price $P_1$ lies below $D_1$. If the firm sets a price lower than $P_1$, what happens?

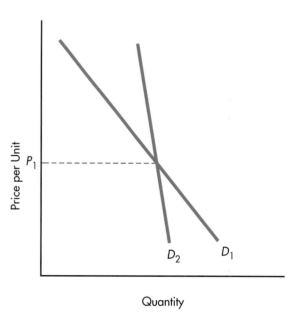

10. The payoff matrix below shows the profit two firms earn if both advertise, neither advertises, or one advertises while the other does not. Profits are reported in millions of dollars. Does either firm have a dominant strategy?

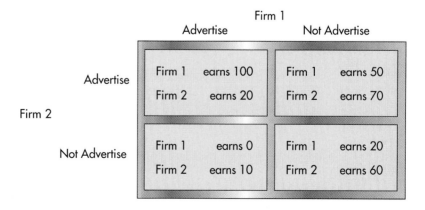

## Internet Exercise

**Use the Internet to familiarize yourself with the FTC and its role in regulating the behavior of large firms.**

Go to the Boyes/Melvin, *Fundamentals of Economics* website accessible through **http://college.hmco.com** and click on the Internet Exercise link for Chapter 7. Now answer the questions that appear on the Boyes/Melvin website.

# Study Guide for Chapter 7

## Key Term Match

**Match each term with its correct definition by placing the appropriate letter next to the corresponding number.**

A. business firm
B. sole proprietorship
C. partnership
D. corporation
E. interdependence
F. prisoner's dilemma
G. dominant strategy
H. cartel
I. facilitating practices
J. cost-plus markup pricing

K. most-favored customer
L. antitrust laws
M. monopolization of a market
N. regulation
O. natural monopolies
P. social regulation
Q. rent

_____ 1. actions that lead to cooperation among rivals
_____ 2. an entity in which resources are combined to produce and sell output
_____ 3. the control of some aspect of business by the government
_____ 4. a business firm owned by two or more persons
_____ 5. market dominance by one firm that is gained unfairly
_____ 6. an alternative that is better than other alternatives, no matter what rivals do
_____ 7. a business firm owned by one person
_____ 8. rules of behavior prescribed by the government
_____ 9. an organization of independent producers that dictates the quantities produced by each member of the organization
_____10. a price set by adding an amount to the per-unit cost of producing and supplying a good or service
_____11. a commitment that the customer will receive a lower price if anyone else receives a lower price
_____12. a business firm owned by many shareholders, who are not liable for the debts of the firm
_____13. a situation in which the best strategy for one firm depends on what another firm does
_____14. a situation in which the best outcome is not selected because actions depend on other firms
_____15. when economies of scale lead to just one firm
_____16. resources used to gain benefits from the government
_____17. government regulation of health, safety, the environment, and employment policies

## Quick-Check Quiz

1  The general term economists use for an organization in which resources are combined to produce an output is a
   a. seller.
   b. business firm.
   c. revenue generator.
   d. sole partnership.
   e. corporate entity.

2  Price discrimination means
   a. making careful decisions about price.
   b. selling different products to people with different skin colors.
   c. charging different customers different prices for the same product.
   d. refusing to serve certain groups of people.
   e. providing different customers with the same product.

3  Price discrimination is worthwhile only when
   a. different people have different price elasticities of demand.
   b. different people live in different places.
   c. business firms don't maximize profits.
   d. business firms have the same costs.
   e. different people like different colors of the product.

4  In markets with interdependent firms, one firm's actions will affect
   a. other firms' demand curves.
   b. other firms' marginal revenue curves.
   c. other firms' profits.
   d. all of the above.
   e. none of the above.

5  Monopolization of a market can be illegal when
   a. the monopoly is gained unfairly.
   b. consumers receive benefits from the monopoly.
   c. the monopolist benefits from economies of scale.
   d. the monopolist makes political contributions.
   e. the government grants the monopoly.

## Practice Questions and Problems

1  In the United States, the most common form of business organization is the _____.

**2** In the United States, the form of business organization that generates the most revenues and profits is the _____.

**3** All pricing strategies are based on the profit-maximization equation _____.

**4** The purpose of price discrimination is to allow a firm to get part of buyers' _____.

**5** Cartels are generally _____ (legal, illegal) in the United States.

**6** Briefly describe how a price-leadership arrangement works.

_____

_____

_____

**7** Briefly explain how cost-plus markup pricing and most-favored-customer agreements facilitate cooperation among rival firms.

_____

_____

_____

**8** Joe's and Moe's are two competing gas stations in town. Both are considering adding a video game parlor to their stations. The following payoff matrix shows the expected daily profits for each gas station:

|  | Joe's Station | |
|---|---|---|
| | **Adds Video Games** | **Doesn't Add Video Games** |
| **Moe's Station** — **Adds Video Games** | Joe's $200 Moe's $500 | Joe's $100 Moe's $300 |
| **Moe's Station** — **Doesn't Add Video Games** | Joe's $250 Moe's $350 | Joe's $180 Moe's $400 |

a. Does Joe have a dominant strategy? If yes, what is it?

_____

b. Does Moe have a dominant strategy? If yes, what is it?

_____

c. If you were Joe, would you add video games, not add video games, or wait to see what Moe does? Explain your answer.

_____

_____

_____

d. If you were Moe, would you add video games, not add video games, or wait to see what Joe does? Explain your answer.

_____

_____

_____

**9** Antitrust laws are enforced by two government agencies: _____ and _____.

**10** Antitrust laws focus primarily on _____ (large, small) businesses.

**11** During the last few decades, _____ (regulation, social regulation) has been out of favor, but _____ (regulation, social regulation) has grown recently.

## Exercises and Applications

**Cartel Behavior**  The key difference between oligopoly and other market structures is that oligopolists are interdependent: the decisions of one affect the others. In many situations, interdependence creates conflicting incentives both to cooperate with others and to "cheat" on one's cooperation.

You can see how this happens in oligopolies by looking at the choices faced by a member of a cartel such as OPEC. Let's make you the oil minister of Scheherazade, a hypothetical small member of OPEC. You are responsible for managing your country's oil output and price, and your objective is to maximize your country's total revenues from oil. (Your marginal cost of producing more oil is so low that you don't have to pay any attention to costs.)

Last week, the OPEC countries met and agreed to charge $25 per barrel for oil. Scheherazade was given an output quota of 300,000 barrels per day. The following graph shows your current position and possible options. $D_1$ is the demand curve for your oil if the rest of OPEC ignores any price changes you make, and $D_2$ is your demand

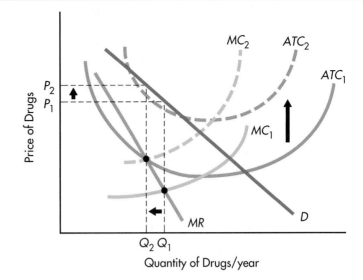

## Figure 5

### The War on Drugs

One demand curve is used along with two sets of cost curves to illustrate the effect of the government's War on Drugs. The result of increased enforcement is increased costs to the cartels, illustrated as an upward shift of the average- and marginal-cost curves. In this case, the increased costs force the supplier to raise its price and sell a lower quantity. In addition, the supplier's profits decline.

The rising costs mean that the suppliers' profits decline, but this is most likely only a temporary setback. Aggressive marketing by the cartels has attracted more young people and created more hard-core users. Drug use among junior high and high school students has increased dramatically since the 1980s. Illicit drug use rose to 40 from 29 percent among high school students. The percentage of the population addicted to illicit drugs today is three times greater than before drug prohibition was implemented in 1920. Thus, although enforcement increased suppliers' costs, the demand for the drugs rose, leading to even higher profits.

The result of the War on Drugs has been to reduce the number of suppliers and to increase the barriers to entry, thereby ensuring that the remaining cartels control the market and earn positive economic profit.

## 2.c. Free Drugs?

Is there an alternative to illicit drug control other than the War on Drugs? The Swiss government provides heroin to hard-core users free and has a very liberal policy regarding drug use by others. In Vancouver, British Columbia, Canada, the government provides drugs, needles, and a safe house in which to administer the heroin. Is this the appropriate policy? The user need not commit crimes to obtain the funds with which to purchase the heroin. The Swiss have found that drug-related crime has declined since they initiated their policy of providing free heroin to hard-core users. The Vancouver experiment is too new for us to know the effects. On the other hand, reducing the price increases the quantity demanded.

## 2.d. Designer Drugs

What about policy regarding the so-called designer drugs, the easily manufactured drugs? Entry into the market for designer drugs is easy. This means that economic profit is driven to zero, and there is no incentive for new suppliers to enter. Suppliers might try to differentiate their product in an attempt to reduce the price elasticity of demand, but the cost of differentiating typically exceeds the possible benefits.

The government's policy of eliminating the drug "factories" and confiscating supplies increases the costs of entry during the increased enforcement or interdiction period. As a result, the supply curve shifts up, the price rises, and the quantity sold declines.

*Now You Try It*

**Rather than focusing on supply, would it be more productive to focus on demand? What policy change might result from focusing on demand?**

Isn't this the desired result—fewer drugs sold? Yes, but it is only a very temporary result. The more difficult entry means that remaining suppliers earn positive economic profit. Potential suppliers line up to enter the market once the enforcement activity is lessened. And enforcement has to be reduced eventually. Otherwise, the costs to the government would rise unabated. No society can afford a continual increase in drug enforcement and interdiction activities.

**RECAP**

1. The market for cocaine and heroin is difficult to enter.
2. The market for designer drugs is easy to enter, and the products are identical.
3. The cocaine and heroin market has few suppliers, who usually cooperate. Cartels dominate the market, dictating prices, quantities, and location.

# 3. DISCRIMINATION

**discrimination:** the practice of treating people differently in a market, based on a characteristic having nothing to do with that market

We've talked about price discrimination many times in this book. Price discrimination is the practice of charging different customers different prices for an identical item. Price discrimination occurs because the different customers have different price elasticities of demand. **Discrimination,** in general, is somewhat different from price discrimination. Discrimination is the practice of treating different people differently in a market, based on some characteristic that has nothing to do with the market. In the labor market, discrimination occurs when someone or some group is receiving favorable treatment for a reason having nothing to do with that person's or group's job performance.

**?**

**3. Does discrimination make economic sense?**

## 3.a. The Market

Discrimination on the basis of characteristics that have nothing to do with one's job performance is costly in a market in which entry is easy. Suppose, for instance, that customers preferred to be served by only a certain kind of individual. Customers would then have to be willing to pay higher prices to be served by the preferred group. This is illustrated in Figure 6.

The firm can supply the good using the services of any employee, along cost curve $MC_A$. The firm can also use the preferred employees, but then the cost of supplying the good is higher, $MC_P$. Those customers who want the product but only if served by the preferred group have to pay $P_P$, whereas those customers choosing to be served by anyone have to pay only $P_A$.

Discrimination requires paying a premium to associate or not to associate with certain groups. As we know from prior chapters, any firm not using resources efficiently will be driven out of the market if entry is easy. When entry is easy, having higher costs due to discrimination could drive the discriminating firm out of the market. If customers are not willing to pay the premium (the difference between $P_P$ and $P_A$), then the firm cannot discriminate.

If a firm has erected strict barriers to entry, then the discrimination may not be costly. A monopoly or even a government agency that does not have to compete with another firm could get away with using resources less efficiently. Managers, employees, and even customers of monopolies or government agencies may be able to discriminate without having more efficient firms drive them out of the market. Indeed, studies have shown that most discrimination takes place in government agencies, firms that do business with the government, and regulated monopolies.

Figure 6

**Discrimination**

The demand by customers for the product is *D*. The supplier has a marginal cost of $MC_P$ to supply the good if the employee is a member of the preferred group and $MC_A$ if the employee is not a member of the preferred group.

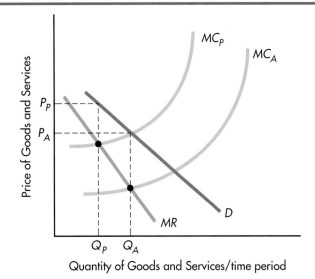

### 3.b. Statistical Discrimination

Discrimination may occur because of a lack of information rather than a taste for or against certain groups. For instance, employers must try to predict the potential value of job applicants to the firm, but rarely do they know what a worker's actual value will be. Often, the only information available when they hire someone is information that may be imperfectly related to value in general and may not apply to a particular person at all. Using characteristics like education, experience, age, and test scores as the basis for selecting among job applicants may keep some very good people from getting a job and may result in hiring some unproductive people.

Suppose two types of workers apply for a word-processing job: those who can process 80 words per minute and those who can process only 40 words per minute. The problem is that these actual productivities are unknown to the employer. The employer can observe only the results of a five-minute word-processing test given to all applicants. How can the employer decide who is lucky or unlucky on the test and who can actually process 80 words per minute? Suppose the employer discovers that applicants from a particular vocational college, the AAA School, are taught to perform well on preemployment tests, but their average overall performance as employees is less than that of the rest of the applicants—some do well and some do not. The employer might decide to reject all applicants from AAA because the good and bad ones can't be differentiated. Is the employer discriminating against AAA? The answer is yes. The employer is **statistically discriminating.** Statistical discrimination can cause a systematic preference for one group over another at the expense of some individuals in the group.

**statistically discriminating:** using characteristics that apply to a group, although not to all individual members of that group, as an allocation device

What is the effect of a ban on statistical discrimination? It would raise the firm's costs. The firm would have to either collect information about each applicant or risk hiring some of the lower-quality word processors. Since costs rise, profits fall. This would induce the firm to reduce its output and to reduce the number of resources used, including labor.

So would a ban on statistical discrimination be a good law even if it raises costs and creates job losses? The answer is determined by comparing the costs and benefits to society of allowing statistical discrimination versus the costs and benefits to society of outlawing statistical discrimination.

1. Discrimination is costly in a market economy when entry into markets is easy.

2. Statistical discrimination occurs due to a lack of information. When the characteristics of a group are imposed on each member of that group whether they apply or not, statistical discrimination occurs.

## 4. MINIMUM WAGES

**minimum wage:** the least amount an employee can be paid according to government mandate

A **minimum wage** is a government policy that requires firms to pay at least a certain wage—the minimum wage. The federal minimum wage in the United States is $5.15 per hour. States may have their own minimum wage if their wages exceed the federal level. In 2004, Washington state's minimum wage was the highest, at $7.16, exceeding Alaska's by one penny. If cities are not happy with the level of either the federal or state minimum wage, they may set their own. More than 100 cities have their own minimum wage ordinances. The highest effective rate in 2004 was $8.50 in Santa Fe, New Mexico, but other cities have proposed equal or higher wage levels. The minimum wage is not just a U.S. phenomenon. Every industrialized country and many developing countries also have a minimum wage.

The arguments in favor of the minimum wage are that a worker must earn at least the minimum wage in order to have a decent standard of living. At $5.15 per hour, 40 hours per week, 50 weeks per year, you would earn $10,300 per year. Currently, the government defines the poverty level of income for a family of four to be $18,811. Thus, at the U.S. federal minimum wage, a family of four with a single wage earner would be below the poverty level of $18,811. The arguments opposed to minimum wages claim that implementation of such minimums will increase unemployment, particularly among the unskilled—teenagers, minorities, and women—and lead to worse cases of poverty.

In a competitive labor market, a worker's wage is equal to the value he or she contributes to the firm. A minimum wage set above the equilibrium wage creates a labor surplus (unemployment). In Figure 7, setting the minimum wage ($W_M$) at $5.15, above the equilibrium wage ($W$) of $4, creates a labor surplus of $Q_S - Q_D$.

**4. Does a minimum wage make economic sense?**

Figure 7

**Minimum Wage**

The imposition of a minimum wage reduces the number of jobs offered to workers and reduces the employment of workers.

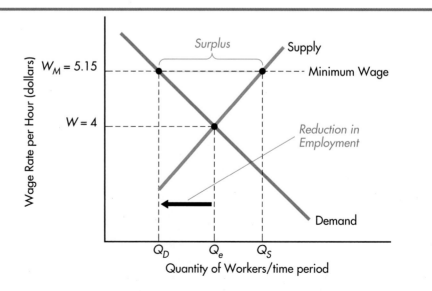

In other words, all the people willing and able to work at $5.15 are unable to get jobs. At the $5.15 per hour wage, $Q_S$ are willing and able to work, but only $Q_D$ are able to find jobs. A surplus of $Q_S - Q_D$ workers is created. Notice also that employment falls from the equilibrium level of $Q_e$ to $Q_D$.

Who is most affected by the surplus? It is those who have the least value to the firm. Studies show that the minimum wage adversely affects teenagers and other low-skilled workers, causing increased unemployment in these groups. A 10 percent increase in the minimum wage is estimated to result in a 1 to 3 percent decrease in teenage employment. The last increase in the minimum wage from $4.35 to $5.15 per hour was an 18 percent increase. This caused somewhere between a 1.8 to 5.4 percent reduction in teenage employment. To reduce the adverse effects on teens, the government has allowed firms to pay a wage to teens that is lower than the minimum wage. The lower wage reduces the negative effects on teenagers. Still, any time an above-equilibrium or minimum wage is imposed, some job loss occurs.

*Now You Try It*

Using Figure 7, indicate what would happen if the minimum wage was increased to $8 per hour. Then indicate what would happen if the minimum wage was lowered to $3 per hour.

RECAP

1. A minimum wage is a government policy requiring firms to pay at least that wage—a wage that is above the equilibrium wage.
2. The effect of a minimum wage is to reduce employment.
3. A minimum wage has the greatest negative effects on the unskilled—usually teenagers, minorities, and women.

**5. Why are incomes not equally distributed?**

## 5. INCOME INEQUALITY AND POVERTY

In a market system, incomes are distributed according to the ownership of resources. Those who own the most highly valued resources have the highest incomes. One consequence of a market system, therefore, is that incomes are distributed unequally. In the United States, as in every country, there are rich and there are poor.

The inequality of income distribution among members of a population can be illustrated as a graph, as shown in Figure 8. The horizontal axis measures the total population in cumulative percentages; as we move along the horizontal axis, we are counting a larger and larger percentage of the population. The numbers end at 100, which designates 100 percent of the population. The vertical axis measures total income in cumulative percentages. As we move up the vertical axis, the percentage of total income being counted rises to 100 percent. The 45-degree line splitting the distance between the axes is called the line of income equality. At each point on the line, the percentage of total population and the percentage of total income are equal. The line of income equality indicates that 10 percent of the population earns 10 percent of the income, 20 percent of the population earns 20 percent of the income, and so on, until we see that 90 percent of the population earns 90 percent of the income, and 100 percent of the population earns 100 percent of the income.

**income distribution:** the ways in which a society's income is divided

**Lorenz curve:** a diagram illustrating the degree of income inequality

Points off the line of income equality indicate an **income distribution** that is unequal. Figure 8 shows the line of income equality and a curve that bows down below the income-equality line. The bowed curve is called a **Lorenz curve.** The Lorenz curve in Figure 8 is for the United States. In the United States, 20 percent of the population receives only 3.6 percent of total income, seen at point *A*. The second 20 percent accounts for another 9.6 percent of income, shown as point *B*, so the bottom 40 percent of the population has 13.2 percent of the income (3.6 percent owned by the first 20 percent of the population plus the additional 9.6 percent owned by the second 20 percent). The third 20 percent accounts for another 15.7 percent of income,

## Figure 8

### The Lorenz Curve

The Lorenz curve illustrates the degree of income inequality. The further the curve bows down, away from the line of equality, the greater the amount of inequality.

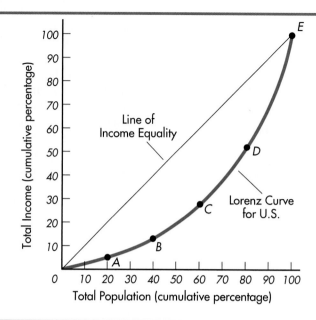

Now You Try It

**With the following data, construct a Lorenz curve.**

| | |
|---|---|
| **Top 20%** | 30 |
| **Next 20%** | 40 |
| **Next 20%** | 20 |
| **Next 20%** | 8 |
| **Lowest 20%** | 2 |

**poverty:** an arbitrary level of income chosen to provide a measure of how well basic human needs are being met

so point *C* is plotted at a population of 60 percent and an income of 28.9 percent. The fourth 20 percent accounts for another 23.4 percent of income, shown as point *D*, where 80 percent of the population receives 52.3 percent of the income. The richest 20 percent accounts for the remaining 47.7 percent of income, shown as point *E*. With the last 20 percent of the population and the last 47.7 percent of income, 100 percent of population and 100 percent of income are accounted for. Point *E*, therefore, is plotted where both income and population are 100 percent.

The farther the Lorenz curve bows down, away from the line of income equality, the greater the inequality of the distribution of income. From 1929 to 1995, the Lorenz curve for the United States moved closer to the line of income equality as incomes became more equally distributed. But from 1995 to 2003, the curve moved farther away from the line of income equality, and the distribution of income became less equal.

Many people argue that the increasing inequality of income in recent years is the result of the increased demand for skilled labor. With skills, people are earning relatively more; without skills, they are earning relatively less. Professional, technical, and managerial jobs accounted for just one-sixth of the work force in 1950. By 2003, that number had risen to more than one-third. This increased demand for skilled labor has placed a much higher premium on educational attainment; generally speaking, workers who have spent more time in training and education earn significantly higher wages. Between 1984 and 2003, employees with post–high school education and training gained more than 11 percent in income while high school dropouts' earnings fell more than 1.5 percent.

The most unequal distributions of income are found in developing countries. On average, the richest 20 percent of the population receives more than 50 percent of income, and the poorest 20 percent receives less than 4 percent. Figure 9 shows two Lorenz curves: one for the United States and one for Mexico. The curve for Mexico bows down far below the curve for the United States, indicating the greater inequality in Mexico.

### 5.a. Poverty

Unequal income means some people are relatively well-off and some are relatively poor. The poorest in the United States are those in **poverty.** Poverty is an arbitrary

Figure 9

**The Lorenz Curves for the United States and for Mexico**

Income is more unequally distributed in Mexico than in the United States. This can be seen as the Lorenz curve for Mexico bows farther away from the line of income equality than the Lorenz curve for the United States.

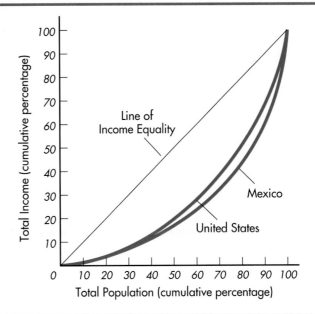

**6. What does it mean to be living in poverty?**

level of income that is supposed to provide a measure of how well basic human needs are being met. The poverty level in the United States, as specified by the federal government, is listed in Table 1. Currently, a family of four with an income less than $18,811 in the United States is considered to be living in poverty. Yet an income of $18,811 per year would be a very high level of income in some countries. Ethiopia, for instance, has a per capita income of only $150 per year.

How many Americans fall below the poverty line? In 2003, more than 34 million U.S. residents received incomes that were lower than the cutoff. Figure 10 compares the *number* of people living in poverty and the *percentage* of the total population living in poverty (the incidence of poverty) for each year from 1960 to 2003. From 1960 to the late 1970s, the incidence of poverty declined rapidly. From the late 1970s until the early 1980s, the incidence of poverty rose; it then began to decline again after 1982. Small upswings in the incidence of poverty occurred in 1968 and 1974, and a large rise occurred between 1978 and 1982. It then fell until 1990, when the United States once again dipped into recession. It continued to rise even as the economy grew in 1993 and 1994 and then fell slightly until 2000, when the economy dipped into recession. The greatest impact on poverty is the health of the economy.

Studies indicate that approximately 25 percent of all Americans fall below the poverty line at some time in their lives. Many of these spells of poverty are relatively short; nearly 45 percent last less than a year. However, more than 50 percent of those in poverty at a particular time remain in poverty for at least 10 years.

Since the young have more trouble finding jobs than the middle-aged, a young person has a much greater chance of falling into poverty. The highest incidence of poverty occurs among those under 18 years old. The second highest occurs among those between 18 and 24.

## 5.b. Income Distribution Over Time

We often hear that the rich get richer and the poor get poorer. Is this statement true? If we look at the income level of the bottom 20 percent of income earners and compare that with the income level of, say, the top 5 percent of income earners, we find that between 1980 and 2002, the income level of the bottom 20 percent rose

**Table 1**

**Average Income Poverty Cutoffs for a Nonfarm Family of Four in the United States, 1959–2003**

| Year | Poverty Level | Year | Poverty Level |
|------|---------------|------|---------------|
| 1959 | $ 2,973 | 1987 | $11,611 |
| 1960 | $ 3,022 | 1988 | $12,090 |
| 1966 | $ 3,317 | 1989 | $12,675 |
| 1969 | $ 3,743 | 1990 | $13,359 |
| 1970 | $ 3,968 | 1991 | $13,924 |
| 1975 | $ 5,500 | 1992 | $13,950 |
| 1976 | $ 5,815 | 1993 | $14,764 |
| 1977 | $ 6,191 | 1994 | $15,200 |
| 1978 | $ 6,662 | 1995 | $15,600 |
| 1979 | $ 7,412 | 1996 | $16,036 |
| 1980 | $ 8,414 | 1997 | $16,276 |
| 1981 | $ 9,287 | 1998 | $16,530 |
| 1982 | $ 9,862 | 1999 | $16,895 |
| 1983 | $10,178 | 2000 | $17,463 |
| 1984 | $10,609 | 2001 | $17,960 |
| 1985 | $10,989 | 2002 | $18,244 |
| 1986 | $11,203 | 2003 | $18,811 |

*Source:* U.S. Bureau of the Census, *Poverty Thresholds,* http://www.census.gov/hhes/poverty/threshold.html.

**Figure 10**

**The Trends of Poverty Incidence**

The number of people classified as living in poverty is measured on the left vertical axis. The percentage of the population classified as living in poverty is measured on the right vertical axis. The number and the percentage declined steadily throughout the 1960s, rose during the recessions of 1969, 1974, 1981, 1990, and 2001, and fell between 1982 and 1990, and again from 1992 to 2000. They continued to rise during 2002 and 2003.
*Source:* www.census.gov/hhes/www/poverty.html.

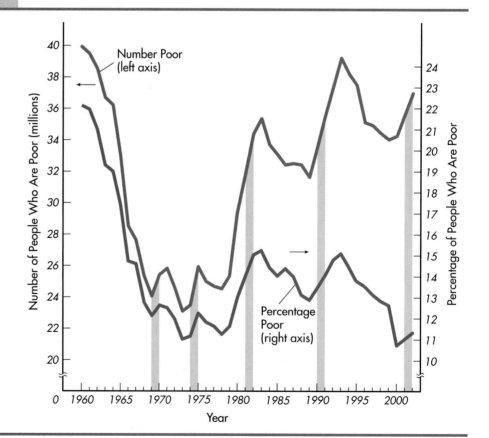

## The Official Poverty Rate

A government employee named Molly Orshansky first figured out the calculation for the U.S. poverty rate. She was a lifetime civil servant who had initially worked for the Department of Agriculture, but in 1963, when she came up with the poverty measure, she was working for the Social Security Administration. She was working on a larger project at the Social Security Administration to try to understand what was happening to children in families without fathers. The result she arrived at became the official poverty standard

because as she was working on this project, the President's Council of Economic Advisers was under a mandate to come up with a plan for fighting what became known as the War on Poverty. At that time, there was no official poverty standard, so how could a war be waged on something that was not being measured? The Office of Economic Opportunity, which was under tremendous political pressure, announced that from that point on it was going to use the poverty measure as the official figure. However, despite its use,

there is widespread agreement among the people who do research on poverty that this is a deeply flawed measure. Some of the common criticisms are that it does not take account of the growth of noncash benefits such as food stamps, does not take account of taxes, and does not take account of differences across geographical areas in the cost of living. Taking these factors into account can have a significant effect on the poverty rate.

13.4 percent while the income of the top 5 percent of income earners rose 46 percent. Clearly, the rich got richer, but the poor also got richer. The difference is in the relative increases—the rich had a greater percentage increase in income than the poor did. In other words, the distribution of income in 2002 was more unequal than it was in 1980.

Is it income inequality, the number of people living in poverty, or something else that is troubling to people? The government has attempted to reduce the number of people living in poverty and the inequality of income for the past 50 years through its transfer programs such as social security, welfare, and unemployment compensation. Yet, as we have just seen, income is more unequal now than it was in 1980.

Figure 11 places the expenditures devoted to reducing poverty alongside the percentages of the U.S. population that are in poverty. It shows that the expenditures seem to have had very little effect on the poverty rate. Could it be that the measures of poverty are misleading? Perhaps one should look at how those defined as poor actually live rather than attempting to measure income levels. In one study, it was found that those officially defined as "poor" were actually doing much better in 1994 than they had in 1984. In this study, the authors examined what household items these poor households owned. It was found that in 1984, 70.5 percent of poor households had a color TV; by 1994, 92.5 percent had one. In 1984, 3.4 percent had a VCR while 59.7 percent did in 1994. In 1984, 64.5 percent of poor families had one or more cars while 71.8 percent did in 1994 (W. Michael Cox and Richard Alm, *Myths of Rich and Poor* [New York: Basic Books, 1999], p. 15). So perhaps the definition of *poverty* (the income levels) needs to be measured differently. Doing so might provide a different picture than the one presented in Figure 11.

Another factor affecting the poverty rate is the age distribution of the population. The United States is becoming older; the elderly make up an increasing percentage of the population. The elderly have smaller incomes than the nonelderly, primarily because many elderly people are retired. In fact, many of the elderly have incomes that are less than the poverty threshold level. As a result, the aging population shows up as an increasing number of people living in poverty on the basis of income. At the same time, many of the elderly have wealth enough to enable them to live very well even though their income is low. It might make more sense to take the wealth and income levels into account when defining *poverty*.

Figure 11

**Spending and Poverty**

Curves representing total government spending in real (1987) billions of dollars on poverty programs since 1960 and the incidence of poverty since 1960 are shown. Total expenditures on antipoverty programs in equal purchasing power terms (real terms) are measured on the left vertical axis, and the percentage of population in poverty is shown on the right vertical axis. During the 1960s, the incidence of poverty decreased as spending increased. Since then, spending has continued to increase, but the incidence of poverty has not declined. *Source:* Department of Commerce, 2004. www.census.gov/hhes/poverty.html.

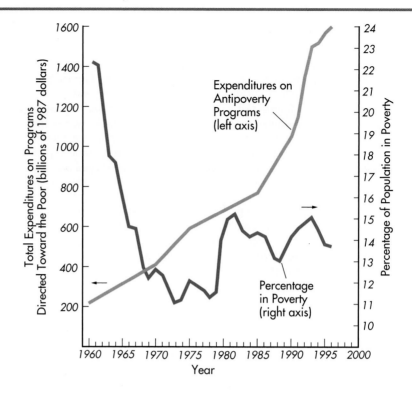

**RECAP**

1. A person's income is determined by the value of the resources a person owns.
2. Since not everyone owns the same resources, incomes are not equal.
3. Income distribution is illustrated by a Lorenz curve.
4. Poverty is defined relative to a society. Someone in poverty in the United States would be considered well-off in Ethiopia.
5. The primary factor leading to poverty is a lack of a job; that is partly determined by whether the economy is growing or is in a recession.

## SUMMARY

**? What does economic analysis have to contribute to the understanding of environmental issues?**

1. Renewable resources are resources that can replenish themselves.

2. Nonrenewable resources are resources whose total amount in existence is limited.

3. The market for resources determines prices at which the rate of use of renewable resources allows the resources to replenish and limits the rate at which the nonrenewable resources are consumed.

4. When an externality occurs, private costs and benefits differ from social costs. Either too much or too little is consumed or produced relative to the quantities that would occur if all costs and benefits were included.

5. An externality may result from the lack of private property rights.

6. Possible solutions to environmental problems include the government's reducing externalities and assigning private property rights.

7. Global environmental problems are more difficult to resolve than domestic ones because of the lack of property rights. When no one government owns the resource being damaged by an externality, then the externality cannot be resolved by any one government.

182

Part Two / Consumers, Firms, and Social Issues

### ? Does the War on Drugs make economic sense?

8. The market for illicit drugs is actually two types of markets: one with barriers to entry and one with free entry.

9. The cocaine and heroin market consists of a few suppliers, who usually cooperate. Cartels dominate the market, dictating prices, quantities, and location.

10. The market for designer drugs is characterized by easy entry.

11. Government policy attempting to control illicit drugs has been flawed in both markets. In the cocaine and heroin market, the government has failed to differentiate between the addict and the experimental user. In the designer drug market, the government has failed to realize that the market is one with free entry and that it must focus on changing demand, not supply.

### ? Does discrimination make economic sense?

12. Discrimination occurs when some factor not related to an individual's value to the firm affects the wage rate that person receives.

13. Discrimination is costly to those who discriminate and should not last in a market economy, at least when entry is easy.

14. Statistical discrimination is the result of imperfect information and can occur as long as information is imperfect.

### ? Does a minimum wage make economic sense?

15. A minimum wage is a wage imposed by government that is greater than the equilibrium wage.

16. In the United States, the current minimum wage is $5.15 per hour.

17. A minimum wage reduces employment.

18. The unskilled, usually teenagers, minorities, and women, bear the costs of a minimum wage.

### ? Why are incomes not equally distributed?

19. The Lorenz curve illustrates the degree of income inequality.

20. If the Lorenz curve corresponds with the line of income equality, then incomes are distributed equally. If the Lorenz curve bows down below the line of income equality, then income is distributed in such a way that more people earn low incomes than high incomes.

21. As a rule, incomes are distributed more unequally in developing countries than in developed countries.

### ? What does it mean to be living in poverty?

22. Poverty is an arbitrary level of income chosen to provide a measure of how well basic human needs are being met.

23. The incidence of poverty decreases as the economy grows and increases as the economy falls into recession.

24. Many people fall below the poverty line for a short time only. However, a significant core of people remain in poverty for at least ten years.

25. The poor are primarily those without jobs. These tend to be people without skills and the youngest members of society.

## KEY TERMS

renewable natural resources
nonrenewable natural resources
private costs
negative externality
social cost
positive externality
private property right

discrimination
statistically discriminating
minimum wage
income distribution
Lorenz curve
poverty

## EXERCISES

1. What is the Lorenz curve? What would the curve look like if income were equally distributed? Could the curve ever bow upward above the line of income equality?

2. Why does the health of the economy affect the number of people living in poverty?

3. What would it mean if the poverty income level of the United States were applied to Mexico?

4. Use the following information to plot a Lorenz curve.

| Percentage of Population | Percentage of Income |
|---|---|
| 20 | 5 |
| 40 | 15 |
| 60 | 35 |
| 80 | 65 |
| 100 | 100 |

5. If the incidence of poverty decreases during periods when the economy is growing and increases during periods when the economy is in recession, what government policies might be used to reduce poverty most effectively?

6. Explain what is meant by the term *discrimination.* Explain what statistical discrimination is.

7. Why do economists say that discrimination is inherently inefficient and therefore will not occur in general?

8. Use the following information to answer these four questions:
   a. What are the external costs per unit of output?
   b. What level of output will be produced?
   c. What level of output should be produced to achieve economic efficiency?
   d. What is the value to society of correcting the externality?

| Quantity | Marginal Costs MC | Marginal Social Costs MSC | Marginal Revenue MR |
|---|---|---|---|
| 1 | $ 2 | $ 4 | $12 |
| 2 | 4 | 6 | 10 |
| 3 | 6 | 8 | 8 |
| 4 | 8 | 10 | 6 |
| 5 | 10 | 12 | 4 |

9. If, in Exercise 8, the *MC* and *MSC* columns were reversed, you would have an example of what? Would too much or too little of the good be produced?

10. Overfishing refers to catching fish at a rate that does not allow the fish to repopulate. What is the fundamental problem associated with overfishing of the oceans? What might lead to underfishing?

11. Elephants eat 300 pounds of food per day. They flourished in Africa when they could roam over huge areas of land, eating the vegetation in one area and then moving on so that the vegetation could renew itself. Now the area over which elephants can roam is declining. Without some action, the elephants will become extinct. What actions might save the elephants? What are the costs and benefits of such actions?

12. What could explain why the value of pollution permits in one area of the country is rising 20 percent per year while in another it is unchanged from year to year? What would you expect to happen as a result of this differential?

*Internet Exercise*

**The Equal Employment Opportunity Commission is charged with overseeing U.S. anti-discrimination laws. Use the Internet to explore the EEOC website.**

Go to the Boyes/Melvin, *Fundamentals of Economics* website accessible through **http://college.hmco.com** and click on the Internet Exercise link for Chapter 8. Now answer the questions that appear on the Boyes/Melvin website.

## Study Guide for Chapter 8

## Key Term Match

Match each term with its correct definition by placing the appropriate letter next to the corresponding number.

A. renewable natural resources
B. nonrenewable natural resources
C. private costs
D. negative externality
E. social cost
F. positive externality
G. private property right
H. discrimination
I. statistically discriminating
J. minimum wage
K. income distribution
L. Lorenz curve
M. poverty

_____ 1. costs borne by individuals not involved in the transaction creating the costs
_____ 2. resources that can replenish themselves
_____ 3. the right to claim ownership of an item
_____ 4. costs borne solely by the individuals involved in a transaction
_____ 5. an arbitrary level of income chosen to provide a measure of how well basic human needs are being met
_____ 6. the practice of treating people differently in a market which is based on a characteristic having nothing to do with that market
_____ 7. using characteristics that apply to a group, although not to all individual members of that group, as an allocation device
_____ 8. a diagram illustrating the degree of income inequality
_____ 9. the ways in which a society's income is divided
_____10. private costs plus external costs
_____11. the least amount an employee can be paid according to government mandate
_____12. resources that cannot replenish themselves
_____13. benefits received by individuals who are not involved in the transaction that creates the benefits

## Quick-Check Quiz

**1** Which of the following is a renewable resource?
- a. coal
- b. the rain forest
- c. uranium
- d. oil
- e. natural gas

**2** Which of the following statements is true?
- a. Suppliers of illicit drugs would like to see these drugs legalized because their costs would decrease.
- b. The markets for cocaine and heroin have barriers to entry.
- c. If illicit drugs were legalized, the drug cartels would make higher profits.
- d. The government's policy of eliminating drug "factories" and confiscating supplies addresses the differences between addicts and experimental users.
- e. Designer drugs are extremely difficult to manufacture.

Use the following graph to answer question 3.

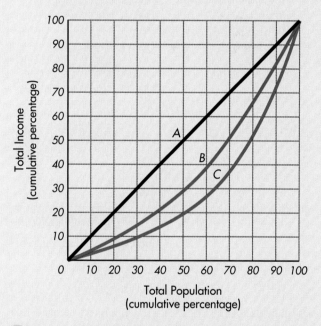

**3** Which of the following statements about these Lorenz curves is correct?
- a. Line *A* shows the most unequally distributed income.
- b. Line *C* shows a more equal income distribution than line *B* does.
- c. Line *A* shows a perfectly equal distribution.
- d. All of the above are correct.
- e. Only a and b are correct.

**4** Relative to developed nations, less-developed nations have
- a. the same income distribution.
- b. a more unequal income distribution.

c. a more equal income distribution.

d. an almost perfectly equal income distribution.

e. an almost perfectly unequal income distribution.

## Practice Questions and Problems

1. When social costs are higher than private costs, the market produces _____ (too much, not enough) of the product.

2. When private property rights are ill-defined, _____ (too much, too little) of a resource is consumed.

3. When positive externalities exist, _____ (too much, too little) of a good is consumed or produced.

4. The demand for illicit drugs by hard-core users is price _____ (elastic, inelastic).

5. Experimental users pay a _____ (higher, lower) price for illegal drugs than do hard-core addicts.

6. The market for designer drugs _____ (is, is not) characterized by ease of entry.

7. Legalizing drugs would _____ (increase, decrease) the costs of production and _____ (increase, decrease) the profits made by drug cartels.

8. The U.S. antidrug effort consists of trying to reduce the _____ (supply of, demand for) illegal drugs.

9. The market for heroin and cocaine is _____ (easy, difficult) to enter.

10. Discrimination based on personal prejudice is usually _____ (costly, profitable) for a firm.

11. When entry is _____ (easy, difficult), having higher costs due to discrimination may drive a firm out of the market.

12. Which groups are likely to suffer unemployment as a result of increases in the minimum wage law? _____

13. An increase in the minimum wage is likely to _____ (increase, decrease) teenage employment.

14. The minimum wage is a price _____ (ceiling, floor).

15. The following table gives income distribution data for the United States and Mexico. On the following graph, draw the Lorenz curves for the two countries. The country with the more equal income distribution is _____.

| | Lowest 20% | Second 20% | Third 20% | Fourth 20% | Highest 20% |
|---|---|---|---|---|---|
| Mexico | 3 | 7 | 12 | 20 | 58 |
| United States | 5 | 12 | 18 | 25 | 40 |

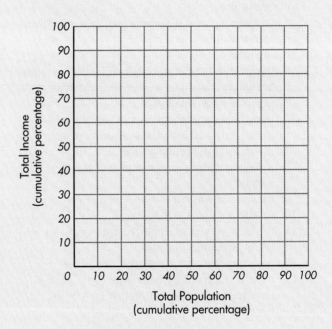

16. In terms of age, the highest incidence of poverty is for _____.

## Exercises and Applications

1. **Comparable Worth and High School Teachers** Labor markets in the United States frequently have resulted in wage patterns that seem discriminatory;

minorities and women, on average, are paid substantially less than white males. One approach (known as *comparable worth*) to making wage patterns more equal is to disregard the market forces of demand and supply and to set wages for jobs based on job characteristics. Using this approach, people who hold jobs that take place in the same sort of environment, that require the same level of responsibility, and that require the same amount of education should receive the same rate of pay.

The job market for high school teachers in most of the United States has worked this way for many years. In most high schools, teachers with the same education and years of experience are paid the same salary, regardless of the subject area they teach. This practice fits the comparable worth idea: The working conditions and demands on English teachers are the same as those for math teachers. But ignoring demand and supply has some economic effects worth looking at.

1. Suppose U.S. high schools decide to improve the training of skilled workers by requiring students to take more math classes. The following graphs show the demand and supply ($D_1$ and $S_1$) for math teachers and English teachers before adding math classes, with both math and English teachers earning $30,000, and a new demand curve ($D_2$) for math teachers after adding more math classes. Mark on graph (a) the old and new equilibrium salary and number of math teachers.

a. The market equilibrium salary for math teachers now is _____ .
b. Using the ideas presented in this chapter and the previous one, explain why the salary has to go up to attract new math teachers.

_____

_____

_____

2. If the schools maintain equal salaries for all teachers, English teachers also will receive a salary of $35,000. Mark on graph (b) the quantity demanded and quantity supplied of English teachers when the salary is $35,000. Explain what will happen in the market for English teachers if their salaries are raised to $35,000.

_____

_____

_____

3. One of the most useful characteristics of a market economy is that price changes signal changes in the relative scarcity of different products and resources and encourage people to respond to those changes. Can you think of any ways that labor markets, by setting salaries based on comparable worth, can do the same thing without having math

**(a) Market for Math Teachers**

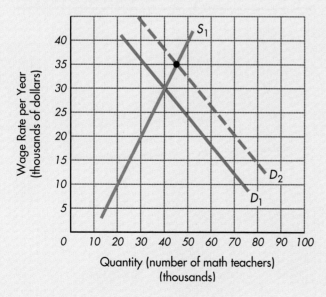

Wage Rate per Year (thousands of dollars)

Quantity (number of math teachers) (thousands)

**(b) Market for English Teachers**

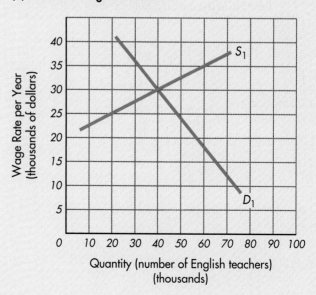

Wage Rate per Year (thousands of dollars)

Quantity (number of English teachers) (thousands)

teachers receiving higher salaries than English teachers?

_____

_____

_____

**II** **Discrimination and Minimum Wage Laws** Walter Williams, an economist and columnist, was quoted in the *Wall Street Journal* as saying, "The brunt of the minimum wage law is borne by low-skilled workers . . . particularly black teenagers." In this chapter, we have found that discrimination in competitive labor markets is usually costly to employers and that minimum wage laws can create a labor surplus in competitive labor markets. Use these two ideas to explain the logic behind Williams's comment. (*Hint:* Think about the effects that a surplus has on the costs of discriminating.)

_____

_____

_____

**III** **Welfare, Workfare, and Incentives to Work** In a story entitled "Problem of the Poor," *New York Newsday* stated:

> Liberal critics and welfare-rights groups point to [New York's] high poverty rate—60 percent above the national average—citing inadequate welfare benefits, a lack of public housing and other holes in the safety net. Yet New York has provided some of the most generous welfare benefits in the country, both in terms of the

amount of benefits offered and the number of people covered. . . . The level of cash benefits in the basic welfare program is 50 percent above that of the median state in the United States.

The article also points out that about 16 percent of the people in New York City receive cash payments from public assistance programs, compared with fewer than 8 percent for the United States as a whole.

1. Use what you have learned in this chapter and in previous chapters about the supply of labor to explain why generous welfare programs in New York City might increase the number of people living in poverty in New York.

_____

_____

_____

2. How would a workfare program change incentives? Do you think workfare is a good idea or a bad idea? Why?

_____

_____

_____

ACE self-test

Now that you've completed the Study Guide for this chapter, you should have a good sense of the concepts you need to review. If you'd like to test your understanding of the material again, go to the Practice Tests on the Boyes/Melvin *Fundamentals of Economics*, 3e website, **economics.college.hmco.com/students.**

# Part Three

**The National and Global Economies**

## Chapter 9

# An Overview of the National and International Economies

**? Fundamental Questions**

1. **What is a household, and what is household income and spending?**
2. **What is a business firm, and what is business spending?**
3. **How does the international sector affect the economy?**
4. **What does government do?**
5. **How do the three private sectors—households, businesses, and the international sector—interact in the economy?**
6. **How does the government interact with the other sectors of the economy?**

*Preview*

You decide to buy a new Toyota, so you go to a Toyota dealer and exchange money for the car. The Toyota dealer has rented land and buildings and hired workers in order to make cars available to you and other members of the public. The employees earn income paid by the Toyota dealer and then use their incomes to buy food from the grocery store. This transaction generates revenue for the grocery store, which hires workers and pays them incomes that they then use to buy groceries and Toyotas. Your expenditure for the Toyota is part of a circular flow. Revenue is received by the Toyota dealer, who pays employees, who, in turn, buy goods and services.

Of course, the story is complicated by the fact that the Toyota is originally manufactured and purchased in Japan and then shipped to the United States before it can be sold by the local Toyota dealer. Your purchase of the Toyota creates revenue for the local dealer as well as for the manufacturer in Japan, which pays Japanese autoworkers to produce Toyotas. Furthermore, when you buy your Toyota, you must pay a tax to the government, which uses tax revenues to pay for police protection, national defense, the legal system, and other services. Many people in different areas of the economy are involved.

An economy is made up of individual buyers and sellers. Economists could discuss the neighborhood economy that surrounds your university, the economy of the city of Chicago, or the economy of the state of Massachusetts. But typically it is the national economy, the economy of the United States, that is the center of their attention. To clarify the operation of the national economy, economists usually group individual buyers and sellers into sectors: households, businesses, government, and the international sector. Since the U.S. economy affects, and is affected by, the rest of the world, to understand how the economy functions, we must include the international sector. In this chapter we examine basic data and information on each individual sector and examine how the sectors interact. ■

## 1. HOUSEHOLDS

A **household** consists of one or more persons who occupy a unit of housing. The unit of housing may be a house, an apartment, or even a single room, as long as it

**household:** one or more persons who occupy a unit of housing

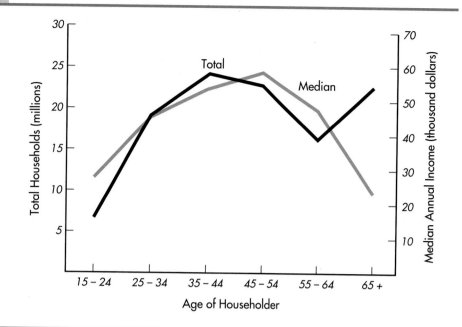

**Figure 1**

**Age of Householder, Number of Households, and Median Household Income in the United States**

The graph reveals that householders aged 35 to 44 make up the largest number of households, and householders aged 45 to 54 earn the highest median annual income.

*Source:* U.S. Department of Commerce, *Income in the United States: 2002,* www.census.gov/.

constitutes separate living quarters. A household may consist of related family members, like a father, mother, and children, or it may comprise unrelated individuals, like three college students sharing an apartment. The person in whose name the house or apartment is owned or rented is called the *householder.*

## 1.a. Number of Households and Household Income

**1. What is a household, and what is household income and spending?**

In 2002, there were more than 109 million households in the United States. The breakdown of households by age of householder is shown in Figure 1. Householders between 35 and 44 years old make up the largest number of households. Householders between 45 and 54 years old have the largest median income. The *median* is the middle value—half of the households in an age group have an income higher than the median, and half have an income lower than the median. Figure 1 shows that households in which the householder is between 45 and 54 years old have a median income of about $59,000, substantially higher than the median incomes of other age groups. Typically, workers in this age group are at the peak of their earning power. Younger households are gaining experience and training; older households include retired workers.

Thirty-three percent of all households, or 34,418,046, are two-person households. The stereotypical household of husband, wife, and two children accounts for only 14 percent of all households. There are relatively few large households in the United States. Of the more than 105 million households in the country, only 1,846,844 (about 1 percent) have seven or more persons.

## 1.b. Household Spending

**consumption:** household spending

Household spending is called **consumption.** Householders consume housing, transportation, food, entertainment, and other goods and services. Household spending (also called *consumer spending*) is the largest component of total spending in the economy—rising to about $7.7 trillion in 2003.

RECAP

1. A household consists of one or more persons who occupy a unit of housing.

2. An apartment or house is rented or owned by a householder.

3. As a group, householders between the ages of 45 and 54 have the highest median incomes.

4. Household spending is called *consumption*.

2. What is a business firm, and what is business spending?

## 2. BUSINESS FIRMS

A business firm is a business organization controlled by a single management. The firm's business may be conducted at more than one location. The terms *company, enterprise,* and *business* are used interchangeably with *firm*.

### 2.a. Forms of Business Organizations

Firms are organized as sole proprietorships, partnerships, or corporations. A sole proprietorship is a business owned by one person. This type of firm may be a one-person operation or a large enterprise with many employees. In either case, the owner receives all the profits and is responsible for all the debts incurred by the business. There is no separation between the owner and the firm in that the owner has unlimited liability for the firm's debts, and profits are taxed at the owner's individual income tax rate. However, the owner also has sole control over business decisions.

A partnership is a business owned by two or more partners who share both the profits of the business and responsibility for the firm's losses. The partners could be individuals, estates, or other businesses. Partners owning a firm have unlimited liability for firm debts and are taxed at individual tax rates.

State law allows the formation of corporations. A corporation is a business whose identity in the eyes of the law is distinct from the identity of its owners. A corporation is an economic entity that, like a person, can own property and borrow money in its own name. The owners of a corporation are shareholders. If a corporation cannot pay its debts, creditors cannot seek payment from the shareholders' personal wealth. The corporation itself is responsible for all its actions. The shareholders' liability is limited to the value of the stock they own. Corporations are taxed at corporate income tax rates. In many corporations there are many shareholders who exercise no control over the firm. A separation of ownership and control may occur when the professional managers of the firm are different individuals than those who own large amounts of stock.

Many firms are global in their operations even though they may have been founded and may be owned by residents of a single country. Firms typically first enter the international market by selling products to foreign countries. As revenues from these sales increase, the firms realize advantages by locating subsidiaries in foreign countries. A **multinational business** is a firm that owns and operates producing units in foreign countries. The best-known U.S. corporations are multinational firms. Ford, IBM, PepsiCo, and McDonald's all own operating units in many different countries. Ford Motor Company, for instance, is the parent firm of sales organizations and assembly plants located around the world. As transportation and communication technologies progress, multinational business activity will grow.

**multinational business:** a firm that owns and operates producing units in foreign countries

### 2.b. Business Statistics

Figure 2(a) shows that in the United States there are far more sole proprietorships than partnerships or corporations. Figure 2(a) also compares the revenues earned by each type of business. The great majority of sole proprietorships are small

Figure 2

**Number and Revenue of Business Firms**

Most sole proprietorships and partnerships are small firms, with nearly 70 percent of all proprietorships falling into the less-than-$25,000 revenue category, and over 50 percent of all partnerships falling into the same lowest revenue category. Corporations are more likely to be larger; 19 percent have revenues exceeding $1 million.

Most sole proprietorship revenues are earned by the larger proprietorships, those in the $100,000 to $499,000 category. By contrast, the small number of partnerships in the top revenue category is enough to account for 89 percent of all partnership revenues.

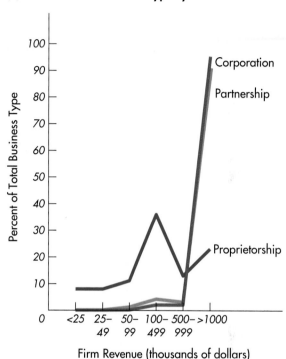

**(a) Number of Business Firms by Revenue Amount**

**(b) Percent of Total Business Type by Revenue Amount**

Source: Statistical Abstract of the United States, 2002 (Washington, D.C.: U.S. Government Printing Office, 2003).

businesses, with revenues under $25,000 a year. Similarly, more than half of all partnerships also have revenues under $25,000 a year, but only 24 percent of the corporations are in this category.

Figure 2(b) shows that the 67 percent of sole proprietorships that earn less than $25,000 a year account for only 8 percent of the revenue earned by proprietorships. The 0.004 percent of proprietorships with revenue of $1 million or more account for 23 percent. Even more striking are the figures for partnerships and corporations. The 53 percent of partnerships with the smallest revenue account for only 0.3 percent of the total revenue earned by partnerships. At the other extreme, the 6 percent of partnerships with the largest revenue account for 91 percent of total partnership revenue. The 24 percent of corporations in the smallest range account for less than 0.1 percent of total corporate revenue, while the 19 percent of corporations in the largest range account for 95 percent of corporate revenue.

The message of Figure 2 is that big business is important in the United States. There are many small firms, but large firms and corporations account for the greatest share of business revenue. Although there are only about one-third as many

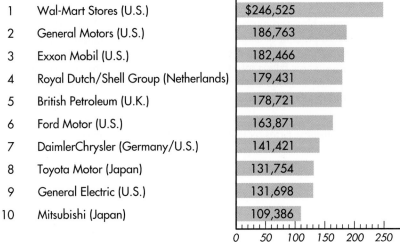

**Figure 3**

**The World's Ten Largest Public Companies**

As shown in the chart, large firms are not just a U.S. phenomenon.

| Rank | Firm (country) | Sales (millions) |
|------|----------------|------------------|
| 1 | Wal-Mart Stores (U.S.) | $246,525 |
| 2 | General Motors (U.S.) | 186,763 |
| 3 | Exxon Mobil (U.S.) | 182,466 |
| 4 | Royal Dutch/Shell Group (Netherlands) | 179,431 |
| 5 | British Petroleum (U.K.) | 178,721 |
| 6 | Ford Motor (U.S.) | 163,871 |
| 7 | DaimlerChrysler (Germany/U.S.) | 141,421 |
| 8 | Toyota Motor (Japan) | 131,754 |
| 9 | General Electric (U.S.) | 131,698 |
| 10 | Mitsubishi (Japan) | 109,386 |

*Source: Fortune* Global 500, http://www.fortune.com, "The World's Ten Largest Public Companies" as it appeared on Fortune.com, 11/9/2001. Reprinted with permission.

corporations as sole proprietorships, corporations have more than 15 times the revenue of sole proprietorships.

## 2.c. Firms Around the World

Big business is a dominant force in the United States. Many people believe that because the United States is the world's largest economy, U.S. firms are the largest in the world. Figure 3 shows that this is not entirely true. Of the ten largest corporations in the world (measured by sales), five are outside the United States. Big business is not just a U.S. phenomenon.

## 2.d. Business Spending

**investment:** spending on capital goods to be used in producing goods and services

**Investment** is the expenditure by business firms for capital goods—machines, tools, and buildings—that will be used to produce goods and services. The economic meaning of *investment* is different from the everyday meaning, "a financial transaction such as buying bonds or stocks." In economics, the term *investment* refers to business spending for capital goods.

Investment spending in 2003 was $1,671 billion, an amount equal to roughly one-fifth of consumption, or household spending. Investment increases unevenly, actually falling at times and then rising very rapidly. Even though investment spending is much smaller than consumption, the wide swings in investment spending mean that business expenditures are an important factor in determining the economic health of the nation.

**RECAP**

1. Business firms may be organized as sole proprietorships, partnerships, or corporations.

2. Large corporations account for the largest fraction of total business revenue.

3. Business investment spending fluctuates widely over time.

# 3. THE INTERNATIONAL SECTOR

**3. How does the international sector affect the economy?**

Today, foreign buyers and sellers have a significant effect on economic conditions in the United States, and developments in the rest of the world often influence U.S. buyers and sellers. We saw in previous chapters, for instance, how exchange rate changes can affect the demand for and supply of U.S. goods and services.

## 3.a. Types of Countries

The nations of the world may be divided into two categories: industrial countries and developing countries. Developing countries greatly outnumber industrial countries (see Figure 4). The World Bank (an international organization that makes loans to developing countries) groups countries according to per capita income (income per person). Low-income economies are those with per capita incomes of $735 or less. Lower-middle-income economies have per capita incomes of $736 to $2,935. Upper-middle-income economies have per capita incomes of $2,936 to $9,075. High-income economies—oil exporters and industrial market economies—have per capita incomes of greater than $9,075. Some countries are not members of the World Bank and so are not categorized, and information about a few small countries is so limited that the World Bank is unable to classify them.

It is readily apparent from Figure 4 that low-income economies are heavily concentrated in Africa while lower-middle-income economies are heavily concentrated in Asia. Countries in these regions have a low profile in U.S. trade, although they may receive aid from the United States. The U.S. trade is concentrated with its neighbors Canada and Mexico, along with the major industrial powers.

**3.a.1. The Industrial Countries**   The richest industrial market economies are listed in the bar chart in Figure 5. The countries listed in Figure 5 are among the wealthiest countries in the world. Not appearing on the list are the high-income oil-exporting nations like Libya, Saudi Arabia, Kuwait, and the United Arab Emirates, which are considered to still be developing.

The economies of the industrial nations are highly interdependent. As conditions change in one nation, business firms and individuals looking for the best return or interest rate on their funds may shift large sums of money from one country to others. As they do, economic conditions in one country spread to other countries. As a result, the industrial countries, particularly the major economic powers like the United States, Germany, and Japan, are forced to pay close attention to each other's economic policies.

**3.a.2. The Developing Countries**   Referring back to Figure 4, we see that the developing countries (sometimes referred to as the less-developed countries, or LDCs) are classified as low or middle income. These countries differ greatly in terms of the provision of basic human needs to the average citizen. A major way that such countries can raise living standards is by selling goods to the rest of the world.

The United States tends to buy, or *import,* primary products such as agricultural produce and minerals from the developing countries. Products that a country buys from another country are called **imports.** The United States tends to sell, or *export,* manufactured goods to developing countries. Products that a country sells to another country are called **exports.** The United States is the largest producer and exporter of grains and other agricultural output in the world. The efficiency of U.S. farming relative to farming in much of the rest of the world gives the United States a comparative advantage in many agricultural products.

**imports:** products that a country buys from other countries

**exports:** products that a country sells to other countries

## 3.b. International Sector Spending

Economic activity of the United States with the rest of the world includes U.S. spending on foreign goods and foreign spending on U.S. goods. Figure 6 shows

## Figure 4

### World Economic Development

The colors on the map identify low-income, middle-income, and high-income economies. Countries have been placed in each group on the basis of GNP per capita and, in some instances, other distinguishing economic characteristics.

Low-income economies
$735 or less

Lower-middle-income economies
$736 to $2,935

Upper-middle-income economies
$2,936 to $9,075

High-income economies
More than $9,075

No data

---

**trade surplus:** the situation that exists when imports are less than exports

**trade deficit:** the situation that exists when imports exceed exports

**net exports:** the difference between the value of exports and the value of imports

how U.S. exports and imports are spread over different countries. Notice that three countries—Mexico, Canada, and Japan—account for 44 percent of U.S. exports and 38 percent of U.S. imports.

When exports exceed imports, a **trade surplus** exists. When imports exceed exports, a **trade deficit** exists. Figure 6 shows that the United States is importing much more than it exports.

The term **net exports** refers to the difference between the value of exports and the value of imports: net exports equals exports minus imports. Positive net exports represent trade surpluses; negative net exports represent trade deficits. In 2003, U.S. net exports were –$495 billion.

RECAP

1. The majority of U.S. trade is with the industrial market economies.
2. Exports are products sold to foreign countries; imports are products bought from foreign countries.
3. Exports minus imports equals net exports.
4. Positive net exports signal a trade surplus; negative net exports signal a trade deficit.

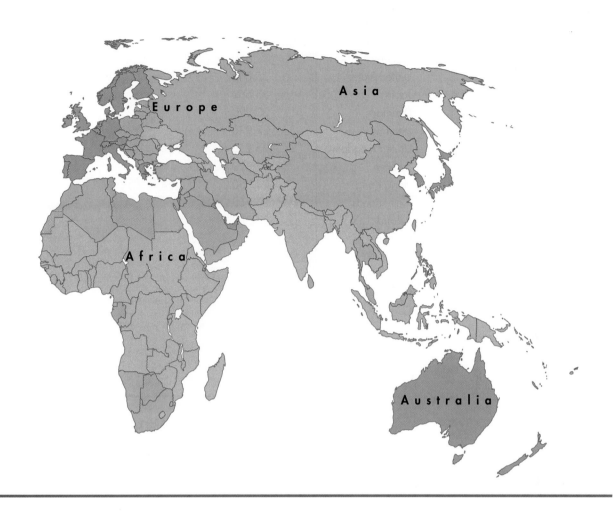

## 4. OVERVIEW OF THE U.S. GOVERNMENT

**4. What does government do?**

When Americans think of government policies, rules, and regulations, they typically think of Washington, D.C., because their economic lives are regulated and shaped more by policies made there than by policies made at the state and local levels.

Who actually is involved in economic policymaking? Important government institutions that shape U.S. economic policy are listed in Table 1. This list is far from inclusive, but it does include the agencies with the broadest powers and greatest influence. Economic policy involves macroeconomic issues like government spending and control of the money supply and microeconomic issues aimed at providing public goods like police and military protection and correcting problems such as pollution.

### 4.a. Government Policy

The government has been given many functions in the economy. These include providing some goods, regulating some firm behaviors, and promoting competition via laws restricting the ability of business firms to engage in certain practices.

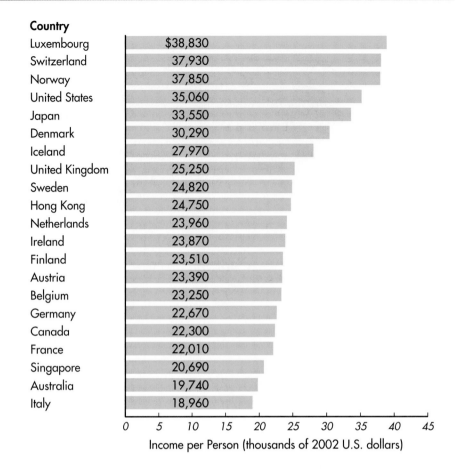

## Figure 5

**The Industrial Market Economies**

The bar chart lists some of the wealthiest countries in the world. Ironically, high-income oil-exporting countries such as Libya, Saudi Arabia, Kuwait, and the United Arab Emirates do not appear on the list because they are still considered to be developing.

**Country**

| Country | Income per Person (thousands of 2002 U.S. dollars) |
|---------|------|
| Luxembourg | $38,830 |
| Switzerland | 37,930 |
| Norway | 37,850 |
| United States | 35,060 |
| Japan | 33,550 |
| Denmark | 30,290 |
| Iceland | 27,970 |
| United Kingdom | 25,250 |
| Sweden | 24,820 |
| Hong Kong | 24,750 |
| Netherlands | 23,960 |
| Ireland | 23,870 |
| Finland | 23,510 |
| Austria | 23,390 |
| Belgium | 23,250 |
| Germany | 22,670 |
| Canada | 22,300 |
| France | 22,010 |
| Singapore | 20,690 |
| Australia | 19,740 |
| Italy | 18,960 |

Income per Person (thousands of 2002 U.S. dollars)

*Source:* World Bank: www.worldbank.org/data/databytopic/GNIPC.pdf

**monetary policy:** policy directed toward the control of money and credit

**Federal Reserve:** the central bank of the United States

Most attention is given to the government's monetary and fiscal policies. **Monetary policy** is policy directed toward the control of money and credit. The major player in this policy arena is the Federal Reserve, commonly called the *Fed*. The **Federal Reserve** is the central bank of the United States. It serves as a banker for the U.S. government and regulates the U.S. money supply.

The Federal Reserve System is run by a seven-member Board of Governors. The most important member of the board is the chairman, who is appointed by the president for a term of four years. The board meets regularly (from 10 to 12 times a year) with a group of high-level officials to review the current economic situation and set policy for the growth of U.S. money and credit. The Federal Reserve exercises a great deal of influence on U.S. economic policy.

**fiscal policy:** policy directed toward government spending and taxation

**Fiscal policy,** the other area of macroeconomic policy, is policy directed toward government spending and taxation. In the United States, fiscal policy is determined by laws that are passed by Congress and signed by the president. The relative roles of the legislative and executive branches in shaping fiscal policy vary with the political climate, but usually it is the president who initiates major policy changes. Presidents rely on key advisers for fiscal policy information. These advisers include cabinet officers such as the secretary of the Treasury and the secretary of state as well as the director of the Office of Management and Budget. In addition, the president has a

## Study Guide for Chapter 9

### Key Term Match

Match each key term with its correct definition by placing the appropriate letter next to the corresponding numbers.

A. household
B. consumption
C. multinational business
D. investment
E. imports
F. exports
G. trade surplus
H. trade deficit
I. net exports
J. monetary policy

K. Federal Reserve
L. fiscal policy
M. transfer payments
N. budget surplus
O. budget deficit
P. private sector
Q. public sector
R. circular flow diagram

_____ 1. spending on capital goods to be used in producing goods and services

_____ 2. products that a country buys from other countries

_____ 3. the shortage that results when government spending is greater than revenue

_____ 4. the situation that exists when imports exceed exports

_____ 5. policy directed toward government spending and taxation

_____ 6. a firm that owns and operates producing units in foreign countries

_____ 7. the excess that results when government spending is less than revenue

_____ 8. the situation that exists when imports are less than exports

_____ 9. income transferred from one citizen who is earning income to another citizen who may not be

_____10. the difference between the value of exports and the value of imports

_____11. a model showing the flow of output and income from one sector of the economy to another

_____12. one or more persons who occupy a unit of housing

_____13. households, businesses, and the international sector

_____14. household spending

_____15. the central bank of the United States

_____16. the government

_____17. products that a country sells to other countries

_____18. policy directed toward the control of money and credit

### Quick-Check Quiz

1. Householders _____ years old make up the largest number of households.
   - a. 15 to 24
   - b. 25 to 34
   - c. 35 to 44
   - d. 45 to 54
   - e. 55 to 64

2. Householders _____ years old have the largest median annual income.
   - a. 15 to 24
   - b. 25 to 34
   - c. 35 to 44
   - d. 45 to 54
   - e. 55 to 64

3. The largest percentage of households consists of _____ person(s).
   - a. one
   - b. two
   - c. three
   - d. four
   - e. five

4. Household spending, or consumption, is the _____ component of total spending in the economy.
   - a. largest
   - b. second largest
   - c. third largest
   - d. fourth largest
   - e. smallest

5. Which of the following is *not* a component of household spending?
   - a. capital goods
   - b. housing
   - c. transportation
   - d. food
   - e. entertainment

6. In _____ the owner(s) of the business is (are) responsible for all the debts incurred by the business and may have to pay those debts from his/her (their) personal wealth.
   - a. a sole proprietorship
   - b. a partnership
   - c. a corporation

    d. sole proprietorships and partnerships

    e. sole proprietorships, partnerships, and corporations

7 _____ are the most common form of business organization, but _____ account for the largest share of total revenues.

    a. Sole proprietorships; partnerships

    b. Sole proprietorships; corporations

    c. Partnerships; corporations

    d. Corporations; sole proprietorships

    e. Partnerships; sole proprietorships

8 The United States tends to import primary products such as agricultural produce and minerals from _____ countries.

    a. low-income

    b. medium-income

    c. high-income

    d. industrial

    e. developing

9 U.S. trade is concentrated with

    a. major industrial powers.

    b. developing countries.

    c. Canada and Mexico.

    d. oil exporters.

    e. a and c.

10 Low-income countries are concentrated heavily in

    a. Central America.

    b. South America.

    c. North America.

    d. Africa.

    e. Western Europe.

11 Combined government spending on goods and services is larger than _____ but smaller than _____.

    a. consumption; net exports

    b. consumption; investment

    c. net exports; investment

    d. investment; net exports

    e. investment; consumption

12 Which of the following is a macroeconomic function of government?

    a. provision of military protection

    b. promotion of competition

    c. determining the level of government spending and taxation

    d. provision of police protection

    e. correction of pollution problems

13 The _____ is (are) responsible for fiscal policy, and the _____ is (are) responsible for monetary policy.

    a. Federal Reserve; Congress

    b. Federal Reserve; Congress and the president

    c. Congress; Federal Reserve

    d. Congress and the president; Federal Reserve

    e. Congress; Federal Reserve and the president

14 Which of the following statements is false?

    a. Households sell the factors of production in exchange for money payments.

    b. Firms buy the factors of production from households.

    c. The value of output must equal the value of income.

    d. The value of input must equal the value of household income.

    e. Money that is saved by households reenters the economy in the form of investment spending.

15 _____ own(s) the factors of production.

    a. Corporations

    b. Partnerships

    c. The international sector

    d. State and local governments

    e. Households

## Practice Questions and Problems

1 The largest component of total spending in the economy is _____ spending.

2 _____ is the expenditure by business firms for capital goods.

3 _____ account for the largest percentage of business revenue.

4 The _____ is an international organization that makes loans to developing countries.

5 _____ equal exports minus imports.

6 _____ net exports signal a trade surplus; _____ net exports signal a trade deficit.

Economists can compute GDP using two methods: the final goods and services method uses the market value of the final good or service; the value-added method uses the value added at each stage of production. Both methods count the value of intermediate goods only once. This is an important distinction: GDP is based not on the market value of *all* goods and services but on the market value of all *final* goods and services.

*Produced in a Year* The GDP measures the value of output *produced in a year*. The value of goods produced last year is counted in last year's GDP; the value of goods produced this year is counted in this year's GDP. The year of production, not the year of sale, determines allocation to GDP. Although the value of last year's goods is not counted in this year's GDP, the value of services involved in the sale is. This year's GDP does not include the value of a house built last year, but it does include the value of the real estate broker's fee; it does not include the value of a used car, but it does include the income earned by the used-car dealer in the sale of that car.

**inventory:** the stock of unsold goods held by a firm

To determine the value of goods produced in a year but not sold in that year, economists calculate changes in inventory. **Inventory** is a firm's stock of unsold goods. If a shirt that is produced this year remains on the retail store's shelf at the end of the year, it increases the value of the store's inventory. A $20 shirt increases that value by $20. Changes in inventory allow economists to count goods in the year in which they are produced whether or not they are sold.

Changes in inventory can be planned or unplanned. A store may want a cushion above expected sales (*planned inventory changes*), or it may not be able to sell all the goods it expected to sell when it placed the order (*unplanned inventory changes*). For instance, suppose Jeremy owns a surfboard shop, and he always wants to keep 10 surfboards above what he expects to sell. This is done so that in case business is surprisingly good, he does not have to turn away customers to his competitors and lose those sales. At the beginning of the year, Jeremy has 10 surfboards and then builds as many new boards during the year as he expects to sell. Jeremy *plans* on having an inventory at the end of the year of 10 surfboards. Suppose Jeremy expects to sell 100 surfboards during the year, so he builds 100 new boards. If business is surprisingly poor so that Jeremy sells only 80 surfboards, how do we count the 20 new boards that he made but did not sell? We count the change in his inventory. He started the year with 10 surfboards and ends the year with 20 more unsold boards for a year-end inventory of 30. The change in inventory of 20 (equal to the ending inventory of 30 minus the starting inventory of 10) represents output that is counted in GDP. In Jeremy's case, the inventory change is unplanned since he expected to sell the 20 extra surfboards that he has in his shop at the end of the year. But whether the inventory change is planned or unplanned, changes in inventory will count output that is produced but not sold in a given year.

**1.a.1. GDP as Output** The GDP is a measure of the market value of a nation's total output in a year. Remember that economists divide the economy into four sectors: households, businesses, government, and the international sector. The total value of economic activity equals the sum of the output produced in each sector. Since GDP counts the output produced in the United States, U.S. GDP is produced in business firms, households, and government located within the boundaries of the United States. Not unexpectedly in a capitalist country, privately owned businesses account for the largest percentage of output: in the United States, 84 percent of the GDP is produced by private firms. Government produces 11 percent of the GDP, and households 5 percent.

In terms of output, GDP is the value of final goods and services produced by domestic households, businesses, and government units. If some of the firms producing in the United States are foreign owned, their output produced in the United States is counted in U.S. GDP.

### 1.a.2. GDP as Expenditures

Here we look at GDP in terms of what each sector pays for goods and services it purchases. The dollar value of total expenditures—the sum of the amount each sector spends on final goods and services—equals the dollar value of output. Household spending is called *consumption*. Households spend income on goods and services to be consumed. Business spending is called *investment*. Investment is spending on capital goods that will be used to produce other goods and services. The two other components of total spending are *government spending* and *net exports*. Net exports are the value of *exports* (goods and services sold to the rest of the world) minus the value of *imports* (goods and services bought from the rest of the world).

$$GDP = consumption + investment + government\ spending + net\ exports$$

Or, in the shorter form commonly used by economists,

$$GDP = C + I + G + X$$

where $X$ is net exports.

Consumption, or household spending, accounts for 68 percent of national expenditures. Government spending represents 18 percent of expenditures, and business investment 17 percent. Net exports are negative ($-3$ percent); this means that imports exceed exports. To determine total national expenditures on *domestic* output, the value of imports, spending on foreign output, is subtracted from total expenditures.

### 1.a.3. GDP as Income

The total value of output can be calculated by adding up the expenditures of each sector. And because one sector's expenditures are another's income, the total value of output also can be computed by adding up the income of all sectors.

Business firms use factors of production to produce goods and services. The income earned by factors of production is classified as wages, interest, rent, and profits. *Wages* are payments to labor, including fringe benefits, social security contributions, and retirement payments. *Interest* is the net interest paid by businesses to households plus the net interest received from foreigners (the interest they pay us minus the interest we pay them). *Rent* is income earned from selling the use of real property (houses, shops, farms). Finally, *profits* are the sum of corporate profits plus proprietors' income (income from sole proprietorships and partnerships).

In terms of income, wages account for 58 percent of the GDP. Interest and profits account for 5 percent and 10 percent of the GDP, respectively. Proprietors' income accounts for 7 percent. Rent (2 percent) is very small in comparison. *Net factor income from abroad* is income received from U.S.-owned resources located in other countries minus income paid to foreign-owned resources located in the United States. Since U.S. GDP refers only to income earned within U.S. borders, we must deduct this kind of income to arrive at GDP ($-0.2$ percent).

The GDP also includes two income categories that we have not discussed: capital consumption allowance and indirect business taxes. **Capital consumption allowance** is not a money payment to a factor of production; it is the estimated value of capital goods used up or worn out in production plus the value of accidental damage to capital goods. The value of accidental damage is relatively small, so it is common to hear economists refer to capital consumption allowance as **depreciation.** Machines and other capital goods wear out over time. The reduction in the value of capital stock due to its being used up or worn out over time is called depreciation. A depreciating capital good loses value each year of its useful life until its value is zero.

Even though capital consumption allowance does not represent income received by a factor of production, it must be accounted for in GDP as income. Otherwise the value of GDP measured as output would be higher than the value of GDP

**capital consumption allowance:** the estimated value of depreciation plus the value of accidental damage to capital stock

**depreciation:** a reduction in value of capital goods over time due to their use in production

$$GDP = C + I + G + X$$

measured as income. Depreciation is a kind of resource payment, part of the total payment to the owners of capital. All of the income categories—wages, interest, rent, profits, and capital consumption allowance—are expenses incurred in the production of output.

**Indirect business taxes,** like capital consumption allowances, are not payments to a factor of production. They are taxes collected by businesses that then are turned over to the government. Both excise taxes and sales taxes are forms of indirect business taxes.

For example, suppose a motel room in Florida costs $80 a night. A consumer would be charged $90. Of that $90, the motel receives $80 as the value of the service sold; the other $10 is an excise tax. The motel cannot keep the $10; it must turn it over to the state government. (In effect, the motel is acting as the government's tax collector.) The consumer spends $90; the motel earns $80. To balance expenditures and income, we have to allocate the $10 difference to indirect business taxes.

To summarize, GDP measured as income includes the four payments to the factors of production: wages, interest, rent, and profits. These income items represent expenses incurred in the production of GDP. From these we must subtract net factor income from abroad in order for the total to sum to GDP. Along with these payments are two nonincome items: capital consumption allowance and indirect business taxes.

$$\text{GDP} = \text{wages} + \text{interest} + \text{rent} + \text{profits} - \text{net factor income from abroad} + \text{capital consumption allowance} + \text{indirect business taxes}$$

The GDP is the total value of output produced in a year, the total value of expenditures made to purchase that output, and the total value of income received by the factors of production. Because all three are measures of the same thing—GDP—all must be equal.

## 1.b. Other Measures of Output and Income

The GDP is the most common measure of a nation's output, but it is not the only measure. Economists rely on a number of others in analyzing the performance of components of an economy.

### 1.b.1. Gross National Product

Gross national product (GNP) equals GDP plus receipts of factor income from the rest of the world minus payments of factor income to the rest of the world. If we add to GDP the value of income earned by U.S. residents from factors of production located outside the United States and subtract the value of income earned by foreign residents from factors of production located inside the United States, we have a measure of the value of output produced by U.S.-owned resources—GNP.

Figure 2 shows the national income accounts in the United States in 2003. The figure begins with the GDP and then shows the calculations necessary to obtain the GNP and other measures of national output. In 2003, the U.S. GNP was $11,031.6 billion.

### 1.b.2. Net National Product

Net national product (NNP) equals GNP minus capital consumption allowance. The NNP measures the value of goods and services produced in a year less the value of capital goods that became obsolete or were used up during the year. Because the NNP includes only net additions to a nation's capital, it is a better measure of the expansion or contraction of current output than is GNP. Remember how we defined GDP in terms of expenditures in section 1.a.2:

$$\text{GDP} = \text{consumption} + \text{investment} + \text{government spending} + \text{net exports}$$

Figure 2

## U.S. National Income Accounts, 2003 (billion dollars)

Gross domestic product plus receipts of factor income from the rest of the world minus payments of factor income to the rest of the world equals gross national product. Gross national product minus capital consumption allowance equals net national product. Net national product minus indirect business taxes equals national income. National income plus income currently received but not earned (transfer payments, personal interest, dividend income) minus income currently earned but not received (corporate profits, net interest, social security taxes) equals personal income. Personal income minus personal taxes equals disposable personal income.

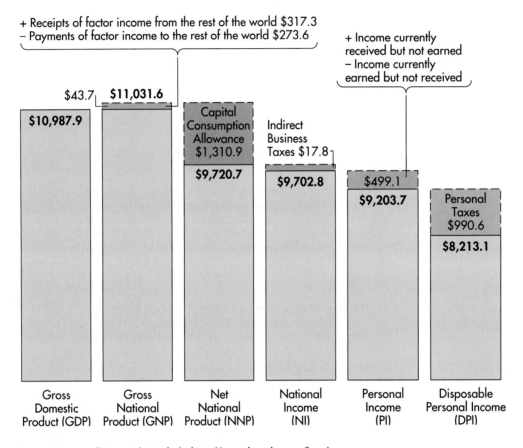

*Source:* Bureau of Economic Analysis, http://www.bea.doc.gov/bea/.

**gross investment:** total investment, including investment expenditures required to replace capital goods consumed in current production

**net investment:** gross investment minus capital consumption allowance

The investment measure in GDP (and GNP) is called **gross investment.** Gross investment is total investment, which includes investment expenditures required to replace capital goods consumed in current production. The NNP does not include investment expenditures required to replace worn-out capital goods; it includes only net investment. **Net investment** is equal to gross investment minus capital consumption allowance. Net investment measures business spending over and above that required to replace worn-out capital goods.

Figure 2 shows that in 2003, the U.S. NNP was $9,720.7 billion. This means that the U.S. economy produced well over $9 trillion worth of goods and services above those required to replace capital stock that had depreciated. Over $1,310 billion in capital was "worn out" in 2003.

**national income (NI):** net national product minus indirect business taxes

**1.b.3. National Income** National income (NI) equals the NNP minus indirect business taxes, plus or minus a couple of other small adjustments. NI captures the costs of the factors of production used in producing output. Remember that GDP

All final goods and services produced in a year are counted in GDP. For instance, the value of a vacation trip to the Grand Canyon would count as part of the national output of the United States. This would include the cost of lodging, transportation, and expenditures on food and activities.

includes two nonincome expense items: capital consumption allowance and indirect business taxes (section 1.a.3). Subtracting both of these items from the GDP leaves the income payments that actually go to resources.

Because the NNP equals the GNP minus capital consumption allowance, we can subtract indirect business taxes from the NNP to find NI, as shown in Figure 2. This measure helps economists analyze how the costs of (or payments received by) resources change.

### 1.b.4. Personal Income

**personal income (PI):** national income plus income currently received but not earned, minus income currently earned but not received

**Personal Income** Personal income (PI) is national income adjusted for income that is received but not earned in the current year and income that is earned but not received in the current year. Social security and welfare benefits are examples of income that is received but not earned in the current year. As you learned in Chapter 9, they are called transfer payments. An example of income that is currently earned but not received is profits that are retained by a corporation to finance current needs rather than paid out to stockholders. Another is social security (FICA) taxes, which are deducted from workers' paychecks.

### 1.b.5. Disposable Personal Income

**disposable personal income (DPI):** personal income minus personal taxes

**Disposable Personal Income** Disposable personal income (DPI) equals personal income minus personal taxes—income taxes, excise and real estate taxes on personal property, and other personal taxes. The DPI is the income that individuals have at their disposal for spending or saving. The sum of consumption spending plus saving must equal disposable personal income.

RECAP

1. Gross domestic product (GDP) is the market value of all final goods and services produced in an economy in a year.

2. GDP can be calculated by summing the market value of all final goods and services produced in a year, by summing the value added at each stage of production, by adding total expenditures on goods and services (GDP = consumption + investment + government spending + net exports), and by using

Use the following information
to find the value of:
a. GDP    d. NI
b. GNP    e. PI
c. NNP    f. DPI

| Consumption | $600 |
| Gross investment | $100 |
| Government spending | $200 |
| Net exports | $100 |
| Income earned but not received | $ 20 |
| Income received but not earned | $ 30 |
| Personal taxes | $200 |
| Capital consumption allowance | $230 |
| Receipts of factor income from the rest of the world | $ 50 |
| Payments of factor income to the rest of the world | $ 50 |
| Indirect business taxes | $ 90 |

the total income earned in the production of goods and services (GDP = wages + interest + rent + profits), subtracting net factor income from abroad, and adding depreciation and indirect business taxes.

3. Other measures of output and income include gross national product (GNP), net national product (NNP), national income (NI), personal income (PI), and disposable personal income (DPI).

**National Income Accounts**

GDP = consumption + investment + government spending
      + net exports

GNP = GDP + receipts of factor income from the rest of the world
      − payments of factor income to the rest of the world

NNP = GNP − capital consumption allowance

NI  = NNP − indirect business taxes

PI  = NI − income earned but not received
      + income received but not earned

DPI = PI − personal taxes

## 2. NOMINAL AND REAL MEASURES

The GDP is the market value of all final goods and services produced within a country in a year. Value is measured in money terms, so the U.S. GDP is reported in dollars, the German GDP in euros, the Mexican GDP in pesos, and so on. Market value is the product of two elements: the money price and the quantity produced.

### 2.a. Nominal and Real GDP

**nominal GDP:** a measure of national output based on the current prices of goods and services

**real GDP:** a measure of the quantity of final goods and services produced, obtained by eliminating the influence of price changes from the nominal GDP statistics

**Nominal GDP** measures output in terms of its current dollar value. **Real GDP** is adjusted for changing price levels. In 1980, the nominal U.S. GDP was $2,796 billion; in 2000, it was $9,872.9 billion—an increase of 250 percent. Does this mean that the United States produced 250 percent more goods and services in 2000 than it did in 1980? If the numbers reported are for nominal GDP, we cannot be sure. Nominal GDP cannot tell us whether the economy produced more goods and services because nominal GDP changes when prices change *and* when quantity changes.

Real GDP measures output in constant prices. This allows economists to identify the changes in actual production of final goods and services: real GDP measures the quantity of goods and services produced after eliminating the influence of price changes contained in nominal GDP. In 1980, real GDP in the United States was $4,901 billion; in 2000, it was $9,224 billion, an increase of 88 percent. The 250 percent increase in nominal GDP in large part reflects increased prices, not increased output.

Since we prefer more goods and services to higher prices, it is better to have nominal GDP rise because of higher output than because of higher prices. We want nominal GDP to increase as a result of an increase in real GDP.

Consider a simple example that illustrates the difference between nominal GDP and real GDP. Suppose a hypothetical economy produces just three goods: oranges, coconuts, and pizzas. The dollar value of output in three different years is listed in the table in Figure 3.

As shown in Figure 3, in year 1, 100 oranges were produced at $.50 per orange, 300 coconuts at $1 per coconut, and 2,000 pizzas at $8 per pizza. The total dollar value of output in year 1 was $16,350. In year 2, prices are constant at the year 1

**2. What is the difference between nominal and real GDP?**

Figure 3

**Prices and Quantities in a Hypothetical Economy**

In year 1, total output was $16,350. In year 2, prices remained constant but quantities produced increased by 10 percent, resulting in a higher output of $17,985. With prices constant, we can say that both nominal GDP and real GDP increased from year 1 to year 2. In year 3, quantities produced remained constant but prices increased by 10 percent, resulting in the same increased output as in year 2, $17,985. Production did not change from year 1 to year 3, however, so though nominal GDP increased, real GDP remained constant.

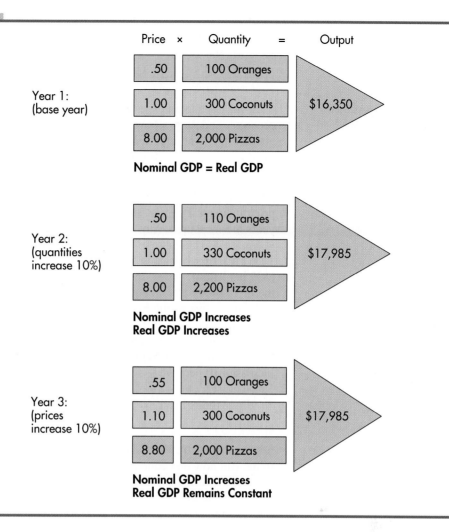

values, but the quantity of each good has increased by 10 percent. The dollar value of output in year 2 is $17,985, 10 percent higher than the value of output in year 1. In year 3, the quantity of each good is back at the year 1 level, but prices have increased by 10 percent. Oranges now cost $.55, coconuts $1.10, and pizzas $8.80. The dollar value of output in year 3 is $17,985.

Notice that in years 2 and 3, the dollar value of output ($17,985) is 10 percent higher than it was in year 1. But there is a difference here. In year 2, the increase in the dollar value of output is due entirely to an increase in the production of the three goods. In year 3, the increase is due entirely to an increase in the prices of the goods.

Because prices did not change between years 1 and 2, the increase in nominal GDP is entirely accounted for by an increase in real output, or real GDP. In years 1 and 3, the actual quantities produced did not change, which means that real GDP was constant; only nominal GDP was higher, a product only of higher prices.

## 2.b. Price Indexes

**3. What is the purpose of a price index?**

The total dollar value of output or income is equal to price multiplied by the quantity of goods and services produced:

$$\text{Dollar value of output} = \text{price} \times \text{quantity}$$

By dividing the dollar value of output by price, you can determine the quantity of goods and services produced:

$$\text{Quantity} = \frac{\text{dollar value of output}}{\text{price}}$$

In macroeconomics, a **price index** measures the average level of prices in an economy and shows how prices, on average, have changed. Prices of individual goods can rise and fall relative to one another, but a price index shows the general trend in prices across the economy.

**price index:** a measure of the average price level in an economy

### 2.b.1. Base Year

The example in Figure 3 provides a simple introduction to price indexes. The first step is to pick a **base year,** the year against which other years are measured. Any year can serve as the base year. Suppose we pick year 1 in Figure 3. The value of the price index in year 1, the base year, is defined to be 100. This simply means that prices in year 1 are 100 percent of prices in year 1 (100 percent of 1 is 1). In the example, year 2 prices are equal to year 1 prices, so the price index also is equal to 100 in year 2. In year 3, every price has risen 10 percent relative to the base-year (year 1) prices, so the price index is 10 percent higher in year 3, or 110. The value of the price index in any particular year indicates how prices have changed relative to the base year. A value of 110 indicates that prices are 110 percent of base-year prices, or that the average price level has increased 10 percent.

**base year:** the year against which other years are measured

Price index in any year = 100 +/− percentage change in base-year prices

### 2.b.2. Types of Price Indexes

The price of a single good is easy to determine. But how do economists determine a single measure of the prices of the millions of goods and services produced in an economy? They have constructed price indexes to measure the price level; there are several different price indexes used to measure the price level in any economy. Not all prices rise or fall at the same time or by the same amount. This is why there are several measures of the price level in an economy.

The price index used to estimate constant dollar real GDP is the **GDP price index (GDPPI),** a measure of prices across the economy that reflects all of the categories of goods and services included in GDP. The GDPPI is a very broad measure. Economists use other price indexes to analyze how prices change in more specific categories of goods and services.

**GDP price index (GDPPI):** a broad measure of the prices of goods and services included in the gross domestic product

Probably the best-known price index is the **consumer price index (CPI).** The CPI measures the average price of consumer goods and services that a typical household purchases. The CPI is a narrower measure than the GDPPI because it includes fewer items. However, because of the relevance of consumer prices to the standard of living, news reports on price changes in the economy typically focus on consumer price changes. In addition, labor contracts sometimes include provisions that raise wages as the CPI goes up. Social security payments also are tied to increases in the CPI. These increases are called **cost of living adjustments (COLAs)** because they are supposed to keep nominal income rising along with the cost of items purchased by the typical household.

**consumer price index (CPI):** a measure of the average price of goods and services purchased by the typical household

**cost of living adjustment (COLA):** an increase in wages that is designed to match increases in the prices of items purchased by the typical household

**producer price index (PPI):** a measure of average prices received by producers

The **producer price index (PPI)** measures average prices received by producers. At one time this price index was known as the *wholesale price index (WPI).* Because the PPI measures price changes at an earlier stage of production than the CPI, it can indicate a coming change in the CPI. If producer input costs are rising, we can expect the price of goods produced to go up as well.

Figure 4 illustrates how the three different measures of prices have changed over time. Notice that the PPI is more volatile than the GDPPI or the CPI. This is

Figure 4

**The GDP Price Index, the CPI, and the PPI**

The graph plots the annual percentage change in the GDP price index (GDPPI), the consumer price index (CPI), and the producer price index (PPI). The GDPPI is used to construct constant dollar real GDP. The CPI measures the average price of consumer goods and services that a typical household purchases. The PPI measures the average price received by producers; it is the most variable of the three because fluctuations in equilibrium prices of intermediate goods are much greater than for final goods.

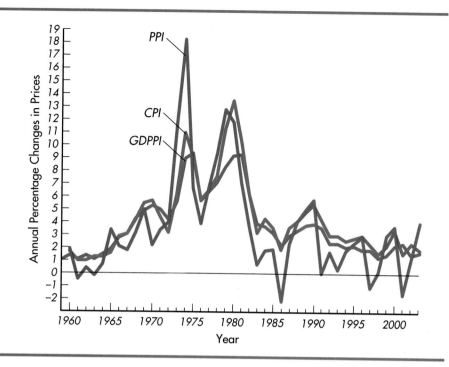

because there are smaller fluctuations in the equilibrium prices of final goods than in those of intermediate goods.

RECAP

1. Nominal GDP is measured using current dollars.
2. Real GDP measures output with price effects removed.
3. The GDP price index, the consumer price index, and the producer price index are all measures of the level of prices in an economy.

## 3. FLOWS OF INCOME AND EXPENDITURES

The GDP is both a measure of total expenditures on final goods and services and a measure of the total income earned in the production of those goods and services. The idea that total expenditures equal total income is clearly illustrated in the circular flow diagram of Chapter 9.

The figure links the four sectors of the economy: households, firms, government, and foreign countries. The arrows between the sectors indicate the direction of the flows. The money flows are both income and expenditures. Because one sector's expenditures represent another sector's income, the total expenditures on goods and services must be the same as the total income from selling goods and services, and those must both be equal to the total value of the goods and services produced.

RECAP

1. Total spending on final goods and services equals the total income received in producing those goods and services.
2. The circular flow model shows that one sector's expenditures represent other sectors' incomes.

# 4. THE FOREIGN EXCHANGE MARKET

**foreign exchange:** currency and bank deposits that are denominated in foreign money

**foreign exchange market:** a global market in which people trade one currency for another

**4. How is money traded internationally?**

**Foreign exchange** is foreign money, including paper money and bank deposits like checking accounts that are denominated in foreign currency. When someone with U.S. dollars wants to trade those dollars for Japanese yen, the trade takes place in the **foreign exchange market,** a global market in which people trade one currency for another. Many financial markets are located in a specific geographic location. For instance, the New York Stock Exchange is a specific location in New York City where stocks are bought and sold. The Commodity Exchange is a specific location in New York City where contracts to deliver agricultural and metal commodities are bought and sold. The foreign exchange market is not in a single geographic location, however. Trading occurs all over the world by telephone or electronically. Most of the activity involves large banks in New York, London, and other financial centers. A foreign exchange trader at Bank of America in New York can buy or sell currencies with a trader at Barclays Bank in London by electronic or telephone communication.

Only tourism and a few other transactions in the foreign exchange market involve the actual movement of currency. The great majority of transactions involve the buying and selling of bank deposits denominated in foreign currency. Currency notes, like dollar bills, are used in a relatively small fraction of transactions. When a large corporation or a government buys foreign currency, it buys a bank deposit denominated in the foreign currency. Still, all exchanges in the market require that monies have a price.

## 4.a. Exchange Rates

An exchange rate is the price of one country's money in terms of another country's money. Exchange rates are needed to compare prices quoted in two different currencies. Suppose a shirt that has been manufactured in Canada sells for 20 U.S. dollars in Seattle, Washington, and for 25 Canadian dollars in Vancouver, British Columbia. Where would you get the better buy? Unless you know the exchange rate between U.S. and Canadian dollars, you can't tell. The exchange rate allows you to convert the foreign currency price into its domestic currency equivalent, which then can be compared to the domestic price.

Table 1 lists exchange rates for April 5, 2004. The rates are quoted in U.S. dollars per unit of foreign currency in the second column, and in units of foreign currency per U.S. dollar in the last column. For instance, the Canadian dollar was selling for $.7606, or a little more than 76 U.S. cents. The same day, the U.S. dollar was selling for 1.3147 Canadian dollars (1 U.S. dollar would buy 1.3147 Canadian dollars).

If you know the price in U.S. dollars of a currency, you can find the price of the U.S. dollar in that currency by taking the reciprocal. To find the reciprocal of a number, write it as a fraction and then turn the fraction upside down. Let's say that 1 British pound sells for 2 U.S. dollars. In fraction form, 2 is 2/1. The reciprocal of 2/1 is 1/2, or .5. So 1 U.S. dollar sells for .5 British pounds. The table shows that the actual dollar price of the pound was 1.8143. The *reciprocal exchange rate*—the number of pounds per dollar—is .5512 (1/1.8143), which was the pound price of 1 dollar that day.

Let's go back to comparing the price of the Canadian shirt in Seattle and Vancouver. The symbol for the U.S. dollar is $. The symbol for the Canadian dollar is C$. The shirt sells for $20 in Seattle and C$25 in Vancouver. Suppose the exchange rate between the U.S. dollar and the Canadian dollar is .8. This means that C$1 costs $0.80.

To find the domestic currency value of a foreign currency price, multiply the foreign currency price by the exchange rate:

$$\text{Domestic currency value} = \text{foreign currency price} \times \text{exchange rate}$$

| Country | U.S. $ per Currency | Currency per U.S. $ |
|---|---|---|
| Argentina (peso) | 0.3494 | 2.8494 |
| Australia (dollar) | 0.7530 | 1.3280 |
| Britain (pound) | 1.8143 | 0.5512 |
| Canada (dollar) | 0.7606 | 1.3147 |
| China (renminbi) | 0.1208 | 8.2790 |
| European (euro) | 1.2009 | 0.8327 |
| Japan (yen) | 0.0095 | 105.34 |
| Mexico (peso) | 0.0897 | 11.154 |
| New Zealand (dollar) | 0.6500 | 1.5386 |
| Russia (ruble) | 0.0350 | 28.543 |
| Singapore (dollar) | 0.5949 | 1.6810 |
| Switzerland (franc) | 0.7663 | 1.3049 |

**Table 1**

**Exchange Rates
April 5, 2004**

Source: Bank of Canada, "Exchange Rates," April 5, 2004, http://www.bank-banque-canada.ca/. Copyright © 2004, Bank of Canada. Reprinted with permission.

In our example, the U.S. dollar is the domestic currency:

$$\text{U.S. dollar value} = \text{C\$25} \times 0.8 = \$20$$

If we multiply the price of the shirt in Canadian dollars (C$25) by the exchange rate (0.8), we find the U.S. dollar value ($20). After adjusting for the exchange rate, then, we can see that the shirt sells for the same price when the price is measured in a single currency.

## 4.b. Exchange Rate Changes and International Trade

Because exchange rates determine the domestic currency value of foreign goods, changes in those rates affect the demand for and supply of goods traded internationally. Suppose the price of the shirt in Seattle and in Vancouver remains the same, but the exchange rate changes from .8 to .9 U.S. dollars per Canadian dollar. What happens? The U.S. dollar price of the shirt in Vancouver increases. At the new rate, the shirt that sells for C$25 in Vancouver costs a U.S. buyer $22.50 (C$25 × 0.9).

A rise in the value of a currency is called *appreciation*. In our example, as the exchange rate moves from $.8 = C$1 to $.9 = C$1, the Canadian dollar appreciates against the U.S. dollar. As a country's currency appreciates, international demand for its products falls, other things equal.

Suppose the exchange rate in our example moves from $.8 = C$1 to $.7 = C$1. Now the shirt that sells for C$25 in Vancouver costs a U.S. buyer $17.50 (C$25 × 0.7). In this case the Canadian dollar has *depreciated* in value relative to the U.S. dollar. As a country's currency depreciates, its goods sell for lower prices in other countries and the demand for its products increases, other things remaining equal.

When the Canadian dollar is appreciating against the U.S. dollar, the U.S. dollar must be depreciating against the Canadian dollar. For instance, when the exchange rate between the U.S. dollar and the Canadian dollar moves from $.8 = C$1 to $.9 = C$1, the reciprocal exchange rate—the rate between the Canadian dollar and the U.S. dollar—moves from C$1.25 = $1 (1/.8 = 1.25) to C$1.11 = $1 (1/0.9 = 1.11). At the same time that Canadian goods are becoming more expensive to U.S. buyers, U.S. goods are becoming cheaper to Canadian buyers.

## 5. THE BALANCE OF PAYMENTS

**5. How do nations record their transactions with the rest of the world?**

**balance of payments:** a record of a country's trade in goods, services, and financial assets with the rest of the world

The U.S. economy does not operate in a vacuum. It affects and is affected by the economies of other nations. This point was brought home to Americans in recent years as newspaper headlines announced the latest trade deficit, and politicians denounced foreign countries for running trade surpluses against the United States. It seemed as if everywhere there was talk of the balance of payments.

The **balance of payments** is a record of a country's trade in goods, services, and financial assets with the rest of the world. This record is divided into categories, or accounts, that summarize the nation's international economic transactions. For example, one category measures transactions in merchandise; another measures transactions involving financial assets (bank deposits, bonds, stocks, loans). These accounts distinguish between private transactions (by individuals and businesses) and official transactions (by governments). Balance of payments data are reported quarterly for most developed countries.

### 5.a. Balance of Payments Accounts

**current account:** the sum of the merchandise, services, investment income, and unilateral transfers accounts in the balance of payments

The balance of payments uses several different accounts to classify transactions (Table 2). The **current account** is the sum of the balances in the merchandise, services, investment income, and unilateral transfers accounts.

**balance of trade:** the balance on the merchandise account in a nation's balance of payments

*Merchandise*    This account records all transactions involving goods. U.S. exports of goods bring money into the country for U.S. exporters. U.S. imports of foreign goods require payments to foreign sellers. When exports exceed imports, the merchandise account shows a surplus. When imports exceed exports, the account shows a deficit. The balance on the merchandise account is frequently referred to as the **balance of trade.**

Table 2

**Simplified U.S. Balance of Payments, 2003 (millions of dollars)**

| Account | Net Balance |
| --- | --- |
| Merchandise | $ − 549,409 |
| Services | $ 59,245 |
| Investment income | $ 16,625 |
| Unilateral transfers | $ − 68,291 |
| **Current account** | $ − 541,830 |
| **Financial account** | $ 575,906 |
| Statistical discrepancy | $ − 34,076 |

*Source:* Data from Bureau of Economic Analysis, http://www.bea.doc.gov/bea/.

In 2003, the merchandise account in the U.S. balance of payments showed a deficit of $549,409 million. In other words, the United States bought more goods from other nations than it sold to them.

*Services*　This account measures trade involving services. It includes travel and tourism, royalties, transportation costs, and insurance premiums. In 2003, the balance on the services account was a $59,245 million surplus.

*Investment Income*　The income earned from investments in foreign countries brings money into the United States; the income paid on foreign-owned investments in the United States takes money out of the United States. Investment income is the return on a special kind of service: it is the value of services provided by capital in foreign countries. In 2003, there was a surplus of $16,625 million in the investment income account.

*Unilateral Transfers*　In a unilateral transfer, one party gives something but gets nothing in return. Gifts and retirement pensions are forms of unilateral transfers. For instance, if a farmworker in El Centro, California, sends money to his family in Guaymas, Mexico, this is a unilateral transfer from the United States to Mexico. In 2003, that unilateral transfers balance was a deficit of $68,291.

The current account is a useful measure of international transactions because it contains all of the activities involving goods and services. The **financial account** is where trade involving financial assets and international investment is recorded. In 2003, the current account showed a deficit of $541,830 million. This means that U.S. imports of merchandise, services, investment income, and unilateral transfers were $541,830 million greater than exports of these items.

If we draw a line in the balance of payments under the current account, then all entries below the line relate to financing the movement of merchandise, services, investment income, and unilateral transfers into and out of the country. Financial account transactions include bank deposits, purchases of stocks and bonds, loans, land purchases, and purchases of business firms. Inflows of money associated with the U.S. financial account reflect foreign purchases of U.S. financial assets or real property like land and buildings, and outflows of money reflect U.S. purchases of foreign financial assets and real property. In 2003, the U.S. financial account showed a surplus of $575,906 million.

**financial account:** the record in the balance of payments of the flow of financial assets into and out of a country

The *statistical discrepancy* account, the last account listed in Table 2, could be called *omissions and errors*. Government cannot accurately measure all transactions that take place. Some international shipments of goods and services go uncounted or are miscounted, as are some international flows of capital. The statistical discrepancy account is used to correct for these omissions and errors. In 2003, measured surpluses exceeded measured deficits, so the statistical discrepancy was −$34,076 million.

Over all of the balance of payments accounts, the sum of surplus accounts must equal the sum of deficit accounts. The bottom line—the *net balance*—must be zero. It cannot show a surplus or a deficit. When people talk about a surplus or a deficit in the balance of payments, they actually are talking about a surplus or a deficit in one of the balance of payments accounts. The balance of payments itself, by definition, is always in balance.

## 5.b. The Current Account and the Financial Account

The current account reflects the movement of goods and services into and out of a country. The financial account reflects the flow of financial assets into and out of a country. In Table 2, the current account shows a deficit balance of $541,830 million. Remember that the balance of payments must *balance*. If there is a deficit in the current account, there must be a surplus in the financial account that offsets that deficit.

What is important here is not the bookkeeping process, the concept that the balance of payments must balance, but rather the meaning of deficits and surpluses in the current and financial accounts. These deficits and surpluses tell us whether a country is a net borrower from or lender to the rest of the world. A deficit in the current account means that a country is running a net surplus in its financial account. And it signals that a country is a net borrower from the rest of the world. A country that is running a current account deficit must borrow from abroad an amount sufficient to finance that deficit. A financial account surplus is achieved by selling more bonds and other debts of the domestic country to the rest of the world than the country buys from the rest of the world.

Figure 5 shows the current account balance in the United States for each year from 1960 to 2003. The United States experienced large current account deficits in

**Figure 5**

**The U.S. Current Account Balance, 1960–2003**

The current account of the balance of payments is the sum of the balances in the merchandise, services, investment income, and unilateral transfers accounts.

the 1980s and then again in the late 1990s and 2000s. Such deficits indicate that the United States consumed more than it produced. Remember that in section 1.a.2 of this chapter GDP is equal to total expenditures, or $GDP = C + I + G + X$, where $X$ is net exports. A country with a current account deficit will have negative net exports. Rewriting the total spending equation as $X = GDP - C - I - G$, a negative $X$ means that domestic spending, $C + I + G$, must be greater than domestic production, GDP. This means that the United States sold financial assets and borrowed large amounts of money from foreign residents to finance its current account deficits. This large foreign borrowing made the United States the largest debtor in the world. A *net debtor* owes more to the rest of the world than it is owed; a *net creditor* is owed more than it owes. The United States was an international net creditor from the end of World War I until the mid-1980s. The country financed its large current account deficits in the 1980s by borrowing from the rest of the world. As a result of this accumulated borrowing, in 1985 the United States became an international net debtor for the first time in almost 70 years. Since that time, the net debtor status of the United States has grown steadily.

RECAP

1. The balance of payments is a record of a nation's international transactions.
2. The current account is the sum of the balances in the merchandise, services, investment income, and unilateral transfers accounts.
3. A surplus exists when money inflows exceed outflows; a deficit exists when money inflows are less than outflows.
4. The financial account is where the transactions necessary to finance the movement of merchandise, services, investment income, and unilateral transfers into and out of the country are recorded.
5. The net balance in the balance of payments must be zero.
6. A deficit in the current account must be offset by a surplus in the financial account. It also indicates that the nation is a net borrower.

## SUMMARY

### ? How is the total output of an economy measured?

1. National income accounting is the system economists use to measure both the output of an economy and the flows between sectors of that economy.
2. Gross domestic product (GDP) is the market value of all final goods and services produced in a year in a country.
3. The GDP also equals the value added at each stage of production.
4. The GDP as output equals the sum of the output of households, business firms, and government within the country.
5. The GDP as expenditures equals the sum of consumption plus investment plus government spending plus net exports.
6. The GDP as income equals the sum of wages, interest, rent, profits, proprietors' income, capital consumption allowance, and indirect business taxes less net factor income from abroad.

7. Other measures of national output include gross national product (GNP), net national product (NNP), national income (NI), personal income (PI), and disposable personal income (DPI).

### ? What is the difference between nominal and real GDP?

8. Nominal GDP measures output in terms of its current dollar values including the effects of price changes; real GDP measures output after eliminating the effects of price changes.

### ? What is the purpose of a price index?

9. A price index measures the average level of prices across an economy.

10. Total expenditures on final goods and services equal total income.

### ? How is money traded internationally?

11. Foreign exchange is currency and bank deposits that are denominated in foreign currency.

12. The foreign exchange market is a global market in which people trade one currency for another.

13. Exchange rates, the price of one country's money in terms of another country's money, are necessary to compare prices quoted in different currencies.

14. The value of a good in a domestic currency equals the foreign currency price times the exchange rate.

15. When a domestic currency appreciates, domestic goods become more expensive to foreigners, and foreign goods become cheaper to domestic residents.

16. When a domestic currency depreciates, domestic goods become cheaper to foreigners, and foreign goods become more expensive to domestic residents.

### ? How do nations record their transactions with the rest of the world?

17. The balance of payments is a record of a nation's transactions with the rest of the world.

18. The current account is the sum of the balances in the merchandise, services, investment income, and unilateral transfers accounts.

19. The financial account reflects the transactions necessary to finance the movement of merchandise, services, investment income, and unilateral transfers into and out of the country.

20. A deficit in the current account must be offset by a surplus in the financial account.

## KEY TERMS

national income accounting

gross domestic product (GDP)

intermediate goods

value added

inventory

capital consumption allowance

depreciation

indirect business taxes

gross national product (GNP)

net national product (NNP)

gross investment

net investment

national income (NI)

personal income (PI)

disposable personal income (DPI)

nominal GDP

real GDP

price index

base year

GDP price index

consumer price index (CPI)

cost of living adjustment (COLA)

producer price index (PPI)

foreign exchange

foreign exchange market

balance of payments

current account

balance of trade

financial account

## EXERCISES

1. The following table lists the stages required in the production of a personal computer. What is the value of the computer in the GDP?

| Stage | Value Added |
|---|---|
| Components manufacture | $ 50 |
| Assembly | 250 |
| Wholesaler | 500 |
| Retailer | 1,500 |

2. What is the difference between GDP and each of the following?
   a. Gross national product
   b. Net national product
   c. National income
   d. Personal income
   e. Disposable personal income

Use the following national income accounting information to do exercises 3–7:

| | |
|---|---|
| Consumption | $400 |
| Imports | 10 |
| Net investment | 20 |
| Government purchases | 100 |
| Exports | 20 |
| Capital consumption allowance | 20 |
| Indirect business taxes | 5 |
| Receipts of factor income from the rest of the world | 12 |
| Payments of factor income to the rest of the world | 10 |

3. What is the GDP for this economy?

4. What is the GNP for this economy?

5. What is the NNP for this economy?

6. What is the national income for this economy?

7. What is the gross investment in this economy?

8. Why has nominal GDP increased faster than real GDP in the United States over time? What would it mean if an economy had real GDP increasing faster than nominal GDP?

9. If a surfboard is produced this year but not sold until next year, how is it counted in this year's GDP and not next year's?

10. What is the price of 1 U.S. dollar in terms of each of the following currencies, given the following exchange rates?
    a. 1 European euro = $.95
    b. 1 Chinese yuan = $.12
    c. 1 Israeli shekel = $.30
    d. 1 Kuwaiti dinar = $3.20

11. A bicycle manufactured in the United States costs $100. Using the exchange rates listed in Table 1, what would the bicycle cost in the currency of each of the following countries?
    a. Argentina
    b. Britain
    c. Canada

12. The U.S. dollar price of a Swedish krona changes from $.1572 to $.1730.
    a. Has the dollar depreciated or appreciated against the krona?
    b. Has the krona appreciated or depreciated against the dollar?

Use the information in the following table on Mexico's international transactions to do exercises 13–15 (the amounts are the U.S. dollar values in millions):

| | |
|---|---|
| Merchandise imports | $96,000 |
| Merchandise exports | 89,469 |
| Services exports | 10,901 |
| Services imports | 10,819 |
| Investment income receipts | 4,032 |
| Investment income payments | 17,099 |
| Unilateral transfers | 4,531 |

13. What is the balance of trade?

14. What is the current account?

15. Did Mexico become a larger international net debtor during this period?

16. If the U.S. dollar appreciated against the euro, what would you expect to happen to U.S. net exports with Germany?

17. Suppose the U.S. dollar price of a British pound is $1.50; the dollar price of a euro is $.90; a hotel room in London, England, costs 120 British pounds; and a comparable hotel room in Hanover, Germany, costs 220 euros.
    a. Which hotel room is cheaper to a U.S. tourist?
    b. What is the exchange rate between the euro and the British pound?

18. Use the national income accounting definition $GDP = C + I + G + X$ to explain what a current account deficit (negative net exports) means in terms of domestic spending, production, and borrowing.

## Internet Exercise

Use the Internet to explore why the CPI doesn't always match an individual's experience with inflation.

Go to the Boyes/Melvin, *Fundamentals of Economics* website accessible through **http://college.hmco.com** and click on the Internet Exercise link for Chapter 10. Now answer the questions found on the Boyes/Melvin website.

## Key Term Match

**Match each term with its correct definition by placing the appropriate letter next to the corresponding number.**

A. national income accounting
B. gross domestic product (GDP)
C. intermediate goods
D. value added
E. inventory
F. capital consumption allowance
G. depreciation
H. indirect business taxes
I. gross national product (GNP)
J. net national product (NNP)
K. gross investment
L. net investment
M. national income
N. personal income

O. disposable personal income
P. nominal GDP
Q. real GDP
R. price index
S. base year
T. GDP price index
U. consumer price index
V. cost of living adjustment
W. producer price index
X. foreign exchange
Y. foreign exchange market
Z. balance of payments
AA. current account
BB. balance of trade
CC. financial account

_____ 1. the difference between the value of the output and the value of the intermediate goods used in the production of that output

_____ 2. taxes that are collected by businesses for a government agency

_____ 3. a measure of the average price level in an economy

_____ 4. the stock of unsold goods held by a firm

_____ 5. national income plus income currently received but not earned, minus income currently earned but not received

_____ 6. a reduction in value of capital goods over time due to their use in production

_____ 7. gross domestic product plus receipts of factor income from the rest of the world minus payments of factor income to the rest of the world

_____ 8. currency and bank deposits that are denominated in foreign money

_____ 9. the sum of the merchandise, services, investment income, and unilateral transfers accounts in the balance of payments

_____10. the market value of all final goods and services produced in a year within a country

_____11. a measure of the quantity of final goods and services produced, obtained by eliminating the influence of price changes from the nominal GDP statistics

_____12. a measure of the average price of goods and services purchased by the typical household

_____13. gross national product minus capital consumption allowance

_____14. a global market in which people trade one currency for another

_____15. a measure of national output based on the current prices of goods and services

_____16. total investment, including investment expenditures required to replace capital goods consumed in current production

_____17. the balance on the merchandise account in a nation's balance of payments

_____18. a record of a country's trade in goods, services, and financial assets with the rest of the world

_____19. net national product minus indirect business taxes

_____20. the year against which other years are measured

_____21. the framework that summarizes and categorizes productive activity in an economy over a specific period of time, typically a year

_____22. an increase in wages that is designed to match increases in the prices of items purchased by the typical household

_____23. the estimated value of depreciation plus the value of accidental damage to capital stock

_____24. the record in the balance of payments of the flow of financial assets into and out of a country

_____25. goods that are used as inputs in the production of final goods and services

_____26. gross investment minus capital consumption allowance

_____27. personal income minus personal taxes

_____28. a broad measure of the prices of goods and services included in the gross domestic product

_____29. a measure of average prices received by producers

## Quick-Check Quiz

**1** Which of the following is counted in GDP?

   a. the value of homemaker services
   b. estimated illegal drug transactions
   c. the value of oil used in the production of gasoline
   d. estimated in-kind wages
   e. the sale of a used automatic dishwasher

**2** A price index equal to 90 in a given year

   a. indicates that prices were lower than prices in the base year.
   b. indicates that the year in question was a year previous to the base year.

c. indicates that prices were 10 percent higher than prices in the base year.

d. is inaccurate—price indexes cannot be lower than 100.

e. indicates that real GDP was lower than GDP in the base year.

**3** Social security payments are tied to the

a. GDP price index.

b. wholesale price index.

c. CPI.

d. nominal GDP.

e. PPI.

**4** The foreign exchange market, like the New York Stock Exchange, is located in a specific building in New York City. _____ (true or false?)

**5** Most foreign exchange transactions involve the movement of currency. _____ (true or false?)

**6** As a country's currency depreciates, international demand for its products _____ (rises, falls), all other things being equal.

**7** If the U.S. dollar drops to 1.1485 euros from 1.1598 euros, then the dollar has

a. appreciated against the euro, and the prices of European cars will increase in the United States.

b. appreciated against the euro, and the prices of European cars will decrease in the United States.

c. depreciated against the euro, and the prices of European cars will increase in the United States.

d. depreciated against the euro, and the prices of European cars will decrease in the United States.

e. depreciated against the euro, and the prices of American cars will increase in Europe.

**8** If a Japanese investor bought the Epic Center office building in Wichita, Kansas, the transaction would be recorded as a _____ in the _____ account.

a. credit; current

b. credit; financial

c. debit; current

d. debit; financial

e. credit; investment income

**9** A country with a deficit in its current account

a. exports more goods and services than it imports.

b. is running a deficit in its financial account.

c. is a net lender to the rest of the world.

d. is a net borrower from the rest of the world.

e. is running a surplus in its merchandise account.

**10** The net balance in the balance of payments

a. is positive if a country is a net creditor to the rest of the world.

b. is negative if a country imports more goods and services than it exports.

c. is negative if the country is a net debtor to the rest of the world.

d. is positive if a country exports more goods and services than it imports.

e. must be zero.

**11** Suppose the dollar ended at 1.4165 Swiss francs today, well above yesterday's 1.4045 francs.

a. The dollar has _____ (appreciated, depreciated) against the franc.

b. Swiss goods are now _____ (more expensive, cheaper) in the United States.

c. As a result of the change in exchange rates, U.S. exports to Switzerland will _____ (increase, decrease), all other things being equal.

**12** You read in the paper that the Finnish markka is expected to depreciate against the dollar. Therefore, the price of a Finnish sweater sold in the United States will _____ (increase, decrease), and the price of U.S. blue jeans sold in Finland will _____ (increase, decrease).

## Practice Questions and Problems

**1** List the three factors of production and the name of the payments each factor receives. What additional three items must be figured in to find gross domestic product?

_____

_____

_____

**2** A lei maker buys flowers from a nursery for $125. She makes 50 leis from the flowers and sells each lei for $3.99. What is the value added for the lei maker?

_____

3 A Kansas farmer sells wheat to a craftsperson to make into decorative ornaments. The farmer sells his wheat to the craftsperson for $300. The craftsperson adds labor, valued at $200, and some ribbons, valued at $50, and produces 110 ornaments. What is the final market value of each ornament? _____

4 Unplanned inventory _____ (is, is not) included in the GDP.

5 Write the formulas for the following:

Gross domestic product as expenditures (GDP):

_____

Gross domestic product as income (GDP):

_____

Gross national product (GNP): _____

Net national product (NNP): _____

National income (NI): _____

Personal income (PI): _____

Disposable personal income (DPI): _____

6 Use the following information to calculate GDP, GNP, NNP, and NI. All figures are in billions of dollars.

| | | | |
|---|---|---|---|
| Capital consumption allowance | 328 | Wages and salaries | 1,803 |
| | | Personal taxes | 398 |
| Corporate profits | 124 | Indirect business taxes | 273 |
| Rents | 6 | | |
| Interest | 264 | Proprietor's income | 248 |
| Net factor income from abroad | 43 | | |

GDP_____ GNP_____

NNP_____ NI_____

7 The following table shows nominal GDP and the implicit GDP deflator for three years. Use this information to calculate the real GDP and to answer the following questions.

| Year | Nominal GDP | Implicit GDP Deflator | Real GDP |
|---|---|---|---|
| 1 | 206 | 98 | _____ |
| 2 | 216 | 100 | _____ |
| 3 | 228 | 115 | _____ |

a. Which year is the base year? _____

b. Prices in year 3 were _____ (higher, lower) than prices in the base year.

c. During year 3, nominal GDP _____ (increased, did not change, decreased)

8 Why isn't nominal GDP a good measure of the strength or weakness of the economy? What measure would be better?

_____

_____

9 If the price index in the current year is 212, then prices have _____ (increased, not changed, decreased) by _____ percent from the base year.

10 What is the price of one U.S. dollar given the following exchange rates?

a. 1 Canadian dollar = $.86610
b. 1 euro = $.8707
c. 1 Japanese yen = $.00677
d. 1 British pound = $1.8155

11 A 35 mm camera manufactured in the United States costs $150. Using the exchange rates listed in the following table, what would the camera cost in each of the following countries?

| Country | U.S. Dollar Equivalent | Currency per U.S. Dollar |
|---|---|---|
| Euro area (euro) | .8707 | 1.1485 |
| Pakistan (rupee) | .0463 | 21.61 |
| Philippines (peso) | .04413 | 22.66 |

a. Euro area _____

b. Pakistan _____

c. Philippines _____

## Exercises and Applications

I **Understanding Price Indexes** Suppose the economy of Strandasville produces only four goods: CDs, pizza, desk chairs, and sweaters. The following tables show the dollar value of output for three different years.

| Year | Number of CDs | Price per CD | Number of Pizzas | Price per Pizza |
|---|---|---|---|---|
| 1 | 1,000 | $5 | 8,000 | $6.60 |
| 2 | 1,000 | $6 | 8,000 | $6.60 |
| 3 | 4,000 | $7 | 10,000 | $6.80 |

| Year | Number of Desk Chairs | Price per Chair | Number of Sweaters | Price per Sweater |
|---|---|---|---|---|
| 1 | 3,000 | $20 | 5,000 | $20 |
| 2 | 3,000 | $25 | 5,000 | $18 |
| 3 | 3,500 | $25 | 4,900 | $15 |

1. Calculate the total dollar value of output for year 1, year 2, and year 3.

_____

_____

2. The dollar value of output in year 2 is higher than the dollar value of output in year 1
   a. entirely because of price changes.
   b. entirely because of output changes.
   c. because of both price and output changes.

3. The dollar value of output in year 3 is higher than the dollar value of output in year 2
   a. entirely because of price changes.
   b. entirely because of output changes.
   c. because of both price and output changes.

**II  The Balance of Payments as an Indicator**  A surplus in the merchandise account means that a nation is exporting more goods than it is importing. This is often interpreted as a sign that a nation's producers can produce at a lower cost than their foreign counterparts. A trade deficit may indicate that a nation's producers are less efficient than their foreign counterparts.

Interpret these statements in terms of what you have read about the United States as the world's largest debtor nation. Can you explain why many analysts viewed the U.S. balance of payments accounts with concern in the mid-1990s?

_____

_____

_____

**III  The Balance of Payments and Exchange Rates**  If U.S. residents lend and invest less in foreign countries than foreigners lend and invest in the United States, the financial account will be in surplus. If U.S. purchases of foreign stocks and bonds exceed foreign purchases of U.S. stocks and bonds, then more funds are leaving the country than entering it, and the financial account will be in deficit. Pretend that you are willing to sell your DVD player to a French resident. Would you prefer to be paid in U.S. dollars or in euros? Since you can't easily spend euros in this country, you would prefer to be paid in U.S. dollars. Therefore, if the French buy more U.S. goods and services, they will need dollars to pay for them, and the dollar will appreciate against the euro. Similarly, if U.S. investors demand more French bonds and stocks, the euro will appreciate.

What impact will a financial account surplus have on domestic currency? If U.S. federal budget deficits continue, what will be the impact on the dollar?

_____

_____

Now that you've completed the Study Guide for this chapter, you should have a good sense of the concepts you need to review. If you'd like to test your understanding of the material again, go to the Practice Tests on the Boyes/Melvin *Fundamentals of Economics,* 3e website, **economics.college.hmco.com/students.**

## Chapter 11

# Unemployment, Inflation, and Business Cycles

1. What is a business cycle?
2. How is the unemployment rate defined and measured?
3. What is the cost of unemployed resources?
4. What is inflation?
5. Why is inflation a problem?

*Preview*

[I]f you were graduating from college today, what would your job prospects be? In 1932, they would have been bleak. A large number of people were out of work (about one in four workers), and a large number of firms had laid off workers or gone out of business. At any time, job opportunities depend not only on the individual's ability and experience but also on the current state of the economy.

All economies have cycles of activity: periods of expansion, when output and employment increase, followed by periods of contraction, when output and employment decrease. For instance, during the expansionary period of the 1990s, fewer than 5 percent of U.S. workers had no job by 1997. But during the period of contraction of 1981–1982, 9.5 percent of U.S. workers had no job. When the economy is growing, the demand for goods and services tends to increase. To produce those goods and services, firms hire more workers. Economic expansion also has an impact on inflation. As the demand for goods and services goes up, the prices of those goods and services also tend to rise. By the late 1990s, following several years of economic growth, consumer prices in the United States were rising by about 3 percent a year. During periods of contraction, as more people are out of work, demand for goods and services tends to fall, and there is less pressure for rising prices. During the period of the Great Depression in the 1930s in the United States, consumer prices fell by more than 5 percent in 1933. Both price increases and the fraction of workers without jobs are affected by business cycles in fairly regular ways. But their effects on individual standards of living, income, and purchasing power are much less predictable.

Why do certain events move in tandem? What are the links between unemployment and inflation? What causes the business cycle to behave as it does? What effect does government activity have on the business cycle and on unemployment and inflation? Who is harmed by rising unemployment and inflation? Who benefits? Macroeconomics attempts to answer all of these questions. ■

# 1. BUSINESS CYCLES

1. **What is a business cycle?**

In this chapter we describe the business cycle and examine measures of unemployment and inflation. We talk about the ways in which the business cycle, unemployment, and inflation are related. And we describe their effects on the participants in the economy.

The most widely used measure of a nation's output is gross domestic product. When we examine the value of real GDP over time, we find periods in which it rises and other periods in which it falls.

## 1.a. Definitions

**business cycle:** pattern of rising real GDP followed by falling real GDP

This pattern—real GDP rising, then falling—is called a **business cycle.** The pattern occurs over and over again, but as Figure 1 shows, the pattern over time is anything but regular. Historically the duration of business cycles and the rate at which real GDP rises or falls (indicated by the steepness of the line in Figure 1) vary considerably.

**recession:** a period in which real GDP falls

Looking at Figure 1, it is clear that the U.S. economy has experienced up-and-down swings in the years since 1959. Still, real GDP has grown at an average rate of approximately 3 percent per year. While it is important to recognize that periods of economic growth, or prosperity, are followed by periods of contraction, or **recession,** it is also important to recognize the presence of long-term economic growth; despite the presence of periodic recessions, in the long run the economy produces more goods and services. The long-run growth in the economy depends on the growth in productive resources, like land, labor, and capital, along with technological advances. Technological change increases the productivity of resources so that output increases even with a fixed amount of inputs. In recent years there has been concern about the growth rate of U.S. productivity and its effect on the long-run growth potential of the economy.

Figure 1

**U.S. Real GDP**

The shaded areas represent periods of economic contraction (recession). The table lists the dates of business-cycle peaks and troughs. The peak dates indicate when contractions began; the trough dates, when expansions began.

| Peaks | Troughs |
| --- | --- |
| April 1960 | February 1961 |
| December 1969 | November 1970 |
| November 1973 | March 1975 |
| January 1980 | July 1980 |
| July 1981 | November 1982 |
| July 1990 | March 1991 |
| March 2001 | November 2001 |

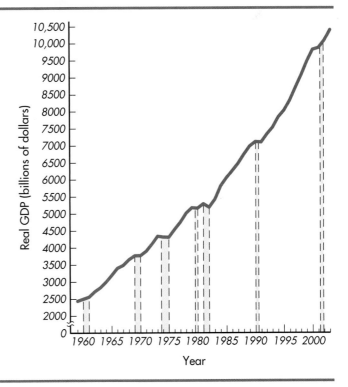

## Figure 2

### The Business Cycle

The business cycle contains four phases: the expansion (boom), when real GDP is increasing; the peak, which marks the end of an expansion and the beginning of a contraction; the contraction (recession), when real GDP is falling; and the trough, which marks the end of a contraction and the beginning of an expansion.

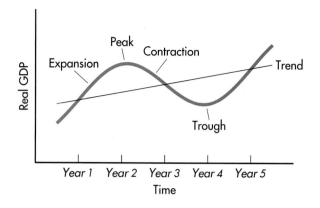

Figure 2 shows how real GDP behaves over a hypothetical business cycle and identifies the stages of the cycle. The vertical axis on the graph measures the level of real GDP; the horizontal axis measures time in years. In year 1, real GDP is growing; the economy is in the *expansion* phase, or *boom* period, of the business cycle. Growth continues until the *peak* is reached, in year 2. Real GDP begins to fall during the *contraction* phase of the cycle, which continues until year 4. The *trough* marks the end of the contraction and the start of a new expansion. Even though the economy is subject to periodic ups and downs, real GDP, the measure of a nation's output, has risen over the long term, as illustrated by the upward-sloping line labeled *Trend*.

If an economy is growing over time, why do economists worry about business cycles? Economists try to understand the causes of business cycles so that they can learn to moderate or avoid recessions and their harmful effects on standards of living.

## 1.b. Historical Record

The official dating of recessions in the United States is the responsibility of the National Bureau of Economic Research (NBER), an independent research organization. The NBER defines a recession as "a period of significant decline in total output, income, employment, and trade, usually lasting from six months to a year, and marked by widespread contractions in many sectors of the economy." People sometimes say that a recession is defined by two consecutive quarters of declining real GDP. This informal idea of what constitutes a recession seems consistent with the past recessions experienced by the United States since every recession through the 1990s has had at least two quarters of falling real GDP. However, this is not the official definition of a recession. The business cycle dating committee of the NBER generally focuses on monthly data. Close attention is paid to the following monthly data series: employment, real personal income less transfer payments, the volume of sales of the manufacturing and wholesale-retail sectors adjusted for price changes, and industrial production. The focus is not on real GDP since it is only measured quarterly and does not permit the identification of the month in which business cycle turning points occur. The NBER has identified the shaded areas in the graph in Figure 1 as recessions and the unshaded areas as expansions. Recessions are periods between cyclical peaks and the troughs that follow them. Expansions are periods between cyclical troughs and the peaks that follow them. There have been 12 recessions since 1929. The most severe was the Great Depression. It occurred between 1929 and 1933, and national output fell by 25 percent. A **depression** is a prolonged period of severe economic contraction. The fact that people refer to "the Depression" when speaking about the recession that began in 1929 indicates the severity of

**depression:** a severe, prolonged economic contraction

| Table 1 | **Leading Indicators** | |
| --- | --- | --- |
| **Indicators of the Business Cycle** | Average workweek | New building permits |
| | Unemployment claims | Delivery times of goods |
| | Manufacturers' new orders | Interest rate spread |
| | Stock prices | Money supply |
| | New plant and equipment orders | Consumer expectations |

| **Coincident Indicators** | **Lagging Indicators** |
| --- | --- |
| Payroll employment | Labor cost per unit of output |
| Industrial production | Inventories to sales ratio |
| Personal income | Unemployment duration |
| Manufacturing and trade sales | Consumer credit to personal income ratio |
| | Outstanding commercial loans |
| | Prime interest rate |
| | Inflation rate for services |

that contraction relative to others in recent experience. There was widespread suffering during the Depression. Many people were jobless and homeless, and many firms went bankrupt. The most recent recession began in March 2001. This business-cycle peak marked the end of a ten-year expansion, the longest in U.S. history.

## 1.c. Indicators

We have been talking about the business cycle in terms of real GDP. There are a number of other variables that move in a fairly regular manner over the business cycle. The Department of Commerce classifies these variables in three categories—leading indicators, coincident indicators, and lagging indicators—depending on whether they move up or down before, at the same time as, or following a change in real GDP (see Table 1).

**leading indicator:** a variable that changes before real output changes

**Leading indicators** generally change before real GDP changes. As a result, economists use them to forecast changes in output. Looking at Table 1, it is easy to see how some of these leading indicators could be used to forecast future output. For instance, new building permits signal new construction. If the number of new permits issued goes up, economists can expect the amount of new construction to increase. Similarly, if manufacturers receive more new orders, economists can expect more goods to be produced.

Leading indicators are not infallible, however. The link between them and future output can be tenuous. For example, leading indicators may fall one month and rise the next while real output rises steadily. Economists want to see several consecutive months of a new direction in the leading indicators before forecasting a change in output. Short-run movements in the indicators can be very misleading.

**coincident indicator:** a variable that changes at the same time that real output changes

**Coincident indicators** are economic variables that tend to change at the same time real output changes. For example, as real output increases, economists expect to see employment and sales rise. The coincident indicators listed in Table 1 have demonstrated a strong tendency over time to change along with changes in real GDP.

**lagging indicator:** a variable that changes after real output changes

The final group of variables listed in Table 1, **lagging indicators,** do not change their value until after the value of real GDP has changed. For instance, as output increases, jobs are created and more workers are hired. It makes sense, then, to expect the duration of unemployment (the average time workers are unemployed) to fall. The duration of unemployment is a lagging indicator. Similarly, the inflation rate for services (which measures how prices change for things like dry cleaners,

As real income falls, living standards go down. This 1937 photo of a Depression-era breadline indicates the paradox of the world's richest nation, as emphasized on the billboard in the background, having to offer public support to feed able-bodied workers who are out of work due to the severity of the business-cycle downturn.

veterinarians, and other services) tends to change after real GDP changes. Lagging indicators are used along with leading and coincident indicators to identify the peaks and troughs in business cycles.

RECAP

1. The business cycle is a recurring pattern of rising and falling real GDP.
2. Although all economies move through periods of expansion and contraction, the duration of expansion and recession varies.
3. Real GDP is not the only variable affected by business cycles; leading, lagging, and coincident indicators also show the effects of economic expansion and contraction.

2. How is the unemployment rate defined and measured?

## 2. UNEMPLOYMENT

Recurring periods of prosperity and recession are reflected in the nation's labor markets. In fact, this is what makes understanding the business cycle so important. If business cycles signified only a little more or a little less profit for businesses, governments would not be so anxious to forecast or to control their swings. It is the human costs of lost jobs and incomes—the inability to maintain standards of living—that make an understanding of business cycles and of the factors that affect unemployment so important.

### 2.a. Definition and Measurement

**unemployment rate:**
the percentage of the labor force that is not working

The **unemployment rate** is the percentage of the labor force that is not working. The rate is calculated by dividing the number of people who are unemployed by the number of people in the labor force:

$$\text{Unemployment rate} = \frac{\text{number unemployed}}{\text{number in labor force}}$$

This ratio seems simple enough, but there are several subtle issues at work here. First, the unemployment rate does not measure the percentage of the total population that is not working; it measures the percentage of the *labor force* that is not working. Who is in the labor force? Obviously, everybody who is employed is part of the labor force. But only some of those who are not currently employed are counted in the labor force.

The Bureau of Labor Statistics of the Department of Labor compiles labor data each month based on an extensive survey of U.S. households. All U.S. residents are potential members of the labor force. The Labor Department arrives at the size of the actual labor force by using this formula:

Labor force = all U.S. residents − residents under 16 years of age
− institutionalized adults − adults not looking for work

So the labor force includes those adults (an adult being 16 or older) currently employed or actively seeking work. It is relatively simple to see to it that children and institutionalized adults (for instance, those in prison or long-term care facilities) are not counted in the labor force. It is more difficult to identify and accurately measure adults who are not actively looking for work.

A person is actively seeking work if he or she is available to work, has looked for work in the past four weeks, is waiting for a recall after being laid off, or is starting a job within 30 days. Those who are not working and who meet these criteria are considered unemployed.

## 2.b. Interpreting the Unemployment Rate

Is the unemployment rate an accurate measure? The fact that the rate does not include those who are not actively looking for work is not necessarily a failing. Many people who are not actively looking for work—homemakers, older citizens, and students, for example—have made a decision to do housework, to retire, or to stay in school. These people rightly are not counted among the unemployed.

But there are people missing from the unemployment statistics who are not working and are not looking for work, yet would take a job if one was offered. **Discouraged workers** have looked for work in the past year but have given up looking for work because they believe that no one will hire them. These individuals are ignored by the official unemployment rate even though they are able to work and may have spent a long time looking for work. Estimates of the number of discouraged workers indicate that in early 2004, about 1.7 million people were not counted in the labor force yet claimed that they were available for work. Of this group, 484,000 people were considered to be discouraged workers. In this case the reported unemployment rate underestimates the true burden of unemployment in the economy because it ignores discouraged workers.

Discouraged workers are one source of hidden unemployment; under employment is another. **Underemployment** is the underutilization of workers—employment in tasks that do not fully utilize their productive potential—including part-time workers who prefer full-time employment. Even if every worker has a job, substantial underemployment leaves the economy producing less than its potential GDP.

The effect of discouraged workers and underemployment is an unemployment rate that understates actual unemployment. In contrast, the effect of the *underground economy* is a rate that overstates actual unemployment. A sizable component of the officially unemployed is actually working. The unemployed construction worker who plays in a band at night may not report that activity because he or she wants to avoid paying taxes on his or her earnings as a musician. This person is officially unemployed but has a source of income. Many officially unemployed individuals have an alternative source of income. This means that official statistics overstate the true magnitude of unemployment. The larger the underground economy, the greater this overstatement. (See the Economic Insight "The Underground Economy.")

**discouraged workers:** workers who have stopped looking for work because they believe no one will offer them a job

**underemployment:** the employment of workers in jobs that do not utilize their productive potential

## The Underground Economy

*Economic Insight*

Official unemployment data, like national income data, do not include activity in the underground economy. Obviously, drug dealers and prostitutes do not report their earnings. Nor do many of the people who supplement their unemployment benefits with part-time jobs. In addition, people like the waiter who reports a small fraction of his actual tips and the house-cleaning person who requests payment in cash in order to avoid reporting taxable income are also part of the underground economy.

Because activity in the underground economy goes unreported, there is no exact way to determine its size. Estimates range from 5 to 33 percent of the gross domestic product. With the GDP at $9 trillion, this places the value of underground activity between $50 billion and $3 trillion.

We will never know the true size of the underground economy, but evidence suggests that it is growing. That evidence has to do with cash. The vast majority of people working in the underground economy are paid in cash. One indicator of the growth of that economy, then, is the rise in currency over time relative to checking accounts. Also, per capita holdings of $100 bills have increased substantially. Certainly, much of the demand for $100 bills is a product of inflation (as the prices of goods and services go up, it is easier to pay for them in larger-denomination bills). But there is also a substantial rise in real holdings of $100 bills as well.

The underground economy forces us to interpret government statistics carefully. We must remember that:

- Official income statistics understate the true national income.
- Official unemployment data overestimate true unemployment.
- When the underground economy grows more rapidly than the rest of the economy, the true rate of growth is higher than reported.

We have identified two factors, discouraged workers and underemployment, that cause the official unemployment rate to underestimate true unemployment. Another factor, the underground economy, causes the official rate to overestimate the true rate of unemployment. There is no reason to expect these factors to cancel one another out, and there is no way to know for sure which is most important. The point is to remember what the official data on unemployment do and do not measure.

### 2.c. Types of Unemployment

Economists have identified four basic types of unemployment:

*Seasonal unemployment.* A product of regular, recurring changes in the hiring needs of certain industries on a monthly or seasonal basis

*Frictional unemployment.* A product of the short-term movement of workers between jobs and of first-time job seekers

*Structural unemployment.* A product of technological change and other changes in the structure of the economy

*Cyclical unemployment.* A product of business-cycle fluctuations

In certain industries, labor needs fluctuate throughout the year. When local crops are harvested, farms need lots of workers; the rest of the year, they do not. (Migrant farmworkers move from one region to another, following the harvests, to avoid seasonal unemployment.) Ski resort towns like Park City, Utah, are booming during the ski season, when employment peaks, but need fewer workers during the rest of the year. In the nation as a whole, the Christmas season is a time of peak employment and low unemployment rates. To avoid confusing seasonal fluctuations in unemployment with other sources of unemployment, unemployment data are seasonally adjusted.

Frictional and structural unemployment exist in any dynamic economy. In terms of individual workers, frictional unemployment is short term in nature. Workers quit

Seasonal unemployment is unemployment that fluctuates with the seasons of the year. For instance, these Santas in training will be employed from fall through Christmas. After Christmas they will be unemployed and must seek new positions. Other examples of seasonal unemployment include farmworkers who migrate to follow the harvest of crops, experiencing unemployment between harvests.

one job and soon find another; students graduate and soon find a job. This kind of unemployment cannot be eliminated in a free society. In fact, it is a sign of efficiency in an economy when workers try to increase their income or improve their working conditions by leaving one job for another. Frictional unemployment is often called *search unemployment* because workers take time to search for a job after quitting a job or leaving school.

Frictional unemployment is short term; structural unemployment, on the other hand, can be long term. Workers who are displaced by technological change (assembly-line workers who have been replaced by machines, for example) or by a permanent reduction in the demand for an industry's output (cigar makers who have been laid off because of a decrease in demand for tobacco) may not have the necessary skills to maintain their level of income in another industry. Rather than accept a much lower salary, these workers tend to prolong their job search. Eventually they adjust their expectations to the realities of the job market, or they enter the pool of discouraged workers.

Structural unemployment is very difficult for those who are unemployed. But for society as a whole, the technological advances that cause structural unemployment raise living standards by giving consumers a greater variety of goods at a lower cost.

Cyclical unemployment is a result of the business cycle. As a recession occurs, cyclical unemployment increases, and as growth occurs, cyclical unemployment decreases. It is also a primary focus of macroeconomic policy. Economists believe that a greater understanding of business cycles and their causes may enable them to find ways to smooth out those cycles and swings in unemployment. Much of the analysis in future chapters is related to macroeconomic policy aimed at minimizing business-cycle fluctuations. In addition to macroeconomic policy aimed at moderating cyclical unemployment, other policy measures—for example, job training and counseling—are being used to reduce frictional and structural unemployment.

### 2.d. Costs of Unemployment

**3. What is the cost of unemployed resources?**

The cost of being unemployed is more than the obvious loss of income and status suffered by the individual who is not working. In a broader sense, society as a

## Figure 3

### The GDP Gap

The GDP gap is the difference between what the economy can produce at the natural rate of unemployment (potential GDP) and actual output (actual GDP). When the unemployment rate is higher than the natural rate, actual GDP is less than potential GDP. The gap between potential and actual real GDP is a cost associated with unemployment. Recession years are shaded to highlight how the gap widens around recessions.

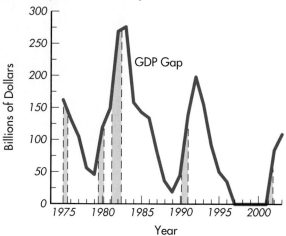

**(a) Potential and Real GDP**

**(b) A Graph of the GDP Gap**

---

whole loses when resources are unemployed. Unemployed workers produce no output. So an economy with unemployment will operate inside its production possibilities curve rather than on the curve. Economists measure this lost output in terms of the *GDP gap:*

$$\text{GDP gap} = \text{potential real GDP} - \text{actual real GDP}$$

**potential real GDP:** the output produced at the natural rate of unemployment

**natural rate of unemployment:** the unemployment rate that would exist in the absence of cyclical unemployment

**Potential real GDP** is the level of output produced when nonlabor resources are fully utilized and unemployment is at its natural rate. The **natural rate of unemployment** is the unemployment rate that would exist in the absence of cyclical unemployment, so it includes seasonal, frictional, and structural unemployment. The natural rate of unemployment is not fixed; it can change over time. For instance, some economists believe that the natural rate of unemployment has risen in recent decades, a product of the influx of baby boomers and women into the labor force. As more workers move into the labor force (begin looking for jobs), frictional unemployment increases, raising the natural rate of unemployment. The natural rate of unemployment is sometimes called the non-accelerating-inflation rate of unemployment, or NAIRU—the idea being that there would be upward pressure on wages and prices in a "tight" labor market when the unemployment rate fell below the NAIRU.

Potential real GDP measures what we are capable of producing at the natural rate of unemployment. If we compute potential real GDP and then subtract actual real GDP, we have a measure of the output lost as a result of unemployment, or the cost of unemployment.

The GDP gap in the United States for recent decades is shown in Figure 3(a). The gap widens during recessions and narrows during expansions. As the gap widens (as the output not produced increases), there are fewer goods and services available, and living standards are lower than they would be at the natural rate of unemployment. Figure 3(b) is a graph of the gap between potential and real GDP, taken from Figure 3(a). One can see that the expansion of the 1990s eliminated the GDP gap by 1997.

Economists used to use the term *full employment* instead of *natural rate of unemployment*. Today the term *full employment* is rarely used because it may be interpreted as implying a zero unemployment rate. If frictional and structural unemployment are always present, zero unemployment is impossible; there must always be unemployed resources in an economy. *Natural rate of unemployment* describes the labor market when the economy is producing what it realistically can produce in the absence of cyclical unemployment.

What is the value of the natural rate of unemployment in the United States? In the 1950s and 1960s, economists generally agreed on 4 percent. By the 1970s, that agreed-on rate had gone up to 5 percent. In the early 1980s, many economists placed the natural rate of unemployment in the United States at 6 to 7 percent. By the late 1980s, some had revised their thinking, placing the rate back at 5 percent. In fact, economists do not know exactly what the natural rate of unemployment is. Over time it varies within a range from around 4 percent to around 7 percent. It will also vary across countries, as labor markets and macroeconomic policies differ.

## 2.e. The Record of Unemployment

Unemployment rates in the United States from 1951 to 2003 are listed in Table 2. Over this period, the unemployment rate for all workers reached a low of

**Table 2**

**Unemployment Rates in the United States**

| | | | Unemployment Rate, Civilian Workers[1] | | | | |
|---|---|---|---|---|---|---|---|
| Year | All Civilian Workers | Males | Females | Both Sexes 16–19 Years | White | Black | Hispanic |
| 1951 | 3.3 | 2.8 | 4.4 | 8.2 | 3.1 | – | – |
| 1955 | 4.4 | 4.2 | 4.9 | 11.0 | 3.9 | – | – |
| 1959 | 5.5 | 5.2 | 5.9 | 14.6 | 4.8 | – | – |
| 1963 | 5.7 | 5.2 | 6.5 | 17.2 | 5.0 | – | – |
| 1967 | 3.8 | 3.1 | 5.2 | 12.9 | 3.4 | – | – |
| 1971 | 5.9 | 5.3 | 6.9 | 16.9 | 5.4 | – | – |
| 1975 | 8.5 | 7.9 | 9.3 | 19.9 | 7.8 | 14.8 | 12.2 |
| 1979 | 5.8 | 5.1 | 6.8 | 16.1 | 5.1 | 12.3 | 8.3 |
| 1983 | 9.6 | 9.9 | 9.2 | 22.4 | 8.4 | 19.5 | 13.7 |
| 1987 | 6.2 | 6.2 | 6.2 | 16.9 | 5.3 | 13.0 | 8.3 |
| 1991 | 6.8 | 7.2 | 6.4 | 18.7 | 6.1 | 12.5 | 10.0 |
| 1995 | 5.6 | 5.6 | 5.6 | 17.3 | 4.9 | 10.4 | 9.3 |
| 1999 | 4.2 | 4.1 | 4.3 | 13.9 | 3.7 | 8.0 | 6.4 |
| 2000 | 4.0 | 3.9 | 4.1 | 13.1 | 3.5 | 7.6 | 5.7 |
| 2001 | 4.7 | 4.8 | 4.7 | 14.7 | 4.2 | 8.6 | 6.6 |
| 2002 | 5.8 | 5.9 | 5.6 | 16.5 | 5.1 | 10.2 | 7.5 |
| 2003 | 6.0 | 6.3 | 5.7 | 17.5 | 5.2 | 10.8 | 7.7 |

[1]Unemployed as a percentage of the civilian labor force in the group specified.

2.8 percent in 1953 and a high of 9.6 percent in 1982 and 1983. The table shows some general trends in the incidence of unemployment across different demographic groups:

*In most years, the unemployment rate for women is higher than it is for men.* Several factors may be at work here. First, during this period, a large number of women entered the labor force for the first time. Second, discrimination against women in the workplace limited job opportunities for them, particularly early in this period. Finally, a large number of women move out of the labor force on temporary maternity leaves.

*Teenagers have the highest unemployment rates in the economy.* This makes sense because teenagers are the least-skilled segment of the labor force.

*Whites have lower unemployment rates than nonwhites.* Discrimination plays a role here. To the extent that discrimination extends beyond hiring practices and job opportunities for minority workers to the education that is necessary to prepare students to enter the work force, minority workers will have fewer opportunities for employment. The quality of education provided in many schools with large minority populations may not be as good as that provided in schools with large white populations. Equal opportunity programs and legislation are aimed at rectifying this inequality.

Although exact comparisons across countries are difficult to make because countries measure unemployment in different ways, it is interesting to look at the reported unemployment rates of different countries. Table 3 lists unemployment rates for seven major industrial nations. The rates have been adjusted to match as closely as possible the U.S. definition of unemployment. For instance, the official Italian unemployment data include people who have not looked for work in the past 30 days. The data for Italy in Table 3 have been adjusted to remove these people. If the data had not been adjusted, the Italian unemployment rates would be roughly twice as high as those listed.

Countries not only define unemployment differently; they also use different methods to count the unemployed. All major European countries except Sweden use a national unemployment register to identify the unemployed. Only those people who register for unemployment benefits are considered unemployed.

**Table 3**

**Unemployment Rates in Major Industrial Countries**

| Year | Civilian Unemployment Rate (percent) | | | | | | |
|------|----------------|--------|--------|-------|-------|-------------------|---------|
|      | United States | Canada | France | Italy | Japan | United Kingdom | Germany |
| 1960 | 5.5 | 6.5 | 1.5 | 3.7 | 1.7 | 2.2 | 1.1 |
| 1965 | 4.5 | 3.6 | 1.6 | 3.5 | 1.2 | 2.1 | .3 |
| 1970 | 4.9 | 5.7 | 2.5 | 3.2 | 1.2 | 3.1 | .5 |
| 1975 | 8.5 | 6.9 | 4.1 | 3.4 | 1.9 | 4.6 | 3.4 |
| 1980 | 7.1 | 7.5 | 6.4 | 4.4 | 2.0 | 7.0 | 2.9 |
| 1985 | 7.2 | 10.5 | 10.4 | 6.0 | 2.6 | 11.2 | 7.5 |
| 1990 | 5.5 | 8.1 | 9.2 | 7.0 | 2.1 | 6.9 | 5.0 |
| 1995 | 5.6 | 9.5 | 11.7 | 12.0 | 3.2 | 8.8 | 6.5 |
| 2000 | 4.0 | 5.7 | 9.6 | 10.6 | 4.7 | 5.5 | 8.3 |
| 2003 | 6.0 | 7.2 | 9.3 | 8.7 | 5.2 | 5.0 | 9.1 |

*Source: Economic Report of the President, 2004 (Washington, D.C.: U.S. Government Printing Office, 2004).*

A problem with this method is that it excludes those who have not registered because they are not entitled to benefits, and it includes those who receive benefits but would not take a job if one was offered. Other countries—among them the United States, Canada, Sweden, and Japan—conduct monthly surveys of households to estimate the unemployment rate. Surveys allow more comprehensive analysis of unemployment and its causes than the use of a register does. The Organization for Economic Cooperation and Development, an organization created to foster international economic cooperation, compared annual surveys of the labor force in Europe with the official register of unemployment data and found that only 80 to 85 percent of those surveyed as unemployed were registered in Germany, France, and the United Kingdom. In Italy, only 63 percent of those surveyed as unemployed were registered.

Knowing their limitations, we can still identify some important trends from the data in Table 3. Through the 1960s and early 1970s, European unemployment rates generally were lower than U.S. and Canadian rates. Over the next decade, European unemployment rates increased substantially, as did the rates in North America. But in the mid-1980s, while U.S. unemployment began to fall, European unemployment remained high. The issue of high unemployment rates in Europe has become a major topic of discussion at international summit meetings. The Global Business Insight "High Unemployment in Europe" discusses this issue further. Japanese unemployment rates, like those in Europe, were much lower than U.S. and Canadian rates in the 1960s and 1970s. However, while Japanese rates remained much lower in the 1980s and 1990s, by 2000, a prolonged economic slowdown in Japan had led to rising unemployment.

**RECAP**

1. The unemployment rate is the number of people unemployed as a percentage of the labor force.

2. To be in the labor force, one must either have or be looking for a job.

3. By its failure to include discouraged workers and the output lost because of underemployment, the unemployment rate understates real unemployment in the United States.

4. By its failure to include activity in the underground economy, the U.S. unemployment rate overstates actual unemployment.

5. Unemployment data are adjusted to eliminate seasonal fluctuations.

6. Frictional and structural unemployment are always present in a dynamic economy.

7. Cyclical unemployment is a product of recession; it can be moderated by controlling the period of contraction in the business cycle.

8. Economists measure the cost of unemployment in terms of lost output.

9. Unemployment data show that women generally have higher unemployment rates than men, that teenagers have the highest unemployment rates in the economy, and that nonwhites have higher unemployment rates than whites.

## 3. INFLATION

**4. What is inflation?**

inflation: a sustained rise in the average level of prices

**Inflation** is a sustained rise in the average level of prices. Notice the word *sustained*. Inflation does not mean a short-term increase in prices; it means prices are rising over a prolonged period of time. Inflation is measured by the percentage change in the price level. The inflation rate in the United States was 1.9 percent in 2003. This means that the level of prices increased 1.9 percent over the year.

# High Unemployment in Europe

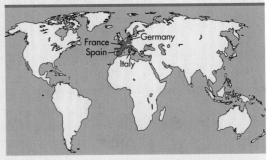

The data in Table 3 indicate that European countries tend to have higher unemployment rates than other industrial countries. This is not true of all European countries, but it is certainly true for the biggest: France, Germany, Italy, and Spain. One factor that contributes to the higher unemployment rates in these countries is government policy with regard to the labor market. Countries that have policies that encourage unemployment should be expected to have more unemployed workers. In a recent speech, a British scholar gave his analysis of why Europe has such high unemployment. One story he told illustrates how government policy aimed at protecting citizens against unemployment can create the very unemployment that is the cause for concern. In Italy, laws require parents to support their adult children who do not work, even if the children are entirely capable of working. The story goes as follows:

> The Italian Court of Cessation ruled that a professor at Naples University, separated from his family, must continue to pay his 30-year-old son €775 per month until he can find himself suitable employment. This despite the fact that the son owns a house and possesses an investment trust fund worth €450,000. The judges said that an adult son who refused work that did not reflect his training, abilities and personal interests could not be held to blame. In particular the judges said[,] "You cannot blame a young person, particularly from a well-off family, who refuses a job that does not fit his aspirations." By contrast, under UK law, a separated father would only have to support his children until they completed full-time education." (Stephen Nickell, 2002)

The government requirement that parents support unemployed adult children encourages the children to remain unemployed.

Among men of prime working age (age 25–54), there are more who are inactive and not participating in the labor force than there are unemployed. The majority of these men are receiving benefits from the government claiming disability or illness. In the 1970s, there were many fewer disabled or ill workers as a fraction of the population. But as social benefits were increased, and the eligibility rules were relaxed, the number claiming to suffer from such problems also increased. The unfortunate truth of human nature is that as you provide better support for those who truly need help, there will be more and more who do not truly need it yet will claim a need. The experience of Denmark is instructive in this regard. Denmark has generous unemployment benefits. But in the 1990s, Danish eligibility requirements were tightened, creating greater incentives for the unemployed to look for work. Danish unemployment rates fell dramatically as a result.

Another effect of government policy is related to a person's loss of job skills while unemployed. Unemployment benefits in Europe are relatively high and can last a long time. Unemployment benefits in the United States are relatively low and have a shorter duration. Given just these facts, one would expect more European unemployment since the unemployed would be out of work for a longer time in Europe than in the United States. If people are not working for a prolonged time, they are more likely to find their work skills deteriorating, so they are less likely to be attractive candidates for jobs if and when they do look for work. Therefore, a longer duration of unemployment benefits, meant to protect workers who lose their jobs, will also contribute to more workers' job skills appearing to be inadequate to employers when the workers do apply for employment.

Other factors contributing to higher unemployment rates in some countries are the restrictions on the ability of firms to terminate workers and the requirement that firms pay high separation costs to workers who are fired. The more difficult it is for firms to adjust their labor force in the face of economic fluctuations, the less likely firms are to hire new workers. If you own a business and your sales increase, you are more likely to hire extra employees to meet the increased demand for your product. However, you cannot be sure that your sales will remain higher permanently, so you would be very conservative about hiring new workers if you would have to pay terminated workers a large amount of money if sales fell and you needed to lay off some of your employees. Such labor market rigidities, aimed at protecting workers from losing jobs, create incentives against hiring so that those who would like to work cannot get hired.

The lesson learned from large European countries is that government policies aimed at protecting workers from unemployment may create a bigger unemployment problem. Then the costs imposed on the economy in terms of taxes and reduced labor market flexibility may exceed the benefits to those who keep their jobs or receive unemployment compensation because of the programs.

*Sources:* Stephen Nickell, "A Picture of European Unemployment: Success and Failure," speech given to CESifo Conference in Munich, December 2002; and Lars Ljungqvist and Thomas Sargent, "The European Unemployment Dilemma," *Journal of Political Economy,* 1998.

### 3.a. Absolute Versus Relative Price Changes

In the modern economy, over any given period, some prices rise faster than others. To evaluate the rate of inflation in a country, then, economists must know what is happening to prices on average. Here it is important to distinguish between *absolute* and *relative* price changes.

Let's look at an example using the prices of fish and beef:

|  | Year 1 | Year 2 |
| --- | --- | --- |
| 1 pound of fish | $1 | $2 |
| 1 pound of beef | $2 | $4 |

In year 1, beef is twice as expensive as fish. This is the price of beef *relative* to fish. In year 2, beef is still twice as expensive as fish. The relative prices have not changed between years 1 and 2. What has changed? The prices of both beef and fish have doubled. The *absolute* levels of all prices have gone up, but because they have increased by the same percentage, the relative prices are unchanged.

Inflation measures changes in absolute prices. In our example, all prices doubled, so the inflation rate is 100 percent. There was a 100 percent increase in the prices of beef and fish. Inflation does not proceed evenly through the economy. Prices of some goods rise faster than others, which means that relative prices are changing at the same time that absolute prices are rising. The measured inflation rate records the *average* change in absolute prices.

### 3.b. Effects of Inflation

**5. Why is inflation a problem?**

To understand the effects of inflation, you have to understand what happens to the value of money in an inflationary period. The real value of money is what it can buy, its *purchasing power:*

$$\text{Real value of \$1} = \frac{\$1}{\text{price level}}$$

The higher the price level, the lower the real value (or *purchasing power*) of the dollar. For instance, suppose an economy had only one good—milk. If a glass of milk sold for $.50, then one dollar would buy two glasses of milk. If the price of milk rose to $1, then a dollar would only buy one glass of milk. The purchasing power, or real value, of money falls as prices rise.

Table 4 lists the real value of the dollar in selected years from 1946 to 2003. The price level in each year is measured relative to the average level of prices over the 1982–1984 period. For instance, the 1946 value, 0.195, means that prices in 1946 were, on average, only 19.5 percent of prices in the 1982–1984 period. Notice that as prices go up, the purchasing power of the dollar falls. In 1946, a dollar bought five times more than a dollar bought in the early 1980s. The value 5.13 means that one could buy 5.13 times more goods and services with a dollar in 1946 than one could in 1982–1984.

Prices have risen steadily in recent decades. By 2003, they had gone up more than 80 percent above the average level of prices in the 1982–1984 period. Consequently, the purchasing power of a 2003 dollar was lower. In 2003, $1 bought just 54 percent of the goods and services that one could buy with a dollar in 1982–1984.

If prices and nominal income rise by the same percentage, it might seem that inflation is not a problem. It doesn't matter whether it takes twice as many dollars now to buy fish and beef as it did before if we have twice as many dollars in income available to buy the products. Obviously, inflation is very much a problem when a household's nominal income rises at a slower rate than prices. Inflation hurts those households whose income does not keep up with the prices of the goods they buy.

In the 1970s in the United States, the rate of inflation rose to near-record levels. Many workers believed that their incomes were lagging behind the rate of inflation,

Table 4

**The Real Value of a Dollar**

| Year | Average Price Level[1] | Purchasing Power of a Dollar[2] |
|------|------------------------|--------------------------------|
| 1946 | 0.195 | 5.13 |
| 1950 | 0.241 | 4.15 |
| 1954 | 0.269 | 3.72 |
| 1958 | 0.289 | 3.46 |
| 1962 | 0.302 | 3.31 |
| 1966 | 0.324 | 3.09 |
| 1970 | 0.388 | 2.58 |
| 1974 | 0.493 | 2.03 |
| 1978 | 0.652 | 1.53 |
| 1982 | 0.965 | 1.04 |
| 1986 | 1.096 | 0.91 |
| 1990 | 1.307 | 0.77 |
| 1994 | 1.482 | 0.67 |
| 1997 | 1.608 | 0.62 |
| 2000 | 1.722 | 0.58 |
| 2003 | 1.840 | 0.54 |

[1] Measured by the consumer price index as given in http://data.bls.gov/.
[2] Found by taking the reciprocal of the consumer price index (1/CPI).

so they negotiated cost-of-living raises in their wage contracts. The typical cost-of-living raise ties salary to changes in the consumer price index. If the CPI rises 8 percent over a year, workers receive an 8 percent raise plus compensation for experience or productivity increases. As the U.S. rate of inflation fell during the 1980s, concern about cost-of-living raises subsided as well.

It is important to distinguish between expected and unexpected inflation. *Unexpectedly high inflation* redistributes income away from those who receive fixed incomes (like creditors who receive debt repayments of a fixed amount of dollars per month) toward those who make fixed expenditures (like debtors who make fixed debt repayments per month). For example, consider a simple loan agreement.

Maria borrows $100 from Ali, promising to repay the loan in one year at 10 percent interest. In one year, Maria will pay Ali $110—principal of $100 plus interest of $10 (10 percent of $100, or $10).

When Maria and Ali agree to the terms of the loan, they do so with some expected rate of inflation in mind. Suppose they both expect 5 percent inflation over the year. In one year it will take 5 percent more money to buy goods than it does now. Ali will need $105 to buy what $100 buys today. Because Ali will receive $110 for the principal and interest on the loan, he will gain purchasing power. However, if the inflation rate over the year turns out to be surprisingly high—say, 15 percent—then Ali will need $115 to buy what $100 buys today. He will lose purchasing power if he makes a loan at a 10 percent rate of interest.

Economists distinguish between nominal and real interest rates when analyzing economic behavior. The **nominal interest rate** is the observed interest rate in the market and includes the effect of inflation. The **real interest rate** is the nominal interest rate minus the rate of inflation:

Real interest rate = nominal interest rate − rate of inflation

If Ali charges Maria 10 percent nominal interest, and the inflation rate is 5 percent, the real interest rate is 5 percent (10 − 5 = 5 percent). This means that Ali

**nominal interest rate:** the observed interest rate in the market

**real interest rate:** the nominal interest rate minus the rate of inflation

will earn a positive real return from the loan. However, if the inflation rate is 10 percent, the real return from a nominal interest rate of 10 percent is zero $(10 - 10 = 0)$. The interest Ali will receive from the loan will just compensate him for the rise in prices; he will not realize an increase in purchasing power. If the inflation rate is higher than the nominal interest rate, then the real interest rate is negative; the lender will lose purchasing power by making the loan.

Now you can see how unexpected inflation redistributes income. Borrowers and creditors agree to loan terms on the basis of what they *expect* the rate of inflation to be over the period of the loan. If the *actual* rate of inflation turns out to be different from what was expected, then the real interest rate paid by the borrower and received by the lender will be different from what was expected. If Ali and Maria both expect a 5 percent inflation rate and agree to a 10 percent nominal interest rate for the loan, then they both expect a real interest rate of 5 percent $(10 - 5 = 5$ percent) to be paid on the loan. If the actual inflation rate turns out to be greater than 5 percent, then the real interest rate will be less than expected. Maria will get to borrow Ali's money at a lower real cost than she expected, and Ali will earn a lower real return than he expected. Unexpectedly high inflation hurts creditors and benefits borrowers because it lowers real interest rates.

Figure 4 shows the real interest rates on U.S. Treasury bills from 1970 through 2003. You can see a pronounced pattern in the graph. In the late 1970s, there was a period of negative real interest rates, followed by high positive real rates in the 1980s. The evidence suggests that nominal interest rates did not rise fast enough in the 1970s to offset high inflation. This was a time of severe strain on many creditors, including savings and loan associations and banks. These firms had lent funds at fixed nominal

Figure 4

**The Real Interest Rate on U.S. Treasury Bills**

The real interest rate is the difference between the nominal rate (the rate actually observed) and the rate of inflation over the life of the bond. The figure shows the real interest rate in June and December for each year. For instance, in the first observation for June 1970, a six-month Treasury bill paid the holder 6.91 percent interest. This is the nominal rate of interest. To find the real rate of interest on the bond, we subtract the rate of inflation that existed over the six months of the bond's life (June to December 1970), which was 5.17 percent. The difference between the nominal interest rate (6.91 percent) and the rate of inflation (5.17 percent) is the real interest rate, 1.74 percent. Notice that real interest rates were negative during most of the 1970s and then turned highly positive (by historical standards) in the early 1980s.

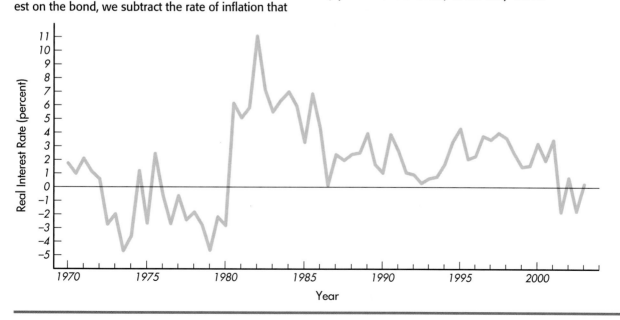

rates of interest. When those rates of interest turned out to be lower than the rate of inflation, the financial institutions suffered significant losses. In the early 1980s, the inflation rate dropped sharply. Because nominal interest rates did not drop nearly as fast as the rate of inflation, real interest rates were high. In this period many debtors were hurt by the high costs of borrowing to finance business or household expenditures.

Unexpected inflation affects more than the two parties to a loan. Any contract calling for fixed payments over some long-term period changes in value as the rate of inflation changes. For instance, a long-term contract that provides union members with 5 percent raises each year for five years gives the workers more purchasing power if inflation is low than if it is high. Similarly, a contract that sells a product at a fixed price over a long-term period will change in value as inflation changes. Suppose a lumber company promises to supply a builder with lumber at a fixed price for a two-year period. If the rate of inflation in one year turns out to be higher than expected, the lumber company will end up selling the lumber for less profit than it had planned. Inflation raises costs to the lumber company. Usually the company would raise its prices to compensate for higher costs. Because the company contracted to sell its goods at a fixed price to the builder, however, the builder benefits at the lumber company's expense. Again, unexpectedly high inflation redistributes real income or purchasing power away from those receiving fixed payments to those making fixed payments.

One response to the effects of unexpected inflation is to allow prices, wages, or interest rates to vary with the rate of inflation. Labor sometimes negotiates cost-of-living adjustments as part of new wage contracts. Financial institutions offer variable interest rates on home mortgages to reflect current market conditions. Any contract can be written to adjust dollar amounts over time as the rate of inflation changes.

### 3.c. Types of Inflation

Economists often classify inflation according to the source of the inflationary pressure. The most straightforward method defines inflation in terms of pressure from the demand side of the market or the supply side of the market. **Demand-pull inflation** is caused by increasing demand for output. Increases in total spending that are not offset by increases in the supply of goods and services cause the average level of prices to rise. **Cost-push inflation** is caused by rising costs of production. Increases in production costs cause firms to raise prices to avoid losses.

Sometimes inflation is blamed on "too many dollars chasing too few goods." This is a roundabout way of saying that the inflation stems from demand pressures. Because demand-pull inflation is a product of increased spending, it is more likely to occur in an economy that is producing at maximum capacity. If resources are fully employed, in the short run it may not be possible to increase output to meet increased demand. The result: existing goods and services are rationed by rising prices.

Some economists claim that rising prices in the late 1960s were a product of demand-pull inflation. They believe that increased government spending for the Vietnam War caused the level of U.S. prices to rise.

Cost-push inflation can occur in any economy, whatever its output. If prices go up because the costs of resources are rising, the rate of inflation can go up regardless of demand.

For example, some economists argue that the inflation in the United States in the 1970s was largely due to rising oil prices. This means that decreases in the oil supply (a shift to the left in the supply curve) brought about higher oil prices. Because oil is so important in the production of many goods, higher oil prices led to increases in prices throughout the economy. Cost-push inflation stems from changes in the supply side of the market.

Cost-push inflation is sometimes attributed to profit-push or wage-push pressures. *Profit-push pressures* are created by suppliers who want to increase their profit margins by raising prices faster than their costs increase. *Wage-push pressures* are created

**demand-pull inflation:** inflation caused by increasing demand for output

**cost-push inflation:** inflation caused by rising costs of production

by labor unions and workers who are able to increase their wages faster than their productivity. There have been times when "greedy" businesses and unions have been blamed for periods of inflation in the United States. The problem with these "theories" is that people have always wanted to improve their economic status and always will. In this sense, people have always been greedy. But inflation has not always been a problem. Were people less greedy in the early 1980s when inflation was low than they were in the late 1970s when inflation was high? Obviously, we have to look to other reasons to explain inflation. We discuss some of those reasons in later chapters.

### 3.d. The Inflationary Record

Many people today, having always lived with inflation, are surprised to learn that inflation is a relatively new problem for the United States. From 1789, when the U.S. Constitution was ratified, until 1940, there was no particular trend in the general price level. At times prices rose, and at times they fell. The average level of prices in 1940 was approximately the same as it was in the late eighteenth century.

Since 1940, prices in the United States have gone up markedly. The price level today is eight times what it was in 1940. But the rate of growth has varied. Prices rose rapidly for the first couple of years following World War II and then grew at a relatively slow rate through the 1950s and 1960s. In the early 1970s, the rate of inflation began to accelerate. Prices climbed quickly until the early 1980s, when inflation slowed.

Annual rates of inflation for several industrial and developing nations are shown in Table 5. Look at the diversity across countries: rates range from –2.0 percent in Japan to 106 percent in Angola.

Table 5

**Rates of Inflation for Selected Countries, 2002**

| Selected industrial | Inflation Rate (Percent) |
|---|---|
| Australia | 2.8 |
| Canada | 2.2 |
| Germany | 1.3 |
| Japan | –2.0 |
| United Kingdom | 2.1 |
| United States | 1.6 |
| **Selected developing** | |
| Angola | 106.0 |
| Botswana | 8.1 |
| Brazil | 8.3 |
| Chile | 2.5 |
| Egypt | 4.3 |
| Hong Kong, China | 3.0 |
| India | 5.4 |
| Israel | 5.7 |
| Mexico | 6.4 |
| Philippines | 3.1 |
| Poland | 1.9 |
| South Africa | 9.9 |
| Venezuela | 31.0 |

*Source:* Data from *The World Factbook*, 2003, http://www.bartleby.com/isi/fields.

**Hyperinflation** is an extremely high rate of inflation. In most cases hyperinflation eventually makes a country's currency worthless and leads to the introduction of a new currency. Argentina experienced hyperinflation in the 1980s. People had to carry large stacks of currency for small purchases. Cash registers and calculators ran out of digits as prices reached ridiculously high levels. After years of high inflation, Argentina replaced the old peso with the peso Argentino in June 1983. The government set the value of 1 peso Argentino equal to 10,000 old pesos (striking four zeros from all prices). A product that sold for 10,000 old pesos before the reform sold for 1 new peso after. But Argentina did not follow up its monetary reform with a noninflationary change in economic policy. In 1984 and 1985, the inflation rate exceeded 600 percent each year. As a result, in June 1985, the government again introduced a new currency, the austral, setting its value at 1,000 pesos Argentino. However, the economic policy associated with the introduction of the austral only lowered the inflation rate temporarily. By 1988, the inflation rate was over 300 percent, and in 1989, the inflation rate was over 3,000 percent. The rapid rise in prices associated with the austral resulted in the introduction of yet another currency, again named peso Argentino, in January 1992, with a value equal to 10,000 australes. This new peso was fixed at a value of 1 peso per 1 U.S. dollar, and this exchange rate lasted for about ten years due to reasonably stable inflation in Argentina. In late 2001, Argentina experienced another financial crisis due to large government budget deficits, and the fixed rate of exchange between the peso and dollar ended, but the peso has remained the currency of Argentina. In coming chapters we will learn how monetrary and fiscal policy of government can create high inflation and how low and stable inflation results from sound macroeconomic policy.

The most dramatic hyperinflation in modern times occurred in Europe after World War I. Table 6 shows how the price level rose in Germany between 1914 and 1924 in relation to prices in 1914. For instance, the value in 1915, 126, indicates that prices were 26 percent higher that year than in 1914. The value in 1919, 262, indicates that prices were 162 percent higher that year than in 1914. By 1924, German prices were more than 100 trillion times higher than they had been in 1914. At the height of the inflation, the mark was virtually worthless.

Table 6

**German Wholesale Prices, 1914–1924**

| Year Index | Price |
| --- | --- |
| 1914 | 100 |
| 1915 | 126 |
| 1916 | 150 |
| 1917 | 156 |
| 1918 | 204 |
| 1919 | 262 |
| 1920 | 1,260 |
| 1921 | 1,440 |
| 1922 | 3,670 |
| 1923 | 278,500 |
| 1924 | 117,320,000,000,000 |

Source: J. P. Young, *European Currency and Finance* (Washington, DC: U.S. Government Printing Office, 1925).

In later chapters, we will see how high rates of inflation generally are caused by rapid growth of the money supply. When a central government wants to spend more than it is capable of funding through taxation or borrowing, it simply issues money to finance its budget deficit. As the money supply increases faster than the demand to hold it, spending increases and prices go up.

**RECAP**

1. Inflation is a sustained rise in the average level of prices.
2. The higher the price level, the lower the real value (purchasing power) of money.
3. Unexpectedly high inflation redistributes income away from those who receive fixed-dollar payments (like creditors) toward those who make fixed-dollar payments (like debtors).
4. The real interest rate is the nominal interest rate minus the rate of inflation.
5. Demand-pull inflation is a product of increased spending; cost-push inflation reflects increased production costs.
6. Hyperinflation is a very high rate of inflation that often results in the introduction of a new currency.

## SUMMARY

### ❓ What is a business cycle?

1. Business cycles are recurring changes in real GDP, in which expansion is followed by contraction.
2. The four stages of the business cycle are expansion (boom), peak, contraction (recession), and trough.
3. Leading, coincident, and lagging indicators are variables that change in relation to changes in output.

### ❓ How is the unemployment rate defined and measured?

4. The unemployment rate is the percentage of the labor force that is not working.
5. To be in the U.S. labor force, an individual must be working or actively seeking work.
6. Unemployment can be classified as seasonal, frictional, structural, or cyclical.
7. Frictional and structural unemployment are always present in a dynamic economy; cyclical unemployment is a product of recession.

### ❓ What is the cost of unemployed resources?

8. The GDP gap measures the output lost because of unemployment.

### ❓ What is inflation?

9. Inflation is a sustained rise in the average level of prices.
10. The higher the level of prices, the lower the purchasing power of money.

### ❓ Why is inflation a problem?

11. Inflation becomes a problem when income rises at a slower rate than prices.
12. Unexpectedly high inflation hurts those who receive fixed-dollar payments (like creditors) and benefits those who make fixed-dollar payments (like debtors).
13. Inflation can stem from demand-pull or cost-push pressures.
14. Hyperinflation—an extremely high rate of inflation—can force a country to introduce a new currency.

## KEY TERMS

business cycle
recession
depression
leading indicator
coincident indicator

lagging indicator
unemployment rate
discouraged workers
underemployment
potential real GDP

natural rate of unemployment

inflation

nominal interest rate

real interest rate

demand-pull inflation

cost-push inflation

hyperinflation

## EXERCISES

1. What is the labor force? Do you believe that the U.S. government's definition of the labor force is a good one—that it includes all the people it should include? Explain your answer.

2. Suppose you are able bodied and intelligent, but lazy. You would rather sit home and watch television than work, even though you know you could find an acceptable job if you looked.

   a. Are you officially unemployed?

   b. Are you a discouraged worker?

3. Does the GDP gap measure all of the costs of unemployment? Why or why not?

4. Why do teenagers have the highest unemployment rate in the economy?

5. Write an equation that defines the real interest rate. Use the equation to explain why unexpectedly high inflation redistributes income from creditors to debtors.

6. Many home mortgages in recent years have been made with variable interest rates. Typically, the interest rate is adjusted once a year based on the current rates on government bonds. How do variable interest rate loans protect creditors from the effects of unexpected inflation?

7. The word *cycle* suggests a regular, recurring pattern of activity. Is there a regular pattern in the business cycle? Support your answer by examining the duration (number of months) of each expansion and contraction in Figure 1.

8. Suppose 500 people were surveyed, and of those 500, 450 were working full time. Of the 50 not working, 10 were full-time college students, 20 were retired, 5 were under sixteen years of age, 5 had stopped looking for work because they believed there were no jobs for them, and 10 were actively looking for work.

   a. How many of the 500 surveyed are in the labor force?

   b. What is the unemployment rate among the 500 surveyed people?

9. Consider the following price information:

| | Year 1 | Year 2 |
|---|---|---|
| Cup of coffee | $ .50 | $1.00 |
| Glass of milk | $1.00 | $2.00 |

   a. Based on the information given, what was the inflation rate between year 1 and year 2?

   b. What happened to the price of coffee relative to that of milk between year 1 and year 2?

10. Use a supply and demand diagram to illustrate:

   a. Cost-push inflation caused by a labor union successfully negotiating for a higher wage

   b. Demand-pull inflation caused by an increase in demand for domestic products from foreign buyers

## Internet Exercise

**Use the Internet to explore unemployment and labor statistics.**

Go to the Boyes/Melvin, *Fundamentals of Economics* website accessible through **http://college.hmco.com** and click on the Internet Exercise link for Chapter 11. Now answer the questions that appear on the Boyes/Melvin website.

## Key Term Match

**Match each term with its correct definition by placing the appropriate letter next to the corresponding number.**

A. business cycle
B. recession
C. depression
D. leading indicator
E. coincident indicator
F. lagging indicator
G. unemployment rate
H. discouraged workers
I. underemployment
J. potential real GDP
K. natural rate of unemployment
L. inflation
M. nominal interest rate
N. real interest rate
O. demand-pull inflation
P. cost-push inflation
Q. hyperinflation

_____ 1. a period in which real GDP falls
_____ 2. a sustained rise in the average level of prices
_____ 3. the nominal interest rate minus the rate of inflation
_____ 4. the pattern of rising real GDP followed by falling real GDP
_____ 5. a variable that changes before real output changes
_____ 6. an extremely high rate of inflation
_____ 7. the unemployment rate that would exist in the absence of cyclical unemployment
_____ 8. inflation caused by increasing demand for output
_____ 9. a severe, prolonged economic contraction
_____10. the observed interest rate in the market
_____11. the percentage of the labor force that is not working
_____12. the output produced at the natural rate of unemployment
_____13. the employment of workers in jobs that do not utilize their productive potential
_____14. a variable that changes at the same time that real output changes
_____15. inflation caused by rising costs of production
_____16. a variable that changes after real output changes
_____17. workers who have stopped looking for work because they believe no one will offer them a job

## Quick-Check Quiz

1  In correct sequence, the four stages of the business cycle are

   a. peak, boom, expansion, and contraction.
   b. peak, contraction, trough, and expansion.
   c. recession, expansion, peak, and boom.
   d. contraction, trough, boom, and expansion.
   e. recession, contraction, peak, and boom.

2  To arrive at the number of workers in the U.S. labor force, we subtract all of the following from the number of all U.S. residents *except*

   a. residents under 16 years old.
   b. institutionalized adults.
   c. adults who are not looking for work.
   d. unemployed adults.
   e. All of the above must be subtracted from the number of U.S. residents to arrive at the number of workers in the labor force.

3  Which of the following cause(s) the unemployment rate to be overstated?

   a. discouraged workers
   b. underground economic activities
   c. part-time employment
   d. underemployment
   e. students who are not looking for work

4  A graduating college basketball star who has one month off before reporting to his new NBA team is an example of

   a. frictional unemployment.
   b. structural unemployment.
   c. cyclical unemployment.
   d. technological unemployment.
   e. a rich, employed person.

5  A person who finds that her skills are no longer needed because she has been replaced by a machine is an example of

   a. frictional unemployment.
   b. seasonal unemployment.
   c. cyclical unemployment.
   d. search unemployment.
   e. structural unemployment.

6  A steelworker who has been laid off during a recession is an example of

   a. frictional unemployment.
   b. seasonal unemployment.
   c. cyclical unemployment.
   d. search unemployment.
   e. structural unemployment.

7  Job training and counseling are policy measures primarily used to fight

   a. frictional unemployment.
   b. seasonal unemployment.
   c. cyclical unemployment.
   d. structural unemployment.
   e. both a and d.

8 Which of the following statements is false?

    a. The GDP gap widens during recessions and narrows during expansions.

    b. The natural rate of unemployment varies over time and across countries.

    c. Men have higher unemployment rates than women because women move out of the labor force to have children.

    d. Teenagers have the highest unemployment rates in the economy.

    e. Nonwhites have higher unemployment rates than whites.

9 If a college professor's income has increased by 3 percent at the same time that prices have risen by 5 percent, the professor's real income has

    a. decreased by 2 percent.

    b. increased by 2 percent.

    c. increased by 7 percent.

    d. decreased by 7 percent.

    e. not changed.

10 Which of the following groups benefits from unexpectedly high inflation?

    a. creditors

    b. retirees on fixed incomes

    c. debtors

    d. workers whose salaries are tied to the CPI

    e. suppliers who have contracted to supply a fixed amount of their product for a fixed price

11 Which of the following could be a cause of demand-pull inflation?

    a. war in the Middle East, which can increase oil prices

    b. drought in the Midwest, which can cause crop failures

    c. suppliers who increase their profit margins by raising prices faster than their costs increase

    d. increased government spending in the absence of increased taxes

    e. labor unions, which can force wage increases that are not justified by increases in productivity

12 Which of the following statements is true?

    a. The higher the price level, the higher the purchasing power of money.

    b. Demand-pull inflation can be a result of increased production costs.

    c. High rates of inflation are generally caused by rapid growth of the money supply.

    d. Unexpectedly high inflation redistributes income away from those who make fixed dollar payments toward those who receive fixed dollar payments.

    e. The real interest rate increases as the rate of inflation increases.

13 A lender who does not expect any change in the price level is willing to make a mortgage loan at a 10 percent rate of interest. If that same lender anticipates a future inflation rate of 5 percent, she will charge the borrower

    a. 5 percent interest.

    b. 10 percent interest.

    c. 15 percent interest.

    d. 2 percent interest.

    e. .5 percent interest.

## Practice Questions and Problems

1 When real GDP is growing, the economy is in the

_____ phase, or boom period, of the business cycle.

2 The _____ marks the end of a contraction and the start of a new business cycle.

3 The _____ marks the end of the expansion phase of a business cycle.

4 Real GDP falls during the contraction, or _____, phase of the business cycle.

5 Which organization has the responsibility of officially dating recessions in the United States?

_____

6 _____ unemployment is a product of business-cycle fluctuations.

7 _____ unemployment is a product of regular, recurring changes in the hiring needs of certain industries over the months or seasons of the year.

8 _____ unemployment is a product of short-term movements of workers between jobs and of first-time job seekers.

**9** _____ unemployment is a product of technological change and other changes in the structure of the economy.

**10** Potential real GDP minus actual real GDP equals the

_____.

**11** The existence of _____ and

_____ causes the official unemployment rate in the United States to be understated.

**12** Economists measure the cost of unemployment in

terms of _____.

**13** The higher the price level, the _____ (higher, lower) the purchasing power of the dollar.

**14** Unexpectedly high inflation hurts _____

(creditors, debtors) and benefits _____ (creditors, debtors) because it lowers real interest rates.

## Exercises and Applications

**I  In or Out of the Labor Force?**  The Department of Labor defines the labor force as all U.S. residents minus residents under 16 years old minus institutionalized adults minus adults who are not looking for work. A person is seeking work if he or she is available to work, has looked for work in the past four weeks, is waiting for a recall after being laid off, or is starting a job within 30 days.

Place an *X* next to the description of those who would be considered part of the labor force.

_____ Per Olsen is a Norwegian citizen who is looking for a job in the United States. He plans to move to the United States to marry his American sweetheart.

_____ Carl Wolcutt is a retired police chief who has recently been offered a position as head of his state's police academy. Mr. Wolcutt is happily raising beagles and has turned down the job.

_____ Blake Stephans has just been laid off from his quality-control job at Boeing. He is waiting for a recall, but the company has just announced it will lay off even more workers.

_____ Thomas Butting is a recent college graduate who quit his part-time job but is taking the summer off before searching for a "real" job.

_____ Joe Shocker, a pitcher on Wichita State University's baseball team, has been selected in the first round of the draft and expects to join the Mets after he finishes playing in the College World Series. In the meantime, he will enjoy the sights and sounds of beautiful downtown Omaha.

**II  Illustrating the Business Cycle**  The horizontal axis measures time, and the vertical axis measures economic activity. Label the points on the following diagram with the appropriate phases of the business cycle.

**III  Economic Reporting**  Assume you are a reporter for *The Wall Street Journal*. Respond to the following developments. You should consider whether the indicator in question leads, lags, or moves with the economy.

1. The Commerce Department has just released its index of leading indicators, which rose only 0.1 percent in April after dropping 1 percent the previous month. What can you tell your readers about the probable growth of the economy?

_____

_____

_____

2. The Commerce Department reported that new plant and equipment orders were flat in April after a 3.7 percent decline in March. What does this news imply about the economy?

_____

_____

3. Stock prices rose in April, up 4.8 percent from March.

_____

_____

_____

4. The Commerce Department originally reported that the economy grew at a 1.8 percent annual rate in the first quarter. What measure was released? The figures were revised after the U.S. trade deficit increased sharply in March. Would your estimate of economic growth be revised upward or downward as a result of the trade figures?

_____

_____

_____

Now that you've completed the Study Guide for this chapter, you should have a good sense of the concepts you need to review. If you'd like to test your understanding of the material again, go to the Practice Tests on the Boyes/Melvin *Fundamentals of Economics*, 3e website, **economics.college.hmco.com/students.**

## Chapter 12

# Macroeconomic Equilibrium: Aggregate Demand and Supply

*Preview*

Total output and income in the United States have grown over time. Each generation has experienced a higher living standard than the previous generation. Yet, as we learned in Chapter 11, economic growth has not been steady. Economies go through periods of expansion followed by periods of contraction or recession, and such business cycles have major impacts on people's lives, incomes, and living standards.

Economic stagnation and recession throw many, often those who are already relatively poor, out of their jobs and into real poverty. Economic growth increases the number of jobs and draws people out of poverty and into the mainstream of economic progress. To understand why economies grow and why they go through cycles, we must discover why firms decide to produce more or less and why buyers decide to buy more or less. The approach we take is similar to the approach we followed in the early chapters of the text using demand and supply curves. In Chapters 2 and 3, demand and supply curves were derived and used to examine questions involving the equilibrium price and quantities demanded and supplied of a single good or service. This simple yet powerful microeconomic technique of analysis has a macroeconomic counterpart—aggregate demand and aggregate supply, which are used to determine an equilibrium price level and quantity of goods and services produced for the *entire economy*. In this chapter we use aggregate demand and supply curves to illustrate the causes of business cycles and economic growth. ■

## 1. AGGREGATE DEMAND, AGGREGATE SUPPLY, AND BUSINESS CYCLES

What causes economic growth and business cycles? We can provide some answers to this important question using aggregate demand (*AD*) and aggregate supply (*AS*) curves. Suppose we represent the economy in a simple demand and supply diagram, as shown in Figure 1. Aggregate demand represents the total spending in the economy at alternative price levels. Aggregate supply represents the total output of the economy at alternative price levels. To understand the causes of business cycles and inflation, we must understand how aggregate demand and supply cause the equilibrium price level and real GDP, the nation's output of goods and services, to

payment by the bond price, or $100/$1,000 = 10 percent. If the price of the bond falls to $900, then the interest rate is equal to the annual interest payment (which remains fixed at $100 for the life of the bond) divided by the new price of $900: $100/$900 = 11 percent. When bond prices fall, interest rates rise, and when bond prices rise, interest rates fall.

If people want more money, and they sell some of their bond holdings to raise the money, bond prices will fall, and interest rates will rise. The rise in interest rates is necessary to sell the larger quantity of bonds, but it causes investment expenditures to fall, which causes aggregate expenditures to fall.

When prices fall, people need less money to purchase the same quantity of goods, so they use their money holdings to buy bonds and other financial assets. The increased demand for bonds increases bond prices and causes interest rates to fall. Lower interest rates increase investment expenditures, thereby pushing aggregate expenditures up.

Figure 4 shows the **interest rate effect,** the relationship among the price level, interest rates, and aggregate expenditures. As the price level rises, interest rates rise, and aggregate expenditures fall. As the price level falls, interest rates fall, and aggregate expenditures rise.

**interest rate effect:** a change in interest rates that causes investment and therefore aggregate expenditures to change as the level of prices changes

### 3.a.3. The International Trade Effect
The third channel through which a price-level change affects the quantity of goods and services demanded is called the **international trade effect.** A change in the level of domestic prices can cause net exports to change. If domestic prices rise while foreign prices and the foreign exchange rate remain constant, domestic goods become more expensive in relation to foreign goods.

**international trade effect:** a change in aggregate expenditures resulting from a change in the domestic price level that changes the price of domestic goods in relation to foreign goods

Suppose the United States sells oranges to Japan. If the oranges sell for $1 per pound, and the yen-dollar exchange rate is 100 yen = $1, a pound of U.S. oranges costs a Japanese buyer 100 yen. What happens if the level of prices in the United States goes up 10 percent? All prices, including the price of oranges, increase 10 percent. The U.S. oranges sell for $1.10 a pound after the price increase. If the exchange rate is still 100 yen = $1, a pound of oranges now costs the Japanese buyer 110 yen (100 × 1.10). If orange prices in other countries do not change, some Japanese buyers may buy oranges from those countries. The increase in the level of U.S. prices makes U.S. goods more expensive relative to foreign goods and causes U.S. net exports to fall; a decrease in the level of U.S. prices makes U.S. goods cheaper in relation to foreign goods and causes U.S. net exports to rise.

When the price of domestic goods increases in relation to the price of foreign goods, net exports fall, causing aggregate expenditures to fall. When the price of domestic goods falls in relation to the price of foreign goods, net exports rise, causing aggregate expenditures to rise. The international trade effect of a change in the level of domestic prices causes aggregate expenditures to change in the opposite direction.

### 3.a.4. The Sum of the Price-Level Effects
The **aggregate demand curve** (*AD*) shows how the equilibrium level of expenditures for the economy's output changes as the price level changes. In other words, the curve shows the amount people spend at different price levels.

**aggregate demand curve:** a curve that shows the different levels of expenditures on domestic output at different levels of prices

Figure 5 displays the typical shape of the *AD* curve. The price level is plotted on the vertical axis, and real GDP is plotted on the horizontal axis. Suppose that initially the economy is at point *A* with prices at $P_0$. At this point, spending equals $500. If prices fall to $P_1$, expenditures equal $700, and the economy is at point *C*. If prices rise from $P_0$ to $P_2$, expenditures equal $300 at point *B*.

Because aggregate expenditures increase when the price level decreases and decrease when the price level increases, the aggregate demand curve slopes down. The aggregate demand curve is drawn with the price level for the *entire economy* on the vertical axis. A price-level change here means that, on average, *all prices in the economy change;* there is no relative price change among domestic goods.

Figure 5

**The Aggregate Demand Curve**

The aggregate demand curve (*AD*) shows the level of expenditures at different price levels. At price level $P_0$, expenditures are $500; at $P_1$, $700; and at $P_2$, $300.

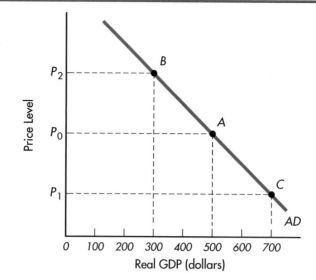

The negative slope of the aggregate demand curve is a product of the wealth effect, the interest rate effect, and the international trade effect.

A lower domestic price level increases consumption (the wealth effect), investment (the interest rate effect), and net exports (the international trade effect). As the price level drops, aggregate expenditures rise.

A higher domestic price reduces consumption (the wealth effect), investment (the interest rate effect), and net exports (the international trade effect). As prices rise, aggregate expenditures fall. These price effects are summarized in Figure 6.

### 3.b. Changes in Aggregate Demand: Nonprice Determinants

The aggregate demand curve shows the level of aggregate expenditures at alternative price levels. We draw the curve by varying the price level and finding out what the resulting total expenditures are, holding all other things constant. As those "other things"—the nonprice determinants of aggregate demand—change, the aggregate demand curve shifts. The nonprice determinants of aggregate demand include all of the factors covered in the discussion of the components of expenditures—income, wealth, demographics, expectations, taxes, the interest rate (interest rates can change for reasons other than price-level changes), the cost of capital goods, capacity utilization, foreign income and price levels, exchange rates, and government policy. A change in any one of these can cause the *AD* curve to shift. In the discussions that follow, we will focus particularly on the effect of expectations, foreign income levels, and price levels, and we will also mention government policy, which will be examined in detail in Chapter 13. Figure 7 summarizes these effects, which are discussed next.

### 3.b.1. Expectations

Consumption and business spending are affected by expectations. Consumption is sensitive to people's expectations of future income, prices, and wealth. For example, when people expect the economy to do well in the future, they increase consumption today at every price level. This is reflected in a shift of the aggregate demand curve to the right, from $AD_0$ to $AD_1$, as shown in Figure 8. When aggregate demand increases, aggregate expenditures increase at every price level.

On the other hand, if people expect a recession in the near future, they tend to reduce consumption and increase saving in order to protect themselves against a greater likelihood of losing a job or a forced cutback in hours worked. As consumption

**?**

**2. What causes the aggregate demand curve to shift?**

Figure 6

**Why the Aggregate Demand Curve Slopes Down**

(a) Wealth Effect (b) Interest Rate Effect (c) International Trade Effect

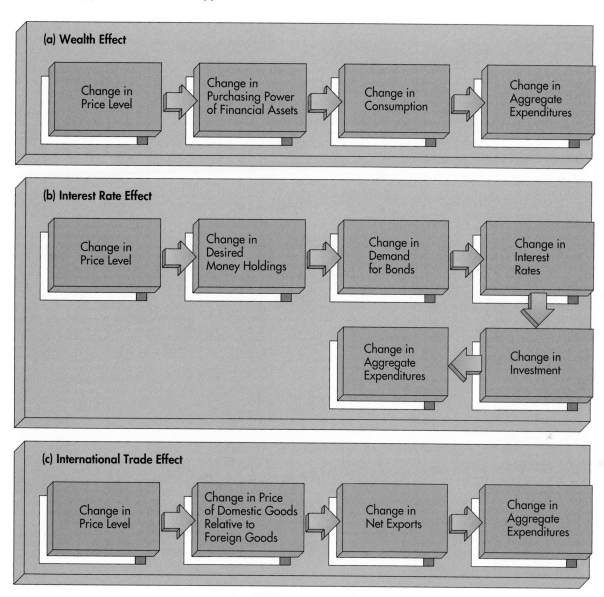

drops, aggregate demand decreases. The *AD* curve shifts to the left, from $AD_0$ to $AD_2$. At every price level along $AD_2$, planned expenditures are less than they are along $AD_0$.

Expectations also play an important role in investment decisions. Before undertaking a particular project, businesses forecast the likely revenues and costs associated with that project. When the profit outlook is good—say, a tax cut is on the horizon—investment and therefore aggregate demand increase. When profits are expected to fall, investment and aggregate demand decrease.

**3.b.2. Foreign Income and Price Levels** When foreign income increases, so does foreign spending. Some of this increased spending is for goods produced in

Figure 7

**Nonprice Determinants: Changes in Aggregate Demand**

(a) Expectations (b) Foreign Income and Price Levels
(c) Government Policy

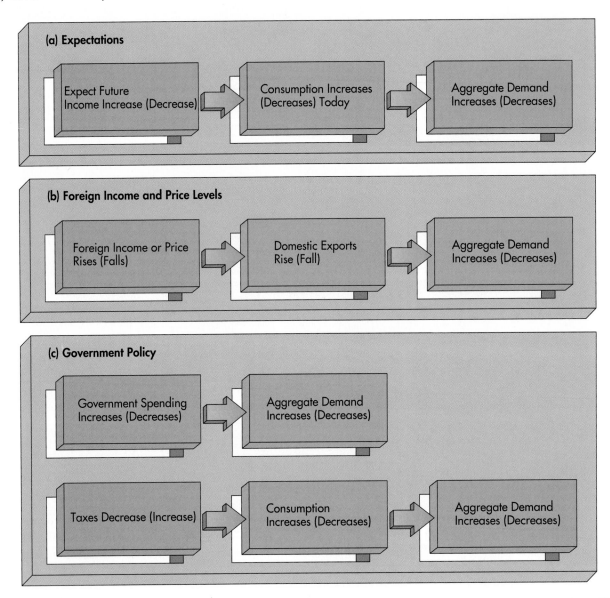

the domestic economy. As domestic exports increase, aggregate demand rises. Lower foreign income has just the opposite effect. As foreign income falls, foreign spending falls, including foreign spending on the exports of the domestic economy. Lower foreign income, then, causes domestic net exports and domestic aggregate demand to fall.

If foreign prices rise in relation to domestic prices, domestic goods become less expensive relative to foreign goods, and domestic net exports increase. This means that aggregate demand rises, or the aggregate demand curve shifts up, as the level of foreign prices rises. Conversely, when the level of foreign prices falls, domestic

Figure 8

**Shifting the Aggregate Demand Curve**

As aggregate demand increases, the *AD* curve shifts to the right, like the shift from $AD_0$ to $AD_1$. At every price level, the quantity of output demanded increases. As aggregate demand falls, the *AD* curve shifts to the left, like the shift from $AD_0$ to $AD_2$. At every price level, the quantity of output demanded falls.

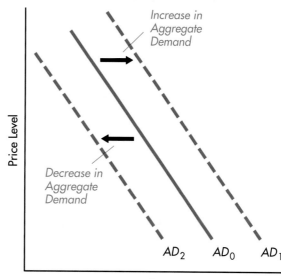

goods become more expensive relative to foreign goods, causing domestic net exports and aggregate demand to fall.

Let's go back to the market for oranges. Suppose U.S. growers compete with Brazilian growers for the Japanese orange market. If the level of prices in Brazil rises while the level of prices in the United States remains stable, the price of Brazilian oranges to the Japanese buyer rises in relation to the price of U.S. oranges. What happens? The U.S. exports of oranges to Japan should rise while Brazilian exports of oranges to Japan fall.

**3.b.3. Government Policy** One of the goals of macroeconomic policy is to achieve economic growth without inflation. For GDP to increase, either *AD* or *AS* would have to change. Government economic policy can cause the aggregate demand curve to shift. An increase in government spending or a decrease in taxes will increase aggregate demand; a decrease in government spending or an increase in taxes will decrease aggregate demand. We devote Chapter 13, "Fiscal Policy," to an examination of the effect of taxes and government spending on aggregate demand. In Chapter 15, "Monetary Policy," we describe how changes in the money supply can cause the aggregate demand curve to shift.

RECAP

1. The aggregate demand curve shows the level of aggregate expenditures at different levels of price.

2. Aggregate expenditures are the sum of consumption, investment, government spending, and net exports.

3. The wealth effect, the interest rate effect, and the international trade effect are three reasons why aggregate demand slopes down. These effects explain movements along a given *AD* curve.

4. The aggregate demand curve shifts with changes in the nonprice determinants of aggregate demand: expectations, foreign income and price levels, and government policy.

# 4. AGGREGATE SUPPLY

**3. What is aggregate supply?**

**aggregate supply curve:** a curve that shows the amount of real GDP produced at different price levels

The **aggregate supply curve** shows the quantity of real GDP produced at different price levels. The aggregate supply (*AS*) curve looks like the supply curve for an individual good, but, as with aggregate demand and the microeconomic demand curve, different factors are at work. The positive relationship between price and quantity supplied of an individual good is based on the price of that good's changing in relation to the prices of all other goods. As the price of a single good rises relative to the prices of other goods, sellers are willing to offer more of the good for sale. With aggregate supply, on the other hand, we are analyzing how the amount of all goods and services produced changes as the level of prices changes. The direct relationship between prices and national output is explained by the effect of changing prices on profits, not by relative price changes.

## 4.a. Changes in Aggregate Quantity Supplied: Price-Level Effects

Along the aggregate supply curve, everything is held fixed except the price level and output. The price level is the price of output. The prices of resources, that is, the costs of production—wages, rent, and interest—are assumed to be constant, at least for a short time following a change in the price level.

If the price level rises while the costs of production remain fixed, business profits go up. As profits rise, firms are willing to produce more output. As the price level rises, then, the quantity of output firms are willing to supply increases. The result is the positively sloped aggregate supply curve shown in Figure 9.

As the price level rises from $P_0$ to $P_1$ in Figure 9, real GDP increases from $300 to $500. The higher the price level, the higher are the profits, everything else held constant, and the greater is the quantity of output produced in the economy. Conversely, as the price level falls, the quantity of output produced falls.

## 4.b. Short-Run Versus Long-Run Aggregate Supply

The curve in Figure 9 is a *short-run* aggregate supply curve because the costs of production are held constant. Although production costs may not rise immediately

---

**Figure 9**

**Aggregate Supply**

The aggregate supply curve shows the amount of real GDP produced at different price levels. The *AS* curve slopes up, indicating that the higher the price level, the greater the quantity of output produced.

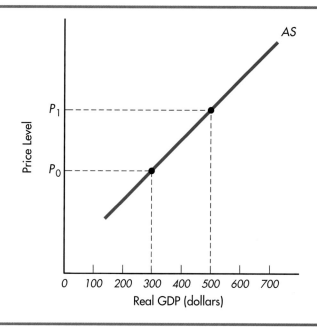

Figure 10

**The Shape of the Short-Run Aggregate Supply Curve**

The upward-sloping aggregate supply curve occurs when the price level must rise to induce further increases in output. The curve gets steeper as real GDP increases since the closer the economy comes to the capacity level of output, the less output will rise in response to higher prices as more and more firms reach their maximum level of output in the short run.

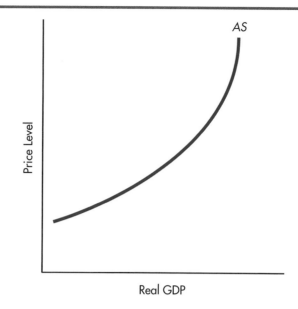

**4. Why does the short-run aggregate supply curve become steeper as real GDP increases?**

**5. Why is the long-run aggregate supply curve vertical?**

long-run aggregate supply curve (LRAS): a vertical line at the potential level of national income

when the price level rises, eventually they will. Labor will demand higher wages to compensate for the higher cost of living; suppliers will charge more for materials. The positive slope of the *AS* curve, then, is a short-run phenomenon. How short is the short run? It is the period of time over which production costs remain constant. (In the long run, all costs change or are variable.) For the economy as a whole, the short run can be months or, at most, a few years.

**4.b.1. Short-Run Aggregate Supply Curve**  Figure 9 represents the general shape of the short-run aggregate supply curve. In Figure 10 you see a more realistic version of the same curve; its steepness varies. The steepness of the aggregate supply curve depends on the ability and willingness of producers to respond to price-level changes in the short run. Figure 10 shows the typical shape of the short-run aggregate supply curve.

Notice that as the level of real GDP increases in Figure 10, the *AS* curve becomes steeper. This is because each increase in output requires firms to hire more and more resources until eventually full capacity is reached in some areas of the economy, resources are fully employed, and some firms reach maximum output. At this point, increases in the price level bring about smaller and smaller increases in output from firms as a whole. The short-run aggregate supply curve becomes increasingly steep as the economy approaches maximum output.

**4.b.2. Long-Run Aggregate Supply Curve**  Aggregate supply in the short run is different from aggregate supply in the long run (see Figure 11). That difference stems from the fact that quantities and costs of resources are not fixed in the long run. Over time, contracts expire and wages and other resource costs adjust to current conditions. The increased flexibility of resource costs in the long run has costs rising and falling with the price level and changes the shape of the aggregate supply curve. Lack of information about economic conditions in the short run also contributes to the inflexibility of resource prices as compared to the long run.

The **long-run aggregate supply curve (*LRAS*)** is viewed by most economists to be a vertical line at the potential level of real GDP or output ($Y_p$), as shown in Figure 11. Remember that the potential level of real GDP is the income level that is produced in the absence of any cyclical unemployment, or when the natural rate of unemployment exists. In the long run, wages and other resource costs fully adjust

Figure 11

**The Shape of the Long-Run Aggregate Supply Curve**

In the long run, the *AS* curve is a vertical line at the potential level of real GDP. This indicates that there is no relationship between price-level changes and the quantity of output produced.

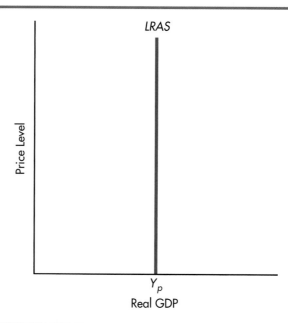

to price changes. The short-run AS curve slopes up because we assume that the costs of production, particularly wages, do not change to offset changing prices. In the short run, then, higher prices increase producers' profits and stimulate production. In the long run, because the costs of production adjust completely to the change in prices, neither profits nor production increases. What we find here are higher wages and other costs of production to match the higher level of prices.

### 4.c. Changes in Aggregate Supply: Nonprice Determinants

The aggregate supply curve is drawn with everything but the price level and real GDP held constant. There are several things that can change and cause the aggregate supply curve to shift. The shift from $AS_0$ to $AS_1$ in Figure 12 represents an increase in aggregate supply. The $AS_1$ curve lies to the right of $AS_0$; this means that at

**?**

**6. What causes the aggregate supply curve to shift?**

Technological advance shifts the aggregate supply curve outward and increases output. An example of a technological advance that has increased efficiency in banking is the automated teller machine (ATM). The photo shows an ATM in Brazil that allows the bank to offer the public a lower-cost way to make withdrawals and deposits than dealing with a bank employee. Such innovations can be important determinants of aggregate supply.

## Figure 12

**Changes in Aggregate Supply**

The aggregate supply curve shifts with changes in resource prices, technology, and expectations. When aggregate supply increases, the curve shifts to the right, like the shift from $AS_0$ to $AS_1$, so that at every price level more is being produced. When aggregate supply falls, the curve shifts to the left, like the shift from $AS_0$ to $AS_2$, so that at every price level less is being produced.

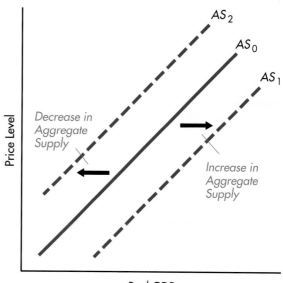

every price level, production is higher on $AS_1$ than on $AS_0$. The shift from $AS_0$ to $AS_2$ represents a decrease in aggregate supply. The $AS_2$ curve lies to the left of $AS_0$; this means that at every price level, production along $AS_2$ is less than along $AS_0$. The nonprice determinants of aggregate supply are resource prices, technology, and expectations. Figure 13 summarizes the nonprice determinants of aggregate supply.

**4.c.1. Resource Prices**   When the price of output changes, the costs of production do not change immediately. At first, then, a change in profits induces a change in production. Costs eventually change in response to the change in prices and production, and when they do, the aggregate supply curve shifts. When the cost of resources—labor, capital goods, materials—falls, the aggregate supply curve shifts to the right, from $AS_0$ to $AS_1$ in Figure 12. This means firms are willing to produce more output at any given price level. When the cost of resources goes up, profits fall, and the aggregate supply curve shifts to the left, from $AS_0$ to $AS_2$. Here, at any given level of price, firms produce less output.

Remember that the vertical axis of the aggregate supply graph plots the price level for all goods and services produced in the economy. Only those changes in resource prices that raise the costs of production across the economy have an impact on the aggregate supply curve. For example, oil is an important raw material. If a new source of oil is discovered, the price of oil falls, and aggregate supply increases. However, if oil-exporting countries restrict oil supplies, and the price of oil increases substantially, aggregate supply decreases—a situation that occurred when OPEC reduced the supply of oil in the 1970s (see the Economic Insight "OPEC and Aggregate Supply"). If the price of only one minor resource changed, then aggregate supply would be unlikely to change. For instance, if the price of land increased in Las Cruces, New Mexico, we would not expect the U.S. aggregate supply curve to be affected.

**4.c.2. Technology**   Technological innovations allow businesses to increase the productivity of their existing resources. As new technology is adopted, the amount of output that can be produced by each unit of input increases, moving the aggregate supply curve to the right. For example, personal computers and word-processing

## Figure 13

**Determinants of Aggregate Supply**

(a) Resource Prices (b) Technology (c) Expectations

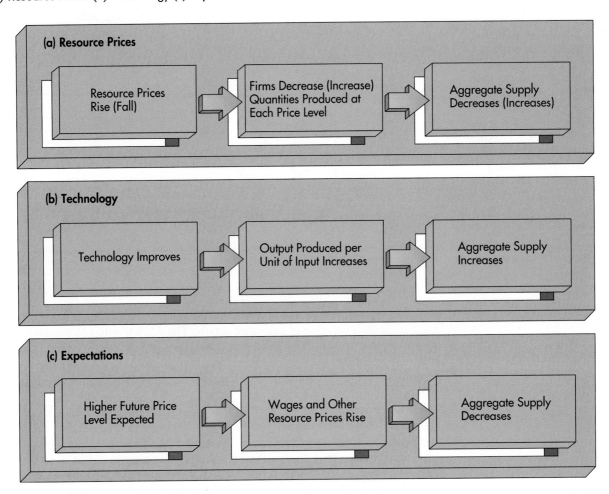

software have allowed secretaries to produce much more output in a day than type-writers allowed.

**4.c.3. Expectations**   To understand how expectations can affect aggregate supply, consider the case of labor contracts. Manufacturing workers typically contract for a nominal wage on the basis of what they and their employers expect the future level of prices to be. Because wages typically are set for at least a year, any unexpected increase in the price level during the year lowers real wages. Firms receive higher prices for their output, but the cost of labor stays the same. So profits and production go up.

If wages rise in anticipation of higher prices, but prices do not go up, the cost of labor rises. Higher real wages caused by expectations of higher prices reduce current profits and production, moving the aggregate supply curve to the left. Other things being equal, anticipated higher prices cause aggregate supply to decrease; conversely, anticipated lower prices cause aggregate supply to increase. In this

Figure 14

**Shifting the Long-Run Aggregate Supply Curve**

Changes in technology and the availability and quality of resources can shift the *LRAS* curve. For instance, a new technology that increases productivity would move the curve to the right, from *LRAS* to *LRAS*₁.

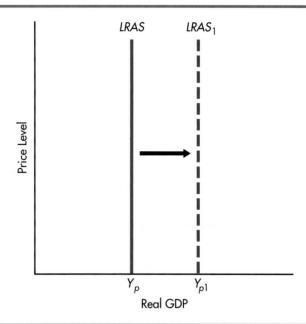

sense, expectations of price-level changes that shift aggregate supply bring about price-level changes.

**4.c.4. Economic Growth: Long-Run Aggregate Supply Shifts**  The vertical long-run aggregate supply curve, as shown in Figure 11, does not mean that the economy is forever fixed at the current level of potential real gross domestic product. Over time, as new technologies are developed, and the quantity and quality of resources increase, potential output also increases, shifting both the short- and long-run aggregate supply curves to the right. Figure 14 shows long-run economic growth by the shift in the aggregate supply curve from *LRAS* to *LRAS*₁. The movement of the long-run aggregate supply curve to the right reflects the increase in potential real GDP from $Y_p$ to $Y_{p1}$. Even though the price level has no effect on the level of output in the long run, changes in the determinants of the supply of real output in the economy do.

**RECAP**

1. The aggregate supply curve shows the quantity of output (real GDP) produced at different price levels.

2. The aggregate supply curve slopes up because, everything else held constant, higher prices increase producers' profits, creating an incentive to increase output.

3. The aggregate supply curve shifts with changes in resource prices, technology, and expectations. These are nonprice determinants of aggregate supply.

4. The short-run aggregate supply curve is upward sloping, showing that increases in production are accompanied by higher prices.

5. The long-run aggregate supply curve is vertical at potential real GDP because, eventually, wages and the costs of other resources adjust fully to price-level changes.

## OPEC and Aggregate Supply

In the late winter of 2003, there was much talk about high oil prices leading to a fall in GDP for oil-importing countries. At the same time that the Bush administration was planning to invade Iraq, a move which would disrupt oil supplies from the Mideast, a strike by Venezuelan oil workers interrupted oil supplies from the world's fifth-largest producer. Oil prices rose dramatically, and the price of gasoline rose from about $1.60 per gallon to more than $2.00 per gallon. The higher oil prices rose, the more talk there was about recession. What is the link between oil prices and real GDP? A look back to recent history can help develop our understanding of this link.

In 1973 and 1974, and again in 1979 and 1980, the Organization of Petroleum Exporting Countries (OPEC) reduced the supply of oil, driving the price of oil up dramatically. For example, the price of Saudi Arabian crude oil more than tripled between 1973 and 1974, and more than doubled between 1979 and 1980. Researchers estimate that the rapid jump in oil prices reduced output by 17 percent in Japan, by 7 percent in the United States, and by 1.9 percent in Germany.*

Oil is an important resource in many industries. When the price of oil increases due to restricted oil output, aggregate supply falls. You can see this in the graph. When the price of oil goes up, the aggregate supply curve falls from $AS_1$ to $AS_2$. When aggregate supply falls, the equilibrium level of real GDP (the intersection of the $AS$ curve and the $AD$ curve) falls from $Y_1$ to $Y_2$.

Higher oil prices due to restricted oil output would decrease not only short-run aggregate supply and current equilibrium real GDP, as shown in the figure, but also potential equilibrium income at the natural rate of unemployment. Unless other factors change to contribute to economic growth, the higher resource (oil) price reduces the productive capacity of the economy.

There is evidence that fluctuations in oil prices have less effect on the economy today than in the past.[†] The amount of energy that goes into producing a dollar of GDP has declined over time so that oil plays a less important role as a determinant of aggregate supply today than in the 1970s and earlier. This means

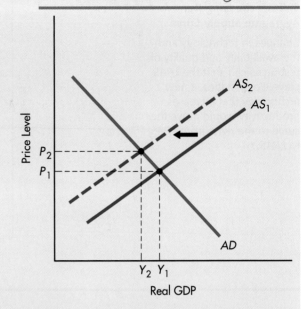

that any given change in oil prices today will be associated with smaller shifts in the $AS$ curve than it would have been in earlier decades.

*These estimates were taken from "Energy Price Shocks, Aggregate Supply, and Monetary Policy: The Theory and the International Evidence," Robert H. Rasche and John A. Tatom, in *Carnegie-Rochester Conference Series on Public Policy,* ed. Karl Brunner and Allan H. Meltzer, no. 14, Spring 1981, pp. 9–93.

[†]See Stephen P. A. Brown and Mine K. Yücel, "Oil Prices and the Economy," in *Southwest Economy,* Federal Reserve Bank of Dallas, July–August 2000.

---

**7. What determines the equilibrium price level and real GDP?**

## 5. AGGREGATE DEMAND AND SUPPLY EQUILIBRIUM

Now that we have defined the aggregate demand and aggregate supply curves separately, we can put them together to determine the equilibrium level of price and real GDP.

### 5.a. Short-Run Equilibrium

Figure 15 shows the level of equilibrium in a hypothetical economy. Initially, the economy is in equilibrium at point 1, where $AD_1$ and $AS_1$ intersect. At this point, the equilibrium price is $P_1$ and the equilibrium real GDP is $500. At price $P_1$, the amount of output demanded is equal to the amount supplied. Suppose aggregate demand increases from $AD_1$ to $AD_2$. In the short run, aggregate supply does not

Figure 15

**Aggregate Demand and Supply Equilibrium**

The equilibrium level of price and real GDP is at the intersection of the AD and AS curves. Initially, equilibrium occurs at point 1, where the AD₁ and AS₁ curves intersect. Here the price level is $P_1$ and real GDP is $500. If aggregate demand increases, moving from AD₁ to AD₂, in the short run there is a new equilibrium at point 2, where AD₂ intersects AS₁. The price level rises to $P_2$, and the equilibrium level of real GDP increases to $600. Over time, as the costs of wages and other resources rise in

response to higher prices, aggregate supply falls, moving AS₁ to AS₂. Final equilibrium occurs at point 3, where the AS₂ curve intersects the AD₂ curve. The price level rises to $P_3$, but the equilibrium level of real GDP returns to its initial level, $500. In the long run, there is no relationship between prices and the equilibrium level of real GDP because the costs of resources adjust to changes in the level of prices.

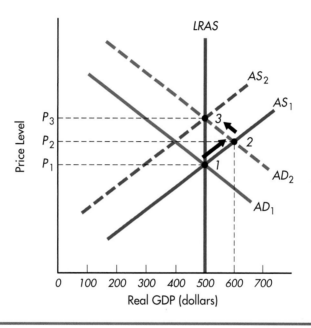

change, so the new equilibrium is at the intersection of the new aggregate demand curve $AD_2$ and the same aggregate supply curve $AS_1$, at point 2. The new equilibrium price is $P_2$, and the new equilibrium real GDP is $600. Note that in the short run, the equilibrium point on the short-run aggregate supply curve can lie to the right of the long-run aggregate supply curve (*LRAS*). This is because the *LRAS* represents the potential level of real GDP, not the capacity level. It is possible to produce more than the potential level of real GDP in the short run when the unemployment rate falls below the natural rate of unemployment.

### 5.b. Long-Run Equilibrium

Point 2 is not a permanent equilibrium because aggregate supply decreases to $AS_2$ once the costs of production rise in response to higher prices. Final equilibrium is at point 3, where the price level is $P_3$ and real GDP is $500. Notice that equilibrium here is the same as the initial equilibrium at point 1. Points 1 and 3 both lie along the long-run aggregate supply curve (*LRAS*). The initial shock to or change in the economy was an increase in aggregate demand. The change in aggregate expenditures initially led to higher output and higher prices. Over time, however, as resource costs rise and profit falls, output falls back to its original value.

*Now You Try It*

What will happen to the equilibrium price level and real GDP when:

1. foreign price levels rise?
2. foreign incomes fall?
3. taxes rise?
4. the use of new computers increases productivity?

We are not saying that the level of output never changes. The long-run aggregate supply curve shifts as technology changes, and new supplies of resources are obtained. But the output change that results from a change in aggregate demand is a temporary, or short-run, phenomenon. The price level eventually adjusts, and output eventually returns to the potential level.

RECAP

1. The equilibrium level of price and real GDP is at the point where the aggregate demand and aggregate supply curves intersect.

2. In the short run, a shift in aggregate demand establishes a temporary equilibrium along the short-run aggregate supply curve.

3. In the long run, the short-run aggregate supply curve shifts so that changes in aggregate demand only affect the price level, not the equilibrium level of output or real GDP.

## SUMMARY

### ? What is aggregate demand?

1. Aggregate demand is the relation between aggregate expenditures and the price level.

2. Aggregate demand is the sum of consumption, investment, government spending, and net exports at alternative price levels.

3. Aggregate expenditures change with changes in the price level because of the wealth effect, the interest rate effect, and the international trade effect. These cause a movement along the *AD* curve.

### ? What causes the aggregate demand curve to shift?

4. The aggregate demand (*AD*) curve shows the level of expenditures for real GDP at different price levels.

5. Because expenditures and prices move in opposite directions, the *AD* curve is negatively sloped.

6. The nonprice determinants of aggregate demand include expectations, foreign income and price levels, and government policy.

### ? What is aggregate supply?

7. Aggregate supply is the relation between the quantity of real GDP produced and the price level.

### ? Why does the short-run aggregate supply curve become steeper as real GDP increases?

8. As real GDP rises, and the economy pushes closer to capacity output, the level of prices must rise to induce increased production.

### ? Why is the long-run aggregate supply curve vertical?

9. The long-run aggregate supply curve is vertical at the potential level of real GDP because there is no effect of higher prices on output when an economy is producing at potential real GDP.

### ? What causes the aggregate supply curve to shift?

10. The nonprice determinants of aggregate supply are resource prices, technology, and expectations.

### ? What determines the equilibrium price level and real GDP?

11. The equilibrium level of price and real GDP is at the intersection of the aggregate demand and aggregate supply curves.

12. In the short run, a shift in aggregate demand establishes a new, but temporary, equilibrium along the short-run aggregate supply curve.

13. In the long run, the short-run aggregate supply curve shifts so that changes in aggregate demand determine the price level, not the equilibrium level of output or real GDP.

## KEY TERMS

wealth effect

interest rate effect

international trade effect

aggregate demand curve

aggregate supply curve

long-run aggregate supply curve (*LRAS*)

## EXERCISES

1. How is the aggregate demand curve different from the demand curve for a single good, like hamburgers?

2. Why does the aggregate demand curve slope down? Give real-world examples of the three effects that explain the slope of the curve.

3. How does an increase in foreign income affect domestic aggregate expenditures and demand? Draw a diagram to illustrate your answer.

4. How does a decrease in foreign price levels affect domestic aggregate expenditures and demand? Draw a diagram to illustrate your answer.

5. How is the aggregate supply curve different from the supply curve for a single good, like pizza?

6. There are several determinants of aggregate supply that can cause the aggregate supply curve to shift.
   a. Describe those determinants and give an example of a change in each.
   b. Draw and label an aggregate supply diagram that illustrates the effect of the change in each determinant.

7. Draw a short-run aggregate supply curve that gets steeper as real GDP rises.
   a. Explain why the curve has this shape.
   b. Now draw a long-run aggregate supply curve that intersects a short-run *AS* curve. What is the relationship between short-run *AS* and long-run *AS*?

8. Draw and carefully label an aggregate demand and supply diagram with initial equilibrium at $P_0$ and $Y_0$.
   a. Using the diagram, explain what happens when aggregate demand falls.
   b. How is the short run different from the long run?

9. Draw an aggregate demand and supply diagram for Japan. In the diagram, show how each of the following affects aggregate demand and supply:
   a. U.S. gross domestic product falls.
   b. The level of prices in Korea falls.
   c. Labor receives a large wage increase.
   d. Economists predict higher prices next year.

10. If the long-run aggregate supply curve gives the level of potential real GDP, how can the short-run aggregate supply curve ever lie to the right of the long-run aggregate supply curve?

11. What will happen to the equilibrium price level and real GDP if:
    a. Aggregate demand and aggregate supply both increase?
    b. Aggregate demand increases and aggregate supply decreases?
    c. Aggregate demand and aggregate supply both decrease?
    d. Aggregate demand decreases and aggregate supply increases?

12. During the Great Depression, the U.S. economy experienced a falling price level and declining real GDP. Using an aggregate demand and aggregate supply diagram, illustrate and explain how this could occur.

13. Suppose aggregate demand increases, causing an increase in real GDP but no change in the price level. Using an aggregate demand and aggregate supply diagram, illustrate and explain how this could occur.

14. Suppose aggregate demand increases, causing an increase in the price level but no change in real GDP. Using an aggregate demand and aggregate supply diagram, illustrate and explain how this could occur.

15. Use an aggregate demand and aggregate supply diagram to illustrate and explain how each of the following will affect the equilibrium price level and real GDP:
    a. Consumers expect a recession.
    b. Foreign income rises.
    c. Foreign price levels fall.
    d. Government spending increases.
    e. Workers expect higher future inflation and negotiate higher wages now.
    f. Technological improvements increase productivity.

16. In the boom years of the late 1990s, it was often said that rapidly increasing stock prices were responsible for much of the rapid growth of real GDP. Explain how this could be true by using aggregate demand and aggregate supply analysis.

17. In 2003, there was much concern that rising oil prices would contribute to a global recession. Use aggregate demand and supply analysis to explain how high oil prices could reduce real GDP.

The length of expansions and contractions in the business cycle is determined by the size and duration of shifts in aggregate demand (*AD*) and aggregate supply (*AS*).

Check out the history of U.S. business cycle fluctuations by going to the Boyes/Melvin, *Fundamentals of Economics* website accessible through **http://college.hmco.com** and clicking on the Internet Exercise link for Chapter 12. Now answer the questions found on the Boyes/Melvin website.

## Key Term Match

**Match each term with its correct definition by placing the appropriate letter next to the corresponding number.**

A. wealth effect
B. interest rate effect
C. international trade effect
D. aggregate demand curve
E. aggregate supply curve
F. long-run aggregate supply curve (LRAS)

_____ 1. a curve that shows the different levels of expenditures on domestic output at different levels of prices

_____ 2. a vertical line at the potential level of national income

_____ 3. a change in the real value of wealth that causes spending to change when the level of prices changes

_____ 4. a curve that shows the amount of real GDP produced at different price levels

_____ 5. a change in interest rates that causes investment and therefore aggregate expenditures to change as the level of prices changes

_____ 6. a change in aggregate expenditures resulting from a change in the domestic price level that changes the price of domestic goods in relation to foreign goods

## Quick-Check Quiz

1 Which of the following would cause an increase in both the equilibrium price level and the equilibrium level of real GDP?

  a. The Fed cuts interest rates.
  b. Business confidence decreases.
  c. Energy prices decrease.
  d. Energy prices increase.
  e. Interest rates fall accompanied by a decline in energy prices.

2 Which of the following will *not* decrease investment?

  a. an increase in the cost of capital goods
  b. an improvement in technology
  c. an increase in interest rates
  d. unfavorable changes in tax policy
  e. rumors that the government will nationalize firms

3 Which of the following will *not* cause an increase in U.S. exports?

  a. European incomes increase.
  b. The dollar depreciates.
  c. A favorable change in tastes.
  d. The dollar appreciates.
  e. A meeting of the WTO results in lowered trade restrictions.

4 Which of the following will *not* decrease U.S. aggregate demand?

  a. Consumers expect a recession.
  b. The dollar depreciates.
  c. Mexican and Canadian incomes decline.
  d. The cost of capital goods increases.
  e. Excess capacity in manufacturing becomes apparent.

5 When prices increase, people and businesses need _____ money. They _____ bonds, causing interest rates to _____ and aggregate expenditures to _____.

  a. more; buy; fall; rise
  b. more; sell; rise; fall
  c. more; sell; fall; rise
  d. less; buy; fall; rise
  e. more; buy; rise; fall

6 The long-run aggregate supply curve is

  a. upward-sloping because of the effect of higher prices on profits.
  b. horizontal, reflecting excess capacity in all parts of the economy.
  c. upward-sloping, reflecting excess capacity in some parts of the economy.
  d. horizontal because there is no relationship between the price level and national income in the long run.
  e. vertical because there is no relationship between the price level and national income in the long run.

7 Which of the following statements is false?

  a. The long-run aggregate supply curve can shift to the right if new technologies are developed.
  b. The long-run aggregate supply curve can shift to the left if the quality of the factors of production decreases.
  c. The long-run aggregate supply curve is fixed at potential output and cannot shift.

d. An increase in long-run aggregate supply will decrease the equilibrium price level.

e. A decrease in long-run aggregate supply will decrease the equilibrium level of real GDP.

**8** Which of the following will increase aggregate supply?

a. Oil prices increase as Saudi Arabia decreases its production.

b. A change in computer chip technology increases productivity.

c. The Consumer Price Index rises.

d. The price level decreases.

e. Consumers anticipate higher prices.

**9** Consumer prices rose at their fastest rate in a year in January 2004, fueled mostly by higher energy prices. This increase in inflation coupled with an increase in unemployment can only result from a(n)

a. increase in aggregate demand.

b. decrease in aggregate demand.

c. increase in aggregate supply.

d. decrease in aggregate supply.

e. decrease in government spending.

**10** Which of the following statements is true?

a. In the long run, the short-run aggregate demand curve shifts so that changes in aggregate supply determine the price level, not the equilibrium level of income.

b. In the long run, the short-run aggregate demand curve shifts so that changes in aggregate supply determine the equilibrium level of income, not the price level.

c. In the long run, the equilibrium level of output never changes.

d. In the long run, there is a positive relationship between the level of prices and the level of output.

e. In the long run, the short-run aggregate supply curve shifts so that changes in aggregate demand determine the price level, not the equilibrium level of income.

## Practice Questions and Problems

**1** _____ inflation is inflation caused by increasing demand for output.

**2** If aggregate demand falls, the equilibrium level of income _____ (rises, falls),

unemployment _____ (rises, falls), and the price level _____ (rises, falls).

**3** A(n) _____ (increase, decrease) in aggregate supply leads to an increase in the equilibrium level of national income, a(n) _____ (increase, decrease) in unemployment, and a(n) _____ (increase, decrease) in the price level.

**4** _____ inflation is an increase in the price level caused by increased costs of production.

**5** If wealth decreases, consumption (spending by households) _____.

**6** As foreign income rises, net exports _____.

**7** If a new trade agreement with Japan succeeds in opening Japanese markets to U.S. goods, net exports will _____.

**8** _____ equal exports minus imports.

**9** All other things being equal, economists expect consumption to _____ (rise, fall, not change) as the population increases.

**10** As taxation increases, consumption _____ (rises, falls, does not change).

**11** _____ is business spending on capital goods and inventories.

**12** As household wealth increases, consumption _____ (increases, decreases).

**13** List the five determinants of consumption.

_____  _____

_____  _____

_____

**14** As the cost of capital goods rises, the amount of investment _____ (rises, falls).

**15** When capacity utilization is high, investment tends to _____ (rise, fall).

16 List the four determinants of investment.

_____  _____

_____  _____

17 When the domestic currency depreciates, imports _____ (rise, fall).

18 The higher the domestic income, the _____ (higher, lower) the net exports.

19 List the four determinants of net exports.

_____  _____

_____  _____

20 As the level of prices increases, the purchasing power of money _____ (increases, decreases), and the real value of assets _____ (increases, decreases). The _____ effect, or real-balance effect, predicts that the real value of aggregate expenditures will then _____ (rise, fall).

21 If domestic prices rise while foreign prices and foreign exchange rates remain constant, domestic goods will become _____ (less expensive, more expensive) for foreigners. Net exports will _____ (rise, fall), causing aggregate expenditures to _____ (rise, fall).

22 If foreign prices fall, foreign goods become _____ (less expensive, more expensive), which causes _____ (a movement along the aggregate demand curve, a shift to the left of the aggregate demand curve).

23 A fall in the domestic price level causes _____ (a movement along the aggregate demand curve, a shift in aggregate demand to the left).

24 Positive expectations about the economy increase _____ and _____, which in turn _____ (increases, decreases) aggregate demand.

25 Higher foreign incomes cause _____ to rise, causing _____ (a movement along the aggregate demand curve, a shift in aggregate demand to the right).

26 If the prices of output increase while all other prices remain unchanged, business profits will _____ (increase, decrease), and producers will produce _____ (more, less) output.

27 List the three nonprice determinants of short-run aggregate supply.

_____

_____

_____

28 When the prices of resources fall, the short-run aggregate supply curve shifts to the _____.

29 In the long run, there _____ (is, is not) a relationship between the level of prices and the level of output.

## Exercises and Applications

1 **Aggregate Demand and Its Determinants** Now that you have finished this chapter, you should be able to predict the effect on aggregate demand when one of its determinants changes. In the following exercise, decide which of the spending components each event affects, whether it increased or decreased the component, and whether it increased or decreased aggregate demand. Remember the determinants of each component of aggregate demand:

Consumption: income, wealth, expectations, demographics, taxes

Investment: interest rate, cost of capital goods, technology, capacity utilization

Government spending: set by government authorities

Net exports: foreign and domestic income and prices, exchange rates, government policy

### Events

1. The Federal Reserve, fearing an upsurge in inflation, increases interest rates.

2. In the wake of the war in Iraq, the dollar depreciates against the euro.
3. In April 2004, Fed Chairman Alan Greenspan opposed a tax increase to contain the deficit and instead proposed scaling back on social security and Medicare. Consider the effects if Greenspan's recommendations are implemented by Congress.

4. Foreign incomes rise.
5. The population increases more quickly.
6. Factories note a decline in the rate of capacity utilization.
7. Congress imposes a nationwide sales tax on retail goods and services.
8. The cost of capital goods decreases.

| *Component* | *Effect on Component* | *Effect on Aggregate Demand* |
|---|---|---|
| 1. Investment | Decrease | Decrease |
| 2. | | |
| 3. | | |
| 4. | | |
| 5. | | |
| 6. | | |
| 7. | | |
| 8. | | |

**II  A Long-Run Analysis of the Effects of a Slump in Productivity**  Many people have been concerned about the slower growth of productivity in recent years. Suppose that the growth of productivity in the United States not only slows but actually decreases. This could result from declines in workers' basic skills that some educators believe are due to a lack of students' adequate preparation in the nation's high schools. What will happen to the equilibrium price level and real GDP in the long run? Use the graph at right to analyze this problem. Be sure to label your axes.

ACE self-test

Now that you've completed the Study Guide for this chapter, you should have a good sense of the concepts you need to review. If you'd like to test your understanding of the material again, go to the Practice Tests on the Boyes/Melvin *Fundamentals of Economics,* 3e website, **economics.college.hmco.com/students.**

## Chapter 13

# Fiscal Policy

**Fundamental Questions**

1. How can fiscal policy eliminate a GDP gap?
2. How has U.S. fiscal policy changed over time?
3. What are the effects of budget deficits?
4. How does fiscal policy differ across countries?

## Preview

Macroeconomics plays a key role in national politics. When Jimmy Carter ran for the presidency against Gerald Ford in 1976, he created a "misery index" to measure the state of the economy. The index was the sum of the inflation rate and the unemployment rate, and Carter showed that it had risen during Ford's term in office. When Ronald Reagan challenged Carter in 1980, he used the misery index to show that inflation and unemployment had gone up during the Carter years. The implication is that presidents are responsible for the condition of the economy. If the inflation rate or the unemployment rate is relatively high coming into an election year, incumbent presidents are open to criticism by their opponents. For instance, many people believe that George Bush was defeated by Bill Clinton in 1992 because of the country's economic conditions. Clinton emphasized the recession that began in 1990—a recession that was not announced as having ended in March 1991 until after the election. As a result, Clinton's campaign made economic growth a focus of its attacks on Bush. Then in 1996, a healthy economy helped Bill Clinton defeat Bob Dole. In the election of 2000, Al Gore supporters made the strong economic growth during the Clinton years a major focal point of their campaign against George W. Bush. Finally, in 2004, the Bush administration was criticized for a lack of job growth, even though the economy was growing. This is more than campaign rhetoric, however. By law the government *is* responsible for the macroeconomic health of the nation. The Employment Act of 1946 states:

"It is the continuing policy and responsibility of the Federal Government to use all practical means consistent with its needs and obligations and other essential considerations of national policy to coordinate and utilize all its plans, functions, and resources for the purpose of creating and maintaining, in a manner calculated to foster and promote free competitive enterprise and the general welfare conditions under which there will be afforded useful employment opportunities, including self-employment for those able, willing, and seeking to work, and to promote maximum employment, production, and purchasing power."

*Fiscal policy* is one tool that government uses to guide the economy along an expansionary path. In this chapter we examine the role of fiscal policy—government spending and taxation—in determining the equilibrium level of income. Then we review the budget process and the history of fiscal policy in the United States. Finally, we describe the difference in fiscal policy between industrial and developing countries. ■

**1. How can fiscal policy eliminate a GDP gap?**

# 1. FISCAL POLICY AND AGGREGATE DEMAND

The GDP gap is the difference between potential real GDP and the equilibrium level of real GDP. If the government wants to close the GDP gap so that the equilibrium level of real GDP reaches its potential, it must use fiscal policy to alter aggregate expenditures and cause the aggregate demand curve to shift.

Fiscal policy is the government's policy with respect to spending and taxation. Since aggregate demand includes consumption, investment, net exports, and government spending, government spending on goods and services affects the level of aggregate demand directly. Taxes affect aggregate demand indirectly by changing the disposable income of households, which alters consumption.

## 1.a. Shifting the Aggregate Demand Curve

Changes in government spending and taxes shift the aggregate demand curve. Remember that the aggregate demand curve represents combinations of equilibrium aggregate expenditures and alternative price levels. An increase in government spending or a decrease in taxes raises the level of expenditures at every level of prices and moves the aggregate demand curve to the right.

Figure 1 shows an increase in aggregate demand that would result from an increase in government spending or a decrease in taxes. Only if the aggregate supply curve is horizontal do prices remain fixed as aggregate demand increases. In Figure 1(a), equilibrium occurs along the horizontal segment (the Keynesian region) of the $AS$ curve. If government spending increases, and the price level remains constant, aggregate demand shifts from $AD$ to $AD_1$; it increases by the horizontal distance from point $A$ to point $B$. Once aggregate demand shifts, the $AD_1$ and $AS$ curves intersect at potential real GDP, $Y_p$.

But Figure 1(a) is not realistic. The $AS$ curve is not likely to be horizontal all the way to the level of potential real GDP; it should begin sloping up well before $Y_p$. And once the economy reaches the capacity level of output, the $AS$ curve should become a vertical line, as shown in Figure 1(b).

If the $AS$ curve slopes up before reaching the potential real GDP level, as it does in part (b) of the figure, expenditures have to go up by more than the amount suggested in part (a) for the economy to reach $Y_p$. Why? Because when prices rise, the effect of spending on real GDP is reduced. This effect is shown in Figure 1(b). To increase the equilibrium level of real GDP from $Y_e$ to $Y_p$, aggregate demand must shift by the amount from point $A$ to $C$, a larger increase than that shown in Figure 1(a), where the price level is fixed.

## 1.b. Multiplier Effects

Changes in government spending may have an effect on real GDP that is a multiple of the original change in government spending; a $1 change in government spending may increase real GDP by more than $1. This is because the original $1 of expenditure is spent over and over again in the economy as it passes from person to person. The government spending multiplier measures the multiple by which an increase in government spending increases real GDP. Similarly, a change in taxes may have an effect on real GDP that is a multiple of the original change in taxes.

If the price level rises as real GDP increases, the multiplier effects of any given change in aggregate demand are smaller than they would be if the price

Figure 1

**Eliminating the Recessionary Gap: Higher Prices Mean Greater Spending**

When aggregate demand increases from $AD$ to $AD_1$ in Figure 1(a), equilibrium real GDP increases by the full amount of the shift in demand. This is because the aggregate supply curve is horizontal over the area of the shift in aggregate demand. In Figure 1(b), in order for equilibrium real GDP to rise from $Y_e$ to $Y_p$, aggregate demand must shift by more than it does in part (a). In reality, the aggregate supply curve begins to slope up before potential real GDP ($Y_p$) is reached, as shown in part (b) of the figure.

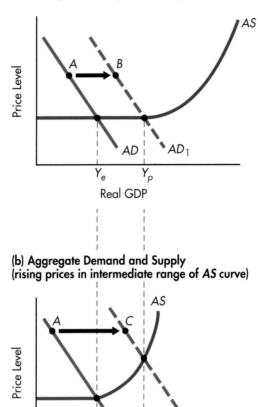

**(a) Aggregate Demand and Supply**
(constant prices in Keynesian range of *AS* curve)

**(b) Aggregate Demand and Supply**
(rising prices in intermediate range of *AS* curve)

level remains constant. In addition to changes in the price level modifying the effect of government spending and taxes on real GDP, there are other factors that affect how much real GDP will change following a change in government spending. One such factor is how the government pays for, or finances, its spending.

Government spending must be financed by some combination of taxing, borrowing, or creating money:

Government spending = taxes + change in government debt
+ change in government-issued money

In Chapter 15 we discuss the effect of financing government spending by creating money. As you will see, this source of government financing is relied on heavily in some developing countries. Here we talk about the financing problem relevant for industrial countries: how taxes and government debt can modify the expansionary effect of government spending on national income.

### 1.c. Government Spending Financed by Tax Increases

Suppose that government spending rises by $100 billion and that this expenditure is financed by a tax increase of $100 billion. Such a "balanced-budget" change in fiscal policy will cause equilibrium real GDP to rise. This is because government spending increases aggregate expenditures directly, but higher taxes lower aggregate expenditures indirectly through consumption spending. For instance, if taxes increase $100, consumers will not cut their spending by $100, but by some fraction, say 9/10, of the increase. If consumers spend 90 percent of a change in their disposable income, then a tax increase of $100 would lower consumption by $90. So the net effect of raising government spending and taxes by the same amount is an increase in aggregate demand, illustrated in Figure 2 as the shift from $AD$ to $AD_1$. However, it may be incorrect to assume that the only thing that changes is aggregate demand. An increase in taxes may also affect aggregate supply.

Aggregate supply measures the output that producers offer for sale at different levels of prices. When taxes go up, workers have less incentive to work because their after-tax income is lower. The cost of taking a day off or extending a vacation for a few extra days is less than it is when taxes are lower and after-tax income is higher. When taxes go up, then, output can fall, causing the aggregate supply curve to shift to the left. Such supply-side effects of taxes have been emphasized by the so-called supply-side economists.

Figure 2 shows the possible effects of an increase in government spending financed by taxes. The economy is initially in equilibrium at point $A$, with prices at $P_1$ and real GDP at $Y_1$. The increase in government spending shifts the aggregate demand curve from $AD$ to $AD_1$. If this were the only change, the economy would be in equilibrium at point $B$. But if the increase in taxes reduces output, the aggregate supply curve moves back from $AS$ to $AS_1$, and output does not expand all the way to $Y_p$. The decrease in aggregate supply creates a new equilibrium at point $C$. Here real GDP is at $Y_2$ (less than $Y_p$), and the price level is $P_3$ (higher than $P_2$).

The standard analysis of government spending and taxation assumes that aggregate supply is not affected by the change in fiscal policy, leading us to expect a greater change in real GDP than may actually occur. If tax changes do affect aggregate supply, the expansionary effects of government spending financed by tax increases are moderated. The actual magnitude of the effect is the subject of debate among economists. Most argue that the evidence in the United States indicates that tax increases have a fairly small effect on aggregate supply.

Figure 2

**The Effect of Taxation on Aggregate Supply**

An increase in government spending shifts the aggregate demand curve from $AD$ to $AD_1$, moving equilibrium from point $A$ to point $B$, and equilibrium real GDP from $Y_1$ to $Y_p$. If higher taxes reduce the incentive to work, aggregate supply could fall from $AS$ to $AS_1$, moving equilibrium to point $C$ and equilibrium real GDP to $Y_2$, a level below potential real GDP.

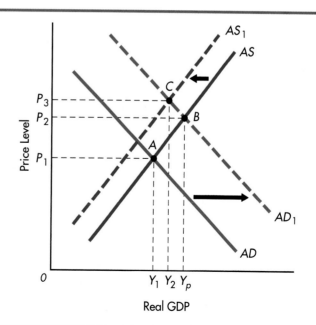

Many government expenditures are unrelated to current economic conditions. For instance, the provision of national defense, a legal system, and police and fire protection are all cases in which government expenditures would not typically fluctuate with the business cycle. These firefighters are employed through booms and recessions in the economy. Although macroeconomists focus typically on the discretionary elements of fiscal policy that may be altered to combat business cycles, the nondiscretionary elements account for the bulk of governments' budgets.

## 1.d. Government Spending Financed by Borrowing

The standard multiplier analysis of government spending does not differentiate among the different methods of financing that spending. Yet you just saw how taxation can offset at least part of the expansionary effect of higher government spending. Borrowing to finance government spending can also limit the increase in aggregate demand.

A government borrows funds by selling bonds to the public. These bonds represent debt that must be repaid at a future date. Debt is, in a way, a kind of substitute for current taxes. Instead of increasing current taxes to finance higher spending, the government borrows the savings of households and businesses. Of course, the debt will mature and have to be repaid. This means that taxes will have to be higher in the future in order to provide the government with the funds to pay off the debt.

Current government borrowing, then, implies higher future taxes. This can limit the expansionary effect of increased government spending. If households and businesses take higher future taxes into account, they tend to save more today so that they will be able to pay those taxes in the future. And as saving today increases, consumption today falls.

## 1.e. Crowding Out

Expansionary fiscal policy can crowd out private-sector spending; that is, an increase in government spending can reduce consumption and investment. **Crowding out** is usually discussed in the context of government spending financed by borrowing rather than by taxing. Though we have just seen how future taxes can cause consumption to fall today, investment can also be affected. Increases in government borrowing drive up interest rates. As interest rates go up, investment falls. This sort of indirect crowding out works through the bond market. The U.S. government borrows by selling Treasury bonds or bills. Because the government is not a profit-making institution, it does not have to earn a profitable return from the money it raises by selling bonds. A corporation does, however. When interest rates rise, fewer corporations offer new bonds to raise investment funds because the cost of repaying the bond debt may exceed the rate of return on the investment.

**crowding out:** a drop in consumption or investment spending caused by government spending

Crowding out is important in principle, but economists have never demonstrated conclusively that its effects can substantially alter spending in the private sector. Still, you should be aware of the possibility to understand the potential shortcomings of changes in government spending and taxation.

## 2. FISCAL POLICY IN THE UNITED STATES

Our discussion of fiscal policy assumes that policy is made at the federal level. In the modern economy this is a reasonable assumption. This was not the case before the 1930s, however. Before the Depression, the federal government limited its activities largely to national defense and foreign policy, and left other areas of government policy to the individual states. With the growth of the importance of the federal government in fiscal policy has come a growth in the role of the federal budget process.

### 2.a. The Budget Process

Fiscal policy in the United States is the product of a complex process that involves both the executive and legislative branches of government (Figure 3). The fiscal year for the U.S. government begins October 1 of one year and ends September 30 of the next. The budget process begins each spring when the president directs the federal agencies to prepare their budgets for the fiscal year that starts almost 18 months later. The agencies submit their budget requests to the Office of Management and Budget (OMB) by early September. The OMB reviews and modifies each agency's request and consolidates all of the proposals into a budget that the president presents to Congress in January.

Once Congress receives the president's budget, the Congressional Budget Office (CBO) studies it, and committees modify it before funds are appropriated. The budget is evaluated in Budget Committee hearings in both the House of Representatives and the Senate. In addition, the CBO reports to Congress on the validity of the economic assumptions made in the president's budget. A budget resolution is passed by April 15 that sets out major expenditures and estimated revenues. (Revenues are estimated because future tax payments can never be known exactly.) The resolution is followed by *reconciliation,* a process in which each committee of Congress must coordinate relevant tax and spending decisions. Once the reconciliation process is completed, funds are appropriated. The process is supposed to end before Congress recesses for the summer, at the end of June. When talking about the federal budget, the monetary amounts of various categories of expenditures are

Figure 3

**The Making of U.S. Fiscal Policy**

The flow chart shows the policymaking process. Start with the president and follow the arrows in order. Although the dates are approximate, the process of setting the federal budget involves these stages and participants.

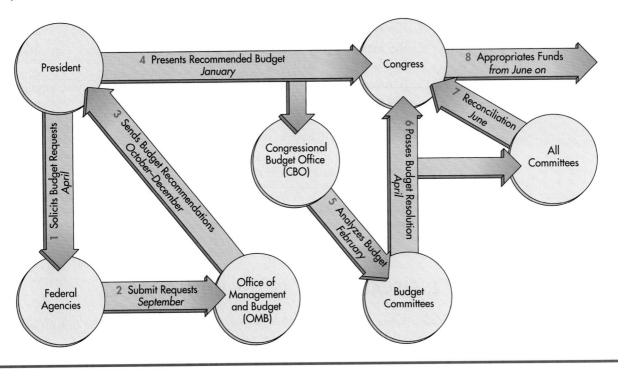

so huge that they are often difficult to comprehend. But if you were to divide up the annual budget by the number of individual taxpayers, you would come up with an average individual statement that might make more sense, as shown in the Economic Insight "The Taxpayer's Federal Government Credit Card Statement."

The federal budget is determined as much by politics as by economics. Politicians respond to different groups of voters by supporting different government programs regardless of the needed fiscal policy. It is the political response to constituents that tends to drive up federal budget deficits (the difference between government expenditures and tax revenues), not the need for expansionary fiscal policy. As a result, deficits have become commonplace.

## 2.b. The Historical Record

**2. How has U.S. fiscal policy changed over time?**

The U.S. government has grown dramatically since the early part of the century. Figure 4 shows federal revenues and expenditures over time. Figure 5 places the growth of government in perspective by plotting U.S. government spending as a percentage of gross domestic product over time. Before the Great Depression, federal spending was approximately 3 percent of the GDP; by the end of the Depression, it had risen to almost 10 percent. The ratio of spending to GDP reached its peak during World War II, when federal spending hit 45 percent of the GDP. After the war, the ratio fell dramatically and then slowly increased to about 18 percent today.

Fiscal policy has two components: discretionary fiscal policy and automatic stabilizers. **Discretionary fiscal policy** refers to changes in government spending and taxation aimed at achieving a policy goal. **Automatic stabilizers** are elements of fiscal policy that automatically change in value as national income changes. Figures 4 and 5 suggest that government spending is dominated by growth over time. But there is

**discretionary fiscal policy:** changes in government spending and taxation aimed at achieving a policy goal

**automatic stabilizer:** an element of fiscal policy that changes automatically as income changes

## The Taxpayer's Federal Government Credit Card Statement

Suppose the U.S. government's expenditures and revenues were accounted for annually to each individual income taxpayer like a credit card statement. For 2004, the statement would look like the one at the right.

**Statement for 2004 Budget Year**

| | |
|---|---|
| **Previous balance, 2003** | **$51,083.64** |

(your average taxpayer share of the publicly held beginning-of-year national debt)

**New purchases during the year**

(your average taxpayer share)

| | |
|---|---|
| Social security | $3,749.66 |
| National defense | 3,428.50 |
| Income security | 2,565.52 |
| Medicare | 2,044.10 |
| Commerce and housing credit | 58.19 |
| Health | 1,840.07 |
| Education, training, and employment | 658.95 |
| Veterans' benefits and services | 457.18 |
| Transportation | 514.61 |
| Natural resources and environment | 239.55 |
| Science, space, and technology | 168.52 |
| International affairs | 258.44 |
| Agriculture | 151.89 |
| Administration of justice | 314.36 |
| General government | 191.94 |
| Community and regional development | 142.07 |
| Energy | 7.56 |

**Payments received—Thank you**

(your average taxpayer share)

| | |
|---|---|
| Individual income taxes | $5,783.94 |
| Corporate income taxes | 1,274.82 |
| Social security taxes | 5,534.57 |
| Other | 994.69 |

| | |
|---|---|
| **Finance charge** | **$1,181.12** |

(your average taxpayer share of net interest on the national debt)

| | |
|---|---|
| **New balance due** | **$56,569.84** |

(your average taxpayer share of the publicly held end-of-year national debt)

## Figure 4

### U.S. Government Revenues and Expenditures

Revenues are total revenues of the U.S. government in each fiscal year. Expenditures are total spending of the U.S. government in each fiscal year. The difference between the two curves equals the U.S. budget deficit (when expenditures exceed revenues) or surplus (when revenues exceed expenditures).

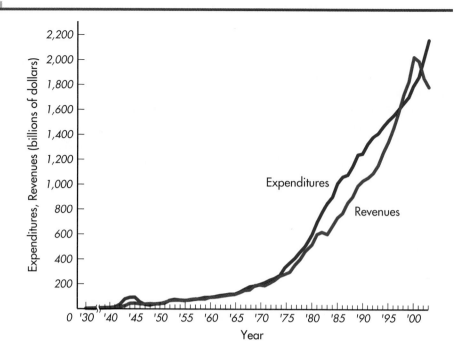

*Source: Economic Report of the President,* 2004 (Washington, D.C.: Govt Printing Office, 2004).

no indication here of discretionary changes in fiscal policy, changes in government spending and taxation aimed at meeting specific policy goals. Perhaps a better way to evaluate the fiscal policy record is in terms of the budget deficit. Government expenditures can rise, but the effect on aggregate demand could be offset by a simultaneous increase in taxes so that there is no expansionary effect on the equilibrium level of national income. By looking at the deficit, we see the combined spending and tax policy results that are missing if only government expenditures are considered.

Figure 6 illustrates the pattern of the U.S. federal deficit and the deficit as a percentage of GDP over time. Figure 6(a) shows that the United States ran close to a

## Figure 5

### U.S. Government Expenditures as a Percentage of Gross Domestic Product

The U.S. federal government spending as a percentage of the GDP reached a high of 45 percent in 1943 and 1944. Discounting wartime spending and cutbacks after the war, you can see no particular trend in U.S. government spending as a share of the GDP over time.

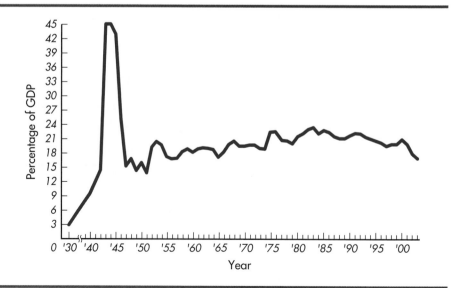

Figure 6

**The U.S. Deficit**

As part (a) shows, since 1940, the U.S. government has rarely shown a surplus. For much of the 1950s and 1960s, the United States was close to a balanced budget. Part (b) shows the federal deficit as a percentage of GDP. The deficits during the 1950s and 1960s generally were small.

The early 1980s were a time of rapid growth in the federal budget deficit, and this is reflected in the growth of the deficit as a percentage of GDP. From the late 1990s into the 2000s, there was a brief period of budget surpluses.

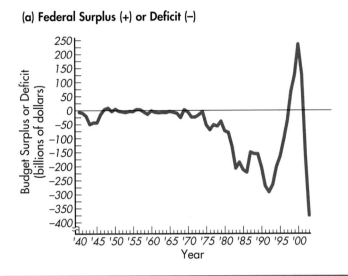

**(a) Federal Surplus (+) or Deficit (−)**

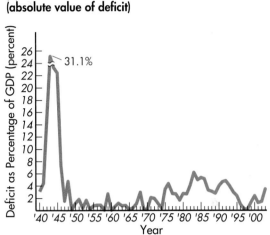

**(b) Federal Deficit as a Percent of GDP (absolute value of deficit)**

balanced budget for much of the 1950s and 1960s. There were large deficits associated with financing World War II and then large deficits resulting from fiscal policy decisions in the 1970s, 1980s, and 1990s. By 1998, however, the first surplus since 1969 was recorded. However, by 2002, budget deficits had returned. Figure 6(b) shows that the deficit as a percentage of GDP was much larger during World War II than in recent years.

The deficit increase in the mid-1970s was a product of a recession that cut the growth of tax revenues. Historically, aside from wartime, budget deficits increase the most during recessions. When real GDP falls, tax revenues go down, and government spending on unemployment and welfare benefits goes up. These are examples of automatic stabilizers in action. As income falls, taxes fall and personal benefit payments rise to partially offset the effect of the drop in income. The rapid growth of the deficit in the 1980s involved more than the recessions in 1980 and 1982, however. The economy grew rapidly after the 1982 recession ended, but so did the fiscal deficit. The increase in the deficit was the product of a rapid increase in government spending to fund new programs and enlarge existing programs while taxes were held constant. The reduction in the deficit in the late 1990s was the result of strong economic growth's generating surprisingly large tax revenue gains combined with only moderate government spending increases. However, with the recession of 2001, the country soon returned to deficits.

### 2.c. Deficits and the National Debt

**3. What are the effects of budget deficits?**

The large federal deficits of the 1980s and 1990s led many observers to question whether a deficit can harm the economy. Figure 6 shows how the fiscal deficit has changed over time. One major implication of a large deficit is the resulting increase in the national debt, the total stock of government bonds outstanding.

Table 1

**Debt of the U.S. Government (dollar amounts in billions)**

| (1) Year | (2) Total Debt | (3) Debt/GDP (percent) | (4) Net Interest | (5) Interest/Government Spending (percent) |
|---|---|---|---|---|
| 1958 | $ 279.7 | 63 | $ 5.6 | 6.8 |
| 1960 | 290.5 | 57 | 6.9 | 7.5 |
| 1962 | 302.9 | 55 | 6.9 | 6.5 |
| 1964 | 316.1 | 50 | 8.2 | 6.9 |
| 1966 | 328.5 | 44 | 9.4 | 7.0 |
| 1968 | 368.7 | 43 | 11.1 | 6.2 |
| 1970 | 380.9 | 39 | 14.4 | 7.4 |
| 1972 | 435.9 | 38 | 15.5 | 6.7 |
| 1974 | 483.9 | 34 | 21.4 | 8.0 |
| 1976 | 629.0 | 37 | 26.7 | 7.3 |
| 1978 | 776.6 | 36 | 35.4 | 7.9 |
| 1980 | 909.1 | 34 | 52.5 | 9.1 |
| 1982 | 1,137.3 | 36 | 85.0 | 11.6 |
| 1984 | 1,564.7 | 42 | 111.1 | 13.2 |
| 1986 | 2,120.6 | 50 | 136.0 | 13.7 |
| 1988 | 2,601.3 | 54 | 151.8 | 14.3 |
| 1990 | 3,206.6 | 59 | 184.2 | 14.7 |
| 1992 | 4,002.1 | 68 | 199.4 | 14.4 |
| 1994 | 4,643.7 | 70 | 203.0 | 13.9 |
| 1996 | 5,181.9 | 69 | 241.1 | 15.5 |
| 1998 | 5,478.7 | 63 | 241.2 | 14.6 |
| 2000 | 5,629.0 | 57 | 223.0 | 12.5 |
| 2001 | 5,769.9 | 58 | 206.2 | 11.1 |
| 2002 | 6,198.4 | 60 | 171.0 | 8.5 |
| 2003 | 6,760.0 | 62 | 153.1 | 7.1 |

Table 1 lists data on the debt of the United States. The total debt more than doubled between 1980 and 1986. Column 3 shows debt as a percentage of GDP. During World War II, the debt was greater than the GDP for five years. Despite the talk of "unprecedented" federal deficits in the 1980s and 1990s, clearly the ratio of the debt to GDP was by no means unprecedented.

We have not yet answered the question of whether deficits are bad. To do so, we have to consider their potential effects.

**2.c.1. Deficits, Interest Rates, and Investment** Because government deficits mean government borrowing and debt, many economists argue that deficits raise interest rates. Increased government borrowing raises interest rates, which in turn can depress investment. (Remember that as interest rates rise, the rate of return on investment drops, along with the incentive to invest.) What happens when government borrowing crowds out private investment? Lower investment means fewer capital goods in the future, so deficits lower the level of output in the economy both today and in the future. In this sense, deficits are potentially bad.

**2.c.2. Deficits and International Trade** If government deficits raise real interest rates (the nominal interest rate minus the expected inflation rate), they also may have an effect on international trade. A higher real return on U.S. securities makes those securities more attractive to foreign investors. As the foreign demand for U.S. securities increases, so does the demand for U.S. dollars in exchange for Japanese yen, British pounds, and other foreign currencies. As the demand for dollars increases, the dollar *appreciates* in value on the foreign exchange market. This means that the dollar becomes more expensive to foreigners while foreign currency becomes cheaper to U.S. residents. This kind of change in the exchange rate encourages U.S. residents to buy more foreign goods and foreign residents to buy fewer U.S. goods. Ultimately, then, as deficits and government debt increase, U.S. net exports fall. Many economists believe that the growing fiscal deficits of the 1980s were responsible for the record decline in U.S. net exports during that period.

The U.S. federal budget deficit rose from $73.8 billion in 1980 to $212.3 billion in 1985. During this time, the dollar appreciated in value from 1.95 German marks per dollar to 3.32 marks per dollar and from 203 Japanese yen per dollar to 260 yen per dollar. (*Note:* German marks were replaced by euros in 2002.) These changes in the dollar exchange rate caused U.S. goods to rise in price to foreign buyers. For instance, a $1,000 IBM personal computer would sell for 1,950 German marks at the exchange rate of 1.95 marks per dollar. But at the rate of 3.32 marks per dollar, the $1,000 computer would sell for 3,320 marks. Furthermore, foreign currencies became cheaper to U.S. residents, making foreign goods cheaper in dollars. In 1980, one German mark sold for $.51. In 1985, one mark sold for $.30. At these prices, a Volkswagen wheel that sells for 100 marks would have changed in dollar price from $51 to $30 as the exchange rate changed. The combination of the dollar price of U.S. imports falling and the foreign currency price of U.S. exports rising caused U.S. net exports to fall dramatically at the same time that the fiscal deficit rose dramatically. Such foreign trade effects are another potentially bad effect of deficits.

### 2.c.3. Interest Payments on the National Debt

The national debt is the stock of government bonds outstanding. It is the product of past and current budget deficits. As the size of the debt increases, the interest that must be paid on the debt tends to rise. Column 4 of Table 1 lists the amount of interest paid on the debt; column 5 lists the interest as a percentage of government expenditures. The numbers in both columns have risen steadily over time and only recently have started to drop.

The steady increase in the interest cost of the national debt is an aspect of fiscal deficits that worries some people. However, to the extent that U.S. citizens hold government bonds, we owe the debt to ourselves. The tax liability of funding the interest payments is offset by the interest income bondholders earn. In this case there is no net change in national wealth when the national debt changes.

Of course, we do not owe the national debt just to ourselves. Over time, the share of U.S. debt held by foreigners has grown. The United States is the world's largest national financial market, and many U.S. securities, including government bonds, are held by foreign residents. In 1965, foreign holdings of the U.S. national debt amounted to about 5 percent of the outstanding debt. By 2003, this figure had risen to about 37 percent. Because the tax liability for paying the interest on the debt falls on U.S. taxpayers, the greater the payments made to foreigners, the lower the wealth of U.S. residents, other things being equal.

Other things are not equal, however. To understand the real impact of foreign holdings on the economy, we have to evaluate what the economy would have been like if the debt had not been sold to foreign investors. If the foreign savings placed in U.S. bonds allowed the United States to increase investment and its productive capacity beyond what would have been possible in the absence of foreign lending, then the country could very well be better off for selling government bonds to foreigners. The presence of foreign funds may keep interest rates lower than they would otherwise be, preventing the substantial crowding out associated with an increase in the national debt.

So while deficits are potentially bad due to the crowding out of investment, larger trade deficits with the rest of the world, and greater interest costs of the debt, we cannot generally say that all deficits are bad. It depends on what benefit the deficit provides. If the deficit spending allowed for greater productivity than would have occurred otherwise, the benefits may outweigh the costs.

## 2.d. Automatic Stabilizers

We have largely been talking about discretionary fiscal policy, the changes in government spending and taxing that policymakers make consciously. *Automatic stabilizers* are the elements of fiscal policy that change automatically as income changes. Automatic stabilizers partially offset changes in income: as income falls, automatic stabilizers increase spending; as income rises, automatic stabilizers decrease spending. Any program that responds to fluctuations in the business cycle in a way that moderates the effect of those fluctuations is an automatic stabilizer. Examples are progressive income taxes and transfer payments.

In our examples of tax changes, we have been using *lump-sum taxes*—taxes that are a flat dollar amount regardless of income. However, income taxes are determined as a percentage of income. In the United States, the federal income tax is a **progressive tax**: as income rises, so does the rate of taxation. A person with a very low income pays no income tax while a person with a high income can pay more than a third of that income in taxes. Countries use different rates of taxation on income. Taxes can be **regressive** (the tax rate falls as income rises) or **proportional** (the tax rate is constant as income rises). But most countries, including the United States, use a progressive tax, with the percentage of income paid as taxes rising with taxable income.

Progressive income taxes act as an automatic stabilizer. As income falls, so does the average tax rate. Suppose a household earning $60,000 must pay 30 percent of its income ($18,000) in taxes, leaving 70 percent of its income ($42,000) for spending. If that household's income drops to $40,000, and the tax rate falls to 25 percent, the household has 75 percent of its income ($30,000) available for spending. But if the tax rate is 30 percent at all levels of income, the household earning $40,000 would have only 70 percent of its income ($28,000) to spend. By allowing a greater percentage of earned income to be spent, progressive taxes help offset the effect of lower income on spending.

Industrial countries all have progressive federal income tax systems. For instance, the tax rate in Japan starts at 10 percent for low-income households and rises to a maximum of 40 percent for high-income households. U.S. individual income taxes start at 10 percent and rise to a maximum of 35 percent. The United Kingdom tax system rises from 10 percent to 40 percent while taxes in Germany rise from 23.9 to 53 percent and in France from 10.5 to 54 percent.

Recall that a transfer payment is a payment to one person that is funded by taxing others. Food stamps, welfare benefits, and unemployment benefits are all government transfer payments: current taxpayers provide the funds to pay those who qualify for the programs. Transfer payments that use income to establish eligibility act as automatic stabilizers. In a recession, as income falls, more people qualify for food stamps or welfare benefits, raising the level of transfer payments.

Unemployment insurance is also an automatic stabilizer. As unemployment rises, more workers receive unemployment benefits. Unemployment benefits tend to rise in a recession and fall during an expansion. This countercyclical pattern of benefit payments offsets the effect of business cycle fluctuations on consumption.

**progressive tax:** a tax whose rate rises as income rises

**regressive tax:** a tax whose rate falls as income rises

**proportional tax:** a tax whose rate is constant as income rises

1. Fiscal policy in the United States is a product of the budget process.

2. Federal spending in the United States has grown rapidly over time, from just 3 percent of the GDP before the Great Depression to approximately 18 percent of the GDP today.

3. Government budget deficits can hurt the economy through their effect on interest rates and private investment, net exports, and the tax burden on current and future taxpayers.

4. Automatic stabilizers are government programs that are already in place and that respond automatically to fluctuations in the business cycle, moderating the effect of those fluctuations.

**4. How does fiscal policy differ across countries?**

# 3. FISCAL POLICY IN DIFFERENT COUNTRIES

A country's fiscal policy reflects its philosophy toward government spending and taxation. In this section we present comparative data that demonstrate the variety of fiscal policies in the world.

## 3.a. Government Spending

Our discussion to this point has centered on U.S. fiscal policy. But fiscal policy and the role of government in the economy can be very different across countries. Government has played an increasingly larger role in the major industrial countries over time. Table 2 shows how government spending has gone up as a percentage of output in five industrial nations. In every case, government spending accounted for a larger percentage of output in 2001 than it did more than 100 years earlier. For instance, in 1880, government spending was only 6 percent of the GNP in Sweden. By 1929, it had risen to 8 percent; and by 2001, to 26 percent.

Historically in industrial countries, the growth of government spending has been matched by growth in revenues. But in the 1960s, government spending began to grow faster than revenues, creating increasingly larger debts for nations.

Developing countries have not shown the uniform growth in government spending found in industrial countries. In fact, in some developing countries (for instance, Chile, the Dominican Republic, and Peru), government spending is a smaller percentage of GDP today than it was 20 years ago. And we find a greater variation in the role of government in developing countries.

One important difference between the typical developed country and the typical developing country is that government plays a larger role in investment spending in the developing country. One reason for this difference is that state-owned enterprises account for a larger percentage of economic activity in developing countries than they do in developed countries. Also, developing countries usually rely more

**Table 2**

**Share of Government Spending in GNP in Selected Industrial Countries, 1880, 1929, and 2001 (percent)**

| Year | France | Germany | Sweden | United Kingdom | United States |
|------|--------|---------|--------|----------------|---------------|
| 1880 | 15 | 10* | 6 | 10 | 8 |
| 1929 | 19 | 31 | 8 | 24 | 10 |
| 2001 | 23 | 19 | 26 | 19 | 14 |

*1881.
*Source:* Data from World Bank, *World Development Report*, Washington, D.C., various issues.

Figure 7

**Central Government Spending by Functional Category**

The charts show the pattern of government spending in an industrial country, the United States; a middle-income developing country, Russia; and a low-income developing country, China. Social programs (education, health, and housing, social security, and welfare) account for 55 percent of federal government expenditures in the United States, but only 37 percent in Russia and 6 percent in China.

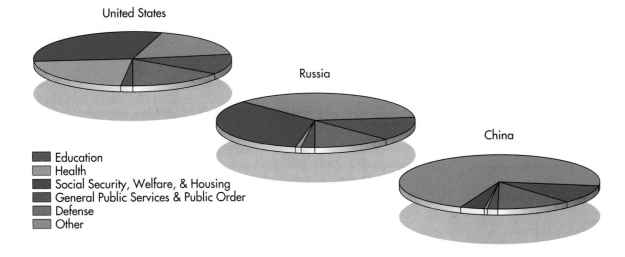

United States

Russia

China

- Education
- Health
- Social Security, Welfare, & Housing
- General Public Services & Public Order
- Defense
- Other

*Source:* Data are drawn from International Monetary Fund, *Government Finance Statistics Yearbook,* 2002.

on government than the private sector to build their infrastructure—schools, roads, hospitals—than do developed countries.

How a government spends its money is a function of its income. Here we find differences not only between industrial and developing countries but also among developing countries. Figure 7 provides data for one industrial country, the United States; and two large developing countries, Russia, a middle-income developing country; and China, a low-income developing country. It clearly illustrates the relative importance of social welfare spending in industrial and developing countries. Although standards of living are lowest in the poorest countries, these countries do not have the resources to spend on social services (education, health, housing, social security, welfare). The United States spends 55 percent of its budget on social programs. Russia spends 37 percent of its budget on social programs. China spends only 6 percent of its budget on these programs.

### 3.b. Taxation

There are two different types of taxes: *direct taxes* (on individuals and firms) and *indirect taxes* (on goods and services). Figure 8 compares the importance of different sources of central government tax revenue across industrial and developing countries. The most obvious difference is that personal income taxes are much more important in industrial countries than in developing countries. Why? Because personal taxes are hard to collect in agricultural nations, where a large percentage of household production is for personal consumption. Taxes on businesses are easier to collect, and thus are more important in developing countries.

That industrial countries are better able to afford social programs is reflected in the great disparity in social security taxes between industrial countries and developing countries. With so many workers living near the subsistence level in the

## Figure 8

**Central Government Tax Composition by Income Group**

When we group countries by income level, the importance of different sources of tax revenue is obvious. Domestic income taxes account for roughly a third of government revenue in industrial and middle-income developing countries and a quarter of government revenue in developing countries. However, personal income taxes are more important in industrial countries while business income taxes are more important in developing countries. Social security taxes are a major source of government revenue in industrial countries; they are less important in developing countries, which cannot afford social programs. International trade taxes represent just 1 percent of tax revenues in industrial countries; developing countries rely heavily on these taxes. (*Note:* Percentages do not total 100 because of rounding.)

*Source:* Data are drawn from *Government Finance Statistics,* 2002.

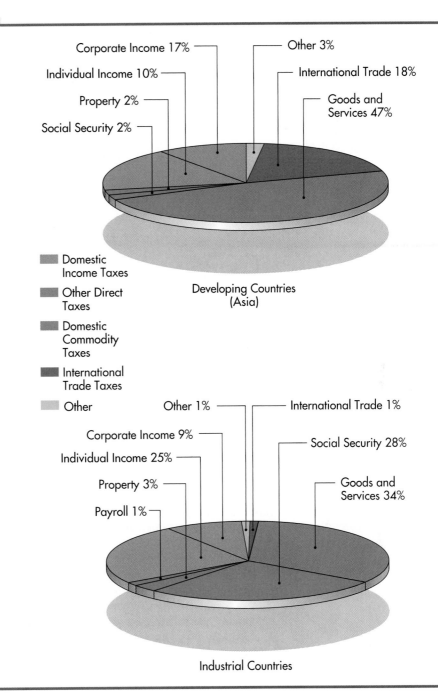

Legend:
- Domestic Income Taxes
- Other Direct Taxes
- Domestic Commodity Taxes
- International Trade Taxes
- Other

Developing Countries (Asia):
- Corporate Income 17%
- Individual Income 10%
- Property 2%
- Social Security 2%
- Other 3%
- International Trade 18%
- Goods and Services 47%

Industrial Countries:
- Other 1%
- International Trade 1%
- Corporate Income 9%
- Individual Income 25%
- Social Security 28%
- Property 3%
- Goods and Services 34%
- Payroll 1%

poorest countries, their governments simply cannot tax workers for retirement and health security programs.

Figure 8 also shows that taxes on international trade are very important in developing countries. Because goods arriving or leaving a country must pass through customs inspection, export and import taxes are relatively easy to collect compared with income taxes. In general, developing countries depend more heavily on indirect taxes on goods and services than do developed countries.

Figure 8 lists "goods and services" taxes. Of these, 65 percent are value-added taxes for industrial countries while 61 percent of developing country commodity taxes come from value-added taxes. A **value-added tax (VAT)** is an indirect tax imposed on each sale at each stage of production. Each seller from the first stage of

**value-added tax (VAT):** a general sales tax collected at each stage of production

## Value-Added Tax

*Global Business Insight*

A value-added tax (VAT) is a tax levied on all sales of goods and services at each stage of production. As implied by the name, the tax applies only to the value added at each stage, and so a firm that pays value-added taxes will pay tax only on the value that it added to the good or service that it sells. If a firm sells melons at a fruit stand, the VAT it pays is based on the difference between the cost the firm paid for the melons and the sales price it charges to its customers who buy the fruit. Of course, the customers bear the cost of the VAT, as it is built into the price they must pay.

As the accompanying map indicates, VATs are very popular around the world. Many countries adopted VATs in the 1990s. It is clear that there are more countries that use VATs than that do not. Such a tax has its advantages. One important consideration is that a VAT is a tax on consumption. Anyone who buys goods and services will contribute to the government's VAT revenue. Thus, VATs are very powerful revenue

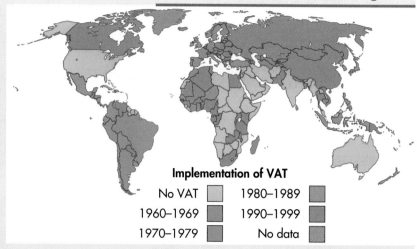

**Implementation of VAT**

| | |
|---|---|
| No VAT | 1980–1989 |
| 1960–1969 | 1990–1999 |
| 1970–1979 | No data |

*Source:* From IMF Survey, *International Monetary Fund,* Fol. 29, No. 9, May 8, 2000, p. 156. Reprinted with permission of International Monetary Fund.

generators. Those individuals who evade income taxes and pay less than their legal obligation will not escape the VAT. For instance, a criminal who earns income illegally and pays no tax on that income will be taxed on all legal goods and services that he or she purchases. In this sense, there is a certain attractiveness to taxing consumption rather than income. But a VAT also acts as a

regressive tax in that a poor person would tend to pay a higher fraction of income as VAT than a rich person. It is important to realize that no country relies strictly on a VAT for government revenue. VATs are part of an overall government tax policy that attempts to incorporate fairness along with a need to raise sufficient revenue to finance public expenditures.

production on collects the VAT from the buyer and then deducts any VATs it has paid in buying its inputs. The difference is remitted to the government. See the Global Business Insight, "Value-Added Tax," for additional details. From time to time, Congress has debated the merits of a VAT in the United States, but has never approved this kind of tax.

**RECAP**

1. Over time, government spending has become more important in industrial countries.

2. Governments in developing countries typically play a larger role in investment spending in their economies than do the governments of developed countries.

3. Developing countries depend more on indirect taxes on goods and services as a source of revenue than on direct taxes on individuals and businesses.

4. Value-added taxes are general sales taxes that are collected at every stage of production.

# SUMMARY

### ❓ How can fiscal policy eliminate a GDP gap?

1. A GDP gap can be closed by increasing government spending or by cutting taxes.

2. Government spending affects aggregate expenditures directly; taxes affect aggregate expenditures indirectly through their effect on consumption.

3. Aggregate expenditures must rise to bring equilibrium real GDP up to potential real GDP—to eliminate the GDP gap.

4. An increase in government spending matched by an increase in taxes raises equilibrium spending and real GDP.

5. If the public expects to pay higher taxes as a result of government borrowing, then the expansionary effects of government deficits may be reduced.

6. Government borrowing can crowd out private spending by raising interest rates and reducing investments.

### ❓ How has U.S. fiscal policy changed over time?

7. Fiscal policy in the United States is a product of the budget process.

8. Federal government spending in the United States has increased from just 3 percent of the GDP before the Great Depression to about 18 percent of the GDP today.

9. Fiscal policy has two components: discretionary fiscal policy and automatic stabilizers.

### ❓ What are the effects of budget deficits?

10. Budget deficits, through their effects on interest rates, international trade, and the national debt, can reduce investment, output, net exports, and national wealth.

11. Progressive taxes and transfer payments are automatic stabilizers, elements of fiscal policy that change automatically as national income changes.

### ❓ How does fiscal policy differ across countries?

12. Industrial countries spend a much larger percentage of their government budget for social programs than do developing countries.

13. Industrial countries depend more on direct taxes and less on indirect taxes than do developing countries.

# KEY TERMS

crowding out
discretionary fiscal policy
automatic stabilizer
progressive tax

regressive tax
proportional tax
value-added tax (VAT)

# EXERCISES

1. What is the role of aggregate demand in eliminating the GDP gap? How does the slope of the *AS* curve affect the fiscal policy actions necessary to eliminate the GDP gap?

2. Briefly describe the process of setting the federal budget in the United States. What is the time lag between the start of the process and the point at which the money is actually spent?

3. In what ways are government deficits harmful to the economy?

4. Define and give three examples of automatic stabilizers.

5. Briefly describe the major differences between fiscal policy in industrial countries and that in developing countries.

6. Why will real GDP tend to rise when government spending and taxes rise by the same amount?

7. How can a larger government fiscal deficit cause a larger international trade deficit?

8. Why do government budget deficits grow during recessions?

9. Taxes can be progressive, regressive, or proportional. Define each and briefly offer an argument for why income taxes are usually progressive.

## Internet Exercise

The national debt and deficit are two highly charged political–economic issues. Use the Internet to find the current level of the debt and the most recent budget deficit.

Go to the Boyes/Melvin, *Fundamentals of Economics* website accessible through **http://college.hmco.com** and click on the Internet Exercise link for Chapter 13. Now answer the questions that appear on the Boyes/Melvin website.

## Key Term Match

Match each term with its corresponding definition by placing the appropriate letter next to the corresponding number.

A. crowding out
B. discretionary
   fiscal policy
C. automatic stabilizer
D. progressive tax
E. regressive tax
F. proportional tax
G. value-added tax

_____ 1. a tax whose rate rises as income rises
_____ 2. a drop in consumption or investment spending caused by government spending
_____ 3. a tax whose rate falls as income rises
_____ 4. an element of fiscal policy that changes automatically as income changes
_____ 5. changes in government spending and taxation aimed at achieving a policy goal
_____ 6. a general sales tax collected at each stage of production
_____ 7. a tax whose rate is constant as income rises

## Quick-Check Quiz

1. Taxes affect the level of aggregate demand primarily through changing the level of _____, which alters _____.
   a. disposable income; consumption
   b. disposable income; investment
   c. disposable income; government spending
   d. government spending; consumption
   e. government spending; investment

2. A(n) _____ in government spending or a(n) _____ in taxes lowers the level of expenditures at every price and shifts the aggregate demand curve to the _____.
   a. decrease; increase; right
   b. decrease; increase; left
   c. increase; decrease; right
   d. increase; decrease; left
   e. decrease; decrease; left

3. A decrease in taxes may cause aggregate supply to shift to the _____, causing the level of prices to _____ and the level of national income to _____.
   a. right; fall; rise
   b. right; fall; fall

c. right; rise; rise
d. left; fall; rise
e. left; rise; fall

4. Increases in government spending financed by _____ may drive _____ interest rates and decrease _____.
   a. taxes; up; consumption
   b. taxes; down; consumption
   c. borrowing; down; investment
   d. borrowing; up; investment
   e. borrowing; down; net exports

5. Expansionary fiscal policy refers to
   a. decreasing government spending and decreasing taxes.
   b. decreasing government spending and increasing taxes.
   c. increasing government spending and increasing taxes.
   d. increasing government spending and decreasing taxes.
   e. increasing government spending and increasing the money supply.

6. Discretionary fiscal policy refers to
   a. government spending at the discretion of the president.
   b. government spending at the discretion of the Congress.
   c. elements of fiscal policy that automatically change in value as national income changes.
   d. government spending at the discretion of the president and the Congress.
   e. changes in government spending and taxation aimed at achieving an economic policy goal.

7. Which of the following is *not* a harmful effect of government deficits?
   a. lower private investment as a result of crowding out
   b. lower net exports as a result of the appreciation of the dollar
   c. increased investment caused by foreign savings placed in U.S. bonds
   d. an increase in saving caused by anticipated future increases in taxes
   e. an increase in imports

8. Which of the following is *not* an example of an automatic stabilizer?

a. unemployment insurance
b. lump-sum taxes
c. progressive taxes
d. food stamps
e. welfare benefits

**9** Which of the following statements is true?

a. Developing countries rely more heavily on direct taxes than do developed countries.
b. Developing countries rely more heavily on indirect taxes than do developed countries.
c. Developing countries rely more heavily on personal income taxes than do developed countries.
d. Developing countries rely more heavily on social security taxes than do developed countries.
e. Developed countries rely more heavily on import and export taxes than do developing countries.

**10** Which of the following statements is true?

a. The United States imposes value-added taxes.
b. An export tax is an example of a direct tax.
c. Developing countries spend more on social programs than industrial nations because their needs are greater.
d. Personal taxes are hard to collect in agricultural nations.
e. Personal income taxes are indirect taxes.

## Practice Questions and Problems

**1** Fiscal policy is changing _____ and _____ .

**2** Taxes affect aggregate expenditures indirectly by changing _____ . This change alters _____ .

**3** Increases in government spending may drive interest rates _____ (up, down), thereby _____ (increasing, decreasing) investment.

**4** If government spending increases by the same amount as taxes, the effect is _____ (expansionary, contractionary).

**5** An increase in government spending or a decrease in taxes causes the aggregate demand curve to shift to the _____ .

**6** List the three ways in which government spending may be financed.

_____

_____

_____

**7** An increase in taxes may shift aggregate supply to the _____ .

**8** A government borrows funds by _____ (buying bonds from, selling bonds to) the public.

**9** Fiscal policy in the United States is a product of the budget process, which involves the _____ and _____ branches of government.

**10** As part of the budget process, federal agencies submit their budgets to the _____ , which reviews and modifies each agency's requests and consolidates all of the proposals into a single budget.

**11** The _____ reports to Congress on the validity of the economic assumptions made in the president's budget.

**12** List the two kinds of fiscal policy.

_____

_____

**13** As income falls, automatic stabilizers _____ spending.

**14** _____ are taxes that are a flat dollar amount regardless of income.

**15** Look at the following tax payment schedules.

Which is progressive? _____

Regressive? _____

Proportional? _____

| | A | B | C |
|---|---|---|---|
| Income | Tax Payment | Tax Payment | Tax Payment |
| $100 | $10 | $50 | $10 |
| 200 | 20 | 80 | 30 |
| 300 | 30 | 90 | 60 |
| 400 | 40 | 100 | 100 |

**16** _____ taxes are an example of an automatic stabilizer.

**17** Government plays a bigger role in investment spending in _____ (developing, industrial) countries. Give two reasons why this should be so.

_____

_____

**18** Low-income countries _____ (do, do not) spend a greater percentage of their budgets on social programs as compared with industrialized countries.

**19** In general, developing countries rely more heavily on _____ (direct, indirect) taxes than do developed countries.

## Exercises and Applications

**I** **Reducing the Deficit**   Your text discusses the possible harmful effects of budget deficits. Since a budget deficit results from government spending that is greater than tax revenues, reducing the deficit implies reducing government spending, increasing taxes, or both. But to quote Publius Syrus, "There are some remedies worse than the disease" (Maxim 301). Since reducing government spending and increasing taxes reduces aggregate demand, the economy might be thrown into a recession if spending cuts and tax increases are adopted.

1. Consider the following graph, in which the economy is at equilibrium at $P_1$ and $Y_1$. Show what will happen if spending cuts and tax increases are implemented.

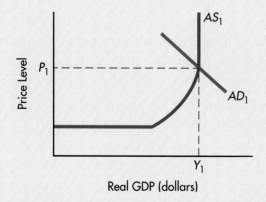

What will happen to equilibrium real GDP and price level?

_____

_____

2. Now consider an economy operating in the vertical region of the aggregate supply curve. Can you draw a curve that illustrates tax increases and spending cuts but does *not* throw the economy into a recession?

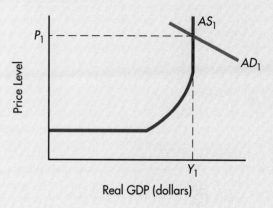

Explain:

_____

_____

**II** **Bush's Economic Stimulus Package**

1. President Bush's initial 2001 budget was referred to as an "economic stimulus package." From what you know about fiscal policy, if the president's goal was economic stimulus, you would expect this package to consist of increases in _____ and decreases in _____.

2. The president proposed cutting capital gains taxes for investors in some small businesses and would have expanded the bill's proposed write-off for businesses' equipment purchases. These tax breaks were intended to _____ (increase, decrease) which component of aggregate expenditures? What effect would that change have on real GDP?

_____

_____

Now that you've completed the Study Guide for this chapter, you should have a good sense of the concepts you need to review. If you'd like to test your understanding of the material again, go to the Practice Tests on the Boyes/Melvin *Fundamentals of Economics*, 3e website, **economics.college.hmco.com/students.**

## Chapter 14

# Money and Banking

## ? Fundamental Questions

1. **What is money?**
2. **How is the U.S. money supply defined?**
3. **How do countries pay for international transactions?**
4. **Why are banks considered intermediaries?**
5. **How does international banking differ from domestic banking?**
6. **How do banks create money?**

*money:* anything that is generally acceptable to sellers in exchange for goods and services

## Preview

Up to this point, we have been talking about aggregate expenditures, aggregate demand and supply, and fiscal policy without explicitly discussing money. Yet money is used by every sector of the economy in all nations and plays a crucial role in every economy. In this chapter we discuss what money is, how the quantity of money is determined, and the role of banks in determining this quantity. In the next chapter, we examine the role of money in the aggregate demand and supply model.

As you will see in the next two chapters, the quantity of money has a major impact on interest rates, inflation, and the amount of spending in the economy. Money is, then, important for macroeconomic policymaking, and government officials use both monetary and fiscal policy to influence the equilibrium level of real GDP and prices.

Banks and the banking system also play key roles, both at home and abroad, in the determination of the amount of money in circulation and the movement of money between nations. After we define *money* and its functions, we look at the banking system. We begin with banking in the United States and then discuss international banking. Someone once joked that banks follow the rule of 3-6-3. They borrow at 3 percent interest, lend at 6 percent interest, and close at 3 PM. If those days ever existed, clearly they do not today. The banking industry in the United States and the rest of the world has undergone tremendous change in recent years. New technology and government deregulation are allowing banks to respond to changing economic conditions in ways that were unthinkable only a few years ago, and these changes have had dramatic effects on the economy. ■

## 1. WHAT IS MONEY?

**Money** is anything that is generally acceptable to sellers in exchange for goods and services. The cash in your wallet can be used to buy groceries or a movie ticket. You simply present your cash to the cashier, who readily accepts it. If you want to use your car to buy groceries or a movie ticket, the exchange is more complicated. You would probably have to sell the car before you could use it to buy other goods and services. Cars are seldom exchanged directly for goods and services (except

**liquid asset:** an asset that can easily be exchanged for goods and services

**1. What is money?**

for other cars). Because cars are not a generally acceptable means of paying for other goods and services, we don't consider them to be money.

Money is the most liquid asset. A **liquid asset** is an asset that can easily be exchanged for goods and services. Cash is a liquid asset; a car is not. How liquid must an asset be before we consider it money? To answer this question, we must first consider the functions of money.

## 1.a. Functions of Money

Money serves four basic functions: it is a *medium of exchange,* a *unit of account,* a *store of value,* and a *standard of deferred payment.* Not all monies serve all of these functions equally well, as will be apparent in the following discussion. But to be money, an item must perform enough of these functions to induce people to use it.

### 1.a.1. Medium of Exchange

Money is a medium of exchange; it is used in exchange for goods and services. Sellers willingly accept money in payment for the products and services they produce. Without money, we would have to resort to *barter,* the direct exchange of goods and services for other goods and services.

For a barter system to work, there must be a *double coincidence of wants.* Suppose Bill is a carpenter and Jane is a plumber. In a monetary economy, when Bill needs plumbing repairs in his home, he simply pays Jane for the repairs using money. Because everyone wants money, money is an acceptable means of payment. In a barter economy, Bill must offer his services as a carpenter in exchange for Jane's work. If Jane does not want any carpentry work done, Bill and Jane cannot enter into a mutually beneficial transaction. Bill has to find a person who can do what he wants and also wants what he can do; there must be a double coincidence of wants.

The example of Bill and Jane illustrates the fact that barter is a lot less efficient than using money. This means that the cost of a transaction in a barter economy is higher than the cost of a transaction in a monetary economy. The use of money as a medium of exchange lowers transaction costs.

The people of Yap Island highly value and thus accept as a medium of exchange giant stones. But in most cultures in order to be an effective medium of exchange, money must be portable—a property the stone money of Yap Island clearly lacks. Another important property of money is *divisibility.* Money must be measurable in both small units (for low-value goods and services) and large units (for high-value goods and services). Yap stone money is not divisible, so it is not a good medium of exchange for the majority of goods bought and sold.

### 1.a.2. Unit of Account

Money is a unit of account; we price goods and services in terms of money. This common unit of measurement allows us to compare relative values easily. If whole-wheat bread sells for a dollar a loaf, and white bread sells for 50 cents, we know that whole-wheat bread is twice as expensive as white bread.

Using money as a unit of account is efficient. It reduces the costs of gathering information on what things are worth. The use of money as a unit of account lowers information costs relative to barter. In a barter economy, people constantly have to evaluate the worth of the goods and services being offered. When money prices are placed on goods and services, their relative value is obvious.

### 1.a.3. Store of Value

Money functions as a store of value or purchasing power. If you are paid today, you do not have to hurry out to spend your money. It will still have value next week or next month. Some monies retain their value better than others. In colonial New England, fish and furs both served as money. But because fish does not store as well as furs, its usefulness as a store of value was limited. An important property of a money is its *durability,* its ability to retain its value over time.

Inflation plays a major role in determining the effectiveness of a money as a store of value. The higher the rate of inflation, the faster the purchasing power of money falls. In high-inflation countries, workers spend their pay as fast as possible because the purchasing power of their money is falling rapidly. It makes no sense to hold on to a money that is quickly losing value. In countries where the domestic money does not serve as a good store of value, it ceases to fulfill this function of money, and people begin to use something else as money, like the currency of another nation. For instance, U.S. dollars have long been a favorite store of value in Latin American countries that have experienced high inflation. This phenomenon—**currency substitution**—has been documented in Argentina, Bolivia, Mexico, and other countries during times of high inflation.

**currency substitution:** the use of foreign money as a substitute for domestic money when the domestic economy has a high rate of inflation

**1.a.4. Standard of Deferred Payment**  Finally, money is a standard of deferred payment. Debt obligations are written in terms of money values. If you have a credit card bill that is due in 90 days, the value you owe is stated in monetary units, for example, dollars in the United States and yen in Japan. We use money values to state amounts of debt and use money to pay our debts.

We should make a distinction here between money and credit. Money is what we use to pay for goods and services. **Credit** is available savings that are lent to borrowers to spend. If you use your Visa or MasterCard to buy a shirt, you are not buying the shirt with your money. You are taking out a loan from the bank that issued the credit card in order to buy the shirt. Credit and money are different. Money is an *asset,* something you own. Credit is *debt,* something you owe.

**credit:** available savings that are lent to borrowers to spend

### 1.b. The U.S. Money Supply

The quantity of money available for spending is an important determinant of many key macroeconomic variables since changes in the money supply affect interest rates, inflation, and other indicators of economic health. When economists measure the money supply, they measure spendable assets. Identifying those assets, however, can be difficult. Although it would seem that *all* bank deposits are money, some bank deposits are held for spending while others are held for saving. In defining the money supply, then, economists must differentiate among assets on the basis of their liquidity and the likelihood of their being used for spending.

The problem of distinguishing among assets has produced several definitions of the money supply: M1, M2, and M3. Economists and policymakers use all three definitions to evaluate the availability of funds for spending. Although economists have tried to identify a single measure that best influences the business cycle and changes in interest rates and inflation, research indicates that different definitions work better to explain changes in macroeconomic variables at different times.

**2. How is the U.S. money supply defined?**

**1.b.1. M1 Money Supply**  The narrowest and most liquid measure of the money supply is the **M1 money supply,** the financial assets that are immediately available for spending. This definition emphasizes the use of money as a medium of exchange. The M1 money supply consists of currency, travelers' checks, demand deposits, and other checkable deposits. Demand and other checkable deposits are **transactions accounts;** they can be used to make direct payments to a third party.

**M1 money supply:** financial assets that are the most liquid

**transactions account:** a checking account at a bank or other financial institution that can be drawn on to make payments

*Currency*  Currency includes coins and paper money in circulation (in the hands of the public). In early 2004, currency represented 51 percent of the M1 money supply. A common misconception about currency today is that it is backed by gold or silver. This is not true. There is nothing backing the U.S. dollar except the confidence of the public. This kind of monetary system is called a *fiduciary monetary system.* Fiduciary comes from the Latin *fiducia,* which means "trust." Our monetary system is based on trust. As long as we believe that our money is an acceptable form of payment for goods and services, the system works. It is not necessary for money to be backed by any precious object. As long as people believe that a money has value, it will serve as money.

The United States has not always operated under a fiduciary monetary system. At one time the U.S. government issued gold and silver coins and paper money that could be exchanged for silver. In 1967, Congress authorized the U.S. Treasury to stop redeeming "silver certificate" paper money for silver. Coins with an intrinsic value are known as *commodity money;* they have value as a commodity in addition to their face value. The problem with commodity money is that as the value of the commodity increases, the money stops being circulated. People hoard coins when their commodity value exceeds their face value. For example, no one would take an old $20 gold piece to the grocery store to buy $20 worth of groceries because the gold is worth much more than $20 today.

*Travelers' Checks*   Outstanding U.S. dollar–denominated travelers' checks issued by nonbank institutions are counted as part of the M1 money supply. There are several nonbank issuers, among them American Express and Cook's. (Travelers' checks issued by banks are included in demand deposits. When a bank issues its own travelers' checks, it deposits the amount paid by the purchaser in a special account that is used to redeem the checks. Because this amount is counted as part of demand deposits, it is not counted again as part of outstanding travelers' checks.) Travelers' checks accounted for less than 1 percent of the M1 money supply in 2004.

*Demand Deposits*   Demand deposits are checking account deposits at a commercial bank. These deposits pay no interest. They are called *demand deposits* because the bank must pay the amount of the check immediately on the demand of the depositor. Demand deposits accounted for 24 percent of the M1 money supply in 2004.

*Other Checkable Deposits*   Until the 1980s, demand deposits were the only kind of checking account. Today there are many different kinds of checking accounts, known as *other checkable deposits (OCDs)*. The OCDs are accounts at financial institutions that pay interest and give the depositor check-writing privileges. Among the OCDs included in the M1 money supply are the following:

*Negotiable orders of withdrawal (NOW) accounts.* These are interest-bearing checking accounts offered by savings and loan institutions.

*Automatic transfer system (ATS) accounts.* These are accounts at commercial banks that combine an interest-bearing savings account with a non-interest-bearing checking account. The depositor keeps a small balance in the checking account; anytime the checking account balance is overdrawn, funds automatically are transferred from the savings account.

*Credit union share draft accounts.* Credit unions offer their members interest-bearing checking accounts called *share drafts*.

*Demand deposits at mutual savings banks.* Mutual savings banks are nonprofit savings and loan organizations. Any profits after operating expenses have been paid may be distributed to depositors.

**1.b.2. M2 Money Supply**   The components of the M1 money supply are the most liquid assets, the assets most likely to be used for transactions. M2 is a broader definition of the money supply that includes assets in somewhat less liquid forms. The M2 money supply includes the M1 money supply plus:

- **Savings deposits** Savings deposits are accounts at banks and savings and loan associations that earn interest but offer check-writing privileges.

- **Small-denomination time deposits** These deposits are often called *certificates of deposit*. Funds in these accounts must be deposited for a specified period of time. (*Small* means less than $100,000.)

■ **Retail money market mutual fund balances** These money market mutual funds combine the deposits of many individuals and invest them in government Treasury bills and other short-term securities. Many money market mutual funds grant check-writing privileges but limit the size and number of checks.

### 1.b.3. M3 Money Supply

The M3 money supply equals the M2 money supply plus:

■ **Large-denomination time deposits** These are deposits of $100,000 or more made for a specified period of time.

■ **Repurchase agreements (RPs)** A repurchase agreement is an agreement between a bank and a customer under which the customer buys U.S. government securities from the bank one day and then sells them back to the bank later at a price that includes the interest earned. Overnight RPs are used by firms that have excess cash one day that may be needed the next.

■ **Eurodollar deposits** These are deposits denominated in dollars but held outside the U.S. domestic bank industry.

■ **Institution-only money market fund balances** These money market mutual funds do not include the balances of individuals.

These additional assets are less liquid than those found in the M1 or M2 money supply. Figure 1 summarizes the three definitions of the money supply.

### 1.c. Global Money

**3. How do countries pay for international transactions?**

So far we have discussed the money supply in a domestic context. Just as the United States uses dollars as its domestic money, every nation has its own monetary unit of account. Japan has the yen, Mexico the peso, Canada the Canadian dollar, and so on. Since each nation uses a different money, how do countries pay for transactions that involve residents of other countries? As you saw in Chapter 10, the foreign exchange market links national monies together so that transactions can be made across national borders. If Sears in the United States buys a home entertainment system from Sony in Japan, Sears can exchange dollars for yen in order to pay Sony in yen. The exchange rate between the dollar and yen determines how many dollars are needed to purchase the required number of yen (¥). For instance, if Sony wants ¥1,000,000 for the component and the exchange rate is ¥100 = $1, Sears needs $10,000 (1,000,000/100) to buy the yen.

Sales contracts between developed countries usually are written (invoiced) in the national currency of the exporter. To complete the transaction, the importer buys the exporter's currency on the foreign exchange market. Trade between developing and developed nations typically is invoiced in the currency of the developed country, whether the developed country is the exporter or importer, because the currency of the developed country is usually more stable and more widely traded on the foreign exchange market than the currency of the developing country. As a result, the currencies of the major developed countries tend to dominate the international medium-of-exchange and unit-of-account functions of money.

### 1.c.1. International Reserve Currencies

Governments hold monies as a temporary store of value until money is needed to settle international debts. At one time gold was the primary **international reserve asset,** an asset used to settle debts between governments. Although gold still serves as an international reserve asset, its role is unimportant relative to that of currencies. Today national currencies function as international reserves. The currencies that are held for this purpose are called **international reserve currencies.**

Table 1 shows the importance of the major international reserve currencies over time. In the mid-1970s, the U.S. dollar made up almost 80 percent of international

**international reserve asset:** an asset used to settle debts between governments

**international reserve currency:** a currency held by a government to settle international debts

Figure 1

**The U.S. Money Supply: M1, M2, M3 (billions of dollars)**

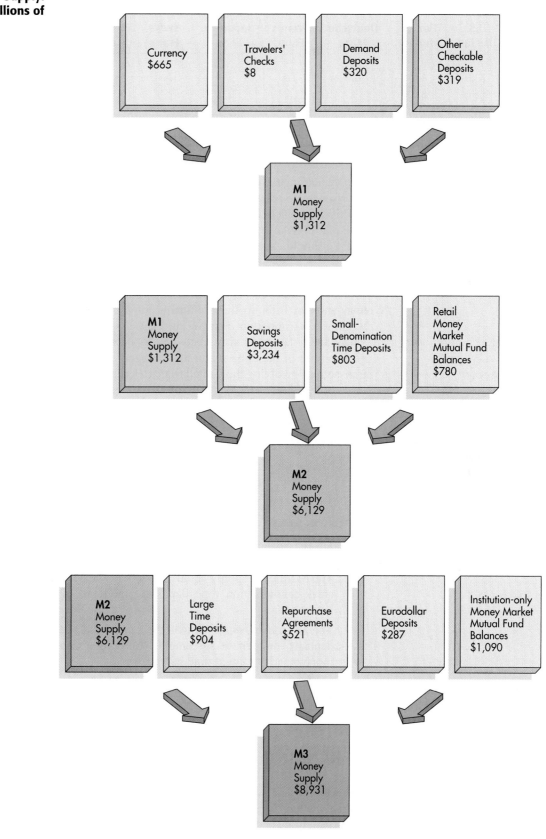

Table 1

**International Reserve Currencies**
**(percentage shares of national currencies in total official holdings of foreign exchange)**

| Year | U.S. Dollar | Pound Sterling | Deutsche Mark | French Franc | Japanese Yen | Swiss Franc | Netherlands Guilder | Euro | Unspecified Currencies |
|------|-------------|----------------|---------------|--------------|--------------|-------------|---------------------|------|------------------------|
| 1976 | 78.8 | 1.0 | 8.7 | 1.5 | 1.9 | 2.1 | 0.8 | — | 5.2 |
| 2002 | 64.8 | 4.4 | — | — | 4.5 | 0.7 | — | 14.6 | 11.0 |

*Source:* Data from International Monetary Fund, *Annual Report,* http://www.imf.org/external/pubs/.

reserve holdings. By 1990, its share had fallen to less than 50 percent, but its share has risen again recently.

Prior to the actual introduction of the euro, there was much discussion about its potential popularity as a reserve currency. In fact, some analysts were asserting that we should expect the euro to replace the U.S. dollar as the world's dominant currency. As Table 1 shows, the euro is now the second most popular reserve currency, but it has much lower use than the dollar. The dominant world currency evolves over time as business firms and individuals find one currency more useful than another. Prior to the dominance of the dollar, the British pound was the world's most important reserve currency. As the U.S. economy grew in importance, and U.S. financial markets developed to the huge size they now have, the growing use of the dollar naturally emerged due to the large volume of financial transactions involving the United States. Perhaps over time, the euro will someday replace the dollar as the world's dominant money.

**RECAP**

1. Money is the most liquid asset.
2. Money serves as a medium of exchange, a unit of account, a store of value, and a standard of deferred payment.
3. The use of money lowers transaction and information costs relative to barter.
4. To be used as money, an asset should be portable, divisible, and durable.
5. The M1 money supply is the most liquid definition of money and equals the sum of currency, travelers' checks, demand deposits, and other checkable deposits.
6. The M2 money supply equals the sum of the M1 money supply, savings and small-denomination time deposits, and retail money market mutual fund balances.
7. The M3 money supply equals the sum of the M2 money supply, large time deposits, repurchase agreements, Eurodollar deposits, and institution-only money market mutual fund balances.
8. International reserve currencies are held by governments to settle international debts.

## 2. BANKING

*Commercial banks* are financial institutions that offer deposits on which checks can be written. In the United States and most other countries, commercial banks are privately owned. *Thrift institutions* are financial institutions that historically offered just savings accounts, not checking accounts. Savings and loan associations, credit unions, and mutual savings banks are all thrift institutions. Prior to 1980, the differences between commercial banks and thrift institutions were much greater than they are today. For example, only commercial banks could offer checking accounts, and those accounts earned no interest. The law also regulated maximum interest rates. In 1980, Congress passed the Depository Institutions Deregulation and Monetary Control Act, in part to stimulate competition among financial institutions. Now thrift institutions and even brokerage houses offer many of the same services as commercial banks.

**?**

**4. Why are banks considered intermediaries?**

**murabaha:** the most popular instrument for financing Islamic investments

## 2.a. Financial Intermediaries

Both commercial banks and thrift institutions are *financial intermediaries,* middlemen between savers and borrowers. Banks accept deposits from individuals and firms, then use those deposits to make loans to individuals and firms. The borrowers are likely to be different individuals or firms from the depositors, although it is not uncommon for a household or business to be both a depositor and a borrower at

---

## Islamic Banking

*Global Business Insight*

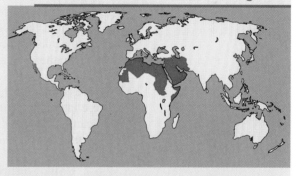

According to the Muslim holy book, the Koran, Islamic law prohibits interest charges on loans. Banks that operate under Islamic law still act as intermediaries between borrowers and lenders. However, they do not charge interest on loans or pay interest on deposits. Instead, they take a predetermined percentage of the borrowing firm's profits until the loan is repaid, then share those profits with depositors.

Since the mid-1970s, more than a hundred Islamic banks have opened, most in Arab nations. Deposits in these banks have grown rapidly. In fact, in some banks deposits have grown faster than good loan opportunities, forcing the banks to refuse new deposits until their loan portfolio could grow to match available deposits. One bank in Bahrain claimed that more than 60 percent of deposits during its first two years in operation were made by people who had never made a bank deposit before.

In addition to profit-sharing deposits, Islamic banks typically offer checking accounts, travelers' checks, and trade-related services on a fee basis. The return on profit-sharing deposits has fluctuated with regional economic conditions. In the late 1970s and early 1980s, when oil prices were high, returns were higher

than they were in the mid-1980s, when oil prices were depressed.

Because the growth of deposits has usually exceeded the growth of local investment opportunities, Islamic banks have been lending money to traditional banks to fund investments that satisfy the moral and commercial needs of both, such as lending to private firms. These funds cannot be used to invest in interest-bearing securities or in firms that deal in alcohol, pork, gambling, or arms. The growth of mutually profitable investment opportunities suggests that Islamic banks are meeting both the dictates of Muslim depositors and the profitability requirements of modern banking.

The potential for expansion and profitability of Islamic financial services has led major banks to create units dedicated to providing Islamic banking services. In addition, there are stock mutual funds that screen firms for compliance with Islamic law before buying their stock. For instance, since most financial institutions earn and pay large amounts of interest, such firms

would tend to be excluded from an Islamic mutual fund.

The most popular instrument for financing Islamic investments is **"murabaha."** This is essentially cost-plus financing in which the financial institution purchases goods or services for a client and then is repaid over time an amount that equals the original cost plus an additional amount of profit. Such an arrangement is even used for financing mortgages on property in the United States. A financial institution will buy a property and then charge a client rent until the rent payments equal the purchase price plus some profit. After the full payment is received, the title to the property is passed to the client.

*Source:* Peter Koh, "The Shari'ah Alternative," *Euromoney,* October 2002. Additional information can be found at http://www.failaka.com/.

---

the same institution. Of course, depositors and borrowers have very different interests. For instance, depositors typically prefer short-term deposits; they don't want to tie their money up for a long time. Borrowers, on the other hand, usually want more time for repayment. Banks typically package short-term deposits into longer-term loans. To function as intermediaries, banks must serve the interests of both depositors and borrowers.

A bank is willing to serve as an intermediary because it hopes to earn a profit from this activity. It pays a lower interest rate on deposits than it charges on loans; the difference is a source of profit for the bank. Islamic banks are prohibited by holy law from charging interest on loans; thus, they use a different system for making a profit (see the Global Business Insight "Islamic Banking").

## 2.b. U.S. Banking

### 2.b.1. Current Structure
If you add together all the pieces of the bar graph in Figure 2, you see that there were 89,096 banking offices operating in the United States in 2003. Roughly half of these offices were operated by *national banks,* banks chartered by the federal government; the other half, by *state banks,* banks chartered under state laws.

An important change that has taken place in the U.S. bank market is the growth of interstate banking. Historically, banks were allowed to operate in just one state. In some states, banks could operate in only one location. This is known as *unit banking.* Today there are still many unit banks, but these are typically small community banks.

Over time, legal barriers have been reduced so that today almost all states permit entry to banks located out of state. In the future, banking is likely to be done on a national rather than a local scale. The growth of automated teller machines (ATMs) is a big step in this direction. The ATM networks give bank customers access to services over a much wider geographic area than any single bank's branches cover. These international networks allow a bank customer from Dallas to withdraw cash in Seattle, Zurich, or almost anywhere in the world. Today more than one-fourth of ATM transactions occur at banks that are not the customer's own bank.

### 2.b.2. Bank Failures
Banking in the United States has had a colorful history of booms and panics. Banking is like any other business. Banks that are poorly managed can fail; banks that are properly managed tend to prosper. Regional

## Figure 2

### U.S. Depository Institutions

There are many more banks and bank branches than there are savings institutions and savings branches.

*Source:* Data are drawn from Federal Deposit Insurance Corporation, *Statistics on Banking,* http://www.fdic.gov.

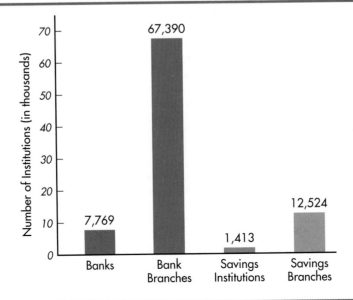

Part Three / The National and Global Economies

Figure 3

**Number of Failed and Uninsured Banks**

The number of banks that went out of business in the 1980s was the highest it had been since the Depression. Unlike the banks that failed in the 1930s, the banks that closed in the 1980s were covered by deposit insurance, so depositors did not lose their money.

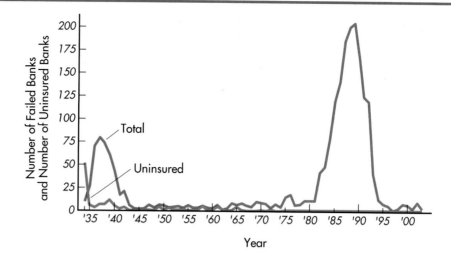

*Source:* Federal Deposit Insurance Corporation, http://www2.fdic.gov/hsob/hsobrpt.asp.

economic conditions are also very important. In the mid-1980s, hundreds of banks in states with large oil industries, like Texas and Oklahoma, and farming states, like Kansas and Nebraska, could not collect many of their loans due to falling oil and agricultural prices. Those states that are heavily dependent on the oil industry and farming had significantly more banks fail than other states did. The problem was not so much bad management as it was a matter of unexpectedly bad business conditions. The lesson here is simple: commercial banks, like other profit-making enterprises, are not exempt from failure.

At one time a bank panic could close a bank. A bank panic occurs when depositors, fearing a bank's closing, rush to withdraw their funds. Banks keep only a fraction of their deposits on reserve, so bank panics often result in bank closings as depositors try to withdraw more money than the banks have on a given day. In the United States today, this is no longer true. The **Federal Deposit Insurance Corporation (FDIC)** was created in 1933. The FDIC is a federal agency that insures bank deposits in commercial banks so that depositors do not lose their deposits when a bank fails. Figure 3 shows the number of failed banks and the number without deposit insurance. In the 1930s, many of the banks that failed were not insured by the FDIC. In this environment, it made sense for depositors to worry about losing their money. In the 1980s, the number of bank failures increased dramatically, but none of the failed banks were uninsured. Deposits in those banks were protected by the federal government. Even though large banks have failed in recent times, the depositors have not lost their deposits.

**Federal Deposit Insurance Corporation (FDIC):** a federal agency that insures deposits in commercial banks

5. How does international banking differ from domestic banking?

**Eurocurrency market (offshore banking):** the market for deposits and loans generally denominated in a currency other than the currency of the country in which the transaction occurs

## 2.c. International Banking

Large banks today are truly transnational enterprises. International banks, like domestic banks, act as financial intermediaries, but they operate in a different legal environment. The laws regulating domestic banking in each nation are typically very restrictive, yet many nations allow international banking to operate largely unregulated. Because they are not hampered by regulations, international banks typically can offer depositors and borrowers better terms than could be negotiated at a domestic bank.

**2.c.1. Eurocurrency Market** Because of the competitive interest rates offered on loans and deposits, there is a large market for deposits and loans at international banks. For instance, a bank in London, Tokyo, or the Bahamas may accept deposits and make loans denominated in U.S. dollars. The international deposit and loan market often is called the **Eurocurrency market,** or **offshore banking.** In the

In many developing countries, informal financial markets play an important role. In this photo, Pakistani currency traders are exchanging Afghan currency. Although these traders operate on the street, they are also part of a worldwide, informal financial market linking money traders around the world. This global network of money agents is able to transfer money from a Pakistani immigrant almost anywhere in the world to relatives in a remote village of Pakistan.

Eurocurrency market, the currency used in a banking transaction generally is not the domestic currency of the country in which the bank is located. (The prefix *Euro-* is misleading here. Although the market originated in Europe, today the market is global and operates with different foreign currencies; it is in no way limited to European currencies or European banks.)

In those countries that allow offshore banking, we find two sets of banking rules: restrictive regulations for banking in the domestic market and little or no regulation of offshore-banking activities. Domestic banks are required to hold reserves against deposits and to carry deposit insurance, and they often face government-mandated credit or interest rate restrictions. The Eurocurrency market operates with few or no costly restrictions, and international banks generally pay lower taxes than domestic banks. Because offshore banks operate with lower costs, they are able to offer better terms to their customers than domestic banks.

The Eurocurrency market exists for all of the major international currencies, but the value of activity in Eurodollars dwarfs the rest. Eurodollars account for about 60 percent of deposit and loan activity in the Eurocurrency market. This emphasizes the important role the U.S. dollar plays in global finance. Even deposits and loans that do not involve a U.S. lender or borrower often are denominated in U.S. dollars.

**2.c.2. International Banking Facilities**   The term *offshore banking* is somewhat misleading in the United States today. Prior to December 1981, U.S. banks were forced to process international deposits and loans through their offshore branches. Many of the branches in places like the Cayman Islands and the Bahamas were little more than "shells," small offices with a telephone. Yet these branches allowed U.S. banks to avoid the reserve requirements and interest rate regulations that restricted domestic banking activities.

In December 1981, the Federal Reserve Board legalized **international banking facilities (IBFs),** allowing domestic banks to take part in international banking on U.S. soil. The IBFs are not physical entities; they are a bookkeeping system set up in existing bank offices to record international banking transactions. The IBFs can receive deposits from and make loans to nonresidents of the United States or other IBFs. These deposits and loans must be kept separate from other transactions because IBFs are not subject to the reserve requirements, interest rate regulations, and FDIC deposit insurance premiums that apply to domestic U.S. banking.

**international banking facility (IBF):** a division of a U.S. bank that is allowed to receive deposits from and make loans to nonresidents of the United States without the restrictions that apply to domestic U.S. banks

The goal of the IBF plan was to allow banking offices in the United States to compete with offshore banks without having to use offshore banking offices. The location of IBFs reflects the location of banking activity in general. It is not surprising that 47 percent of IBFs are located in New York State, the financial center of the country. New York also receives over 75 percent of IBF deposits.

## 2.d. Informal Financial Markets in Developing Countries

In many developing countries, a sizable part of the population has no access to formal financial institutions like banks. In these cases, it is common for informal financial markets to develop. Such markets may take different forms. Sometimes, they take the form of an individual making small loans to local residents. Sometimes, groups of individuals form a self-help group where they pool their resources to provide loans to each other. To give some idea of the nature of these sorts of arrangements, a few common types are reviewed here.

A common form of informal financial arrangement is rotating savings and credit associations or **ROSCAS.** These tend to go by different names in different countries. For example, *tandas* in Mexico, *susu* in Ghana, *hui* in China, or *chits* in India are like savings clubs where members contribute money every week or month into a common fund, and then each month one member of the group receives the full amount contributed by everyone. This usually operates for a cycle of as many months as there are members in the group. For instance, if there were 12 members in the group contributing $10 a month, then a cycle would last 12 months; each month a different member of the group would receive the $120 available. So the ROSCAS are vehicles for saving in which only the last member of the group to receive the funds has saved over the full 12-month period before having use of $120. The determination of who receives the funds in which month is typically determined by a random drawing at the beginning of the cycle. Therefore, ROSCAS are a means of saving that allows all but one member in each cycle to receive funds faster than they could save on their own.

The informal market in many countries is dominated by individual lenders who tend to specialize in a local area and make loans primarily for the acquisition of seeds, fertilizer, or mechanical equipment needed by farmers. Surveys in China indicate that about two-thirds of farm loans to poor rural households are made by informal lenders. Such informal lenders are distinct from friends and relatives who can also be important in poor-household lending. The interest rate charged by informal lenders is typically significantly higher than that charged by banks or government lending institutions. The higher interest rates may reflect a higher risk associated with the borrower, who may have no collateral (goods or possessions that may be transferred to the lender if the borrower does not repay).

Informal loans among friends or relatives are typically one-time loans for purposes like financing weddings or home construction. If your cousin lends you money today in your time of need, then you are expected to lend to him at some later time if he has a need. Repeat loans, like those to a farmer in advance of the harvest each year, tend to be made by individuals who are unrelated to the borrower and in the business of providing such financing.

A form of informal financial market that gained much publicity after the September 11, 2001, terrorist attack on New York City's World Trade Center is the **hawala** network. In much of the developing world with heavy Muslim populations, people can send money all over the world using the hawala network. Let's say a Pakistani immigrant working as a taxi driver in New York wants to send money to a relative in a remote village of Pakistan. He can go to a hawala agent and give the money to the agent, who writes down the destination location and the amount of money to be sent. The agent then gives the taxi driver a code number and the location of an agent in Pakistan that the driver can pass along to his relative. The agent in the United States then calls a counterpart agent in Pakistan and informs that person of the amount of money and the code number. The Pakistani agent then pays

**ROSCAS:** rotating savings and credit associations

**hawala:** a network for transferring money, popular in Muslim countries

the money to whoever walks in his door with the code number. Since no names or addresses of the source of the money or the recipient exists, it is clear how such a network can be an effective source of financing terrorist activities. For this reason, the hawala network was a source of much investigation following the 2001 terrorist attacks in the United States. Of course, such a network serves many more people than just terrorists and is an important part of the informal financial market operating in many countries. For poor people without bank accounts, such informal markets allow some access to financial services.

**RECAP**

1. The Depository Institutions Deregulation and Monetary Control Act (1980) eliminated many of the differences between commercial banks and thrift institutions.

2. Banks are financial intermediaries.

3. In the United States, banks can be chartered as either national or state banks.

4. Since the FDIC began insuring bank deposits in commercial banks, bank panics are no longer a threat to the banking system.

5. The international deposit and loan market is called the Eurocurrency market, or offshore banking.

6. With the legalization in 1981 of international banking facilities, the Federal Reserve allowed international banking activities on U.S. soil.

7. Informal financial markets play an important role in developing countries.

## 3. BANKS AND THE MONEY SUPPLY

Banks create money by lending money. They take deposits, then lend a portion of those deposits in order to earn interest income. The portion of deposits that banks keep on hand is a *reserve* to meet the demand for withdrawals. In a **fractional reserve banking system,** banks keep less than 100 percent of their deposits on reserve. If all banks hold 10 percent of their deposits as a reserve, for example, then 90 percent of their deposits are available for loans. When they loan these deposits, money is created.

**fractional reserve banking system:** a system in which banks keep less than 100 percent of the deposits available for withdrawal

### 3.a. Deposits and Loans

Figure 4 shows a simple balance sheet for First National Bank. A *balance sheet* is a financial statement that records a firm's assets (what the firm owns) and liabilities (what the firm owes). The bank has cash assets ($100,000) and loan assets ($900,000). The deposits placed in the bank ($1,000,000) are a liability (they are an asset of the depositors).[1] Total assets always equal total liabilities on a balance sheet.

Banks keep a percentage of their deposits on reserve. In the United States the reserve requirement is set by the Federal Reserve Board (which will be discussed in detail in the next chapter). Banks can keep more than the minimum reserve if they choose. Let's assume that the reserve requirement is set at 10 percent and that banks always hold actual reserves equal to 10 percent of deposits. With deposits of $1,000,000, the bank must keep $100,000 (.10 × $1,000,000) in cash reserves held in its vault. This $100,000 is the bank's **required reserves,** as the Federal Reserve requires the banks to keep 10 percent of deposits on reserve. This is exactly what First National Bank has on hand in Figure 4. Any cash held in excess of $100,000 would represent **excess reserves.** Excess reserves can be loaned by the bank.

**required reserves:** the cash reserves (a percentage of deposits) a bank must keep on hand

**excess reserves:** the cash reserves beyond those required, which can be loaned

---

[1]In our simplified balance sheet, we assume there is no net worth, or owner's equity. Net worth is the value of the owner's claim on the firm (the owner's equity) and is found as the difference between the value of assets and nonequity liabilities.

## Figure 4

**First National Bank Balance Sheet, Initial Position**

The bank has cash totaling $100,000 and loans totaling $900,000, for total assets of $1,000,000. Deposits of $1,000,000 make up its total liabilities. With a reserve requirement of 10 percent, the bank must hold required reserves of 10 percent of its deposits, or $100,000. Because the bank is holding cash of $100,000, its total reserves equal its required reserves. Because it has no excess reserves, the bank cannot make new loans.

### First National Bank

| Assets | | Liabilities | |
|---|---|---|---|
| Cash | $100,000 | Deposits | $1,000,000 |
| Loans | 900,000 | | |
| Total | $1,000,000 | Total | $1,000,000 |

Total reserves = $100,000
Required reserves = 0.1 ($1,000,000) = $100,000
Excess reserves = 0

---

**6. How do banks create money?**

A bank is *loaned up* when it has zero excess reserves. Because its total reserves equal its required reserves, First National Bank has no excess reserves and is loaned up.

$$\text{Excess reserves} = \text{total reserves} - \text{required reserves}$$
$$= \$100,000 - \$100,000$$
$$= 0$$

The bank cannot make any new loans.

What happens if the bank receives a new deposit of $100,000? Figure 5 shows the bank's balance sheet right after the deposit is made. Its cash reserves are now $200,000, its deposits $1,100,000. With the additional deposit, the bank's total reserves equal $200,000. Its required reserves are $110,000 (.10 × $1,100,000), so its excess reserves are $90,000 ($200,000 − $110,000). Since a bank can lend its excess reserves, First National Bank can loan an additional $90,000.

Suppose the bank lends someone $90,000 by depositing $90,000 in the borrower's First National account. At the time the loan is made, the money supply

---

## Figure 5

**First National Bank Balance Sheet After $100,000 Deposit**

A $100,000 deposit increases the bank's cash reserves to $200,000 and deposits to $1,100,000. The bank must hold 10 percent of deposits, $110,000, on reserve. The difference between total reserves ($200,000) and required reserves ($110,000) is excess reserves ($90,000). The bank now has $90,000 available for lending.

### First National Bank

| Assets | | Liabilities | |
|---|---|---|---|
| Cash | $200,000 | Deposits | $1,100,000 |
| Loans | 900,000 | | |
| Total | $1,100,000 | Total | $1,100,000 |

Total reserves = $200,000
Required reserves = 0.1 ($1,100,000) = $110,000
Excess reserves = $90,000

## Figure 6

**Balance Sheets After a $90,000 Loan Made by First National Bank Is Spent and Deposited at Second National Bank**

Once First National Bank makes the $90,000 loan, its cash reserves fall to $110,000, and its loans increase to $990,000. At this point the bank's total reserves ($110,000) equal its required reserves (10 percent of deposits). Because it has no excess reserves, the bank cannot make new loans.

Second National Bank receives a deposit of $90,000. It must hold 10 percent, or $9,000, on reserve. Its excess reserves equal total reserves ($90,000) minus required reserves ($9,000), or $81,000. Second National Bank can make a maximum loan of $81,000.

First National Bank

| Assets | | Liabilities | |
|--------|--------|--------|--------|
| Cash | $110,000 | Deposits | $1,100,000 |
| Loans | 990,000 | | |
| Total | $1,100,000 | Total | $1,100,000 |

Total reserves = $110,000
Required reserves = 0.1 ($1,100,000) = $110,000
Excess reserves = 0

Second National Bank

| Assets | | Liabilities | |
|--------|--------|--------|--------|
| Cash | $90,000 | Deposits | $90,000 |
| Total | $90,000 | Total | $90,000 |

Total reserves = $90,000
Required reserves = 0.1 ($90,000) = $9,000
Excess reserves = $81,000

increases by the amount of the loan, $90,000. By making the loan, the bank has increased the money supply. But this is not the end of the story. The borrower spends the $90,000, and it winds up being deposited in the Second National Bank.

Figure 6 shows the balance sheets of both banks after the loan is made, and the money is spent and deposited at Second National Bank. First National Bank now has loans of $990,000 and no excess reserves (the required reserves of $110,000 equal total reserves). Therefore, First National Bank can make no more loans until a new deposit is made. Second National Bank has a new deposit of $90,000 (to simplify the analysis, we assume that this is the first transaction at Second National Bank). Its required reserves are 10 percent of $90,000, or $9,000. With total reserves of $90,000, Second National Bank has excess reserves of $81,000. It can make loans up to $81,000.

Notice what has happened to the banks' deposits as a result of the initial $100,000 deposit in First National Bank. Deposits at First National Bank have increased by $100,000. Second National Bank has a new deposit of $90,000, and the loans it makes will increase the money supply even more. Table 2 shows how the initial deposit of $100,000 is multiplied through the banking system. Each time a new loan is made, the money is spent and redeposited in the banking system. But each bank keeps 10 percent of the deposit on reserve, lending only 90 percent, so the amount of money loaned decreases by 10 percent each time it goes through another bank. If we carried the calculations out, you would see that the total increase in deposits associated with the initial $100,000 deposit is $1,000,000. Required reserves would increase by $100,000, and new loans would increase by $900,000.

### 3.b. Deposit Expansion Multiplier

Rather than calculate the excess reserves at each bank, as we did in Table 2, we can use a simple formula to find the maximum increase in deposits given a new

Table 2

**The Effect on Bank Deposits of an Initial Bank Deposit of $100,000**

| Bank | New Deposit | Required Reserves | Excess Reserves (new loans) |
|------|-------------|-------------------|------------------------------|
| First National | $ 100,000 | $ 10,000 | $ 90,000 |
| Second National | 90,000 | 9,000 | 81,000 |
| Third National | 81,000 | 8,100 | 72,900 |
| Fourth National | 72,900 | 7,290 | 65,610 |
| Fifth National | 65,610 | 6,561 | 59,049 |
| Sixth National | 59,049 | 5,905 | 53,144 |
| ⋮ | ⋮ | ⋮ | ⋮ |
| TOTAL | $1,000,000 | $100,000 | $900,000 |

**deposit expansion multiplier:** the reciprocal of the reserve requirement

**Now You Try It**

What is the deposit expansion multiplier if the reserve requirement is each of the following?

a. 5 percent
b. 25 percent
c. 33 percent
d. 50 percent

deposit. The **deposit expansion multiplier** equals the reciprocal of the reserve requirement:

$$\text{Deposit expansion multiplier} = \frac{1}{\text{reserve requirement}}$$

In our example, the reserve requirement is 10 percent, or .10, so the deposit expansion multiplier equals 1/.10, or 10. An initial increase in deposits of $100,000 expands deposits in the banking system by 10 times $100,000, or $1,000,000. The maximum increase in the money supply is found by multiplying the deposit expansion multiplier by the amount of the new deposit. With no new deposits, the banking system can increase the money supply only by the multiplier times excess reserves:

Deposit expansion multiplier × excess reserves

= maximum increase in money supply

The deposit expansion multiplier indicates the *maximum* possible change in total deposits when a new deposit is made. For the effect to be that large, all excess reserves must be loaned out, and all of the money that is deposited must stay in the banking system.

If banks hold more reserves than the minimum required, they lend a smaller fraction of any new deposits, which reduces the effect of the deposit expansion multiplier. For instance, if the reserve requirement is 10 percent, we know that the deposit expansion multiplier is 10. If a bank chooses to hold 20 percent of its deposits on reserve, the deposit expansion multiplier equals 5 (1/.20).

If money (currency and coin) is withdrawn from the banking system and kept as cash, deposits and bank reserves are smaller, and less money exists to be loaned out. This *currency drain*—removal of money—reduces the deposit expansion multiplier. The greater the currency drain, the smaller the multiplier. There is always some currency drain as people carry currency to pay for day-to-day transactions. However, during historical periods of bank panic when people lost confidence in banks, large currency withdrawals contributed to declines in money supply.

Remember that the deposit expansion multiplier measures the *maximum* expansion of the money supply by the banking system. Any single bank can lend only its excess reserves, but the whole banking system can expand the money supply by a multiple of the initial excess reserves. Thus, the banking system as a whole can increase the money supply by the deposit expansion multiplier times the excess reserves of the system. The initial bank is limited to its initial loan; the banking system generates loan after loan based on that initial loan. A new deposit can increase the money supply by the deposit expansion multiplier times the new deposit.

**RECAP**

1. The fractional reserve banking system allows banks to expand the money supply by making loans.
2. Banks must keep a fraction of their deposits on reserve; their excess reserves are available for lending.
3. The deposit expansion multiplier measures the maximum increase in the money supply given a new deposit; it is the reciprocal of the reserve requirement.
4. A single bank increases the money supply by lending its excess reserves.
5. The banking system can increase the money supply by the deposit expansion multiplier times the excess reserves in the banking system.

## SUMMARY

### ? What is money?

1. Money is anything that is generally acceptable to sellers in exchange for goods and services.
2. Money serves as a medium of exchange, a unit of account, a store of value, and a standard of deferred payment.
3. Money, because it is more efficient than barter, lowers transaction costs.
4. Money should be portable, divisible, and durable.

### ? How is the U.S. money supply defined?

5. There are three definitions of money based on its liquidity.
6. The M1 money supply equals the sum of currency plus travelers' checks plus demand deposits plus other checkable deposits.
7. The M2 money supply equals the sum of the M1 money supply plus savings and small-denomination time deposits, and retail money market mutual fund balances.
8. The M3 money supply equals the M2 money supply plus large time deposits, repurchase agreements, Eurodollar deposits, and institution-only money market mutual fund balances.

### ? How do countries pay for international transactions?

9. Using the foreign exchange market, governments (along with individuals and firms) are able to convert national currencies to pay for trade.

10. The U.S. dollar is the world's major international reserve currency.

### ? Why are banks considered intermediaries?

11. Banks serve as middlemen between savers and borrowers.

### ? How does international banking differ from domestic banking?

12. Domestic banking in most nations is strictly regulated; international banking is not.
13. The Eurocurrency market is the international deposit and loan market.
14. International banking facilities (IBFs) allow U.S. domestic banks to carry on international banking activities on U.S. soil.

### ? How do banks create money?

15. Banks can make loans up to the amount of their excess reserves, their total reserves minus their required reserves.
16. The deposit expansion multiplier is the reciprocal of the reserve requirement.
17. A single bank expands the money supply by lending its excess reserves.
18. The banking system can increase the money supply by the deposit expansion multiplier times the excess reserves in the system.

## KEY TERMS

money

liquid asset

currency substitution

credit

# Part Four

## Macroeconomic Policy

## Chapter 15

# Monetary Policy

## Fundamental Questions

1. **What does the Federal Reserve do?**
2. **How is monetary policy set?**
3. **What are the tools of monetary policy?**
4. **What role do central banks play in the foreign exchange market?**
5. **What are the determinants of the demand for money?**
6. **How does monetary policy affect the equilibrium level of real GDP?**
7. **What does the ECB do?**

*Preview*

I n the previous chapter, we saw how banks "create" money by making loans. However, that money must get into the system to begin with. Most of us never think about how money enters the economy. All we worry about is having money available when we need it. But there is a government body that controls the U.S. money supply, and in this chapter we will learn about this agency—the Federal Reserve System and the Board of Governors that oversees monetary policy.

The amount of money available for spending by individuals or businesses affects prices, interest rates, foreign exchange rates, and the level of income in the economy. Thus, having control of the money supply gives the Federal Reserve powerful influence over these important economic variables. As we learned in Chapter 13, fiscal policy, or the control of government spending and taxes, is one of two ways by which government can change the equilibrium level of real GDP. Monetary policy as carried out by the Federal Reserve is the other mechanism through which attempts are made to manage the economy. In this chapter we will also explore the tools of monetary policy and see how changes in the money supply affect the equilibrium level of real GDP. ■

## 1. THE FEDERAL RESERVE SYSTEM

The Federal Reserve is the central bank of the United States. A *central bank* performs several functions: accepting deposits from and making loans to commercial banks, acting as a banker for the federal government, and controlling the money supply.

### 1.a. Structure of the Fed

Congress created the Federal Reserve System in 1913, with the Federal Reserve Act. Bank panics and failures had convinced lawmakers that the United States needed an agency to control the money supply and make loans to commercial banks when those banks found themselves without sufficient reserves. Because Americans tended to distrust large banking interests, Congress called for a decentralized central bank. The Federal Reserve System divides the nation into 12 districts, each with its own Federal Reserve bank (Figure 1).

Figure 1

**The Federal Reserve System**

The Federal Reserve System divides the country into 12 districts. Each district has its own Federal Reserve bank, headquarters for Fed operations in that district. For example, the first district bank is in Boston; the twelfth is in San Francisco. There are also branch banks in Los Angeles, Miami, and other cities.

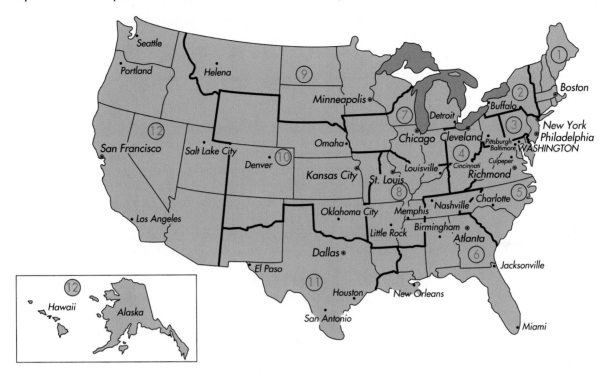

Source: *Federal Reserve Bulletin* (Washington, D.C.).

**1.a.1. Board of Governors** Although Congress created a decentralized system so that each district bank would represent the special interests of its own region, in practice the Fed is much more centralized than its creators intended. Monetary policy is largely set by the Board of Governors in Washington, D.C. This board is made up of seven members, who are appointed by the president and confirmed by the Senate.

The most visible and powerful member of the board is the chairperson. In fact, the chairperson of the Board of Governors has been called *the second most powerful person in the United States.* This individual serves as a leader and spokesperson for the board and typically exercises more authority in determining the course of monetary policy than do the other governors.

The chairperson is appointed by the president to a four-year term. In recent years most chairs have been reappointed to an additional term (Table 1). The governors serve 14-year terms, the terms being staggered so that every two years a new position comes up for appointment. This system allows continuity in the policy-making process and is intended to place the board above politics. Congress created the Fed as an independent agency: monetary policy is supposed to be formulated independent of Congress and the president. Of course, this is impossible in practice because the president appoints and the Senate approves the members of the board. But because the governors serve 14-year terms, they outlast the president who appointed them.

Table 1

**Recent Chairmen of the Federal Reserve Board**

| Name | Age at Appointment | Term Began | Term Ended | Years of Tenure |
|---|---|---|---|---|
| William McChesney Martin | 44 | 4/2/51 | 1/31/70 | 18.8 |
| Arthur Burns | 65 | 1/31/70 | 2/1/78 | 8.0 |
| G. William Miller | 52 | 3/8/78 | 8/6/79 | 1.4 |
| Paul Volcker | 51 | 8/6/79 | 8/5/87 | 8.0 |
| Alan Greenspan | 61 | 8/11/87 | | |

**1.a.2. District Banks**  Each of the Fed's 12 district banks is formally directed by a nine-person board of directors. Three directors represent commercial banks in the district, and three represent nonbanking business interests. These six individuals are elected by the Federal Reserve System member banks in the district. The three remaining directors are appointed by the Fed's Board of Governors. District bank directors are not involved in the day-to-day operations of the district banks, but they meet regularly to oversee bank operations. They also choose the president of the bank. The president, who is in charge of operations, participates in monetary policymaking with the Board of Governors in Washington, D.C.

**Federal Open Market Committee (FOMC):** the official policymaking body of the Federal Reserve System

**1.a.3. The Federal Open Market Committee**  The **Federal Open Market Committee (FOMC)** is the official policymaking body of the Federal Reserve System. The committee is made up of the 7 members of the Board of Governors plus 5 of the 12 district bank presidents. All of the district bank presidents, except for the president of the Federal Reserve Bank of New York, take turns serving on the FOMC. Because the New York Fed actually carries out monetary policy, that bank's president is always on the committee.

**1. What does the Federal Reserve do?**

## 1.b. Functions of the Fed

The Federal Reserve System offers banking services to the banking community and the U.S. Treasury, and supervises the nation's banking system. The Fed also regulates the U.S. money supply.

**1.b.1. Banking Services and Supervision**  The Fed provides several basic services to the banking community: it supplies currency to banks, holds their reserves, and clears checks. The Fed supplies U.S. currency (Federal Reserve notes) to the banking community through its 12 district banks. (See the Economic Insight "What's on a 20-Dollar Bill?") Commercial banks in each district also hold reserves in the form of deposits at their district bank. In addition, the Fed makes loans to banks. In this sense, the Fed is the *bankers' bank*. And the Fed clears checks, transferring funds to the banks where checks are deposited from the banks on which the checks are drawn.

The Fed also supervises the nation's banks, ensuring that they operate in a sound and prudent manner. And it acts as the banker for the U.S. government, selling U.S. government securities for the U.S. Treasury.

**1.b.2. Controlling the Money Supply**  All of the functions the Federal Reserve carries out are important, but none is more important than managing the nation's money supply. Before 1913, when the Fed was created, the money supply did not change to meet fluctuations in the demand for money. These fluctuations can stem from changes in income or seasonal patterns of demand. For example, every year during the Christmas season, the demand for currency rises because people

Figure 4

**The Dollar-Yen Foreign Exchange Market**

The demand is the demand for dollars arising out of the Japanese demand for U.S. goods and services. The supply is the supply of dollars arising out of the U.S. demand for Japanese goods and services. Initially, the equilibrium exchange rate is at the intersection of the demand curve ($D_1$) and the supply curve ($S_1$), where the exchange rate is ¥100 = $1. An increase in the U.S. demand for Japanese goods increases $S_1$ to $S_2$ and pushes the equilibrium exchange rate down to point B, where ¥90 = $1. If the Fed's target exchange rate is ¥100 = $1, the Fed must intervene and buy dollars in the foreign exchange market. This increases demand to $D_2$ and raises the equilibrium exchange rate to point C, where ¥100 = $1.

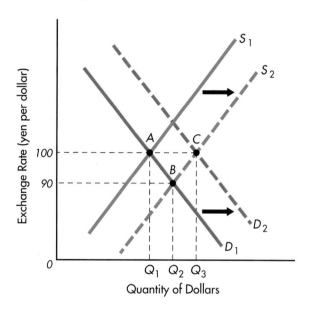

The initial equilibrium exchange rate is at point A, where the demand curve ($D_1$) and the supply curve ($S_1$) intersect. At point A, the exchange rate is ¥100 = $1, and $Q_1$ dollars are exchanged for yen. Suppose that over time, U.S. residents buy more from Japan than Japanese residents buy from the United States. As the supply of dollars increases in relation to the demand for dollars, equilibrium shifts to point B. At point B, $Q_2$ dollars are exchanged at a rate of ¥90 = $1. The dollar has *depreciated* against the yen, or, conversely, the yen has *appreciated* against the dollar.

When the dollar depreciates, U.S. goods are cheaper to Japanese buyers (it takes fewer yen to buy each dollar). The depreciated dollar stimulates U.S. exports to Japan. It also raises the price of Japanese goods to U.S. buyers, reducing U.S. imports from Japan. Rather than allow exchange rates to change, with the subsequent changes in trade, central banks often seek to maintain fixed exchange rates because of international agreements or desired trade in goods or financial assets.

Suppose the Fed sets a target range for the dollar at a minimum exchange rate of ¥100 = $1. If the exchange rate falls below the minimum, the Fed must intervene in the foreign exchange market to increase the value of the dollar. In Figure 4, you can see that the only way to increase the dollar's value is to increase the demand for dollars. The Fed intervenes in the foreign exchange market by buying dollars in exchange for yen. It uses its holdings of Japanese yen to purchase $Q_3 - Q_1$ dollars, shifting the demand curve to $D_2$. Now equilibrium is at point C, where $Q_3$ dollars are exchanged at the rate of ¥100 = $1.

The kind of intervention shown in Figure 4 is only temporary because the Fed has a limited supply of yen. Under another intervention plan, the Bank of Japan would support the ¥100 = $1 exchange rate by using yen to buy dollars. The Bank of Japan could carry on this kind of policy indefinitely because it has the power to create yen. A third alternative is *coordinated intervention,* in which both the Fed and the Bank of Japan sell yen in exchange for dollars to support the minimum yen-dollar exchange rate.

**2.c.2. Effects of Intervention** Intervention can be used to shift the demand and supply for currency and thereby change the exchange rate. Foreign exchange market intervention also has effects on the money supply. If the Federal Reserve wanted to increase the dollar price of the euro, it would create dollars to purchase euros. Thus, when foreign exchange market intervention involves the use of domestic currency to buy foreign currency, it increases the domestic money supply. The expansionary effect of this intervention can be offset by a domestic open market operation, in a process called **sterilization.** If the Fed creates dollars to buy euros, for example it increases the money supply, as we have just seen. To reduce the money supply, the Fed can direct an open market bond sale. The bond sale sterilizes the effect of the intervention on the domestic money supply.

**sterilization:** the use of domestic open market operations to offset the effects of a foreign exchange market intervention on the domestic money supply

RECAP

1. The ultimate goal of monetary policy is economic growth with stable prices.
2. The Fed controls GDP indirectly through its control of the money supply.
3. The equation of exchange ($MV = PQ$) relates the quantity of money to nominal GDP.
4. The quantity theory of money states that with constant velocity, changes in the quantity of money change nominal GDP.
5. Every six to eight weeks, the Federal Open Market Committee issues a directive to the Federal Reserve Bank of New York that defines the FOMC's monetary targets and policy tools.
6. The Fed controls the nation's money supply by changing banks' excess reserves.
7. The tools of monetary policy are reserve requirements, the discount rate, and open market operations.
8. The money supply tends to increase (decrease) as the reserve requirement falls (rises), the discount rate falls (rises), and the Fed buys (sells) bonds.
9. Each FOMC directive defines its short-run operating target in terms of the federal funds rate.
10. Foreign exchange market intervention is the buying and selling of foreign money by a central bank to achieve a targeted exchange rate.
11. Sterilization is the use of domestic open market operations to offset the money supply effects of foreign exchange market intervention.

# 3. MONETARY POLICY AND EQUILIBRIUM INCOME

To see how changes in the money supply affect the equilibrium level of real GDP, we incorporate monetary policy into the aggregate demand and supply model. The first step in understanding monetary policy is understanding the demand for money. If you know what determines money demand, you can see how monetary policy is used to shift aggregate demand and change the equilibrium level of real GDP.

4  The most important function of the Fed is

_____.

5  The _____ has been called the second most powerful person in the United States.

6  Write the formula for the equation of exchange.

_____

7  The _____ of money is the average number of times each dollar is spent on final goods and services in a year.

8  The _____ states that if the money supply increases, and the velocity of money is constant, nominal GDP must rise.

9  List the three tools the Fed uses to change reserves.

_____    _____    _____

10  The Fed can reduce the money-creating potential of the banking system by _____ (raising, lowering) the reserve requirement.

11  The _____ rate is the rate of interest the Fed charges banks. In other countries, this rate is often called the _____ rate.

12  If the Fed wants to increase the money supply, it _____ (raises, lowers) the discount rate.

13  To increase the money supply, the Fed _____ (buys, sells) bonds.

14  If the Fed wants the dollar to appreciate against the yen, it will buy _____ (dollars, yen).

15  If the Fed wishes to support a foreign currency, it _____ (increases, decreases) the domestic money supply unless offsetting operations are undertaken.

16  The demand for money depends on _____ and _____.

17  There is a(n) _____ relationship between the interest rate and the quantity of money demanded.

18  The greater the nominal income, the _____ (greater, smaller) the demand for money.

19  The supply of money _____ (does, does not) depend on interest rates and nominal income.

20  Norm and Debbie keep 1.5 months' income in a NOW account for emergencies. This is an example of the _____ demand for money.

21  A young couple cashes in a bond to buy a crib and changing table to prepare for the birth of their first child. This is an example of the _____ demand for money.

22  If nominal income increases, the demand for money _____ (shifts to the left, does not change, shifts to the right).

23  You read in the *Wall Street Journal* that the bond markets rallied yesterday (bond prices increased). Interest rates must have _____ (increased, decreased).

24  A decrease in the money supply causes interest rates to _____ (rise, fall), which causes consumption and investment to _____ (rise, fall). The changes in consumption and investment cause aggregate demand to _____ (increase, decrease), which causes equilibrium income to _____ (rise, fall). Use the following graphs to illustrate the sequence of events following a decrease in the money supply.

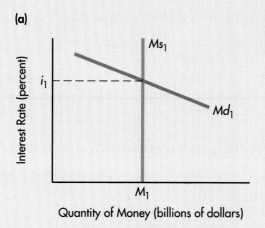

(a)

Interest Rate (percent)

$i_1$

$Ms_1$

$Md_1$

$M_1$

Quantity of Money (billions of dollars)

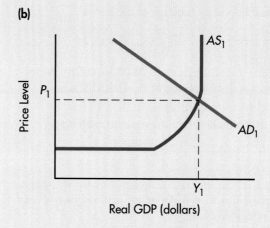

(b)

Price Level

$P_1$

$AS_1$

$AD_1$

$Y_1$

Real GDP (dollars)

# Exercises and Applications

**I  More on Foreign Exchange Market Intervention**
If the Fed feels that the price of the dollar in terms of U.K. pounds is unacceptably high, it may choose to intervene directly in the foreign exchange markets. To

bolster the pound, the Fed will _____ (buy, sell) pounds. In the process, the domestic money

supply will _____ (increase, decrease).

In the absence of any sterilization actions by the

Fed, domestic interest rates will _____ (increase, decrease) as a result of the change in the money supply. The change in domestic interest rates

will _____ (increase, decrease) the demand for U.S. securities. The dollar will

_____ (appreciate, depreciate) in value. The effect of the change in the money supply

has _____ (reinforced, opposed) the Fed's actions in the foreign exchange market.

**II  Bond Prices and Interest Rates**  Fill in the gaps in these typical quotations from articles from the *Wall Street Journal.*
a. "The benchmark 10-year Treasury bond rose more than 1/4 point to 106, a gain of more than $2.50

for a bond with a $1,000 face amount. Its yield,

which moves in the _____ (same, opposite) direction from the price,

_____ (rose, fell) to 6.65% . . ."

b. "More investors and economists are beginning to believe that interest rates are headed higher, although many think long-term bond yields won't move as fast as short-term rates. . . . Mr. Olsen . . . believes there will be a significant sell-off in the bond market."

Why would higher interest rates precipitate a significant sell-off in the bond market?

_____

_____

_____

_____

_____

ACE self-test

Now that you've completed the Study Guide for this chapter, you should have a good sense of the concepts you need to review. If you'd like to test your understanding of the material again, go to the Practice Tests on the Boyes/Melvin *Fundamentals of Economics,* 3e website, **economics.college.hmco.com/students.**

## Chapter 16

# Macroeconomic Policy, Business Cycles, and Growth

**? Fundamental Questions**

1. Is there a tradeoff between inflation and the unemployment rate?
2. How does the trade-off between inflation and the unemployment rate vary from the short to the long run?
3. What is the relationship between unexpected inflation and the unemployment rate?
4. How are macroeconomic expectations formed?
5. Are business cycles related to political elections?
6. How do real shocks to the economy affect business cycles?
7. How is inflationary monetary policy related to government fiscal policy?
8. How are economic growth rates determined?
9. What is productivity?

**Phillips curve:** a graph that illustrates the relationship between inflation and the unemployment rate

## Preview

**M**acroeconomics is a dynamic discipline. Monetary and fiscal policies change over time. And so does our understanding of those policies. Economists debate the nature of business cycles and economic growth, and what, if anything, government can do about them. Some economists argue that policies that lower the unemployment rate tend to raise the rate of inflation. Others insist that only unexpected inflation can influence real GDP and employment. If the latter economists are right, does government always have to surprise the public in order to improve economic conditions?

Some economists claim that politicians manipulate the business cycle to increase their chances of reelection. If they are right, we should expect economic growth just before national elections. But what happens after the elections? What are the long-term effects of political business cycles? Because of these issues, the material in this chapter should be considered somewhat controversial. ■

## 1. THE PHILLIPS CURVE

In 1958, a New Zealand economist, A. W. Phillips, published a study of the relationship between the unemployment rate and the rate of change in wages in England. He found that over the period from 1826 to 1957, there had been an inverse relationship between the unemployment rate and the rate of change in wages: the unemployment rate fell in years when there were relatively large increases in wages and rose in years when wages increased relatively little. Phillips's study started other economists searching for similar relationships in other countries. In those studies, it became common to substitute the rate of inflation for the rate of change in wages.

Early studies in the United States found an inverse relationship between inflation and the unemployment rate. The graph that illustrates this relationship is called a **Phillips curve.** Figure 1 shows a Phillips curve for the United States in the 1960s. Over this period, lower inflation rates were associated with higher unemployment rates, as shown by the downward-sloping curve.

The slope of the curve in Figure 1 depicts an inverse relationship between the rate of inflation and the unemployment rate: as the inflation rate falls, the unemployment rate rises. In 1969, the inflation rate was relatively high, at 5.5 percent, while the unemployment rate was relatively low, at 3.5 percent. In 1967, an inflation rate of 3.1 percent was consistent with an unemployment rate of 3.8 percent; and in 1961, 1 percent inflation occurred with 6.7 percent unemployment.

Figure 1

**A Phillips Curve, United States, 1961–1969**

In the 1960s, as the rate of inflation rose, the unemployment rate fell. This inverse relationship suggests a tradeoff between the rate of inflation and the unemployment rate.

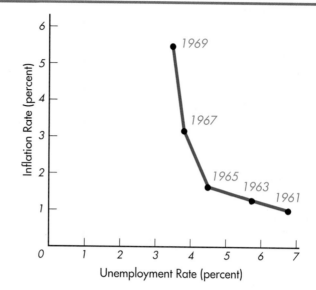

*Source:* Data from *Economic Report of the President, 1995* (Washington, D.C.: U.S. Government Printing Office, 1995).

The downward-sloping Phillips curve seems to indicate a tradeoff between unemployment and inflation. A country could have a lower unemployment rate by accepting higher inflation, or a lower rate of inflation by accepting higher unemployment. Certainly this was the case in the United States in the 1960s. But is the curve depicted in Figure 1 representative of the tradeoff over long periods of time?

## 1.a. An Inflation-Unemployment Tradeoff?

**1. Is there a tradeoff between inflation and the unemployment rate?**

Figure 2 shows unemployment and inflation rates in the United States for several years from 1955 to 2000. The points in the figure do not lie along a downward-sloping curve like the one shown in Figure 1. For example, in 1955, the unemployment rate was 4.4 percent, and the inflation rate was −0.4 percent. In 1960, the unemployment rate was 5.5 percent, and the inflation rate was 1.7 percent. Both unemployment and inflation rates had increased since 1955. Moving through time, you can see that the inflation rate tended to increase along with the unemployment rate through the 1960s and 1970s. By 1980, the unemployment rate was 7.1 percent, and the inflation rate was 13.5 percent.

The scattered points in Figure 2 show no evidence of a tradeoff between unemployment and inflation. A downward-sloping Phillips curve does not seem to exist over the long term.

## 1.b. Short-Run Versus Long-Run Tradeoffs

**2. How does the tradeoff between inflation and the unemployment rate vary from the short to the long run?**

Most economists believe that the downward-sloping Phillips curve and the tradeoff it implies between inflation and unemployment are short-term phenomena. Think of a series of Phillips curves, one for each of the points in Figure 2. From 1955 to 1980, the curves shifted out to the right. In the early 1980s, they shifted in to the left.

Figure 3 shows a series of Phillips curves that could account for the data in Figure 2. At any point in time, a downward-sloping Phillips curve indicates a tradeoff between inflation and unemployment. Many economists believe that this kind of tradeoff is just a short-term phenomenon. Over time, the Phillips curve shifts so that the short-run tradeoff between inflation and unemployment disappears in the long run.

## Figure 2

**Unemployment and Inflation in the United States, 1955–2000**

The data on inflation and unemployment rates in the United States between 1955 and 2000 show no particular relationship between inflation and unemployment over the long run. There is no evidence here of a downward-sloping Phillips curve.

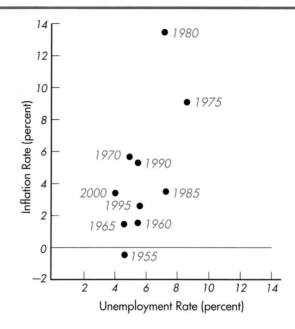

*Source:* Data from *Economic Report of the President, 2001.*

## Figure 3

### The Shifting Phillips Curve

We can reconcile the long-run data on unemployment and inflation with the downward-sloping Phillips curve by using a series of Phillips curves. (In effect, we treat the long run as a series of short-run curves.) The Phillips curve for the early 1960s shows 5 percent unemployment and 2 percent inflation. Over time, the short-run curve shifted out to the right. The early 1970s curve shows 5 percent

unemployment and 6 percent inflation. And the short-run curve for the late 1970s shows 5 percent unemployment and 10 percent inflation. In the early 1980s, the short-run Phillips curve began to shift down toward the origin. By the late 1980s, 5 percent unemployment was consistent with 4 percent inflation.

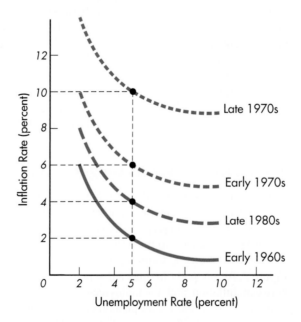

On the early 1960s curve in Figure 3, 5 percent unemployment is consistent with 2 percent inflation. By the early 1970s, the curve had shifted up. Here 5 percent unemployment is associated with 6 percent inflation. On the late 1970s curve, 5 percent unemployment is consistent with 10 percent inflation. For more than two decades, the tradeoff between inflation and unemployment worsened as the Phillips curves shifted up so that higher and higher inflation rates were associated with any given level of unemployment. Then, in the 1980s, the tradeoff seemed to improve as the Phillips curve shifted down. On the late 1980s curve, 5 percent unemployment is consistent with 4 percent inflation.

The Phillips curves in Figure 3 represent changes that took place over time in the United States. We cannot be sure of the actual shape of a Phillips curve at any time, but an outward shift of the curve in the 1960s and 1970s and an inward shift during the 1980s are consistent with the data. Later in this chapter we describe how changing government policy and the public's expectations about that policy may have shifted aggregate demand and aggregate supply and produced these shifts in the Phillips curves.

**1.b.1. In the Short Run**   Figure 4 uses aggregate demand and supply analysis to explain the Phillips curve. Initially, the economy is operating at point 1 in both diagrams. In part (a), the aggregate demand curve ($AD_1$) and aggregate supply curve ($AS_1$) intersect at price level $P_1$ and real GDP level $Y_p$, the level of potential real GDP. Remember that potential real GDP is the level of income and output generated at the natural rate of unemployment, the unemployment rate that exists in the absence of cyclical unemployment. In part (b), point 1 lies on Phillips curve I, where the inflation rate is 3 percent and the unemployment rate is 5 percent. We assume that the 5 percent unemployment rate at the level of potential real GDP is the natural rate of unemployment ($U_n$).

What happens when aggregate demand goes up from $AD_1$ to $AD_2$? A new equilibrium is established along the short-run aggregate supply curve ($AS_1$) at point 2. Here the price level ($P_2$) is higher, as is the level of real GDP ($Y_2$). In part (b), the increase in price and income is reflected in the movement along Phillips curve I to point 2. At point 2, the inflation rate is 6 percent, and the unemployment rate is 3 percent. The increase in expenditures raises the inflation rate and lowers the unemployment rate (because national output has surpassed potential output).

Notice that there appears to be a tradeoff between inflation and unemployment on Phillips curve I. The increase in spending increases output and stimulates employment so that the unemployment rate falls. And the higher spending pushes the rate of inflation up. But this tradeoff is only temporary. Point 2 in both diagrams is only a short-run equilibrium.

**1.b.2. In the Long Run**   As we discussed in Chapter 12, the short-run aggregate supply curve shifts over time as production costs rise in response to higher prices. Once the aggregate supply curve shifts to $AS_2$, long-run equilibrium occurs at point 3, where $AS_2$ intersects $AD_2$. Here, the price level is $P_3$, and real GDP returns to its potential level $Y_p$.

The shift in aggregate supply lowers real GDP. As income falls, the unemployment rate goes up. The decrease in aggregate supply is reflected in the movement from point 2 on Phillips curve I to point 3 on Phillips curve II. As real GDP returns to its potential level ($Y_p$), unemployment returns to the natural rate ($U_n$), 5 percent. In the long run, as the economy adjusts to an increase in aggregate demand, and expectations adjust to the new inflation rate, there is a period in which real GDP falls and the price level rises.

Over time there is no relationship between the price level and the level of real GDP. You can see this in the aggregate demand and supply diagram. Points 1 and 3 both lie along the long-run aggregate supply curve (*LRAS*) at potential real

## Figure 4

### Aggregate Demand and Supply and the Phillips Curve

The movement from point 1 to point 2 to point 3 traces the adjustment of the economy to an increase in aggregate demand. Point 1 is initial equilibrium in both diagrams. At this point potential real GDP is $Y_p$ and the price level is $P_1$ in the aggregate demand and supply diagram, and the inflation rate is 3 percent with an unemployment rate of 5 percent (the natural rate) along short-run curve 1 in the Phillips curve diagram.

If the aggregate demand curve shifts from $AD_1$ to $AD_2$, equilibrium real GDP goes up to $Y_2$ and the price level rises to $P_2$ in the aggregate demand and supply diagram. The increase in aggregate demand pushes the inflation rate up to 6 percent and the unemployment rate down to 3 percent along Phillips curve I. The movement from point

1 to point 2 along the curve indicates a tradeoff between inflation and the unemployment rate.

Over time the $AS$ curve shifts in response to rising production costs at the higher rate of inflation. Along $AS_2$, equilibrium is at point 3, where real GDP falls back to $Y_p$ and the price level rises to $P_3$. As we move from point 2 to point 3 in part (b), we shift to short-run Phillips curve II. Here the inflation rate remains high (at 6 percent) while the unemployment rate goes back up to 5 percent, the rate consistent with production at $Y_p$. In the long run, then, there is no tradeoff between inflation and unemployment. The vertical long-run aggregate supply curve at the potential level of real GDP is associated with the vertical long-run Phillips curve at the natural rate of unemployment.

### (a) Aggregate Demand and Supply

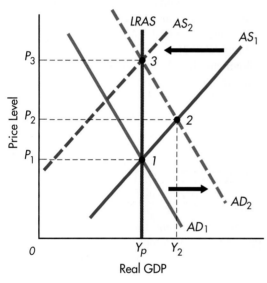

### (b) Phillips Curve

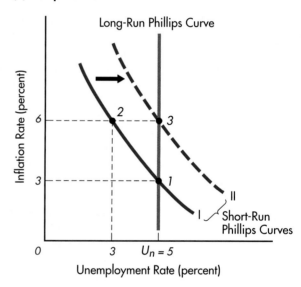

GDP. The *LRAS* curve has its analogue in the long-run Phillips curve, a vertical line at the natural rate of unemployment. Points 1 and 3 both lie along this curve.

---

**RECAP**

1. The Phillips curve shows an inverse relationship between inflation and unemployment.
2. The downward slope of the Phillips curve indicates a tradeoff between inflation and unemployment.
3. Over the long run that tradeoff disappears.
4. The long-run Phillips curve is a vertical line at the natural rate of unemployment, analogous to the long-run aggregate supply curve at potential real GDP.

## 2. THE ROLE OF EXPECTATIONS

The data and analysis in the previous section indicate that there is no long-run tradeoff between inflation and unemployment. But they do not explain the movement of the Phillips curve in the 1960s, 1970s, and 1980s. To understand why the short-run curve shifts, you must understand the role that unexpected inflation plays in the economy.

### 2.a. Expected Versus Unexpected Inflation

**3. What is the relationship between unexpected inflation and the unemployment rate?**

Figure 5 shows two short-run Phillips curves like those in Figure 4. Each curve is drawn for a particular expected rate of inflation. Curve I shows the tradeoff between inflation and unemployment when the inflation rate is expected to be 3 percent. If the actual rate of inflation (measured along the vertical axis) is 3 percent, the economy is operating at point 1, with an unemployment rate of 5 percent (the natural rate). If the inflation rate unexpectedly increases to 6 percent, the economy moves from point 1 to point 2 along Phillips curve I. Obviously, unexpected inflation can affect the unemployment rate. There are three factors at work here: wage expectations, inventory fluctuations, and wage contracts.

#### 2.a.1. Wage Expectations and Unemployment
Unemployed workers who are looking for a job choose a **reservation wage,** the minimum wage they are willing to accept. They continue to look for work until they receive an offer that equals or exceeds their reservation wage.

**reservation wage:** the minimum wage a worker is willing to accept

Wages are not the only factor that workers take into consideration before accepting a job offer. A firm that offers good working conditions and fringe benefits can pay a lower wage than a firm that does not offer these advantages. But other things being equal, workers choose higher wages over lower wages. We simplify our analysis here by assuming that the only variable that affects the unemployed worker who is looking for a job is the reservation wage.

The link between unexpected inflation and the unemployment rate stems from the fact that wage offers are surprisingly high when the rate of inflation is surprisingly high. An unexpected increase in inflation means that prices are higher than

**Figure 5**

**Expectations and the Phillips Curve**

Short-run Phillips curve I shows the tradeoff between inflation and the unemployment rate as long as people expect 3 percent inflation. When the actual rate of inflation is 3 percent, the rate of unemployment ($U_n$) is 5 percent (point 1). Short-run Phillips curve II shows the tradeoff as long as people expect 6 percent inflation. When the actual rate of inflation is 6 percent, the unemployment rate is 5 percent (point 3).

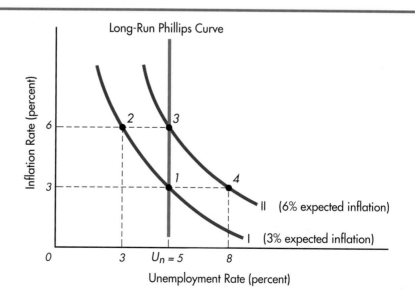

Figure 6

**Inflation, Unemployment, and Wage Expectations**

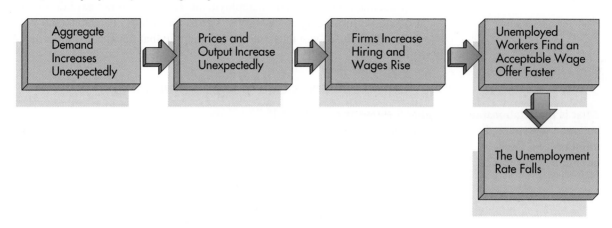

anticipated, as are nominal income and wages. If aggregate demand increases unexpectedly, then, prices, output, employment, and wages go up. Unemployed workers with a constant reservation wage find it easier to obtain a satisfactory wage offer during a period when wages are rising faster than the workers expected. This means that more unemployed workers find jobs, and they find those jobs quicker than they do in a period when the rate of inflation is expected. So the unemployment rate falls during a period of unexpectedly high inflation (Figure 6).

In Figure 5, an expected increase in inflation moves us from point 1 on curve I to point 3 on curve II. When increased inflation is expected, the reservation wage reflects the higher rate of inflation, and there is no tradeoff between inflation and the unemployment rate. Instead, the economy moves along the long-run Phillips curve, with unemployment at its natural rate. The clockwise movement from point 1 to point 2 to point 3 is the pattern that follows an unexpected increase in aggregate demand.

What if the inflation rate is lower than expected? Here we find a reservation wage that reflects higher expected inflation. This means that those people who are looking for jobs are going to have a difficult time finding acceptable wage offers, the number of unemployed workers is going to increase, and the unemployment rate is going to rise. This sequence is shown in Figure 5, as the economy moves from point 3 to point 4. When the actual inflation rate is 6 percent, and the expected inflation rate is also 6 percent, the economy is operating at the natural rate of unemployment. When the inflation rate falls to 3 percent, but workers still expect 6 percent inflation, the unemployment rate rises (at point 4 along curve II). Eventually, if the inflation rate remains at 3 percent, workers adjust their expectations to the lower rate, and the economy moves to point 1 on curve I. The short-run effect of unexpected *disinflation* is rising unemployment. Over time the short-run increase in the unemployment rate is eliminated.

As long as the actual rate of inflation equals the expected rate, the economy remains at the natural rate of unemployment. The tradeoff between inflation and the unemployment rate comes from unexpected inflation.

**2.a.2. Inventory Fluctuations and Unemployment** Businesses hold inventories based on what they expect their sales to be. When aggregate demand is

Figure 7

**Inflation, Unemployment, and Inventories**

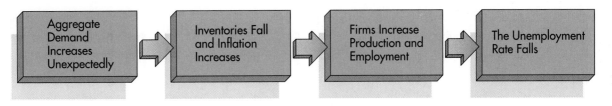

greater than expected, inventories fall below targeted levels. To restore inventories to the levels wanted, production is increased. Increased production leads to increased employment. If aggregate demand is lower than expected, inventories rise above targeted levels. To reduce inventories, production is cut back, and workers are laid off from their jobs until sales have lowered unwanted inventories. Once production increases, employment rises again.

Inventory, production, and employment all play a part in the Phillips curve analysis (Figure 7). Expected sales and inventory levels are based on an expected level of aggregate demand. If aggregate demand is greater than expected, inventories fall and prices rise on the remaining goods in stock. With the unexpected increase in inflation, the unemployment rate falls as businesses hire more workers to increase output to offset falling inventories. This sequence represents movement along a short-run Phillips curve because there is a tradeoff between inflation and the unemployment rate. We find the same tradeoff if aggregate demand is lower than expected. Here inventories increase, and prices are lower than anticipated. With the unexpected decrease in inflation, the unemployment rate goes up as workers are laid off to reduce output until inventory levels fall.

### 2.a.3. Wage Contracts and Unemployment
Another factor that explains the short-run tradeoff between inflation and unemployment is labor contracts that fix wages for an extended period of time. When an existing contract expires, management must renegotiate with labor. A firm facing lower demand for its products may negotiate lower wages in order to keep as many workers employed as before. If the demand for a firm's products falls while a wage contract is in force, the firm must maintain wages, which means it is going to have to lay off workers.

In the national economy, wage contracts are staggered; they expire at different times. Each year only 30 to 40 percent of all contracts expire across the entire economy. As economic conditions change, firms with expiring wage contracts can adjust *wages* to those conditions; firms with existing contracts must adjust *employment* to those conditions.

How do long-term wage contracts tie in with the Phillips curve analysis? The expected rate of inflation is based on expected aggregate demand and reflected in the wage that is agreed on in the contract. When the actual rate of inflation equals the expected rate, businesses retain the same number of workers they had planned on when they signed the contract. For the economy overall, when actual and expected inflation rates are the same, the economy is operating at the natural rate of unemployment. That is, businesses are not hiring new workers because of an unexpected increase in aggregate demand, and they are not laying off workers because of an unexpected decrease in aggregate demand.

Figure 8

**Inflation, Unemployment, and Wage Controls**

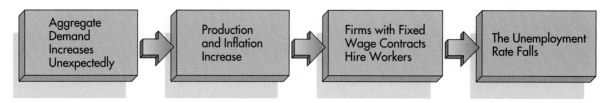

When aggregate demand is higher than expected, those firms with unexpired wage contracts hire more workers at the fixed wage, reducing unemployment (Figure 8). Those firms with expiring contracts have to offer higher wages in order to maintain the existing level of employment at the new demand condition. When aggregate demand is lower than expected, those firms with unexpired contracts have to lay off workers because they cannot lower the wage while those firms with expiring contracts negotiate lower wages in order to keep their workers.

If wages were always flexible, unexpected changes in aggregate demand might be reflected largely in *wage* rather than in *employment* adjustments. Wage contracts force businesses to adjust employment when aggregate demand changes unexpectedly. The Global Business Insight "Why Wages Don't Fall in Recessions" addresses this issue further.

## Why Wages Don't Fall in Recessions

*Global Business Insight*

A look at macroeconomic data across countries reveals that when economies experience recessions, unemployment rates rise, but wages fall very little, if at all. If we think of a supply and demand diagram for labor, we would think that as demand for labor falls in a recession, the equilibrium quantity of labor would fall as well as the equilibrium price, the wage rate. We do see the quantity effect as workers lose their jobs, and the unemployment rate rises. Why don't we see wages also falling?

The text discusses long-term labor contracts as one reason that wages may be relatively inflexible over time. Beyond the presence of contracts, recent research points to human behavior as a contributing factor.* Surveys of firms and workers indicate that worker morale is a major reason that wages are not

reduced during recessions. Workers would view a wage cut as an indication that the firm does not value their work as much, and they may, as a result, suffer lower morale and expend less effort. When some workers are laid off, these workers suffer from the job loss, but they are no longer at the firm and cannot harm others' morale and work effort. Only in the case in which the very survival of the firm is clearly at stake do wage cuts appear to be acceptable to workers.

Thus, wages are "sticky downwards" because this strategy promotes good worker effort and ensures that workers and firms share the same goals of efficient production

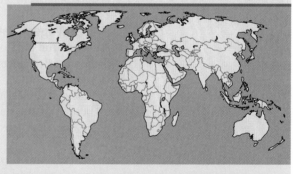

and profit maximization. Rather than keeping all workers when demand falls by paying lower wages to all, it may be better for the firm to lay off some workers and keep paying the remaining employees the same wage as before.

*Sources: Truman F. Bewley, *Why Wages Don't Fall During a Recession* (Cambridge, MA: Harvard University Press, 1999); Peter Howitt, "Looking Inside the Labor Market: A Review Article," *Journal of Economic Literature XL* (March 2002): 125–138.

4. How are macroeconomic expectations formed?

**adaptive expectation:** an expectation formed on the basis of information collected in the past

**rational expectation:** an expectation that is formed using all available relevant information

## 2.b. Forming Expectations

Expectations play a key role in explaining the short-run Phillips curve, the tradeoff between inflation and the unemployment rate. How are these expectations formed?

### 2.b.1. Adaptive Expectations

Expectations can be formed solely on the basis of experience. **Adaptive expectations** are expectations that are determined by what has happened in the recent past.

People learn from their experiences. For example, suppose the inflation rate has been 3 percent for the past few years. On the basis of past experience, then, people expect the inflation rate in the future to remain at 3 percent. If the Federal Reserve increases the growth of the money supply to a rate that produces 6 percent inflation, the public will be surprised by the higher rate of inflation. This unexpected inflation creates a short-run tradeoff between inflation and the unemployment rate along a short-run Phillips curve. Over time, if the inflation rate remains at 6 percent, the public will learn that the 3 percent rate is too low and will adapt its expectations to the actual, higher inflation rate. Once public expectations have adapted to the new rate of inflation, the economy returns to the natural rate of unemployment along the long-run Phillips curve.

### 2.b.2. Rational Expectations

Many economists believe that adaptive expectations are too narrow. If people look only at past information, they are ignoring what could be important information in the current period. **Rational expectations** are based on all available relevant information.

We are not saying that people have to know everything in order to form expectations. Rational expectations require only that people consider the information they believe to be relevant. This information includes their past experience along with what is currently happening and what they expect to happen in the future. For instance, in forming expectations about inflation, people consider rates in the recent past, current policy, and anticipated shifts in aggregate demand and supply that could affect the future rate of inflation.

If the inflation rate has been 3 percent over the past few years, adaptive expectations suggest that the future inflation rate will be 3 percent. No other information is considered. Rational expectations are based on more than the historical rate. Suppose the Fed announces a new policy that everyone believes will increase inflation in the future. With rational expectations the effect of this announcement will be considered. Here, when the actual rate of inflation turns out to be more than 3 percent, there is no short-run tradeoff between inflation and the unemployment rate. The economy moves directly along the long-run Phillips curve to the higher inflation rate while unemployment remains at the natural rate.

If we believe that people have rational expectations, we do not expect them to make the same mistakes over and over. We expect them to learn and react quickly to new information.

**RECAP**

1. Wage expectations, inventory fluctuations, and wage contracts help explain the short-run tradeoff between inflation and the unemployment rate.

2. The reservation wage is the minimum wage a worker is willing to accept.

3. Because wage expectations reflect expected inflation, when the inflation rate is surprisingly high, unemployed workers find jobs faster, and the unemployment rate falls.

4. Unexpected increases in aggregate demand lower inventories and raise prices. To increase output (to replenish shrinking inventories), businesses hire more workers, which reduces the unemployment rate.

5. When aggregate demand is higher than expected, those businesses that have wage contracts hire more workers at the fixed wage and thereby lower unemployment.

6. If wages were always flexible, unexpected changes in aggregate demand would be reflected in wage adjustments rather than in employment adjustments.

7. Adaptive expectations are formed on the basis of information about the past.

8. Rational expectations are formed using all available relevant information.

## 3. SOURCES OF BUSINESS CYCLES

In Chapter 13 we examined the effect of fiscal policy on the equilibrium level of real GDP. Changes in government spending and taxes can expand or contract the economy. In Chapter 15 we described how monetary policy affects the equilibrium level of real GDP. Changes in the money supply also produce booms and recessions. Besides the policy-induced sources of business cycles covered in earlier chapters, there are other sources of economic fluctuations that economists have studied. One is the election campaign of incumbent politicians; when a business cycle results from this action, it is called a *political business cycle*. Macroeconomic policy may be used to promote the reelection of incumbent politicians. We also examine another source of business cycles that is not related to discretionary policy actions, the *real business cycle*.

**5. Are business cycles related to political elections?**

### 3.a. The Political Business Cycle

If a short-run tradeoff exists between inflation and unemployment, an incumbent administration could stimulate the economy just before an election to lower the unemployment rate, making voters happy and increasing the probability of reelection. Of course, after the election, the long-run adjustment to the expansionary policy would lead to higher inflation and move unemployment back to the natural rate.

Figure 9 illustrates the pattern. Before the election, the economy is initially at point 1 in parts (a) and (b). The incumbent administration stimulates the economy by increasing government spending or increasing the growth of the money supply. Aggregate demand shifts from $AD_1$ to $AD_2$ in part (a). In the short run, the increase in aggregate demand is unexpected, so the economy moves along the initial aggregate supply curve ($AS_1$) to point 2. This movement is reflected in part (b) of the figure, in the movement from point 1 to point 2 along short-run Phillips curve I. The pre-election expansionary policy increases real GDP and lowers the unemployment rate. Once the public adjusts its expectations to the higher inflation rate, the economy experiences a recession. Real GDP falls back to its potential level ($Y_p$), and the unemployment rate goes back up to the natural rate ($U_n$), as shown by the movement from point 2 to point 3 in both parts of the figure.

An unexpected increase in government spending or money growth temporarily stimulates the economy. If an election comes during the period of expansion, higher incomes and lower unemployment may increase support for the incumbent administration. The long-run adjustment back to potential real GDP and the natural rate of unemployment comes after the election.

Economists do not agree on whether a political business cycle exists in the United States. But they do agree that an effort to exploit the short-run tradeoff between inflation and the unemployment rate would shift the short-run Phillips curve out as shown in part (b) of Figure 9.

Figure 9

**The Political Business Cycle**

Before the election, the government stimulates the economy, unexpectedly increasing aggregate demand. The economy moves from point 1 to point 2, pushing equilibrium real GDP above $Y_p$ (part [a]) and the unemployment rate below $U_n$ (part [b]). The incumbent politicians hope that rising incomes and lower unemployment will translate into votes. After the election comes adjustment to the higher aggregate demand as the economy moves from point 2 to point 3. The aggregate supply curve shifts to the left, and equilibrium real GDP falls back to $Y_p$. Unemployment goes back up to $U_n$, and the rate of inflation rises.

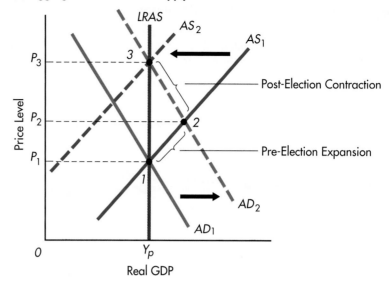

(a) Aggregate Demand and Supply

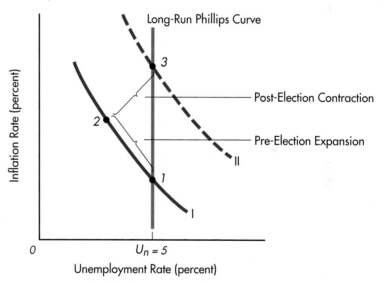

(b) Phillips Curve

**6. How do real shocks to the economy affect business cycles?**

shock: an unexpected change in a variable

## 3.b. Real Business Cycles

In recent years economists have paid increasing attention to real **shocks**—unexpected changes—in the economy as a source of business cycles. Many believe that it is not only fiscal or monetary policy that triggers expansion or contraction in the economy but also technological change, change in tastes, labor strikes, weather, war and terrorism, or other real changes. A real business cycle is one that is generated by a change in one of those real variables.

Interest in the real business cycle was stimulated by the oil price shocks in the early 1970s and the important role they played in triggering the recession of 1973–1975. At that time, many economists were focusing on the role of unexpected changes in monetary policy in generating business cycles. They argued that

Figure 10

**The Impact of Real Shocks on Equilibrium Real GDP**

A labor strike in a key industry can shift the aggregate supply curve to the left, like the shift from $AS_1$ to $AS_2$. This pushes equilibrium real GDP down from $Y_1$ to $Y_2$.

If good weather leads to a banner harvest, the aggregate supply curve shifts to the right, like the shift from $AS_1$ to $AS_2$, raising equilibrium real GDP from $Y_1$ to $Y_2$.

**(a) A Labor Strike in the Steel Industry**

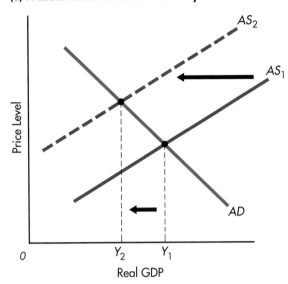

**(b) A Surprisingly Large Agricultural Harvest**

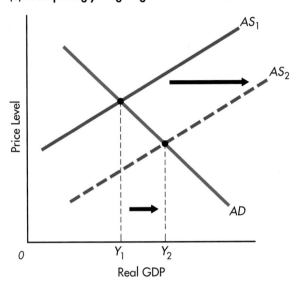

these kinds of policy changes (changes in a nominal variable, the money supply) were responsible for the shifts in aggregate demand that led to expansions and contractions. When OPEC raised oil prices, it caused major shifts in aggregate supply. Higher oil prices in 1973 and 1974, and in 1979 and 1980, reduced aggregate supply, pushing the equilibrium level of real GDP down. Lower oil prices in 1986 raised aggregate supply and equilibrium real GDP.

An economywide real shock, like a substantial change in the price of oil, can affect output and employment across all sectors of the economy. Even an industry-specific shock can generate a recession or expansion in the entire economy if the industry produces a product used by a substantial number of other industries. For example, a labor strike in the steel industry would have major recessionary implications for the economy as a whole. If the output of steel fell, the price of steel would be bid up by all the industries that use steel as an input. This would shift the short-run aggregate supply curve to the left, as shown in part (a) of Figure 10, and would move equilibrium real GDP from $Y_1$ down to $Y_2$.

Real shocks can also have expansionary effects on the economy. Suppose that the weather is particularly good one year and that harvests are surprisingly large. What happens? The price of food, cotton, and other agricultural output tends to fall, and the short-run aggregate supply curve shifts to the right, as shown in Figure 10(b), raising equilibrium real GDP from $Y_1$ to $Y_2$.

Real business cycles explain why national output can expand or contract in the absence of a discretionary macroeconomic policy that would shift aggregate demand. To fully understand business cycles, we must consider both policy-induced changes in real GDP, as covered in Chapters 13 and 15, and real shocks that occur independent of government actions.

Those who were around in the 1970s can remember the long lines and shortages at gas stations and the rapid increase in the price of oil that resulted from the oil embargo imposed by the Organization of Petroleum Exporting Countries. There was another effect of the oil price shock—the aggregate supply curve in the United States and other oil-importing nations shifted to the left, lowering the equilibrium level of real GDP while raising the price level. Such "real" sources of business cycles can explain why national output can rise or fall in the absence of any discretionary government macroeconomic policy.

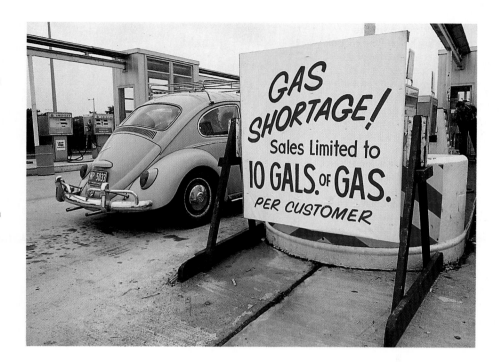

**RECAP**

1. The political business cycle is a short-term expansion stimulated by an administration before an election to earn votes. After the election comes the long-term adjustment (rising unemployment and inflation).

2. A real business cycle is an expansion and contraction caused by a change in tastes or technology, strikes, weather, war and terrorism, or other real factors.

## 4. THE LINK BETWEEN MONETARY AND FISCAL POLICIES

In earlier chapters we have described how monetary and fiscal policies determine the equilibrium level of prices and national income. In our discussions we have talked about monetary policy and fiscal policy individually. Here we consider the relationship between them.

In some countries, monetary and fiscal policies are carried out by a single central authority. Even in the United States, where the Federal Reserve was created as an independent agency, monetary policy and fiscal policy are always related. The actions of the central bank have an impact on the proper role for fiscal policy, and the actions of fiscal policymakers have an impact on the proper role for monetary policy.

For example, suppose the central bank follows a monetary policy that raises interest rates. That policy raises the interest cost of new government debt, in the process also increasing government expenditures. On the other hand, a fiscal policy that generates large fiscal deficits could contribute to higher interest rates. If the central bank has targeted an interest rate that lies below the current rate, the central bank could be drawn into an expansionary monetary policy. This interdependence between monetary and fiscal policy is important to policymakers as well as to business people and others who seek to understand current economic developments.

Some aspects of the macro-economy are beyond the control of the government. This photo depicts the damage done in Kobe, Japan, following an earthquake. Natural disasters, such as earthquakes or bad weather, sometimes play a role in determining the price level and national output in the short run. A major earthquake will lower national output and raise the price level. However, such effects should be important only in the short run as other determinants of the equilibrium price level and real GDP will dominate the forces of nature in normal times.

The *government budget constraint* clarifies the relationship between monetary and fiscal policies:

$$G = T + B + \Delta M$$

where

$$G = \text{government spending}$$

$$T = \text{tax revenue}$$

$$B = \text{government borrowing}$$

$$\Delta M = \text{the change in the money supply}[1]$$

The government budget constraint always holds because there are only three ways for the government to finance its spending: by taxing, by borrowing, and by creating money.

We can rewrite the government budget constraint with the change in $M$ on the left-hand side of the equation:

$$\Delta M = (G - T) - B$$

In this form you can see that the change in government-issued money equals the government fiscal deficit $(G - T)$ minus borrowing. This equation is always true. A government that has the ability to borrow at reasonable costs will not have the incentive to create rapid money growth and the consequent inflation that results in order to finance its budget deficit.

In the United States and other industrial nations, monetary and fiscal policies are conducted by separate, independent agencies. Fiscal authorities (Congress and the president in the United States) cannot impose monetary policy on the central bank. But in typical developing countries, monetary and fiscal policies are controlled by

**7. How is inflationary monetary policy related to government fiscal policy?**

___

[1]The $M$ in the government budget constraint is government-issued money (usually called *base money,* or *high-powered money*). It is easiest to think of this kind of money as currency, although in practice base money includes more than currency.

a central political authority. Here monetary policy is often an extension of fiscal policy. Fiscal policy can impose an inflationary burden on monetary policy. If a country is running a large fiscal deficit, and much of this deficit cannot be financed by government borrowing, monetary authorities must create money to finance the deficit.

RECAP

1. The government budget constraint ($G = T + B + \Delta M$) defines the relationship between fiscal and monetary policies.
2. The implications of fiscal policy for the growth of the money supply can be seen by rewriting the government budget constraint as $\Delta M = (G - T) - B$.

## 5. ECONOMIC GROWTH

Although much of macroeconomics is aimed at understanding business cycles—recurring periods of prosperity and recession—the fact is that over the long run, most economies do grow wealthier. The long-run trend of real GDP in the United States and most other countries is positive. Yet the rate at which real GDP grows is very different across countries. In this section we examine the determinants of economic growth to understand what accounts for the different rates of growth across countries.

### 5.a. The Determinants of Growth

**?**

**8. How are economic growth rates determined?**

The long-run aggregate supply curve is a vertical line at the potential level of real GDP ($Y_{p1}$). As the economy grows, the potential output of the economy rises. Figure 11 shows the increase in potential output as a rightward shift in the long-run aggregate supply curve. The higher the rate of growth, the farther the aggregate supply curve moves to the right. To illustrate several years' growth, we would show several curves shifting to the right.

Figure 11

**Economic Growth**

As the economy grows, the long-run aggregate supply curve shifts to the right. This represents an increase in the potential level of real GDP.

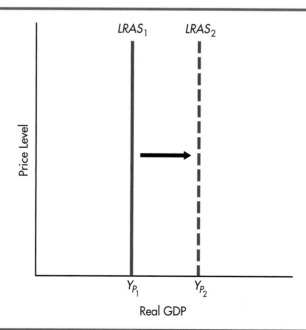

To find the determinants of economic growth, we must turn to the determinants of aggregate supply. In Chapter 12, we identified three determinants of aggregate supply: resource prices, technology, and expectations. Changes in expectations can shift the aggregate supply curve, but changing expectations are not a basis for long-run growth in the sense of continuous rightward movements in aggregate supply. The long-run growth of the economy rests on growth in productive resources (labor, capital, and land) and technological advances.

**5.a.1. Labor** Economic growth depends on the size and quality of the labor force. The size of the labor force is a function of the size of the working-age population (16 and older in the United States) and the percentage of that population in the labor force. The labor force typically grows more rapidly in developing countries than in industrial countries because birthrates are higher in developing countries. Between 1990 and 2001, the population grew at an average annual rate of 2.0 percent in low-income developing countries and 0.7 percent in high-income industrial countries.

Solely on the basis of growth in the labor force, it seems that developing countries are growing faster than industrial countries. But the size of the labor force is not all that matters; changes in productivity can compensate for lower growth in the labor force, as we discuss in section 5.b.

**5.a.2. Capital** Labor is combined with capital to produce goods and services. A rapidly growing labor force by itself is no guarantee of economic growth. Workers need machines, tools, and factories to work. If a country has lots of workers but few machines, then the typical worker cannot be very productive. Capital is a critical resource in growing economies.

The ability of a country to invest in capital goods is tied to its ability to save. A lack of current saving can be offset by borrowing, but the availability of borrowing is limited by the prospects for future saving. Debt incurred today must be repaid by not consuming all output in the future. If lenders believe that a nation is going to consume all of its output in the future, they do not make loans today.

The lower the standard of living in a country, the harder it is to forgo current consumption in order to save. It is difficult for a population living at or near subsistence level to do without current consumption. This in large part explains the low level of saving in the poorest countries.

**5.a.3. Land** Land surface, water, forests, minerals, and other natural resources are called *land*. Land can be combined with labor and capital to produce goods and services. Abundant natural resources can contribute to economic growth, but natural resources alone do not generate growth. Several developing countries, like Argentina and Brazil, are relatively rich in natural resources but have not been very successful in exploiting these resources to produce goods and services. Japan, on the other hand, has relatively few natural resources but showed dramatic economic growth for decades until a recession in the 1990s. The experience of Japan makes it clear that abundant natural resources are not a necessary condition for economic growth.

**technology:** ways of combining resources to produce output

**5.a.4. Technology** A key determinant of economic growth is **technology,** ways of combining resources to produce goods and services. New management techniques, scientific discoveries, and other innovations improve technology. Technological advances allow the production of more output from a given amount of resources. This means that technological progress accelerates economic growth for any given rate of growth in the labor force and the capital stock.

Technological change depends on the scientific community. The more educated a population, the greater its potential for technological advances. Industrial countries have better-educated populations than developing countries do. Education gives industrial countries a substantial advantage over developing countries in

## Key Term Match

Match each term with its correct definition by placing the appropriate letter next to the corresponding number.

A. Phillips curve
B. reservation wage
C. adaptive expectation
D. rational expectation
E. shock
F. technology
G. total factor productivity (TFP)

_____ 1. ways of combining resources to produce output
_____ 2. an expectation that is formed using all available relevant information
_____ 3. the ratio of the economy's output to its stock of labor and capital
_____ 4. an expectation formed on the basis of information collected in the past
_____ 5. an unexpected change in a variable
_____ 6. the minimum wage a worker is willing to accept
_____ 7. a graph that illustrates the relationship between inflation and the unemployment rate

## Quick-Check Quiz

**1** Which of the following could *not* cause a movement along the Phillips curve?

a. a change in inflation that is not expected by workers
b. an unexpected increase in inflation that causes inventories to decline
c. wage contracts that did not correctly anticipate the inflation rate
d. an anticipated rise in nominal wages
e. All of the above cause movements along the short-run Phillips curve.

**2** Which of the following is an example of rational rather than adaptive expectations?

a. The crowd expects a 95 percent free-throw shooter to sink the free throw to win the state basketball championship.
b. A professor has been 10 minutes late to class three times in a row. Students come to the fourth class 10 minutes late.
c. The fans of a pro football team that had four wins, ten losses, and one tie last year find another team to root for this year.
d. Stockholders of a firm that had losses three years in a row sell off their stocks.

e. A company with a poor earnings record over the past five years finds itself swamped by investors when word of its new superproduct leaks out.

**3** Which of the following is false?

a. The short-run effect of unexpected disinflation is rising unemployment.
b. The short-run Philips curve assumes a constant reservation wage and a constant expected rate of inflation.
c. The tradeoff between inflation and unemployment comes from expected inflation.
d. Inventory fluctuations may cause a movement along the Phillips curve.
e. If wages were flexible, unexpected changes in aggregate demand might be reflected more in wage adjustments than in employment adjustments.

**4** Unexpected increases in aggregate demand

_____ inventories and _____

prices. Unemployment _____.

a. lowers; raises; decreases
b. lowers; raises; increases
c. lowers; lowers; increases
d. raises; lowers; increases
e. raises; lowers; decreases

**5** Which of the following would *not* be a cause of a real business cycle?

a. a decrease in government borrowing
b. a drought in the Midwest
c. oil prices skyrocketing as a result of an accident on the world's largest offshore oil rig
d. a labor strike that cripples the steel industry
e. an improvement in the technology for solar energy that yields a lightweight solar battery that can be used to power cars for long trips

**6** The existence of a political business cycle implies that, prior to the election, the incumbent administration would

a. increase aggregate demand by increasing government spending and the money supply.
b. increase aggregate demand by increasing government spending and decreasing the money supply.
c. increase aggregate demand by decreasing government spending and the money supply.
d. decrease aggregate demand by increasing government spending and the money supply.

e. decrease aggregate demand by increasing government spending and decreasing the money supply.

**7** A drought in the Midwest would cause _____ to shift _____, which would _____ real GDP.

    a. aggregate demand; left; decrease
    b. aggregate demand; right; increase
    c. aggregate supply; left; increase
    d. aggregate supply; left; decrease
    e. aggregate supply; right; increase

**8** Which of the following is false?

    a. In most developed countries, monetary and fiscal policies are conducted by separate independent agencies.
    b. Fiscal policy can impose an inflationary burden on monetary policy.
    c. In typical developing countries, monetary and fiscal policies are controlled by the same central authority.
    d. Using money to finance deficits has produced severe deflation in many countries.
    e. Monetary control is not possible until fiscal policy is under control.

**9** An abundance of natural resources

    a. is always necessary for economic growth.
    b. is necessary for economic growth only in capitalist countries.
    c. is necessary for economic growth only in developing countries.
    d. has no effect on economic growth.
    e. can contribute to economic growth but is not necessary for growth.

**10** Growth in a country's capital stock is tied to

    a. increases in the amounts of natural resources available.
    b. current and future saving.
    c. improvements in technology.
    d. increases in the amount of labor available.
    e. decreases in the labor force participation ratio.

**11** Which of the following is *not* one of the determinants of economic growth?

    a. the size and quality of the labor force
    b. the amount of capital goods available
    c. technology
    d. natural resources
    e. the shape of the aggregate demand curve

## Practice Questions and Problems

**1** The _____ illustrates the inverse relationship between inflation and the unemployment rate.

**2** The Phillips curve tradeoff between inflation and unemployment _____ (does, does not) persist over the long run.

**3** The downward slope of the short-run Phillips curve is caused by shifts in _____, with _____ remaining constant.

**4** List the two assumptions underlying the short-run Phillips curve.

_____

_____

**5** If people's expectations about inflation do not change, the short-run effect of disinflation is rising _____.

**6** Unexpected inflation can affect the employment rate in the following three ways:

_____

_____

_____

**7** Your economics professor bases her first exam solely on material from the textbook. Before the second exam, she announces that this exam will be based primarily on lecture material. If you only study the textbook, you are acting on the basis of _____ expectations.

**8** When the inflation rate is unexpectedly high, unemployment _____.

**9** Write the equation for the government budget restraint.

_____

**10** The government can finance its spending by _____, _____, or _____.

**11** Economic growth shifts the aggregate _____ (demand, supply) curve to the _____ (right, left).

**12** The long-run growth of the economy rests on growth in productive resources such as _____, _____, _____, and _____, and on advances in _____.

**13** The size of country's labor force is determined by the _____ and the _____ of the population in the labor force.

**14** Growth in a country's capital stock depends on current and future _____.

**15** What are two factors that cause developing countries to lag behind in the development and implementation of new technology?

_____

_____

**16** Productivity is the ratio of _____ to the amount of _____.

**17** _____ is the nation's real GDP divided by its stock of labor and capital.

**18** In the United States, labor receives about 70 percent of national income, and capital receives about 30 percent. If total factor productivity increases by 1 percent, labor increases by 1 percent, and capital increases by 3 percent, by what percentage will national income increase? _____

## Exercises and Applications

**I** **War on Inflation** The leader of a developing nation has declared war on inflation by issuing a series of belt-tightening measures. Capital gains taxes will be enforced, lending and deposit rates at banks will be raised, and government spending will be slashed.

Use the government's budget constraint to explain how these measures will affect inflation.

_____

_____

**II** **Government Policy and Growth** Government policies that hold down interest rates have adverse effects on economic growth in developing countries. Although low interest rates are intended to make it cheaper for local businesses to invest in new capital goods, they have the effect of drying up the supply of savings since savers can get a higher return by taking their money out of the country or by making less productive investments on their own. Similar policies are sometimes followed in other economic sectors, with similarly bad results.

For example, many developing countries require farmers to sell their crops to the government, which resells the food to city dwellers. To keep the city dwellers happy, the prices charged for food are set very low, as are the prices paid to farmers. Think about the farmers' opportunity costs of growing food for sale and predict what is likely to happen to the food supply in countries adopting this policy.

_____

_____

_____

**ACE self-test** Now that you've completed the Study Guide for this chapter, you should have a good sense of the concepts you need to review. If you'd like to test your understanding of the material again, go to the Practice Tests on the Boyes/Melvin *Fundamentals of Economics,* 3e website, **economics.college.hmco.com/students.**

## Chapter 17

# Issues in International Trade and Finance

**? Fundamental Questions**

1. What determines the goods a nation will export?
2. What are the sources of comparative advantage?
3. Why do countries restrict international trade?
4. How do countries restrict the entry of foreign goods and promote the export of domestic goods?
5. What kinds of exchange rate arrangements exist today?

**?**

1. What determines the goods a nation will export?

## Preview

The world is a global marketplace, and all nations are interdependent. An understanding of international trade and finance is critical to understanding the modern economy. While earlier chapters have frequently considered international implications of various topics, in this chapter we delve more deeply into the global economic linkages.

Besides studying the determinants of international trade and how and why nations restrict such trade, we also will learn about the variety of exchange rate regimes that exist in the world today. Some countries allow the value of their currency to float with the free market forces of supply and demand while other countries choose to fix the value of their currency at some constant value against another currency. Still other countries choose some sort of hybrid exchange rate system. Since exchange rates are the prices that link the currencies of the world, we better understand the interrelationships among countries when we understand the current exchange rate environment. ■

## 1. AN OVERVIEW OF WORLD TRADE

Recall from Chapter 1 that trade occurs because it makes people better off. International trade occurs because it makes people better off than they would be if they could consume only domestically produced products. Who trades with whom, and what sorts of goods are traded? The underlying reasons for trade are found in comparative advantage.

### 1.a. Comparative Advantage

In Chapter 1, you learned that *comparative advantage* is the ability to produce a good or service at a lower opportunity cost than someone else. This is true for countries as well as for individuals. Comparative advantage is found by comparing the relative costs of production in each country. We measure the cost of producing a particular good in two countries in terms of opportunity costs—what other goods must be given up in order to produce more of the good in question.

Table 1 presents a hypothetical example of two countries, the United States and India, that both produce two goods, wheat and cloth. The table lists the amount of each good that could be produced by one worker. This example assumes that labor productivity differences alone determine comparative advantage. In the United States,

| Table 1 | Output per Worker per Day in Either Wheat or Cloth | |
| --- | --- | --- |
| **An Example of Comparative Advantage** | U.S. (units) | India (units) |
| Wheat | 8 | 4 |
| Cloth | 4 | 3 |

one worker can produce either 8 units of wheat or 4 units of cloth. In India, one worker can produce 4 units of wheat or 3 units of cloth.

**absolute advantage:** an advantage derived from one country's having a lower absolute input cost of producing a particular good than another country

The United States has an **absolute advantage**—greater productivity—in producing both wheat and cloth. Absolute advantage is determined by comparing the absolute productivity in different countries of producing each good. Since one worker can produce more of either good in the United States than in India, the United States is the more efficient producer of both goods.

It might seem that since the United States is the more efficient producer of both goods, there would be no need for trade with India. But absolute advantage is not the critical consideration. What matters in determining the benefits of international trade is comparative advantage. To find the comparative advantage—the lower opportunity cost—we must compare the opportunity cost of producing each good in each country.

The opportunity cost of producing wheat is what must be given up in cloth using the same resources, like one worker per day. Look again at Table 1 to see the production of wheat and cloth in the two countries. Since one U.S. worker can produce 8 units of wheat or 4 units of cloth, if we take a worker from cloth production and move him to wheat production, we gain 8 units of wheat and lose 4 units of cloth. The opportunity cost of producing wheat equals 4/8, or 1/2, unit of cloth and is represented as

$$\frac{\text{Output of cloth given up}}{\text{Output of wheat gained}} = \begin{matrix}\text{opportunity cost of} \\ \text{producing 1 unit of wheat} \\ \text{(in terms of cloth given up)}\end{matrix}$$

$$4/8 = 1/2$$

Comparative advantage is based on what a country can do relatively better than other countries. This photo shows a woman in Sri Lanka picking tea leaves. Sri Lanka is one of the few countries that export a significant amount of tea. Due to favorable growing conditions (a natural resource), these countries have a comparative advantage in tea production.

Applying the same thinking to India, we find that one worker can produce 4 units of wheat or 3 units of cloth. The opportunity cost of producing 1 unit of wheat in India is 3/4 unit of cloth.

A comparison of the domestic opportunity costs in each country will reveal which one has the comparative advantage in producing each good. The U.S. opportunity cost of producing 1 unit of wheat is 1/2 unit of cloth; the Indian opportunity cost is 3/4 unit of cloth. Because the United States has a lower domestic opportunity cost, it has the comparative advantage in wheat production and will export wheat. Since wheat production costs are lower in the United States, India is better off trading for wheat rather than trying to produce it domestically.

The comparative advantage in cloth is found the same way. Taking a worker in the United States from wheat production and putting her in cloth production, we gain 4 units of cloth and lose 8 units of wheat per day. Therefore, the opportunity cost is

$$\frac{\text{Output of wheat given up}}{\text{Output of cloth gained}} = \begin{array}{l}\text{opportunity cost of}\\ \text{producing 1 unit of cloth}\\ \text{(in terms of wheat given up)}\end{array}$$

$$8/4 = 2$$

In India, moving a worker from wheat to cloth production means that we gain 3 units of cloth but lose 4 units of wheat, so the opportunity cost is 4/3, or $1\frac{1}{3}$, units of wheat for 1 unit of cloth. Comparing the U.S. opportunity cost of 2 units of wheat with the Indian opportunity cost of $1\frac{1}{3}$ units, we see that India has the comparative advantage in cloth production and will therefore export cloth. In this case, the United States is better off trading for cloth than producing it since India's costs of production are lower.

In international trade, as in other areas of economic decision making, it is opportunity cost that matters; and opportunity costs are reflected in comparative advantage. Absolute advantage is irrelevant because knowing the absolute number of labor hours required to produce a good does not tell us if we can benefit from trade. We benefit from trade if we are able to obtain a good from a foreign country by giving up less than we would have to give up to obtain the good at home. Because only opportunity cost can allow us to make such comparisons, international trade proceeds on the basis of comparative advantage.

### 1.b. Sources of Comparative Advantage

We know that countries specialize and trade in accordance with comparative advantage, but what gives a country a comparative advantage? Economists have suggested several theories of the source of comparative advantage. Let us review these theories.

#### 1.b.1. Productivity Differences

The example of comparative advantage showed the United States to have a comparative advantage in wheat production and India to have a comparative advantage in cloth production. Comparative advantage was determined by differences in the labor hours required to produce each good. In this example, differences in the *productivity* of labor accounted for comparative advantage.

For over two hundred years, economists have argued that productivity differences account for comparative advantage. In fact, this theory of comparative advantage is often called the *Ricardian model,* after David Ricardo, a nineteenth-century English economist who explained and analyzed the idea of productivity-based comparative advantage. Variation in the productivity of labor can explain many observed trade patterns in the world.

Although we know that labor productivity differs across countries—and that this can help explain why countries produce the goods they do—there are factors other

2. **What are the sources of comparative advantage?**

than labor productivity that determine comparative advantage. Furthermore, even if labor productivity were all that mattered, we would still want to know why some countries have more productive workers than others. The standard interpretation of the Ricardian model is that technological differences between countries account for differences in labor productivity. The countries with the most-advanced technology would have a comparative advantage with regard to those goods that can be produced most efficiently with modern technology.

### 1.b.2. Factor Abundance

Goods differ in terms of the resources, or factors of production, required for their production. Countries differ in terms of the abundance of different factors of production: land, labor, and capital. It seems self-evident that countries would have an advantage in producing those goods that use relatively large amounts of their most abundant factor of production. Certainly countries with a relatively large amount of farmland would have a comparative advantage in agriculture, and countries with a relatively large amount of capital would tend to specialize in the production of manufactured goods.

In many cases, factor abundance has served well as an explanation of observed trade patterns. However, there remain cases in which comparative advantage seems to run counter to the predictions of the factor abundance theory. In response, economists have suggested other explanations for comparative advantage.

### 1.b.3. Other Theories of Comparative Advantage

New theories of comparative advantage have typically come about in an effort to explain the trade pattern in some narrow category of products. They are not intended to serve as general explanations of comparative advantage, as do factor abundance and productivity. These supplementary theories emphasize human skills, product cycles, and preferences.

*Human Skills* This approach emphasizes differences across countries in the availability of skilled and unskilled labor. The basic idea is that countries with a relatively abundant stock of highly skilled labor will have a comparative advantage in producing goods that require relatively large amounts of skilled labor. This theory is similar to the factor abundance theory except that here the analysis rests on two segments (skilled and unskilled) of the labor factor.

The human skills argument is consistent with the observation that most U.S. exports are produced in high-wage (skilled-labor) industries, and most U.S. imports are products produced in relatively low-wage industries. Since the United States has a well-educated labor force relative to that of many other countries, we would expect the United States to have a comparative advantage in industries requiring a large amount of skilled labor. Developing countries would be expected to have a comparative advantage in industries requiring a relatively large amount of unskilled labor.

*Product Life Cycles* This theory explains how comparative advantage in a specific good can shift over time from one country to another. This occurs because goods experience a *product life cycle*. At the outset, development and testing are required to conceptualize and design the product. For this reason, the early production will be undertaken by an innovative firm. Over time, however, a successful product tends to become standardized, in the sense that many manufacturers can produce it. The mature product may be produced by firms that do little or no research and development, specializing instead in copying successful products invented and developed by others.

The product life cycle theory is related to international comparative advantage in that a new product will be first produced and exported by the nation in which it was invented. As the product is exported elsewhere, and foreign firms become familiar with it, the technology is copied in other countries by foreign firms seeking to produce a competing version. As the product matures, comparative advantage shifts away from the country of origin if other countries have lower manufacturing costs using the now-standardized technology.

The history of color television production shows how comparative advantage can shift over the product life cycle. Color television was invented in the United States, and U.S. firms initially produced and exported color TVs. Over time, as the technology of color television manufacturing became well known, countries like Japan and Taiwan came to dominate the business. Firms in these countries had a comparative advantage over U.S. firms in the manufacture of color televisions. Once the technology is widely available, countries with lower production costs due to lower wages can compete effectively against the higher-wage nation that developed the technology.

*Preferences*   The theories of comparative advantage we have looked at so far have all been based on supply factors. It may be, though, that the demand side of the market can explain some of the patterns observed in international trade. Seldom are different producers' goods exactly identical. Consumers may prefer the goods of one firm to those of another firm. Domestic firms usually produce goods to satisfy domestic consumers. But since different consumers have different preferences, some consumers will prefer goods produced by foreign firms. International trade allows consumers to expand their consumption opportunities.

Consumers who live in countries with similar levels of development can be expected to have similar consumption patterns. The consumption patterns of consumers in countries at much different levels of development are much less similar. This suggests that firms in industrial countries will find a larger market for their goods in other industrial countries than in developing countries.

Another feature of international trade that may be explained by consumer preference is **intraindustry trade,** a circumstance in which a country both exports and imports goods in the same industry. The fact that the United States exports Budweiser beer and imports Heineken beer is not surprising when preferences are taken into account. Supply-side theories of comparative advantage rarely provide an explanation of intraindustry trade since they would expect each country to export only those goods produced in industries in which a comparative advantage exists. Yet the real world is characterized by a great deal of intraindustry trade.

We have discussed several potential sources of comparative advantage: labor productivity, factor abundance, human skills, product cycles, and preferences. Each of these theories, summarized in Figure 1, has proven useful in understanding certain trade patterns. Each has also been shown to have limitations as a general theory applicable to all cases. Once again we are reminded that the world is a very complicated place. Theories are simpler than reality. Nevertheless, they help us to understand how comparative advantage arises.

**intraindustry trade:** simultaneous import and export of goods in the same industry by a particular country

RECAP

1. Comparative advantage can arise because of differences in labor productivity.
2. Countries differ in their resource endowments, and a given country may enjoy a comparative advantage in products that intensively use its most abundant factor of production.
3. Industrial countries may have a comparative advantage in products requiring a large amount of skilled labor. Developing countries may have a comparative advantage in products requiring a large amount of unskilled labor.
4. Comparative advantage in a new good initially resides in the country that invented the good. Over time, other nations learn the technology and may gain a comparative advantage in producing the good.
5. In some industries, consumer preferences for differentiated goods may explain international trade flows, including intraindustry trade.

government subsidizes General Motors in its attack on the bus market, the German government is likely to subsidize BMW rather than lose the entire bus market to a U.S. producer. As a result, taxpayers in both nations will be subsidizing two firms, each producing too few buses to earn a profit.

## 2.b. Tools of Policy

**4. How do countries restrict the entry of foreign goods and promote the export of domestic goods?**

Commercial policy makes use of several tools, including tariffs, quotas, subsidies, and nontariff barriers like health and safety regulations that restrict the entry of foreign products. Since 1945, barriers to trade have been reduced. Much of the progress toward free trade may be linked to the *General Agreement on Tariffs and Trade,* or *GATT,* that began in 1947. In 1995, the World Trade Organization (WTO) was formed to incorporate the agreements under GATT into a formal permanent international organization that oversees world trade. The WTO has three objectives: help global trade flow as freely as possible, achieve reductions in trade restrictions gradually through negotiation, and provide an impartial means of settling disputes. Nevertheless, restrictions on trade still exist, and this section will review the most commonly used restrictions.

**tariff:** a tax on imports and selected exports

**2.b.1. Tariffs** In Chapter 3 we defined a **tariff** as a tax on imports—goods and services purchased from foreign suppliers. Every country imposes tariffs on at least some imports. Some countries also impose tariffs on selected *exports* as a means of raising government revenue. Brazil, for instance, taxes coffee exports. The United States does not employ export tariffs, which are forbidden by the U.S. Constitution.

Tariffs are frequently imposed in order to protect domestic producers from foreign competition. The dangers of imposing tariffs are well illustrated in the Economic Insight "Smoot-Hawley Tariff." The effect of a tariff is illustrated in

### Smoot-Hawley Tariff

### *Economic Insight*

Many economists believe that the Great Depression of the 1930s was at least partly due to the Smoot-Hawley Tariff Act, signed into law by President Herbert Hoover in 1930. Hoover had promised that, if elected, he would raise tariffs on agricultural products to raise U.S. farm income. Congress began work on the tariff increases in 1928. Congressman Willis Hawley and Senator Reed Smoot conducted the hearings.

In testimony before Congress, manufacturers and other special interest groups also sought protection from foreign competition. The resulting bill increased tariffs on over 12,000 products. Tariffs reached their highest levels ever, about 60 percent of average import values.

Only twice before in U.S. history had tariffs approached the levels of the Smoot-Hawley era.

Before President Hoover signed the bill, 38 foreign governments made formal protests, warning that they would retaliate with high tariffs on U.S. products. A petition signed by 1,028 economists warned of the harmful effects of the bill. Nevertheless, Hoover signed the bill into law.

World trade collapsed as other countries raised their tariffs in response. Between 1930 and 1931, U.S. imports fell 29 percent, but U.S. exports fell 33 percent. By 1933, world trade was about one-third of the 1929 level. As the level of trade fell, so did income and prices. In 1934, in an effort to correct the mistakes of Smoot-Hawley, Congress

passed the Reciprocal Trade Agreements Act, which allowed the president to lower U.S. tariffs in return for reductions in foreign tariffs on U.S. goods. This act ushered in the modern era of relatively low tariffs. In the United States today, tariffs are about 5 percent of the average value of imports.

Many economists believe the collapse of world trade and the Depression to be linked by a decrease in real income caused by abandoning production based on comparative advantage. Few economists argue that the Great Depression was caused solely by the Smoot-Hawley tariff, but the experience serves as a lesson to those who support higher tariffs to protect domestic producers.

Figure 2

**The Effects of a Tariff**

The domestic equilibrium price and quantity with no trade are $P_d$ and $Q_d$, respectively. The world price is $P_w$. With free trade, therefore, imports will equal $Q_2 - Q_1$. A tariff added to the world price reduces imports to $Q_4 - Q_3$.

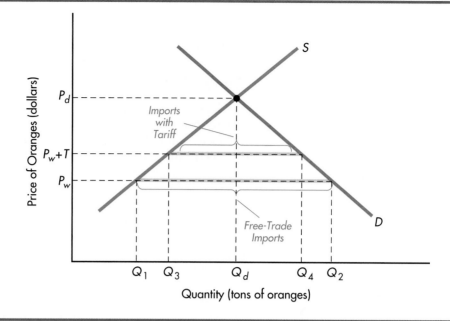

Figure 2, which shows the domestic market for oranges. Without international trade, the domestic equilibrium price $P_d$ and quantity $Q_d$ demanded are determined by the intersection of the domestic demand and supply curves. If the world price $P_w$ of oranges is lower than the domestic equilibrium price, this country will import oranges. The quantity imported will be the difference between the quantity $Q_1$ produced domestically at a price of $P_w$ and the quantity $Q_2$ demanded domestically at the world price of oranges.

When the world price of the traded good is lower than the domestic equilibrium price without international trade, free trade causes domestic production to fall and domestic consumption to rise. The domestic shortage at the world price is met by imports. Domestic consumers are better off since they can buy more at a lower price. But domestic producers are worse off since they now sell fewer oranges and receive a lower price.

Suppose a tariff of $T$ (the dollar value of the tariff) is imposed on orange imports. The price paid by consumers is now $P_w + T$, rather than $P_w$. At this higher price, domestic producers will produce $Q_3$, and domestic consumers will purchase $Q_4$. The tariff has the effect of increasing domestic production and reducing domestic consumption, relative to the free trade equilibrium. Imports fall accordingly, from $Q_2 - Q_1$ to $Q_4 - Q_3$.

Domestic producers are better off since the tariff has increased their sales of oranges and raised the price they receive. Domestic consumers pay higher prices for fewer oranges than they would with free trade, but they are still better off than they would be without trade. If the tariff had raised the price paid by consumers to $P_d$, there would be no trade, and the domestic equilibrium quantity $Q_d$ would prevail.

The government earns revenue from imports of oranges. If each ton of oranges generates tariff revenue of $T$, the total tariff revenue to the government is found by multiplying the tariff by the quantity of oranges imported. In Figure 2, this amount is $T \times (Q_4 - Q_3)$. As the tariff changes, so does the quantity of imports and the government revenue.

Figure 3

**The Effects of a Quota**

The domestic equilibrium price with no international trade is $P_d$. At this price, 250 tons of oranges would be produced and consumed at home. With free trade, the price is $P_w$ and 300 tons will be imported. An import quota of 100 tons will cause the price to be $P_q$, where the domestic shortage equals the 100 tons allowed by the quota.

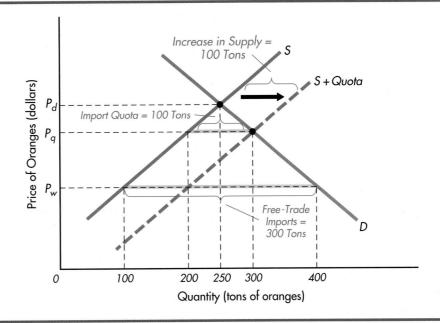

**quantity quota:** a limit on the amount of a good that may be produced

**value quota:** a limit on the monetary value of a good that may be imported

**2.b.2. Quotas** Quotas are limits on the quantity or value of goods imported and exported. A **quantity quota** restricts the physical amount of a good. For instance, through 1994, the United States allowed only 2.5 million tons of sugar to be imported. Even though the United States is not a competitive sugar producer compared with other nations like the Dominican Republic or Cuba, the quota allowed U.S. firms to produce about 6 percent of the world's sugar output. A **value quota** restricts the monetary value of a good that may be traded. Instead of a physical quota on sugar, the United States could have limited the dollar value of sugar imports.

Quotas are used to protect domestic producers from foreign competition. By restricting the amount of a good that may be imported, they increase its price and allow domestic producers to sell more at a higher price than they would with free trade. Figure 3 illustrates the effect of a quota on the domestic orange market. The domestic equilibrium supply and demand curves determine the equilibrium price and quantity without trade to be $P_d$ and 250 tons, respectively. The world price of oranges is $P_w$. Since $P_w$ lies below $P_d$, this country will import oranges. The quantity of imports is equal to the amount of the domestic shortage at $P_w$. The quantity demanded at $P_w$ is 400 tons, and the quantity supplied domestically is 100 tons, so imports will equal 300 tons of oranges. With free trade, domestic producers sell 100 tons at a price of $P_w$.

But suppose domestic orange growers convince the government to restrict orange imports. The government then imposes a quota of 100 tons on imported oranges. The effect of the quota on consumers is to shift the supply curve to the right by the amount of the quota, 100 tons. Since the quota is less than the quantity of imports with free trade, the quantity of imports will equal the quota. The domestic equilibrium price with the quota occurs at the point where the domestic shortage equals the quota. At price $P_q$, the domestic quantity demanded (300 tons) is 100 tons more than the domestic quantity supplied (200 tons).

Quotas benefit domestic producers in the same way that tariffs do. Domestic producers receive a higher price ($P_q$ instead of $P_w$) for a greater quantity (200 instead of 100) than they do under free trade. The effect on domestic consumers is also similar to that of a tariff: they pay a higher price for a smaller quantity than they would with free trade. A tariff generates government tax revenue; quotas do not (unless the government auctioned off the right to import under the quota). Furthermore, a tariff only raises the price of the product in the domestic market. Foreign producers receive the world price, $P_w$. With a quota, both domestic and foreign producers receive the higher price, $P_q$, for the goods sold in the domestic market. So foreign producers are hurt by the reduction in the quantity of imports permitted, but they do receive a higher price for the amount they sell.

### 2.b.3. Other Barriers to Trade

Tariffs and quotas are not the only barriers to the free flow of goods across international borders. There are three additional sources of restrictions on free trade: subsidies, government procurement, and health and safety standards. Though often enacted for reasons other than protection from foreign competition, a careful analysis reveals their import-reducing effect.

Before discussing these three types of barriers, let us note the cultural or institutional barriers to trade that also exist in many countries. Such barriers may exist independently of any conscious government policy. For instance, Japan has frequently been criticized by U.S. officials for informal business practices that discriminate against foreigners. Under the Japanese distribution system, goods typically pass through several layers of intermediaries before appearing in a retail store. A foreign firm faces the difficult task of gaining entry to this system to supply goods to the retailer. Furthermore, a foreigner cannot easily open a retail store. Japanese law requires a new retail firm to receive permission from other retailers in the area in order to open a business. A firm that lacks contacts and knowledge of the system cannot penetrate the Japanese market.

In the fall of 1989, the U.S. toy firm Toys "R" Us announced its intent to open several large discount toy stores in Japan. However, local toy stores in each area objected to having a Toys "R" Us store nearby. The U.S. government has argued that the laws favoring existing firms are an important factor in keeping Japan closed to foreign firms that would like to enter the Japanese market. Eventually, Toys "R" Us opened stores in Japan.

*Subsidies*  **Subsidies** are payments by a government to an exporter. Subsidies are paid to stimulate exports by allowing the exporter to charge a lower price. The amount of a subsidy is determined by the international price of a product relative to the domestic price in the absence of trade. Domestic consumers are harmed by subsidies in that their taxes finance the subsidies. Also, since the subsidy diverts resources from the domestic market toward export production, the increase in the supply of export goods could be associated with a decrease in the supply of domestic goods, causing domestic prices to rise.

Subsidies may take forms other than direct cash payments. These include tax reductions, low-interest loans, low-cost insurance, government-sponsored research funding, and other devices. The U.S. government subsidizes export activity through the U.S. Export-Import Bank, which provides loans and insurance to help U.S. exporters sell their goods to foreign buyers. Subsidies are more commonplace in Europe than in Japan or the United States.

*Government Procurement*  Governments are often required by law to buy only from local producers. In the United States, a "buy American" act passed in 1933 required U.S. government agencies to buy U.S. goods and services unless the domestic price was more than 12 percent above the foreign price. This kind of policy allows domestic firms to charge the government a higher price for their products than they charge consumers; the taxpayers bear the burden. The United States is by no means alone in the use of such policies. Many other nations also use such policies to create larger markets for domestic goods.

*Health and Safety Standards*  Government serves as a guardian of the public health and welfare by requiring that products offered to the public be safe and

**subsidy:** a grant of money given to help produce or purchase a specific good or service

fulfill the use for which they are intended. Government standards for products sold in the domestic marketplace can have the effect (intentional or not) of protecting domestic producers from foreign competition. These effects should be considered in evaluating the full impact of such standards.

The government of Japan once threatened to prohibit foreign-made snow skis from entering the country for reasons of safety. Only Japanese-made skis were determined to be suitable for Japanese snow. Several western European nations announced that U.S. beef would not be allowed into Europe because hormones approved by the U.S. government are fed to U.S. beef cattle. In the late 1960s, France required tractors sold there to have a maximum speed of 17 miles per hour; in Germany, the permissible speed was 13 mph, and in the Netherlands it was 10 mph. Tractors produced in one country had to be modified to meet the requirements of the other countries. Such modifications raise the price of goods and discourage international trade.

Product standards may not eliminate foreign competition, but standards different from those of the rest of the world do provide an element of protection to domestic firms.

---

**RECAP**

1. Government restrictions on foreign trade are usually aimed at protecting domestic producers from foreign competition.

2. Import restrictions may save domestic jobs, but the costs to consumers may be greater than the benefits to those who retain their jobs.

3. Advocates of "fair trade," or the creation of a level playing field, call for import restrictions as a means of lowering foreign restrictions on markets for domestic exports.

4. The national defense argument in favor of trade restrictions is that protection from foreign competition is necessary to ensure that certain key defense-related industries continue to produce.

5. The infant industries argument in favor of trade restriction is to allow a new industry a period of time in which to become competitive with its foreign counterparts.

6. Strategic trade policy is intended to provide domestic increasing-returns-to-scale industries an advantage over their foreign competitors.

7. A tariff is a tax on imports or exports. Tariffs protect domestic firms by raising the prices of foreign goods.

8. Tariffs are an important source of revenue in many developing countries.

9. Quotas are government-imposed limits on the quantity or value of an imported good. Quotas protect domestic firms by restricting the entry of foreign products to a level less than the quantity demanded.

10. Subsidies are payments by the government to domestic producers. Subsidies lower the price of domestic goods.

11. Governments are often required by law to buy only domestic products.

12. Health and safety standards can also be used to protect domestic firms.

## 3. EXCHANGE RATE SYSTEMS AND PRACTICES

**5. What kinds of exchange rate arrangements exist today?**

The world today consists of some countries with fixed exchange rates, whose governments keep the exchange rates between two or more currencies constant over time; other countries with floating exchange rates, which shift on a daily basis according to the forces of supply and demand; and still others whose exchange rate systems lie somewhere in between. Table 3, which lists the exchange rate

Table 3

**Exchange Rate Arrangements
(as of 2003)**

| Crawling Pegs (5) | Exchange Rates Within Crawling Bands (5) | Managed Floating with No Preannounced Path for Exchange Rate (48) | Independently Floating (37) |
|---|---|---|---|
| Bolivia | Belarus | Afghanistan | Albania |
| Costa Rica | Honduras | Algeria | Armenia |
| Nicaragua | Israel | Angola | Australia |
| Solomon Islands | Romania | Argentina | Brazil |
| Tunisia | Slovenia | Azerbaijan | Canada |
| | | Burundi | Chile |
| | | Cambodia | Colombia |
| | | Croatia | Congo, Dem. Rep. of |
| | | Czech Rep. | Georgia |
| | | Dominican Rep. | Guinea |
| | | Egypt | Iceland |
| | | Ethiopia | Japan |
| | | Gambia, The | Korea |
| | | Ghana | Liberia |
| | | Guatemala | Madagascar |
| | | Guyana | Malawi |
| | | Haiti | Mexico |
| | | India | Mozambique |
| | | Indonesia | New Zealand |
| | | Iran | Norway |
| | | Iraq | Papua New Guinea |
| | | Jamaica | Peru |
| | | Kazakhstan | Philippines |
| | | Kenya | Poland |
| | | Kyrgyz Rep. | Sierra Leone |
| | | Lao P.D.R. | Somalia |
| | | Mauritania | South Africa |
| | | Mauritius | Sri Lanka |
| | | Moldova | Sweden |
| | | Mongolia | Switzerland |
| | | Myanmar | Tanzania |
| | | Nigeria | Turkey |
| | | Pakistan | Uganda |
| | | Paraguay | United Kingdom |
| | | Russian Federation | United States |
| | | Rwanda | Uruguay |
| | | Serbia and Montenegro | Yemen |
| | | Singapore | |
| | | Slovak Rep. | |
| | | São Tomé and Principe | |
| | | Sudan | |
| | | Tajikistan | |
| | | Thailand | |
| | | Trinidad and Tobago | |
| | | Ukraine | |
| | | Uzbekistan | |
| | | Vietnam | |
| | | Zambia | |

## Key Term Match

**Match each key term with its correct definition by placing the appropriate letter next to the corresponding number.**

A. absolute advantage
B. intraindustry trade
C. commercial policy
D. strategic trade policy
E. increasing-returns-to-scale industry
F. tariff
G. quantity quota
H. value quota
I. subsidies

_____ 1. simultaneous import and export of goods in the same industry by a particular country

_____ 2. the use of trade restrictions or subsidies to allow domestic firms with decreasing costs to gain a greater share of the world market

_____ 3. an advantage derived from one country's having a lower absolute input cost of producing a particular good than another country

_____ 4. a tax on imports and selected exports

_____ 5. an industry in which the costs of producing a unit of output fall as more output is produced

_____ 6. government policy that influences international trade flows

_____ 7. a limit on the monetary value of a good that may be imported

_____ 8. a limit on the amount of a good that may be produced

_____ 9. a grant of money given to help produce or purchase a specific good or service

## Quick-Check Quiz

**1** A nation has an absolute advantage in producing a good when

a. it can produce a good for a lower input cost than other nations can.
b. the opportunity cost of producing a good, in terms of the forgone output of other goods, is lower than that of other nations.
c. it can produce a good for a higher input cost than other nations can.
d. the opportunity cost of producing a good, in terms of the forgone output of other goods, is higher than that of other nations.
e. the nation's export supply curve is below its import demand curve.

**2** A nation has a comparative advantage in producing a good when

a. it can produce a good for a lower input cost than other nations can.
b. the opportunity cost of producing a good, in terms of the forgone output of other goods, is lower than that of other nations.
c. it can produce a good for a higher input cost than other nations can.
d. the opportunity cost of producing a good, in terms of the forgone output of other goods, is higher than that of other nations.
e. the nation's export supply curve is below its import demand curve.

**3** The productivity-differences explanation of comparative advantage stresses

a. differences in labor productivity among countries.
b. the advantage that comes to a country that is the first to develop and produce a product.
c. the relative amounts of skilled and unskilled labor in a country.
d. differences in the amounts of resources countries have.
e. differences in tastes within a country.

**4** The factor-abundance explanation of comparative advantage stresses

a. differences in labor productivity among countries.
b. the advantage that comes to a country that is the first to develop and produce a product.
c. the relative amounts of skilled and unskilled labor in a country.
d. differences in the amounts of resources countries have.
e. differences in tastes within a country.

**5** The human-skills explanation of comparative advantage stresses

a. differences in labor productivity among countries.
b. the advantage that comes to a country that is the first to develop and produce a product.
c. the relative amounts of skilled and unskilled labor in a country.
d. differences in the amounts of resources countries have.
e. differences in tastes within a country.

**6** The product-life-cycle explanation of comparative advantages stresses

a. differences in labor productivity among countries.

b. the advantage that comes to a country that is the first to develop and produce a product.

c. the relative amounts of skilled and unskilled labor in a country.

d. differences in the amounts of resources countries have.

e. differences in tastes within a country.

7 The consumer-preferences explanation of comparative advantage stresses

a. differences in labor productivity among countries.

b. the advantage that comes to a country that is the first to develop and produce a product.

c. the relative amounts of skilled and unskilled labor in a country.

d. differences in the amounts of resources countries have.

e. differences in tastes within a country.

8 The basic objective of commercial policy is to

a. promote free and unrestricted international trade.

b. protect domestic consumers from dangerous, low-quality imports.

c. protect domestic producers from foreign competition.

d. protect foreign producers from domestic consumers.

e. promote the efficient use of scarce resources.

9 Using trade restrictions to save domestic jobs

a. usually forces consumers to pay higher prices.

b. usually redistributes jobs from other industries to the protected industry.

c. may provoke other countries to restrict U.S. exports.

d. does all of the above.

e. does only b and c.

10 Some arguments for trade restrictions have economic validity. Which of the following arguments has *no* economic validity?

a. the infant industry argument

b. the national defense argument

c. the government revenue creation from tariffs argument

d. the creation of domestic jobs argument

e. All of the above have some economic validity.

11 In the world today, exchange rates are determined by

a. the United Nations.

b. the government of the United States.

c. the same method in all countries.

d. one of two methods.

e. several diverse methods.

12 The two main methods of determining exchange rates are

a. set and non-set exchange rates.

b. fixed and floating exchange rates.

c. monetary and fiscal exchange rates.

d. dollar and non-dollar exchange rates.

e. European and Asian exchange rates.

13 The exchange rate system whereby central banks try to influence exchange rates by intervening in floating foreign exchange markets is called

a. a managed floating exchange rate.

b. a manipulated fixed exchange rate.

c. the multiplied-float arrangement.

d. the EMS.

e. a clean float.

14 The exchange rate system in which the exchange rate is fixed against a major currency or some basket of currencies is called

a. crawling pegs.

b. managed floating.

c. a fixed peg.

d. horizontal bands.

e. a currency board.

## Practice Questions and Problems

1 The following table shows the output per worker per day in either mangoes or papayas in Samoa and in Fiji.

|  | Samoa | Fiji |
|---|---|---|
| Mangoes (in tons) | 6 | 2 |
| Papayas (in tons) | 12 | 6 |

a. The country that has an absolute advantage in producing mangoes is _____.

b. The country that has an absolute advantage in producing papayas is _____.

c. The opportunity cost of 1 ton of papayas in Samoa is _____.

d. The opportunity cost of 1 ton of papayas in Fiji is _____.

e. The country that has a comparative advantage in papayas is _____.

f. The opportunity cost of 1 ton of mangoes in Samoa is _____.

g. The opportunity cost of 1 ton of mangoes in Fiji is _____.

h. The country that has a comparative advantage in mangoes is _____.

i. The limits on the terms of trade are 1 ton of mangoes for between _____ and _____ tons of papayas.

2. Name the comparative-advantage theory that matches each of the following explanations of comparative advantage.

a. Differences in labor productivity among countries: _____

b. The advantage that comes to a country that is the first to develop and produce a product: _____

c. The relative amounts of skilled and unskilled labor in a country: _____

d. Differences in the amounts of resources countries have: _____

e. Differences in tastes within a country: _____

3. Governments can generate revenues by restricting trade through _____; this is a common tactic in _____ (industrial, developing) countries.

4. The argument that new industries should receive temporary protection is known as the _____ argument.

5. Trade restrictions usually _____ (create more, redistribute) domestic jobs within the economy.

6. Tariffs are _____ on imports or exports. In the United States, tariffs on _____ (imports, exports) are illegal under the Constitution.

7. A country is said to _____ its currency when the value of its currency is tied to another country's currency.

8. What type of exchange rate system does the United States use? _____

## Exercises and Applications

I. **Saving Jobs by Restricting Imports: Is it Worth the Cost?** One area of the U.S. economy that has been protected from international competition is the food and beverage industry. According to a study by the Institute for International Economics in Washington, D.C., the cost to U.S. consumers of this protection is about $2,947,000,000 per year that U.S. consumers have paid in higher prices for food and beverages. That's about $10 per person in the U.S. per year. That might look like a reasonable price to pay to protect jobs, but let's look more closely.

1. The trade restrictions on food and beverages save about 6,039 jobs per year. How much does it cost U.S. consumers every year for each job saved?

_____

2. Some people who work in the food and beverage industry may make a lot of money, but they don't average almost $500,000 per year! How much money would U.S. consumers save if the United States got rid of the trade restrictions and paid the 6,039 people in the food and beverage industry protected by trade restrictions each $100,000 per year to sit at home and watch TV?

_____

3. If U.S. consumers took the money they would save if the United States removed trade restrictions on food and beverages and instead spent it buying other things, do you think that this spending would create other jobs? _____

4. Instead of paying the 6,039 workers each $100,000 per year to stay home and watch TV, is there something else that the United States could do to help these people that would cost only a small fraction of the almost $3 billion a year currently spent on trade protection in the food and beverage industry? (Hint: It's what you are doing in your economics class now.) _____

II. **Tax Effects of Import Restrictions** According to *Newsweek:*

Lower-income families are hit hardest by trade restrictions, because they spend a far greater share of their earnings at the store. In a recent year, for example, households earning more than $50,000 laid out 3.3 percent of their disposable incomes on clothing, but households in the $20,000-to-$30,000 bracket spent 4.6 percent—and families earning $10,000 to $15,000 spent 5.4 percent. The quotas and tariffs that force import prices up to protect U.S. apparel jobs don't matter much in Beverly Hills, but they put a big dent in pocketbooks in Watts.[*]

Let's look more closely at the effects of tariffs and quotas on apparel purchased by different income groups. Assuming that 20 percent of the price of clothing is due to tariffs and quotas, calculate the dollar cost of tariffs and quotas on families making the following incomes. Then calculate the percentage of its income that each family pays because of tariffs and quotas.

[*]*Source: Newsweek, July 12, 1993, p. 45.*

1. Family income = $50,000; cost: _____;

   percentage of income: _____

2. Family income = $25,000; cost: _____;

   percentage of income: _____

3. Family income = $10,000; cost: _____;

   percentage of income: _____

4. Do tariffs and quotas hit lower-income families the

   hardest, as *Newsweek* maintains? _____

 **ACE self-test**

Now that you've completed the Study Guide for this chapter, you should have a good sense of the concepts you need to review. If you'd like to test your understanding of the material again, go to the Practice Tests on the Boyes/Melvin *Fundamentals of Economics,* 3e website, **economics.college.hmco.com/students.**

## Chapter 18

# Globalization

## Fundamental Questions

1. What is globalization?
2. What are the arguments against globalization?
3. What are the arguments in support of globalization?
4. How has globalization affected economic growth and poverty?
5. Can recent financial crises be linked to globalization?

1. What is globalization?

*Preview*

I n every chapter we have discussed the international aspects of the topics covered. However, we have not yet considered the implications of closer links among economies internationally. The so-called *globalization* of the world's economies has become an issue that is rich in controversy. Thousands have gathered to protest globalization in Washington, D.C., and Seattle in the United States; in Johannesburg, South Africa; in Davos, Switzerland; and in many other places. This chapter will provide an introduction to the potential costs and benefits of globalization and offer an analysis of the historical record regarding the effects of globalization.

It is important to recognize that the debate over globalization continues and involves political and social as well as economic dimensions. Intelligent people disagree about the impact of globalization on rich as well as poor countries. The reader should keep in mind that the issue is unsettled and much can change in the coming years. ■

## 1. THE MEANING OF GLOBALIZATION

Globalization is characterized by an increased cross-border flow of trade in goods, services, and financial assets, along with an increased international mobility of technology, information, and individuals. As globalization progresses, countries become less isolated, so we can think more in terms of a global economy and its implications for individuals and nations.

### 1.a. Globalization Is neither New nor Widespread

Globalization is not new. The forces that drive globalization have existed as long as humans have been around. Everyone has a natural desire to improve his or her well-being, so interest in trade has always existed. As we learned in earlier chapters, trade based on comparative advantage raises living standards. Even primitive societies engaged in trade so that their living standards would be higher than would otherwise have been possible. As circumstances permitted a greater range of travel, trade with more remote regions became possible. International trade is not a new phenomenon. World trade as a fraction of world GDP was about the same at the end of the nineteenth century as it is today. However, between World

financial crisis may come as a surprise to all but the insiders in a troubled firm. Similarly, if the government does not disclose its international reserve position in a timely and informative manner, investors may be taken by surprise when a devaluation occurs. The lack of good information on government and business activities serves as a warning sign of potential future problems.

This short list of warning signs provides an indication of the sorts of variables an international investor must consider when evaluating the risks of investing in a foreign country. This list is also useful to international organizations like the International Monetary Fund when monitoring countries and advising them on recommended changes in policy.

So far we have not explicitly considered how globalization may contribute to crises. The analysis of Figure 3 provides a hint. If there is free trading in a country's currency, and the country has globalized financial markets so that foreign investors trade domestic financial assets, there is a greater likelihood of a crisis than in a country that is not globalized. The money that comes into the developing country from foreign investors can also flow back out. This points out an additional factor to be considered:

- *Short-term international investment.* The greater the amount of short-term money invested in a country, the greater the potential for a crisis if investors lose confidence in the country. So if foreigners buy large amounts of domestic stocks, bonds, or other financial assets, they can turn around and sell these assets quickly. These asset sales will depress the value of the country's financial markets, and as foreigners sell local currency for foreign currency, like U.S. dollars, the local currency will also fall in value. Too much short-term foreign investment may serve as another warning sign for a financial crisis.

Of course, a country can always avoid financial crises by not globalizing—keeping its domestic markets closed to foreigners. However, such a policy costs more than it is worth. As discussed earlier in this chapter, globalization has paid off with faster economic growth and reductions in poverty. To avoid globalization in order to avoid financial crises is to remain in poverty as the rest of the world grows richer. We should think of globalization and financial crises in these terms: A closed economy can follow very bad economic policies for a long time, and the rest of the world will have no influence in bringing about change for the better. A country with a globalized economy will be punished for bad economic policy as foreign investors move money out of the country, contributing to financial market crises in that country. It is not globalization that brings about the crisis. Instead, globalization allows the rest of the world to respond to bad economic policies in a way that highlights the bad policy and imposes costs on the country for following such policies. In this sense, globalization acts to discipline countries. A country with sound economic policy and good investment opportunities is rewarded with large flows of savings from the rest of the world to lower the cost of developing the local economy.

**RECAP**

1. The 1990s saw financial crises in Mexico, Indonesia, South Korea, Malaysia, the Philippines, and Thailand.

2. Fixed exchange rates encouraged speculative attacks and ultimate devaluations of the currencies of the countries involved in these crises.

3. Exchange rate devaluations raised the cost of debts that were denominated in foreign currency and imposed large losses on debtor firms.

4. Factors contributing to the financial crises included fixed exchange rates, falling international reserves, a lack of transparency to investors, and a high level of short-term international investment.

# SUMMARY

## ❓ What is globalization?

1. Globalization involves an increased cross-border flow of trade in goods, services, and financial assets, along with increased international mobility of technology, information, and individuals.

2. The process of globalization has always existed because of its potential to raise living standards.

3. The rapid pace of globalization in recent decades has been made possible by technological advances.

## ❓ What are the arguments against globalization?

4. Free trade increases corporate profits but harms people.

5. International organizations and the agreements they are associated with serve corporate interests and harm people.

6. Globalization occurs at the cost of environmental quality.

7. Globalization encourages harmful labor practices.

## ❓ What are the arguments in support of globalization?

8. Those who lose their jobs to more efficient producers in other countries will be harmed, but the benefits to all consumers far outweigh the losses of those workers and firms that are harmed by globalization.

9. International organizations are funded by governments, not firms, and such organizations serve the interests of all nations in that they provide a setting where grievances must be heard and policy changes can be implemented.

10. Globalization has not resulted in a "race to the bottom," in which labor practices suffer and environmental decay results.

## ❓ How has globalization affected economic growth and poverty?

11. Globalizers have faster economic growth and less poverty than nonglobalizers.

## ❓ Can recent financial crises be linked to globalization?

12. Globalization allows for international financial flows that punish countries that follow bad economic policy.

# KEY TERMS

"race to the bottom"
Asian tigers

NICs
speculative attack

# EXERCISES

1. What is globalization?

2. Comment on the following statement: "Globalization is an event of the 1980s and 1990s. Prior to this time, we never had to worry about globalization and its effects."

3. Write a script for two speakers arguing about globalization and its effects. Give each speaker a name and then write a script for a debate between the two. The debate should be no longer than two pages, double-spaced. Each speaker should make a few key points, and the other speaker should offer a reply to each point the first speaker makes.

4. Why has the pace of globalization quickened since the 1950s?

5. If you wanted to compare countries on the basis of how globalized they are, how could you construct some numerical measures that would allow a cross-country comparison?

6. What are the major arguments against globalization?

7. What are the major arguments in favor of globalization?

8. What is the difference between "fair" and "free" trade?

9. What is the WTO? Where is it located, and what does it do?

10. Suppose we find that multinational firms are paying much lower wages in some poor countries than they would have to pay in the United States. Would this be

sufficient evidence that these firms are exploiting the workers in the poor countries? Why or why not?

11. How can globalization reduce poverty? What does the evidence suggest about globalization and poverty?

12. There were several major international financial crises in the 1990s. What role did globalization play in these crises?

13. Using a supply and demand diagram, explain how central banks maintain a fixed exchange rate. What can cause an end to the fixed exchange rate regime?

14. Using a supply and demand diagram, explain how speculative attacks occur in the foreign exchange market.

15. If you were forecasting the likelihood of a financial crisis for a major international bank, what key variables would you want to monitor for the countries you are studying? Why would you want to monitor these variables?

## Internet Exercise

**Use the Internet to learn more about globalization and the World Trade Organization.**

Go to the Boyes/Melvin, *Fundamentals of Economics* website accessible through **http://college.hmco.com** and click on the Internet Exercise link for Chapter 18. Now answer the questions that appear on the Boyes/Melvin website.

## Key Term Match

**Match each term with the correct definition by placing the appropriate letter next to the corresponding number.**

A. "race to the bottom"    C. NICs
B. Asian tigers    D. speculative attack

_____ 1. a situation in which private investors sell domestic currency and buy foreign currency, betting that the domestic currency will be devalued

_____ 2. Hong Kong, South Korea, Singapore, and Taiwan—countries that globalized during the 1960s and 1970s and experienced fast economic growth

_____ 3. with globalization, countries compete for international investment by offering low or no environmental regulations or labor standards

_____ 4. newly industrialized countries

## Quick-Check Quiz

**1** Which of the following has *not* been a factor in the increased pace of globalization since the 1950s?

   a. increased governmental barriers to immigration
   b. reduced costs of international communications
   c. formation of the European Union
   d. reduced costs for information processing
   e. the desire to improve living standards

**2** Which of the following would be a sign of increased globalization?

   a. Norway, Denmark, and the United Kingdom decide to adopt the euro as their common currency.
   b. Out of concern for safety, businesses conduct teleconferences in place of face-to-face meetings.
   c. Global foreign direct investment decreases.
   d. Poor countries, enraged by U.S. farm subsidies, stall trade negotiations at the World Trade Organization meetings.
   e. The number of countries participating in U.N. peacekeeping missions declines.

**3** Which of the following is an argument against globalization?

   a. Poor countries compete for multinational firms by allowing lax environmental standards.
   b. Multinational firms tend to pay higher wages than local firms.

   c. The benefits of globalization to all consumers greatly outweigh the loss of jobs to international competition.
   d. Removal of restrictions against agricultural products would increase incomes in poor countries.
   e. The increased integration of the world's economies has been associated with economic growth in most countries.

**4** Which of the following is an argument in favor of globalization?

   a. There is evidence of a "race to the bottom" in labor standards as multinational firms search the world for the lowest labor costs.
   b. Multinational firms produce goods for international markets at the expense of local markets.
   c. Multinational firms are attracted by the prospects of consumer markets in developing countries.
   d. World organizations provide a forum for corporate elites to secure legislation that will benefit them.
   e. Poor countries compete for multinational corporations by permitting lax labor standards.

**5** Which of the following is *not* an argument against globalization?

   a. Free trade benefits corporate profits but hurts people.
   b. Globalization encourages hurtful environmental practices because governments block costly environmental regulations to provide a cheaper location for large global firms.
   c. Specialization according to comparative advantage raises the living standards of the trading partners.
   d. People in developed countries lose their jobs to people in poor countries who are willing to work for substandard wages.
   e. International organizations like the World Trade Organization usurp the economic decision-making powers of local authorities.

**6** Which of the following is true?

   a. Some individuals and firms are harmed by free trade agreements.
   b. There is widespread evidence of a "race to the bottom" by which multinational firms move production to countries with lax environmental standards.

c. Multinational companies usually locate production units in developing countries, exploit the local labor supply, and then sell the products in rich countries.

d. The fact that wages are lower in developing countries than they are for the same work in Western countries is evidence of worker exploitation.

e. International organizations are funded by corporations and are tools of those corporations.

7 The World Bank tracked the performance of countries that had undergone varying degrees of globalization since the 1960s. Which of the following was *not* a conclusion of the study?

a. The process of globalization widened the gap between rich countries and poor countries.

b. The growth rates of globalizing countries were higher than the growth rates of nonglobalizers.

c. The fraction of the very poor declined in newly globalized economies.

d. Except for China, globalization did not increase income inequality.

e. Poverty has been reduced in newly globalized countries.

8 Which of the following was characteristic of the Asian tigers after they globalized in the 1960s and 1970s?

a. They experienced annual growth rates of 1.4 percent.

b. Environmental standards declined.

c. Unemployment rose as workers lost their jobs because lower-cost imports displaced domestic products.

d. Worker safety regulations were relaxed.

e. Living standards increased dramatically.

9 A speculative attack

a. cannot occur if central banks maintain a fixed exchange rate.

b. cannot occur if exchange rates are allowed to float.

c. is more likely to occur if the domestic currency is appreciating in value.

d. can force a central bank to revalue its currency.

e. can be precipitated by an unprecedented increase in the demand for domestic goods and services.

10 Which of the following is an indicator of a potential financial crisis?

a. floating exchange rates

b. falling international reserves

c. transparency in government activities

d. a high level of long-term international investment

e. bank loans as a small percentage of GDP

11 Which of the following statements is an accurate characterization of the relationship between financial crises and globalization?

a. A country with a globalized economy is more vulnerable to financial crises than a country with a closed economy.

b. The greater the amount of short-term money invested in a country, the greater the potential for a crisis if investors lose confidence in the country.

c. An open economy will be punished for bad economic policy as foreign investors move money out of the country.

d. A globalized country with sound economic policies will be rewarded with large flows of savings from the rest of the world.

e. All these statements are accurate characterizations of the relationship between financial crises and globalization.

## Practice Questions and Problems

1 True or false? The growth of international trade is a new phenomenon. _____

2 World trade as a fraction of world GDP is _____ (larger than, smaller than, about the same as) it was at the end of the nineteenth century.

3 Barriers to immigration _____ (increase, decrease) globalization.

4 List the four broad categories used by *Foreign Policy* magazine to measure the degree of globalization in individual nations.

_____

_____

5 _____ plays an important role in determining the pace of globalization.

**6** _____ (Rising, Constant, Falling) transportation costs increase the pace of globalization.

**7** Critics view international organizations such as _____, _____, and _____ as undemocratic organizations that have usurped the economic decision-making powers that rightly belong to local authorities.

**8** The _____ comes under criticism for funding resource extraction projects and dams, which critics say benefit the corporations that do the work while also destroying the environment.

**9** The role of the _____ is to provide a venue for negotiating international trade agreements and to enforce international trade rules.

**10** List three arguments against globalization.

_____

_____

_____

**11** List three arguments in favor of globalization.

_____

_____

_____

**12** International organizations such as the WTO are funded by _____, not corporations.

**13** List the four Asian tigers that opened their economies in the 1960s and 1970s and experienced rapid growth and dramatic increases in their living standards.

_____ _____ _____ _____

**14** The increased globalization of the world's economies has been associated with economic _____ (growth, stagnation) and _____ (growth, reduction) of poverty in most countries.

**15** Globalizing countries find that income inequality _____ (does, does not) increase as the pace of globalization increases.

**16** The gap between rich countries and globalized developing countries has _____ (shrunk, widened).

**17** Each of the recent international financial crises has involved _____ exchange rates.

**18** A speculative attack cannot occur in countries with _____ exchange rates.

**19** List four factors that may serve as indicators of potential financial crises.

_____

_____

_____

_____

**20** The greater the amount of short-term money invested in a country, the _____ (greater, less) potential for a crisis if investors lose confidence in the country.

## Exercises and Applications

**1** **Flexible versus Fixed Exchange Rates** In September 2003, the *Wall Street Journal* reported that the Group of Seven's finance ministers and central bank governors released the following statement: "We emphasize that more flexibility in exchange rates is desirable for major countries or economic areas to promote smooth and widespread adjustments in the international financial system, based on market mechanisms." At the time, Japan and China were frequently intervening in the currency market to keep their currencies from gaining too much *strength* against the dollar. These Asian countries preferred to keep their currency weak to promote their export industries.

1. At the time the statement was released, Japan and China were tying their currencies to the dollar at a rate designed to help their export industries. Since this amounts to a fixed-exchange-rate system, were China and Japan in danger from speculative attacks?

_____

_____

_____

# CHAPTER 12

*Key Term Match*
  **1.** d  **2.** f  **3.** a  **4.** e  **5.** b  **6.** c

*Quick-Check Quiz*
  **1.** a  **2.** b  **3.** d  **4.** b  **5.** b  **6.** e  **7.** c  **8.** b  **9.** d
  **10.** e

*Practice Questions and Problems*
  **1.** Demand-pull  **2.** falls; rises; falls  **3.** increase; decrease;
decrease  **4.** Cost-push  **5.** decreases  **6.** increase
**7.** increase  **8.** Net exports  **9.** rise  **10.** falls
**11.** Investment  **12.** increases  **13.** income; wealth;
expectations; demographics; taxes  **14.** falls  **15.** rise
**16.** interest rate; technology; cost of capital goods; capacity
utilization  **17.** fall  **18.** lower  **19.** foreign and domestic
income; foreign and domestic prices; exchange rates;
government policy  **20.** decreases; decreases; wealth; fall
**21.** more expensive; fall; fall  **22.** less expensive; a shift to
the left of the aggregate demand curve  **23.** a movement
along the aggregate demand curve  **24.** consumption;
investment; increases  **25.** exports; a shift in aggregate
demand to the right  **26.** increase; more  **27.** resource
prices; technology; expectations  **28.** right  **29.** is not

*Exercises and Applications*
### I. Aggregate Demand and Its Determinants

|    | Component | Effect on Component | Effect on Aggregate Demand |
|----|-----------|---------------------|----------------------------|
| 1. | Investment | Decrease | Decrease |
| 2. | Net exports | Increase | Increase |
| 3. | Government spending | Decrease | Decrease |
| 4. | Net exports | Increase | Increase |
| 5. | Consumption | Increase | Increase |
| 6. | Investment | Decrease | Decrease |
| 7. | Consumption | Decrease | Decrease |
| 8. | Investment | Increase | Increase |

### II. A Long-Run Analysis of the Effects of a Slump in Productivity
A decrease in productivity causes the
long-run aggregate supply curve to shift to the left. If
aggregate demand does not change, equilibrium real
GDP will be lower and the price level will be higher—a
very sorry prospect indeed.

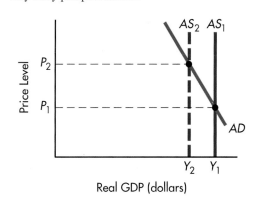

# CHAPTER 13

*Key Term Match*
  **1.** d  **2.** a  **3.** e  **4.** c  **5.** b  **6.** g  **7.** f

*Quick-Check Quiz*
  **1.** a  **2.** b  **3.** a  **4.** d  **5.** d  **6.** e  **7.** c  **8.** b  **9.** b
  **10.** d

*Practice Questions and Problems*
  **1.** taxation; government spending  **2.** disposable income;
consumption  **3.** up; decreasing  **4.** expansionary  **5.** right
**6.** taxes; changes in government debt (borrowing); changes
in the stock of government-issued money  **7.** left
**8.** selling bonds to  **9.** legislative; executive  **10.** Office of
Management and Budget  **11.** Congressional Budget Office
**12.** discretionary fiscal policy; automatic stabilizers
**13.** increase  **14.** Lump-sum taxes  **15.** C; B; A
(To determine what kind of tax it is, we must first calculate
the tax *rate* at each level of income. Since A's tax *rate* is
constant at .10, A is a proportional tax schedule. B's tax
*rate* decreases with income, so B is a regressive tax. C's tax
*rate* increases with income, so C is a progressive tax
schedule.

| | A | | B | | C | |
|--------|-------------|----------|-------------|----------|-------------|----------|
| Income | Tax Payment | Tax Rate | Tax Payment | Tax Rate | Tax Payment | Tax Rate |
| $100 | $10 | .10 | $ 50 | .50 | $ 10 | .10 |
| 200 | 20 | .10 | 80 | .40 | 30 | .15 |
| 300 | 30 | .10 | 90 | .30 | 60 | .20 |
| 400 | 40 | .10 | 100 | .25 | 100 | .25 |

*Note:* If you look at just the *dollar* amount of taxes paid, all
three schedules look "progressive" because the dollar
amount of tax payments increases as income increases. But
we classify these taxes according to how the tax *rate*
changes as income increases.)

**16.** Progressive  **17.** developing; State-owned enterprises
account for a larger percentage of economic activity in
developing countries as compared with industrial countries.
Also, developing countries rely on their governments, as
opposed to private investment, to build their infrastructure.
**18.** do not  **19.** indirect

*Exercises and Applications*
### I. Reducing the Deficit
  **1.** Government spending cuts and tax increases both
     decrease aggregate demand. If the economy is
     operating in the Keynesian or intermediate regions,
     decreasing aggregate demand will decrease real GDP.
     If the economy is in the intermediate range, the price
     level will decline. If it is in the Keynesian region,
     there will be no change in the price level. These are
     the dire results that economic analysts fear.

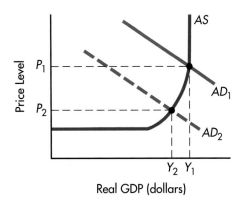

Real GDP (dollars)

2. If the economy is operating in the vertical region of short-run aggregate supply (above), a decrease in aggregate demand may bring only a decrease in the price level with no decrease in real GDP.

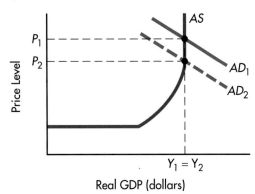

Real GDP (dollars)

## II. Bush's Economic Stimulus Package

1. government spending; taxes
2. increase; These tax breaks are intended to increase investment, thereby increasing aggregate demand and equilibrium real GDP.

## CHAPTER 14

*Key Term Match*

**1.** d  **2.** g  **3.** e  **4.** q  **5.** n  **6.** c  **7.** r  **8.** f  **9.** m
**10.** h  **11.** b  **12.** o  **13.** l  **14.** j  **15.** a  **16.** p  **17.** k
**18.** i

*Quick-Check Quiz*

**1.** c  **2.** d  **3.** c  **4.** e  **5.** c  **6.** a  **7.** a  **8.** b  **9.** e

*Practice Questions and Problems*

**1.** medium of exchange; unit of account; store of value; standard of deferred payment  **2.** currency; travelers' checks; demand deposits; other checkable deposits (OCDs)  **3.** share drafts  **4.** Mutual savings banks  **5.** M1; savings deposits; small denomination time deposits (certificates of deposit, or CDs); retail money market mutual fund balances  **6.** repurchase agreement  **7.** Eurodollar  **8.** Savings  **9.** certificates of deposit  **10.** Retail money market mutual fund balances  **11.** savings and loans; mutual savings banks; credit unions  **12.** Offshore  **13.** more risky  **14.** panic  **15.** 1/reserve requirement  **16.** maximum  **17.** currency drain  **18.** excess reserves  **19.** making loans

## I. How Banks Create Money

**a.** Required reserves = .01 ($500,000) = $5,000. Excess reserves = $5,000 − $5,000 = 0.

**b.** $99,000 (Cash = $105,000. Deposits = $600,000. Required reserves = .01($600,000) = $6,000. Excess reserves = $105,000 − $6,000 = $99,000.)

**c.** $9,900,000 (Deposit expansion multiplier = 1/.01 = 100. Maximum amount of money that can be created = deposit expansion multiplier × excess reserves = 100($99,000) = $9,900,000.)

## II. The Components of the Monetary Aggregates

| | |
|---|---|
| **M1** | = Currency + travelers' checks + demand deposits + other checkable deposits |
| | = 357.3 + 8.1 + 406.5 + 420.0 |
| | = 1,191.9 |
| **M2** | = M1 + savings deposits + small-denomination time deposits + retail money market mutual funds |
| | = 1,191.9 + 1,135.0 + 826.9 + 372.1 |
| | = 3,525.9 |
| **M3** | = M2 + large time deposits + RPs + Eurodollars + institution-only money market mutual funds |
| | = 3,525.9 + 356.7 + 100.8 + 52.2 + 178.0 |
| | = 4,213.6 |

## CHAPTER 15

*Key Term Match*

**1.** j  **2.** m  **3.** a  **4.** h  **5.** k  **6.** b  **7.** g  **8.** c  **9.** i
**10.** f  **11.** l  **12.** n  **13.** o  **14.** d  **15.** e

*Quick-Check Quiz*

**1.** b  **2.** e  **3.** a  **4.** b (Answer a is false, and the others are true only if certain assumptions are made. For c to be true, velocity must be constant and the economy must be at full employment, so that $Q$ cannot rise. For d to be true, velocity must be constant and there must be some unemployment in the economy. Answer e may be true if velocity is constant.)
**5.** d  **6.** c  **7.** d  **8.** d  **9.** a  **10.** d  **11.** e  **12.** b
**13.** d  **14.** c

*Practice Questions and Problems*

**1.** decentralized  **2.** Board of Governors  **3.** president; 4; 14  **4.** controlling the money supply  **5.** Fed chairperson  **6.** $MV = PQ$  **7.** velocity  **8.** quantity theory of money  **9.** reserve requirement; discount rate; open market operations  **10.** raising  **11.** discount; bank  **12.** lowers  **13.** buys  **14.** dollars  **15.** increases  **16.** nominal income; interest rates  **17.** inverse  **18.** greater  **19.** does not  **20.** precautionary  **21.** transactions  **22.** shifts to the right  **23.** decreased  **24.** rise; fall; decrease; fall

**(a)**

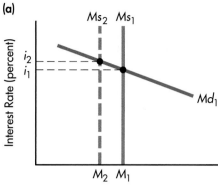

**(b)**

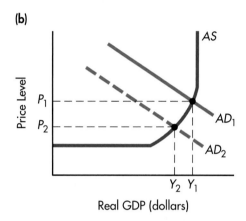

## Exercises and Applications

**I. More on Foreign Exchange Market Intervention**
buy; increase; decrease; decrease; depreciate; reinforced

**II. Bond Prices and Interest Rates** **a.** opposite; fell
**b.** Bond prices drop as interest rates rise. If owners of bonds expect higher interest rates, they will want to sell their bonds before the prices of the bonds decrease.

## CHAPTER 16

*Key Term Match*
**1.** f  **2.** d  **3.** g  **4.** c  **5.** e  **6.** b  **7.** a

*Quick-Check Quiz*
**1.** d (Only unanticipated inflation makes the inflation-unemployment tradeoff possible.)  **2.** e  **3.** c  **4.** a  **5.** a
**6.** a  **7.** d  **8.** d  **9.** e  **10.** b  **11.** e

*Practice Questions and Problems*
**1.** Phillips curve  **2.** does not  **3.** aggregate demand; aggregate supply (Note that aggregate supply does shift in the long run.)  **4.** constant expected rate of inflation; constant reservation wage  **5.** unemployment  **6.** wage expectations; inventory fluctuations; wage contracts
**7.** adaptive  **8.** decreases  **9.** $G = T + B + \Delta M$
**10.** taxing; borrowing; creating money  **11.** supply; right
**12.** labor; capital; natural resources; technology
**13.** working-age population; percentage  **14.** saving
**15.** low levels of education; limited funds for research and development  **16.** output produced; inputs  **17.** Total factor productivity  **18.** 2.6 percent (Growth is growth in TFP plus

growth in each resource $\times$ that resource's share of national income. For this case, growth = 1 (TFP growth) + .7 (1 percent growth in labor $\times$ labor's .7 share of national income) + .9 (3 percent growth in capital $\times$ capital's .3 share of national income.)

*Exercises and Applications*
**I. War on Inflation** $\Delta M = (G - T) - B$. If $G$ is decreased and $T$ is increased, $(G - T)$ will be smaller. If there is no change in government borrowing, the change in the money supply will be negative and inflation will decrease.
**II. Government Policy and Growth** If the price paid for food crops is low enough, farmers will decide to do something else with their resources than grow food crops. They may switch to cash crops sold for export or just take more leisure, growing only enough to feed themselves and their families. Either way, the amount of food produced for sale to city dwellers will drop substantially. The low prices charged to city dwellers will not help them much when there is no food available for sale.

## CHAPTER 17

*Key Term Match*
**1.** b  **2.** d  **3.** a  **4.** f  **5.** e  **6.** c  **7.** h  **8.** g  **9.** i

*Quick-Check Quiz*
**1.** a  **2.** b  **3.** a  **4.** d  **5.** c  **6.** b  **7.** e  **8.** c  **9.** d
**10.** d  **11.** e  **12.** b  **13.** a  **14.** c

*Practice Questions and Problems*
**1. a.** Samoa (One Samoan worker can produce more mangoes than one worker in Fiji.)  **b.** Samoa (One Samoan worker can produce more tons of papaya than one worker in Fiji.)  **c.** 1/2 ton of mangoes (6 mangoes = 12 papayas, so 12/12 papayas = 6/12 mangoes)  **d.** 1/3 ton of mangoes (2 mangoes = 6 papayas, so 6/6 papayas = 2/6 mangoes)
**e.** Fiji (Fiji has the lower opportunity cost; it has to give up only 1/3 ton of mangoes to get a ton of papayas, whereas Samoa has to give up 1/2 ton.)  **f.** 2 tons of papayas (6 mangoes = 12 papayas, so 6/6 mangoes = 12/6 papayas)
**g.** 3 tons of papayas (2 mangoes = 6 papayas, so 2/2 mangoes = 6/2 papayas)  **h.** Samoa (Samoa has the lower opportunity cost; it has to give up only 2 tons of papayas to get a ton of mangoes, whereas Fiji has to give up 3 tons.)
**i.** 2; 3  **2. a.** productivity differences  **b.** product life cycle  **c.** human skills  **d.** factor abundance  **e.** consumer preferences  **3.** tariffs; developing  **4.** infant industry
**5.** redistribute  **6.** taxes; exports  **7.** peg  **8.** Independently Floating

*Exercises and Applications*
**I. Saving Jobs by Restricting Imports: Is It Worth the Cost?**
1. $487,995 (the $2,947,000,000 total cost divided by the 6,039 jobs saved)
2. $2,343,100,000 (the $2,947,000,000 total cost minus (6,039 $\times$ $100,000))
3. yes
4. Get an education. As you learned in Chapter 3, workers with more skills usually get paid better.

## II. Tax Effects of Import Restrictions

1. $330 (3.3 percent of $50,000 = $1,650 spent on clothing; 20 percent of $1,650 = $330); 0.66 percent ($330/$50,000 = .0066 = 0.66 percent)
2. $165 (4.6 percent of $25,000 = $1,150 spent on clothing; 20 percent of $1,150 = $230); 0.92 percent ($230/$25,000 = .0092 = 0.92 percent)
3. $108 (5.4 percent of $10,000 = $540 spent on clothing; 20 percent of $540 = $108); 1.08 percent ($108/$10,000 = .0108 = 1.08 percent)
4. Yes. (The percentage of income paid in the "tax" is highest for low-income families and then decreases for higher-income families.)

## CHAPTER 18

*Key Term Match*

1. d  2. b  3. a  4. c

*Quick-Check Quiz*

1. a  2. a  3. a  4. c  5. c  6. a  7. a  8. e  9. b  10. b
11. e

*Practice Questions and Problems*

1. false  2. about the same as  3. decrease  4. economic integration; technology; personal contact; political engagement  5. Technology  6. Falling  7. The World Trade Organization; the World Bank; the International Monetary Fund  8. World Bank  9. World Trade Organization  10. Free trade is harmful to people who might lose their jobs if lower-cost foreign producers are permitted to compete with domestic producers. Globalization results in countries competing for international investment by offering little or no environmental regulations or labor standards. International organizations are the tools of multinational corporations, who use them to generate profits without regard for the interests of the citizens of the world.  11. Free trade based on comparative advantage raises living standards everywhere. International organizations are funded by governments, not corporations; they are tools of governments in achieving international agreements that benefit their people. Environmental quality and wages tend to improve after globalization.  12. governments
13. Hong Kong; South Korea; Singapore; Taiwan
14. growth; reduction  15. does not  16. shrunk  17. fixed
18. floating  19. fixed exchange rates; falling international reserves; lack of transparency; short-term international investment  20. greater

*Exercises and Applications*

### I. Flexible Versus Fixed Exchange Rates

1. No. To help their export industries, China and Japan were encouraging their currencies to be weak. If they had been trying to prop up their currencies, they would have been vulnerable to a speculative attack.
2. The yen and yuan were artificially weak, which made foreign products expensive. If Japan and China let their currencies float, U.S. exports would be cheaper for the Chinese and Japanese.
3. Japan and China were protecting their export industries. A weak currency makes exports cheap for foreigners.

### II. U.S. Steel Tariffs

Industries that use steel as an input would be hurt by not having access to cheaper steel. As these industries raised their prices to cover increasing costs, they would lose customers. Industries that would have been allowed to trade with the European Union would also be hurt by being denied access as a result of European Union retaliation against the tariffs.

# Glossary

**absolute advantage** an advantage derived from one country having a lower absolute input cost of producing a particular good than another country (17)

**accounting profit** total revenue less total costs except for the opportunity cost of capital; revenue less costs except opportunity costs of owner's capital (5)

**adaptive expectation** an expectation formed on the basis of information collected in the past (16)

**aggregate demand curve** a curve that shows the different equilibrium levels of expenditures at different price levels (12)

**aggregate supply curve** a curve that shows the amount of production at different price levels (12)

**antitrust laws** rules of behavior prescribed by the government (7)

**Asian tigers** Hong Kong, Korea, Singapore, and Taiwan; countries that globalized in the 1960s and 1970s and experienced fast economic growth (18)

**automatic stabilizer** an element of fiscal policy that changes automatically as income changes (13)

**average revenue** per unit revenue, total revenue divided by quantity (4)

**average total costs (ATC)** total cost divided by the total output per unit costs, total costs divided by quantity (5)

**balance of payments** a record of a country's trade in goods, services, and financial assets with the rest of the world (10)

**balance of trade** the balance on the merchandise account in the U.S. balance of payments; the balance on the merchandise account in a nation's balance of payments (10)

**barter** the direct exchange of goods and services without the use of money; trade without the use of money (1)

**base year** the year against which other years are measured (10)

**budget deficit** the shortage that results when government spending is greater than revenue (9)

**budget surplus** the excess that results when government spending is less than revenue (9)

**business cycle** the recurrent pattern of rising real GDP followed by falling real GDP; pattern of rising real GDP followed by falling real GDP (11)

**business firm** a business organization controlled by a single management; an entity in which resources are combined to produce an output (7)

**capital** products such as machinery and equipment that are used in production; the equipment, machines, and buildings used to produce goods and services (1)

**capital consumption allowance** the estimated value of depreciation plus the value of accidental damage to capital stock (10)

**cartel** an organization of independent firms whose purpose is to control and limit production and maintain or increase prices and profits; an organization of independent producers that dictates the quantities produced by each member of the organization (7)

**circular flow diagram** a model showing the flow of output and income from one sector to another (9)

**coincident indicator** a variable that changes at the same time that real output changes (11)

**commercial policy** government policy that influences international trade flows (17)

**comparative advantage** the ability to produce a good or service at a lower opportunity cost than someone else (1)

**compensating wage differential** wage differences that make up for the higher risk or poorer working conditions of one job over another; wage differences due to different risks or job characteristics (3)

**complementary goods** goods that are used together [as the price of one rises, the demand for the other falls]; items that are used together [as the price of one rises, demand for the other falls] (2)

**consumer price index (CPI)** a measure of the average price of goods and services purchased by the typical household (10)

**consumer surplus** the difference between what the consumer is willing to pay for a unit of a good and the price that the consumer actually has to pay; the difference between what consumers would be willing to pay and what they have to pay to purchase some item (6)

**consumption** household spending (9)

**corporation** a legal entity owned by shareholders whose liability for the firm's losses is limited to the value of the stock they own; a business firm owned by many shareholders [owners are not liable for debts of a corporation] (7)

**cost of capital** the opportunity cost of the funds used to purchase capital; the cost of debt plus the cost of equity (5)

**cost of living adjustment (COLA)** an increase in wages that is designed to match increases in prices of items purchased by the typical household (10)

**cost-plus markup pricing** a pricing policy whereby a firm computes its average cost of producing a product and then sets the price at some percentage above this cost; a price set by adding an amount to the per-unit cost of producing and supply a good or service (7)

**cost-push inflation** inflation caused by rising costs of production (11)

**credit** available savings that are lent to borrowers to spend (14)

**crowding out** a drop in consumption or investment spending caused by government spending (13)

**currency substitution** the use of foreign money as a substitute for domestic money when the domestic money has a high rate of inflation; the use of foreign currency as a substitute for domestic money when the domestic economy has a high rate of inflation (14)

**current account** the sum of the merchandise, services, investment income, and unilateral transfers accounts in the balance of payments (10)

**deadweight loss** the reduction of consumer surplus without a corresponding increase in monopoly profit when a perfectly competitive firm is monopolized; the loss of consumer and producer surplus when entry is restricted (6)

**debt** loans; funds owed to lenders by borrowers (5)

**demand** the quantities of a well-defined commodity that consumers are willing and able to buy at each possible price during a given period of time, ceteris paribus the amount of a product that people are willing and able to purchase at every possible price (2)

**demand curve** a graph of a demand schedule that measures price on the vertical axis and quantity demanded on the horizontal axis (3); a graph showing the law of demand (2)

**demand-pull inflation** inflation caused by increasing demand for output (11)

**demand schedule** a list or table of the prices and the corresponding quantities demanded of a particular good or service; a table listing the quantity demanded at each price (2)

**deposit expansion multiplier** the reciprocal of the reserve requirement (14)

**depreciation** a reduction in the value of capital goods over time due to their use in production (10)

**depression** a severe, prolonged economic contraction (11)

**determinants of demand** factors other than the price of the good that influence demand-income, tastes, prices of related goods and services, expectations, and number of buyers; things that influence demand other than the price (2)

**determinants of supply** factors other than the price of the good that influence supply-prices of resources, technology and productivity, expectations of producers, number of producers, and the prices of related goods and services; those factors that affect supply other than price (2)

**discount rate** the interest rate the Fed charges commercial banks when they borrow from it (15)

**discouraged workers** workers who have stopped looking for work because they believe no one will offer them a job (11)

**discretionary fiscal policy** changes in government spending and taxation aimed at achieving a policy goal (13)

**discrimination** prejudice that occurs when factors unrelated to marginal productivity affect the wages or jobs that are obtained; the practice of treating people differently in a market, based on a characteristic having nothing to do with that market (8)

**diseconomies of scale** the increases of unit costs as the quantity of production increases and all resources are variable; per-unit costs rise when all resources are increased (6)

**disposable personal income (DPI)** personal income minus personal taxes (10)

**dominant strategy** a strategy that produces better results no matter what strategy the opposing firm follows; when one alternative is better than other alternatives no matter what rivals do (7)

**economic profit** total revenue less total costs including all opportunity costs; revenue less all costs, including opportunity costs of owner's capital (5)

**economies of scale** the decrease of unit costs as the quantity of production increases and all resources are variable; per-unit costs decline when all resources are increased (6)

**efficiency** the measure of how well an allocation system satisfies people's wants and needs (2)

**elastic** price elasticity greater than 1 (4)

**equation of exchange** an equation that relates the quantity of money to nominal GDP (15)

**equilibrium** the point at which quantity demanded and quantity supplied are equal for a particular price; the price and quantity at which demand equals supply (2)

**equity** shares of stock; value of a firm less debt (5)

**Eurocurrency market (offshore banking)** the market for deposits and loans generally denominated in a currency other than the currency of the country in which the transaction occurs; also called offshore banking (14)

**excess reserves** the cash reserves beyond those required, which can be loaned (14)

**exchange rate** the price of one country's money in terms of another country's money; the price at which one currency is exchanged for another (1)

**exports** products that a country sells to other countries (9)

**facilitating practices** actions by oligopolistic firms that can contribute to cooperation and collusion even though the firms do not formally agree to cooperate; actions that lead to cooperation among rivals (7)

**fallacy of composition** the faulty logic that what's true for the individual or the single business is true for the whole economy (1)

**Federal Deposit Insurance Corporation (FDIC)** a federal agency that insures deposits in commercial banks (14)

**federal funds rate** the interest rate a bank charges when it lends excess reserves to another bank (15)

**Federal Open Market Committee (FOMC)** the official policymaking body of the Federal Reserve System (15)

**Federal Reserve** the central bank of the United States (9)

**financial account** the record in the balance of payments of the flow of financial assets into and out of a country (10)

**financial capital** the money used to purchase capital; stocks and bonds; the stocks and bonds used to purchase capital (1)

**fiscal policy** the policy directed toward government spending and taxation (9)

**fixed costs** costs of fixed resources; costs that do not change as output changes (5)

**FOMC directive** instructions issued by the FOMC to the Federal Reserve Bank of New York to implement monetary policy (15)

**foreign exchange**  foreign currency and bank deposits that are denominated in foreign money (10)

**foreign exchange market**  a global market in which people trade one currency for another (10)

**foreign exchange market intervention**  the buying and selling of currencies by a government or central bank to achieve a specified exchange rate; the buying and selling of foreign exchange by a central bank to move exchange rates up or down to a targeted level (15)

**fractional reserve banking system**  a system in which banks keep less than 100 percent of the deposits available for withdrawal (14)

**free good**  a good for which there is no scarcity (1)

**gains from trade**  the additional amount traders get relative to what they could produce without trade (1)

**GDP price index**  a broad measure of the prices of goods and services included in the gross domestic product (10)

**gross domestic product (GDP)**  the market value of all final goods and services produced in a year within a country (10)

**gross investment**  total investment, including investment expenditures, required to replace capital goods consumed in current production (10)

**gross national product (GNP)**  gross domestic product plus receipts of factor income from the rest of the world minus payments of factor income to the rest of the world (10)

**hawala**  a network for transferring money, popular in Muslim countries (14)

**household**  one or more persons who occupy a unit of housing (9)

**hyperinflation**  an extremely high rate of inflation (11)

**imports**  products that a country buys from other countries (9)

**income distribution**  the ways in which a society's income is divided (8)

**increasing-returns-to-scale industry**  an industry in which the costs of producing a unit of output fall as more output is produced (17)

**indirect business tax**  a tax that is collected by businesses for a government agency (10)

**inelastic**  price elasticity less than 1 (4)

**inferior goods**  goods that people buy less of as their income rises (2)

**inflation**  a sustained rise in the average level of prices (11)

**interdependence**  a situation in which the best strategy for one firm depends on what another firm does (7)

**interest rate effect**  a change in interest rates that causes investment and therefore aggregate expenditures to change as the level of prices changes (12)

**intermediate good**  a good that is used as an input in the production of final goods and services (10)

**intermediate target**  an objective used to achieve some ultimate policy goal (15)

**international banking facility (IBF)**  a division of a U.S. bank that is allowed to receive deposits from and make loans to nonresidents of the United States without the restrictions that apply to domestic U.S. banks (14)

**international reserve asset**  an asset used to settle debts between governments (14)

**international reserve currency**  a currency held by a government to settle international debts (14)

**international trade effect**  the change in aggregate expenditures resulting from a change in the domestic price level that changes the price of domestic goods in relation to foreign goods (12)

**intraindustry trade**  the simultaneous import and export of goods in the same industry by a particular country (17)

**inventory**  the stock of unsold goods held by a firm (10)

**investment**  spending on capital goods to be used in producing goods and services (9)

**labor**  the physical and intellectual services of people, including the training, education, and abilities of the individuals in a society; the general category of resources encompassing all human activity related to the productive process (1)

**lagging indicator**  a variable that changes after real output changes (11)

**land**  all the natural resources, such as minerals, timber, and water, as well as the land itself; the general category of resources encompassing all natural resources, land, and water (1)

**law of demand**  as the price of a good or service rises (falls), the quantity of that good or service that people are willing and able to purchase during a particular period of time falls (rises), ceteris paribus inverse relationship between price and quantity demanded (2)

**law of diminishing marginal returns**  when successive equal amounts of a variable resource are combined with a fixed amount of another resource, marginal increases in output that can be attributed to each additional unit of the variable resource will eventually decline as quantity of variable resources is increased; output initially rises rapidly, the more slowly, and eventually may decline (5)

**law of supply**  as the price of a good or service that producers are willing and able to offer for sale during a particular period of time rises (falls), the quantity of that good or service supplied rises (falls), ceteris paribus as the price rises, the quantity supplied rises and vice versa (2)

**leading indicator**  a variable that changes before real output changes (11)

**legal reserves**  the cash a bank holds in its vault plus its deposit in the Fed (15)

**liquid asset**  an asset that can easily be exchanged for goods and services (14)

**long run**  a period of time long enough that the quantities of all resources can be varied; period of time just long enough that all resources are variable (6)

**long-run aggregate supply curve (LRAS)**  a vertical line at the potential level of GDP; a vertical line at the potential level of national income (12)

**Lorenz curve**  a curve measuring the degree of inequality of income distribution within a society; a diagram illustrating the degree of income inequality (8)

**M1 money supply** the financial assets that are most liquid (14)

**marginal costs (MC)** the additional costs of producing one more unit of output; incremental costs; change in total costs divided by change in quantity (5)

**marginal revenue** incremental revenue, change in total revenue divided by change in quantity (4)

**market demand** the sum of individual demands (2)

**market failure** a circumstance in which the market is unable to allocate scarce goods, services, or resources (2)

**minimum wage** a government-imposed wage defining the least someone can be paid (8)

**monetary policy** the policy directed toward the control of the money supply; policy directed toward control of money and credit (9)

**money** anything that is generally acceptable to sellers in exchange for goods and services (14)

**monopoly** a market structure in which there is just one firm and entry by other firms is not possible. The firm produces a good with no close substitutes (6)

**monopolistic competition** a market structure characterized by a large number of firms, easy entry, and differentiated products (6)

**monopolization of a market** market dominance by one firm gained unfairly (7)

**most-favored customer (MFC)** a customer who receives a guarantee of the lowest price and all product features for a certain period of time; a commitment that the customer will receive a lower price if anyone else receives a lower price (7)

**multinational business** a firm that owns and operates producing units in foreign countries (9)

**murabaha** the most popular instrument for financing Islamic investments (14)

**national income (NI)** net national product minus indirect business taxes (10)

**national income accounting** the process that summarizes the level of production in an economy over a specific period of time, typically a year; the framework that summarizes and categorizes productive activity in an economy over a specific period of time, typically a year (10)

**natural monopolies** a monopoly that emerges because of economies of scale when economies of scale lead to just one firm (7)

**natural rate of unemployment** the unemployment rate that would exist in the absence of cyclical unemployment (11)

**negative economic profit** total revenue that is less than total costs when total costs include all opportunity costs; revenue does not pay for all opportunity costs (5)

**negative externality** costs of a transaction that are borne by someone not directly involved in the transaction (2, 8)

**net exports** exports minus imports; the difference between the value of exports and the value of imports (9)

**net investment** gross investment minus capital consumption allowance (10)

**net national product (NNP)** gross national product minus capital consumption allowance (10)

**NICs** newly industrialized countries (18)

**nominal GDP** a measure of national output based on the current prices of goods and services (10)

**nominal interest rate** the observed interest rate in the market (11)

**nonrenewable natural resources** resources that cannot be replaced or renewed; resources that cannot replenish themselves (8)

**normal accounting profit** zero economic profit (5)

**normal goods** goods that people buy more of as their income rises (2)

**oligopoly** a market structure in which there are few firms—more than one, but few enough so that each firm alone can affect the market (6)

**open market operations** the buying and selling of government bonds by the Fed to control bank reserves and the money supply (15)

**opportunity costs** the highest-valued alternative that must be forgone when a choice is made (1)

**partnership** a business with two or more owners who share the firm's profits and losses; a business firm owned by two or more persons (7)

**perfect competition** a market structure characterized by a very large number of firms producing an identical (undifferentiated) product, with easy market entry (6)

**perfectly elastic** price elasticity is infinite (4)

**perfectly inelastic** price elasticity is zero (4)

**personal income (PI)** national income plus income currently received but not earned, minus income currently earned but not received (10)

**Phillips curve** a graph that illustrates the relationship between inflation and the unemployment rate (16)

**positive economic profit** total revenue that is greater than total costs when total costs include all opportunity costs; revenue exceeds all opportunity costs (5)

**positive externality** benefits of a transaction that are received by someone not directly involved in the transaction (2, 8)

**potential real GDP** the output produced at the natural rate of unemployment (11)

**poverty** an arbitrary level of income chosen to provide a measure of how well basic human needs are being met (8)

**precautionary demand for money** the demand for money to cover unplanned transactions or emergencies (15)

**price ceiling** a situation where the price is not allowed to rise above a certain level; price is not allowed to rise above a specific level (3)

**price discrimination** charging different customers different prices for the same product (4)

**price elasticity of demand** the percentage change in the quantity demanded of a product divided by the percentage change in the price of that product (4)

**price floor** a situation where the price is not allowed to decrease below a certain level; price is not allowed to fall below a specific level (3)

**price index** a measure of the average price level in an economy (10)

**prisoner's dilemma** a situation in which the best outcome is not selected because the actions depend on other firms (7)

**private costs** costs borne by the individual in the transaction that created the costs; costs borne solely by the individuals involved in the transaction (8)

**private property right** the limitation of ownership to an individual; the right to claim ownership of an item (8)

**private sector** households, businesses, and the international sector (9)

**producer price index (PPI)** a measure of average prices received by producers (10)

**producer surplus** the difference between the price firms would have been willing to accept for their products and the price they actually receive; the difference between what suppliers would require to supply some item and the price they actually receive (6)

**production possibilities curve (PPC)** a graphical representation showing the maximum quantity of goods and services that can be produced using limited resources to the fullest extent possible; shows the maximum output that can be produced using resources fully and efficiently (app 1)

**progressive tax** a tax whose rate rises as income rises (13)

**proportional tax** a tax where rate is constant as income rises (13)

**public sector** the government (9)

**quantity demanded** the amount of a product that people are willing and able to purchase at a specific price (2)

**quantity quota** a limit on the amount of a good that may be imported (17)

**quantity theory of money** with constant velocity, changes in the quantity of money change nominal GDP (15)

**"race to the bottom"** with globalization, countries compete for international investment by offering low or no environmental regulations or labor standards (18)

**rational expectation** an expectation that is formed using all available relevant information (16)

**real GDP** a measure of the quantity of goods and services produced, adjusted for price changes; a measure of the quantity of final goods and services produced, obtained by eliminating the influence of price changes from the nominal GDP statistics (10)

**real interest rate** the nominal interest rate minus the rate of inflation (11)

**recession** a period in which the real GDP falls (11)

**regressive tax** a tax where rate falls as income rises (13)

**regulation** the control of some aspect of business by the government (7)

**renewable natural resources** resources that can be replaced or renewed; resources that can renew themselves (8)

**rent** or **benefit seeking** the use of resources simply to transfer wealth from one group to another without increasing production or total wealth; resources used to gain benefits from the government (7)

**required reserves** the cash reserves (a percentage of deposits) a bank must keep on hand or on deposit with the Federal Reserve (14)

**reservation wage** the minimum wage a worker is willing to accept (16)

**resources** goods used to produce other goods, i.e., land, labor, capital, and entrepreneurial ability inputs used to create goods and services (1)

**ROSCAS** rotating savings and credit associations (14)

**scarcity** the shortage that exists when less of something is available than is wanted at a zero price; occurs when the quantity people want is greater than the quantity available (1)

**shock** an unexpected change in a variable (16)

**shortage** a quantity supplied that is smaller than the quantity demanded at a given price the quantity demanded is greater than the quantity supplied (2)

**short run** a period of time short enough that the quantities of at least some of the resources cannot be varied; a period of time just short enough that at least one resource is fixed (5)

**social cost** the private and external costs of a transaction; private costs plus external costs (8)

**social regulation** the prescribing of health, safety, performance, and environmental standards that apply across several industries; government regulation of health, safety, the environment, and employment policies (7)

**sole proprietorship** a business owned by one person who receives all the profits and is responsible for all the debts incurred by the business; a business firm owned by one person (7)

**speculative attack** a situation in which private investors sell domestic currency and buy foreign currency betting that the domestic currency will be devalued (18)

**speculative demand for money** the demand for money created by uncertainty about the value of other assets (15)

**statistically discriminating** discrimination that results when an indicator of group performance is incorrectly applied to an individual member of the group using characteristics that apply to a group, although not all individual members of that group may have those characteristics, as an allocation device (8)

**sterilization** the use of domestic open market operations to offset the effects of a foreign exchange market intervention on the domestic money supply (15)

**strategic trade policy** the use of trade restrictions or subsidies to allow domestic firms with decreasing costs to gain a greater share of the world market (17)

**subsidy** a grant of money given to help produce or purchase a specific good or service; subsidies may take the form of grants to individuals to reward certain types of behavior, or government payments to domestic firms to encourage exports (3, 17)

**substitute goods** goods that can be used in place of each other [as the price of one rises, the demand for the other rises] (2)

**sunk costs** cost that cannot be recouped (6)

**supply** the amount of a good or service that producers are willing and able to offer for sale at each possible price during a period of time, ceteris paribus the quantities suppliers are willing and able to supply at each price (2)

**supply curve** a graph of a supply schedule that measures price on the vertical axis and quantity supplied on the horizontal axis; a plot of the supply schedule (2)

**supply schedule** a list or table of prices and corresponding quantities supplied of a particular good or service; a list of prices and quantities supplied (2)

**surplus** a quantity supplied that is larger than the quantity demanded at a given price; the quantity demanded is less than the quantity supplied (2)

**tariff** a tax imposed on goods and services purchased from foreign suppliers (i.e., imports); can also be levied on exports (3, 17)

**technology** ways of combining resources to produce output (16)

**total factor productivity (TFP)** the ratio of the economy's output to its stock of labor and capital (16)

**total revenue (TR)** TR = P × Q; price times quantity sold (4)

**trade deficit** the situation that exists when imports exceed exports (9)

**trade surplus** the situation that exists when imports are less than exports (9)

**tradeoffs** the act of giving up one good or activity in order to obtain some other good or activity; what must be given up to acquire something else (1)

**transaction costs** the costs involved in making an exchange (2)

**transactions account** a checking account at a bank or other financial institution that can be drawn on to make payments (14)

**transactions demand for money** the demand to hold money to buy goods and services (15)

**transfer payments** the income transferred from one citizen, who is earning income, to another citizen (9)

**underemployment** the employment of workers in jobs that do not utilize their productive potential (11)

**unemployment rate** the percentage of the labor force that is not working (11)

**unit elastic** price elasticity equal to 1 (4)

**value added** the difference between the value of output and the value of the intermediate goods used in the production of that output (10)

**value-added tax (VAT)** a general sales tax collected at each stage of production (13)

**value quota** a limit on the monetary value of a good that may be imported (17)

**variable costs** costs that vary as output varies (5)

**velocity of money** the average number of times each dollar is spent on final goods and services in a year (15)

**wealth effect** a change in the real value of wealth that causes spending to change when the price level changes (12)

**zero economic profit** the result when total revenue equals total costs where total costs include all opportunity costs; revenue just pays all opportunity costs (5)

# Index